SUHARTO

A POLITICAL BIOGRAPHY

Suharto is synonymous with modern Indonesia. He came to the leadership of Indonesia amidst extreme social upheaval and mass violence in 1966 and established an enduring regime known as the 'New Order'. He remained in command of the world's fourth most populous country until his dramatic fall from power in 1998. This book provides fascinating insights into a man who rose from humble beginnings to exert extraordinary power over a complex and volatile nation. He presented himself as an infallible father of Indonesia, yet he remained a mysterious and puzzling figure. He sought to transform Indonesia into a strong, united and economically prosperous nation, but he is remembered today for human rights abuses and profound corruption. The system of power he created collapsed with his decline, and he left a problematic legacy for Indonesia's current leaders as they seek to create a new beginning for their country.

R. E. ELSON is Professor in the School of Asian and International Studies at Griffith University, Brisbane. One of the leading historians of Indonesia and Southeast Asia, he has written on the social impact of the sugar industry in Java, a general history of the peasantry in Southeast Asia and was a contributor to *The Cambridge History of Southeast Asia.*

For Thee Kian Wie
– a true Indonesian

SUHARTO

A POLITICAL BIOGRAPHY

R. E. Elson

CAMBRIDGE
UNIVERSITY PRESS

PUBLISHED BY THE PRESS SYNDICATE OF THE UNIVERSITY OF CAMBRIDGE
The Pitt Building, Trumpington Street, Cambridge, United Kingdom

CAMBRIDGE UNIVERSITY PRESS
The Edinburgh Building, Cambridge CB2 2RU, UK
40 West 20th Street, New York, NY 10011–4211, USA
10 Stamford Road, Oakleigh, VIC 3166, Australia
Ruiz de Alarcón 13, 28014 Madrid, Spain
Dock House, The Waterfront, Cape Town 8001, South Africa

http://www.cambridge.org

First published 2001

Printed in Australia by Brown Prior Anderson

Typeface Garamond (*Adobe*) 10/12 pt. *System* QuarkXPress® [BC]

A catalogue record for this book is available from the British Library

National Library of Australia Cataloguing in Publication data
Elson, R. E. (Robert Edward).
Suharto: a political biography.
Bibliography.
Includes index.
ISBN 0 521 77326 1
1. Soeharto, 1921– . 2. Politicians – Indonesia –
Biography. 3. Indonesia – Politics and government – 1945– .
4. Indonesia – History – 1945– . I. Title.
959.803092

ISBN 0 521 77326 1 hardback

Contents

Preface

In a curious way, it is unfortunate that Suharto fell from power so dramatically, in so violent a context, and with such immediately perturbing consequences for Indonesia. Because he ruled so long and, at his height, with such complete and magisterial authority, Indonesia's multiple and apparently intractable problems at the end of the 1990s were laid at his door. It was he who had created a closed and fearful system of institutionalised state authoritarianism, he who had clothed his people in the immobilising ideological torpor of Pancasila, he who had fleeced the country for the sake of his horrible children and his cronies and flunkies. He, indeed, was the reason why Indonesia needed *reformasi total* and a new and more humane beginning. His going presented the long-awaited opportunity to cast off and forever commit to oblivion a shameful chapter in modern Indonesian history.

Such a view is unfortunate not just because the popular foregrounding of his sullied reputation makes longer-term assessment of his legacy more difficult. More important, it renders an analysis of his extraordinary rule, and the means by which he achieved it, strangely irrelevant. Indonesia, it seems, just wants to forget Suharto and his works, and to rationalise the New Order as an aberration from a more wholesome historical trajectory.

This is an understandable attitude. It is also superficial. Whatever moral judgements one might wish to cast on his methods and behaviour, Suharto was undeniably one of the most significant figures of twentieth-century Asia. Within his domestic domain, according to one commentator, 'Suharto has done more to shape Indonesian society than any other figure in the country's history'.[1] He came to power, unknown and unexpectedly, in controversial and chaotic circumstances. Slowly, cautiously, deliberately, he constructed a wholly new Indonesia, one with a growing sense of its identity and purpose, with an economy which developed at a rate and (some hiccups aside) with a constancy which astounded the world. He contrived, with a sense of destiny, a steely purpose and an unwavering will, and seemingly against all the odds, to transform his sinking, impoverished, dishevelled, politically polarised and culturally fragmented country into something that appeared to be, at the height of his power, a dynamic and formidable success story and a shining example of hope to other developing nations.

That he could so wholly and completely bring so erratic, long-suffering and fabricated a nation as Indonesia to his purpose was an extraordinary achievement. That he could do so for so long seems, on the surface, miraculous. This book attempts to tell the story of how Suharto managed such a feat and – because he came to personify so much of the way in which the modern Indonesian polity came to work – in so doing to portray something of the essential nature of modern Indonesian political practice.

The prospect of a long and defining Suharto era seemed unlikely when the 44-year-old emerged from relative obscurity in the wake of the carnage and uproar caused by the events of 1 October 1965. Despite his military seniority (the rank of major-general and the status of standing deputy to the army commander, Achmad Yani), Suharto was seen as a reserved, introspective and quietly undemonstrative man. Of lowly Javanese background and limited education, he had a reputation as a tough and successful field officer and troop commander, but he seemed to lack any trace of charisma, political flair or social gaiety. He seemed the kind of man more visionary types like to have on hand to get their dreams implemented: dour, reliable, uncomplaining, a person who, properly instructed and mandated, would carry through a designated task to a successful completion. He seemed not at all to be a leader.

Yet lead he did, gathering confidence, demonstrating hitherto unappreciated skills of charm and persuasion and, eventually, decisiveness, and also tactical and strategic skills of the highest order. They allowed him to climb to the top of the mountain, and to stay at the peak for more than three decades. Before age and weariness, together with a gathering arrogance, robbed him of his political acumen, it seemed that Indonesia was unimaginable without the presence of its rotund, ever-smiling president and, more important, that its future was inextricably identified with his own enduring mastery. He became one of the most famous and successful political leaders in the world, as comfortable and competent with the mighty and powerful as he was with his own citizenry.

Even at the very heights of his power and visibility, however, Suharto remained enigmatic. For so prominent a figure, one whose professional life was wholly led in the public domain, his remoteness and inaccessibility were astounding. He was the most privately silent of public men. No one, not even the closest of his working colleagues, knew with any certainty what drove him; no one could safely predict how he might react to particular circumstances, what he might be thinking, or what tactical moves he was hatching behind those strong eyes. His personality remained elusive, masked by an impeccable charm and the broad smile which became his trademark. He proved just as cryptic to the journalists and academics who tried to understand him. One experienced foreign commentator found 'the president himself … the most difficult and least accessible area of analysis in Indonesia',[2] while a scholar remarked in the early 1990s that, 'even after twenty-five years of thoroughly dominating his "New Order" regime, President Soeharto enjoys only a spectral presence in the social science literature on Indonesia'.[3]

Different writers have employed different approaches in their efforts to penetrate the wall of unknowing that surrounded Suharto. Some saw him in terms of ruthless and all-encompassing political ambition; thus, in one account, 'Indonesian politics since 1965 are best understood in terms of a totalitarian ambition'.[4] His relentless, unscrupulous drive for power above everything else shapes such analyses. Others have chosen culture and tradition as their analytical gateway to the ineffably Javanese Suharto. Typically, in such accounts, Javanese culture is 'the well-spring not just for the style of the current president and his government, but also for … the conceptions that underpin the logic of the Indonesian state'.[5] Despite their usefulness, there sometimes appears in such culturally grounded accounts the tendency to regard Javanese culture as 'an all-purpose explanation for complex and opaque behaviour'.[6] Others again have come to see him as a creator and natural centre of a certain kind of bureaucratic patrimonialism, so that 'meaningful power [was] obtained through interpersonal competition in the elite circle in closest physical proximity to the president'.[7]

All these approaches have their merits, but none of them seems of itself capable of making incisive inroads into the complexity and hiddenness of the man. The fundamental assumption of this book is that Suharto can be understood, and that the best tool for that analysis is narrative history – the detailed, nuanced exposition of the complex and changing dialectic of idea, circumstance and milieu in Suharto's life and career. The reader, therefore, will find no explicit theoretical formulations or models to drive the analysis; there is, rather, a reflectiveness on how and why Suharto mapped, negotiated and organised the changing circumstances of his life and how those circumstances imposed themselves on him.

THE HISTORIOGRAPHY OF SEARCHING FOR SUHARTO

Given Suharto's centrality to Indonesia and its politics – 'no study of contemporary Indonesian politics can fail to consider President Soeharto who has dominated Indonesian national life for thirty years'[8] – it is in one way surprising that he has received so little systematic biographical attention. But tracking and probing Suharto is no simple matter. The range and flavour of the sources mirror his personal elusiveness, notwithstanding the renown he came to enjoy. The documentary record is uneven, to say the least. He appears not at all until the middle 1940s, and then only as an insignificant figure in the greater drama of the revolutionary struggle, occasionally mentioned in newspaper reports, and his name routinely listed in the fastidiously organised (if pretentiously titled) Dutch military intelligence reports of the Indonesian Army's 'order of battle'.[9] His shadowy and patchy appearances in the Indonesian newspaper record of the 1950s tell us little about him. His rise to public notability – even then a limited notability – came only with his leading role in the military side of the West Irian campaign. Only with his decisive intervention on the morning of 1 October 1965 does he obtain real prominence, but again he enjoys only a ghostly presence in the contemporary reporting. Thereafter, of course, he is famous; no day goes by without his being mentioned in some capacity, greeting heads of state, delivering speeches, conferring with colleagues.

But as his New Order grew in authoritarian intensity, and as we learn more of his daily activities and read ever-longer reports of his utterances, the mystery of the man remains. It is a mystery heightened by the New Order's propaganda machine, which shielded him almost completely from criticism and which, especially from the time of his true ascendancy from the early 1980s, began to magnify him into a figure of singular, remote and heroic proportions. Such efforts reached their height in his 1989 autobiography, *My thoughts, words, and deeds*, in which he appears as in a lonely moonscape populated only by himself, in which he alone is the fount of wisdom and the source of Indonesia's true direction.[10] The six-volume collection of his 'diaries', running from 1965 to 1993, performs a similar hagiographic task.[11] Suharto's effort at self-aggrandisement, however, is not as self-serving as he would have wished; in presenting himself so fully formed, so much in control, he denies us insights into his true strengths: his nimbleness of mind, his patiently modulated indecisiveness, his voracious capacity to learn from his personal past and from his contemporaries.

How might one escape from what might otherwise be the strangling, dutiful and dreary prose of New Order reporting to search for the real man? There are, unfortunately, no archives accessible which might detail his thinking and the base mechanics of his politics and policies. Their absence can be compensated for, partly at least, by interviews (both the direct and reported kinds) with his contemporaries, but they present their own difficulties. Past interactions are distorted through the lenses of current interests and the natural tendency to recreate the past to magnify the interviewee's influence (or, as the case may be, to diminish it). The difficulty becomes the greater because the period in which the research for this book was undertaken is neatly divided by the dramatic events of May 1998. While it might be expected that interviews conducted under New Order orthodoxy might reveal little compared to those done in the unfettered atmosphere of the post-Suharto era, in fact the scrambling for self-justification and distancing from problematic pasts engaged in by many elite players in the post-fall period make the information gleaned from them just as problematic. To this problem, one scholar remarks with considerable justification, must be added the fact that 'Indonesian politics and public debate had always had an element of untruthfulness, lack of factual evidence, wilful distortion, plotting, double-dealing, and groundless insinuation in it'.[12] There is, fortunately, a considerable quantity of high-quality foreign analysis of modern and contemporary Indonesia, both of a journalistic and academic kind (much of it the work of Australians), against which such material can be read.

In the end, however, historians must view this mountain of grist with a jaundiced, critical and sensitive eye, and do their best to draw balanced, measured and sensible conclusions from it. I have sought to achieve this goal but am embarrassingly conscious both of the limitations of my data gathering (pursuing all that has been written and spoken about Suharto would devour many lifetimes) and even more of the halting and provisional nature of my conclusions. I can but hope that this early, stumbling attempt to explore the significance of Suharto's remarkable life for the history of Indonesia may generate other efforts to comprehend and evaluate so elusive a personality. No matter how many Indonesians may wish to forget him, there is no escaping his profound and far-reaching legacy. Indonesians must seek to understand and be reconciled with that legacy before they can move forward.

To conclude on a technicality: the spelling of Indonesian personal names is a difficult matter. For the sake of simplicity and consistency I have rendered them in the text (but not in the Acknowledgements) according to the current mode of spelling (thus, Suharto not Soeharto, Selo Sumarjan not Selo Soemardjan). Readers should be aware that under this spelling regime 'c' is pronounced as 'ch'.

Acknowledgements

SEARCHING FOR SO large and imposing a subject as Suharto has placed me in the debt of a proportionately large and often imposing group of people and institutions. The Australian Research Council granted me the resources needed for travel and to free me for periods of uninterrupted reflection and writing. Numerous archives and libraries provided access to rich collections, and assisted me in finding my way through them: The Centraal Archievendepot of the Ministerie van Defensie, Rijswijk (especially S. Martijn), the Sectie Militaire Geschiedenis, Koninklijk Landmacht, The Hague (especially P. M. H. Groen), the Ministerie van Buitenlandse Zaken, The Hague (especially R. J. H. van Laak), the Nederlands Instituut voor Oorlogsdocumentatie, Amsterdam (especially Elly Touwen), the Algemeen Rijksarchief, The Hague (especially Francien van Aanrooij and Sierk Plantinga), the Library of the Koninklijk Instituut voor Taal-, Land- en Volkenkunde, Leiden, the Griffith University Library (especially Christine Cordwell), the University of Queensland Library, the National Library of Australia (especially Ralph Sanderson), the Menzies Library at the Australian National University (especially George Miller), the Monash University Library (especially Helen Soemardjo), the Perpustakaan Nasional Republik Indonesia, Jakarta (especially Paul Permadi), and the Library of the Centre for Strategic and International Studies, Jakarta. I thank them all for their enthusiastic and skilled assistance.

A great army of people has helped me along the way in Indonesia, in Australia, in the Netherlands, in Germany and, virtually, in the United States and I am indebted to them for their wisdom, their expertise and their generosity. I mention them, in no particular order, as a means of recording my gratitude to them: Kresno Adji Djayandaru, Ali Alatas, Anthony Reid, Anton Tabah, Arief Budiman, Ben Anderson, Bill Case, Julia Howell, Andrew MacIntyre, J. D. Legge, Clara Joewono, Daniel Dhakidae, David Jenkins, Deliar Noer, Dewi Fortuna Anwar, Gerry van Klinken, Goenawan Mohamad, Greg Earl, Greg Poulgrain, Hadi Soesastro, the late Hardi, Harold Crouch, Harry Tjan Silalahi, Hasnan Habib, Herb Feith, Christiane Sie, John Butcher, Kate McGregor, A. Kemal Idris, Ken

Ward, Ewan Ward, Kevin Evans, L. B. Murdani, Liem Soei Liong, Linda Reeves, M. Ryaas Rasyid, J. A. C. Mackie, Marzuki Darusman, Merle Ricklefs, Kees van Dijk, Muchtar Pakpahan, Nazaruddin Sjamsuddin, Simone Dennis, Patrick Walters, Phillipa McGuinness, Sharon Tickle, Emil Salim, Don Greenlees, Frans Seda, Andi Mallarangeng, Margaret Pearce, Wimar Witoelar, Ramadhan K. H., Rod and Mita Brazier, Salim Said, Philip Flood, Alan Atwell, Sarwono Kusumaatmadja, Selo Soemardjan, Sri Mulyani Indrawati, Steve Irvine, Subroto, Sumarsono, Aristides Katoppo, Sumiskum, Thee Kian Wie and Tjoe, Ulf Sundhaussen, Wiryono Sastrohandoyo, Yoga Sugomo, Ikrar Nusa Bhakti, C. P. F. Luhulima, the late A. M. W. Pranarka, Shigeru Sato, Onghokham, Colin England, Henk Schulte-Nordholt, Akiko Yamada, Honor Lawler, and, as well, a number of serving officials who did not wish to be identified.

Any errors are, of course, my own doing.

On a personal note, I want to record my deepest gratitude to my beloved wife and children, Elizabeth, Charles, Kathryn, Brigid, Jane, Gretchen and Jerome, who put up with me, and without me, as I wrestled with Suharto.

Timeline

1921	
8 June	Suharto born in Kemusuk (Central Java), to Kertosudiro and Sukirah
1923	
23 August	Birth of Siti Hartinah, future wife of Suharto
1940	
1 June	Suharto accepted at KNIL military school, Gombong; assigned to Battalion XIII at Rampal, near Malang; duty at Gresik
2 December	Suharto accepted at Military Cadre School, Gombong
1942	
March	Japanese invasion of Java
1 November	Suharto joins Japanese-sponsored police force, Yogyakarta
1943	
October	Suharto joins Peta; undertakes platoon commander course, Yogyakarta
1944	
c. April	Suharto undertakes company commander course, Bogor
1945	
17 August	Indonesian proclamation of independence
29 September	Arrival of Allied troops in Java
October	Suharto joins BKR; involved in clashes with Allied troops
1946	
January?	Suharto appointed lt. col. and commander of Regiment III
2–3 July	Suharto involvement in 3 July affair
12 November	Linggarjati agreement
November	Suharto commander of 22nd Regiment, Division III (Yogya)
1947	
21 July	First Dutch 'police action'
26 December	Suharto marries Siti Hartinah

1948

17 January	Renville agreement
18 September	Madiun revolt
19 December	Second Dutch 'police action'

1949

23 January	Birth of daughter Siti Hardiyanti Hastuti (Tutut)
1 March	General assault on Yogyakarta
7 May	Rum-Van Royen agreement
27 December	Sovereignty transferred to Republic of the United States of Indonesia

1950

January?	Suharto confirmed as lt. col. of TNI
26 April	Suharto commander of Garuda Mataram Brigade, Makasar
17 August	Formation of unitary Republic of Indonesia
September	Suharto commander of Prince Mangkubumi Brigade, Yogya

1951

1 May	Birth of son Sigit Haryoyudanto
15 November	Suharto commander of Pragola Brigade, Salatiga
8 December	Rebellion of Battalion 426

1952

October	17 October affair

1953

1 March	Suharto commander of Infantry Regiment 15, Solo
23 July	Birth of son Bambang Trihatmojo

1955

February	Army reconciliation conference in Yogya
April	Afro-Asian conference in Bandung
September	First parliamentary elections

1956

1 March	Suharto chief of staff of Diponegoro Division, Semarang
September	Suharto assumes command of Diponegoro Division
December	Regional military coups in Sumatra

1957

1 January	Suharto promoted to colonel
2 March	Proclamation of Permesta in Sulawesi
March	Army-led councils take over in East Indonesia
14 March	Declaration of State of War and Siege
May	Establishment of National Council by emergency decree
29 November	West Irian vote fails in UN; seizure of Dutch businesses

1958

15 February	Proclamation of PRRI
17 February	Permesta rebellion

1959

14 April	Birth of daughter Siti Hediyati Haryadi (Titiek)

5 July	Constituent Assembly dissolved; 1945 Constitution reintroduced
9 July	Sukarno appoints 43-member cabinet with self as prime minister
October	Suharto removed from Diponegoro command and posted to SSKAD

1960

1 January	Suharto promoted to brigadier-general
5 March	Sukarno suspends elected parliament
25 June	Installation of newly appointed DPR
September	Sukarno appoints provisional MPR; Suharto commander of Army Reserve Corps I
December	Suharto deputy I (operations) to army chief of staff

1961

1 March	Suharto appointed commander of Caduad
June	Suharto's first overseas trip
1 October	Suharto commander of Army Air Defence Command

1962

9 January	Suharto appointed Mandala commander, promoted to maj.-gen.
23 January	Suharto deputy commander of East Indonesia Territory
15 July	Birth of son Hutomo Mandala Putra (Tommy)
15 August	Agreement on West Irian transfer to Indonesia
late	Beginning of Confrontation against Malaysia

1963

1 March	Suharto commander of Kostrad
May	MPRS makes Sukarno President for Life

1964

23 August	Birth of daughter Siti Hutami Endang Adiningsih (Mamiek)

1965

1 January	Suharto first deputy commander, Kolaga; Indonesia leaves UN
1 October	'Coup attempt' of 30 September Movement
10 October	Formation of Kopkamtib
14 October	Suharto appointed army commander, promoted to lt. gen.
25 October	Formation of student action front (KAMI)
October	Beginning of massacres

1966

10 January	KAMI campaign of demonstrations begins
11 March	Supersemar
12 March	PKI banned
18 March	Arrest and dismissal of 15 cabinet ministers
27 March	New cabinet, headed by 6-man team
25 July	Ampera cabinet; Suharto appointed chair of presidium
28 July	Suharto promoted to general
11 August	Normalisation of Indonesia–Malaysia relations
28 September	Indonesia readmitted to UN
3 October	Economic stabilisation measures

1967	
10 January	Foreign Investment Law
22 February	Sukarno transfers powers to Suharto
12 March	Suharto appointed acting president by MPRS
August	Indonesia founding member of ASEAN
October	Freezing of relations with China
1968	
27 March	Suharto sworn in as full president
6 June	First Development Cabinet appointed
1969	
1 April	First Five-Year Development Plan begins
July–August	'Act of free choice' in West Irian
16 September	West Irian declared an autonomous region of Indonesia
22 November	General Election law passed by DPR-GR
1970	
January	Student protests against corruption
31 January	Appointment of Commission of Four on Corruption
21 June	Death of Sukarno
6 September	Suharto attends Non-Aligned Movement conference in Lusaka
1971	
5 July	First New Order parliamentary elections, won by Golkar (62.8%)
1973	Beginning of oil boom
8 January	Muslim parties merged into PPP
10 January	Non-Muslim parties merged to form PDI
23 March	Suharto inaugurated by MPR as president for second term (Sultan of Yogyakarta, vice-president)
27 March	Second Development Cabinet formed
5 August	Anti-Chinese riots in Bandung
1974	
15 January	Malari riots on visit of Japanese Prime Minister Tanaka
1975	
10 August	UDT coup in Dili
6 October	Beginning of Indonesian covert war in East Timor
28 November	Fretilin declares independence of East Timor
7 December	Formal Indonesian invasion of East Timor
1976	
3 March	Ibnu Sutowo dismissed as Pertamina director
17 July	East Timor integrated into Indonesia as 27th province
September	Sawito plot uncovered
1977	
2 May	Second New Order elections: Golkar (62.1%), PPP (29.3%), PDI (8.6%)
1978	
20 January	Closure of leading newspapers; troops sent onto campuses

22 March — Suharto president for third term (Adam Malik, vice-president); MPR approves decree on Pancasila (P-4)
29 March — Third Development Cabinet formed
15 November — Devaluation of rupiah

1980
14 March — Death of Hatta
13 May — Petition of 50

1982
18 March — Election riot, Banteng Square (Golkar rally)
4 May — Third New Order elections: Golkar (64.2%), PPP (28%), PDI (7.9%)

1983
March — Beginning of 'mysterious killings' (Petrus)
10 March — MPR names Suharto 'Father of Development'
11 March — Suharto president for fourth term (Umar Wirahadikusumah, vice-president)
16 March — Fourth Development Cabinet formed
30 March — Devaluation of rupiah by 27.6%

1984
12 September — Unrest and shootings in Tanjung Priok (Jakarta)

1985
May — All social organisations required to adopt Pancasila as sole foundation
14 November — Suharto addresses FAO meeting in Rome

1986
12 September — Devaluation of rupiah
9 November — Suharto names Sukarno and Hatta independence proclamation heroes

1987
23 April — Fourth New Order elections: Golkar (73.2%), PPP (16%), PDI (10.9%)

1988
11 March — Suharto president for fifth term (Sudharmono, vice-president)
March — Fifth Development Cabinet formed
5 September — Kopkamtib replaced by Bakorstanas
27 October — Deregulation of banking
December — East Timor declared opened

1989
23 February — Suharto meets Chinese Foreign Minister Qian Qichen
September — Suharto visits Soviet Union

1990
8 August — Normalisation of relations with China
16 August — Suharto speech on democracy and openness
5 December — ICMI established

1991	
April	Establishment of Democracy Forum
June	Suharto pilgrimage to Mecca
September	Indonesia chosen as leader of Non-Aligned Movement
12 November	Massacre at Santa Cruz cemetery in Dili, East Timor
1992	
9 June	Fifth New Order elections: Golkar (68.1%), PPP (17%), PDI (14.9%)
1993	
11 March	Suharto begins sixth term as president (Try Sutrisno, vice-president)
March	Sixth Development Cabinet formed
May	Xanana Gusmao sentenced to life imprisonment (later commuted to 20 years)
December	Megawati voted chair of PDI; finally endorsed
1994	
April	Riots in Medan
22 June	Banning of *Tempo, De Tik*, and *Editor*
November	Indonesia hosts APEC summit
1995	
18 December	Indonesia signs defence pact with Australia
1996	
28 April	Death of Suharto's wife, Ibu Tien
20–22 June	Megawati ousted from PDI leadership (Suryadi elected leader)
27 July	Anti-PDI (Megawati) disturbances in Jakarta
October	Nobel Peace Prize to Bishop Carlos Belo and Jose Ramos Horta
26 December	Anti-Chinese riots in Tasikmalaya
1997	
30 January	Anti-Chinese riots in Rengasdengklok
January–February	Dayak massacres of Madurese in West Kalimantan
23 May	Election riot in Banjarmasin; shopping mall fire kills >100
29 May	Sixth New Order elections: Golkar (74%), PPP (23%), PDI (3%)
July	Beginning of currency crisis and severe economic slump
July–November	Forest fires in Sumatra and Kalimantan
October	IMF bailout package
December	Suharto suffers mild stroke
1998	
15 January	Second IMF bailout package
11 March	Suharto president for seventh term (B. J. Habibie, vice-president)
March	Seventh Development Cabinet formed
12 May	Four students shot dead at Trisakti University
13–15 May	Violent riots in Jakarta

18 May	Suharto's resignation called for; students occupy DPR/MPR
21 May	Suharto resigns; Habibie sworn in as president
November	MPR calls for investigation into Suharto's wealth

1999

7 June	Elections for parliament and local assemblies
20 October	Abdurrahman Wahid elected president (Megawati, vice-president)

2000

April	Suharto placed under city arrest
29 May	Suharto under house arrest
August	Charges of corruption laid against Suharto
28 September	Charges dismissed on grounds of ill health

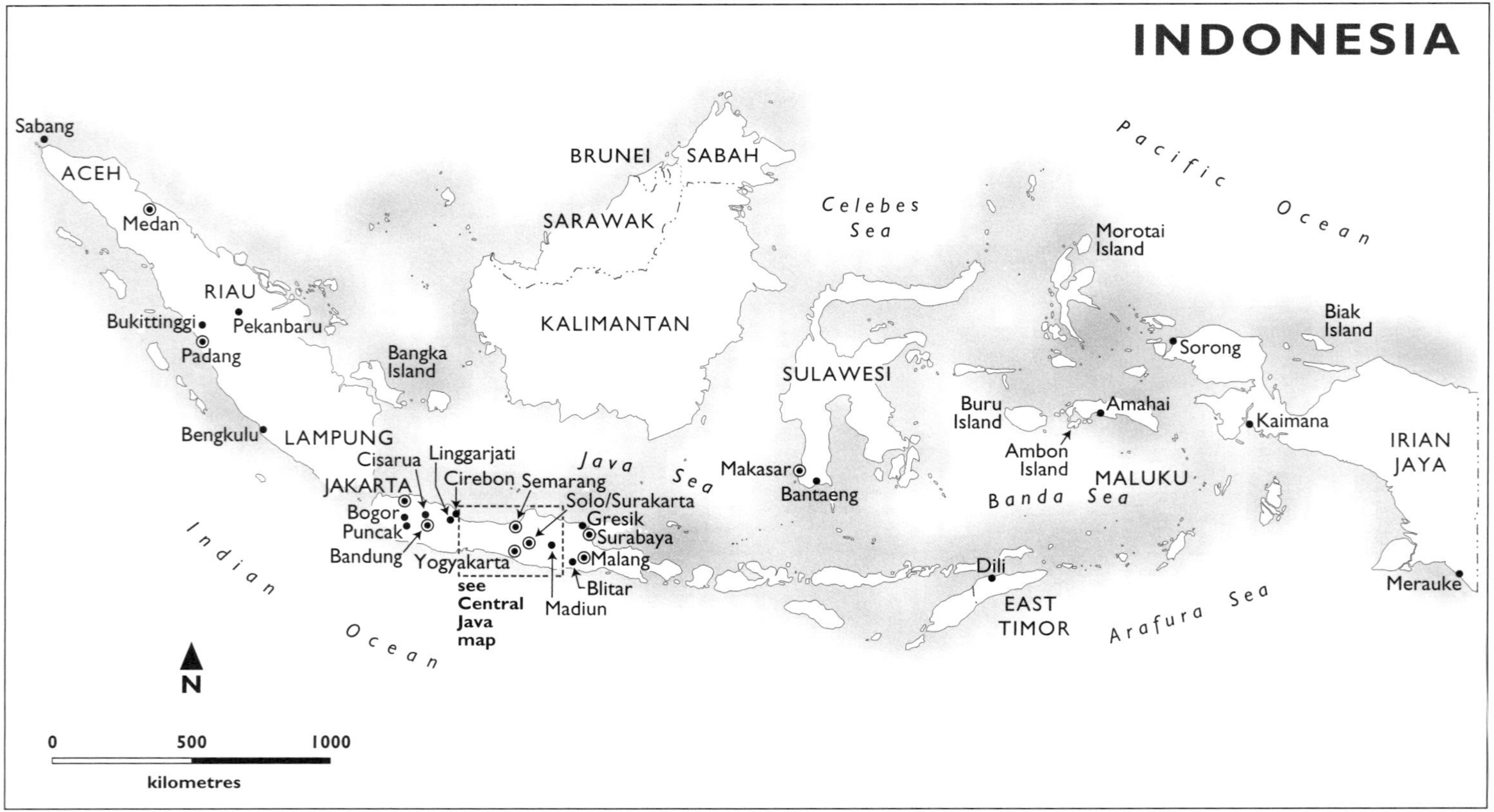
INDONESIA
Sabang
ACEH
Medan
RIAU
Bukittinggi
Pekanbaru
Padang
Bangka Island
Bengkulu
LAMPUNG
BRUNEI
SABAH
SARAWAK
KALIMANTAN
Celebes Sea
Pacific Ocean
Morotai Island
Biak Island
Sorong
SULAWESI
Buru Island
Amahai
Kaimana
IRIAN JAYA
Ambon Island
MALUKU
Banda Sea
Java Sea
Makasar
Bantaeng
Cisarua
Linggarjati
Cirebon
Semarang
Solo/Surakarta
JAKARTA
Bogor
Puncak
Bandung
Yogyakarta
Gresik
Surabaya
Malang
Blitar
Madiun
see Central Java map
Dili
EAST TIMOR
Arafura Sea
Merauke
Indian Ocean
N
0
500
1000
kilometres

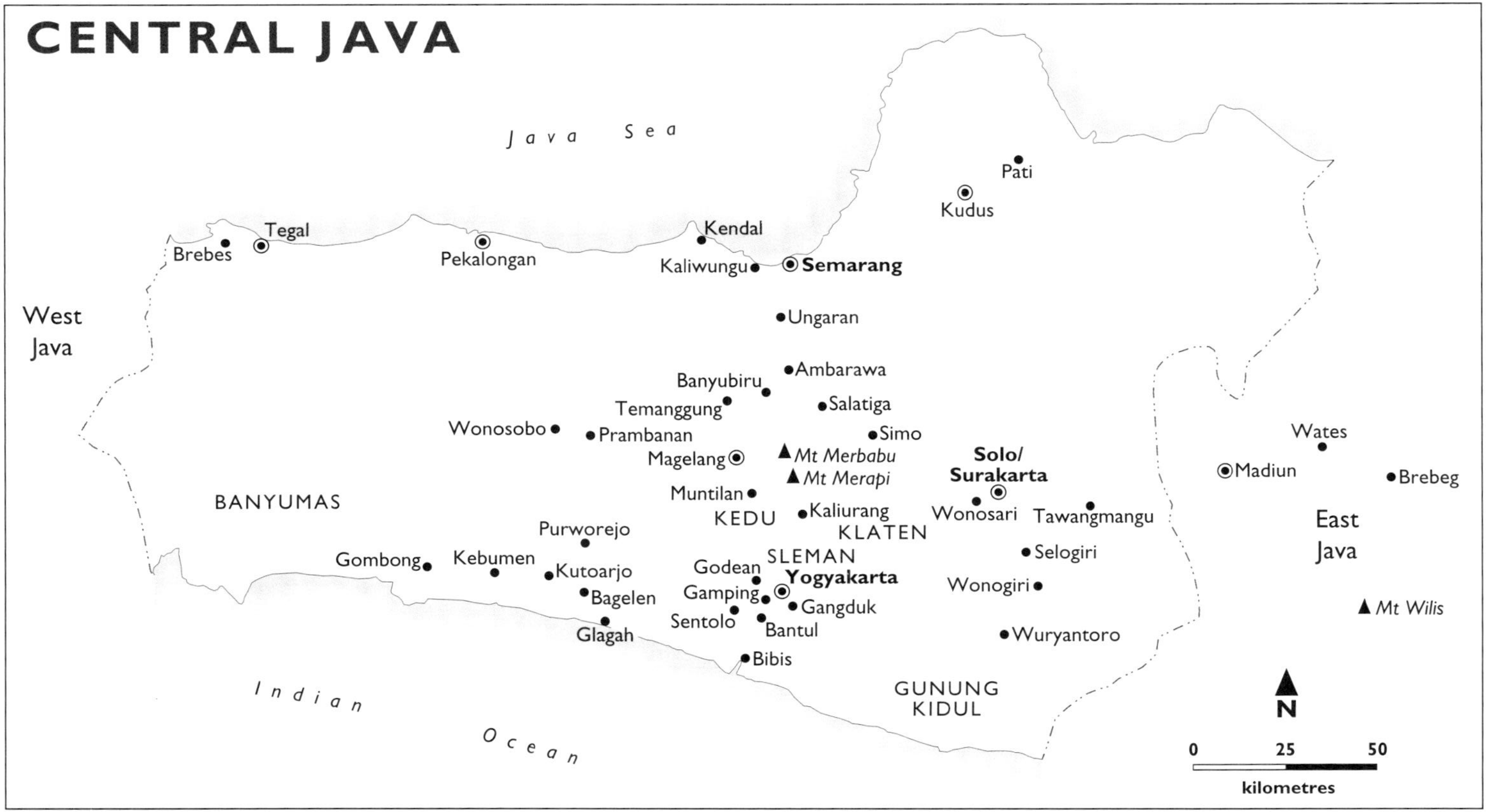
CENTRAL JAVA
Java Sea
West Java
Brebes
Tegal
Pekalongan
Kendal
Kaliwungu
Semarang
Kudus
Pati
Ungaran
Ambarawa
Banyubiru
Temanggung
Salatiga
Wonosobo
Prambanan
Simo
Magelang
Mt Merbabu
Mt Merapi
Solo/
Surakarta
Muntilan
Kaliurang
Wonosari
Tawangmangu
BANYUMAS
KEDU
KLATEN
Purworejo
SLEMAN
Selogiri
Gombong
Kebumen
Kutoarjo
Godean
Yogyakarta
Wonogiri
Bagelen
Gamping
Gangduk
Sentolo
Bantul
Glagah
Wuryantoro
Bibis
GUNUNG
KIDUL
Indian
Ocean
Wates
Madiun
Brebeg
East
Java
Mt Wilis
N
0
25
50
kilometres

1 Beginnings and youth

Suharto's long reign as President of the Republic of Indonesia ended on 21 May 1998 in confusion and controversy. Equally, though not so dramatically, confusion and controversy surround his origins.

HE WAS BORN, official and semi-official accounts eventually agreed, on 8 June 1921, in the hamlet of Kemusuk, part of the larger village of Godean, about 15 kilometres due west of Yogyakarta.[1] He was 'just a mere village boy, born of a poor farming family'.[2] His mother was Sukirah, previously unmarried, from the northern part of the hamlet (Kemusuk lor). His father, already the father of two children from his first marriage, was named Kertosudiro (on the occasion of his second marriage he had changed his name from Kertorejo, the name he used during his first marriage; like many Javanese, Kertosudiro changed his name numerous times during his life to denote consequential changes to his circumstances). Kertosudiro, resident in the southern part of the hamlet, Kemusuk kidul, earned his living as an irrigation official, responsible for allocating irrigation water to the different fields of the village and for the general upkeep of the irrigation channels which were so vital for village agriculture. In return for his official duties, Kertosudiro had been granted a small piece of land, a hectare or so, called *lungguh*, to grow food for his family. (By the standards of the day, this was an unusually large amount of land.) He had no other land, nor cattle. He and his family lived in a small bamboo-walled house with a palm-leaf roof, without running water or electricity. Suharto's father and mother never left the hamlet of Kemusuk.

It was, the publisher of his autobiography tells us, 'a not so glittering childhood'.[3] More bluntly, McDonald remarks, 'Suharto's early life was a remarkably disturbed one', even by Javanese standards where divorce was common and children encouraged to reach autonomy rapidly. Suharto himself acknowledged his early years as troubled: 'I had to endure much suffering which perhaps others have not experienced'.[4] Amongst the earliest of them was the breakdown of his parents' marriage; they divorced just over five weeks after his birth; he was their only offspring. His father married another woman, who bore him four more children. Two years after her divorce, Sukirah also remarried, to a villager of Kemusuk named Pranomo, nicknamed Nomo, who took the name Atmoprawiro at his marriage to Sukirah. Together they had seven further children, the fourth of whom was Probosutejo, later to play a significant and controversial role in New Order business.

Neither Kertosudiro nor Sukirah appears to have played a direct and continuing role in Suharto's rearing; his father seems to have disappeared from his life – for the time being at least – after the divorce, while his mother appears to have suffered from severe emotional difficulties, perhaps a nervous breakdown, following his birth. Before the child Suharto was forty days old, and following a family quarrel, Sukirah withdrew into herself. Apparently partaking of the ascetic practice of *ngebleng*, she had sought refuge in the inner area of a village house.[5] Silent and unable to be found for a week, and with the family in a panic, at last she was discovered in a badly weakened condition. In such circumstances, with Sukirah unable to nurse her child and little immediate prospect of her raising him, Suharto was given over to his paternal great-aunt, the wife of Kromodiryo, herself the midwife who had delivered him. Her daughter, Amat Idris, cared for him. His great-uncle, Kromodiryo, looked after him while the women were busy – Suharto seemed to hold him in particular affection – and took the young boy to the fields with him where he worked as a farmer. On one such occasion, Suharto remembers, he badly gashed his foot when a sickle he was using to cut grass detached from its handle.

Suharto returned to the house of his mother only after her remarriage, when he himself was aged about 4. Schooling began, at an unusually early age, in the nearby village of Pulihan, close to the house of his maternal grandparents, where his mother and her husband lived. But when his mother moved to the southern part of the hamlet (presumably to establish a separate household), Suharto moved school to the village of Pedes, attending class in the morning until around 11 a.m. and doing agricultural work such as tending cattle in the afternoons for his grandfather, Atmosudiro. On one occasion, he recalled, he allowed a buffalo he was leading across a dyke in the rice-fields to fall into a ditch, and cried when he found himself unable to extract it.

In 1929, at the age of 8, in order to continue his schooling Suharto was obliged to move to the house of his paternal aunt, married to Mas Ngabei Prawirowiharjo, a senior agricultural official in Wuryantoro, a small settlement 12 kilometres south of Wonogiri. The move seems to have been a ploy by his father, who was apparently unhappy with Suharto's circumstances; Sukirah, it seems, was so preoccupied by her rapid series of pregnancies to her new husband that Suharto received little by way of attention, either physical or material. Convinced that Suharto's mother would not approve such a move, Kertosudiro took him, without her knowledge, by train, bus and taxi to Wuryantoro via Yogyakarta (where they stopped to outfit Suharto with new clothes) and Wonogiri. The youngster was warmly received by his new family, and later spoke with great fondness about his adoption by Bapak Prawirowiharjo 'as his own son' – indeed, the eldest son – in a family already well endowed with children, one of whom, Sudwikatmono, later became a prominent New Order business figure. There he was 'treated the same as the other children', and continued his primary-level schooling in Wuryantoro. After a year or so, however, apparently as a result of a calculated ploy which involved promises by his mother of an early return to Wuryantoro, he was brought back to Kemusuk by his stepfather, Atmoprawiro, to be with his mother, and attended school at Tiwir – the third school he had attended in the Kemusuk region. He stayed in Kemusuk for less than a year. The tug of war between parents continued and, this time 'with the knowledge of my father and mother', the Prawirowiharjos returned Suharto to Wuryantoro.[6]

A QUESTION OF ORIGINS

This representation of the simple peasant boy, struggling alone from the very earliest years in a hostile and unforgiving world, was to become a constant motif in Suharto's perception of himself; more important, it came to shape a certain moral view of the world, with its associated imperatives, and took on a more far-reaching import for his fellow Indonesians, as we shall later see. The story of his early years, as Suharto told it at the height of his power, served a political purpose as a kind of moral primer for his people; it spoke of inner strength in resisting the worst effects of the hand of fate, of the need for developing disciplined self-control, of the eventual triumph of perseverance over unpromising circumstances. 'If', Suharto later noted, 'I remember the suffering of my childhood and youth, it could make me sad. But if one thinks of the benefits, it is precisely because of these sufferings since I was small that I have become a man. I have become a person who thinks, who has feelings, because I have suffered'.[7]

It was for this reason, amongst others, that in 1974 a story in the sensationalist Jakarta magazine, *POP*,[8] sent Suharto into a fury. The report, mirroring long-circulating gossip about Suharto's origins,[9] claimed that he was the offspring of Padmodipuro, an aristocratic descendant of Hamengkubuwono II, Sultan of Yogyakarta (r. 1792–1810, 1811–12, 1826–28), who had unloaded the 6-year-old Suharto and his mother onto the villager Kertorejo because of an obligation to marry the daughter of an influential district chief. Calling a press conference at his Bina Graha office rather than his home, Suharto made an extended address to the hundred or so domestic and foreign journalists and senior officials in attendance, during which he attempted to lay the rumours to rest; he presented to the press a bevy of aged relatives and acquaintances who could testify to the truth of what he said: 'I am a child born in the village of Kemusuk and, indeed, the son of a farmer from Kemusuk'. In Suharto's view, the allegations made in the *POP* article were of such a kind as to raise serious disputation and differences within society, since they provided a 'good opportunity for subversion' and disturbing national stability, and would bring shame on the nation and create distrust in its leader.[10]

Notwithstanding Suharto's 1974 elucidation, numerous aspects of the story of his birth and early life remain elusive and unclear. There are some puzzling discrepancies and oddities in these official and semi-official accounts.[11] For example, Roeder names Kertosudiro's mother as the midwife at Suharto's birth; Suharto himself names his father's uncle's wife as his midwife. An official account from 1973 relates that Sukirah endured a seclusion of forty days after her divorce, not the week mentioned in other sources. Again, in his account in 1974, Suharto states that his father separated from his first wife and married Sukirah; in his autobiography, however, he states that his father's first wife died. Roeder dates the separation of Suharto's parents to a time two years after Suharto's birth; Suharto's own account makes it clear that it happened soon after his birth. Roeder implies that Suharto was reared in the house of his paternal grandmother after his parents' separation; Probosutejo, however, claims that he lived with his maternal grandmother. Roeder places Suharto's move to live with his aunt and her family at age 9, while the genealogy in Suryohadi (p. 8) makes him 8 years old. Roeder also mysteriously calls Suharto's mother 'Fatimah', rather than Sukirah, an error that came about, Suharto suggests, 'because the name Fatimah is the name of the younger sister of my mother'. Roeder gives Tiwir as the place where Suharto began school; Suharto himself later states that it was in the village of Pulihan. In Roeder's account, and Suharto's recent autobiographical recounting, Suharto's father took him to the Prawirowiharjo family in Solo (a place in which Suharto is said to have taken great delight), and only later did the family move to Wuryantoro; in Suharto's 1974 account, the journey was made directly to the Prawirowiharjos' home in Wuryantoro. Roeder makes no mention whatsoever of Suharto's being brought back from Wuryantoro to live in Kemusuk.

There are other matters as well which require explanation. How was it, for example, that a man so apparently poor as Kertosudiro could afford to send his child to school at so young an age, and at a time when only a tiny proportion of Indonesians received any kind of formal education? How could it be that Suharto's father remains such a shadowy figure, appearing at the time of his birth, and then disappearing (apart from those times when they 'met occasionally'), coming into the picture again only at times when Suharto's best interests needed catering for, or in the guise of the friendly gift-giver, donating a goat – an expensive present for a poor, landless peasant – to the young boy Suharto?

It is at least conceivable that the true story varies considerably from this official tale. At the outset, it seems very unlikely that Suharto himself was closely related to any person with royal blood in the Yogya *kraton* (palace), although Notosudiro, Suharto's maternal great-grandfather, had taken for his wife a woman descended, by a distance of five generations, from the princely son of Hamengkubuwono V by his first concubine. But the picture of shadowy parents, an obviously distraught mother, a father who disappears almost immediately after Suharto's birth but who nonetheless keeps a watching brief on his progress, is certainly in accord with the notion that Suharto was an illegitimate child. If this notion is true, it is possible that Suharto's real father was a person of some means, certainly not just a village irrigation official who was so poor that 'he did not himself own even an inch of land'.[12] He may well have enjoyed a higher official post. He may have been someone outside the village who arranged for Kertosudiro to play a father's role – admittedly in a limited way – and to ensure Suharto's overall progress. Indeed, Suharto's former neighbour and close associate, Mashuri, later expressed the view that Suharto's father was a peripatetic village trader of Chinese descent.[13]

Whatever the case – and in my view the notion of illegitimacy is perhaps the most compelling one – Suharto was anything but the simple son of a villager.

While he played a part in village life, it was essentially an ancillary job to his major occupation as student, and his romantic remembrances of village life – eating eels, tending cattle – have the strained quality of one trying one's best to be what one is not. Education of the kind Suharto enjoyed over many years was exceptional for most Javanese peasants; generally speaking, their labour was so valuable that it could not be wasted in such dubious activities as schooling.

What, then, can we conclude about Suharto's earliest days? It seems reasonable to conclude that he was the illegitimate child of a well-placed villager, probably one with connections beyond the village, or someone of some means who might come in continuing contact with villagers. He was, in fact, farmed out to relatives from an early age and, indeed, taken out of the village. The opportunities he enjoyed for education were extraordinary by the standards of village life at the time. From the age of about 8 – notwithstanding later reports of his youth spent within the village environment[14] – whatever close contact he had with village life was effectively ended, when he joined the family of a lower Javanese official living in a town and saw village life from the perspective of officialdom on those occasions when he accompanied Prawirowiharjo on his inspection tours.

WURYANTORO

Once finally established in Wuryantoro, Suharto seems to have experienced a more settled existence. He continued his primary school education (apparently riding a bicycle part way to the school), began to receive formal religious instruction – though his circumcision was delayed until he was 14, allegedly because of lack of funds – joined the Hizbul wathon scouts, and seems to have modelled himself on the moral pattern set by his foster-father, Prawirowiharjo. Judging from his later accounts, he was a persistent but not brilliant student; there is no sense that he was developing a sophisticated view of the world from his studies. Rather, his fundamentalist mental universe was best represented by his increasing attachment to aphorism, something that was to mark his life thereafter. Put simply, he developed the view that useful knowledge could be encapsulated into a collection of wise sayings that were timeless and which, if followed, would provide their own reward. Thus,

> At that time I learned about the three 'don'ts': 'don't be startled [that is, troubled], don't be surprised, don't be arrogant'. These later became the guiding principles of my life, which stiffened me in facing problems which might have shaken me. I always remember the teachings of our ancestors: 'respect for God, teacher, government and both parents'. Even after I became President, I have not changed in this matter in the slightest. I hold these teachings in high esteem and I believe in their truth.[15]

The demands of Suharto's education soon brought yet another change of domicile. In 1931, in order to attend the first year of junior high school (*schakelschool*) at Wonogiri, he moved, together with Prawirowiharjo's second son Sulardi, to Selogiri, a few kilometres outside Wonogiri. There he stayed with another relative; Sulardi's elder brother, Sudiarto, was already in residence. At Wonogiri's Hollandsch-Inlandsche School (Dutch-Native school), Sulardi was joined in class in 1933 by the daughter of the newly arrived district chief of Wonogiri, R. M. Sumoharyomo. Siti Hartinah, two years younger than Suharto, became a social associate of Sulardi; she would later become Suharto's wife. According to Abdul Gafur, Siti Hartinah's biographer, the Sumoharyomo family developed a strong and close relationship with the Prawirowiharjo family once they moved to Wuryantoro around 1937. Suharto may have come to know his future wife then, even though he did not return to live with the Prawirowiharjos until the late 1930s.

After a period at Selogiri, Suharto, now aged about 13, was forced to move yet again, this time taken by his father to Wonogiri because of a family break-up at Selogiri; in Wonogiri, he lived with the childless family of a relative of his father, Harjowiyono, a retired railway worker. In these circumstances, Suharto was required to perform many tasks around the house, 'like a house boy',[16] ranging from cleaning to cooking, shopping, and collecting water; these, he later reflected, saw him become 'a worker, someone who could stand on his own feet if necessary' and 'learn many things quickly'.[17] There is some indication that he was treated rather badly at his Wonogiri home, receiving no pay and feeding himself from the family's leftover meals.

Through Pak Harjo, Suharto became acquainted with the locally well-known Javanese mystic and religious teacher Kiai Daryatmo, who also worked as an irrigation official. Both in the company of Pak Harjo and, later, on his own, he was a frequent visitor to Daryatmo's house, hanging about the place, absorbing the discussions and teachings he overheard when Daryatmo entered into discussion with or gave advice to those who came to consult him about religious, philosophical or medical matters. The relationship with Daryatmo was a special one, and it seems clear that Suharto, already apparently predisposed to devotional practices, absorbed a great deal of spiritual backboning from him. Daryatmo remained in Suharto's life long after; he was consulted for advice by Suharto in the early 1950s when he was a regimental commander in Salatiga, and regularly afterwards as well.

The difficulty of finding sufficient money for the regulated school clothing at Wonogiri was the reason, according to Suharto, for still another move, this time back to Kemusuk, whence he rode each day by bicycle to continue his higher school studies at a Muhammadiyah school – 'more extended lower education', as the Dutch called it – in the city of Yogyakarta where, it seems, there were no such clothing regulations and where he completed the second grade.[18] Suharto has little to remark about his experiences in Yogyakarta, which, according to a leading nationalist figure, 'was well known as the centre of the movement for national independence' in the late 1920s.[19] He notes that it was there that he first heard of indigenous protest at the colonial order, and about the organisation of meetings to discuss matters. His reaction was that of most of his fellows at the time who took little interest in strange and potentially dangerous new movements: 'All this did not yet make a strong impression on me'.[20]

When he finally completed his schooling in 1939, Suharto was around 17 years old. In the context of the times and the fate of his fellows, this was an extraordinarily privileged level of educational achievement, even though formally he had not reached a high standard of schooling. It is, moreover, curious that he relates that his father and others could afford to educate him no longer, and that he had finally to embark on the world of work.[21] Notwithstanding the difficulties caused by his early fragmented life, Suharto appears to have borne no animosity to those who reared him and shows a genuine regard or fondness for them; fate had dealt him this life, and he himself had to face and solve fate's consequences:

> My ideas about life are based on belief in God, belief in His Power. Thus, I firmly believe that whatever God wills is certain to happen. Because of this, I believe that the fate of humankind is traced by God. Every single thing which God wills for humankind and for the entire world will happen. Therefore, there is no point in being regretful or troubled. We just leave it all to fate. There is no need to be shocked. The fact that some people seem to have been the subject of special treatment should not be a cause of astonishment. There is no need for us to be wide-eyed and say, 'That's terrific'. Just see God's hand in it, and we won't be astonished. If we have position, wealth and have something more than others, don't forget that in time it can change if God so wills it. Therefore, if we have a high position we should not act arbitrarily, and those with abundant riches should not forget where they came from.[22]

Suharto's intensely self-regarding autobiography reveals little of the human side of his youth. Apart from his clear distaste with his experiences living with Pak Harjo in Wonogiri, we have no everyday sense of his life: his social relations, his daily routines, the material circumstances of his life in various places, his remembrance of emerging maturity. He mentions that he played soccer with his friends at Wuryantoro, but names only a couple of boyhood friends: Kamin and Warikin.[23] The latter later reminisced that Suharto played in defence, but often scored goals; 'he could run fast, his muscles were as strong as rattan, his body tough. He attacked the ball and played hard'.[24]

We know nothing about his other social interests and leisure pursuits, although he later reminisced about his foster-father in Wuryantoro taking him along on his agricultural inspection trips and to the Sunday market to check out prices.[25] Nor do we have much sense of his evolving intellectual capacities and interests – what he learned in school and what he thought of it or his sense of place and history. He was, we can safely assume, no reader; there is no mention of anything like the 'hundreds of [Dutch] children's books and novels' which the renowned nationalist leader, Syahrir, read in his childhood,[26] nor anything approximating the claim of Sukarno, Indonesia's first president, that 'all my time was spent reading. While others played, I studied. I pursued knowledge beyond mere lessons'.[27] Suharto's social life and education had been solely monolingual; there is no evidence that he learned Dutch or other languages or knew anything of them. There is, indeed, no sense of his ever having experienced any Europeans, although he must have done, or espousing any interest in European traditions; there is, equally, no sense or acknowledgement of the fact of the colonised status of his land.

The emotional and material trials of his childhood and youth shaped an introspective and exceedingly self-reliant turn of mind, what McIntyre calls 'an emotional autarchy'; 'I always remember the experiences and difficulties of my childhood', Suharto later remarked, 'and that is why I always stress the importance of knowing and being true to oneself'.[28] His characteristic mode of examining and solving confusion, puzzles and problems of self-esteem was to look inward, not outward.

FROM SCHOOL TO WORK

Suharto found it difficult to find work in Kemusuk (although he gives no indication of the kind of work he was seeking), and decided to try his luck in Wuryantoro (presumably living once more with the family of his aunt), where 'I knew a lot of people who I hoped would be able to open doors for me'. He was, finally, successful in obtaining a job as a clerical assistant in the local village bank (*Volksbank*) in Wuryantoro, accompanying the bank clerk as he did his rounds by bicycle, in full Javanese dress, collecting applications for credit. While Suharto claims not to have enjoyed the work and to have found it uninteresting, he managed to master book-keeping by studying at night, and he also took to reading the newspapers and magazines that came through the office. However, an accident which tore his clothes – which, he claims, rather strangely, his aunt could not afford to replace – cost him his job.[29]

Upon leaving his employment at the village bank, Suharto first thought to enlist in the Dutch navy but, on his account, quickly changed his mind when he discovered (perhaps remembering his Wonogiri experiences) that he had been nominated to be a cook. He sought work without success in Solo, and returned once more to Wuryantoro where he worked as a labourer on infrastructure projects. Finally, and probably with some desperation, he sought a three-year enlistment in the KNIL (Royal Netherlands Indies Army).[30] The opportunity probably arose simply because, with the threat of approaching war, the Dutch were recruiting heavily for their colonial army, which numbered about 35,000 in 1938. Suharto was not the first, nor the last, to throw in his lot with the army when other prospects looked bleak. He began his service on 1 June 1940.

Suharto's basic military training was conducted at the KNIL school at Gombong, west of Yogyakarta, where 'we trained from morning till night' and where, he later claimed, he began to study Dutch.[31] Having passed the training course 'first in my class' – not the last time, truthfully or not, he was to make this claim – Suharto was assigned to Battalion XIII at Rampal, near Malang, late in 1940 or early in 1941.[32] A short stint of night-guard duty at Gresik saw him contract malaria; after returning to Malang, he had a recurrence which caused him to be hospitalised for about two weeks. Thereafter he returned to Gombong, where he was accepted into the cadre school for training as a sergeant.

WAR

Once he had completed training and been promoted to sergeant, the outbreak of war saw Suharto attached to the Reserves at army headquarters in Bandung. A week after he took up his posting at Cisarua, the Dutch surrendered to the invading Japanese. Rather than run the risk of being captured and interned, he abandoned his uniform and fled back to Wuryantoro, where he immediately succumbed to another bout of malaria. Unable to find work in Wuryantoro, he moved to Yogyakarta, tried to learn typing, and fell ill with malaria again; 'I really had to learn patience, gaining a mastery of myself which would be useful later on'.[33]

Once recovered, on 1 November 1942 – the date on which police affairs were formally passed from the *Kempeitai* (Japanese military police) to the newly structured occupation police force – Suharto availed himself of an opportunity to join the police force. Presumably his uncle, Prawirowiharjo, made use of his connections to help Suharto gain the position since, according to Roeder, Suharto heard of the chance to join while still in Wuryantoro. Once enlisted, he was dispatched for a three-month training course in Yogyakarta, which he 'passed, first in the class' because of his previous experience in the KNIL. He was assigned as assistant to the Yogyakarta chief of police, apparently at the rank of *keibuho* (assistant inspector). It is not clear just what Suharto did in the occupation police force, although he mentions that 'because I passed first in the class I was made a courier and then told to learn Japanese'.[34] Given the emphasis of the police on the maintenance of internal security ('criminal matters became a secondary problem; what was most important were matters of a political kind'),[35] he may there have had his first experience of intelligence work. Equally, he may simply have served in a routine administrative role.

At the suggestion of his Japanese chief of police, he sought to joint the Peta (Defenders of the Fatherland), a Japanese-trained and Indonesian-officered self-defence force, formed in October 1943. Peta's professedly defensive intent, to hold the line against threatening Allied attack and invasion, was reflected in its limited and localised structures: it was essentially a collection of local battalions (*daidan*), with no higher organisational structure, nor horizontal contact with other local battalions. Presumably, Suharto's desire to join Peta was opportunistically rather than ideologically driven; his political consciousness at the time was still minimal, and his choice driven by the chance to continue his previously interrupted military career.

Upon his acceptance into Peta – he was, he claimed, one of only two selected from 500 applicants – Suharto was sent on a platoon commander's (*shodancho*) course, which he found 'quite difficult'.[36] Given his background, and the fact that most candidate Peta officers had *priyayi* backgrounds or were at least the products of the upper echelons of village society, his selection probably indicates the benefits of patronage and his rank within the occupation police force, as well as providing further indication of his unusual level of educational achievement; generally, shodancho candidates were required to have at least a junior high school education. Moreover, given that 'the criteria for selecting the candidate-shodancho were usually evidence of leadership qualities, "spirit" (*semangat*) and physical fitness',[37] Suharto must already have given some evidence of the traits the Japanese required in their Peta officers. Presumably he began his shodancho training – lasting about nine weeks – in mid-October, before the first Peta battalions (most of them formed in southern Java) were created in December 1943.

The Peta training regime was grim and highly disciplined, and Suharto, 'thin and small' at the time, found it hard going.[38] It emphasised the attainment of physical fitness and spiritual strength and toughness. It was a '"translation" of the Japanese *bushido* into Indonesian lore. The Japanese instructors sincerely gave their Indonesian pupils all the warrior's values which they themselves have received at their military schools'.[39]

For the first time, it appears, ideas of a nationalist kind began to impress themselves upon the young trainee Suharto; indeed, he describes Japanese efforts at indoctrination as creating a 'fighting spirit among us, as sons of Indonesia, to defend our own land'.[40] The Japanese captain responsible for Suharto's Peta company later recalled that Suharto was 'a very patriotic young man'.[41] This development in his consciousness and values was not just a reflection of crude and counterproductive Japanese ideologising – even then, Japanese propaganda appears to have evoked a large measure of cynicism in him – but, more important, their racist attitudes towards the Javanese, and the harsh treatment which he both witnessed and experienced personally under their rule ('the desire grew within me to fight back against these people who had hurt us so deeply').[42] Equally important, perhaps – since Suharto was never one to push new and untried ideas in environments where their acceptance might be contentious – was the fact that such notions were becoming common currency amongst those with whom he mixed. Nugroho remarks that 'the roots [of patriotism] could be found in the *ksatrian* (barracks) of the *daidan*'.[43] This was an environment that Suharto much enjoyed, and discussions of matters of this kind were common amongst Peta troops. Accordingly, as Kahin remarks, 'by 1944 the average Peta member was consciously strongly nationalist, anti-Japanese, anti-Dutch', while Anderson adds that 'it was not only the experience of being in the Peta but the specific ideological training the institution provided that created and heightened the nationalist political consciousness of its members'.[44] It is important, as well, to note that Peta remained entirely free from any civilian control or authority, something later reflected both in the reluctance of former Peta officers during the revolution to submit to civilian direction and in the development of a model of the socio-political positioning of the Armed Forces within Indonesian society.

It was a matter of policy that Peta members should serve in their own regions in order to enhance their enthusiasm to defend against Allied attack. Thus, his training course successfully completed, Suharto – presumably dress-uniformed in the Peta officer's white shirt, green jacket, green riding trousers and green cap, together with a smaller version of the Japanese sword – found himself transferred to a battalion in Wates, near Yogyakarta, where his duties included a stretch of coastal defence at Glagah, south of Yogya; shortly thereafter he was admitted to a company commander's (*chudancho*) course at Bogor, a three-month training stint which he probably began in April 1944 and finished in August. Upon its completion, he was sent to Peta headquarters in Solo, where he was kept busy conducting training, and then to Jakarta for similar work, before returning to Peta headquarters, now situated in Madiun. Thereafter he was dispatched south to Brebeg, to an uninhabited stretch of the slopes of Mt Wilis, in order to train Peta *bundancho*[45] to replace those executed by the Japanese after the failed revolt of Peta units at Blitar in February 1945. That Suharto was selected to assist in re-establishing the Blitar battalion in a context of significant Japanese concern about local security is an indication that he enjoyed considerable esteem amongst the Japanese for his reliability and, perhaps, that he held no deep sympathy for the Indonesian victims of the failed revolt.

The last months of the Japanese occupation were extraordinarily trying for the inhabitants of Java, with rampant inflation, severe unemployment, local food production deficits (in part the result of Japanese forced delivery policies and the maladministration to which they were subject), epidemics, large-scale forced labour under desperate conditions, the distribution channels for food and other essentials twisted or emptied by gathering official corruption, and want evident almost everywhere. There was 'a sense of moral crisis, of the traditional order's being upturned, of a transvaluation of normal values'.[46] The practice (not policy) of strict Residency-level independence in food supplies brought a proliferating culture of corruption and black marketeering. It may well be that this was Suharto's first experience of the need to find his own sources of supply for his troops, and his first dabblings in the market.

It was in Brebeg that Suharto first heard the news of the Japanese surrender and the proclamation of Indonesian independence in Jakarta by the nationalist leaders Sukarno and Mohammad Hatta. The proclamation, hurriedly and perfunctorily performed on the morning of 17 August as Sukarno and Hatta, after some persuasion, seized the historical opportunity presented by the surrender, was to invoke a period of decisive and often chaotic change in the lives of Indonesians. Suharto, as we shall see, was strongly affected; he later recalled his reaction: 'Hey, this is a call to duty'.[47] His close involvement with Japanese-sponsored organisations provides some clues to the development of his political and social thinking. According to Kahin, speaking of Indonesian youth between about 15 and 25, 'the sustained and intense Japanese propaganda left its mark. It narrowed and intensified their nationalist sentiments. Few developed a pro-Japanese orientation, but many developed an extremely militant nationalism with a strong, emotional anti-Western bias which frequently verged on sheer hatred'.[48] Anderson speaks, in somewhat exaggerated terms, of the theatrically romantic aspects of the style of Japanese occupation politics;[49] perhaps they had their own emotional impact on Suharto, seemingly confirming in him a desire to fight tenaciously in the cause of a nationalist ideal with which he had hardly been acquainted in the pre-war years.

CONCLUSION

At the end of the Japanese occupation of Java, the 24-year-old Suharto was no more than a moderately promising member of a ragged volunteer army. With a few brief exceptions, he had spent all his life within the uninspiring confines of rural and small-town south-central Java. He had endured a long but unexciting education, drawing more from his association with Daryatmo than from his formal teachers. But he enjoyed what he did, and he did it well enough to draw the attention of his superiors; the regimented life of barracks and field gave him a compass for his life, and a sense of surety and purpose which he had hitherto lacked. He had, as well, been strongly influenced by Japanese ideas of service and devotion to country, in ways, perhaps, that only recent converts to faith might appreciate. Suharto was well placed to take creative advantage of the larger forces that were to shape the fate that awaited his country and people.

2 Soldier in the revolution

DURING HIS LONG presidential rule, Suharto made much of the central national symbolism of the Indonesian Republic's battle against the returning Dutch from 1945 to 1949. In the larger picture, however, his personal role in the revolution was neither significant nor decisive, notwithstanding the later efforts of New Order historians, and Suharto himself, to embellish it.[1] However, like many of his generation, his vision of what Indonesia should be was shaped in fundamental ways by the many-faceted and complex struggles, political as well as military, and internally as well as externally oriented, of the revolutionary period. It was, as Feith remarks, 'a peculiarly central experience for all those who were actively involved in it',[2] and it was to prove for Suharto amongst the most fertile phases of his life.

ORGANISING FOR STRUGGLE

Soon after the Japanese surrender on 15 August 1945, Japanese forces in Java began the process of arranging military affairs for the imminent arrival of Allied troops. Suharto, like other Peta soldiers, found himself dismissed and his arms and equipment seized by the Japanese. Probably confused and uncertain at what this rapid sequence of events might mean and what it might presage, he returned to Yogyakarta to stay with a relative. He was, however, caught up with the tumult of post-proclamation fervour – not the last time that he was to capitalise upon events not of his making and turn them to good effect. Amongst his involvements was one with a group of students, activists, fighters and intellectuals, led by Dayno and centred around the Pathuk district of Yogya, which counted amongst its numbers a certain figure later known as Syam Kamaruzzaman, who was central to the 1965 'coup attempt'.[3] At about the same time, Suharto assisted in calling together former Peta comrades to form a fighting unit of around company size, under the leadership of Umar Slamet, a former chudancho in Bantul, with Suharto himself serving as his deputy. This group may have been part of a broader force, 'a militant youth organisation with a military bent' and with a membership including schoolchildren: the General Guard Unit, established by Slamet, Siswondo Parman and Sudharto in the days immediately after the proclamation.[4]

This organisation soon rolled into the Yogyakarta branch of the BKR (People's Security Body), established by the government as a quasi-police force on 22 August. On 5 October 1945 the government, finally emboldened to establish its own hierarchically organised military force in place of the BKR units which were both confused as to their proper role and function and uncontrolled from above, took the step, post-factum, of creating an Indonesian army: the TKR (People's Defence Army).[5] Notwithstanding such formalities, indigenous armed power remained determinedly local, territorially based and mostly uncoordinated, as well as poorly armed, and was subject to little central control. Many of these bands took the form of spontaneously developed *lasykar rakyat* (popular militias), irregular and localised auxiliary paramilitary groups, under no wider or more systematic control, which, in Yogyakarta, developed 'largely on the initiative of the Sultan of Jogjakarta'.[6] Others were the newly formed paramilitary wings of political organisations like Pesindo (Indonesian Socialist Youth) or Masyumi (Council of Indonesian Muslim Associations).

The efforts of the first chief of the General Staff, Urip Sumoharjo, to create an orderly and efficient hierarchy were no match for the forces from below which shaped institutions according to their, not Urip's, liking. His efforts, perforce, were more akin to divining the shape of the creature he was attempting to capture and placing authority on those who emerged by a kind of armed popular choice; it was no accident that the formal shape of the Army changed so much and so pervasively in the early months of the revolutionary period. Indonesian armed power at this time has been nicely characterised as 'a swarming mass of heterogeneous armed groups that grew up from the bottom on the basis of personal loyalties and fighting experience'.[7]

The immediately necessary task of such armed bodies was to wrest arms and equipment from the Japanese. Suharto claims to have led a number of attacks in and around Yogyakarta which had this aim in view, and which enjoyed varying degrees of success.[8] They included a battle on 7 October with the Japanese garrison at Kotabaru, on the north-eastern fringe of the city, which ended with a Japanese surrender to republican forces. Suharto's own account of his experiences as a military leader in the early days of the revolution, like his later tales, does not suffer from a surfeit of modesty. He portrays himself as a wise strategist, as well as a fearless fighter with more than a touch of bravado.

It is unclear what drove him at this time. His experiences from the time of his enlistment in the Dutch colonial army in 1940 had confirmed his liking for the hierarchy, discipline, order, and close and trusted fellowship of military life. He knew it fitted him well and allowed him to give expression to his personal talents. He had been, in the past, a loyal and obedient servant of both Dutch and Japanese military masters, even when neither had the interests of Indonesians as their first priority, and his motives for enlisting in the service of the current authority were probably strongly and calculatedly self-interested. As we have seen, however – the heavily ideological thrust of Peta training and his experiences in wartime Java were doubtless important here – he was also well imbued, like many of his fellows, with an emotional and unsophisticated attachment to the utterly new concept of Indonesia, and the romanticism of the struggle to achieve it. In Suharto's case, emotion and the calculus of personal advantage dovetailed neatly.

Gradually, and not without considerable resistance from armed elements who prized their independence, the Army began to develop its organisational systems and practices. In the case of Yogyakarta, this development manifested itself in the first weeks of October in the formation of Division IX (Istimewa), comprising two regiments, under the command of the former Yogya region police chief and local powerbroker Colonel Sudarsono, into which Suharto's bands, as well as other local elements, were incorporated to form Battalion X. Within a few weeks of the proclamation, and certainly by October, Suharto's work in assisting in the establishment and organisation of local armed forces apparently led to his promotion to major and to command of Battalion X of Regiment I, stationed at Kotabaru. Suharto's ability to recruit and stand at the head of such a band – one of his recruits was a school student, Y. B. Mangunwijaya, later to become a celebrated Catholic priest and activist in Central Java – was, even then, a sign of his leadership capacities. Mangunwijaya later described him at that time in the following terms:

> Pak Harto was just a major. Still a bachelor, aloof [*anggun*], of good bearing, fearsome, his performance was good … As a leader he was certainly aloof, calm, never gossipy, never engaging in jokes. Even when he was chatting in a relaxed way with his officers, he was in charge. I was very impressed. His way of dressing was also neat.[9]

There was in Yogyakarta, as elsewhere in Java at this time, a gathering tendency, usually inspired by youth groups and combining self-righteousness with rebelliousness, to seize control of the symbols of civilian administration against the confused attempts of the Japanese (anxious, above all, to maintain law and order and looking to their own repatriation) to maintain the status quo. By late September 1945, Yogyakarta was effectively under Indonesian control. Notwithstanding cases of fierce fighting between Japanese and Indonesian forces, the Japanese authorities for the most part cooperated with Indonesian wishes, often handing over arms and equipment to Indonesian groupings in the process.

The policy of the Allied forces arriving in Java was limited in scope; it sought to release prisoners interned by the Japanese, to disarm and repatriate Japanese forces, and to secure law and order before handing back authority to the Dutch. In the highly limiting circumstances they faced, however, Allied forces restricted themselves to capturing the key port cities of Jakarta, Semarang and Surabaya, and then pushing into the hinterland areas where most of the internment camps lay. When the limited and badly stretched Allied troops first arrived in the Central Java city of Semarang on 20 October, they brought with them elements of the Netherlands Indies Civil Administration (NICA), itself a manifestation of Allied policy to restore the *status quo ante bellum* and a direct challenge to Indonesian sovereignty. An Allied advance team had already discovered in Central

Java 'evidence of the strength and purpose of the Nationalist movement ... everywhere. Not a house, nor a public building lacked its Indonesian flag'.[10] Allied efforts to press into the hinterland to release Dutch wartime internees in camps around Ambarawa and Magelang (where 24,000 prisoners-of-war and Dutch internees were thought to be held) brought armed resistance from militant Indonesian forces, including many irregular struggle groups, which had suffered grievously through the previous week in fierce and unsuccessful battles with Japanese troops to regain control of Semarang city. Allied forces pushed south with as much speed as they could muster; Gurkha units took Magelang on 26 October. Indonesian anxieties about Allied intentions, however, and rumours of vindictive behaviour by a Dutch officer, led to clashes between Allied forces and local Indonesian groups, the latter reinforced by their fellows from the south. A truce brokered by newly anointed President Sukarno and cabinet minister Amir Syarifuddin lasted only until the second week of November, when news of the major battle of Surabaya caused tensions to flow over in fighting once more. By 21 November the Allies had been forced to withdraw from Magelang, and from Ambarawa in mid-December. Suharto's Battalion X, part of a regiment commanded by Lt. Col. Sarbini, was involved in clashes at Magelang which forced the Allies back to Ambarawa. There, as well, Suharto was involved in fighting aimed at pushing Allied forces further back. The Indonesian resistance, in this 'period of total war',[11] succeeded in forcing the Allies to retreat to the confines of Semarang; 'the rest of Central Java was left completely in the hands of the Republic'.[12]

Suharto's actions in this fighting, as he recalls, brought him to the attention of the newly installed commander of the TKR, Sudirman, a former Peta *daidancho* (battalion commander). When Sudirman reorganised the Armed Forces at the end of 1945, Suharto was appointed commander of the Third Regiment, comprising four battalions, based in the Yogyakarta area (probably at Wiyoro, a village about 5 kilometres south-east of the city) and promoted to the rank of lieutenant colonel, probably early in 1946. It seems likely that Suharto, notwithstanding his generally apolitical attitude at the time, drew inspiration from Sudirman's efforts to construct an Indonesian army with a populist flavour which emphasised the institution's separateness from and disdain for the comings and goings of civilian politicians and which celebrated the virtue of unalloyed struggle for the national goal of independence.

By March 1946 the violence of the last months of 1945 had slackened, the lines of opposition between Dutch and republican fighters had settled, and the republican government was busily pursuing a diplomatic rather than military solution to conflict. At that time, according to Dutch intelligence, Suharto commanded Regiment III, Division IX (Istimewa), with three battalions (X, under Major Sujono; XX, under Major Sarjono; and XXV, under Major Basyuni). His regiment seems to have numbered about 2,250 men. As a result of a further army reorganisation announced in late May 1946, Java's ten divisions were reduced to seven, and an amalgamation of former divisions V (Pekalongan-Kedu) and IX produced Division III, under Major-General Sudarsono's command, with front responsibility for the Pekalongan, Kedu and Yogyakarta areas; Suharto's troops were incorporated into the new division. Around the same time, Dutch forces in Semarang assumed authority from Allied troops on 17 May 1946, presaging the development of a heightened state of tension and fighting along the front, with each side probing for advantage and weakness. The Dutch T ('Tiger') Brigade attempted to push south from Semarang, again the occasion of further republican armed resistance around Kendal, in which Suharto was involved, and which succeeded in stopping the Dutch advance. Suharto and selected units under his command continually moved back and forth from their bases to man the front line.

It was about this time in 1946 that Suharto learned that his mother was ill, and he claims to have visited her before moving to the front lines to help repel Dutch attacks.[13] When his mother died shortly thereafter as a result of a stomach tumour, Suharto was on duty at the front and therefore unable to see or mourn her. 'But she [had been] able to see her son become an officer, and also to become a battalion commander in Yogyakarta.'[14] Strangely, he notes in his autobiography that he 'went quickly to the village of Kemusuk to my mother's grave',[15] even though she had been buried at the gravesite of the Notosudiro and Atmosudiro families at Gunung Pale.

There were already signs that Suharto's military reputation was growing. In December 1945, the lack of coordination between various fighting units during battles to the south of Semarang had led to a series of meetings between commanders which resulted in the formation of a Battle Leadership Headquarters (MPP). In early June 1946, when Lt. Col. Sunarto Kusumodirjo took command of the MPP, he included Suharto among a number of officers asked to provide working guidelines ('clear and practical') for the use of the MPP.

THE 3 JULY AFFAIR

The Republic's armed opposition to the reimposition of Dutch colonial rule masked serious divisions with the civilian political elite. Because of his prior association with the Japanese, Sukarno himself had been forced to hand over effective power to a prime minister, Sutan Syahrir, as the infant Republic adopted a new form of government in which the prime minister was responsible to an appointed semi-parliament: the KNIP (Central Indonesian National Committee). Other forces of a more revolutionary kind, however, were unhappy at the conservative cast of the republican government, and even less content at its apparent readiness to persist with negotiations with the returning Dutch rather than to adopt the course of relentless struggle for independence. Such forces, which had their champions in both the civilian and military spheres, coalesced around the charismatic figure of Tan Malaka, an old-time revolutionary from colonial days who had returned to the Indies in 1942. Groups amongst them conspired, in the early months of 1946, to attempt to force Sukarno to adopt a more forthright policy: an immediate and, if necessary, violent seizure of independence in its fullness.

Suharto found himself, probably incidentally, directly involved in the continuing internal strife between these radical forces and the cautious and hesitant government led by Syahrir and Amir Syarifuddin which had set its course on a diplomatic settlement with the Dutch. In this battle of minds and worlds, Sudirman and other senior military figures were much attracted by the first camp. The extraordinarily convoluted struggle came to a climax with the kidnapping of Prime Minister Syahrir in the Central Java city of Solo on the night of 27 June 1946, a strategy carried out, as one of its champions (Adam Malik, later the New Order foreign minister) later asserted, 'with the blessing of general Sudirman'.[16] Strong government reaction to Syahrir's arrest brought his almost immediate release. The government then moved to arrest the kidnap plotters, who included Sudarsono, allegedly sympathetic to the thinking of Tan Malaka and the leading military figure in the anti-Syahrir conspiracy. Indeed, it had been on his authority that Syahrir had been kidnapped by his collaborator, A. K. Yusuf, commander of Battalion 63, Yogya's city guard.

What followed exceeded in complexity anything that had already transpired. Messages ordering the arrest of Sudarsono and Yusuf were conveyed to Suharto at Wiyoro. According to his autobiography, he received two separate orders: one conveyed orally by a Yogya youth leader named Sunjoyo, the other a written instruction from Sukarno himself. According to this account, Suharto, confronted with the daunting task of arresting his acclaimed divisional commander who, it appears, had assumed the support or at least neutrality of Suharto in the affair, baulked at the assignment and returned the written orders to Sukarno, requesting that they be issued through Sudirman. Suharto's precise relationship with Sudarsono is not clear; quite possibly he was broadly sympathetic with the general drift of the anti-government movement, and he doubtless felt a strong sense of loyalty to his commander, 'the hero of Yogyakarta in the days when the pemuda [young people] wrested arms from the Japanese'.[17]

However, Suharto's testimony at Sudarsono's 1948 trial was rather different from his autobiographical account. In that testimony, he stated that, having been made aware of the arrest order on Sudarsono, he called a meeting of his battalion commanders which 'unanimously' agreed to carry out the arrest of Sudarsono on their own (*atas dirinya*), 'with the utmost prudence and discretion'.[18] Suharto set up surveillance and patrols to 'prevent bloodshed', and suggested a strategy to his divisional chief of staff, Umar Joi, that would maintain the unity of the Division and secure the arrest of Sudarsono and Yusuf in a manner which would not rob them of their dignity. Yusuf was brought to Wiyoro by Sarjono, one of Suharto's battalion commanders; Suharto explained to Yusuf that he was forced to detain him, and that it was better that he remain at Wiyoro. Suharto also proposed to Umar Joi that he 'suggest' to Sudarsono that he 'take a break' at Wiyoro; once he had arrived, Suharto explained that it was his intention to protect him.

Of the two accounts, the second seems more probable. It is highly unlikely that a junior officer like Suharto, especially one with a narrow-minded sense of duty, would flatly refuse to obey a presidential order. It is much more probable that he went through the motions of 'arresting' Sudarsono, probably conniving with Umar Joi in so doing, while he waited to gain a clearer sense of where Sudirman stood in the contest and what the likely outcome might be. His experience of the chaotic, comical goings-on of Sudarsono's party at Wiyoro on the evening of 2–3 July could not have filled him with confidence at the ultimate success of Sudarsono's plot. Once he became aware that Sudirman had distanced himself from Sudarsono, and that support for Sudarsono's group was not high amongst armed groups in Yogya, he quickly adopted a pose of outright support for the status quo.

So things turned out. When Sudarsono on 2 July sought protection from the commander of Regiment IV, Lt. Col. Sukandar, headquartered in the city, a battalion from Suharto's regiment was one of the two units called up to guard divisional headquarters. Still feeling insecure, Sudarsono, at the suggestion either of Suharto or Umar Joi, followed Umar to Suharto's regimental headquarters at Wiyoro, apparently confident that he would be safe there. Sudarsono then set off for Solo in answer to a summons from Sudirman, who was angered at the government's arrests of other plotters on 1 July. Rightly or wrongly, Sudarsono took from his meeting with Sudirman an understanding that Sudirman wished him to secure the release of the plotters from the Wirogunan jail in Yogyakarta and to press the case with the President for thoroughgoing changes in the cabinet.

It seems likely, as Suharto asserts, that there were communications between Sudirman and a Suharto increasingly perplexed at the sequence of events unfolding before him through the night of 2–3 July.[19] Sudirman, for his part, probably had become alarmed that Sudarsono and the other radicals had moved beyond their earlier manoeuvrings to a higher and less inhibited plane of intensity, and wished to distance himself from the complication of being identified too closely with their actions. Suharto's view of the significance of Sudarsono's action hardened from its earlier prevarication and uncertainty that evening, something almost certainly attributable to advice from Sudirman that he himself was not a party to the plot, and that it had exceeded the bounds of acceptability.

Arriving back in Yogya about 3 a.m. on 3 July, Sudarsono ordered the release of the fourteen recently arrested prisoners, loaded them in a truck and sent them, under Yusuf's care, to the Wiyoro headquarters of a now-sleeping Suharto. Earlier in the night at Suharto's headquarters, while Sudarsono was busying himself with his conversations with Sudirman, his release of the Wirogunan prisoners, and, later still, another trip to Yogya to organise military support and neutralise potential military opposition, Sudarsono's civilian accomplices hurriedly drafted four proclamations, framed in Sukarno's name, which called for the sacking of Syahrir's cabinet, the handover of Sukarno's defence and security powers to Sudirman and a 'Political Leadership Council', and the appointment of a fresh cabinet.[20]

In the midst of all these activities, Suharto later claimed, his suspicions were aroused by Sudarsono's behaviour, especially his instruction to Yusuf to telephone Tawangmangu (where Tan Malaka was imprisoned) and to fetch (that is, kidnap) Hatta and Amir, and he became convinced that 'they were going to carry out actions which were not right'.[21] He himself went to Yogya to alert Battalion X to prevent Yusuf carrying out his kidnapping mission. As it turned out, he was too late, but Amir had in any case escaped kidnap and Yusuf was later captured by the battalion.

Around 7 a.m. on 3 July, all the plotters entered Yogyakarta and proceeded to the presidential palace. Sudarsono, apparently claiming to be acting under the authority of Sudirman, requested Sukarno to sign the prepared instruments. Suharto alleges in his autobiography that he alerted Sukarno about what was afoot, but the fact that he did not make this claim in his 1948 testimony at the trial of the plotters leads one to suspect that he did no such thing. In any event, Sukarno, probably kept abreast of events by Sudirman, as well as others in Yogya whose suspicions and fears had been aroused by the activities of Sudarsono and Yusuf, responded by arresting the unfortunate Sudarsono, whose military backing had failed to materialise at the palace. Suharto himself closed off the city of Yogyakarta to outside forces.

With the scandal of Sudarsono's arrest, disarray set into Division III, especially over the question of the future divisional commander. Sukarno placed Suharto in charge of the Division on a temporary basis, presumably because the events of early July had demonstrated his loyalty to the government, and a flurry of other regimental commanders put themselves forward for the job. After much dispute and confusion, and with Suharto refusing to accept the divisional command on a continuing basis, the post was finally given, under pressure from junior officers and much against the wishes of Sudirman and Urip (who attempted unsuccessfully to appoint another senior officer, Gen. Maj. Sudiro), to an outsider: Col. Susalit from Cirebon. Suharto was probably mightily relieved to have escaped from the collateral taint of his apparent 'protection' of Sudarsono at Wiyoro – a press statement expressing Division III's profound regret about and ignorance of Sudarsono's actions was published in *Kedaulatan Rakyat* on 8 July 1946, over the name of Umar Joi as deputy (*wakil*) commander (*panglima*), Division III – and saw no immediate future for himself as the senior commander in so confused an atmosphere. No doubt he took valuable lessons from the affair's denouement: the importance of wariness when the stakes were high and the lines of disputation unclear, the need to commit only when the winning side was evident, the necessity of holding one's nerve under pressure, the merit of keeping the favour of antagonistic forces until the last possible moment. Equally, qualities that were to become characteristic of him later were already on view: caution, coolness, calculated decisiveness when the time was right.

HOLDING THE LINE

Perhaps as a result of the internal tumult occasioned by the 3 July affair, Division III took on a new organisational shape in early August 1946, with six regiments divided into two brigades. VII Brigade contained the 17th and 18th regiments, and VIII Brigade the 19th, 20th, 22nd and 23rd regiments. Suharto's name, however, does not appear in any regimental command position in Dutch intelligence reports at the time. Indeed, his name does not appear at all in such reports of the Republican Order of Battle until 15 November 1946, when he was mentioned as commander of the 22nd Regiment of the Third ('Diponegoro') Division stationed at Yogyakarta; command of that regiment had previously been reported as being held by Lt. Col. Sukandar. It may well be that before the middle of 1946 Dutch intelligence was neither sufficiently extensive nor effective to provide detail of this kind – the reports are very sketchy to that time – but, from early July until October, Sukandar was probably acting in the place of Suharto after 3 July, releasing Suharto for the task of temporary command of the Division, and of working through and negotiating the backwash of the affair with other senior officers.

By late 1946, Division III was responsible for the defence of the west and south-western fronts against Dutch attack. Suharto's 22nd Regiment was one of three responsible for the western front. At first the defence front, two battalions strong, comprised a collection of companies from the three regiments, but because of leadership problems it was later decided to send battalions rather than companies. Leadership of the front rotated amongst regimental commanders and was headquartered at Kaliwungu. The front around Semarang remained a site of frequent clashes, although less fierce than had been the case in mid-year. Nonetheless, a certain stability and routinisation had descended upon the scene, as both the Republic and the Dutch adopted a more conciliatory tone which led to successful negotiations in November at the North Java hill town of Linggarjati, whereby the Dutch recognised the de facto authority of the Republic in Java and Sumatra and both parties agreed to work together to establish a federal United States of Indonesia.

Notwithstanding the successful discussions and the fact that, following Sudirman's cease-fire order of February 1947, 'the situation of the [Semarang] front was very quiet',[22] the front had still to be manned by troops rotating from their hinterland bases. Suharto's men were heavily involved. In early 1947, Dutch records note that the 22nd Regiment, IX Brigade, headquartered in Yogyakarta under Suharto's command, still comprised three battalions: one (Battalion III) probably stationed at Yogyakarta, another (Battalion IV) with two of its companies serving on the Semarang front (these 600 men having just been dispatched), and a third (Battalion VI) of uncertain location. By mid-1947, Suharto's 22nd Regiment, headquartered at Wiyoro, had grown to four battalions: I, under Major Sujono (Yogyakarta); II, under Major Sumiyarsono, at Kaliurang; III, under Sarjono, at Tanjungtirto; and IV, under Basyuni, at Wonosari.

Conditions in the republican areas were extremely difficult; according to one Dutch intelligence report, they were indeed a reason for a strong ebbing in support for the republican cause: 'People suffer hunger, lack of clothing and footwear, while disease is spreading. In some kampung people willingly let go of the idea of "Merdeka" [freedom] in return for better food with the Dutch'.[23] Presumably these same material conditions to some extent affected the troops under Suharto's care, although there is no direct evidence relating how he went about securing supplies of food, clothing and arms for them. Perhaps a clue can be gleaned from a later Dutch intelligence report from September 1949, which noted that 'great quantities of opium are regularly smuggled out of Yogya into the occupied areas. On the part of the Republicans there is on the whole no control exercised over this; on the contrary, Commander CPM Yogya, Major Dirgo and Lt. Col. Suharto,

Commander X Brigade, lend their cooperation to this smuggling'.[24] Certainly, Diponegoro officers had to adopt entrepreneurial modes of action in procuring the needs of their troops, a good part of which – arms, ammunition, clothing, food, medical supplies – was ferried in by such men as the Kudus-based Sino-Indonesian trader, Liem Siu Liong. The Fukien-born Liem was 20 years old when he arrived in Java and joined a family concern, eventually establishing his own clove trading business and expanding his range of activities, which, assisted by useful political connections – notably Sukarno's father-in-law, Hasan Din – came to include trade between his north coast headquarters and Diponegoro commanders in the Central Java hinterland.

THE FIRST 'POLICE ACTION'

Dutch exasperation at the unwillingness of the Republic to agree on its understanding of the purport of the Linggarjati agreement led, with a directness that verged on inevitability, to a Dutch 'police action', aimed at destroying the Republic as a political and military entity. The Dutch action, launched on 21 July 1947, was devastatingly effective, punching through republican lines at all points. Suharto played a role in the defence against this attack, relieving Major Sarjono as leader of 'Red' battalion, facing Ambarawa, after the republican front was pushed back rapidly by Dutch armour which claimed Ambarawa, Salatiga and Banyubiru. The republican government made a paper response to the threat posed to Yogyakarta by establishing it as a special military area, and naming General Urip Sumoharjo as military governor; amongst the ten-member staff appointed to assist him were Lt. Col. Suharto and the Sultan of Yogyakarta.

While the Dutch police action pushed back republican troops everywhere and secured much more extensive Dutch territorial control in Java, it failed to destroy the Republic's ability to resist and endure. It was stalled by the intervention of the United Nations, which pressured the Dutch government to a cease-fire beginning at midnight of 4 August. For their part the battered and demoralised Diponegoro forces established a new front line centred on Kedu. Suharto rotated with other regimental commanders as front commander of the north Kedu sector, serving there in September–October 1947, January–February 1948, and July 1948. Dutch reports in October 1947 noted the strenuous efforts made by the republican front commanders 'to rekindle fighting spirit amongst their demoralised troops'.[25]

Diplomatic brokerage by the United Nations led to a resumption of negotiations between the Dutch and the Republic which, limpingly, resulted in the signing of the Renville agreement in January 1948, so named from the American troopship moored in the harbour in Jakarta upon which it was signed. Renville, however, even more than its predecessors, was haunted by lack of trust and by substantive differences in interpretation between the parties, and laced with humiliation for the Republic; it emerged only after considerable pressure on the Republic by the United States. Its signing led to the fall of the Republic's government under Prime Minister Amir Syarifuddin, replaced by a presidential cabinet led by Prime Minister Mohammad Hatta. Under Hatta, the rationalisation of the Republic's armed forces, already approved in principle by the Indonesian parliament for reasons of order and finance in December 1947, proceeded, albeit in a halting and confused way. Rationalisation sparked further disaffection within sections of the Army and amongst other armed groups, which shared considerable distaste at efforts substantially to reduce in size and to professionalise the Army, and at the associated loss of revolutionary élan. Ever-fermenting debate about the proper direction of the revolution intensified sharply, led, ironically, by the recently ousted Amir Syarifuddin, himself the architect of the Renville agreement.

MARRIAGE

As these larger matters developed towards the end of 1947, Suharto, who had been living in Yogya with his half-brother, Probosutejo, began to contemplate the prospect of marriage at the suggestion of his foster-mother, Ibu Prawirowiharjo. On Suharto's own account, his marriage to the plain and plumpish Siti Hartinah, schoolmate of his cousin in Wonogiri fourteen years before, was arranged through Ibu Prawirowiharjo's good offices.[26] Ibu Prawiro, according to Roeder, knew a woman who was 'well-acquainted with that family'.[27] According to Gafur, however, this female intermediary ('a meat seller') seems only to have played an investigative role – to establish Siti Hartinah's marital availability and intentions, and to seek an audience for Ibu Prawirowiharjo with her mother – and it was Suharto's foster-mother who used her close relationship with Siti Hartinah's mother to propose the marriage.[28] There is considerable mystery about how such a marriage, between a woman of some social substance – her family, as Suharto himself notes, 'was well regarded and respected in the city [of Solo]', and she was distantly related to the Mangkunegaran royal house of Solo[29] – and an army officer who, despite his dashing good looks, was of lowly, even uncertain, parentage, could have been arranged. The union suggests a meeting of downwardly mobile hereditary minor aristocracy with the newly upward social mobility which military service provides in a period of revolution. In any event, the two were married on 26 December 1947 in a traditional ceremony in Solo (whence Suharto travelled in a battered De Soto sedan). If they were not in love at the time of their marriage, their mutual devotion developed rapidly thereafter. Suharto later noted matter-of-factly that 'I had developed the principles which would guide our boat on the high seas'.[30] What exactly they were and whence they came is left unsaid, although it is unlikely that the sturdy-minded Siti Hartinah was not involved in their evolution. Three days after their marriage, Suharto took his bride to Yogyakarta, to his house at Jl. Merbabu 2. Probosutejo returned to his parental home in Kemusuk.

RENVILLE, RATIONALISATION AND TURMOIL

The time of Suharto's marriage was a period of relative military quiet, as the Republic and the Dutch intensified the negotiations that would soon lead to the

Renville agreement. In February 1948, the commander of Division III ordered a parade in Magelang of newly formed regiments, as well as components of the 21st and 22nd regiments, 'to give expression to the unity of purpose of Army and people and as a public show of force'.[31] To make a stronger impression, each regiment was required to send a fully armed company to the parade, at which Lt. Col. Pranoto Reksosamudro, commander of the 21st Regiment and a later enemy of Suharto, served as parade commander. About the same time, Suharto spent a period as commander of the Kedu North Front, headquartered at Temanggung. There are no details of what his troops did on the line, but it is likely that, like other similar troops, they engaged in 'infiltrations, shootings, minings, and acts of sabotage'.[32] At the same time, the arrival of troops from West Java's Siliwangi Division into Central Java, moving from their bases as a consequence of the provisions of the Renville agreement (which called for the withdrawal of republican forces to republican territory), was the cause of shortages of a logistical kind, as well as a sharpening of inter-divisional hostilities.

The rationalisation and reorganisation of the Army continued in a clumsily persistent way, and in the face of Sudirman's opposition. Apart from the need, for political purposes, to bring 'irregular forces and army units of dubious loyalty to the central command' under control,[33] the rationalisation and reorganisation, under the influence of the young Dutch-trained Sumatran Siliwangi officer Abdul Haris Nasution, looked to the development of two different strands of soldiery: mobile troops, able to move rapidly anywhere in the archipelago, and territorial troops confined to specific places. By April 1948 the reorganisation of Division III was reported to be 'in full swing'.[34] A new Division I, comprising troops from the former II and III divisions, but with its total size planned for reduction from 16,000 to 7,000 men, was established following presidential decree 14/1948 of early May. It comprised four brigades and three battalions, with Suharto as commander of III Brigade. This new Division was part of a new Central Java Defence Staff; in late July, the Defence Staff, under the command of Bambang Supeno, had authority over eight brigades, including Suharto's. Just how effectively the rationalisation was implemented is doubtful; Dutch intelligence reported that it left 'much to be desired … one does not get the impression of a decline in troop strength nor an improvement in the quality of the troops'.[35] Suharto himself managed to escape the fate of being lowered one rung in rank, notwithstanding that such was a general prescription of the reorganisation.

Suharto's brigade, like others in the new Division, comprised four battalions, themselves requiring formation. His brigade's task was described as 'the defence of the Regency of Bagelen'.[36] The following month, similar reports mentioned Suharto as commander of III Brigade, III Division, headquartered at Yogyakarta, and noted him as 'ex-Kedu south front'. His chief of staff was Major Reksosiswo, and he commanded four battalions: I Battalion, under Major Sarjono, headquartered at Kebumen; II Battalion, under Major Sudarmo, at Purworejo; III Battalion, under Major Sruhardoyo, also at Purworejo; and IV Battalion, at Yogyakarta, under Sujono.[37]

In mid-year, a conference of all territorial and brigade commanders, convened by Sudirman, was held at Yogyakarta to plan military affairs in the event of another effort by the Dutch to overwhelm the Republic militarily. At the urging of Nasution, the notion emerged of 'total defence', a full-scale guerrilla offensive, should the Republic be overrun and occupied. The strategy involved dividing republican territory into defence zones, called *Wehrkreise* (defined as 'an independent military, political and economic defence area ... under a single command'), offering only token defence of cities, pursuing scorched-earth tactics, infiltrating 'Federal' (that is, Dutch) territory and, most important of all, falling back to already prepared guerrilla bases in forested and mountainous terrain. Indeed, the establishment of such dumps had already commenced in 1948. As Dutch intelligence later noted, 'it was the Republic's intention that the best tactic was a long-term armed opposition, especially with the goal to give time and opportunity for well-intentioned foreign countries to intervene'.[38]

No amount of army reorganisation or preparation could mask the desperate situation of the Republic at this time. Political violence was widespread; Yogyakarta itself was often 'the scene of disunity between parties and struggle organisations ... giving occasion to violent shooting battles'.[39] More immediately important, material conditions were in serious decline. The Dutch blockade, as well as the huge influx of refugees following the first Dutch police action (variously estimated at one million and six million people),[40] had turned the areas under republican control into food deficit areas. The population of Yogya itself was estimated by mid-1948 to have tripled from 300,000 to 900,000 people. To undernourishment in both rural and urban areas could be added the lack of essential supplies, especially of a medical kind, and ever-increasing inflation. There were 'many unemployed', mainly because of the large number of evacuees in the city, estimated towards the end of 1947 as being in the tens of thousands; people in the surrounding countryside were 'mostly using clothing made of palm leaves and jute'.[41] Around September 1948, the Dutch reported that cloth and yarn were being flown into Yogyakarta from Jambi (Sumatra). Between mid-November and mid-December 1948, the market price of rice in Yogya almost doubled.

THE MADIUN AFFAIR

In a context of rapidly intensifying internal tension, hostilities broke out in Solo (where, according to Nasution, a '"Wild West" atmosphere' had been gathering for some time).[42] The combatants were armed forces dismayed at the rationalisation plans and sympathetic to the radical line now taken by Amir Syarifuddin (and, from August, championed by the returned communist leader Musso, whose presence invigorated the Indonesian Communist Party (PKI)), and troops loyal to the republican government, especially those from the Siliwangi Division now quartered in Central Java. Suharto himself was not a participant in such antagonisms and seems to have been unsympathetic to the invasion of internecine politics onto the field of the revolution; 'as a young officer at that time, I decided not to involve myself in politics. I read about various political happenings and quietly analysed them'.[43]

Notwithstanding his professed wishes, and in a manner resonant of his earlier involvement in the 3 July affair, Suharto found himself pulled headlong into the problem. Returning to Yogyakarta from a trip to East Java, he stopped by Solo, presumably to witness for himself the rising revolutionary mood of that city. There he was for a short time arrested by Siliwangi troops, apparently mistaken for a Major Suharto, then a battalion commander in the Senopati Division based in Solo, a unit heavily populated by supporters of the anti-government PKI. Shortly after Siliwangi forces had brought Solo under control in mid-September, armed forces of the PKI-aligned Pesindo took control of the East Java city of Madiun, and Sumarsono, Pesindo's leader, was proclaimed military governor of the Madiun region. Musso and Amir, hearing the news of this 'coup' at Madiun, felt constrained to rush to the city in support of their revolutionary comrades. Sukarno, in turn, hastened to condemn the Madiun revolt, and when Musso responded acrimoniously to the President's address, the matter was destined for violent resolution.

Back in Yogyakarta, Nasution first heard of the troubles on 18 August from Education Minister Ali Sastroamijoyo, who came to Nasution's house with the news. That evening Nasution called a meeting of various commanders in Yogyakarta, including Suharto, to make preparations for whatever military operations might be needed to quell the rebelliousness in Madiun. At 7 o'clock the next morning, Nasution, accompanied by Suharto (at Sudirman's request), reported to Sudirman, who, having drawn up the broad operational guidelines, was forced through illness to hand over operational authority in the matter to Nasution in his capacity as chief of staff. Sudirman was most anxious to avoid a collision between the leftist forces at Madiun and the Siliwangi troops, and Suharto's neutrality afforded him an opportunity to achieve that end.

On 22 September, Col. Jokosuyono, appointed by newly installed acting Resident Supardi as military governor of the city of Madiun, issued an invitation to all East Java TNI commanders to a conference in Madiun, scheduled for 24 September. The government responded by announcing that all those who accepted the invitation would be regarded as being in revolt against the Republic of Indonesia. Suharto was ordered by Sudirman, eager for a compromise between the contending forces, to travel to Solo to warn the commander of the Senopati Division, Lt. Col. Suadi, not to be seduced into supporting the rebellion. Having finally met with Suadi in Wonogiri, Suharto accepted his invitation to travel to Madiun to inspect the situation there for himself. Arriving on 22 September, he toured the city with Sumarsono, met Musso and, on the orders of Sudirman, attempted to broker a truce to prevent the otherwise inevitable bloodletting.

The outcome of the discussions is a matter of considerable controversy. According to his autobiographical account, Suharto failed to convince Musso of the virtue of ending the rebellion, despite his best efforts. Having made his way back to Yogyakarta by a circuitous route in order to avoid being intercepted by either communist or Siliwangi troops, he reported to Sudirman the contents of his unproductive discussions with Musso.[44] According to Salim Said's account of a 1984 Suharto interview, Suharto in fact persuaded Musso to cease hostilities, provided 'certain conditions' were met, but failed to make it back to Yogya with this message before forces loyal to the government attacked Madiun.[45] A third account, that of Sumarsono, claims that Suharto discovered in the course of his visit, and especially after a day-long tour of the city in the company of Sumarsono himself, that the situation in Madiun was very different and more peaceful than he had been led to believe, that it was not in fact a rebellion (*pemberontakan*) at all, and that Musso's forces were eager for a peaceful accommodation with the government in Yogya.[46] When Suharto returned to Yogya with this news, his message was ignored in the rush by a conservative government to crush what it saw as treasonous communist rebels.

The truth probably lies somewhere between the second and third accounts. Sudirman was perennially keen to prevent internecine disunity between components of the Armed Forces; the Madiun rebels, knowing they would be confronted with crack Siliwangi troops, were eager for a peaceful resolution in which their concerns about key aspects of government policy – notably the pronounced tendency of the government to follow a path of diplomacy rather than struggle with the Dutch, and the army rationalisation plan – could be revisited. It is clear that the government was eager from the outset to use the revolt as a pretext for smashing the serious resistance the rebels presented to its chosen course. Salim Said notes that 'when he learned of Suharto's mission, Hatta reportedly was very angry with Sudirman'.[47] In the event, Sudirman's efforts to avoid the impending conflict failed. Government forces in the form of a Siliwangi battalion entered Madiun on 30 September. The town fell soon thereafter, and the PKI 'rebellion', if such it was, was ruthlessly crushed.

The events at Madiun inevitably spilled over into Solo and Yogyakarta as well. In the city of Yogyakarta itself, about 200 leftist/communist leaders were arrested on 19 September, the day after the Madiun rebellion had broken out. The head office of Pesindo was attacked and the principal leaders of the PKI trade union federation (SOBSI) were arrested. A Dutch intelligence report from early October noted that 'southeast of Yogya, the "red" [so-called communist] revolution is quickly expanding, with Wonosari (26 km southeast of Yogya) as the central point; armed bands occupy villages and eliminate Republican civilian officials … In the surrounds of Magelang Republican troops are still carrying out clearing operations against rebels'.[48] As in 1946, once the lines of battle had been unambiguously drawn and the real disposition of power clear, Suharto the careful mollifier became Suharto the professional soldier. Whatever his views about the reality or otherwise of Madiun's rebelliousness, he immediately fell into line with the republican government's policy and orders. Troops from his brigade occupied Wonosari. His men were also heavily involved in the clearing operation in the eastern part of Yogyakarta, around Wonogiri, aimed at defeating communist-sympathising troops. Troops from Major Sudarmo's II Battalion at Purworejo were sent towards Yogyakarta and Magelang to combat '"red" troops'; together with III Battalion, they assisted in disarming 'communist' troops led by Major Sunarto, formerly battalion commander at Kutoarjo.[49]

THE SECOND DUTCH 'POLICE ACTION'

The internal agitation within the Republic heightened fears that the Dutch would take advantage of its political and military disarray and mount a decisive strike. Accordingly, as the year approached its end, there was an increasing sense of the need to mount pressure upon the Dutch. Dutch intelligence reported in December 1948 plans to infiltrate republican troops into so-called 'Federal' areas, including Battalion III from Suharto's III Brigade, under the command of Sruhardoyo. By late 1948, the Diponegoro Division had completed its reorganisation, and the disposition of its troops was more or less settled. Suharto himself was responsible for the defence of the Yogyakarta region. He had for this task two of his four battalions, with a small and motley collection of other troops from other stations, including cadets from the Military Academy, elements from Brigade XVI, trainees from Brigade XVII, and army and navy units, some military police, and some ex-lasykar remnants from the demobilised 'Martono' Brigade. His two other battalions, under Sudarmo and Sruhardoyo, were charged with the defence of Bagelen.

Fears of Dutch attack proved real enough. On the morning of 19 December 1948 the Dutch, impatient at the lack of an appropriate solution to what they called 'the Indonesian problem',[50] launched a second 'police action' aimed at destroying the military power of the Republic and securing its political collapse. Dutch forces attacked republican territory by air and by land. Parachutists quickly captured the Maguwo airfield, 6 kilometres to the east of Yogyakarta, allowing troop-carrying planes to land and their erstwhile occupants to march on Yogyakarta. With the assistance of troops advancing from the north, the city was completely in their hands by that evening, with minimal losses. Around 2 p.m., Lt. Col. Abdul Latief Hendraningrat, the commander of the Yogya city garrison, had successfully urged Sudirman to quit the city as Dutch forces began to enter it. The civilian leaders of the Republic, including Sukarno and Hatta, were captured without any effort at resistance or flight. The Sultan of Yogyakarta, for his part, refused to see Gen. Maj. J. K. Meijer, the Dutch commander of Central Java, pleading illness.

It had never been the Republic's intention to defend Yogyakarta in the case of Dutch attack; 'what had priority was to save and to evacuate manpower and leadership', according to the policy approved by cabinet more than six weeks before.[51] Nonetheless, despite long-held fears of a pre-emptive Dutch strike, the attack caught the Republic completely unprepared; 'barring a pitiful handful', Sukarno later noted, 'our entire Army was outside the town on maneuvers'.[52] Republican forces rapidly fell back and, with the population in panic, the resistance offered to the advancing Dutch troops was negligible; the Dutch themselves reported losses of only one dead and three wounded. Suharto, with the small number of troops remaining – just two sections of his brigade and some police and military students – attempted, by constructing a perimeter defence east of the city on a 4-kilometre-wide front, to slow the advance of Dutch troops from Maguwo until mid-afternoon, when the city was finally abandoned to the enemy.

The retreat of Suharto's forces from the city seems to have been ragged and poorly prepared, indeed, extemporised. The weak resistance must, at least in part, be sheeted home to Suharto; a Dutch report penned a few days later noted that the attack was a 'complete surprise' for the Republic and that 'very certainly, the city would not have been captured so easily and with so few losses if there had been at least some *organised army* concentration in and around the city'.[53] Indeed, Nasution later criticised Suharto for being 'slow to implement orders, indecisive'.[54] According to Suharto's account, clearly an effort to put the best face on things, the TNI troops had 'withdrawn themselves out of the city' before the attack and were stationed in Purworejo to the west, while he himself had spent the night of 18 December at home with his heavily pregnant wife.[55] Later, he admitted that 'I know how very disappointed were the people of Yogya at that time in Brigade-10, that the capital city of the struggle could be snatched away in such a way by the Dutch'.[56]

GUERRILLA WARFARE

Leaving Siti Hartinah in Yogya, Suharto retreated to Gangduk, where he spent the night of 19 December, and subsequently moved to Gunungpiring and then Bibis, where he established a new headquarters at the house of the village chief, named Harjowiyadi. The villages around Yogyakarta became the 'basis of the guerrilla resistance'.[57] Republican troops, dependent upon villagers for sustenance and support, were quartered three to five in a village house, with the householder responsible for their upkeep. Fighters entered as best they could into the life of the village, assisting in work projects and generally making themselves useful. In Bibis, the village chief established a public kitchen, partly funded by Suharto himself, to feed Suharto's troops; villagers contributed vegetables, oil and meat to the operation. The republican government had neither the money nor the logistical competence to supply these troops, so that 'in practice, each area would have to find its own resources'.[58] With the Republic now under military governance, some commanders contrived their own local tax arrangements and imposed them upon villagers in order to secure the resources they needed for supplies. While there is no evidence that Suharto instituted measures of this kind on behalf of his soldiers, he must have made some arrangements to procure what his troops needed; Nasution himself noted that it had become 'customary for each unit for troops to have its own goods for exchange obtained by its own efforts, and consisting of all kinds of materials and commodities. In this way those troops were able to stand on their own'.[59]

Ensconced in villages, republican troops were able to melt into the surroundings. A captured document from the republican defence headquarters in Bantul, entitled 'Village defence', gives a good indication of the system of intelligence and early warning networks employed in villages to assist republican forces.[60] Guerrilla resistance was the order of the day. According to T. B. Simatupang, 'had the Dutch in fact faced only the TNI, without the territorial organization which allowed it to move everywhere like "fish in water", then they might have achieved their goal of eliminating our army'.[61]

Out in the hills surrounding Yogyakarta, Suharto heard of the birth on 23 January 1949 of his first child, a daughter. Shortly before this time, on 7 January, his stepfather, Atmoprawiro, then aged 45, had been shot dead by Dutch troops undertaking a sweep, 'possibly', according to Suharto, 'in pursuit of me, because at the time of the police action I was battle commander of the Yogyakarta area'. He continues:

> Indeed, at that time, I had just passed through the western side of the village of Kemusuk on patrol, when there was a sweep [*pembersihan*] and my stepfather was shot with many inhabitants of the village of Kemusuk, because the Dutch knew that the battle commander of Yogya was a son of Kemusuk.[62]

On 30 January, Suharto appeared without warning in Kemusuk and asked Probosutejo to take a letter to his wife in Yogyakarta, containing the name of the couple's new baby: Siti Hardiyanti Hastuti, nicknamed Tutut.

At the end of December 1948, 'in order to bring the scattered and spread Republican units once more under an organisational unity', Military Governor Col. Bambang Sugeng divided III Division's territory into three defence zones (the wehrkreises mentioned earlier). Wehrkreise III was the Yogya region, 'where two battalions [I and IV] of X Brigade operate under the direct command of Lt. Col. Suharto'.[63] Suharto's second and third battalions were deployed to strengthen Wehrkreise II, operating on the south Kedu front under the command of Lt. Col. Sarbini. Wehrkreise I comprised Banyumas, Pekalongan and Wonosobo.

Adjusting to the new situation of guerrilla resistance did not come easily to the republican troops; shocked at the violence of the Dutch assault, disordered, and with their morale severely dented, they had to accommodate themselves to new arrangements, new tactics, and new ways of thinking. There was, in addition, the well-worn problem that the continuing presence of large numbers of irregular troops, as well as leaders with their own ideas of strategy and little sympathy for the restraints of command discipline, made things difficult for putative commanders. Suharto, for example, like other TNI commanders in Central Java, had difficulty reining in the likes of the strongly self-willed and uncompromising Bugis-Makassarese leader, Kahar Muzakkar, deputy commander of Brigade XVI. Nonetheless, it seems clear that Suharto much enjoyed the challenges now presented him and took to them with great eagerness. His experience could not have done much to enhance his opinion of the indispensability of civilian leadership for the infant Republic, especially in time of crisis.

Suharto's Wehrkreise III was headquartered in the Menoreh hills at Bantul, immediately south of Yogyakarta. It was further divided into six sub-Wehrkreise (SWK): one was responsible for the area immediately around the city, two for the region around Bantul, another two for the Sleman area, and the sixth for the regions of Wonosari and Maguwo. For the most part, his troops remained in these areas, sometimes approaching the fringes of the city and sometimes even entering it. Suharto moved his own headquarters from place to place; when Simatupang visited him, it was established at Gamping, near the western limits of the city.

As I have suggested, the ease of the Dutch conquest of Yogyakarta in December 1948 caused a sense of guilt in Suharto, something he attempted to assuage by mounting a series of counter-attacks upon the occupied city as a means of demonstrating to its inhabitants, and to the Dutch, that there still existed a strong and capable Indonesian resistance to Dutch power.[64] According to his own account, and notwithstanding that he was outranked by other TNI leaders, he was the inspiration, as well as the consolidator and organiser, of the Indonesian troops in the hills outside the city. The attacks were supposedly carried out on the nights of 29 December, 9 January, mid-January and again in February, although reports vary. The Dutch judged those of 29–30 December and 9–10 January to have been 'obviously planned beforehand', which meant that 'the morale of the enemy was very good'. In February, they reported that 'around Yogya there are still very many active bands. Their morale is good, which is probably attributable to the fact that they are given more active leadership than is the case elsewhere'.[65]

There were also attacks on other occupied urban centres, almost certainly not the work of Suharto's forces. On the night of 15 January, a group of about thirty men attempted to blow up and burn down the tax record building in Magelang. In the early morning of 20 January, about 400 republican troops attacked Temanggung and succeeded in penetrating into the city before being repulsed with heavy losses. Between 1 January and 30 June 1949, attacks on military posts in the areas controlled by the Dutch 'T' Brigade (Yogyakarta, Magelang, Temanggung) averaged almost fourteen per week, while clashes between Dutch patrols and Indonesian fighters averaged over twenty-two per week in the same period.

Other military activity was of a more regular and low-level kind: the laying of mines (which often proved very effective, according to Dutch reports of vehicles lost through mine strikes), barricading roads and destroying bridges, small-scale attacks against Dutch patrols and convoys (sometimes by villagers armed with bamboo spears, but sometimes, too, by bands of as many as 100 republican troops, armed with automatic weapons), sniper-fire, and attacks on Dutch posts. This sort of activity, according to a Dutch report, achieved its aims in terms of morale 'by each day reminding the city's residents that the opposition remains active'. Activity such as this was 'in no small way supported by a well operating information and observation system, which makes it very difficult to use the element of surprise'. It also depended strongly on the support of local people: 'the very rapid and repeated barricading and destruction of large stretches [of road] can only be done if the people actively cooperate, either as a consequence of a continual barrage of propaganda, or under the direct pressure of the bands and remnants of the TNI still roaming around. The attacks which the people, for the most part armed with bamboo spears and clubs, carry out on our patrols here speak for themselves'.[66] There was, finally, another kind of military activity. In February, the Sultan of Yogyakarta had entrusted to Suharto the task of quelling violence and looting within the city itself. How Suharto was meant to achieve this goal is not explained.

There can be little doubt that this continual pressure on the Dutch troops had its effect, notwithstanding Meijer's assertion in late February that 'guerrilla activity is gradually decreasing'.[67] 'T' Brigade's troop losses between 19 December and 12 January amounted to 28 dead, and 54 wounded, 11 seriously; by early February these numbers had risen to 44 dead and 129 wounded. This situation, together with the sickness and exhaustion which came from operating in the tropical conditions of Central Java, the lack of sufficient reserves, the need for continual vigilance, and a growing sense of insecurity wore down the physical and moral reserves of Dutch troops. Further, their material losses were not insignificant; because of mine damage and the need for other repairs, less than half of the brigade's armoured vehicles were able to be deployed. The result was that 'we can scarcely begin the task of an immediately effective restoration of security and law and order'.[68] Moreover, the diplomatic disaster of 28 January, when the UN Security Council passed a resolution requiring the Dutch to restore the republican leadership to Yogyakarta as the first step in a process of establishing an interim federal government of Indonesia, cannot have served to heighten their spirits. Nonetheless, republican losses were very severe whenever Dutch forces made more than sporadic contact with them.

Suharto's characteristically immodest claim to have been the mastermind and guiding hand of guerrilla activities such as these needs to be treated with some caution. There is, for example, a complete neglect in his reminiscences of his relationship with Nasution, who established a command headquarters near Prambanan, who directed the overall military operations, and who had established contact with Suharto. However, it needs to be acknowledged that 'in practice Nasution's headquarters was unable to coordinate activity even in Java, and initiative rested more than ever with the unit commander'.[69] Nasution himself recognised that 'in practice some brigades of their own initiative have organised mobile attacking units which have determinedly conducted actions day after day, attacking by day and night, on and on, as a continuous operation'.[70] Suharto similarly ignores the role of Bambang Sugeng in coordinating guerrilla military activity. Moreover, a considerable amount of the activity outlined above was carried out by troops outside Suharto's immediate control, and probably on their own initiative. According to Kahin, who was present in the city at the time (ensconced, under Dutch guard, on the top floor of the Grand Hotel), the attack on Yogyakarta on the night of 9 January was made 'by a heavy battalion of the Republic's crack Mobile Police Brigade supported by a KRIS company of the Republican army', which reached the middle of the city, the Grand Hotel, and fought there for two hours before being repulsed.[71] KRIS (*Kebaktian Rakyat Indonesia Sulawesi* – Devotion of the Indonesian People of Sulawesi) was a unit based around Menadonese who were in Java at the time of the outbreak of war (Abdul Kahar Muzakkar served as its secretary).

Nonetheless, Suharto's leadership skills should not be underestimated. According to one Dutch source, 'the enemy military activity against Yogya is, according to available information, chiefly directed from Bantul, where the headquarters of the X guerrilla (Tentara Pelajar) is located'. Bantul, of course, was Suharto's headquarters around this time. In February it was reported that 'enemy bands are more frequent [*dichter*] about the road from Kebumen to Purworejo ... Among these are units of the former 2nd and 3rd Battalion of the X Brigade ... Attacks on the road will have to be expected in the future, as well as road blockages of various kinds'. The same report noted that republican forces in the environs of Yogyakarta were 'stubborn and have many times shown that they have good morale'. Indeed, the people south and south-east of Yogyakarta were thought by the Dutch to be 'wholly under the influence of the enemy'.[72]

THE ATTACK OF 1 MARCH 1949

Supposedly disappointed that these attacks had not achieved their public purpose of demonstrating the continuing strength and tenacity of the republican resistance, Suharto later claimed to have generated the idea of mounting a large daylight attack on the capital, 'for a political purpose, so that the world would know that the TNI was still able to mount a resistance'.[73] The significance of the city was well known; the Dutch themselves acknowledged that 'Yogya is still seen by every Republican as a symbol and the influence of what happens in this city makes an impression over the whole of Java and even further afield'.[74]

That the attack was solely Suharto's creative initiative is a notion that gained in strength with the years. However, Roeder's early account, unlike Suharto's later autobiography, speaks of Suharto's secret meetings with the sultan in the Yogyakarta kraton, at one of which 'a bold decision was taken to launch a general attack on Jogjakarta'.[75] Nasution, for his part, asserted that 'the Panglima of the [Third] Division [Bambang Sugeng] ordered the attack'. Simatupang's account suggests that the idea for the attack arose out of his own discussions with Bambang.[76] Salim Said writes that the sultan claimed authorship of the idea in an interview in 1984.[77] On the face of it, it seems highly unlikely that the idea of an attack of this dimension and strategic significance originated with Suharto, a relatively junior officer whose foreshortened experience probably left him in invincible ignorance of the diplomatic aspects of the struggle,[78] and even more of the sophisticated world of international politics. More likely the idea was the product of the sultan's subtle and seasoned grasp of the intertwined nature of politics and military activity. So he later claimed.[79]

The Dutch were highly suspicious of the sultan's attitude towards them, almost to the point of paranoia. They strongly suspected that he would attempt to leave the kraton and join the republican troops in the hills, and they gathered intelligence to the effect that he planned to escape on 1 March. Dutch fears of the sultan's immediate intentions, fuelled perhaps by the awe in which they held him, gave rise to larger thoughts of sultanic conspiracy: they became enamoured of the curious idea that he aimed to establish Yogya as an independent or autonomous region, and that he eyed the chance of becoming the leader of the Republic. A Dutch report of 6 May claimed that 'the Sultan is striving for complete autonomy for his region, and is assisted in that by Col. Jatikusumo and Col. Suharto'.[80] In fact, the sultan never provided any evidence that he was being attracted to such a course, and every sign that he was thoroughly committed to the republican cause.

According to Nasution, Suharto spent a great deal of time preparing for the attack, 'especially conducting research inside the city and economising on the equipment of the troops'. He had also to take account of possible reprisals by the Dutch. He faced quite unusual difficulties in that his troops had no experience in fighting in large groups; 'they knew how to fight only in the context of a platoon, or at most a company'.[81] Having begun preparations for what was to be called the 'General Offensive' (*Serangan Umum*) with a series of minor raids upon Dutch military posts outside the city to instil a false sense of security into the Dutch command, Suharto proceeded to organise a large-scale attack, with a strength of about 2,000 troops, for the morning of 1 March 1949. The tactics included the gradual infiltration of small groups of troops into the city up to two weeks before the attack. Suharto recalled Sarjono's battalion from its station around Purworejo and gave it responsibility for the sector south of Yogyakarta. He organised the western sector from a base near Godean, installing KRIS Major H. N. Ventje Sumual as commander of that sector. To the north, he brought together various groupings of troops from disparate fighting bodies, under the command of Major Kusno, while he placed the eastern sector in the hands of Sujono's battalion. Marsudi and Amir Murtono were placed in charge of the city sector, with the task of 'organising the people in the city to help and facilitating the movement of troops into the city'.[82] The Dutch, for their part, notwithstanding their supreme confidence in their military superiority, recognised in late February that republican military activity was intensifying, 'perhaps as a consequence of the recent resolutions of the Security Council'.[83]

The attack, allegedly presaged by a mistaken republican attack the previous morning, was launched at 6 a.m. on 1 March, at the sound of the siren announcing the end of the curfew. Suharto led the attack from the west, with troops moving in from all sides, complementing the activities of those troops already infiltrated ('in a courageous and skillful manner')[84] into the city under cover of darkness. Suharto, armed with his favourite Owen gun, led his troops – he later claimed they thought him invulnerable to bullets[85] – to the centre of the city, the border of Jalan Malioboro. The official history of the Diponegoro Division describes the attack:

> The city of Yogya was attacked from four sides. Troops from SWK 102 entered from the south under the command of Major Sarjono, troops from SWK 103 came from the west led by Lt. Col. Suhut [Suhud]. Troops from SWK 104 came from the north led by Major Sukasno ... Troops from SWK 105 were earmarked to occupy Tanjungtirto with the minimal task of isolating Dutch troops there so that they could not join together with other troops.[86]

The attacking troops were identified by the yellow coconut leaves worn on their shoulders. Because of the tactical difficulties Suharto's forces faced, the attack was, in fact, no more than a combination of a large number of coordinated small-scale raids. Inhabitants of the city supported the troops, leaving food and drink in front of their houses and providing security as the troops moved about their tasks. The Dutch, Suharto claims, were 'shocked' and, he further claims, the republican troops were able to capture the entire city and hold it until 12 noon, when the reinforcements ordered by the commander of the 'T' Brigade, Colonel van Langen, finally arrived from Semarang in the shape of the 'Red Elephant' unit commanded by Colonel van Zanten.[87] At that point, or perhaps a little later in the afternoon, around 2 p.m., Suharto gave the signal for his troops to withdraw, his point having been successfully made.

Other sources have been equally lyrical in their praise of the attack's achievements. The Republic's radio broadcasts were enthusiastic in their claims for success. RRI (*Radio Republik Indonesia*) Sumatra Utara announced that Yogyakarta had been captured from the Dutch and that troops were shooting from the trees in the city. 'The red and white flag flutters again, and our troops are conducting clearing operations against remnants of the Dutch troops around Yogyakarta.' A more modest commentary from the Republic's Sumatra-based Radio Rimba Raya about two days later noted that 'the attack on Yogyakarta and the occupation of the city [was] a magnificent feat of arms, but it could not be maintained'.[88] According to Roeder, the attack made 'good progress', with troops reaching the centre of the town and capturing a munitions factory (from which they seized 'five tons of ammunition and light arms'), and a small tank, all with casualties mentioned as 'light'.[89] The official history of the Diponegoro Division relates that KNIL troops guarding a munitions plant handed over large quantities of ammunition and arms to the attacking republican forces, 'the result of our underground movement being able to make contact with the KNIL troops there'.[90] The Army Staff College history of the attack remarks that 'in a short time almost every corner of the city was overpowered by the TNI. Jalan Malioboro up to Tugu was full of guerrilla troops'.[91] Salim Said asserts that 'the Republican army very nearly captured Yogyakarta'. Siti Hartinah's biographer reported that 'the Red and White colours of the national flag fluttered from all corners of the city while the people courageously shouted "freedom, freedom"'.[92] The author of an army history wrote that 'it can be said that we were easily able to take over almost all the city, together with the important objectives'. A later hagiographer claimed somewhat effusively that the event 'shook the world' and that, during it, Suharto 'paralysed the Dutch military after which he occupied Yogyakarta for six hours'.[93] Sources sympathetic to the republican cause tended to accept the official republican view; thus, Kahin, clearly influenced by republican information, wrote that 'the Republican army had very nearly captured Jogjakarta', while Reid claims that Suharto 'held most of the city for six hours before Dutch reinforcements arrived'.[94]

Dutch accounts of the scale and success of the attack are, understandably, somewhat more muted:

> In the early morning the enemy began a coordinated attack on Yogya with its main thrust from the west-south-west, assisted in this by troops infiltrated under cover of darkness, including a large enemy concentration in the environs of the kraton [*de buiten-Kraton*]. These [troops] were captured and searched by our troops. In the western part of Yogya the enemy groups offered obstinate resistance. The opposition was cleared away, and the situation is in hand.[95]

The Dutch, with a much inferior strength of a single battalion and some armoured units, were taken by surprise by the attack which, prefaced by light fire on perimeter posts around the city from about 4 a.m., came from the south and west, and was concentrated on their command posts and troop encampments, such as the large one near Tugu railway station. It appeared, they later admitted, 'to have been intelligently arranged', with 'good coordination' which 'gives a strong indication of central leadership'.[96] Dutch forces initially encountered difficulties in locating republican troops because of their camouflage and the early morning light. In one part of the city, Dutch troops encountered streets barricaded with furniture and timber, and came under heavy fire from houses as they attempted clearing operations in these confined spaces, causing them to suspend operations and call for reinforcements. The reinforced sweep continued operations until 2.30 p.m., reporting republican losses as 118 killed as against 5 Dutch wounded. There were Dutch reports that republican troops were within the environs of the kraton, that some republican firing came from the top of trees within the kraton, and that when Dutch troops pursued republican forces from the area directly north of the kraton, those troops had disappeared into the kraton. As a consequence, Dutch troops had entered the kraton. By 1.30 p.m. 'all organised opposition in the city [was] completely broken', and the city was peaceful with the exception of a little sniper-fire.[97] A relief convoy arrived in Yogyakarta at 4.30 p.m.

The losses to Suharto's troops were substantial, variously reported as ranging from 192 to 375. On the other hand, the weapons captured were insignificant: 3 carbines, 4 rifles [*geweren*], 5 pistols, and some ammunition. Dutch losses were very light (six killed and several wounded), considering the size of the operation and the intensity of the fighting.

The Dutch account of matters was substantially endorsed by the report of the UN military observers.[98] They reported the outbreak of heavy shooting at 6 a.m., concentrated in the western part of the town around the railway station. The Dutch response was rapid; already by 7 a.m., according to the UN report, armoured cars and Bren carriers were moving through the streets, with Dutch infantry behind and patrolling the narrow side streets off the main road. The shooting had lessened by 11 a.m., and patrolling continued, accompanied by light tanks. By 2 p.m., the shooting had died away still more. Neither Dutch military reports nor UN observers' reports noted any significant threat to Dutch control of the city – nor any support for the republican claims of success, which must be dismissed as highly exaggerated.

Some republican armed activity continued on 2 March, in which seven Indonesian soldiers were killed. On the same day, notwithstanding Suharto's claim to the contrary ('They did not have enough troops for cleaning-up operations in the city. Our people in the city were saved from Dutch reprisal'),[99] the Dutch began a series of clearing sweeps within the city, in one of which 47 Indonesians were killed and 25 arrested, and a small quantity of arms seized. Another sweep the next day resulted in the death of 7 republican troops and the capture of 7 more. On the night of 2 March, about midnight, the Dutch encountered a large group of Indonesians in the south-eastern part of the town and inflicted heavy casualties on them. Clearing sweeps by Dutch patrols on the eastern edge of the city saw 19 Indonesians killed and 7 captured. On 5 March, 25 Indonesian troops were killed in sweeps through the kampungs to the south-east of the city. Two days later a sweep of the kampung area south of the Tugu railway station resulted in the arrest of 37 'suspected' people.

In a curious aside, Suharto remarks that the news of the assault was broadcast world-wide by the republican radio transmitter at Playen, Wonosari,[100] and that the Dutch conducted sweeps to discover this transmitter, thus drawing off troops who might otherwise have conducted reprisal attacks on areas surrounding Yogya.[101] The Dutch did indeed undertake a large-scale attack on Gading/ Wonosari on 10 March, including 300 paratroopers and three rifle companies, with air support. As things turned out, they encountered only very light opposition; on 21 March a patrol discovered one-and-a-half tons of 'radiomateriaal'. But there were numerous other clearing exercises conducted by the Dutch, such as one undertaken through Muntilan on 13 March and through Sentolo on 18 March; such operations were alleged to have caused significant civilian casualties.

Subsequently, Suharto organised smaller attacks on sites west of Yogyakarta around early April in order 'to confuse the Dutch even more'.[102] According to Nasution, after the 1 March attack 'guerrilla war raged in the city of Yogya. There were often early morning clashes, so that thousands of [Indonesian] Chinese left the city. Even politicians and high officials of the Republic of Indonesia themselves often left the city to look for a more secure abode in Surabaya, Semarang, Jakarta and Bandung'.[103] Some of the Dutch, however, saw things differently; in early April the situation in the area of the 'T' Brigade was 'in general favourable', something attributed 'to the fact that, for example, in the environs of Yogya, enemy groups have effectively been scattered, but also to the circumstance that the large-scale capture of ammunition and weapons causes the struggle groups great difficulties'.[104] But the UN military observers at the end of the third week of March were of the view that 'guerrilla activity is increasing as can readily be seen by the more intensified active military operations taken by the Dutch forces during this period'.[105] A disciplined guerrilla attack on Yogyakarta ('which did not last long') was reported on the night of 14 March.[106] Dutch intelligence itself reported rumours of a republican plan to launch another attack on Yogya on 15 April, to be led by Col. Jatikusumo, assisted by Suharto and others.[107] Shortly thereafter, the sultan was thought by the Dutch to be planning a further attack on Yogyakarta, scheduled for 24 April.

Suharto's and others' accounts claim that the attack of 1 March was a significant demonstration of the continued existence and vitality of the TNI; 'we were able to show that the TNI was still intact as an army and could go out and enter a city any time we wanted to'. The 'political and psychological effects' of this demonstration, so it was argued, had an important effect upon the international deliberations on the 'Indonesian question' at that time.[108] 'Simply and solely we wished to show the world that the TNI and the Indonesian people were still actually capable of facing the Dutch colonial side at every moment.'[109] In Suharto's view, the attack 'was extremely influential',[110] causing the Security Council to place pressure on the Dutch to cease operations and re-embark upon negotiations with the Republic. The sultan himself later remarked that 'the general offensive in Yogyakarta opened the Security Council's eyes to the fact that the TNI was certainly still alive. That was very important, I feel'.[111]

These, it must be said, are generous interpretations, which accord no importance to the crucial role of the United States in exerting severe political and financial pressure upon the Dutch to desist from their efforts to maintain their colonial possession. Domestically, however, the attack had a considerable and important impact. Kahin, for example, relates that the reports of the offensive had a significant effect on the attitude of leaders of the Dutch-inspired 'Federal' states, as well as the attitude of the civilian republican leaders then in Dutch detention on the island of Bangka; it 'stiffened the spines of many ['Federal'] leaders'[112] – and caused them to change their previous attitude of cooperation with the Beel plan for a Dutch-dominated Indonesian federation. No doubt it contributed significantly to the morale of republican forces themselves.

Ironically, Suharto's exaggerated effusiveness about the consequences of his work masks the very real skill which was brought to bear in organising the attack. He received letters and reports from commanders in other regions testifying to the morale-boosting impact on their forces as a result of the action he had led. The attack was, as the UN military observers noted, the result of long and considered planning, and a coordination which 'could only be carried out by a man who enjoyed a relative authority, knows the town, and has the means necessary for liaison and has sufficient authority to impress his will on the chiefs of varied units'.[113] Sudirman, in a letter to Nasution, was even more laudatory; Suharto was, he said, 'a flower of battle'.[114]

PREPARING FOR VICTORY

It was clear by March that the Dutch – their hopes for the destruction or minimalisation of the Republic dashed, their aggressive tactics having failed to win the support of the federal states they had created as counterweights to the Republic, and the Americans having irrevocably withdrawn their support – had lost the will to pursue what had become an impossible project. Further negotiations between the Dutch and the Republic resulted in the Rum-Van Royen agreement of 7 May 1949, which provided for a cease-fire, the release of the republican leaders, including Sukarno and Hatta, the withdrawal of Dutch troops from Yogyakarta, and the holding of a roundtable conference in The Hague to arrange the transfer of sovereignty to a federal Indonesia which would effectively be dominated by the Republic.

The continuing republican military pressure upon Dutch forces was significant in the gestation and delivery of these arrangements. By April 1949, three battalions of Suharto's Brigade X were operating in reasonably defined areas. I Battalion, under the command of Major Sarjono, operated to the west of the city of Yogyakarta, and was headquartered around Panggeng. Battalions II and III, commanded respectively by Major Sudarmo and Major Sruhardoyo, were operating respectively around Kebumen and Purworejo. A later report mentions a fourth battalion, commanded by Major Sujono. All these forces seem to have operated with a large degree of independence, and they continued to harass the occupying forces in the regions to the south and south-west of Yogyakarta. Nasution notes the frustration which faced Dutch efforts to pacify the area: 'Roads which [the Dutch] had cleared of obstacles in the morning were the following night full of all kinds of obstructions put there by the guerrilla groups together with the people who often rendered assistance'. Suharto himself was reported in late April to have established his brigade headquarters at Karangmontong, where he seems to have remained at least until early June. On 16 April it appears that he held a meeting of his battalion commanders and other officers commanding troops to the south and west of Yogyakarta at Sorogedong, which issued an instruction for increased infiltration into Yogyakarta. A Dutch report in May noted an increase in shooting, sabotage, reprisals and a general heightening of 'terror'. An intelligence report from early June noted a meeting at Jiwosari between Jatikusumo, Nasution, Suharto and all Wehrkreise commanders around Yogya. At this meeting, it was unanimously agreed to intensify the struggle; 'there was no one who was certain of the advantages of a cease-fire order, and we were doubtful about the results of diplomacy. The strongest impression in that conference was our belief in the efficacy of the guerrilla struggle'.[115] By early June, with the handover of the city imminent, small-scale incidents seem to have increased; 'at present in the city of Yogya virtually every night there is, for longer or shorter periods, shooting at [Dutch] posts'.[116]

It was one thing to maintain pressure, but a more subtly difficult problem for the Republic to ensure an orderly restoration of republican power in Yogya. Despite its success in grinding down the Dutch military effort, its internal political and military situation was even more chaotic than usual. The exigencies of guerrilla warfare had weakened already tenuous threads of military and political authority, while the uncertainties about the political fate of the Republic had proven fertile grounds for numerous competing political interests and the tensions and strange rumours that proliferated about them. According to Nasution, wild rumours of all kinds spread about what the future might bring; one of them was that Suharto was intending to form a 'federal' [that is, pro-Dutch] army.[117] Again, according to a captured republican report, there were efforts made by leftist groups in Yogyakarta to agitate against the agreement of 7 May. The leftist Sukarni was said to have enquired about approaching leading army figures, including Suharto, to give their backing to these moves, but 'their efforts were discovered by the TNI leadership, whereby their plan failed'.[118]

At this time of stress and uncertainty, Suharto's strongest relations were with his commander, Sudirman, and, especially, with the sultan, a figure of unmatched pre-eminence in Central Java at that time. It seems that Suharto kept in reasonably frequent contact with Sudirman and, indeed, that he served as an intermediary for communications between Sudirman and the sultan. A Dutch intelligence report noted that, around 6 May, Suharto had visited Sudirman in the environs of Sentolo, where Suharto reported on the weak state of the republican troops around

Yogya.[119] On 13 June, a meeting was held at Bantul between Sudirman, Suhud (commander of SWK 103), Suharto, and Selo Ali (military sub-territory commander), which discussed the future shape of the republican army, and especially Sudirman's position in it; amongst the matters raised were the long-time differences between Sudirman and Nasution.

One measure of Suharto's increasing stature is that he is regularly mentioned in Dutch reports in 1949 as a senior military figure. More important, he increasingly enjoyed the sultan's confidence, attributable perhaps to the steady growth of his authority and reputation in the Yogya region since the beginning of the guerrilla war. Such confidence was manifested in two ways. Suharto was, it appears, given responsibility by the sultan to destroy or contain those forces which threatened republican-sponsored order in the lead-up to the Dutch return of Yogyakarta. A report from early March, noting the presence around Yogya of 'strong bands' of communist-affiliated troops, mentioned 'the attempts of Col. Latief [Hendraningrat], ex-commander of Yogya, and Lt. Col. Suharto, ex-commander X Brigade, which would be supported financially by the Sultan, to form troops to support the Sultan and as a counterweight against the PKI bands united against him'.[120] Responding on 11 May to a suggestion that there might be a flare-up of communist activity in the process of Yogyakarta's being returned to the Republic, the sultan noted that on that same day he had given an order to Suharto to begin immediately to disarm 'all irresponsible elements' outside the places occupied by Dutch troops in the region of Yogyakarta, and was confident that he could, with the assistance of Suharto's troops and others, maintain order and security.

It appears that Suharto proceeded to his work with relish; a Dutch report from early June noted that 'the order given by the Sultan on or about 11 May to disarm as many PKI troops as possible has indeed led to the imprisonment and disarming of PKI troops and other bands. In addition to the PKI, KRIS and troops from the strongly communist-infected BPRI-Yogya were also disarmed'.[121] KRIS troops, under the leadership of Major Sumual, were opposed to the Dutch–Indonesian agreement and were ordered by Suharto to leave the Residency; Sumual ignored this order and, according to this report, Suharto intended to attack his troops. In July, another Dutch report noted that Suharto had forced communist groups east of the Yogya region into Dutch lines. Suharto seems to have kept up the pressure on communist forces; in September it was reported that IV Battalion of his brigade, under Major Sujono, had been sent to the Solo region to combat the PKI.

Suharto was also – although, as we shall see, not without controversy – entrusted with the task of re-asserting and maintaining authority and order in Yogyakarta at the Dutch handover and thereafter. Apparently by late March or early April it had been decided that, in the event of the return of Yogya, Suharto and his troops would play a key role in the security of the city, with a City Defence Headquarters (*Markas Pertahanan Kota*) under the joint leadership of the mayor, Sudarisman, and Suharto, and plans were advanced regarding the disposition of troops and authority. Another Dutch report dated 13 May noted that 'Lt. Col. Suharto [then thought to be south-east of Yogya around Terong] has been appointed Commander of the Republican troops which will have the responsibility for the security of Yogya once the handover of authority takes place'.[122]

Things were not, in fact, as neat as these reports suggest. Suharto strenuously objected to a proposal that the Dutch formally transfer authority over the city to the police, and he made known his objections to the sultan.[123] In his view, the Dutch had never been in control of Yogya; they should, therefore, simply leave without ceremony. He also objected to security over the reclaimed city being entrusted to the police. It was, he thought, appropriate and right that the TNI, which had continually harassed Dutch defences, should assume control of the city once the Dutch had left and then, after a short but eloquent interval, formally transfer power to the police. It seems that a difference of opinion had developed between Suharto and Jen Mohammed, commander of the Police Mobile Brigade, about who was to ensure the maintenance of peace and security after the Dutch withdrawal. Jen and the sultan were of the view that it should be done by the police; Suharto, however, thought that he, as 'Battle Commander of the Yogya region', should bear this responsibility with his troops.[124] In both these disputes, Suharto had the better of the argument. The Dutch began a staged withdrawal from the city without incident or fanfare on 29 June 1949; at Suharto's order, the police marched into the city in ceremonial style, while TNI forces ('most of them not wearing a specific uniform or shoes') simply emerged into the city.[125] Suharto, for his part, took the opportunity to visit his wife and baby child in the kraton. On 6 July, the Republic's political leaders returned to Yogyakarta. On 17 July, Suharto, in the presence of the Pakualam, representing the sultan, officially handed authority over the city to the police commander, Jen.

It appears, however, that the controversy may have been, at least in part, of a rather different and more subtle kind than the one reported by Suharto.[126] According to contemporary reports, there was a 'serious difference' between Col. Jatikusumo, scion of the princely house of Solo, former chief of staff of the Army and commander of the Yogya Military Academy, and Suharto over who was to command the republican troops in Yogyakarta after its return to the Republic. It appears that the sultan, having originally appointed Suharto as commander of TNI troops for the reoccupation of Yogya and the subsequent maintenance of authority in the city, decided instead to use other troops, notably police and mobile brigade forces, under Jatikusumo's command, for the purpose, a decision with which Suharto was far from pleased. His response seems to have been to heighten his military activities around the city, apparently in an attempt to demonstrate the importance of his forces to the sultan. Indeed, so serious was the dispute that there were fears of clashes between the troops of the two commanders. There was even mention that the controversy between Jatikusumo and Suharto had led to a failed attempt by Suharto to disarm Jatikusumo's troops.

Suharto's complaint to the sultan apparently made an impression. Whereas, in early June, the plan was that the takeover of the city would be done by 600 men from the Mobile Brigade from the west and south, and 750 assorted police and non-TNI troops from the north, with the troops of X Brigade held in reserve, a Dutch report of 1 July mentioned a recent meeting of commanders at Jiwosari to settle troop dispositions for the takeover and noted that 'there appear to have been some changes in the composition of the occupation troops'. They now included Sarjono's Battalion I from Suharto's X Brigade, and none of the troops in question were under Jatikusumo or Jen; 'thus it would appear that Lt. Col. Suharto has won the battle with the Sultan, and has managed to keep his rivals outside the city'.[127] Once the Dutch had departed, Suharto remarks bluntly, 'it was me who made the regulations'.[128] Of the 2,000 republican troops lodged in the city after the handover, 600 were TNI troops, 'selected and well disciplined', according to the sultan, under the command of Suharto.[129]

These incidents confirm the observation made by Sukarno in 1946 about Suharto's obstinacy. But this was a different style of obstinacy to that, born of caution and naive uncertainty, displayed by Suharto at Wiyoro in July 1946. This was a stubbornness that came from a confident view of what was right and proper. In his mind, it was the TNI that had carried the lion's part of the struggle after the ignominious surrender of the civilian politicians on 19 December; it was the Army which should therefore be accorded the laurels of success when the Republic returned to the revolutionary capital. This jaundiced view of civilian politicians became common currency amongst military leaders; Reid remarks that 'military respect for civilian authority was gravely weakened during this period, with results that have been obvious ever since'.[130]

Suharto, then, had changed significantly from the young, inexperienced and unsophisticated regimental commander of 1946. His relative seniority of rank and position, the reputation he had carved out for himself as an imaginative, tough, brave, experienced and competent military commander,[131] his increasing familiarity with the political machinations of high-ranking military officers and politicians, and the 'narrow but intense'[132] relations with colleagues produced by the revolutionary experience in general and the guerrilla period in particular had all schooled in him an undemonstrative persistence and a confidence in his own abilities, a narrowly construed and brooding sense of what he thought was his by right, and a suspicious cynicism about the proclaimed motives of those outside his own intimate circle, especially the weak and squabbling civilian politicians. Later years would see these tendencies confirmed.

THE FINAL MONTHS

Suharto was reported to be in the environs of Tojono around early July 1949, where he seems to have established his headquarters with a staff of about sixty men. The other units of his brigade, described as having 'very mobile' headquarters, were operating, respectively, south-west of the city of Yogyakarta (I Battalion, under the command of Major Sarjono), in the environs of Kebumen (II Battalion, about 300 men, half of them with arms, under the command of Major Sudarmo), in SWK 103 (III Battalion, under the command of Major Sruhardoyo), and around Wonosari (IV Battalion, commanded by Major Sujono). Notwithstanding the results of negotiations between the Dutch and the Republic, military operations continued; III Battalion, under Major Sruhardoyo, was reported as a limiting factor for the Dutch military situation.

Suharto's final task in the revolution was to escort the Army commander, Sudirman, back to Yogyakarta. As Suharto tells it, Sudirman had not responded to pleas by the sultan and by Col. Gatot Subroto to return after the withdrawal of the Dutch, because he was not sympathetic with the outcome of the Rum-Van Royen talks and was intensely suspicious of Dutch intentions. Suharto himself was finally detailed to escort Sudirman back to the city. His task, on his account, was to persuade Sudirman, apparently unwilling to return to the city while the struggle continued elsewhere, wary of Dutch trickery, and distrustful of the Republic's civilian politicians, that he should come back to lead his troops from the Republic's capital. Suharto met Sudirman on 8 July in the village of Krejo, Ponjong Kecamatan. After some hours of discussion, he successfully prevailed upon him to return, and on 9 July Sudirman, seriously ill with tuberculosis and able to be moved only on a sedan chair, left his mountain redoubt near Wonosari. Suharto went before him to prepare his welcoming parade in Yogya. Sudirman was carried in his sedan chair as far as the Opak river, where he was met on 10 July by Simatupang and Suharjo Harjowardoyo, who came with a car and a Land Rover to convey him the rest of the way. Suharto himself led the welcoming parade provided by Brigade X for the returning Panglima Besar.[133]

It may well be that Suharto has exaggerated his own importance in all this; as he paints the picture, it is he who is Sudirman's confidant, who receives praise from the commander for his actions in the 1 March attack and thereafter, and who makes wise suggestions to Sudirman about how he should comport himself on his arrival in Yogya and where he should go. Nonetheless, there is a certain poignancy about Suharto's account which reveals the depth of his esteem for his commander; in terms of values and views, there was perhaps no other military figure with whom he identified more closely. On Sudirman's death early in 1950, it was Suharto's task to lead his funeral procession from Magelang to Yogyakarta, and to lead the officers' parade which committed Sudirman's body to the ground.[134]

In the last months of 1949, with a cease-fire finally in place, as the civilian politicians prepared themselves for the final negotiations in The Hague which would lead to the transfer of sovereignty to a federal Indonesia, Suharto was securely headquartered in Yogyakarta, his command responsible for the Residency of Yogyakarta as well as the *kabupaten* (district) of Kebumen and Purworejo. In October, divisions II and III were merged to form a larger Division III, with seven brigade commands (including Suharto's Brigade X in Yogya), and with Gatot Subroto as panglima and military governor. Suharto's four battalions, numbering about 800 men each and headquartered, respectively, at Tempel (I Battalion), Gombong (II Battalion), Pengempong (III Battalion), and Bulokerto (IV Battalion), were each divided into four companies. The disposition of his troops was based on a territorial concept, so that troops were spread in battalions and, under them, companies, with defined areas of control and operations. The solidity and symmetry of this organisational pattern was one measure of how far the Armed Forces had come from their ragged beginnings in mid-1945.

Suharto himself had progressed a long way as well. His revolutionary training ground had provided him with a compressed and complex schooling which had shaped him in ways that would be crucial for the later history of his nation. In a little over four years, the socially mobilising forces of the revolution had propelled an otherwise ordinary man from the obscurity of a dusty training ground on the Madiun periphery to the centre stage of Indonesian power in Yogya, where he moved, not yet prominently and not yet altogether easily, in the close and sometimes intimate circles of presidents, sultans, prime ministers and generals. His experiences had also begun to shape a political consciousness, albeit still covert, which emphasised the absolute necessity of unity in the attainment of political success,[135] engendered a certain suspicion of those who sought by force or threat to insert their own fundamental conceptions of the meaning of Indonesia, and magnified his distrust at the latent fissiparousness of the Indonesian people. In addition, his experiences had embossed upon him the importance of hierarchy and knowing one's place in it; in particular, they underlined his sense that the people needed (and respected) leadership, and formed in him a certain sense of duty towards them. Moreover, they left him unimpressed with the qualities of civilian politicians and their lack of respect for the Army's achievement.[136] Other than that, Suharto had not been captured by any particular stream of political thinking and, judging from the brokerage role demanded of him, was generally thought of as someone able to broach and negotiate differences in thinking amongst others. He emerged from the revolution with a significant reputation for efficient field leadership, together with political reliability and a stubborn steadiness. These qualities would, if not immediately, assist his gradual advance over the coming years.

3 Central Java commands, 1950–1959

THE ARMY THAT emerged from the independence struggle was, in some senses, the most powerful institution in the new nation. As a result of its successful prosecution of the anti-colonial war in the face of civilian surrender and apparently overwhelming odds, it enjoyed significant prestige. However, its political ambitions remained undeveloped. With the death of the charismatic Panglima Besar Sudirman in January 1950 (and with him notions that the Army might exert a more defining role in state-building), the Army came firmly under the control of young, Western-influenced and politically inexperienced officers like Nasution and Simatupang, who prized technical adeptness over political engagement and adroitness, and who acceded to the notion of army subordination to civilian control. The Army had not developed any alternative to the Western-style democracy adopted by the new state; as well, it faced more pressing and immediate problems in terms of developing its internal unity, reconfiguring its own size, shape, and command structures, and adjusting to the humdrum situation of peace.

Suharto, his rank of lieutenant colonel confirmed following the transfer of sovereignty, had no thought of leaving the Army following the conclusion of hostilities with the Dutch. His army career had provided him, as we have seen, with an undreamt-of rise in terms of social standing, influence and proximity to power. Like many of his comrades-in-arms, his lack of advanced formal education made him unfit for a civil service position of similar status and prestige, and he showed no inclination to embark full-time upon the world of private business in which he was similarly unschooled, if not altogether unpractised. His customary caution and his visceral demand for security did not incline him to abandon the legacy of almost a decade of military service and experience for the unknown. He began, therefore, to attune himself to the routine life of the professional soldier in a peacetime democracy, probably with little regard or concern for the civilian politicians already scrabbling for the spoils of power in Jakarta. They were the products of Western education, of wealthy or aristocratic families, often cosmopolitan in culture, and they were worlds apart from the small sphere of Central

Java which was virtually all that Suharto knew. His vision, such as it was, was then inward, limited and modest.

TO MAKASAR

Suharto was not long to enjoy a measured peacetime routine in his Yogya post. The formal transfer of sovereignty by the Dutch in December 1949 had been made not to the Republic of Indonesia but to a Republic of the United States of Indonesia (RIS), comprising sixteen states of which the Republic was, morally and in terms of population, prestige and influence, the dominant component. Within weeks of the transfer, other states of the RIS began to fold themselves into the Republic; by early April 1950, the RIS had been reduced to just four entities: the Republic, and the states of East Indonesia, East Sumatra and West Kalimantan. Of the last three, East Indonesia was the oldest and largest and, because of its historic attachment to Dutch authority, the most strongly minded to retain its sovereignty. It was also heavily populated with KNIL troops, with few republican soldiers on its soil.

The Hague agreement of December 1949 governing the transfer of sovereignty had stipulated that the 65,000 KNIL troops in the country would be absorbed into either the RIS army or (a much smaller number) the Dutch army (KL), or demobilised. East Indonesia, with a well-founded belief that the Republic was straining to incorporate it, had opposed a RIS decision to station RIS (in effect, republican) troops in South Sulawesi as a counterweight to KNIL forces. In early April 1950, ex-KNIL troops under the command of Buginese Captain Andi Azis, at the behest of the East Indonesia Minister for Justice Dr Soumokil, staged a coup in Makasar, arresting the newly appointed TNI military commander, Lt. Col. Mokaginta, just prior to the arrival of 900 RIS troops (from East Java's Brawijaya Division), and forcing those troops to move off. While the state of East Indonesia, which Azis professed to be defending, refused to endorse his actions, it had no forces to rein him in. As a consequence, the East Indonesian government fell, later to be replaced by a pro-republican government. Lawlessness flared, a result of clashes in South Sulawesi between pro-republican guerrilla forces lodged in the countryside who attempted to exact vengeance on formerly pro-Dutch ruling groups and as yet not-demobilised KNIL troops.[1]

In response to the crisis, Sukarno formally named Andi Azis as an insurgent on 13 April and called on RIS troops to restore order. Azis was finally persuaded to come to Jakarta for discussions, arriving on 16 April to find himself summarily arrested. A Division-strength expeditionary force of RIS troops, comprising three Java brigades and one battalion, under the command of the Christian Menadonese Lt. Col. A. E. Kawilarang, had already been commissioned to restore RIS authority. Included in the hurriedly prepared force were two combat battalions of Suharto's Brigade III of the Diponegoro Division, under his command, and bearing the designation Garuda Mataram Brigade. The inclusion of Suharto's brigade was presumably a sign that his efforts in the recently concluded struggle for independence had been favourably noted by his superiors, particularly the newly installed Minister of Defence, Sultan Hamengkubuwono IX. Suharto's force, numbering 1,851 in all, moved off from Yogya on 14 April, took ship from Semarang on 21 April and landed without incident at Makasar harbour on 26 April, by which time Makasar had already fallen to other elements of the expeditionary force.

Suharto's brigade was stationed in the town of Makasar and Suharto given the task of commanding the Makasar sector, that is, the town itself and regions to the north and south. He deployed most of his troops to seal off KNIL encampments in the town. Given the circumstances, the posting was relatively uneventful but not entirely free of incident. Predictably, rising tension between RIS and KNIL/KL troops manifested itself in shooting incidents of considerable severity in mid-May; two days of fighting cost APRIS (Armed Forces of the Republic of the United States of Indonesia) ten dead and twenty wounded. The violence petered out quickly once Suharto, on orders from above, had ordered and enforced a ceasefire and, together with KL/KNIL leaders, laid down strict demarcation lines limiting the movements of the respective forces.

There were also difficulties in bringing the often fractious, squabbling and undisciplined local pro-republican guerrilla forces, numbering around 4,000 in South Sulawesi, such as the *Harimau Indonesia* (Indonesian Tigers), under some semblance of control and coordination. As a general rule, the government's army rationalisation policy made it difficult for many poorly educated irregular troops to be admitted into the regular Army. However, APRIS policy was that such forces, where possible and appropriate, and after a two-month period of training, should be inducted formally into the RIS Armed Forces.[2] On 20 May, Suharto issued an order to round up guerrilla troops in his sector. Of the 3,428 collected, 1,044 managed to pass the physical, intellectual and attitudinal checks made upon them and were eventually formed into an APRIS battalion stationed at Bantaeng. Suharto officially inaugurated the battalion, named 'Depot II', on 25 June 1950.

Some guerrilla groups refused to be treated in this way, including a KGSS (Union of South Sulawesi Guerrillas) battalion and troops of the 'Mobile Brigade Ratulangi' (MBR) under Arief Rate, and sought, rather, to remain as integrated fighting units rather than be atomised in APRIS, something Suharto refused to countenance. Having fled from the efforts to bring them under control, they faced attack from Suharto's forces. Retreating to the jungle, they reappeared after the outbreak of hostilities between APRIS and the KL/KNIL in early August (see below), apparently to support the APRIS forces. Conflict arose, however, when a company under the command of a Mataram Brigade captain, Abdul Latief, summarily executed Arief Rate and another MBR leader. The tumult that consequently arose was 'settled only after hard fighting' and resulted in the destruction of Arief's battalion, 'against the will and the order of Lieutenant-Colonel Soeharto'. The incident 'provoked bitter feelings among the population against "the Javanese". One of Soeharto's basic principles had been violated – not to act precipitately'.[3]

Suharto's problems with the incorporation of guerrilla irregulars into the TNI brought him into contact once more with Kahar Muzakkar, who had been permitted to return to Makasar in June to assist in the negotiations with guerrilla groups over incorporation into the regular Army, and who held ambitions to be appointed military commander of South Sulawesi. As we have seen, Suharto had had some personal experience of Kahar during the revolutionary struggle and was clearly unimpressed by his spirited sense of independence, his heightened perception of his own importance, and his well-developed capacity to stir up discontent wherever he trod. Therefore, according to Roeder, Suharto 'opposed Headquarters' decision [to return Kahar to Makasar] very strongly. "Kahar never keeps his promises. He will create more trouble in the area", Soeharto warned'.[4] Kahar indeed proceeded to join the guerrillas, reflecting a popular belief that the TNI was not well disposed towards the local population, and eventually led a major rebellion against the government.

It was during his sojourn in Makasar that Suharto came to know the Habibie family, whose ten members included the 14-year-old Bacharuddin Yusuf Habibie (who in 1998 would succeed him as president). The family 'lived across the road, in front of the Mataram Brigade', and Suharto seems to have become close to them and visited their house often. He tells of his enjoyment at listening to the Javanese stories of Mrs Habibie, a native of Yogyakarta, of his presence at the death by heart attack of Mr Habibie ('I had the opportunity to close his eyes while praying to God Almighty for his forgiveness'), of the brigade's helping with the burial, and of his acting in Mr Habibie's place when one of his captains married one of the Habibie daughters.[5]

In July, Suharto's wife (and child) visited him for a week, and Suharto joined her on her return flight to Jakarta, since he had been ordered to report to army headquarters. Within an hour of his return to Makasar on the afternoon of 5 August, his brigade headquarters was suddenly subjected to a fierce attack from KNIL and KL troops, employing armour and mortar-fire. This incident was the result of a sudden increase in tension between APRIS and KL/KNIL troops, arising out of an apparently unintended transgression of the demarcation line by a newly arrived republican soldier a few days before, which had resulted in his being shot dead by KL/KNIL troops. Suharto managed to quell the offensive, calling on troops from outside the city and counter-attacking with the assistance of land and sea artillery and air support. Another KL/KNIL attack launched on the morning of 7 August developed into a battle that lasted into the night, and ended with the rebel forces on the defensive from a 'well coordinated' TNI counter-attack.[6] Hostilities the following day followed a similar course of attack and counter-attack, with the KL/KNIL forces finally and suddenly conceding defeat. The ferocity of the battle is evidenced by reports that over a thousand civilians were killed and more than 300 houses destroyed.[7]

Under these circumstances, Suharto was naturally reluctant to allow a ceasefire, notwithstanding the wishes of his commanding officer, Kawilarang, relayed to him by a staff officer. Indeed, Suharto ignored the order to cease fire, fearing that it was an enemy ruse. Only when Kawilarang personally confronted him to assure him that the enemy really wished to surrender did the shooting finally cease. A subsequent meeting between Kawilarang and the commander of the KNIL troops at the City Hotel in Makasar (not attended by Suharto, perhaps an indication of his unhappiness at Kawilarang's readiness to negotiate) hammered out an agreement which led, after further negotiation, to the KL/KNIL troops being disarmed and their equipment confiscated, and allowed to leave Makasar by late August.[8] Their primary mission accomplished – but their reputation, and that of the TNI in general, sullied amongst the people of South Sulawesi by the Arief Rate debacle – Suharto's troops returned to Yogya on 17 September 1950, having lost seventeen men in the course of the expedition. In the meantime, the state of East Indonesia had been dissolved into the unitary Republic of Indonesia proclaimed on 17 August 1950.[9]

RETURN TO CENTRAL JAVA

Suharto returned to an army in the midst of a thoroughgoing process of rationalisation and restructuring which sought not just to reduce its size but also to provide it with a more coherent command structure. In July 1950, as a first attempt to flesh out Nasution's concept of a territorial force, the country had been divided into seven military regions (TT), similar in kind to, if on a much larger scale than, the Wehrkreise of the anti-Dutch guerrilla war. The reorganisation itself was something of a compromise. On the one hand, it sought to rationalise and regularise command structures so that the bifurcation of loyalties and confusing multiplicity of commands within specific areas were diminished, particularly by integrating non-TNI elements into the structure and preventing local command overlap. At the same time, regularisation could not be allowed to proceed too far, since the very concept of a territorial structure, which presumed strong local civilian collaboration with army units in times of war, required that 'as far as possible, all units [be] staffed by soldiers from the region they were charged to defend'.[10] This pragmatic policy also recognised the reality of the powerful regional identification of troop formations forged during the struggle against the Dutch, and ignored for the time being the problem of the national unification of the Army.

In pursuit of these broad goals, in September 1950 Gatot Subroto, panglima of the Diponegoro Division (now identified as TT IV, the Fourth Army Territory, and based in Semarang), rationalised the number of Central Java brigades from eight to five. Suharto was placed in command of one of them, Brigade O, with seven battalions, recently renamed the Prince Mangkubumi Brigade. This brigade was responsible for the regions of Kebumen, Purworejo, Magelang, Temanggung, Wonosobo, Sleman, Gunung Kidul, Bantul, Wates and Wonosari. It appears as well that some of Suharto's troops were employed assisting Achmad Yani's brigade in combating armed gangs in the Central Java mountains of the Merapi–Merbabu complex.

How Suharto, following his return from Makasar, handled the delicate and painful problem of troop demobilisation is difficult to know. It was a particularly sensitive issue, given the close personal relations between commander and troops which had developed in the unruly circumstances of the revolutionary period, and

Suharto found it 'psychologically difficult' to force his friends to leave the Army.[11] Presumably he, like other commanders, was reluctant to release men to an uncertain future outside the Armed Forces. For those he was unable to retain, however, he apparently put in place mechanisms to assist them in making the transition to civilian life. According to Gafur, he made 'efforts to assist in the setting up of some business for ex-members of his unit who could not be absorbed anymore in a military formation'.[12] The business was a 'transport enterprise established with Army vehicles in Jogjakarta to provide jobs for his veterans', for which he received a reprimand from his divisional commander, Gatot Subroto.[13] Suharto, stung and hurt by the criticism, 'was so thoroughly disheartened that he almost decided to quit the military service and pursue another profession, if need be [he] was prepared to become a taxi driver'. He was, in Gafur's account, only moved from this course of action by the suasions of his wife: 'I told him that I did not marry a taxi driver, I married a soldier. I furthermore urged him to face all these tribulations with a cool head although a mutinous heart'.[14] Her sentiments, perhaps, were influenced by the fact that their family, now housed in new lodgings at Jl. Pungung, Kotabaru, was growing; on 1 May 1951, Siti Hartinah gave birth to their second child and first son – Sigit Haryoyudanto – apparently conceived during her brief interlude in Makasar in 1950.

On 1 November 1951, Brigades Q and R (Pragola I and II), responsible for the regions of Semarang and Pati, were merged; a couple of weeks thereafter, Suharto was moved from his longstanding station in Yogyakarta to take command of the enlarged Pragola Brigade in Salatiga, swapping commands with Lt. Col. Sarbini. The nine new battalions of his enlarged brigade formed a rather motley crew with wildly different origins, symptomatic of the broader problems of army integration within the new nation. They included 'three original TNI battalions, three battalions of former KNIL troops, three battalions of ex-Hizbullah troops, and the battalion of Muladi Yusuf, formerly of the leftist Pesindo'. Together with the general problems he shared with colleagues of sustaining troop morale in a context of miserly military budgeting, Suharto's immediate task, in line with the prevailing need for demobilisation and rationalisation of troop strengths, was 'to establish four battalions from the existing nine'.[15]

THE REVOLT OF BATTALION 426

This institutional re-engineering was a task requiring considerable delicacy, especially since rationalisation of this kind inevitably meant the reduction in rank and function of officers. Ironically, it was made easier in the end for Suharto by the revolt of one of his battalions (426), a former Hizbullah unit stationed at Kudus, which proclaimed its allegiance to the Darul Islam movement in late 1951. 'It seemed that God gave me a way because Battalion 426 led by Major Munawar and his deputy Captain Sofyan went into revolt. In facing and quelling the rebellion of Battalion 426 I was able to make a natural selection of personnel.'[16]

Darul Islam had developed great strength in its base in the southern and eastern parts of West Java, following the withdrawal of the Siliwangi Division to Central

Java in line with the stipulations of the Renville agreement of early 1948. The movement sought, above all else, the achievement of an Islamic state; indeed, in August 1949 its leader, S. M. Kartosuwiryo, formally proclaimed a *Negara Islam Indonesia* (Islamic State of Indonesia). Elements of the Siliwangi Division returning at the end of 1948 suddenly found themselves contested by Darul Islam forces, originally Hizbullah and Sabillilah units which had refused to abide by the conditions of the Renville agreement to depart West Java, in areas they had previously called their own. Once the greater part of the Siliwangi troops returned, following the capture of Yogyakarta in December 1949, battle was soon joined with Kartosuwiryo's TII (Islamic Army of Indonesia). Already by late 1948, Hizbullah units under Amir Fatah had moved from West Java into the north-central *kabupaten* (districts) of Brebes and Tegal, and a Central Java Islamic state had been proclaimed in April 1949; one of Suharto's battalions, under the leadership of Sarjono, was one of the two battalions ordered in late 1949 to engage in sweeps against it.

Diponegoro staff already harboured suspicions of Darul Islam influence in two of Suharto's Pragola battalions, 423 and 426. Members of Battalion (Bn) 426, mostly Hizbullah troops originating from the region of Klaten, had made something of a name for themselves for the ferocity with which they had assisted in dispatching troops associated with the 1948 Madiun rebellion. Their enthusiasm for violent retribution against 'communists' had drawn the hostility of TNI commanders, notably Slamet Riyadi in Solo, and led to occasional clashes with regular republican troops. They were, moreover, unhappy with their incorporation into Suharto's Pragola Brigade in the regular army. Suharto himself had already reported his own suspicions about the potential for unrest in Bn 426.[17] Suspicions rose to new heights when three officers from Bn 423, mostly comprising former Hizbullah troops, arrested and interrogated after the finding of incriminating documents on the body of a Darul Islam officer killed south of Brebes, eventually revealed plans by Captain Sofyan of Bn 426 for a Darul Islam uprising. Refusing an order to appear before the Diponegoro panglima, Sofyan escaped arrest in the early morning of 8 December, outwitting Suharto's detailed plan for his capture by another Pragola battalion and fleeing his encampment, a disused *kretek* cigarette factory about one kilometre out of Kudus, with three companies of his troops, about 300 men; two other companies of the battalion, stationed in Magelang under Captain Alip, also joined the revolt.

Together with a small number of defectors from Bn 427 based at Semarang, these units began a campaign of terror in the countryside. Suharto, in Salatiga, ordered his troops to pursue and intercept the rebels as they moved southwards towards their home territory of Klaten. Not for the first time, Suharto felt the intrusive hand of civilian politicians; according to a report in a local Semarang newspaper, Masyumi Prime Minister Sukiman had attempted to have one of Suharto's battalion commanders tread softly against the Muslim rebels.[18] The intervention seems to have been ignored, notwithstanding a later plea by Minister for Defence Sewaka that the Army should act with 'justice, humanity and not offend religious feelings'.[19]

Around early January 1952, Suharto succeeded Lt. Col. Bachrun as commander of a task force ('Operasi Merdeka Timur V') established to pursue and crush the rebellious battalion.[20] The job of destroying the rebellion, in which the TNI employed tank, artillery and air power, proved long and difficult; early in January the Diponegoro commander substantially increased the civil powers of the operation's commander, but the revolt nonetheless continued to gain momentum. In a battle at Tanggalan, Sofyan, clad in a white gown and turban, was mortally wounded; in another fierce encounter at Simo, east of Salatiga, on 25 January, in which the Armed Forces employed air support, the rebels suffered serious losses. Alip's Magelang rebels, meanwhile, who had ranged across the lower southern slopes of Mt Merapi, suffered similar pursuit; Alip was killed on 30 January. These extended operations, during which 'all the main roads around Yogyakarta and Surakarta were closed', were allegedly sometimes marked by ruthless and tactless actions by republican forces against prisoners, the local population and mosques.[21] According to Van Dijk, 'one of the districts of Klaten that suffered most was the *kewedanaan* [sub-district] Jatinom. Here 425 houses were damaged or destroyed, and 46 civilians killed and 37 badly wounded'.[22] The remaining rebels scattered north and west, linking with Darul Islam forces in West Java and north-west Central Java or taking their place with the thugs, misfits, revolutionaries, fanatics, escapees and outlaws operating in the mountainous regions of the Merapi–Merbabu complex.

Suharto's frustrated efforts to destroy the rebellious cohorts of Bn 426 attracted barely veiled criticism from the press; *Siasat* remarked drily that 'people are very surprised at how it is that a problem which in the beginning was seen as trifling, up to now has still not been able to be solved'.[23] Nasution was also critical, and the difficulties provided him with ammunition in his urgings to civilian politicians to adopt a more professional attitude to army formation.[24] Suharto, for his part, makes no substantive comment on the performance of his troops during the operation; he was content to remark, as he had earlier suggested, that 'once the rebellion of Battalion 426 had been crushed, consolidation of the Pragola Brigade could be carried out easily without causing any flare-up, and four strong battalions were assembled'.[25]

Suharto's pained efforts to destroy Bn 426 stood in sharp contrast to the strategy later pursued by his fellow brigade commander, Achmad Yani, in his pursuit of Darul Islam forces (including remnants of Bn 426) in north-west Central Java, the so-called GBN area.[26] There, in October 1951, Yani took over from the earlier efforts led by Sarbini and Bachrun, and in June 1952 personally developed an elite band of troops, known as the Banteng Raiders, to pursue the Darul Islam in the GBN area, especially around Brebes. When the Raiders developed from their original two-company strength to battalion size, a certain Ali Murtopo, previously a member of Yani's brigade staff and a veteran of the guerrilla struggle of the revolution, became a company commander in Bn 431. The Raiders, often personally led by the dashing Yani, were able to clear the region of significant Darul Islam activity by 1957.

While Suharto's attention was engaged by his pursuit of Bn 426, Nasution announced further changes to TT IV early in 1952; the area of Central Java was sub-divided into four sub-territories, and Suharto's Pragola Brigade, eight battalions comprising 6,159 troops, was redesignated as the Fourteenth Infantry Regiment, headquartered at Salatiga and responsible for the Semarang and Pati regions. His battalions were 420, 421, 423, 424 and 428. In 1953, further reorganisation created battalion 440 (from the former 421 and 427), 441 (from 420), 442 (from 424), 443 (from 428) and 448 (from 408). Battalion 423, stained by its involvement with the Darul Islam, was eliminated, and 426, as we have seen, had rebelled.

In 1952, Suharto's father died of malaria, and Suharto returned to Kemusuk with his wife (whom we shall hereafter term 'Ibu Tien') for the burial in the family burial compound situated behind his house in Kemusuk kidul.[27] It seems odd in the extreme both that Suharto was apparently not informed of his father's serious condition, and that his assessment of his death is so brief, peremptory and unemotional. Such behaviour makes greater sense, however, if one considers how peripheral Kertosudiro had always been to his son's life, even though, Suharto claims, 'he always visited his grandchildren to bring them all their needs'.[28] His lack of emotion may, indeed, reflect that Suharto had come to realise that Kertosudiro was not in fact his real father. That must remain an open question in the absence of further evidence, but it is clear that Suharto had little attachment of an emotive kind with his purportedly natural father and had learned, simply, to live without him.

THE BROADER FIELD OF POLITICS

Suharto appears at this time to have evinced little interest in the wider developing drama of Indonesian politics, as a rapid succession of civilian governments, working according to a Western-style model of democracy which enjoyed neither broad nor deep legitimacy in elite circles, stumbled from problem to problem without achieving any significant success in their solution. A general sense of disappointment and disillusionment that independence had not produced the expected fruits of progress, prosperity and an enhanced sense of community began to surface. At the same time, leading elements in the Army, increasingly unhappy with civilian governments that did not accord them appropriate respect, manifested the first stirrings of serious army discontent with the political system in the so-called affair of 17 October 1952.

The affair resulted from tensions between the 'professional' military leadership, centred in Jakarta and Bandung, which sought a smaller, more efficient and more technically adept army, and the group of army members who relied either on Peta training or revolutionary experience for their credentials and who were afraid of being set aside or marginalised by army rationalisation. This latter group, itself not especially enamoured of the parliamentary system, found support amongst opposition parliamentarians who sought to stop the rationalisation program. The professional group, wounded at what it saw as civilian interference in internal army affairs, attempted to bring pressure upon Sukarno to dissolve parliament by organising a large-scale demonstration, including a threatening military presence, outside the presidential palace on 17 October. Sukarno's refusal to accommodate the wishes of the 'professional officers' resulted in Nasution's downfall as army chief of staff, and quashed any prospect for the development of an army entirely subservient to civilian control.[29]

Suharto was both uninvolved in and apparently unconcerned by the 17 October affair:

> I had absolutely no understanding about what that incident was really about since I was busy fighting the rebellion … In retrospect, I think that what had happened had come from too much overacting. Placing cannons facing the Palace, I think, was not good tactics. It was said that those who went to the Palace had the intention of delivering a message to the President, as the Supreme Commander. But to do it in such a way with heavy guns facing the Palace was excessive. Indeed, just being ready, ready to face anything that might happen, would have been enough.[30]

Such comment seems like thinly veiled criticism of Nasution, who was heavily involved in the affair, and of the style of those officers who sought to place pressure upon the parliament. Indeed, according to McVey, the affair was the occasion of some tension within the Diponegoro Division, as 'Diponegoro regimental commanders pressed the panglima, Lt. Col. Bachrun, to state his position on the October 17 Affair'. Bachrun, it appears, was sympathetic to the 'professionals' and found himself having to state his support for the government without much conviction.[31] Suharto's role in this local contretemps, if any, is unknown, but it seems likely that he bore greater sympathy to the anti-rationalisation forces.

The denouement left the Army seriously split and its high command badly weakened. In such circumstances, local support became pre-eminently important in commanders maintaining their positions, and local room for manoeuvre and policy-making was greatly strengthened. The demise of the Nasution group left army headquarters enfeebled and directionless just at the time when the civilian arm of politics was exhibiting similar institutional frailty. This pattern of disarray in central authority was exacerbated by the precipitate decline in government funding for the Army after 1952, diminishing the prospects of the high command employing patronage to win support, and encouraging local commanders to explore more vigorously independent avenues of revenue-raising to support their troops and sustain their commands.

Just what Suharto made of these developments is difficult to say. Given his oft-demonstrated close affinity with his troops, and his sure understanding of the necessity for close attention to their needs, he had no need to change his pattern of behaviour. There is no indication, moreover, that any of these developments impinged much on his consciousness, certainly not in a way that might have stimulated him to take a more active role in events. He demonstrated no desire to impress himself or his own ideas on a wider audience, and seemed content to restrain the exercise of his energies to his allotted role as a regimental commander.

TO SOLO

At the conclusion of nearly eighteen months of solid but not especially distinguished service in Salatiga, Suharto was posted to Solo on 1 March 1953, as commander of Infantry Regiment 15 (comprising elements of the former Panembahan Senopati Division). His regiment, four battalions strong following still another reorganisation, comprised 3,704 troops. Elements of two of his battalions were involved in operations against the TII in the GBN area, and units of two others with Operation Twitunggal against allegedly communist-provoked politico-criminal bands in the Merapi–Merbabu complex.

Suharto's Solo experience does not appear to have been especially happy, notwithstanding that within a few months of his arrival, on 23 July 1953, his third child, a son named Bambang Trihatmojo, was born. The region, as we have seen, had long been a site of fierce ideological tension and confrontation and strong leftist politics, especially in comparison with the more staid atmosphere of Yogya where Suharto had served for most of his military career; leftist leanings were pervasive in the troops now under his command. To his evident dismay he discovered that one of his battalions, the Digdo Battalion at Kleco, was even receiving ideological education from the veteran communist leader, Alimin; amongst the members of that battalion were Untung and Suradi, who 'led the G.30.S/PKI [the 'coup attempt'] in 1965'.[32] Untung was a company commander in Bn 444 in Solo while Suharto was commander. Perhaps in response to this situation, Suharto appears to have dedicated special attention to the troops under his command in order to improve their professionalism. Always a stickler for training and practice, he prided himself on his skill as a trainer of troops, but, according to Roeder, he 'succeeded only partly in the elimination of ideological quarrels among the soldiers'.[33]

In addition to attempting to improve the regiment's fighting capacity by training and reorganisation, Suharto also put his mind to the perennial problem of funding for his troops and sought to establish cooperatives to assist them, much as he had done for his Yogya unit. While he later claimed that 'the experience of developing cooperatives within Regiment 15 in Solo was really a great benefit in development of the soldiers' morale and peace within their families', Roeder noted that, 'later, Soeharto complained in particular about the stagnation of the Army co-operative movement which he had promoted'.[34] Roeder's assertion is perhaps a reference to the opposition that Suharto's ideas about development as a means of combating radicalism may have encountered in Solo from the continuing vitality of leftist thinking in the Army (later to emerge in the form of Central Java support for the 30 September Movement). Ibu Tien, for her part, turned her hand to business in a way that suggests she was not unacquainted with its practices; she helped out with family finances by making and selling Solo batik and retailing discounted factory cloth to the wives of soldiers.

During his Solo interlude, Suharto began, perhaps for the first time, to apply himself systematically to different areas of study, apparently to compensate for his relative lack of education and in the realisation that study was both appropriate and necessary to sustain his career. He took part in military courses of an equivalent standing to high school, sharpened his social skills by joining the Brigade Club, and even took flying lessons at the Aero Club, clocking up forty hours solo in a Piper until his doctor, reportedly worried about his heart, ended his flying career. As well, he served a term as vice-president of a local soccer club.

THE ARMY AND POLITICS

By 1955, the long-festering scar of disunity within the Army, both manifested and exaggerated by the 17 October affair, had begun to heal. At a conference held in Yogyakarta in February 1955, attended by some 270 high officers, there came a ceremonial reconciliation, at the grave of General Sudirman, between factions within the Army. If they could agree on nothing else, it was that parliamentary-based government was divisive and had been crudely intrusive in arenas which the Army considered within its own competence. The Army subsequently refused to accept the government's appointment of the junior Colonel Bambang Utoyo as chief of staff; the government consequently lost the confidence of the parliament and was forced to resign.

As a consequence of these developments, 'many officers had clearly become very receptive to the view that the parliamentary system should be abandoned and replaced by a system permitting the Army to play a more active political role'.[35] Two interlocked tendencies began to develop within the Army: the first, most closely identified with elements of the Siliwangi, involved efforts to bring down the government directly by means of a coup; the other, 'for what seems to have been the first time in our period',[36] was the increasingly common practice amongst local commanders outside Java of pursuing their local interests in defiance of central government policy, especially with regard to illicit smuggling activities for local fund-raising purposes.

Suharto was not strongly involved in this flexing of army muscle. I have found no direct evidence that he took part in the famous unity meeting of army officers in Yogyakarta in 1955 – although, given that there were eighty-one lieutenants colonel present, it would be surprising if he had not – and his thoughts on the re-appointment of Nasution as army chief of staff in November 1955 can only be guessed at. If Suharto was present, he was not elected, as was his colleague Sarbini (commander of Regiment 13) and a number of other officers of equal or lower rank, to take part in a smaller meeting, beginning on 21 February, closed to the most senior officers and established to discuss 'problems connected with the Army'.[37] More generally, he paid only passing and unimpressed attention to events of broader national or international significance: 'the Asia–Africa Conference took place in Bandung in April 1955, and in September the first General Elections were held. They were special events in themselves, but not relevant to my own particular activities'.[38]

These words appear to sum up Suharto's attitude to politics and the development of national policy at this phase of his career. He was, and perceived himself to be, primarily a professional soldier, a field officer engaged in developing and training troops for action. While he had his own views about various developments on the broader national stage, he kept them much to himself and made no special effort to engage with these issues. He remained, at this time, a man of seriously foreshortened vision and thoroughgoing conservatism, attached in a deep but probably unexplored way to such dogmas as the soldier's oath of duty and Pancasila – the five principles articulated by Sukarno in June 1945: belief in one God, a just and civilised humanity, Indonesian unity, democracy through representative deliberation, and social justice. He was probably also increasingly unhappy with the threat of social upheaval which leftist ideas presented. But he found no particular motivation for extending himself beyond his accustomed sphere. With a few minor exceptions, all of his adult life had been spent soldiering in Central Java. He was a man of practicality who, notwithstanding his beliefs, set himself to solving only those problems which were within his ambit and competence. He was not necessarily politically naive – his revolutionary experiences had taught him some vital lessons of politics – but he was, at this stage, politically unambitious. According to Roeder, 'Soeharto [in 1957] had no intimate contacts with the top leaders of the country; he was alien to party politics and he was not ambitious to play a role in social life'.[39]

Meanwhile, under Nasution's revived leadership, the Army intensified its struggle for self-identification and to carve out its proper role, with the beginnings of a new sense of strategic purpose in the army high command. Nasution's policies had three major thrusts: the first was to strengthen the high command's control of the Army by means of a deliberate 'tour of duty' policy of senior officer placements, designed to break up comfortable and strongly entrenched local affiliations and enhance professionalism. The British journalist James Mossman had observed that 'the Indonesian Army is not a united force but a coalition of local commanders, most of whom are at present obedient to their Chief of Staff [Nasution] but all of whom could change their loyalties overnight if the political situation favoured their doing so or if Nasution interfered too openly with their private rackets'.[40] Nasution sought to set this to rights by establishing plans for a large-scale program of transfers of command, a process completed by February 1956. A conference in early August 1956 saw Nasution and senior officers schedule a series of important transfers of command, aimed at asserting the authority of army headquarters and developing a sense of broader united purpose amongst territorial commanders.

The second of Nasution's thrusts was to develop a centralised and regular form of army training to inculcate desired values amongst troops and officers in place of, or ancillary to, the local instruction and value inculcation provided by panglima up to 1956, and to 'ultimately … orient ambitious officers away from the cultivation of a local power base and towards the pursuit of expertise and the favor of the center'.[41] The third, rather more diffuse at this time, was to seek a greater prominence and respect for the Army, to be reflected in such things as increased levels of government funding and a greater independence in matters within its own jurisdiction; 'every army officer felt that the budget allocation for defense was entirely inadequate, and the contrast was frequently drawn between the smallness of this allocation and the apparent generosity of the cabinet with funds for a number of other projects'.[42]

By the end of 1956, the feeling of impending crisis, even chaos, was thick in the air. The Siliwangi group, marshalled under Col. Zulkifli Lubis, failed to mount its planned coup, in circumstances as surreal as they were comical. A spate of army-sponsored regional dissidence flared in the second half of 1956. Sukarno, skilfully deploying an increasingly nationalist/revolutionary rhetoric, found in the Army an ally of convenience in the struggle to assert his mastery over the political process and the gathering crescendo of unrest and confusion. His answer – the gradual development of the notion of 'Guided Democracy' – struck a chord with an army disenchanted with Western parliamentary democracy and ready to entertain a more authentically nationalist and authoritarian mode of rule which would allow it to play a more directly influential role in the realm of politics.

Together, Sukarno and the Army conspired to deliver the 'death blow' to parliamentary democracy, in the face of only token opposition by the political parties – a sign of the flaccidity of party politics and the fact that, in their discredited condition, they were no longer the pivot of politics. With the resignation of the second Ali Sastroamijoyo cabinet on 14 March 1957 and the immediate proclamation, after considerable prompting by Nasution and his deputy Gatot Subroto, of a State of War and Siege (SOB), both Sukarno and the Army had the means to inject themselves legally into the political system in order to save the country, to restrict what had formerly been a lively range of political activities, and to lay the foundations of a new political regime.[43] Under the close supervision of Sukarno, a new non-party cabinet was formed under the leadership of the respected technocrat Juanda Kartawijaya.

DIVISIONAL COMMAND

Suharto, for long a musing but essentially uninterested bystander in the drama of capital-city politics, was catapulted into a position of increasing influence with his appointment to the leadership of the Diponegoro Division. It was also to transform him deeply and serve as the vehicle for his articulation to the realm of national politics and policy.

At the beginning of 1956, Suharto's long career with the Diponegoro had been ended, albeit temporarily, with his call to Jakarta for his first taste of staff work. There he worked to the army chief of staff for planning of the General Staff. Within three months, however, he was assigned back to the Diponegoro Division, this time as divisional chief of staff in Semarang. By early September he had succeeded to the post of acting panglima of the Division, replacing Bachrun; an 'unforgettable'[44] transfer ceremony was held on 3 September in Magelang in the presence of Nasution, acting Defence Minister Ali Sastroamijoyo, and a host of senior civilian officials and officers. Accepting his new appointment, Suharto

-GEHEIM-
12

Onderdeel	Commandant	Locatie	Hoofdkwartier	Dat.en Eval.	Sterkte en bewapening
III Brigade	Lt.Kol.SOEHARTO	Zuid-KEDOE	DJOCJA (WA9020)	22/10 A2	C.S. Maj. REKSO
I Bataljon	Maj.SARDJONO	Omg.v.DJOCJA ?	KEDOEMEN (WA1238)	13/8	
II Bataljon	Maj.SOEDARMO	?	POERWOREDJO (WA5132)	13/8	C.S. Kapt. IKSAN SOEGIARTO A2. Dit Bat. heeft deelgenomen aan de ontwapening van de communistische troepen olv Maj. SOENARTO (ex Cdt CLXXI Bat te KOETOARDJO).
III Bataljon	Maj.SHROEHARDOJO	POERWOREDJO-stad	POERWOREDJO (WA5132)	13/9	Dit Bat. heeft deelgenomen aan de ontwapening van de communistische troepen olv Maj. SOENARTO (ex Cdt CLXXI Dat.te KOETOARDJO). Bew. 90%. Sterkte ca. 500 man. Wnd.Cdt. Kapt. SOEBIANDONO.
IV Bataljon	Maj.SOEDJONO	Medan Brig.III	DJOCJA (WA9020)	13/8	Het Medan Brig. III (front Brig. III) omvat het gebied langs de S.Q.-lijn tussen JAVA's Zuidkust en het Regentschap BANDJARNEGARA.
Depot Bataljon	Kapt.SOEKARJADI	?	MAGELANG (WA7457)	21/9 A2	
IV Brigade	Lt.Kol.MARTONO BROTOKOESOMO	N.W.-KEDOE	DJOCJA (WA9020)	6/8 A2	Deze Brig.is opgeh.Lt.Kol.BROTO-KOESOMO is nog steeds voortvluchtig.
I Bataljon (ex Lasjkar-troepen)	Maj. SOEGIRI	?	KEDJADJAR (WA4583)	27/9 A2	Op 7/10'48 is Maj. SOEGIRI met zijn staf naar Ned. gebied gevlucht. 11/10. A2.
II DIVISIE	Lt.Kol.GATOT SOEBROTO (Goebernoer Militer 2)	DAERAH MILITER ISTIMEWA II (REMBANG, SOLO, MADIOEN en GROBOGAN)	SOLO (WB4147)	2/11 A2	C.S. Maj. SOEPRAPTO. A2. De Mil.Gouverneur II heeft in alle opzichten de leiding als cdt en als Hfd. van het militair gezag in de ressorten PATI en MADIOEN. Ook voeren de door de Mil.Gouverneur aangestelde Cdtn het tactisch Co bij alle acties over alle eenheden, inclusief de eenheden van I Div. in hun resp. ressorten. A2.

Dutch intelligence document from mid-November 1948, mentioning Suharto and his battalion leaders. (Netherlands Ministry of Defence)

Suharto and his guerrilla fighters, June 1949, shortly before his return to Yogyakarta. (Ipphos)

Suharto looks on as the Sultan discusses affairs with military observers of the United Nations Commission on Indonesia, upon the Republic's return to Yogya, July 1949. (Ipphos)

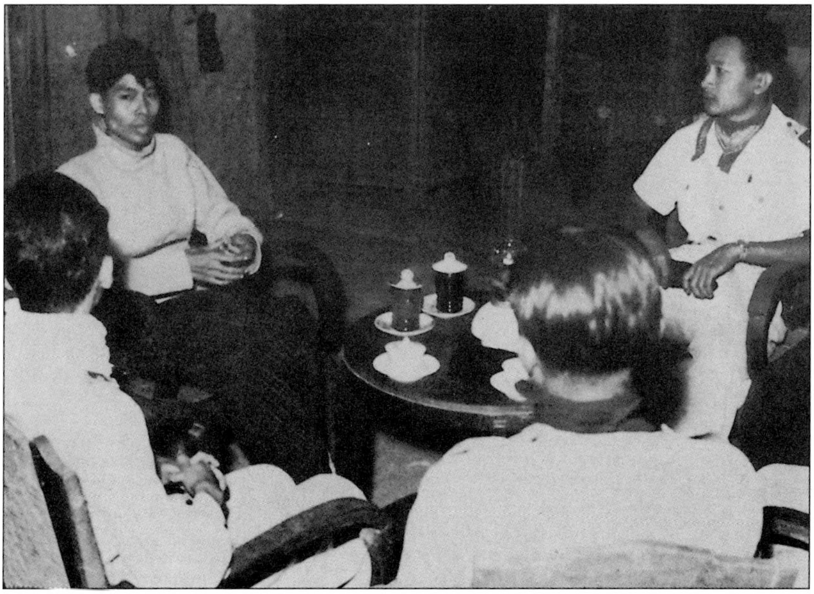

Suharto meeting with Sudirman before the latter's return to Yogya, July 1949. (Ipphos)

Suharto with his commander, Col. Alex Kawilarang, in Makasar, c. August 1950. (Ipphos)

Suharto in discussion with Lt. Col. Bachrun during the campaign against the rebel Bn 426 in Central Java, c. January 1952. (Ipphos)

remarked that 'the struggle of our nation is not yet finished'; he spoke of the need 'to perfect duty and strengthen unity with a spirit of cooperation'. At a reception held in Semarang two days later, he explained that his duties as acting panglima did not spare him 'from the task of development. And the task of development cannot proceed smoothly without the help of the people'. He repeated these sentiments, including an assertion of the 'need to continue the unfinished revolution', in an Order of the Day issued to commemorate Armed Forces Day on 5 October 1956. His Order of the Day on National Heroes' Day (10 November) was more specific and bleak: 'an attitude of provincialism, greed and corruption has broken out in all areas. It seems as though we have lost balance. Lost the direction of life which we outlined when we proclaimed independence'. Placing his stamp on the Division, Suharto organised a meeting of regimental commanders and other senior figures early in November, aimed at discussing 'routine problems' within the Division as well as 'to look for points of agreement in thinking to solidify [*menkonkretisir*] the integrity of the Diponegoro Division and which, it is hoped, can be extended to the integrity of the whole Army'.[45]

Suharto was raised to the rank of acting colonel in November and confirmed in the panglima's post, at the rank of colonel, at the beginning of 1957. Unlike many of his colleagues, like Yani, Suharto was never selected for further training in the United States. The reasons are not clear but perhaps relate to his relative lack of sophistication, his inability to speak English, and perhaps a perception in Jakarta that his career would never rise to significant heights. In this he was somewhat exceptional; 'between 1956 and 1959 more than 200 high ranking officers were trained in the U.S. while low ranking officers were trained by the hundreds'.[46]

Suharto's appointment to the crucial position of Diponegoro commander was itself a demonstration of the power of local interests and the fragility of central army authority. Perhaps on the recommendation of Bachrun, the army high command had planned that he be replaced as panglima by the East Javanese Bambang Supeno, a close associate of Zulkifli Lubis. Having heard that this recommendation merely awaited Sukarno's signature, Yoga Sugama, the Japanese- and British-trained assistant I (intelligence) on Bachrun's staff, not wanting to have the Diponegoro Division drawn into the vortex of army politics and disunity, especially at a time of growing communist strength within army ranks in Central Java, moved quickly to block it. Yoga proceeded to contact all senior Diponegoro officers, as well as sounding out opinion amongst junior officers, including Captain Ali Murtopo, then still commanding a Banteng Raiders unit. An all-night meeting of regional commanders of the Division at Kopeng, near Salatiga, attended as well by Semarang headquarters staff such as Munadi (assistant V), agreed to oppose the appointment of Bambang and to endorse Yoga's proposal that Suharto ('an officer who had a calm way about him and a modest bearing, which brought him great respect from those below him') be appointed instead.[47]

All but the most senior officer at the meeting signed a statement to that effect, and Yoga and Major Suryosumpeno were detailed the task of conveying the message to the army leadership in Jakarta. Before leaving on their errand, the two officers met with Suharto – who must have known of the movement on his behalf but who had apparently not attended the senior officers' meeting, presumably to avoid the accusation that he had engineered the move against Bambang – to explain the attitude of the officers in proposing him as panglima. In Jakarta, Yoga and Suryosumpeno met with Lubis, a former commanding officer of Yoga; Yoga argued that the appointment of Bambang would cause serious dissension in Central Java, with the threat that the centre might lose control there. His view won the day; Suharto was appointed as panglima, and his rank raised to colonel. His appointment entrenched the emerging custom that control of the Diponegoro must go to a 'Yogya' man, rather than one from Solo, Semarang or further afield.

THE BUSINESS OF DEVELOPMENT IN CENTRAL JAVA

Suharto was now the commander of the Division which had been born in the region of his own birth, a place he knew intimately and whose language, Javanese, rather than Indonesian or Dutch, was the common mode of intercourse amongst officers and men. He had always professed a keen interest in the welfare of the soldiers under him, as well as that of the general populace, and a sense of indebtedness towards both groups developed by his revolutionary experiences. More specifically, he had come to a shrewd if unsophisticated realisation that the kind of political quietude which he deemed to be the proper mode of life could most easily be accomplished in the face of the threat presented by the PKI – and other disruptive forces – if society were empowered to develop the material conditions of life, at the same time solidifying the strength and unity of the nation.

Accordingly, he began a systematic attempt to raise funds for the welfare both of his troops and of the general population of Central Java, parts of which region were notorious for their high levels of poverty and malnutrition. Semarang, the site of his headquarters, had long enjoyed a reputation as a central node of Java's commerce; in addition to its port and its role as a central receiving and distribution point for the trade and produce of Central Java, it was home to a large population of Sino-Indonesian traders. It was, then, a likely site for someone with Suharto's commercial proclivities. The Diponegoro Division's finance and economic planning division, popularly known as Finek, had the task 'not only to keep the books but to raise cash'.[48]

Suharto's vision of his role – the pursuit of economic development in Central Java as the means of promoting the general prosperity upon which his vision of the ideal (that is, static, hierarchical, organic and quietistic) polity could be based – was, as we shall see, an early manifestation of a broader concern within the Army. Conscious of the relationship between poverty itself and popular attachment to the solutions presented by the communists to address poverty, he sought in his capacity as regional commander to take steps to address these larger social concerns through the technique of territorial guidance. His program attracted many younger officers to his staff to assist in developing the concept. Yoga was already a strong supporter and served Suharto as assistant (intelligence) as well as chief of staff of the Daily Regional War Authority under martial law. He in turn recruited Ali Murtopo, who held similar views, to serve as assistant V (territorial) on Suharto's headquarters staff. Another recruit was a highly experienced and well-connected finance officer, Sujono Humardani.

In his efforts in this direction, Suharto's arm was immeasurably strengthened by the emergency powers available to regional army commanders by virtue of the declaration of SOB (State of War and Siege). It had the immediate effect of allowing Armed Forces officers to intervene in what had previously been wholly civilian matters, and to assume new powers of a political, administrative and economic kind. The powers available to territorial commanders under the SOB provisions were, according to one authority, 'immense'; indeed, 'through the structure and authority of the army under martial law, a kind of *de facto* federal arrangement evolved'.[49] Immediately upon the announcement of SOB, Suharto (as commander TT IV) attended a senior commanders' meeting at army headquarters in Jakarta from 15 to 20 March which had been convened to discuss matters of national importance, including 'the effort to reassert state authority, the implementation of the state of siege, unity within the army, the problem of the Dwi Tunggal [the governing partnership between Sukarno and Hatta, which had dissolved in 1956], the destruction of corruption and smuggling',[50] as well as the recently decreed State of War and Siege.

The Army did not seek to take complete control from civilian territorial authorities – indeed, there was often a close cultural affinity, an identity of conservative interests, a shared distaste for the political parties, and a sense of mutual support between army men and the elite corps of *pamong praja* (civilian territorial officials) – but officers were not slow to intervene as and where they judged it necessary, and they were swift to assume control in key spheres of the regional economies, notably, as we shall see in the case of Suharto, in economic affairs. In short, 'the martial law administration was enabled to intervene anywhere and at any time it chose'. The result, according to one authority, 'was a growing number of dysfunctions in the governance of the country. For the relationship between the new martial law administration and civil government was unclear, and there was little effective coordination of the two'.[51]

Immediately upon his return to Semarang, Suharto issued an Order of the Day.[52] Noting the less-than-happy history of the Republic since its proclamation ('disorder, smuggling, corruption, subversive activities, unequal competition, and conflicts ... have hindered efforts to develop the nation'), he exhorted his troops, the local state apparatus and the people in general to work to bring the state and nation into a 'national constructive' (*nasional konstruktif*) direction. While the SOB legislation was indeed a colonial relic, its purpose in this case was to protect the people:

> SOB is not power, but firmness. Therefore, accept SOB as a firm tool for completing our unfinished struggle. With SOB we must be firm in upholding the authority of the State of the Republic of Indonesia which we proclaimed on 17 August 1945. With SOB we must endeavour to fulfill the wish of the people for life in a just and prosperous society. With SOB we must firmly break through a byzantine bureaucracy in order to create a dynamic way of working.

Finally, he exhorted members of the Diponegoro Division to make the situation into an opportunity of service for the state and nation, and not to think that the Armed Forces had taken hold of power. The notion that the nation was suffering a serious diminution in its attachment and loyalty to the values of the revolution, and a weakening of its unity from the activities of sectional interests, remained a central theme in his subsequent addresses, as well as the need to work in unison in the interests of development and prosperity.[53]

Suharto also convened a meeting with his civilian counterparts, including the governor of Central Java, the head of the special region of Yogyakarta (Sultan Hamengkubuwono IX), and police and judicial officers. During the meeting, which lasted more than three hours, he 'explained the meaning and intention' of the state of siege.[54] The new powers seemed to fit comfortably into what he construed as his realm of competence, thus a report in April 1957 that he was to release prisoners held under the provisions of SOB as an end-of-fasting month (*Lebaran*) gesture.[55] Under the new arrangements, Suharto assumed the role of Regional War Authority (Peperda). Another Jakarta meeting of territorial commanders, together with civilian governors, took place on 26–28 April. It sought to tackle more steadfastly a number of the issues raised at the conference in March by setting up special sections to deal with specific national problems; one section, on defence, under the leadership of Col. Ibnu Sutowo, called for strong and effective measures against smuggling and corruption. From 17 to 20 June, Suharto attended a smaller conference, a follow-on from the April one, to discuss matters of state finance and planning with other regional commanders and officials from the ministries of finance and trade; the results of their discussions were meant to feed into discussions in the Constituent Assembly on financial affairs. The similarity of the situation obtaining under the SOB provisions and those in force in the post-December 1948 revolutionary period is clear. In both cases, military rule was supreme and rapid executive authority available without recourse to tiresome civilian processes. Suharto was in his element on both occasions.

Suharto's keen interest in the material development of his region had already been made clear.[56] The key element of his strategy was the establishment of the Fourth Territory Development Foundation (YPTE), created in July 1957, which was the vehicle for 'all sorts of efforts in the areas of economy and finance to make it possible to help the farmers, the people in the villages',[57] and which 'worked in various areas of the economy and other endeavours which were intended to help the people'.[58] Another smaller foundation, the Fourth Territory Foundation (YTE), already in operation by June 1957, was intended to raise money specifically to help pay for and improve the conditions of Suharto's troops, and to assist retired military personnel of the Division. By the end of that year, with Sujono's return to Semarang from a stint in Bandung to the post of deputy head of Finek, the foundations began to develop rapidly, investing funds in a multiplicity of activities.

The basis of foundation activities was their capacity to place levies on goods and services – for example, ownership of a radio or use of electricity – and to expect charitable assistance from established companies who saw that their interests would best be served by close association with the pre-eminent force in regional affairs. In respect of YPTE, funds would be provided to peasants in the form of loans, to be repaid over long periods from the income gained from their investment.[59] When YPTE began, under the operational control of Lt. Sunarso, a member of Finek's staff, it had already amassed Rp419,352, partly from a copra levy and partly a gift from the Kudus Cigarette Manufacturing Association. By the end of the year, it had reserves of more than Rp16 million, planned expenditures of more than Rp18 million, and an expectation from Suharto that it could raise its working capital to Rp25 million.[60] By early 1959 it had capital amounting to Rp35,381,935 (then equivalent to US$786,265).

Under Suharto's prompting and Sujono's tireless attention, the foundations began a rapid process of investment into private companies concerned with the distribution of primary commodities, in association with prominent business figures. In December 1957, Sujono and two other officers representing YTE provided a small amount of capital in the establishment of NV Garam. A few days later, these three officers joined with five junior retired officers to establish a company with interests in marketing, transportation and industry in Salatiga; although YTE provided the lion's share of the capital, it was entitled to only 10 per cent of the firm's profits. A venture of much the same structure was established in Solo in January 1958. In May the same year, Sujono and the head of Finek, Lt. Col. Sutomo, purchased half the shares in PT Dwi Bakti; the Jakarta businessman Sukaca and local Sino-Indonesian businessman and foster-son of Gatot Subroto, Mohammad 'Bob' Hasan, purchased the remaining shares. Eight months thereafter, Sujono and Sutomo transferred their interests to Hadisubeno Sosrowerdoyo, the tough, aristocratic and fiercely anti-communist PNI mayor of Semarang. Capital investments by Finek, Hasan and another businessman established an inter-island shipping line, PT Pangeran Lines, in June 1958.

In August, YPTE, represented by a retired civilian official, contributed half of the capital needed to establish NV Pusat Pembelian Hasil Bumi, a company aimed at purchasing and selling agricultural produce; the remaining capital was provided by indigenous traders in Central Java. Hadisubeno was himself also active, purchasing shares in PT Dwi Dasa Karya on behalf of Suharto and the Republic of Indonesia. In companies like this, Sujono and his military and civilian associates were allocated positions which entitled them to percentages of profits. Also in August 1958, the government fishing service received a dredge, the private construction of which had been funded by YPTE. At the beginning of 1959, YPTE lent Rp1 million to develop small-scale industry in the region. In August 1959, apparently as part of a broader scheme of establishing state enterprises as a means of government income, YPTE invested Rp15 million in the purchase of the Pakis sugar factory, which was then handed over to the provincial government. As far as I am aware, Suharto himself was not directly involved in such matters, and there is no evidence that connects him directly to a share in the profits of these businesses.

Suharto's autobiographical discussion of these activities is the soul of vagueness; he mentions a number of 'commercial enterprises', established for the sake of YPTE, which were assisted by Lt. Col. Munadi, Major Sujono Humardani, and

'Bob' Hasan. The results of this enterprise were that 'we succeeded in providing agricultural tools, seeds and fertiliser for farmers, [and] allocating food and clothing to the families of soldiers who also took part in the activities of that foundation'. He also persisted with the establishment of cooperatives amongst his troops, as he had done in Solo. In order to attend to 'the problem of food shortages', he devised a scheme of appropriating sugar from the Central Java sugar factories and, through the agency of YPTE and particularly Hasan, exchanging it for rice from Thailand via Singapore – in direct contravention of government regulations forbidding barter.[61] He was also able to arrange the appointment of army officers to the boards of local state-owned companies such as the Permigan oil company.

Contrary to popular legend, there is no evidence that Suharto developed an especially close relationship with the Kudus-based Sino-Indonesian entrepreneur Liem Siu Liong. According to Liem, he first met Suharto during the 1950s in Semarang, when 'he had not yet become panglima of the Diponegoro'. Given that Suharto did not move to Semarang until 1956, it seems likely that it was only at that time that they first made formal acquaintance. Liem also noted that, 'although I was active in supplying his Kodam [Military Regional Command], I do not exactly remember what his rank was at that time – perhaps colonel'.[62] Given Liem's longstanding connections with the supply and marketing of commodities for the Diponegoro Division, it is highly likely he was well known to Sujono, if as yet not formally acquainted with Suharto. It is probable that the eventual connection came via Sujono, who 'knew Liem as a sufficiently trustworthy and honest entrepreneur to be invited to collaborate in the sphere of business'.[63] The nature of that business remains unclear; McDonald's vague account asserts that Liem 'met Suharto and other officers in the Diponegoro Division, forming a co-operative arrangement in setting up light industries and marketing their produce'.[64] I have found no evidence of such activities directly connected to Suharto. Whatever the case, Liem's focus at that time was elsewhere. In 1954 he had established Bank Windu Kencana, which proved relatively unsuccessful and was 'so it seems, not efficient', and in October 1956 he set up NV Bank Asia, later to develop into the giant Bank Central Asia.[65] Whatever Liem's role in commerce with Suharto, it appears to have been limited in time because in 1957 Liem left Kudus and moved to Jakarta, where he devoted himself to the textile and textile-finishing business.

Such business relationships indicate the skill of Suharto and his staff in insinuating themselves into fruitful relationships with broad sectors of the Central Javanese business and bureaucratic worlds. This was a world, as Sujono later remarked, where 'personal relations are very smooth. It is a small country. Relations tend to be like family relations'.[66] This was the old-style world of order and hierarchy, of appropriate behaviour, of lack of overt discord and disruption and, in Suharto's case in all probability, 'respect for the social superiority of the civilian elite'.[67] It was a world in which Suharto and Hadisubeno had much in common in opposing the disruptive roughness and aggression of the potentially ascendant forces of communism.

The skill of Suharto and his operatives allowed the relevant divisional staff to make arrangements to conduct business and promote development. Sujono, for example, organised the illegal barter trade between Central Java and Singapore, exchanging the region's sugar for much-needed rice. Profits from such enterprise, Sujono later claimed, were used to benefit the ordinary farmer through the provision of fertiliser and the expansion of certain crops, like cotton.[68] Yoga Sugama pointed to the Army's provision of pumping facilities for rice growing and the provision of enhanced electricity supply, and related the development plans to the need to maintain the security of the region. Suharto himself, as he was later to do as president, organised inspection tours – 'crossing a small river still in flood, passing along dykes and swampy land which came halfway up to his knees' – to see for himself the progress villagers were making as a result of his funding.[69] On one occasion, Finek even established a mobile shop to travel around areas now free from guerrillas, selling sugar, textiles and salt to the population at low prices, even presenting gifts to the people in gratitude for their assistance.

It is difficult to know the extent to which Suharto himself profited from these schemes, but his subordinates certainly did, as well as those many civilians who had benefited from his patronage role in the development of new or expanded opportunities. As well as providing a source of funding for village development, he did not neglect the political and social dimensions of improvement; Ali Murtopo was busy developing neighbourhood and kampung associations to promote communal solidarity in the form of community efforts at self-development. Suharto also paid 'special attention … to the social welfare of his men', working not only to develop his long-held dream of an army cooperative movement ('I often pointed out to my staff and those around me [in Semarang], that cooperative activities needed to be established amongst all the units of TT IV/Diponegoro … As Commander of the Diponegoro Division I pressed that point'),[70] but also joining with his wife to create an Army Wives Association 'to work for social advancement and social help'.[71]

The importance of such activities, tying military overlordship to bureaucratic and commercial circuits in Central Java, became evident in July 1957 with the Central Java regional elections. Across the territory, the PKI had made great advances, partly because of the growing disillusionment with parties which had enjoyed government. The party had particular success in the city of Semarang, although Hadisubeno managed to hang on to his position as mayor. Suharto's gathering concern with the expansion of communist influence – and what that might signal for an overturning of the normal and accepted pattern of life – was manifested in his crude efforts to alert Sukarno to the danger.

Suharto relates in his autobiography an interchange with Sukarno on the latter's visit to Semarang to join the celebrations for the Diponegoro Division's tenth anniversary. Suharto took the liberty of raising the question of the growing power and threat of the PKI. His reward was a scolding from Sukarno: 'You, Suharto, you are a soldier. Political problems are my department, leave them to me'. It was perhaps on the same occasion that Sukarno delivered Suharto a lecture on 'his [Sukarno's] wish to make the PKI into a Pancasila PKI. I [Suharto] asked him if that was really possible. Bung Karno was bent on showing that it could be done. That is how the idea of Nasakom [Nationalism, Islam, Communism] was born'.[72] Suharto's response was that, 'as far as I'm concerned … because I don't believe that the PKI can be Pancasilaised [*di-Pancasila-kan*], I am working to separate the PKI from the people by taking steps to develop the region'. Sukarno's apparently distracted response, according to Suharto, was 'Yes, that's good, you keep on going with that'.[73]

THE REGIONALIST CRISIS

Suharto's rise to divisional command coincided with the outbreak of regional rebelliousness in the outer provinces of the country, many of them supported, and some led, by local army commanders, with the result that 'at the beginning of 1957 practically the whole of Sumatra except Medan was in open revolt against the Ali cabinet'.[74] By early 1958, unrest in Sumatra had climaxed in the establishment of a rebellious counter-government, the Revolutionary Government of the Republic of Indonesia (PRRI) based in Bukittinggi, a situation which greatly exacerbated the problems presented by the proclamation on 2 March 1957 by Lt. Col. Sumual (the same officer who had fought with Suharto in Central Java following the capture of Yogyakarta in late 1948) of a movement of 'total struggle' (Permesta) in Sulawesi and Eastern Indonesia.

Suharto, as we have seen, was a strong proponent of national unity. His own elevation as panglima had been partly attributable to a local desire to contain regional unrest, and he himself had refused to cater to local dissatisfactions which might threaten that unity in his own area of command. Indeed, during his period as chief of staff of the Division, he had sent Yoga Sugama on a mission to Jakarta to attempt to persuade Lubis to desist from his support of the regional forces in Sumatra, notwithstanding their shared reservations about the leftward tendencies of the Jakarta government and, presumably, their shared tolerance of smuggling as a means of creating revenue for the purposes of local development. Accordingly, Suharto had no sympathy for those engaging in regional unrest, or for their cause, and was disappointed that army commanders had involved themselves. His response was simple and unambivalent: 'I saw this development as the beginning of the emergence of splits in the unity of the nation … I thought that we must be firm and loyal to the legitimate government … the unity of the Republic should not be disturbed'. Nonetheless, he claims, he remained uninvolved; 'I did not want to become involved in political matters, which were outside my area of specialisation'. This attitude, he declares, was important in ensuring that Central Java was untainted by the unrest.[75] It was perhaps because of this that he was reluctant to commit his troops for possible involvement in Sumatra in 1957 when, as Hatta later alleged, Nasution had 'twice tried to mobilize an expeditionary force against West Sumatra, but in each case the military commanders in Java had refused to cooperate, saying that they would not participate in a situation in which Indonesian fought Indonesian'.[76]

His stand on this matter of regional unrest was a reflection of the narrowly construed, dogmatically held and one-dimensional orthodoxies which had by now crystallised as his political philosophy. His determination to uphold them, however, was unflinching should matters come to a head. It was starkly expressed in the Munas (National Conference) held on 9–14 September 1957 in Jakarta, 'attended by political and military figures from all parts of the country'.[77] There, as Lev says, he 'made it clear that he regarded appeasement of the dissidents in Sumatra and Sulawesi as perverse partiality. He pointed out that the 54 million people of Java would feel unjustly treated should the Government relax its development efforts there in order to permit the obstreperous regions to catch up'.[78] His views on the general direction of the country were expressed just as forcefully in his 1957 end-of-year message. Having rehearsed the problems of the year, notably the continuing regional crisis, he pointed to some hopeful signs, such as the establishment of the Functional Cabinet and the National Council, and the holding of the national conferences. Those hopes, however, were shaken at the end of the year

> by events which heated up the atmosphere. There was great turbulence in the Constitution Building with regard to the settling of the basis of our State. Because of the heated atmosphere the debates had to be postponed or stopped for a while. In the field of diplomacy we experienced great disappointment with the rejection by the United Nations General Assembly of the resolution on West Irian. To this can be added the incident that badly frightened the whole country, the assassination attempt on our Head of State, President Sukarno, in Cikini, Jakarta ... Now we face a new year in a heated atmosphere. Not because of chaos, and not because of dissension, but because of the flaring up of the spirit of the people, which no longer puts up with seeing barriers to the revolution, that is, colonial remnants which still exist in our country. The government realises this situation.[79]

Suharto, now sporting a pencil moustache, was clearly relishing his position and responsibilities as panglima and regional military authority. He was developing an interest in larger matters than the purely mundane military affairs which had previously satisfied him. When, early in 1958, the time came for the government to assert itself militarily in the face of the rebellion, Suharto was the most eager of the Java panglima to send troops to assert central government control over the dissident regions and by early March had made available 'about three battalions', which, according to the US Embassy, were 'heavily Communist infiltrated and led by a Communist Sundanese soldier'.[80] A Diponegoro Raider battalion, Bn 432, made up part of 'Operasi Tegas', which secured the Central Sumatran oilfields. Yani, appointed as assistant II and then, in 1957, first deputy (with the rank of colonel) to Nasution following his return from training at Fort Leavenworth from late 1955 to mid-1956, was commissioned to lead a force, named 'Operasi 17 Agustus', against the rebels in West Sumatra. His troops, including Bn 438 and Bn 440 from the Diponegoro Division, under the leadership of Lt. Col. Suwito Haryoko, successfully attacked Padang on 17 April 1958.

By year's end, the Diponegoro Division had dispatched six battalions to the West Sumatra theatre, according to the estimation of the Sultan of Yogyakarta. Ironically, Diponegoro commanders in West Sumatra found that, once they had destroyed the rebel forces, they had to employ communist civilians to assist in running the civil administration, so widespread was PRRI sentiment.

In contrast to this full-blooded engagement, East Java commander and former Diponegoro brigade commander Sarbini was slow to employ his troops for the operation, while the response of the Siliwangi of West Java was positively timid, making available just one infantry battalion for operations against the rebels. While it was heavily caught up in the struggle against the Darul Islam, its commanders shared some of the perspectives of the rebels, particularly an Islamic identity, disdain for Javanese supremacy, and distrust of the parliamentary system. The Siliwangi caution was shared by the Sultan of Yogyakarta, who thought 'the Government's uncompromising policy on the rebellion' misguided and insufficiently flexible.[81] One can only reflect on the division of opinion between Suharto and the sultan on this crucial matter – the hard-nosed and unyielding professional commander versus the sophisticated and sensitive politician. Sukarno, for his part, used the occasion of a visit to Semarang in April 1958 to congratulate TT IV, its troops and the families for their contribution 'to defending the unity of the Republic of Indonesia'.[82]

Suharto's support of military action against the rebels was as sustained as it was weighty. At the beginning of 1959, a second battle regiment (RTP II), 6,500 strong and under the command of Yoga Sugama, arrived in West Sumatra. When Yoga's chief of staff was moved to Riau shortly after arrival in Bukittinggi, Yoga's suggestion that he be replaced by Ali Murtopo was accepted by Suharto, and Ali given the rank of acting major. In late August and early September, Suharto and six other officers inspected the military region of West Sumatra, where large numbers of Diponegoro troops were 'taking an eminent role in the rebel-stamping campaign'. Accompanied by the commander of Operasi 17 Agustus, Lt. Col. Suryosumpeno, and local governors, Suharto 'gave explanations on the return to the 1945 Constitution and on the cabinet's programs'.[83]

THE ARMY, SUKARNO AND POLITICS

As Suharto busily attended to his local region and developed his interests in broader national themes, Sukarno and Nasution were together conspiring to introduce a new framework for Indonesian politics. The opposition they faced from the orthodox parties was neither strong nor united, especially with the demise of Masyumi and the PSI (Indonesian Socialist Party) with the shambles of the regionalist rebellions; indeed, 'except for the PKI, nearly all the parties energetically helped to emasculate themselves'.[84] With the fall of the second Ali cabinet, parliament declined in importance, and the National Council, created in May 1957, contrived to usurp its place as a policy reference body, if not its proper role, in supporting the Juanda cabinet. The Constituent Assembly, elected in 1955 to draft a new constitution, proved unable to agree on the shape of the new state and reluctant to embrace the revolutionary Constitution of 1945. Sukarno, in the eyes of one Western journalist, had 'become more and more obsessed by the belief that he alone can solve Indonesia's problems'.[85] Nasution, notably in his famous 'middle way' speech at Magelang in 1958[86] – Suharto was in the audience – was the mouthpiece for an increasingly influential strand of thinking amongst senior army officers that contested the notion that government was the prerogative of civilians. Such thinking was based on a rosy view of the Army's revolutionary struggle, its exhilarating success in preventing the dissolution of the nation through regional revolt, its enhanced unity as a result of that success, and a keen apprehension of current political circumstances.

Sukarno's 5 July 1959 decree, which returned the nation to the 1945 Constitution, effectively ushered in the period of authoritarian Guided Democracy, through which, in their respective ways, both the President and the Army inscribed themselves indelibly on politics in ways unimaginable a few years before. Sukarno increasingly arrogated to himself the role of ideological mentor for the nation, while Nasution, appointed minister of defence in Sukarno's first presidential cabinet in July 1959 (while retaining his post as army chief of staff), sought to build on the enhanced central control over the Army resulting from the successful attacks on the regional rebels, as well as shaping a new and more influential role for the military in government and presiding over an enormously developed national military capability. The greatly enhanced role of the Army in government was reflected in the fact that it received almost one-third of the seats in the new cabinet (it had had none in any cabinet before 1957). It also secured a significant voice in the deliberative organs prescribed by the 1945 Constitution: the MPRS (Provisional People's Consultative Assembly), and the reshaped parliament, the DPR (People's Representative Council).

Participating in the various commanders' conferences which Nasution called to strengthen his arm in the struggles to create a new system of governance, Suharto was in all likelihood in broad agreement with Nasution's views that the country had been seriously damaged by its indulgence with liberal democracy, that firmer and more decisive leadership was required, that the Army had a right to engage in the job of ruling and guiding the nation, and that the 1945 Constitution was the most appropriate vehicle to carry these aspirations forward.

SUHARTO AND POLITICS

At the time of his transfer to the Army Staff and Command School (SSKAD) late in 1959,[87] Suharto's political thinking, and especially his thinking about the proper form and nature of the state, had probably advanced little, except by way of unconscious affirmation, beyond the ideas he had come to hold in the revolutionary period. They included a strong but not particularly reflective attachment to the idea of a united Indonesian nation, a generally conservative view of the world which sought to find ways to progress within the existing scheme rather than any desire for fundamental change, a certain cynicism about the actual and potential achievements of civilian politicians, and a respect for order, hierarchy and professionalism. Above all, Indonesia was to be based on the ideals of the independence proclamation, which forswore any divisions to the fabric of Indonesia.

For the TNI, Suharto remarked, the return to the 1945 Constitution meant 'a return to the original spirit of identity … a renewal of the spirit of struggle for the sake of completing the national revolution'.[88] Nonetheless, it seems likely that he saw no substantial role for the military in politics, except to act as a dynamising force to assist (and, where necessary, to push and prod) civilian government to a better performance of its tasks. 'The armed forces', he noted in an announcement on the eve of the 1957 regional elections, 'is not a tool of intimidation, but is an organ which invigorates life, prioritising the interests of society over its own interests'.[89] At the same time, he was ever more strongly attached to the notion that economic problems were best solved by directed collectivist solutions, evidenced not just by his foundation activities but also by his fierce protection of state-sponsored monopolies like the Central Java Copra Cooperative. These ideas, notwithstanding their lack of sophistication, depth and nuance, were held with his characteristic pugnacity and strength.

Like many of his officer fellows, Suharto was developing a strong antipathy to communism. Notwithstanding his initial appreciation of the meaning and purport of the 1948 Madiun affair, he had taken with relish to the task of clearing communists and their sympathisers from his Central Java sectors. More fundamentally, however, his essentially conservative cast of mind was offended by views, such as that of Communist Party chairman D. N. Aidit, that 'the August Revolution [1945] did not complete the implementation of the two basic tasks of the revolution at once, that is the task of the anti-imperialist national revolution and the task of the democratic anti-feudal revolution'.[90] Completing the revolution, in Suharto's view, did not involve wholesale social reordering. At a more practical level, he probably saw the extraordinary success of the PKI in the regional elections of 1957 as a direct challenge to his own authority and power. The PKI was unlike other parties in that it made a genuine effort to reach out to its constituency and listen to it. By contrast, 'many party leaders [other than the communists] felt that they had a well defined clientele, requiring only a certain minimum of attention, and that this entitled them to participate in the government without challenge'.[91]

The PKI, however, proclaimed that its 'activities are not confined to parliamentary work alone but also and especially include activities among the masses … aimed at changing the balance of forces between the imperialists, the landlord class and the compradores on the one hand and the forces of the people on the other'.[92] A program which aimed to invert and eventually re-invent the social system of Java seemed highly dangerous, and the popular method to be employed as doubly so for someone in Suharto's position; the communists therefore 'threatened not only the other parties but the entire traditional elite'.[93] Accordingly, Suharto formed a close association with Hadisubeno Sosrowerdoyo, mayor of Semarang, chairman of the PNI in Central Java, influential member of the party's National Council and, as we have seen, staunch anti-communist.

Hadisubeno had already earned the hostility of the government over his anti-communism, as well as his efforts as local chairman of the pamong praja association in Central Java to defend the rights and privileges of that special group of administrators. He successfully outlasted a longstanding effort by the minister for home affairs to move him to Jakarta. Hadisubeno represented a growing mood within the PNI that the PKI represented a profound threat to its own role and success. Semarang itself was a strong centre of PKI activity; indeed, it, and especially its railways, had been the birthplace of the PKI in the 1910s. The success enjoyed by the PKI in the 1955 elections in Central Java meant that relations between Hadisubeno and the communists were 'constantly strained'.[94]

'TRANSFER'

In time, Suharto's business activities led to allegations of corruption. Nasution, conscious of the mounting civilian criticism of military-sponsored corruption, and himself of puritanical bent, had been endeavouring to purify the Armed Forces since at least 1956, when he had established an army inspectorate-general as his 'right hand'. In April 1957 he had issued a regulation concerning corruption and instigated investigations of the activities of territorial commands, including TT IV. From time to time, various warnings were made about the improper activities of army personnel, and occasional punitive actions taken against officers, such as that against Ibnu Sutowo early in 1959. Indeed, Nasution regarded smuggling as 'a breach of military discipline and a disgrace to the Army'.[95]

In 1959, following the reintroduction of the 1945 Constitution, his anti-corruption drive intensified, apparently in response to criticisms that martial law had provided the opportunity for the military to engage in far-reaching corruption. On 17 July, he appealed for discipline, simplicity and austerity in the lifestyle of army members. On 5 August, he delivered a stiff speech exhorting members of the Armed Forces to set themselves as examples of right behaviour by 'purging ourselves of any impurities for the sake of the country's improvement'; in a subsequent interview, the army information officer stated that 'drastic actions' would be taken 'against Army personnel engaged in activities degradating [*sic*] the TNI's (Army) reputation before the public'. Shortly thereafter, the deputy minister of defence issued an instruction which forbade 'members of the Armed Forces to take part in looking for profits in organisations which directly or indirectly have any contact with the Armed Forces'.[96]

Suharto's varied activities, especially those to do with barter trade in which private entrepreneurs were involved, had drawn the keen attention of army headquarters in Jakarta. On 18 July 1959, according to an *Antara* report, 'an Army Inspection group headed by Army Inspector-General Brig.-Gen. Sungkono arrived at Semarang from Djakarta ... to check the policies of the Central Java War Authority in the financial-economic field. The accounts of the Fourth Army Territory's Development Foundation and financial aspects of the transfer of Dutch enterprises in the region will be personally inspected by a special section led by Lt. Col. Sumantri'.[97] His investigations complete, Sungkono released a statement to the press in Semarang on 13 October detailing his findings on the activities of YPTE and YTE. He revealed that YPTE, established 'for the purpose of paying back the debt of gratitude to the common people who in the periods of the beginning of the revolution gave much assistance in general to the government',[98] held funds of Rp42,174,300, in addition to an amount of Rp33,576,500 already given 'to buy water pumps, tractors, fertiliser, and so on'. These funds had been obtained from a huge variety of levies on production and service industries, many of them government-run. YPTE was, Sungkono remarked, the only one of its kind in all the territorial commands in the country. He also found that YTE had been established 'to assist Army welfare and carries on activities for former members of the Army and the organisation League of Families of Army Members (IKAT) which is intended to work for the basic needs of its members, such as rice, sugar, soap and which organises aid if there are deaths, marriages and so on amongst the members'.

Suharto, possibly still affected by a nose operation a month earlier which had prevented him attending the mid-September commanders' conference in Jakarta, was informed that he would be removed from his command of the Diponegoro Division (shortly before retitled as Kodam VII/Diponegoro) and was ordered to attend the second intake of the C-course at SSKAD, scheduled to begin on 1 November 1959. There was, Ibu Tien's biographer claims, no formal hand-over ceremony to the new commander, Suharto's chief of staff, Lt. Col. Pranoto Reksosamudro, something interpreted by Ibu Tien as a deliberate and painful slight. While Suharto left, alone, for Bandung, his wife was forced to quit the official residence at short notice and move her family into the house of a friend.[99]

There is something puzzling about all this. While Suharto's transfer was related to his commercial activities in Semarang, notably his involvement in the sugar barter, it is not obvious why action was taken against him when so many of his fellows were engaged in similar commercial pursuits. Mossman pointed to 'the difficulty of preventing corruption in the army' and noted that 'there have been hundreds of cases of blatant smuggling by central government officers entrusted with control over former rebel areas, as well as in Java itself'.[100] Moreover, there was a general sense amongst his fellow officers that Suharto was not engaged in activities aimed to enrich himself personally. Years later, Sumitro remarked that 'I do not perceive Pak Harto as being corrupt … When he was the Military Area Commander in Semarang it is true enough that there was a lot of bartering done, but it was other people that were profiting. And Pak Harto was able to build barracks for his unit. His home in Semarang was a modest one'.[101] His former intelligence officer, Marsudi, recalled that 'Pak Harto was very simple [in his tastes]'.[102] In any case, the punishment allocated to him was not especially severe; the C-course was designed to be a normal component of the education of senior officers. Nor was the smooth upward progression of his career trajectory affected, with a promotion to the rank of brigadier-general in January 1960; as McVey notes, 'the jump between colonel and brigadier general is the principal one in the Indonesian as in most armies'.[103]

The explanation probably lies in a constellation of factors. It seems clear that considerable tension had arisen within Suharto's Diponegoro staff in Semarang, and especially between Suharto and Pranoto. Pranoto, a strong supporter of Sukarno and his policies notwithstanding his indeterminate character, did not share Suharto's antipathy to the rise of the communist party and was indeed thought by Suharto's group to be in sympathy with the PKI. Pranoto, while he originally claimed to support Suharto's business and development ventures, was one of a group of senior Diponegoro officers that came to oppose them. Perhaps he was distressed at Suharto's lack of sympathy for the PKI and for Sukarno's hopes of domesticating it, and at Suharto's active association with Hadisubeno's vigorous efforts to contain the party; perhaps, as well, he was distressed at the sheer scale and depth of the business empire Suharto and his associates were constructing. Whatever the case, it seems that he was the source of the original complaints about Suharto's behaviour; his complaint may have been part of what Yoga later labelled a 'planned move' to rid the Diponegoro Division of the Suharto group.[104]

Nasution, of course, was not obliged to take action, even when his inspector-general had uncovered the details of Suharto's business dealings. However, Nasution was himself engaged about this time in a dispute with Sukarno, whose newly appointed attorney-general, Gatot Tarunamiharja, was attempting to have Ibnu Sutowo and Lt. Col. Sukendro brought to trial for their role in the Tanjung Priok corruption affair. Nasution's response was to order the arrest of Gatot Tarunamiharja, presumably because he wished to keep the affair out of the public gaze. He may well have thought that in these circumstances he had no option but to act against Suharto to preserve something of his own credibility. Indeed, Nasution was under some pressure from Sukarno to bring Suharto to trial, perhaps at the urging of Pranoto (whom Sukarno would have preferred in such an important and sensitive regional command, and who apparently kept Sukarno informed about these matters) and with a view to damaging Hadisubeno as well.

While Nasution thought there was sufficient evidence against Suharto, he decided after discussions with Gatot Subroto and Yani not to proceed. There were, he reasoned, larger cases of corruption which had not been taken up. Suharto's barter operations were 'small in relation to all that and Panglima Suharto's intentions were good, that is, his projects [were] for the welfare of his troops and the development of the region'.[105] Nonetheless, he had no option but to yield, even if mildly, in this case, and to terminate Suharto's appointment and dispatch him to SSKAD for a period of study. Gatot, a previous commander and long-time associate of Suharto, and 'a known admirer of Nasution',[106] very likely exerted considerable influence on the army chief of staff to ensure that Suharto's punishment was gentle and that his future prospects were unharmed. Gatot's feelings for his protégé to one side, his foster-son, 'Bob' Hasan, was deeply involved in the Diponegoro businesses; moreover, Gatot himself was probably broadly in sympathy with what Suharto had sought to establish in Central Java during his term as panglima. Indeed, in 1960, Gatot bought into PT Wasesa Lines, previously PT Pangeran Lines.

Suharto's own clearly fictitious account of the affair attempts to muddy the issues and absolve himself of any wrongdoing. He claims that rumours 'that I had committed corruption in the rice trade and had enriched myself from the proceeds of the sugar barter' surfaced only after his transfer to SSKAD, and that as a result he was summoned to Jakarta by Gatot Subroto and investigated by a special team. The result was that 'finally Pak Gatot decided there was nothing doubtful or blameworthy in my actions and I was ordered to continue my education at SSKAD until I had completed it'.[107] It is worthy of note that, in Roeder's account, the reasons for Suharto's move to Bandung are not even broached.[108]

The victory of the Pranoto group meant the end of what the PKI was said to have called 'the Suharto clique' in Diponegoro headquarters.[109] In the words of Ali Murtopo, 'the three of us [Suharto, Yoga and himself] were gotten rid of out of Central Java'.[110] Yoga, having returned to Semarang early in 1960 from his service in West Sumatra, was effectively sidelined; he was given six months in Magelang to write up a report on his West Sumatran activities, a task he completed within two months. He was then sent to Seskoad (the renamed SSKAD) to undertake a regular course, along with his former Diponegoro staff colleagues Sutanto (assistant III) and Hernomo (assistant IV), before accepting, on the advice of Gatot Subroto, a posting as military attaché to Yugoslavia in February 1962. Sujono, it seems, wanted to leave Diponegoro when Suharto was removed, but remained for another year because Suharto had 'ordered him to stay on and clear matters up'.[111] Sujono was then appointed vice-deputy III (finance) to the army chief of staff in Jakarta, perhaps as a result of some string-pulling by his former boss, and promoted to lieutenant colonel in 1961. Ali Murtopo remained with the Division until he received the call to join his old boss in Jakarta in 1961.

For his part, Pranoto explained to an informal meeting of journalists two days after his appointment that he would 'continue the plans and develop the seeds sown by Panglima Col. Suharto, while those things that were lacking would be improved'. In relation to YPTE, Pranoto explained that he would 'consider the results which were directly useful for the people's interests'. His major task, he said, was to emphasise the interests of the people, and to enhance and guard the identity (*kepribadian*) of his troops.[112] Suharto's business and development initiatives in the region were soon a thing of the past.

CONCLUSION

The period of just over three years in which Suharto commanded the Diponegoro Division was a key creative phase of his life. For the first time, he was in a position of independent power and serious responsibility, and he wasted no time in putting that authority to effect. The ideas or, to put it more precisely, reflections on experience in the context of a certain restricted view of the world which were gradually developing, uninterrogated, in his mind, were given their first application. He could only have been satisfied with his success in deploying them, even if angered at the manner in which his enjoyment of his prowess was suddenly brought to a stop with his transfer to Bandung.

These Semarang days were clearly amongst the happiest and most fulfilling of Suharto's life. His family grew further with the addition of his second daughter and fourth child, Siti Hediyati Haryadi, born on 14 April 1959. He was in his own realm, virtually supreme. His post as divisional commander also had its rewards. Thus it was, for example, that he supervised the burial ceremony for the revered nationalist leader and teacher, Ki Hadjar Dewantoro, in Yogya in April 1959. He treasured as well his appointment on 1 September 1957 as a member of the board of trustees of the National Military Academy at Magelang. During this time it appears that he also took advantage of some educational opportunities. He mentions 'the military knowledge' gained at the academy, as well as at the first and second courses for senior officers.[113]

Suharto brought to his period as Diponegoro panglima a long-held and fatherly attachment to the welfare of his troops. In a speech given at the Division's anniversary celebrations in 1958, he remarked that 'the power of a leader is not absolute. Power has its roots in the confidence given to the leader by the men and the people he is leading. Without this confidence, true leadership is impossible'.[114] He had gained a reputation as a 'tough but impartial master',[115] who enjoyed the confidence of the troops under him because he valued their service and took efforts to ensure that their physical well-being and that of their families was looked after, both before and after retirement.

Suharto's attachment to his troops was that of the generous and concerned lord towards his servant. He demonstrated, perhaps for the first time, a different kind of affective behaviour towards the small group of senior officers who coalesced around him; they shared, to a remarkable degree, his general values, hopes and outlook. He trusted them implicitly and gave them considerable autonomy in the carrying out of their duties; in turn, they afforded him an extraordinary and long-lasting affection, devotion and loyalty. The success achieved by this small and closely knit team was a harbinger of a future, and usually similarly successful, style of management practised by Suharto. It was no accident that the three closest to him in the Diponegoro – Yoga Sugama, Ali Murtopo and Sujono Humardani – were all to play highly important and creative roles in the New Order; even less established figures, such as Munadi, Hernomo, Sutanto and Suprapto, filled positions of significance during that era.

With his move to Bandung, Suharto moved forever from the small-town world of Central Java. His varieties of experience and opportunity there, however, had served to prepare him well for coping with the larger demands of the greater and more complex world of Jakarta.

4 High office, 1959–1965

SUHARTO BEGAN HIS studies at the Army Staff and Command School (SSKAD) in Bandung on 1 November 1959. His reflections on his efforts there carry a combative air: struggle with an unfamiliar arena, persistence and, almost inevitably, triumph. 'In the beginning, I had great difficulties in following the military education at Seskoad',[1] a result of his lack of formal military education, but he found that his experience of tactics and strategy during the revolution stood him in good stead. He later characterised himself at SSKAD as quiet and lacking in confidence, one who listened to the conversations of others and, if invited, displayed a special skill in summarising and concluding discussions.[2] He completed the course – yet again, he claims, 'with the top ranking' – at the end of 1960.[3]

This period at SSKAD, at that time the lively hub of army reflection on its ideology and political future, moved Suharto's mind into new and unfamiliar territory. There he came to know Col. Suwarto, an extraordinarily able and influential PSI-leaning Siliwangi officer who was at that time deputy commander of the school. In these pivotal years of early Guided Democracy, Suharto was one of those students who, under Suwarto's influence, began developing a set of ideas 'that greatly extended the Army's political role and brought it into a position to challenge the fast-expanding Communist Party'.[4] Suwarto grounded his thinking in the view that 'the situation of our nation is still one of technical and economic underdevelopment, although it does not neglect the elements of progressivity and modernisation'. In countries at this point in development, 'the army is required as a tool of stabilisation and a tool of stiffening [*kekerasan*] because in general such countries have not yet achieved stability in the political, economic and cultural spheres'. From this it was a short step to the notion of the need for a close identification of the Army with the people: 'our strength is not placed in the power of resistance, but rather in the power of binding together'.[5]

Taking as their starting-point the idea of a territorial army ensconced with the people, set out by Nasution in the late 1940s and after, Suwarto's group drew out its implications for the Army's relationship with Indonesia's broader society. The notion was not just that the Army should be amongst the people, but that it should also seek to *manage* affairs within its territorial areas, including the idea that there should be developed a parallel army administration side by side with the civilian territorial administration controlled by the Ministry of Home Affairs, with a mandate to check and supervise those authorities. There also emerged the idea of the Army's 'civic mission', that is, that it should enter into the life of the people it claimed to serve by providing practical assistance for them in development programs; such work would serve to enhance internal security by assisting in alleviating poverty and a sense of injustice, and would unite the Army with the people. The Army should function as 'an agency for national security ... an agency for nation building ... an agency for national growth and national prosperity'.[6] Suharto, as a member of this second cohort in the C-course, participated in a pathbreaking SSKAD seminar in December 1960 at which these developing concepts were elaborated.

Seskoad Seminar I, on the problem of defence, was held on 9–15 December 1960 and attended by Seskoad students and C-course Seskoad students, graduates from the first C-course, and 'important officials from all of Indonesia, including the Army, Air Force and Navy'.[7] The seminar was designed both as an educational tool for those who took part and as a means of publicising and stimulating further debate about the ideas developed within the college. Students were placed in research groups and required to submit the results of their research on specified problems. Suharto, as leader of Group I, presented a paper on 'Territorial warfare as a conception of Indonesian defence'.[8]

Beginning with a brief survey of classic thinkers on the science of war, such as Clausewitz and Liddell Hart, Suharto moved quickly to a discussion of his subject. He noted that Indonesia, based on the ideology of Pancasila, had been born 'from the depths of the struggle against colonialism'; having achieved independence, it needed to defend itself against threats from within and without, as well as to give content to its independence and become 'a nation both secure and peaceful from Sabang to Merauke, with a just and prosperous society based on Pancasila'. Given the geographic, economic, political and spiritual context, the Armed Forces had a role not just in defence but also 'as a pioneer of struggle and as a pioneer of development'. Surveying the range of possible threats, he concluded that 'we must follow a doctrine of "region-by-region defence"', in which 'the regions of defence form strategic compartments which must have the ability on their own to carry out the activities of war while the nation is in a state of war'. He proceeded to divide Indonesia into three defence areas, further divided into smaller battle areas, a concept which presupposed and depended upon a close relationship between army and a people readied 'mentally and morally' for their defence role. Such a strategy, Suharto concluded, rested upon political stability, the consciousness of Pancasila as the single ideology, a united, authoritative and experienced leadership, and complete integration between the three armed forces.[9] The seminar was in general agreement with the ideas he and his team put forward.

In addition to the question of territorial defence, the seminar also discussed the role of the military in internal security. It considered the different streams of thought and movements which 'have taken shape in a multi-party system, with excesses which cannot be restrained' and which were a source of confusion for the people. As well, there were weaknesses in governance, in the economy and in military unity; there needed to be greater coordination of military and non-military efforts in political, economic and social fields, and a greater sense of unanimity in ideology, to which the military could contribute by propagating Pancasila.[10] Indeed, Suharto's group thought that military power might be employed 'to assist in all activities in political, social and economic spheres'.[11]

The major fields of intellectual endeavour at SSKAD were the military arts – strategy and tactics, planning, staff organisation, logistics – but, under Suwarto's influence, considerable amounts of time were also devoted to such matters as national ideology, social anthropology, development economics, international law and guided democracy and economy; indeed, the amount of such contextual studies in society, politics, culture and economics was increased for Suharto's cohort. Suharto's time of study was also notable for the fact that he also came into contact with civilian economics lecturers who, at Suwarto's invitation, routinely lectured at SSKAD and who 'helped to refine the Territorial Management concept'.[12] Their matter-of-fact ideas about Indonesia's development apparently struck a chord with Suharto.

While it might have been intended as a mild chastisement for Suharto, SSKAD in fact proved to be a turning-point in his career. He later acknowledged that his attendance and success at the course 'made me proud and increased my belief in myself',[13] but it did much more than that. It opened his eyes to worlds of thinking previously unknown to him, and to the cutting edge of army reflection about its role in society, providing him at the same time with an opportunity to contribute to this crucial process of army self-refinement and self-determination, and fundamentally shaping his attitude to the role of the Army in the development of Indonesian society. Perhaps of even greater importance, it expanded his still sharply limited realm of social experience by bringing him into everyday, collegial and intimate contact with a new and influential range of acquaintances from different regions and backgrounds, amongst them the brightest and best of his contemporaries. Suharto himself mentions a number of fellow student officers, including Sarbini (former panglima of the East Java Brawijaya Division, whom Suharto knew well) and Amirmachmud. Also in the course were Col. U. Rukman from the Siliwangi, Col. Achmad Tahir and, 'one of [his] best friends',[14] Lt. Col. Sutoyo, later to be amongst the generals murdered on 1 October 1965.

As we have seen, Suharto was promoted to the rank of brigadier-general shortly after beginning his SSKAD education. Upon completing his course on 17 December 1960, he was assigned to army headquarters in Jakarta and received an appointment as deputy I (operations) to the army chief of staff, Nasution. Settling in Jakarta at an official residence at Jl. Haji Agus Salim no. 98, in the elite suburb of Menteng, he was joined by his wife and family who had stayed on in Semarang after his move to Bandung. Shortly thereafter, presumably at his own instigation, he was joined in Jakarta by his former assistant, Ali Murtopo, appointed to Suharto's staff as his deputy I. Soon after his appointment to Jakarta,

Suharto was caught up in the ideological performance of Guided Democracy, named as head of the Army's ad hoc retooling committee in December 1960.

CADUAD

In March 1961, Suharto received extra responsibilities in addition to those he already held, with his appointment as commander of the Army General Reserve (Caduad). This appointment was to prove the key step in accelerating his thus far relatively modest career. Caduad was an attempt by Nasution to create, for the first time, a highly skilled and trusted mobile force for national needs, directly at the behest of the General Staff, rather than reliant upon having to persuade and cajole local segments of the territorially organised army to throw their forces behind nationally determined goals. Upon the announcement on 27 December 1960 of his plans to establish and place a high priority on Caduad, Nasution had set up a special seven-man working group, chaired by Suharto and including the Siliwangi veterans Achmad Wiranatakusumah and Lt. Col. Amirmachmud, both of whom Suharto had come to know at Seskoad, and Lt. Col. Munadi from his old Diponegoro staff, to develop the concept.

Their work led to the establishment on 6 March 1961 of what was termed the First Army Corps/Caduad, abbreviated to Korra I/Caduad. Its strength and organisational structure were announced shortly thereafter; Suharto was appointed panglima of the new force from 1 March 1961, with Col. Achmad Wiranatakusumah as his chief of staff, Amirmachmud as deputy chief of staff, another former Seskoad colleague, Col. Rukman, as panglima of Division II of the First Army Corps, and a sprinkling of former Diponegoro colleagues in senior positions, including Munadi and Sruhardoyo. Major Ali Murtopo also joined the Caduad staff in 1961, as assistant to the chief of staff, Division II/ Korra I/Caduad, as did Hernomo.

As it was for Suharto, the creation of Caduad was a decisive initiative for the army central command. Caduad took the strongest fighting units from the three Java Kodam (military regions), trained them for paracommando duties and held them ready for immediate dispatch, with RPKAD units (the army commando regiments over which Caduad also enjoyed command), anywhere in the archipelago where trouble threatened. When not on Caduad duty, units assigned to Caduad remained under the direct authority of their panglima and were not posted with a specific territorial responsibility or merged with a larger organisation entity. Caduad, however, retained the right to summon them at any time it judged necessary. Amongst the units assigned to Caduad were Diponegoro's Battalion (Bn) 454, a Banteng Raiders unit, Bn 530 from East Java's Brawijaya Division, and Kujang Bn 328 from the Siliwangi.

Nasution's choice of Suharto for the important Caduad post was a reflection of Suharto's long and generally distinguished career as a battle leader and a former commander of troops, as well as of Nasution's confidence in Suharto's loyalty, the orthodoxy of his ideas, and his general sense, exemplified in his attitude to the PRRI crisis, that national needs must always outweigh local ones. As well, it almost certainly reflected the general estimation within both senior army and civilian circles that Suharto was a professional soldier above all, politically unambitious, tractable and unthreatening, perhaps one of the few amongst his peers who, it could safely be assumed, did not aspire to higher things.[15]

Almost certainly because of Suharto's new appointment – and at the suggestion of Yani, who wanted up-and-coming senior officers to gain some experience – he joined Nasution in June 1961 for his first overseas trip. Following the Eisenhower administration's failure to accede to Nasution's personal request for arms in October 1960, he was forced, albeit reluctantly, to turn to other sources of supply. Already in January 1961, Indonesia had entered a military supply deal with Moscow for US$400 million in armaments, and this mission was aimed at finalising arrangements for the purchases, presumably the reason for Suharto's presence on the trip. Suharto did not leave with Nasution – he was still busy assembling his Caduad staff and organising troops – and joined him only for the Belgrade, Paris and Bonn legs of what was a much more extensive bout of tripping by the army chief of staff.

While in Germany, Suharto met again with B. J. Habibie, who at that time had just completed his undergraduate engineering studies and was in the early stages of doctoral studies in aeronautical engineering at Aachen Institute of Technology. Their meeting left an impression on Suharto: 'I realised Ir. Habibie's spirit in facing up to his area of expertise, the world of technology and industry which were well beyond the reach of our nation. I remember speaking with him which spelled out hope for us in coming days'.[16] Suharto himself is silent about the impact his first foray into the wider world made upon him. Perhaps he was simply bemused by it all; more likely, however, it indicates that, at the age of 40, his personality and way of perceiving the world were more or less settled, or at least not easily disturbed.

In 1 October that year, Suharto took command of the Army's newly created Air Defence Command (Kohanudad). This appointment seems to have been an outcome both of his new Caduad responsibilities and a long-held interest in airborne fighting capacity; according to McVey:

> [they] led him to take a particular interest in the development of an airborne central strike force. The Armed Forces in general and the Army in particular, he argued, must become 'Para-minded'. It was the ambition of Suharto and other air-minded Army leaders to create an Airborne division for the Army, but at the time the Mandala Command began military operations in January 1962 only the RPKAD and Infantry Brigade III were so qualified.[17]

Around mid-1964, Suharto demonstrated his enthusiasm and fascination for airborne combat by undertaking successfully the paratroopers' jump course and earning his jumper's wings from the Air Force.

THE WEST IRIAN CAMPAIGN

As Suharto's career grew in both scope and stature through 1961, tensions were sharpening over the long-running dispute between Indonesia and the Netherlands over the fate of West Irian, 'a thorn in the flesh of the Republic of Indonesia', as Suharto later termed it.[18] The Indonesian claim to the territory, which the Dutch had refused to include in the 1949 transfer of sovereignty, was fuelled by an ever more strident nationalism driven and modulated by Sukarno in the context of Guided Democracy; in turn, the Dutch response gained more urgency, both in its efforts to develop an indigenous elite which might be the vehicle for the emergence of an independent New Guinea under Dutch patronage, and in its defence preparation, which included the dispatch of the aircraft carrier *Karel Doorman*, a symbol of the Dutch determination not to relinquish its controlling hand in the territory. Suharto was appointed to a small inter-service planning committee established in April 1961 to develop a military operations plan for the liberation of West Irian.

In a speech on 19 December 1961, Sukarno announced the Trikora, the three commands of the people, as he put it. They were, 'first, to crush the Dutch colonial effort to build a puppet Papuan state, second, to raise the Indonesian flag in West Irian as part of Indonesia, third, to prepare for a general mobilisation to defend the freedom and unity of Indonesia'.[19] On 2 January 1962, a Theatre Command for the Liberation of West Irian was created, the 'Mandala' command, and on 9 January the appointment of Suharto as commander was announced.[20] He was, at the same time, raised in rank to major-general. Being appointed Mandala commander made Suharto extremely proud: 'It was a real challenge, and an extraordinary honour for a *Sapta Marga* soldier'.[21] An editorial in *Merdeka* noted that 'this has been a long-awaited appointment, because with the appointment of the "Panglima Mandala" or "Theatre Commander" more concrete provisioning has again been given to the apparatuses for the liberation of West Irian'. It added that, on the basis of his experiences, including his leadership role in the 1 March attack on Dutch forces in Yogyakarta in 1949, 'Brigadier General Suharto is obviously a good field officer'.[22] A resumé of his career, published in *Duta Masyarakat* under the heading 'Brig. Gen. Suharto destroyed the Dutch at the time of the Yogya clash', emphasised his military feats, including his defence of Yogya from the Dutch attack on 19 December 1948, his leadership of the attack of 1 March, and his Makasar exploits.[23]

In a discussion with journalists the day after his appointment, Suharto invited them to take up their pens in the struggle for West Irian. In the spate of publicity surrounding his appointment, he had been given the nickname 'bogeyman of the Dutch'. In a light-hearted interchange with the journalists, when asked how he had come to earn this nickname, he smiled and said 'Yes, how?', and proceeded to play down his recent promotion to major-general. He was described as 'clean-faced, indeed, sometimes as if he is always smiling. His hair is wavy and finely combed to the back, his skin the yellow colour of the Lansium fruit'.[24]

Suharto's Mandala appointment also led to his assuming the role as deputy commander for the East Indonesian region, a post previously held by Yani. The handover ceremony, presided over by Gatot Subroto with Yani in attendance, took place in a drizzly Makasar on 23 January 1962. In his comments at the ceremony, Gatot remarked that Suharto's appointment was a very fitting one; he had known Suharto personally since 1945; because of this, the choice of Sukarno and Nasution was exactly right. Suharto was 'known from the Dutch side as a bogeyman, and from the Indonesian side as one who does not indulge in self-aggrandisement, is concerned with society, and is honest'.[25] In his first Order of the Day, Suharto called on all the Armed Forces and people in eastern Indonesia 'to increase and extend even more their energies, internal and external, to prepare themselves to face the heavy and sacred tasks' involved in carrying out the Trikora.[26]

Some have evinced surprise at Suharto's elevation to a station of such national importance. For Nasution's purposes, the appointment was motivated by similar considerations to those that had governed his appointment to Caduad. It was, indeed, all of a piece with the earlier one: the Mandala command called for strategic planning ability, a broader view of Indonesia's strategic environment, a high level of professionalism, and a cautious and systematic personality, especially in the context of Indonesian military weakness in relation to the Dutch. Moreover, as McDonald admits, Suharto 'posed little political threat to his superiors'.[27]

Ritual completed, Suharto took to his tasks. According to presidential instruction 10/1962, they were twofold: first, 'to plan, prepare and carry out military operations with the aim of returning the region of West Irian to the authority of the State of the Republic of Indonesia'; and, second, 'to develop the military situation in the region of the province of West Irian in conformity with the levels of struggle in the political sphere so that in the shortest time possible there can be created in the region of the province of West Irian de facto free areas and/or elements of the authority of the regional government of the Republic of Indonesia'.[28]

Suharto headed the Mandala command from his Caduad headquarters until he moved his headquarters to the city of Makasar on 12 March 1962. The notion of the Mandala command involved the idea of a war theatre in which elements of land, sea and air power could be combined for operational purposes. His command covered land units in Kodam XIII/Merdeka (Central Sulawesi), XIV/Hasanuddin (South and Southeast Sulawesi), XV/Pattimura (Nusa Tenggara), XVI/Udayana (Maluku), Kodamar V, Kodamar VI, Korud II and Korud IV, a total of about 42,000 troops; his authority covered an area of about 5 million square kilometres. In other words, Suharto's Mandala command embraced the whole of eastern Indonesia. He was immediately assisted by two deputy panglima, Col. Subono from the Navy and Col. Leo Wattimena from the Air Force, and provided with a Joint Mandala Staff. His chief of staff was a former fellow-student at SSKAD, Col. Achmad Tahir, and a chief of information was appointed to assist Suharto 'to coordinate and organise all media information'.[29] Amirmachmud commanded Operational Staff (G-2) within the Joint Staff, while Munadi commanded the Joint Territorial Staff and Popular Resistance (G-5). Col. Sudomo, of whom we shall hear more later, was appointed panglima of the Mandala naval forces.[30] Suharto was also accorded the title of Mandala military governor, which provided him with effective martial law authority over the Mandala territory, his responsibilities included raising food production and preparing the civil administration of West Irian for post-liberation duties.

According to Suharto, 'it was laid down that by 17 August 1962 at the latest, the Red and White [flag] would be flying in West Irian. That meant that I was given only seven months'. Moreover, he was starting from nothing. 'There was no base, there were no units, because the task had been set in a short time.'[31] Indeed, shortly after his appointment, the Dutch navy had attacked three Indonesian torpedo craft, killing the Navy's deputy chief of staff, Yos Sudarso, in the process. In this unpromising situation, on 2 March Suharto presented a report to the Operational Staff amidst Indonesian hopes that the West Irian matter could still be settled peacefully. Soon thereafter it was reported that volunteers were arriving at the front lines and undergoing training exercises. Two weeks later, Suharto was again in Jakarta to present another report on the smooth development of his preparations, returning to his post on 18 March. It seems that these visits to Jakarta were occasions for him to issue a generalised call for the people to remain alert and ready to carry out orders. Shortly thereafter, he escorted Nasution around the different regions of eastern Indonesia on a ten-day inspection tour.

With the intervention of US Attorney-General Robert Kennedy, hopes for a peaceful settlement led to initial secret discussions near Washington between Dutch and Indonesian delegations, begun on 20 March, under the facilitation of Ellsworth Bunker, a retired American diplomat appointed to the task by UN Secretary-General U Thant. The talks broke down, however, mainly because the Dutch 'kept pressing for qualifications which would establish the right of self-determination for the Papuans more strongly'.[32] Following the collapse of the March talks, Bunker developed a new set of proposals, involving a short transition period of UN supervision of the territory, to be followed by Indonesian administration and a plebiscite by the Irianese on their future at some future date. The Dutch initially refused to countenance the Bunker plan because it did not, in their eyes, provide sufficient guarantees of the right of the Irianese to self-determination.

Suharto's style in Makasar mirrored that developed during his Diponegoro days. It was characterised by the clique-like group of officers that he drew about him, in whom he invested considerable scope for initiative in their allotted tasks and who responded to him with respect and intense loyalty. Chief amongst this group was Sudomo, appointed as panglima of the Mandala Naval Forces, while Ali Murtopo was placed in the field to develop Mandala's (and, *a fortiori*, Caduad's) capacity in the field of intelligence and operations, notably infiltration. There were, as well, other participants in the operation who would later become notable. Suharto's former SSKAD colleague Rukman worked closely with him at Mandala headquarters and was, in September 1963, to succeed him in command of the territory of East Indonesia. Major Untung, a former subordinate in Solo and now a member of Bn 454, was commander of the West Irian Guerrillas, while Major Benny Murdani served as a commando. Suharto's other field characteristic, his capacity to inspire loyalty amongst his troops by careful attention to the details of their needs, was also in evidence.

In the midst of the campaign, in June 1962, Suharto learned of the sudden death of his mentor, Lt. Gen. Gatot Subroto, at the age of 54. With senior officers and family members, he accompanied Gatot's flag-draped casket on its flight to

Semarang for its burial in Ungaran. The following month, his personal news was more joyous; Tien, who had visited Suharto at his Makasar headquarters, gave birth to the couple's fifth child, a son, on 15 July 1962. Suharto named him Hutomo Mandala Putra, an indication of the significance that he attached to the duties with which he had been commissioned. The boy's nickname was Tommy. A little over two years later, Ibu Tien delivered their sixth and last child, a girl, Siti Hutami Endang Adiningsih, on 23 August 1964, the same birthdate as her (then) 41-year-old mother.

The plan Suharto employed to achieve his military goals was a complicated one, a combined strategy involving sea, air and land forces (the last of which included such Caduad units as Bn 454 from the Diponegoro and the Brawijaya's Bn 530). It involved three phases, the first one, of infiltration, designed to last until the end of 1962. In this phase, ten companies would be introduced into West Irian 'with specific targets to create a "de facto" liberated area' as a base for guerrilla operations to draw out and tie up Dutch forces and carry out sabotage operations; they would expand this area, involving the Irianese themselves in the struggle, and providing a useful diplomatic bargaining chip in the process. Phase 2, beginning in 1963, would involve open attacks against the main Dutch forces, 'occupying all important defence posts'.[33] Phase 3 would be one of consolidation. The major thrust was to come from the tactic of infiltrating elite troops by sea or by air, to force the Dutch to bring their reserves forward and lay the basis for a later main-force assault. Bases were established at Morotai, Amahai, Letfuan and Ambon.

The infiltration of paratroops was generally disastrous. While Suharto was under considerable political pressure from Sukarno to get things moving, his efforts seem to have been poorly planned and implemented. Most of his paratroops were dropped into harsh and inhospitable thickly jungled territory along the swampy reaches of the southern coast, away from Dutch troop concentrations. Many failed to survive the jump, killed by their landing or drowning under the weight of their equipment. Those who survived achieved little militarily. Many were killed or captured; instead of being welcomed as liberators by the West Irianese, they were received coldly and usually handed over to Dutch troops. Those earlier spirited in by small boat did no better. Suharto put the best face on things; in late July, he reported at a press conference in Makasar that the guerrillas inserted into West Irian had made 'satisfactory progress in the task of liberating West Irian'; 'in essence, our guerrillas have done a fine job, even if they have experienced difficulties in the situation in which they have found themselves. But this is not a problem because they obtain full support from the local people'.[34]

Suharto's difficulties were not restricted to the sphere of field operations. In the midst of his planning, the influential politician and ideologue Mohammad Yamin brought forth the suggestion – presumably as a result of the Indonesian torpedo boat disaster in which Yos Sudarso had been lost – that Indonesia should seek to sink Dutch ships, for political reasons. Suharto opposed this with some vehemence, apparently of the view that such a move might escalate hostilities and see the introduction of larger Dutch forces, which would jeopardise his plans. He reluctantly agreed to follow Sukarno's order on this point, demanding at the same time 'a guarantee that thereby Irian will become part of our territory'.[35] Yamin's idea was eventually dropped. Here was evidence once more of Suharto's fixedness of purpose and obduracy, and a hint of his lack of patience at civilian interference in what he saw as a purely military issue. He admits that his acceptance and implementation of the plan were done with reservations.

Dutch intransigence at the negotiating table led Suharto, no doubt at the behest of his superiors who were desperate in the context of continuing negotiations to demonstrate the depth of their commitment to 'liberate' West Irian, to formulate an extremely adventurous and hazardous offensive. The plan, codenamed Jayawijaya, called for an amphibious assault on Biak, which boasted a large Dutch military establishment and the area's only large airstrip (although Suharto sought to deceive the Dutch into thinking that the main amphibious assault would be at Kaimana). For the assault, he gathered a force of two parachute brigades (7,000 men), a 4,500-man marine brigade with amphibious capability, and four infantry brigades totalling almost 13,000 men. The plan was to knock out Dutch observation systems, use parachutists and marines to form a bridgehead, and then proceed to land the infantry by means of a large flotilla of more than a hundred ships. The riskiness of the plan was increased by the fact that the Dutch had already become aware of the target, the attack flotilla's course having been plotted by Dutch Neptune reconnaissance aircraft, so 'the Indonesians ... would undoubtedly have suffered heavy losses before achieving their goal'.[36] The logistics of the planned landing, directed in the first place at a series of uninhabited islands south of Biak because of Indonesian fears of Dutch troop strength on Biak itself, were themselves extremely fragile.

Suharto himself recognised that the proposed attack was 'a very dangerous action, since the Indonesian forces were limited, including the air cover for the first assault'.[37] He admitted to his own troops that 'we have only one opportunity to bring together the strike power of land, sea and air forces; we can't manage more than that. We have no reserves'. He thought of it like a boxing match: 'one punch with all the strength we have and the enemy is knocked out'.[38] Nonetheless, he 'hoped we could overrun the enemy within one week after landing, according to plan. And I was confident that the enemy too had only limited forces'.[39]

Suharto arrived at the assembly point at Peleng, in the island group off the coast of Central Sulawesi, on 5 August 1962. He had originally set the date for the Biak offensive for 9 August, but his forces were not in readiness and the date for the amphibious attack was postponed until 14 August. Apparently as part of a continuing effort to confuse the Dutch, there were large paradrops of around 500 men at Sorong, Kaimana, Teminabuan and Merauke on both 13 and 14 August. As Suharto was setting out for the mission, however, he received orders to postpone operations. Under heavy US pressure to adopt the Bunker plan, fuelled by fears that Indonesia would move into the communist camp if they were denied West Irian, and themselves concerned about the prospects of a large-scale Indonesian attack, the Dutch had been persuaded that their efforts to keep West New Guinea were destined to be fruitless.

While he was probably puzzled and annoyed that he had been permitted to advance so far without a clear sense of the momentum of the parallel negotiations, Suharto was relieved that 'a very great sacrifice of lives and property' had been avoided. Perhaps miffed at being stopped in his tracks, he later strove to inflate the importance of his mission: 'if our attack had really taken place, the West would have been stunned at the time. There would have been an incident like that in 1905 between Japan and Russia at Vladivostok'. To him, 'the Jayawijaya Operation broke through the diplomatic logjam and resulted in West Irian being brought under the care of the Republic of Indonesia'.[40] The agreement with the Dutch, reached on 15 August, saw control over West Irian handed to the United Nations on 1 October 1962 until 1 May 1963, when Indonesia would assume administrative control of the territory. A cease-fire came into effect at one minute past midnight GMT on 18 September.

With hostilities over, Suharto, now assisted by a new chief of staff in the person of Amirmachmud, saw his task as 'ensuring that the agreement can proceed as well as possible'. What needed attention, he went on, was 'whether the Dutch really wanted to carry out the agreement, or would still engage in tactics of incitement, playing off people against each other and so on, as we came to experience in the formerly colonised areas like Maluku with its RMS, Jabar [West Java] with its APRA, and so on'.[41] Suharto took the opportunity to travel extensively through West Irian, checking in typical fashion on the condition of his soldiers, gathering impressions of the region, and making preparations for civic mission activities there. Because of his close involvement with the West Irian problem, the matter of its development remained his strong concern. 'West Irian was 17 years behind other parts of Indonesia, which made it a very backward territory indeed … Because of that, when the New Order government began its development program, I paid special attention to Irian Jaya'.[42] For the rest, apart from ceremonial duties such as formally closing an exhibition of Mandala photographs in Jakarta in late November, attending a flag-raising ceremony in West Irian at the end of 1962, and being present at ceremonies for the decoration and promotion of troops who had served in the conflict (including RPKAD Major Benny Murdani and Major Untung), he was involved in winding up the Mandala command, which was formally disbanded by Sukarno in Makasar on 6 May 1963.

At the dissolution ceremony, Suharto presented a brief report of his achievements, making mention of those who had fallen in the campaign. Suharto, Commodores Subono and Sudomo, Air Commodore Wattimena, and Brig.-Gen. Tahir all received the Bintang Dharma decoration in recognition of their services. Two weeks later, for the first time in the capacity of acting minister and army commander, Suharto presented decorations to 249 members of Bn 454 in a ceremony in Semarang. In his address, he noted that the incorporation of West Irian did not mean that the revolution was over:

> There are still two broad goals of the revolution which we have to achieve … They are a just and prosperous society and friendship with other countries for the sake of world peace … We must continue to struggle, and a heavy burden still

> weighs on the shoulders of the armed forces: guaranteeing security, as well as its task of contributing to the achievement of these two goals.[43]

A few days later, still in his acting capacity, he issued an Order of the Day in relation to the serious bouts of racial rioting and destruction then taking place in Java, warning members of all ranks of the Army not to allow themselves to be influenced in ways which could damage the good name of the Army, the state and the country, and to be vigilant in facing those situations in which military assistance was required; 'the government', he warned, 'has taken strong action to prevent the incidents from spreading or being repeated'.[44]

Suharto emerged from the Mandala campaign both personally and institutionally enhanced. On the personal side, he had gained a broader reputation as a determined and successful battle commander. He was, moreover, one who seemed to go to unusual lengths to see to the welfare of the men under him, manifest in his inspection visits and his establishment in 1962 of a special foundation under his direction, the Trikora Orphan Foundation, to look after those families who had lost husbands and fathers in the conflict, which established strong bonds of affiliation amongst his men. On the institutional level, he stood, as Caduad commander, over troops who had gone to battle not as members of a local fighting organisation but of Jakarta's first centrally controlled command. They had, moreover, emerged triumphant, experienced and better equipped, all of which they could attribute to the fact of centralised command.

KOSTRAD: A BASE FOR POWER

The successful resolution of the West Irian crisis allowed Suharto to return to his post as commander of the General Reserve, reconstituted in February 1963 as Kostrad (Army Strategic Reserve Command), of which he was formally appointed panglima on 1 March 1963. He was now amongst the most senior of Indonesia's army officers. In mid-1962 there were thirty generals in the Army on active military or government service. Only one, Nasution, was a four-star general, and only two (Hidayat and Jatikusumo) were lieutenants general. Suharto was one of eight majors-general (with him were Yani, Sungkono, Azis Saleh, Bambang Sugeng, Suprayogi, Satrilo and Sudirman). Below him stood nineteen brigadiers-general. From April 1963, when Lt. Gen. Hidayat was appointed minister for communications, Suharto became the senior active officer below the army commander, and he routinely stood in for Yani when the latter was absent. In that same month, as we have seen, he acted for the first time as minister/army commander when Yani was overseas for a month in Manila and elsewhere. From that time on, it became routine for Suharto to stand in for Yani while the latter was away, one more indication of his being seen as someone not threateningly covetous of higher station; in January the following year, for instance, he assumed Yani's responsibilities while the chief of staff was accompanying Sukarno overseas.

A further indication of his enhanced standing was his appointment in July 1963 as deputy head (to Maj.-Gen. Sudirman) of a new body, Wanjakti (Advisory

Council for Assignments and Ranks for the Senior Level of the Army), created by Yani to make recommendations to him on senior promotions, awards and placements. This role allowed Suharto an important say in the determination of rewards and tasks for officers at the most senior level, and became a position of significant influence with the passage of time, even if Suharto was, it appears, unsuccessful in his efforts to have Yoga Sugama appointed as panglima of the Diponegoro Division. In what was, in retrospect, to be a prophetic rehearsal, Suharto's stature was further recognised when he was designated to take charge of Kostrad's participation in the occasion of the 1963 Armed Forces Day celebration, which took the form of a spectacular simulated airborne attack upon an area close by the Halim air base in Jakarta called Lubang Buaya.

Suharto's Kostrad appointment was pivotal to his career. It provided him with a base even more fertile than his earlier Diponegoro command to develop a closely knit group of like-minded colleagues and to create a quasi-independent seat of power. Notwithstanding the serious economic difficulties faced by the state, Kostrad did not suffer the budget tightening endured by regular army formations following the successful conclusion of the West Irian campaign. On the contrary, 'it expanded very rapidly, adding cavalry and artillery brigades, upgrading its infantry components, and strengthening the RPKAD'.[45] In one sense, the heightened political tensions which emerged in late 1963 made his role all the more important because he commanded the centre's mobile military muscle for handling both foreign and domestic crises. At the same time, Kostrad provided him with an institutional base to develop a business and intelligence network which was to serve him well then and, more important, in later times.

As he had during his time as Diponegoro commander, Suharto sought, with a close circle of trusted advisers, to develop a lucrative source of income for Kostrad and its members. On 28 April 1964, he established the Kostrad Dharma Putra Social Welfare Foundation, with start-up capital of Rp40,000 and the aim of promoting the economic and cultural interests of its members and their families.[46] The board of the new foundation included Suharto himself, together with Achmad Wiranatakusumah, Cokropranolo, and A. P. Nasution. Over time, the foundation, and Kostrad members at various levels of the military hierarchy, became involved in a raft of businesses, such as banking, film production, transport, industry, and food production intensification projects. As we shall see, Kostrad also developed strong interests in the illegal smuggling of primary produce from production centres in North Sumatra to Singapore.

LEFTWARD POLITICS

1963 was a time of increasingly mobilised politics in Jakarta. 'Domestic political conditions', Suharto was later to reflect, 'had grown increasingly uncertain'.[47] Following the crises caused by the collapse of parliamentary politics and the regional rebellions, and Sukarno's fears of the growing power of the Army, and of Nasution in particular, politics had become framed as a subtle contest between three forces: Sukarno (named President for Life by the MPRS in 1963), the Army, and the PKI. Other formal institutions, such as the parliament and the cabinet, became much less crucial to the political process than this defining contest. Given the charismatic Sukarno's apparently unimpeachable position, and the physical power and relative cohesion in crisis which the Army could muster, the PKI eagerly sought advantage wherever it could find it. The party found a colourful and highly useful character in Sukarno himself, then reaching the pinnacle of his anti-Western and anti-liberal ideologising. Nonetheless, while they often drove the increasingly exuberant ideological campaigns, real power continued to elude the communists. They remained only a tiny fraction of the cabinet, an object of deep suspicion on the part of more established political groups in Jakarta, and had no counterweight to the massive physical threat of the Army. To assuage their vulnerability, they sought to develop a vast membership and set alight a mood of growing revolutionary fervour, perhaps in the hope of coming to power by acclamation.

Sukarno, for his part, was increasingly fearful of the Army's political role. Apart from attempting to bolster the influence of the PKI, and employing his extraordinarily powerful rhetoric and uncanny ability both to manufacture and represent the public mood to set the political agenda, he sought to weaken the Army internally. In a cunning move, he managed to sideline Nasution in mid-1962 by appointing him to the new position of chief of staff of the Armed Forces – essentially an assignment of no operational significance which, combining ceremonial duties with paper-shuffling, undercut Nasution's own central position in the Army – and replacing him as army chief of staff with Yani, whom, notwithstanding his impressive military credentials, he saw as a more malleable character than the flinty, opinionated and staunchly anti-communist Nasution. Yani soon became distant from Nasution, a reflection not just of the circumstances of political fortune (and Yani's acquiescence in them) but also of lifestyle: Yani had a well-developed and well-exercised taste for good living and pretty women.

Suharto was clearly unhappy with the increasingly aggressive and confrontational style of domestic politics, including Sukarno's gathering promotion of the PKI, the raft of ideologising which sought to divide rather than unite (although, according to Roeder, Suharto 'had accepted for some time a general non-committed NASAKOM'),[48] the growing subordination of the Armed Forces to new political agendas and, from 1963, the sidling up to Beijing. Suharto's attitude at this time seems to have been to attempt to play the part of the non-politicised professional military man, aware of the mounting tension between the increasingly pressing Communist Party on the one hand, and military and Muslim groups on the other, but unsure how best to cope on his own initiative. He even claims to have toyed with the idea of resigning 'to become a taxi driver or farmer',[49] a suggestion that drew laughter from his friends. Given his stellar rise to eminence since 1961, we can safely dismiss his purported suggestion as the statement of one self-possessedly in command.

CONFRONTATION WITH MALAYSIA

Suharto's Kostrad appointment coincided with growing tensions surrounding the proposed formation of Malaysia. Plans to create a Malaysian federation had gone virtually unremarked upon in Indonesia until the end of 1962, when a 'trivial, almost Gilbertian'[50] revolt in Brunei drew Indonesian support to the side of those opposing the idea. The highly complex and confusing interrelationship between foreign policy and the accelerating theatre of tension in domestic politics which vitalised Indonesia's pursuit of Confrontation from late 1962 onwards, and which culminated after September 1963 in the campaign to 'crush' Malaysia, need not concern us here.[51] Inevitably and eventually, however, Suharto, by dint of his strategic posting, was drawn into it.

As Confrontation moved into a relatively more purposeful stage in 1964, army misgivings about the policy began to surface. At an earlier stage, it had offered the Army certain political advantages, especially after the ending of martial law on 1 May 1963. It had shielded it from the severe budget cuts which would have accompanied the proposed economic stabilisation scheme,[52] allowed it to continue its equipment enhancement, and provided it with a legitimising context to assert its claim for a larger role in politics. Now, however, there emerged grave misgivings in army ranks that the PKI stood to gain most from the pursuit of Confrontation, as it had with the Irian campaign, and that the Army itself was ill prepared to take on British and Commonwealth arms.

Early in May 1964, Sukarno proclaimed the Dwikora (the Double Command of the People), and two weeks later created a combat command, Koga (Vigilance Command), headed by Air Marshal Omar Dhani, to pursue the confrontation of Malaysia. The creation of Koga was a matter for some alarm to army leaders. Although Brig.-Gen. Achmad Wiranatakusumah, Suharto's Kostrad chief of staff, was appointed deputy II to Koga, the command's creation was viewed 'as a move to reduce their capacity to restrain the military side of the campaign'.[53] Omar Dhani was a man who grew vigorously in Sukarno's shadow, and the move was seen as further evidence of Sukarno's wish to divide the Armed Forces in the interests of advancing and consolidating his own political purposes. Yani, loyal to Sukarno but by no means his lapdog, was able up to about mid-1964 to ensure that Koga's military activities against Malaysia were restricted for the most part to what Mackie calls 'low-posture quasi-guerrilla operations'.[54] However, small-scale seaborne and parachute landings of poorly prepared troops on the Malay peninsula in mid-August and early September 1964 – actions undertaken without the backing of army leaders – were disastrous failures, and the lamentable military performance was used by Yani from October 1964 onwards as a means of asserting a more significant degree of direction by the Army over military operations. Indeed, according to Crouch, army leaders 'had in fact lost interest in the Confrontation campaign since the latter part of 1964'.[55] In an important concession to army sentiment on the conduct of the campaign, perhaps fuelled by the impression that the Army wished to assume a more enthusiastic role in Confrontation,

Suharto and other senior Diponegoro division figures. From left, Lt. Col. Slamet Riyadi; Suharto; Lt. Col. Suadi Suromiharjo; Lt. Col. Sarbini; Col. Gatot Subroto; Lt. Col. M. Bachrun and Lt. Col. Achmad Yani. (Ipphos)

Sukarno and Suharto in Semarang, probably in 1958. (Ipphos)

Suharto in training for his paratroop qualification, c. 1964.
(State Secretariat, Indonesia)

Suharto watches the raising of the generals' bodies at Lubang Buaya, 4 October 1965.
(Department of Information, Indonesia)

Suharto at the funeral of the slain generals, 5 October 1965. (Department of Information, Indonesia)

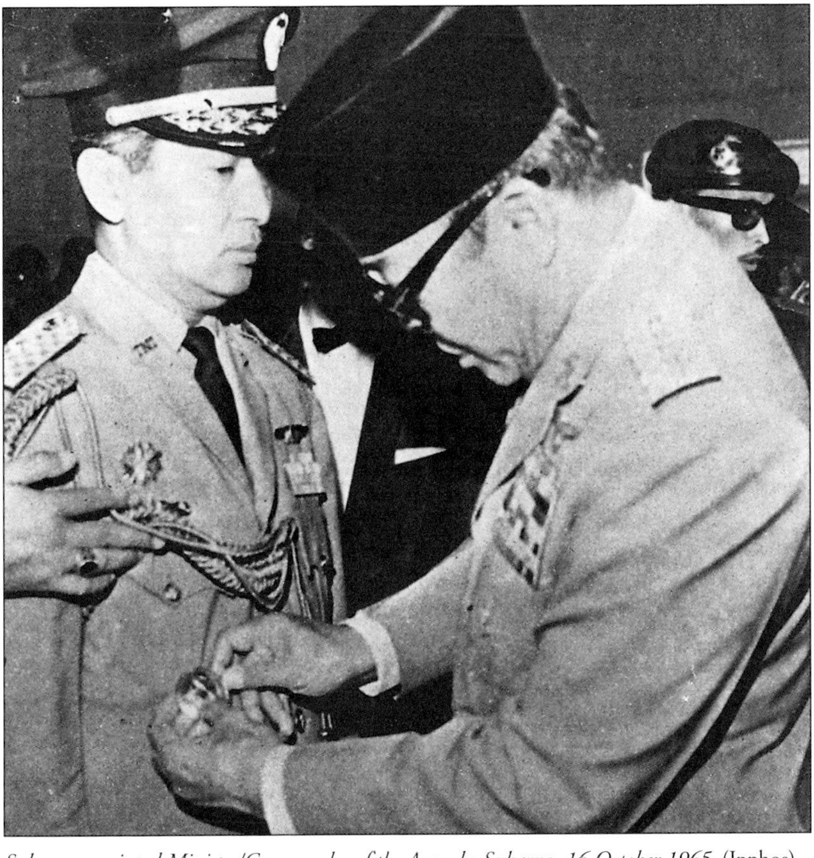

Suharto appointed Minister/Commander of the Army by Sukarno, 16 October 1965. (Ipphos)

Suharto, Sukarno, and Nasution, c. 1967. (State Secretariat, Indonesia)

Suharto appointed Acting President. (Department of Information, Indonesia)

in October Sukarno agreed to the reorganisation of Koga as an area command, Kolaga (Alert Theatre Command), similar to the integrated structure of the former Mandala command and encompassing all military operations in Sumatra and Kalimantan. On 1 January 1965 Suharto, partly on the basis of his earlier Mandala experience, was appointed deputy I commander under Dhani and given the key responsibility for operational affairs. His appointment to a deputy position he interpreted as an indication that Sukarno 'did not completely trust his officer Soeharto'.[56]

It is, as well, highly likely that Suharto himself had an important role in the new appointment. Notwithstanding the view he had expressed in a speech at Lubang Buaya in July 1964 that 'there is now no other road for the Army than to make greater the execution of the Dwikora to heighten the defence of our revolution and also to assist the struggle of the peoples in Malaya, Singapore and North Kalimantan in dissolving the neo-colonialist project of "Malaysia"',[57] Suharto, like Yani, was increasingly dubious about the Confrontation exercise and concerned where it might lead. His apprehension had apparently been heightened by mid-year advice from his Opsus (Special Operations) intelligence unit of the possibility of a move against the army leadership by Sukarno and the PKI and the danger of denuding Java of its best and most reliable forces for the Confrontation effort in a context of serious political tension and uncertainty. It seems, as well, that he soon formed the view that Confrontation was no more than a tactic by the PKI to gain the ideological initiative and enhance its support. The reluctance of Suharto and Yani to commit themselves forthrightly to the Confrontation campaign was deepened by their scepticism about the chance of military success, their scornfulness about the campaign's leadership – at one meeting with Sukarno, Suharto described Dhani as an 'inappropriate' leader[58] – their fears that the campaign would soil Indonesia's international standing, their anger at the losses and dishonour suffered by troops sent on missions doomed from the outset, and their well-founded concern that any success would be claimed by the PKI. With Yani, Suharto conspired to ensure that a tight lid was kept on military activity within the newly established theatre of operations.

Suharto characterises the military effort under Dhani's Koga as one of 'confusion'; together with Yani, Suharto appears to have exerted himself vigorously to ensure that Kolaga presented no significant military threat to Malaysia. Following his appointment as deputy I, he undertook tours of inspection in North Kalimantan and North Sumatra, the planned launching places for attacks on Malaysia. What he found did not please him; 'I saw various things which were not in order and I tried to straighten out the tangled situation'. While the operations in progress could not be stopped, he eventually managed to halt the air drops, which had been a dreadful failure.[59] Furthermore, brakes were applied to further significant troop build-ups. Under the new Kolaga theatre arrangements, all troops designated for service in Sumatra or Kalimantan had to be transferred first to Kostrad, under Suharto's direct command, before being dispatched to the theatre. Even though, as Kostrad commander, he held command of all troops in the Kolaga theatre, he seemed unable to provide sufficient troops for the front in Kalimantan, 'ostensibly because of inadequate equipment and transport, but possibly also because of deliberate obstruction to their despatch for essentially political reasons'.[60] The Kolaga arrangements required that, because the theatre was limited just to Sumatra and Kalimantan, the addition of troops from Java had to be requested; requests were not always complied with, unprepared troops were sent while battle-ready troops remained in Java, and prescribed command structures were ignored. In North Sumatra, Col. Kemal Idris, short, blunt and tough, and no lover of communists, was placed in command of the putative invasion units, apparently with the brief, perhaps tacit, that no invasion should take place. Brig.-Gen. M. S. Suparjo, a left-leaning Siliwangi officer and ardent Sukarnoist, was placed in charge of the Kalimantan battle command in late 1964, but was surrounded by trusted local commanders and never adequately provided with well-prepared army units.

The curiously indeterminate nature of the campaign, as well as the brakes applied by the army high command, therefore prevented any significant escalation of hostilities; 'it was a very minor war if measured in terms of the casualties involved'.[61] Nonetheless, Suharto was adept at maintaining the appearance of the busy commander. In August 1965, for example, he remarked that enemy forces in North Kalimantan were 'in a panic', and 'all their attacks a total failure'. Seemingly unaware of the contradiction, he called for assistance in the form of medicine and clothing for those living in the border areas, who had suffered their houses and schools being burned down, and a general lack of security, because of enemy attacks.[62]

It appears that no one was sufficiently judicious or daring to oppose Suharto's efforts to stall frontal military activity against Malaysia, although Sukarno, and the Air Force and the Navy which were bearing a disproportionate share of Confrontation operations, were aware of the Army's lack of enthusiasm for the campaign. But even before he had put the holding operation in place, Suharto determined, 'probably with the approval of General Yani',[63] on a new and more subtle strategy, designed to appear as a continuation of Confrontation by other means but, in fact – whether originally by design or simply, at this stage, to keep options open[64] – the first steps in negotiating an end to Indonesia's bellicosity. As early as August–September 1964, under the leadership and direction of Suharto's Kostrad intelligence assistant Ali Murtopo (around that time brought back to Jakarta from his intelligence work as assistant I Kopur II in North Sumatra), and doubtless with the knowledge and agreement of Yani, together with Murdani (recently transferred from RPKAD to Kostrad) and Lt. Col. Abdul Rachman Ramly, both members of Murtopo's Opsus team, efforts were directed towards establishing covert contacts with Malaysia. Through expatriate intermediaries formerly associated with the PRRI rebellion – such as Des Alwi, Bandanese foster-son of the then-imprisoned Sutan Syahrir and on the payroll of the Malaysian Foreign Ministry, and Sumitro Joyohadikusumo – ties were initiated with senior Malaysian figures such as Tun Abdul Razak and Malaysian Foreign Ministry head Ghazalie Shafie. The purpose was simple: to assure the Malaysian government and its British sponsors that the support of the Indonesian Armed Forces for the conflict was neither born of conviction nor conducted with enthusiasm, and that it had no wish for a more intense level of conflict, and to seek ways of opening discussions with the Malaysians about ending the dispute. In November, Murtopo and another close Kostrad aide, Col. Cokropranolo, conducted secret negotiations with Malaysian officials to ensure that the lid was kept on any possible escalation of the conflict by either side. In early 1965, Yoga Sugama, on the point of completing his tour of duty as military attaché in Yugoslavia, was recruited by Suharto to rejoin and head his intelligence team, replacing Hernomo as assistant I Kostrad. With Suharto and Ali Murtopo, Yoga completed the team which took the negotiations forward.

Working on another level, Suharto later claimed, he 'changed [the strategy] first by forming pockets of resistance [in Malaysia] to contact Malaysians who were pro-Republic',[65] apparently an effort to infiltrate from the rear. Relying strongly on his intelligence team, in early 1965 he ordered the establishment of an agency in Bangkok, where Benny Murdani posed as a Garuda ticketing officer. Murdani made a few desultory attempts to send agents into Malaysia, with almost no success. It seems highly likely that these efforts were designed not to enhance the Confrontation drive but to cover the deeper and more nuanced negotiations taking place at the same time. In the meantime, international diplomatic efforts to find a negotiated solution to the dispute waxed and waned, without significant success.

Suharto's Confrontation responsibilities also served commercial purposes. His position as deputy I Kolaga and Kostrad commander placed him in effective control of the produce of large plantation areas in North Sumatra and Kalimantan, and the capability of smuggling large quantities of this produce to Malaysia, at a time when formal commercial links had been cut with the formation of Malaysia in September 1963. It is perhaps no coincidence that Ibu Tien visited North Sumatra during the period of Confrontation. Through his Opsus team, Suharto developed lucrative commercial activities, apparently under the cover of Ali Murtopo's Medan-based intelligence activities with Kopur II, which carried rubber and other primary agricultural goods to Malaya. The official Kostrad history notes that '95 per cent of the resources used for carrying out this task [that is, intelligence activities] were Chinese fishermen; our volunteers went with them disguised as traders'.[66] The close operational association between intelligence and trade may, indeed, have been the occasion of a confusion of priorities. According to McDonald, 'the commerce did not go completely unnoticed. At one cabinet meeting of the time, Trade Minister Adam Malik flourished a wad of Singapore customs clearance papers at military men, accusing the Army of undermining Confrontation'.[67] It may be, indeed, that Suharto's half-brother Probosutejo was involved in this commerce; living in Medan in the early 1960s as a schoolteacher, he had left that career and established business connections with a Chinese businessman.

THE ARMY, THE PKI AND SUHARTO

The gathering heat and momentum of the Confrontation drive in 1964 and early 1965 had been skilfully modulated and exploited by the PKI for its own advantage. With the enthusiastic encouragement of the President, and with the Army apparently unsure about how to assert itself in the political realm, the party made great progress. Throughout 1965, the political temperature in Jakarta continued to rise. The increasing tensions in the body of Indonesian politics were moving towards flashpoint, with 'a widespread feeling ... that the political system could not last as it was for very much longer'.[68] The signs of impending crisis and collapse were everywhere. In the economic field – to a considerable extent, the result of the drain of the Irian and Confrontation campaigns – inflation gained pace, the country's physical infrastructure frayed and decayed, output dipped, and what little international confidence remained in Indonesia's economic future was further sapped; no realistic or serious attempt was made thereafter to improve matters. The administrative infrastructure showed similar signs of disarray, overtaken by bottlenecks and increasingly widespread corruption. Sukarno's revolutionary rhetoric became increasingly frenetic and lent further tension to the situation, especially since any kind of departure or demur from total support for his views became unacceptable. On the broader international front, Indonesia's increasingly shrill and aggressive policies were coupled with a move to a more intimate relationship with China, then distancing itself from the Soviet Union, and a sharpening move away from the United States.

The PKI seemed bent on making serious inroads into the seats of power, with its suggestion in January 1965 that peasants and workers be armed and trained, a notion which later took shape as a plan for a 'fifth force' alongside the three services and the police, and its plans for a 'Nasakomisation' of the Armed Forces.[69] More broadly, PKI criticisms of so-called 'bureaucratic capitalists' were interpreted, correctly, as attacks against the growing self-interested business interests of many top-ranking army men. The Army seemed increasingly on the defensive and uncertain how to react, as Sukarno appeared more and more to take the side of the PKI in the cause of the 'continuing revolution', itself most likely a tactical move to keep the Army on the back foot and perhaps even to tempt army leaders to modify their ideas about the nation's direction.[70] Given that he lacked any substantive institutional vehicle to get his way in the face of the various vested interests in elite politics, Sukarno's approach manifested itself most strongly in the symbolic aspects of foreign policy, and in solidarity-building domestically. Indonesia withdrew from the United Nations on 1 January 1965. On top of everything else, Sukarno himself was beginning to show the first signs of physical deterioration, so much so that real fears were held for his life, itself a cause of the escalating domestic political tensions.

It was precisely because of the growing political threat of the PKI that army leaders strove to develop a more coherent sense of the Army's role in the nation's political life and a clearer sense of tactics and purpose. While the Army held a monopoly in terms of force of arms, its leaders recognised that the threat of force was a weak political instrument because it had the potential to shatter the Army's still weakly constructed internal unity. Many of its senior members held the President in the highest awe, there were strong ideological tensions at lower levels of the army structure, and the high command had no strong sense of its own strategic direction. Moreover, there was significant leftist sentiment in the other services, notably the Air Force. Consequently, the Army had to be satisfied with an anxious holding operation, with its real influence on the course of events limited by the conundrum it faced. Enjoying considerable but far from determinate influence in the institutions of governance, the Army had perforce to accommodate itself to the prevailing ideological temper of politics, however reluctantly. Its problem 'was not whether it should resist the PKI but when and where to draw the line'.[71]

Suharto's position probably reflected the general sentiment of growing alarm and confusion in the army high command; he himself must have been perturbed by the dismissal of his old friend Hadisubeno from his party post by a PNI leadership strongly under communist influence. According to Roeder's melodramatic account of these days, Suharto 'was often approached by his men for information and advice. His answer was "I'm not blind. I have reported to my superiors about the serious situation. There was no reaction. What can I do as a soldier?" The man who had found a solution to difficulties even in the darkest hours of his military life confessed: "I'm without hope"'.[72] While, as we have seen, he was no champion of Sukarno's inflammatory foreign policy, Suharto had to accede, albeit in a foot-dragging way, to its overall contours. At the same time, while not a Sukarno loyalist, like most senior officers he held the President in reverential regard. His seniority, and the crucial importance of the positions he held, placed him in an influential position to attempt to resolve the running conflicts within the Army itself. Outside his own strong attachments to his Kostrad staff, he himself was part of no clique or group and was generally conceived to be something of a loner. Apparently, unlike many of the other Jakarta generals who preferred expensive luxury hotel lunches, Suharto customarily went home to lunch with his wife.

In the matter of attachment to Sukarno and his views, Suharto stood somewhere between the sceptical group of officers around Nasution who thought Yani uncomfortably subservient to Sukarno's views and policies, and those more closely associated with and kindly disposed towards the President, grouped around Yani. Suharto, of course, had had his differences with Nasution, who had transferred him in 1959, and with Yani in 1963 over the appropriate organisational structure of Kostrad, but was perhaps closer in intellectual tenor and certainly in lifestyle to Nasution. Around the beginning of 1965, Suharto, along with other senior officers, visited Nasution, apparently in an effort to persuade him to modify his critical attitude towards Sukarno. Shortly thereafter, on 13 January, apparently at Nasution's request, Suharto – and four other officers attached to neither faction, Achmad Sukendro, Sarbini Martodiharjo, Basuki Rachmat and Sudirman – attended a meeting with members of Yani's headquarters group in an effort to ameliorate the differences between Nasution and Yani; Suharto and his fellows apparently represented Nasution's view of things to Yani's people. The meeting was unsuccessful in persuading Yani's circle to adopt a more distanced attitude to Sukarno, and resolved merely to conduct an army seminar, scheduled for April 1965, as a forum both to discuss the current political situation and to provide an opportunity for the Army to reflect upon and develop further the ideological basis for its political and economic role; it claimed both a military role and a role as an independent 'socio-political force', with an integral involvement in areas as diverse as religion and the economy.[73] According to Subandrio, Suharto was the initiator of the doctrine, 'Tri Ubaya Sakti', which emerged from the seminar.[74]

The army high command, notwithstanding its internal differences and its considerable confusion about the way ahead, had – perhaps precisely because of the threat of the gathering shadow of the PKI – forged agreement on some basic principles. All of its members looked askance at the growing influence of the communists and were determined that the party should not accede to power in its own right. This mood was reflected in the inflexible opposition of Yani to the idea of the 'fifth force'.[75] Suharto himself was also 'dead against this plan'.[76]

Suharto's experiences of the tortuous politics of these later years of Guided Democracy – in which nuance, suggestion, the word left unsaid, the strategic utterance, and shifting intrigue were the common currency of political manoeuvre – must have influenced him deeply. Like many of his fellow-officers who only a few years ago had been unschooled in high politics, he became a skilled and adroit operator in the sometimes surreal politics of the period. Moreover, since Yani did not enjoy the stature and independent authority of his predecessor (partly because of the circumstances of his appointment as army chief of staff), Suharto and other senior officers such as the Siliwangi commander Ibrahim Ajie were from time to time able to exert their own policy influence. Indeed, Suharto had become one of the most powerful people in the country. His position as founding commander of Kostrad, his repute as a battle commander, his senior rank and operational command within Kolaga, his standing deputy role to Yani as minister/commander of the Army and his stature as the most senior commander on active duty had brought him to the top echelon of influence in the capital. He was party to numerous high-ranking discussions and strategy meetings, especially in matters relating to national security and the Armed Forces.

One effect of the gathering concern of the army command about the direction of domestic politics was the development of an army-sponsored body of 'functional groups' in late 1964: the Sekber Golkar (Joint Secretariat of Functional Groups).[77] Suharto's friend and next-door neighbour, Mashuri, was one of those developing the idea, and it is tempting to think that Suharto himself may have been involved in these discussions. Yani, for his part, ordered regional commanders to put their weight behind the establishment of local Sekber Golkar organisations.

TOWARDS 1 OCTOBER

A particular reflection of the escalating tensions of early 1965 and, perhaps more specifically, the stiffening of the collective army resolve against PKI advances, was the rumour that developed some months into 1965 of a so-called Council of Generals (*Dewan Jenderal*). This notion, much popularised by the PKI, was that such a council had been formed amongst senior generals who aimed to seize power at an appropriate moment. The controversy surrounding the Council of Generals was ignited with the discovery of the so-called Gilchrist letter, allegedly found in the villa of an American film distributor and suspected CIA agent at Puncak when it was attacked on 1 April by a communist youth group. The document, purportedly a secret telegram from the British ambassador in Jakarta, Sir Andrew Gilchrist, to his London superiors, mentioned possible future cooperation between the British and 'our local army friends'.[78]

Sukarno, his fears about the Army's intentions apparently having been aggravated by the Gilchrist letter, sought clarification from Yani at a specially convened meeting of the four service commanders on the morning of 26 May. In response, Yani confirmed that two of his staff, Parman and Sukendro, kept contact with both British and American embassies and that senior officers had met at his house to express their views about the political situation. Further, he acknowledged the existence of a generals' council, Wanjakti, the body he had created in 1963 to recommend senior placements and promotions, but denied the existence of anything more furtive. Nonetheless, the rumours that a group of top generals were plotting to take power into their own hands strengthened from May onwards, fuelled by an apparent stiffening of Yani's resolve to block the PKI's advance, and perhaps, too, by a sense that the Americans as well were eager for a political change of course in Indonesia. By August and September such rumours were common currency in Jakarta. Sukarno himself seems to have been deeply disturbed by Yani's firmness on such matters as the 'fifth force' and 'Nasakomisation'. According to Crouch, 'the president naturally began to think of replacing Yani with a more pliable army commander'; indeed, 'it is not unlikely that [Sukarno] often spoke of "taking action" to be rid of him'.[79]

No indisputable evidence has ever emerged to substantiate the notion that a Council of Generals was plotting a coup. However, given the high temperature of politics through 1965, it is likely that senior army officers around Yani, those who were to form the core group of victims of the 30 September Movement, were accustomed to meeting to discuss the state of political play and, perhaps, to map out plans of action under a variety of scenarios. Sukendro, a member of the close group of headquarters advisers around Yani, himself later admitted as much.[80] According to Hughes, 'it is difficult to believe that Indonesia's top generals did not, in fact, have some plan laid to assume power. In the atmosphere of those days, they would have been remarkably naive if they had not made some preparations'.[81]

In the highly fraught and confused atmosphere of the time, however, perceptions often counted more than realities. There is no doubt that, whether or not a Council of Generals existed, the PKI leadership thought that it did, just as the party realised that its existence presaged a sudden and fierce move against the communists. The party itself began to make serious plans to forestall this fearful possibility. Around the same time, lower ranked elements in the Armed Forces began to make their dissatisfactions felt with the conduct of the army elite in Jakarta: its high living, its comfortable tenures of plum positions, its preoccupation with political machinations, its lack of interest in what they saw as the foundational values of the Army and the state. The confluence of interests between these two groups was to result in the rapid emergence of what became known as the 30 September Movement. The groundwork had already been in progress for some time, notably through the work of Syam Kamaruzzaman, an aide of the PKI leader D. N. Aidit, who by 1965 had ripened a network of contacts between the PKI's 'Special Bureau' and a small number of officers, mainly in Central Java, and in East Java as well. Fears about the intentions of the Army, heightened by an increasing alarm about the health and longevity of its patron, Sukarno, who suffered a brief collapse on 5 August, were the motives which moved leadership elements within the PKI to seek practical ways of merging their interests with different Armed Forces groups, ranging from the disaffected junior officers in Central Java to deeply devoted Sukarno loyalists in the Air Force, to stave off what they saw as the serious likelihood of a pre-emptive army strike against Sukarno, aimed especially at the destruction of the party.

Suharto, meanwhile, had been appointed in his Kostrad capacity as officer-in-charge of the grand celebrations – to match those held earlier in May for the PKI's forty-fifth birthday – planned for the commemoration of Armed Forces Day on 5 October. Those celebrations would never take place.

5 The coup attempt

On the morning of 30 September 1965, Suharto, as Kostrad commander, had been busy inspecting the troops he had brought in from East, Central and West Java which were exercising at Senayan stadium for the large march past scheduled for 5 October, Armed Forces Day. That night, from about 9 p.m. onwards, he joined his wife in keeping vigil at the bedside of their 3-year-old son, Tommy, scalded by boiling soup which had 'splashed over his whole body' two days before at home, causing him to be taken to Gatot Subroto hospital for attention.[1] Around 10 p.m., Suharto noted an old acquaintance, Col. Abdul Latief, commander of Infantry Brigade I of the Jakarta Military Command, who had apparently dropped by to enquire about Tommy's condition. About midnight, according to Ibu Tien, she asked Suharto to return home, since Mamiek, their 1-year-old daughter, had been left alone in the house, with only a servant in attendance.[2] This he did, and immediately went to bed.

He was awoken about 4.30 a.m. by a visit from a television cameraman named Hamid Syamsuddin, who reported hearing shooting in the city area. Suharto later recalled that he 'didn't think much of this at the time'.[3] Half an hour later, his neighbour Mashuri, chief of the local neighbourhood association, came to him conveying the same story, so that he 'began to give this rather more thought'.[4] Before 6 a.m. he had been brought the news that several senior army officers had been kidnapped. He immediately began to dress in his field uniform. About the same time, Lt. Col. Sujiman, an emissary from the commander of the Jakarta Military Garrison, Maj.-Gen. Umar Wirahadikusumah, arrived at the house with reports of unidentified troops in position in the central part of the city, close by the National Monument and the Merdeka Palace. It is highly likely, as well, that Umar conveyed information to Suharto concerning the identities of the kidnapped generals.

Suharto immediately sent a message via Sujiman to Umar that he was on his way to Kostrad headquarters, located at the northern end of Jalan Merdeka Timur. Beginning to comprehend the huge hole blown in the army high command by the capture of so many generals in one swoop, he 'realized that the Army was in danger and I decided to assume the leadership of the Army'.[5] In doing so, he mobilised the by now long-established practice of his acting in Yani's stead in the latter's absence. Having conveyed this decision to Umar, he proceeded to drive himself, alone, to Kostrad headquarters, dressed in his army fatigues, in his Toyota Jeep. Along the way he noticed troops in position around the National Monument in Merdeka Square, close by his headquarters. Upon his arrival – the trip could have taken no more than fifteen minutes – he was reportedly informed that Sukarno was not at the palace and was on his way to the Halim air base. It was still shortly before 7 a.m.

Soon after 7 a.m., following the normal morning news, Radio Republik Indonesia (RRI) broadcast a report of the activities of a group identifying itself as the '30 September Movement'. The announcement revealed that troops under the leadership of Lt. Col. Untung, commander of a battalion of the Cakrabirawa Regiment which operated as a palace guard, had taken measures to forestall a planned coup by a 'Council of Generals', itself sponsored by the CIA. Untung's action was 'solely a movement within the Army directed against the Council of Generals'.[6] These generals and their followers, the statement continued, 'have neglected the lot of their men and who above the accumulated sufferings of their men have lived in luxury, led a gay life, insulted our women and wasted government funds'. This news, Suharto later recounted, immediately gave him 'a sense of foreboding. Moreover, I knew who Lt. Col. Untung was. I remembered that he was very close to the PKI, in fact he had become a disciple of Alimin, the PKI figure'.[7] Whatever foreboding Suharto experienced was probably magnified by the fact that the Movement's initial broadcast made no effort to claim that it enjoyed the personal support of Sukarno himself.

TAKING CHARGE

By this time, Suharto had been joined at Kostrad by members of his staff, including Ali Murtopo and Yoga Sugama. Yoga, like Suharto and, presumably, Ali Murtopo, knew Untung from Central Java days; Untung had been a member of Yoga's RTP (Battle Regiment) II in West Sumatra in 1959. Suharto later recounted that when he arrived at Kostrad, 'among all my staff officers, there was not one who knew anything about the affair'.[8] In what must have been a confused and confusing environment, he set to establishing his military situation. Having ascertained that no Kostrad officer had ordered the movement of troops to the city's central square, Suharto ordered Ali Murtopo and Brig.-Gen. Sabirin Mochtar, a former battalion commander in Brawijaya, to make contact with the commanders in charge of the 2,000 or so troops around the monument, now identified as battalions 454 (Central Java) and 530 (East Java), which were in Jakarta at Suharto's order for the impending thirtieth anniversary celebration of Armed Forces Day. The emissaries carried instructions for the battalion commanders to report to Suharto. At 8.30 a.m., Ali and Sabirin reported back that the commanders in question were not with their troops but at the palace. Suharto immediately ordered Ali and Sabirin to have the deputy commanders of the battalions report to him. They arrived at Kostrad around 9 a.m. and explained to him that their mission was to protect the President against an imminent coup by the Council of Generals. Suharto immediately determined to take strong action. He advised the officers that their action was 'a revolt' and that he had determined to oppose it. He gave them until 6 p.m. to submit their forces to Kostrad or face the prospect of attack from his own troops.

According to Crouch, Suharto's desire to employ persuasion rather than immediate force was a result of a careful calculation of numerous factors: the fact that he did not want to start operations against other army troops, and especially not right in the middle of the city; the possible reaction by the Air Force; and the fact that Sukarno was physically with the Movement's leaders.[9] Such a view perhaps credits Suharto with too much tactical awareness, not to mention knowledge of the real situation, at this point. More likely at this time – still the early morning – he was simply acting in this way because he knew so little about what the situation was, and his cautious nature refused to allow him to push forward more strongly until he knew better the disposition and cast of mind of the troops he faced and, more important, whose orders they were following and why. To this end, he preferred to employ bluff – a mixture of enticement and bare-faced threats – rather than violence.

Upon dismissing the battalion deputies, Suharto immediately called a staff conference around 9.15 a.m., attended by Yoga Sugama (assistant, intelligence), Col. Wahono (assistant, operations), Col. Joko Basuki (assistant IV), Col. Sruhardoyo (assistant III), and his chief of staff, Brig.-Gen. Achmad Wiranatakusumah. Suharto, so he later recounted, explained that he had long known Untung, 'who has been a disciple of the PKI figure Alimin since 1945'; there was, moreover, no such thing as a Council of Generals. He later related putting his view of what had happened: 'In my view this is not merely a movement to confront the so-called Council of Generals, but something rather different. They have organised a coup to seize the power of the state by force. And the PKI is definitely behind it'. Warming to his theme, he argued that the Movement should be opposed not just because of its attack on the generals, but also because it 'threatened the state and Pancasila'.[10] Without hesitation, it seems – a reflection, perhaps, of the solidarity of the group Suharto had drawn around him – all his assistants agreed to support him in strenuously opposing the Movement. The meeting broke up about 10 a.m.

The generals targeted by the 30 September Movement included Yani (minister/commander of the Army), Nasution (minister/coordinator of defence and security), and key members of the General Staff (SUAD): Maj.-Gen. Suprapto (deputy II, administration), Maj.-Gen. Haryono (deputy III, finance and public relations), Maj.-Gen. S. Parman (assistant I, intelligence), Brig.-Gen. D. I. Panjaitan (assistant IV, logistics), and Brig.-Gen. Sutoyo Siswomiharjo (prosecutor general of the Army). It appears that the assailants, mostly a combination of troops from Latief's I Brigade of the Jakarta regional command (Kodam V/Jaya) and Untung's Cakrabirawa men, told the generals that they were required by the President at the palace. Most of them refused to believe this story, and some resisted. Yani,

Haryono and Panjaitan were killed at their houses; the others were captured alive and carried back to the Movement's base at the Halim air force complex, a few kilometres south-east of Jakarta. Nasution, however, managed to escape the intruders by scaling the fence of his house and hiding in the garden of the Iraqi ambassador's residence next door. The attackers captured one of his aides, Lt. Pierre Tendean, and took him with them, apparently mistaking him in the stress of the moment for Nasution. Nasution's daughter, Ade Irma Suryani, was seriously wounded by gunshot during the assault. Once at Halim, the three surviving generals, together with the unfortunate Tendean, were killed at about 6.30 a.m.

By late morning, however, Suharto was still unaware of the fate of the captured generals. He knew only that six had been kidnapped, that Nasution had escaped, and that Sukarno had gone to Halim, now established as the base of the rebel forces. Having decided to pursue a path of unrelenting opposition to the 30 September Movement, Suharto proceeded to organise his forces and to map out a strategy, making use of the short-wave communications facilities at Kostrad headquarters. He sent an emissary in an armoured car for Col. Sarwo Edhie, commander of the Army's paracommando force (RPKAD) headquartered at Cijantung, just south of Jakarta, but experienced some difficulty bringing Sarwo onside. He also contacted the commanders of the other services. Unable to reach Air Marshal Omar Dhani, he spoke with Air Commodore Leo Wattimena (air force deputy, operations). According to the semi-official army account, 'when [Suharto] finally reached Air Commodore Leo Wattimena at Halim air base, he received vague statements'.[11] Suharto's message to the service leaders was clear: a plot had been launched against the state, and he intended to oppose it with all his strength. To this end, he had temporarily assumed command of the Army, and he sought their cooperation in confining their forces to barracks and activating them only at Kostrad's express command. All of the commanders assured him of their understanding and support, although Wattimena 'expressed the wish to meet me at Kostrad to obtain clarification and to learn the background of the movement that had taken place'.[12]

Suharto's success in convincing the service leaders to commit their support in so confused and perilous a situation speaks volumes not just for his capacity for persuasive negotiation, but also for the respect he enjoyed as a field commander and his position as Kostrad chief. To be sure, he had little by way of serious competition for his self-appointed task; with Nasution's whereabouts and condition uncertain, the only officers of comparable standing were the SUAD officers Mursyid (deputy I) and Major-General Pranoto Reksosamudro (assistant III, personnel), both viewed as strongly Sukarnoist in orientation. Finally, Suharto also arranged for orders to be sent to regional commanders, informing them of the morning's events and instructing them that troop movements must be coordinated through Kostrad.

Having contacted the base of the Kostrad troops encamped at Senayan to discover which units were missing, Suharto was able to establish the general dimensions of the forces arrayed against him. Equally, he could now count the troops whose loyalty he commanded in Jakarta. Apart from Jakarta garrison troops loyal to Latief, he had Umar's forces at his call, as well as those Kostrad troops who had been brought to Jakarta for Armed Forces Day and who had not assisted the Untung group, notably the Siliwangi paracommando Battalion 328 and the Second Cavalry Battalion. Once Sarwo Edhie showed his hand – according to Suharto, Sarwo's troops rolled into Kostrad headquarters around 11 a.m. to receive Suharto's order to retake the RRI and Telecommunications facilities – the RPKAD was Suharto's as well.[13] He now enjoyed an overwhelming preponderance of force over the troops loyal to the 30 September Movement, which had no armour. He had also learned, via Umar, that Suparjo was at the palace looking for Sukarno – some-thing of a surprise for Suharto, since Suparjo should have been in Kalimantan commanding Kopur IV – and probably surmised that he was involved with the coup forces.

What of Sukarno? The previous evening he had addressed delegates to the National Conference on Technology at the indoor Senayan sports stadium. Afterwards, he had gone to the house of Ratna Sari Dewi, his third wife, at Wisma Yaso on Jl. Gatot Subroto. Around 6.30 a.m., apparently having been informed of the shootings at the houses of some of the targeted generals, Sukarno left Dewi's house and attempted to get to the palace; apparently deterred from this aim by news of troops in Merdeka Square, he then travelled to the house of his fourth wife, Haryati, in the suburb of Grogol. Thereafter, reportedly having been informed of Nasution's escape, he determined to go to Halim where a plane awaited him in case of emergency, arriving there at about 9.30 a.m.[14]

Around midday, RRI broadcast a decree of the Untung group which announced the formation of a 'Revolutionary Council' to 'constitute the source of all authority' in the Republic until the holding of elections.[15] In the meantime, the cabinet would enjoy only 'demissionary status' (*berstatus demisioner*), with ministers empowered to undertake only day-to-day activities. No mention was made of the role that Sukarno might play in the proposed new order of things. Two decisions by Untung immediately followed. The first announced the composition of the Revolutionary Council: a curious and apparently hastily manufactured concoction of names (the great majority of whose owners had not been consulted about their appointment), preponderantly Javanese and Sundanese in ethnic origin, which included Umar, busily working at that very moment to destroy the Movement, as well as other anti-communist generals like Amirmachmud, but which omitted both Sukarno and Suharto. The second decision abolished all ranks above that of lieutenant colonel – Untung's rank – and accorded a one-rank promotion to all NCOs and privates who supported the Movement, and two ranks if they actually participated in it. A statement on behalf of Sukarno was broadcast around 1.30 p.m., noting that he was safe and well and remained in control of the state and the revolution.

The announcement of the existence and composition of the Revolutionary Council must have had a profound effect upon Suharto, still struggling to get on top of events and still uncertain about the whereabouts and fate of the President. Indeed, according to one source, he contacted the Sultan of Yogyakarta to discuss the possibility of establishing a counter-government under the sultan, a course from which the sultan reportedly dissuaded him.[16] The Movement's continuing failure to produce clear evidence that the President supported its actions – a compelling sign that Sukarno was already distancing himself from the conspiracy and its proposed political agenda – can only have strengthened Suharto's resolution to oppose it.

SUKARNO REBUFFED, SUHARTO IN CHARGE

At Halim, where he was briefed within an hour of his arrival by Suparjo, Sukarno was himself considering both his responsibilities and his options. Already aware of Nasution's escape, and having received a report by Cakrabirawa commander Sabur that Panjaitan had been killed and bloodstains found at Yani's house, Sukarno immediately instructed Suparjo to cease all violent actions. Amidst frequent bouts of resting, he then began to address the task of appointing an army commander to replace Yani. Suharto's name was amongst those (including Mursyid and Basuki Rachmat) proposed to him by the group of senior ministers and service commanders who had been rapidly assembled at Halim, but Sukarno – just as he had on the occasion of the 3 July 1946 affair – thought him 'too stubborn'.[17] Suparjo, permitted to join the discussion, initially proposed Pranoto or Basuki Rachmat but, on consulting with Untung and other leaders of the Movement, he plumped for Pranoto. Eventually, around 4 p.m., Sukarno decided to assume command himself and appoint an army caretaker for day-to-day matters; his choice was Pranoto Reksosamudro.

Sukarno's refusal to countenance Suharto may have been because he was aware that Suharto had taken control of things in the city centre, and that he was unwilling to give him any kind of endorsement under such circumstances until the picture became clearer. Especially at this time, he wanted someone who was senior, well respected but relatively pliable, someone who was known to be inimical towards Nasution, someone sympathetic to his own political and ideological views, someone not obsessively anti-PKI, and who could exercise some authority over the Diponegoro troops in Central Java, where a regional variety of the 30 September Movement had emerged by midday. Pranoto was all these things. Moreover, Sukarno almost certainly knew of the bad feeling between Pranoto and Suharto, and probably designed the appointment so as to place his own distinctive mark upon the Army and to give a clear rebuff to Suharto – a warning to know his place and keep to it.

Meanwhile, on the home front, Tien, with Tommy, and accompanied by Probosutejo (returned from Medan with his 'resources … depleted' and sharing a room in Suharto's house with two of Tien's brothers) and Suharto's junior ADC Wahyudi, had left the hospital in the early afternoon, having heard news of the mysterious happenings in the city. She arrived home to find a message from Suharto to move herself and the children to Wahyudi's residence in the satellite suburb of Kebayoran Baru, where she stayed one night.[18]

A 12.30 staff meeting at Kostrad headquarters decided on the need to attack and recapture Halim air base. Shortly thereafter, according to Suharto's account which, curiously, severely telescopes the events of the afternoon, Sukarno's adjutant, Col. Bambang Wijanarko, arrived from Halim. He informed Suharto that Sukarno was safe and well, and the exact place at Halim where he was situated. Suharto gave Wijanarko to realise that he should ensure Sukarno's retreat before midnight, since an attack on the air base was planned.[19] Other more credible accounts, however, place Wijanarko's arrival to the late afternoon; more important, as these accounts make clear, his arrival was not just to report on the President's well-being, but also to require that Pranoto, then at Kostrad headquarters, report to Sukarno at Halim in relation to Sukarno's aim to place him in charge of day-to-day affairs in the Army.[20] Suharto, for his part – he was, as we have seen earlier, no friend of Pranoto – refused to let Pranoto go to Halim; he also refused to allow Umar, earlier ordered by Sukarno to join him there, to proceed to the coup headquarters.

Suharto's rationale was reasonable enough: he did not want to lose any more generals, and Halim remained in enemy hands. His response to Wijanarko – 'clearly an act of insubordination', according to Crouch[21] – was the crucial turning-point of the day. Suharto had decided to pursue his own counsel in the face of the express wish of his president. In his defence, of course, he had no way of knowing Sukarno's relationship with the plotters or the degree of freedom of action he maintained. For their part, the plotters must have known that they had lost in this dangerous game of bluff and counter-bluff; Suharto's refusal to accommodate Sukarno's wishes on the appointment of Pranoto could only have sprung from his confidence that he held the important military cards and was preparing to play them for all they were worth.

By late afternoon, matters were beginning to fall decisively Suharto's way, doubtless heightening his confidence in his decision to take matters into his own hands. Omar Dhani's Order of the Day – issued mid-morning but broadcast only in mid-afternoon – that the 30 September Movement had conducted a 'cleansing in the body' of the Army in order to protect and save the revolution and the Great Leader of the Revolution from CIA subversion, left no doubt about air force involvement.[22] Shortly thereafter, Suharto received word that Battalion 530 had left its post in the central square and turned itself in at Kostrad. It seems that Maj.-Gen. Basuki Rachmat, commander of the Brawijaya Division, together with other senior officers, was able to persuade the Brawijaya battalion to submit itself to Suharto around 4 p.m. The failure of the coup group to organise food and drink for these troops was, it appears, an important factor in their surrender. The Diponegoro Battalion 454, by contrast, had continued its rebelliousness, notwithstanding the efforts of Ali Murtopo to persuade it otherwise, and had decided to leave the palace area and strike out for Halim about 6 p.m. Its bloodless departure no doubt came as a relief to Suharto, who now absolutely controlled the city's key points. As these events were taking place, around 5.30 p.m. Nasution appeared at Kostrad headquarters ('at my request', according to

Suharto),[23] weary and distressed about the fate of his wounded daughter. He had left the Iraqi ambassador's yard after dawn and spent most of the day in a hiding place near his headquarters. Notwithstanding some desultory attempts to assert his authority and, it appears, some supportive advice to Suharto on how to respond to Sukarno's appointment of Pranoto, he was effectively ignored by Suharto and his anti-coup group.

Suharto's style, however, remained as cautious as it was calculating. Worried that a precipitate daytime attack upon the RRI and Telecommunications buildings would result in 'many victims', he ordered Sarwo Edhie to delay his planned move on the facilities.[24] Shortly thereafter, Sarwo was instructed to begin preparations for an assault upon Halim as well. Soon after nightfall, the bid to retake the RRI and Telecommunications facilities on the western and southern sides of the square began, a task accomplished quickly without the firing of a single shot, and according to Suharto's timetable. Suharto now controlled all of the major facilities in the centre of Jakarta, and all enemy forces had either surrendered or straggled away. Once RRI was in his hands, it immediately broadcast a statement he had pre-recorded at 3 p.m. It was short and to the point, reciting the rapidly paced happenings of the day: the kidnapping of the generals, the traitorous claims of the 'counter-revolutionary' 30 September Movement, the fact that the President was safe and sound, the unity of the Army, Navy and Police behind Suharto, his assumption of temporary command, and his determination, with the support of the people, to crush the Movement.[25]

Sukarno, already informed of Suharto's intentions by Bambang Wijanarko, left for his Bogor Palace in the late evening, perhaps having been warned by Suharto not to remove to Central Java. Around midnight, or perhaps a little earlier, and satisfied that Sukarno had left Halim – 'he recognized the grave consequences of anything happening to the President which might be considered his responsibility'[26] – Suharto ordered Sarwo Edhie's forces, a combination of RPKAD and Siliwangi paracommandos, to attack the Halim air base. Proceeding with caution out of fear that an air attack might be launched against the city from Halim, and with only minor initial losses and inflicting little damage themselves, by about 6 a.m. on 2 October Sarwo's troops had negotiated the seizure of the now virtually abandoned base of the coup group. Around 10 p.m. on 1 October, Suharto had issued a statement vigorously denouncing the Movement and asserting that the senior officers included in the Revolutionary Council had been named without their prior knowledge. He also took steps to countermand the orders of the rebel group then ensconced in Semarang, and even found time to sign orders for the dishonourable discharge of Untung and Suparjo. Just before midnight, he temporarily moved Kostrad headquarters to Senayan, 'because there was information that the Air Force would launch an air raid' on the headquarters.[27] Now that he was more or less in control of the situation within the capital, army units began sweeping the city in search of communist members, and all leftist newspapers were banned from publication.

The 30 September Movement had also made a pre-emptive strike in Central Java. Around 1 p.m. on 1 October, a radio announcement had declared that the head of intelligence of the Diponegoro Division, Col. Suherman, had been placed in charge of the Movement in Central Java and that the Division's panglima, Brig.-Gen. Suryosumpeno, had been replaced by Lt. Col. Usman Sastrodibroto. Suryosumpeno, having earlier left for Salatiga, which he found in the control of the Movement, returned to Semarang to discover the conspirators in charge there as well. He then took refuge in Magelang, which remained free of the conspiracy, and used it as a base to launch a counter-attack against the rebel headquarters in Semarang; he achieved his aim without violence on the morning of 2 October. In Yogya, the Movement captured Col. Katamso, commander of the 72nd military region (Korem) and his chief of staff, Lt. Col. Sugiyono, and killed them in the early hours of 2 October; Sugiyono had been Suharto's aide at the time of the 1 March 1949 attack on Yogya, had earlier served under him around Yogya in Brigade X and after the revolution in Brigade O. In other parts of Central Java, a number of local commanders were replaced by those sympathetic to the Movement; indeed, 'of the seven infantry battalions in Central Java on October 1, five were under rebel command by the evening'.[28] But the Central Java movement, having reached its peak by the evening of 1 October, just as the Jakarta plot was collapsing, dissolved almost as quickly as its counterpart in Jakarta and was effectively dead by 3 October, even though, once the deposed Suryosumpeno had re-asserted control on 2 October, tension remained high and loyalties uncertain because of the 'delicate balance of allegiances within his own command'.[29] Outside Jakarta and Central Java, however, there were virtually no disturbances of a similar kind.

TENSE POLITICS

On 2 October, Suharto was advised around 11 a.m. by radio of the President's wish to see him at a meeting of service commanders; presumably Sukarno's well-developed instincts for survival made him conscious of the need to re-assert his authority – especially over the Army – rather than remain passive in the face of the unfolding events. Suharto delayed, taken up with Umar and awaiting a report from Sarwo Edhie on his operations; according to McDonald, 'in the first of a series of studied gestures, Suharto sent word he was too busy to come immediately'.[30] Finally, he drove to Bogor by jeep, with an armoured escort, arriving about 2 p.m. There ensued a long and tense discussion with Sukarno, attended by Leimena, Chaerul Saleh, Pranoto, Mursyid, Leo Wattimena, Omar Dhani, and other service commanders. Sukarno sought to play down the significance of the happenings of the previous day; 'things like this are normal in revolutions', Suharto later reported him as saying. Suharto, by his own account, sought to press the involvement of the Air Force in the events of the previous day, contradicting Sukarno's attempt to absolve it from blame.[31] Suharto, struggling to keep his composure with the tension of the moment, resisted Sukarno's insistence on placing army matters in the hands of Pranoto, offering to surrender the title of provisional leader of the Army which he had assumed on the morning of 1 October and to take no further responsibility for the maintenance of security.

Suharto's persistence was rewarded with the undertaking by Sukarno, alarmed and probably frightened at what such a step might signal to the Army which Suharto had rallied so rapidly, that Suharto would retain responsibility for security and order, even though Pranoto remained as day-to-day caretaker, with the leadership of the Army remaining formally in Sukarno's hands. Suharto also insisted that the President publicly proclaim his formal responsibilities through a radio broadcast, made at about 1.30 the following morning. He himself made a subsequent broadcast on 3 October which reiterated the substance of Sukarno's message, acknowledging that the army leadership was in the hands of the President who had enjoined him to restore security. Suharto's reluctant acceptance of this state of affairs is an indication, perhaps, of his unwillingness to challenge his president further at this time, and of his uncertainty about what the next steps in the drama might be. Upon his return, he was met by Sarwo Edhie, who had followed him to Bogor and himself met with Sukarno. Sarwo reported that Sukarno had issued an order to stop the shooting, an order addressed to Suparjo.

The meeting at Bogor inaugurated a long, tense and complex battle between the President, determined to minimise the significance of the events of 1 October, and the Army, effectively under the control of Suharto, who saw those events as a crucial juncture which had transformed the nation's political terrain. Despite its air of apparent compromise, the meeting was in fact a decisive victory for Suharto. He could no longer resist the appointment of Pranoto as he had the previous day by reference to the uncertainty surrounding Sukarno's freedom of action at Halim. But his attitude was firm and combative; he knew that he now enjoyed a position of supremacy within the Army and that Sukarno could not discount him without serious political consequences; the concession he forced from Sukarno was in fact an official endorsement of his pre-eminence and, equally, a sign that a simple return to the old order of things would not be tolerated by the Army. Sukarno's capacity to exploit his charisma and prestige had been seriously damaged; he was no longer inviolate from attacks from the Army. The process of reshaping the prevailing pattern of Indonesian politics had begun.

THE MURDERED GENERALS

Late in the afternoon of 3 October, Suharto's men learned from Sukitman, a policeman captured by the plotters outside Panjaitan's house who had subsequently escaped, of the fate of the generals, their dead bodies dumped down a camouflaged 10-metre-deep dry well at Lubang Buaya ('Crocodile Hole'), on the outskirts of the Halim air base. This news was immediately reported to Suharto, who instructed that the well and its surrounds be placed under tight guard. The recovery of the remains was begun next morning; Suharto arrived at 9 a.m. to supervise proceedings. He lost no opportunity to exploit the gruesome proceedings to the full. According to Crouch, 'the exhumation of the corpses … was delayed until a full battery of journalists, photographers, and television cameramen had been assembled'.[32] When the last body, that of Panjaitan, had been brought to the surface shortly after 2 p.m., Suharto himself delivered a blunt speech about the involvement of the Air Force and the PKI. He even went so far as to cast aspersions on Sukarno's attempt, in a speech broadcast at 1 a.m. that morning, to dissociate the Air Force from involvement in the 30 September Movement. His message was unmistakably defiant: he would do what was necessary to cleanse the body politic of those who had attacked it, even in the face of the opposition of the President.

Photographs taken at the well site show a grim-faced Suharto, clad in camouflage fatigues and wearing sunglasses (and, at one stage, a face mask to alleviate the stench of the decomposing bodies), hands on hips and looking into the middle distance. The grim proceedings were a traumatic episode which, Suharto claims, brought tears to his eyes, as the bodies of the six generals, as well as that of Pierre Tendean (the first to emerge), were brought to the surface. According to his account, the bodies of Suprapto and Parman were tied together, as were those of Yani, Haryono and Sutoyo, and 'all the bodies were in a damaged condition as a result of torture'. 'I will never forget this, truly I will never forget this', Suharto went on. 'Who', he later noted, 'could forget something as barbaric as this?' The discovery of the bodies seems to have spurred a cold decisiveness in him, a desire to ensure that the perpetrators were punished, no matter what the political and social cost. Already he held profound doubts about Sukarno's version of the affair; what he had now found, and the intelligence reports coming in about the participation in the affair by PKI groups and the Air Force, steeled him for more decisive action. 'Since witnessing with my own eyes what had been discovered at Lubang Buaya, my primary duty was to crush the PKI, to smash their resistance everywhere, in the capital, in the regions, and in their mountain hide-outs'. He did not, however, wish to involve the Army directly in such conflict, except in a limited way. 'I preferred to lend aid to the people … to cleanse the respective regions of these evil seeds.'[33]

The bodies were removed to the army central hospital and then laid in state at army headquarters, where Suharto kept vigil through the night; 'his normally placid face was heavy with anger', according to one correspondent.[34] He cancelled the great celebrations planned for the next day, 5 October. Instead, he organised a funeral, a public ceremony of grief for the victims of the 30 September Movement. At army headquarters, Nasution's funeral address, solemn, sad and heartfelt, spoke of duty and continuing struggle, and of justice, truth and human frailty. The murdered generals' coffins, each mounted atop an armoured car, were escorted in military procession through the streets on a winding 20-kilometre-long journey to the Kalibata Heroes' Cemetery in south Jakarta. Thousands lined the streets along the way on a cloudy, drizzling day. Suharto wore the same style of clothing that he had worn since the morning of 1 October: camouflage fatigues and dark glasses. Sukarno himself did not attend the funeral because, he later alleged, of concerns for his security at such an event.[35] But his absence was clearly calculated to demonstrate his view that the happenings of 1 October were not especially significant, just as it served to anger senior army leaders.

Suharto's performance during these dramatic days was nothing short of startling. His capacity to move coolly and in carefully measured ways was outdone only by his extraordinary ability to modulate his action with a keen sensitivity to the context in which the drama was being played out. There are numerous examples of his tactical vision at this time. His early decision to assume temporary command of the Army, his capacity in gaining the confidence of key army and other service commanders on the morning of the coup, his measured refusal to accede to Sukarno's naming of Pranoto as caretaker commander, and his subsequent refusal to withdraw from the scene gracefully, his theatrical handling of the recovery of the generals' bodies and the staged funerals the following day are perhaps the most obvious examples. He was no doubt helped in all this by the unquestioning support of his staff – especially the wily Ali Murtopo, who advised on strategy and tactics, and Sujono, who, according to Sumitro, 'was of great service to Pak Harto due to his skill in mystic and spiritual matters'.[36]

SUHARTO AND THE COUP

The foregoing account has been written over the shoulder, as it were, of Suharto, and with certain assumptions about his role in the affair. Since the events of 1 October 1965 were so fundamental for the future course of Indonesian history, they have generated an enormous literature seeking to explain them. From amongst those attempts, some of them ranging from the implausible to the incredible,[37] to understand the coup, three major interpretations have emerged.

The first, the version cultivated by the New Order regime, was that the coup attempt was the work of the Indonesian Communist Party, which recruited dissident members of the Army and the Air Force – after a long period of 'managing' them – to assist it in its efforts to destroy its influential opponents amongst the General Staff and seize power.[38] The second was that the attempt was orchestrated by dissident members of the Armed Forces, with PKI members only peripherally and incidentally involved; this view has been most famously presented in the so-called 'Cornell Paper', which argued that 'the October 1st coup was essentially an internal Army affair, stemming from a small clique in the Diponegoro Division, which attempted to use both Sukarno and the PKI leadership for its own ends, and succeeded merely in damaging irremediably the moral and political authority of the one, and causing the physical destruction of the other'.[39] The third saw the 'coup attempt' as a coordinated and more-or-less shared effort by members of the PKI in cooperation with dissident junior army men, each acting from different motives, to destroy, or at least cripple, the corrupt General Staff.[40]

It seems unlikely that the whole truth about the events of 1 October will ever be known; the interests to be protected are too great, the lies told too many, the anger too deep. The closed politics of the New Order period and, even more, the desire of the New Order regime to use the events of that day as a foundation stone for its own political purposes have shaped the evidence since presented in unhelpful ways. At the same time, the New Order's opponents, frustrated at their impotence, have sometimes resorted to exaggerated speculations in the search for an audience, any audience. Nonetheless, it is reasonable to suggest that the most plausible scenario is that the coup attempt was a coordinated effort by some PKI leaders and junior officers closely connected with the Diponegoro Division and the Air Force to seize those generals whom they strongly suspected were about to launch a pre-emptive move against the President, the PKI, or both. The purpose seems to have been limited in scale and defensive in intent: to seize the generals, bring them to the President, secure the President's endorsement of the Movement's action against the Council of Generals, and bring the generals down by sacking or downgrading them. According to Latief, there was no plan to kill the generals, and he and Suparjo were 'shocked' to learn they had been done to death.[41] The later endorsement of the Movement by the PKI (if such it was) and the Air Force, and the military actions in Central Java within the Diponegoro Division, best sit with this scenario. Had the attempt been successful, the PKI would have been seen as a champion in the fight against counter-revolutionary elements, the Air Force's role strengthened, and the newly installed leaders endorsed and rewarded for their efforts in purging themselves of officers who were acting in disloyal and scandalous ways.

As we know, things began to go awry almost from the start. While it seems certain that the generals were to have been captured alive, three of them were shot down or bayoneted in their homes by jittery troops, probably unclear as to the precise rules of engagement for their planned activity and doubtful of their authority should it be questioned by such senior officers. The murders immediately brought the incident to a new and more dangerous plane. While it was conceivable that the Army might have caved in, at least in the short term, in the face of the humiliating dismissal of its senior leaders, it was quite another matter that those officers had been put to death, something the Army could never have been expected to stomach. Second, the kidnappers, in an extraordinary display of carelessness, first allowed Nasution to escape, made no significant effort to track him down, and then made off with his adjutant in the belief that he was Nasution. Even then, had Sukarno endorsed the action in mid-morning after arriving at Halim and being appraised of the situation, the plotters may well have held the day.

But Sukarno's finely tuned political instincts must have shrieked at him that, with the death of three generals and the escape of Nasution, the political conflict had reached a new, uncharted and much more dangerous phase. Doubtless racing to piece together the confused patterns of events and their potential significance once he had arrived at the airbase, he realised that under the circumstances facing him he could not support the coup attempt and would have to try to patch matters by temporising and negotiation. Once he gave the fateful order to Suparjo to cease spilling blood, the fate of the Movement was sealed. Without Sukarno's endorsement, the coup could never succeed. The conspirators' lack of a fall-back position when things began to go horribly wrong is just another indication of how hastily prepared and badly disorganised was their attempt to change the course of the nation's politics.

There are other theories as well. One puts Sukarno in the role of key actor, encouraging and controlling the work of others to rid himself of the troublesome generals. Roeder, probably echoing a notion put about by Suharto himself, maintained that

> only after years, the interrogation of officers involved in the putsch revealed orders of Sukarno to the Commander of his Tjakrabirawa Guard on September 28, 1965 to arrest the obstinate leaders of the Army. It's still unclear whether these orders were not fulfilled because of the Tjakrabirawa Commander's hesitation or because of the murder of the Army leaders during the night of September 30/October 1, 1965.[42]

According to another version of this account, Sukarno conspired with the PKI to stage a coup to rid them both of the 'obstructionist generals';[43] in another version, he is thought to have encouraged the Untung group, without significant involvement on the side of the PKI.

A fundamentally different line of interpretation is of more immediate interest for our story. Simply put, it suggests that Suharto himself was deeply involved in the plot – 'the one who conceived the whole thing as a provocation which would, at one stroke, eliminate his rivals in the Army, annihilate the Communist Party and remove President Sukarno from power'[44] – or at least had foreknowledge of its occurrence, did nothing about it, and therefore was able to take advantage of the removal of the senior General Staff and the political chaos that accompanied and succeeded it.[45]

This latter view – which had smouldered in the background, occasionally fanned by forced expatriates and foreign critics of the Suharto regime, for almost three decades before springing back to reinvigorated life following Suharto's resignation on 21 May 1998 – was a consequence of some central unsolved enigmas relating to the events of the coup. They included the fact that Suharto was not targeted by the conspirators, that his Kostrad headquarters was ignored by the troops who took over facilities in Jakarta's central square in the early morning of 1 October, that Suharto himself was well known and previously connected to both Untung and Latief, and that he was able to rally his forces so rapidly and effectively that day. Most intriguing of all was the fact that, on the previous evening, Latief had gone to the hospital where Suharto was visiting his son.

These puzzles, mostly ignored during the period of Suharto's ascendancy, gained renewed pertinence with the opening of Cipanang prison shortly after his fall in May 1998. Ex-colonel Latief was interviewed during an extraordinary 'open day' at the prison and repeated claims, made earlier at his 1978 trial, that he had told Suharto that an attack upon a senior group of generals was imminent, and that Suharto had done nothing to prevent it. Indeed, Latief claimed that he had visited Suharto at his house on Jl. Haji Agus Salim on 28 September and asked him about the Council of Generals. Suharto had brushed off the question, saying he would look into it later. Latief repeated these claims thereafter in numerous interviews both before and after his release in March 1999.[46] Indeed, his claims are still the subject of sensationalist reporting.

Suharto's response was predictable: 'That is nonsense, it is absolutely not true'. He vigorously denied having spoken to Latief at the hospital, although he acknowledged the visit to his home on 28 September, and having seen him in the distance at the hospital on the evening of 30 September.[47] Moreover, he added, 'there are those who wish to exploit the disturbances of the era of reformasi at this time by distorting the history of G-30-S/PKI. They deliberately try to blur the facts as though they were not guilty. Whereas according to clear and firm testimony, they have carried out a barbaric revolt, butchering the nation's best sons in the national tragedy of G-30-S/PKI'.[48]

Suharto's absence from the list of generals certainly requires explanation. Those who allege that he was little known at the time ignore the fact that he was the senior army officer in active service, the standing deputy to Yani, and the founding commander of the Army's Strategic Reserve. Nonetheless, it seems clear that the conspirators were targeting those General Staff officers close to Yani, thought to be both fundamentally opposed to the PKI's push for enhanced power and increasingly inimical towards Sukarno, and involved in the day-to-day political battles and intrigue of Guided Democracy. Suharto himself, while he enjoyed good relations with some of the targeted officers (he claimed, as we have seen, Sutoyo as a special friend, having studied with him at SSKAD), was certainly not one of their number and inhabited a very different social and psychological world. Anderson and McVey themselves noted that Suharto, 'with little formal education, psychologically close to the "Diponegoro world," largely speaking and thinking in Javanese, disciplined and upright ... managed to disassociate himself from the "renegade" Diponegoro men whom Djakarta had absorbed. It seems to have been this which preserved him from becoming a target of the conspirators of the September 30 movement'.[49] Suharto's dislike of publicity, and his taciturn and ungregarious nature, meant that he had not stamped himself as belonging to any particular camp within the fierce factionalisms of the Army and therefore did not present himself as a target; indeed, he had made an art of making his political views, such as they were, indistinctive. The fact that he was well acquainted with some of the major conspirators may also have led them to believe that he presented no serious threat to their designs, even perhaps supportive of what they had in mind.

Latief himself had served with Suharto during the latter days of the revolution. Background details about him, however, are vague and contradictory. In a 1998 interview, he claimed to have known Suharto from the beginning of 1948 and to have served as a company commander in Suharto's Brigade X from 1948.[50] According to another source, Latief was a former Pesindo member taken into Suharto's brigade after the fall of Yogya to the Dutch in late 1948.[51] At his trial in 1978, Latief strongly rebutted accusations that he had been involved in the 1948 Madiun affair, and claimed to have been commander of Medan Brigade IV around Wonosobo in late 1947. During the army rationalisation program of 1948, he was demoted from major to captain and became a company commander. His troops were transferred to the Yogya City Military Command around the time of the Dutch attack. Thereafter, he took part in the guerrilla war, including participation in the attack of 1 March 1949 on Yogya, reporting to Suharto on his actions. It is not clear from his trial documents whether the company Latief commanded at this time was part of Brigade X, or simply subordinate to it in the organisationally ragged situation of the guerrilla war, although that position seems to have been formalised afterwards with the incorporation of his company into

Sujono's battalion. Latief claimed at his trial that he was an 'anak buah [close subordinate] [of Suharto] … directly under his leadership'. He claimed to have enjoyed Suharto's confidence in the guerrilla war, that Suharto sought to recruit him as a para commander, and that Suharto proposed him a few months before the coup attempt to command a task force in East Kalimantan, an idea rejected by his commander, Umar. Suharto and his wife, he claimed, came to Latief's house to celebrate the circumcision of Latief's son.[52]

Untung, as well, was a Diponegoro man who had served under Suharto's direct command in the mid-1950s and been decorated for his bravery during the Mandala campaign, probably at Suharto's behest. So high, indeed, was Suharto's esteem for Untung that he had gone out of his way to attend Untung's wedding in 1964 in Kebumen in Central Java. According to documents attached to Latief's trial statement, Suharto was very unhappy (*marah-marah*) with Untung's transfer to the Cakrabirawa, since he apparently wanted to retain him amongst his Kostrad forces.[53] Brig.-Gen. Suparjo, as we have seen, was in charge of a Kolaga battle command in West Kalimantan under Suharto's overall command; in mid-August 1965, just a couple of weeks before the coup attempt, Suparjo had accompanied Suharto, acting in his Kolaga capacity, on a helicopter tour of the border regions of North Kalimantan. There is, however, no evidence that the two were personally close. The mysterious Syam, the leader of the PKI's 'Special Bureau', had been known to Suharto from 1945 when both were involved in the Pathuk group in Yogyakarta, although Suharto's role in this group was distant and fleeting, to say the least.

Given Suharto's record – he had made his mark as a practising soldier rather than as an ambitious political operator, and had no public history of political opposition to Sukarno – the conspirators could have been forgiven for thinking that he was unlikely to move rapidly and violently against them once they had secured the President's support, notwithstanding the demise of the captured generals. Indeed, given the nature of the conspiracy, it would have made little sense to include Suharto on the list of those to be kidnapped.

It might be thought that a key tactic of the conspirators would have been to neutralise potential armed opposition to their attack on the generals. As one scholar commented, 'the Kostrad-building … was strangely enough not attacked at all by the units of the 30 September Movement'.[54] Another thought that the failure to 'do away with' Suharto and Umar was 'one of the great mysteries of the affair'.[55] A third wondered why 'no arrangements were attempted or even – so far as has been revealed – considered to block action by the RPKAD, or to interfere with the headquarters of Kostrad, which controlled it'.[56] In addition, it was well known that Kostrad possessed a national military radio communications system. However, this problem assumes that the conspirators expected that there might be significant armed opposition to their move from either or both of the two generals in a position to provide it: Suharto himself or Umar, commander of the Jakarta garrison, the only other senior officer in command of troops. More likely, the conspirators did not anticipate that such an eventuality would arise.

What they had planned was a lightning strike against a group of generals they had reason to believe was plotting a real coup. Their strike was pre-emptive, and its purposes limited. They sought to kidnap Nasution, Yani and the five staff generals, in the expectation that Sukarno would quickly throw his support behind the conspiracy. Had the plan gone smoothly, it is likely that it would have been safely completed by mid-morning on 1 October, with the kidnapped generals disgraced and removed from their positions, and the goals both of the army conspirators and the PKI leaders achieved. The option of exercising military power to oppose the Movement would simply not have arisen. The very disposition of the troops in the central square seems to endorse this view; they seized key communications facilities and had a presence at the palace. The first aim was to control communications with the general populace, the second to control the movements of Sukarno. But there was no effort to assert any kind of military control over potential opposition, presumably because it was thought to be dangerous and in any case unnecessary.

What, then, of the visit by Latief to the hospital while Suharto was there? Notwithstanding some suggestions to the contrary (notably Wertheim's curious assertion that 'Colonel Latief had … been one of [Suharto's] closest collaborators')[57] and the fact that the two had long known each other, there is no strong evidence that Latief and Suharto were very close. Accordingly, it seems unlikely that Latief's visit was purely of a social kind, to lend support to the Suharto family at a time of trial. His visit, then, must have been connected with the impending action of the 30 September Movement. It seems that there are two possibilities which might explain the visit. The first is that Latief was simply checking that Suharto was indeed preoccupied with his son's condition, and that he was unlikely to be in a position to take rapid action against the conspirators. It appears that Latief also visited Nasution's house that evening in order to establish the pattern of his early morning movements. The second is that he sought out Suharto to inform him that the planned action against the generals was about to take place. Latief himself explained that he had been told by Untung and Suparjo, who had visited him on 30 September, to inform Suharto of the intended action in order to seek his cooperation; they themselves were unable to relay the message because they had 'other work' to do. Latief continued:

> That night, I came to the Gatot Subroto Hospital, because Pak Harto was in fact at that time watching over Tommy, who had been splashed with soup. As it turned out, there were a lot of visitors there. Then I greeted Ibu Tien and Pak Harto, but there was not yet an opportunity to talk because there were so many visitors. Again and again I sought an opportunity to talk. When that opportunity presented itself, I said, 'As well as conveying my concerns on your son's misfortune, I also want to tell you that tomorrow morning seven generals will be brought before the President' … He just nodded his head, and asked who the leader was. I answered 'Lt. Col. Untung'. Immediately I said this, another visitor arrived. I waited for a reaction from [Suharto], to see if he would make a decision or not. But Pak Harto just kept silent, until I took my leave and went home.[58]

If what Latief reported is true – that he passed on information about the impending action to Suharto, something which, as we have seen, Suharto strongly denied – we need to explain why he should want to share this knowledge with Suharto. It seems strange that a leading figure in a serious conspiracy should want to inform a senior general that his colleagues were about to be targeted, especially an experienced field officer in control of highly trained and battle-ready troops. If this is in fact what Latief did, it could only have been because he trusted that Suharto would not act – indeed, that he was expecting that his information would cause Suharto not to react precipitately when he heard news of the action the following morning. Latief himself explained that he reported the news to Suharto because 'I thought he was very loyal to Bung Karno. As it turns out, I was wrong'. His coming to the hospital was agreed upon earlier that evening in a meeting with Suparjo and Untung and was aimed at seeking Suharto's assistance. But, as Latief remarked, 'he whom we hoped would become a loyal assistant of [Sukarno] became instead his enemy [*menjadi berobah memusuhnya*]'.[59]

If Latief's account is essentially accurate, Suharto's failure to act in the face of such a threat to the senior leadership of the Army requires explanation. A number of possible avenues are available. The first is that Suharto did not take Latief's warning seriously and simply discounted it. This explanation has some cogency – especially in the crisis-ridden atmosphere of the time when talk of coups was always in the air, and in which at least some generals were aware of rumours of a pre-emptive strike against the army leadership – but seems ultimately unsatisfactory. There is no evidence that Suharto was accustomed to receiving advice of this kind, and he knew that both Untung and Latief, in charge of local troops, had the ready means to carry out what they threatened; his caution probably would not have allowed him simply to ignore the advice presented to him.

Second, it is also possible that Latief's advice was so vaguely worded, with that characteristic Indonesian preference for the passive voice, that Suharto misunderstood its real thrust. He may have thought that the proposed action was not unusual and not worthy of further action on his part. Put another way, he may have understood that Latief intended that the generals would simply be summoned to the palace (a common occurrence for senior figures at that time, and often at unusual times) for a discussion, a dressing-down or a diatribe from the President; under such circumstances, it would not be unusual for Untung, as a Cakrabirawa man, to present presidential summonses to the generals in question. According to this explanation, Suharto, on the basis of Latief's information, was not alerted to the gravity and scale of the proposed operation, much less to the chance that it might plunge out of control.

A third explanation might be that Suharto recognised the gravity of the situation but chose to do nothing. This explanation has some force; Suharto was not close to Nasution, somewhat distant from Yani – there was, indeed, some animosity and probably some competition between the two – and certainly not a member of Yani's inner circle. It is conceivable that Suharto saw an opportunity, even a vague one, for rapid personal advancement and determined – just as he had done at Wiyoro during the 3 July 1946 affair – to wait to see how the contending forces played themselves out before committing himself. It is possible that his thinking went further than this; he might have calculated that he would give the Untung group the chance to carry out its plan before bringing to bear his own forces to crush the 30 September Movement, destroy the communists, take Sukarno with them, and himself ride to power. Latief himself, at his 1978 trial, took pains to show that Suharto's foreknowledge of the coup attempt meant in effect that he was involved (*terlibat*).[60]

Fourth, a darker embellishment of the previous explanation, is that Suharto was himself deeply involved in the coup attempt. In this context, much has been made of the fact that Latief, Untung and Suparjo were well known to him, as was Syam. Such an interpretation, however, must remain sheer speculation. There is no direct evidence to support it, and much circumstantial evidence which flies in the face of it. As we have seen, while Suharto seems to have enjoyed cordial, perhaps even friendly, relations with Latief and Untung, there is no evidence that he was especially close to them, much less Suparjo, nor that he had any specific relationship with Syam. His alleged closeness with Untung and Latief has been much exaggerated. Neither is there any reason to think that he shared the vaguely leftish political views of the army conspirators and even less their keenness to neutralise the senior staff, even if his prudishness had something in common with their puritanical ideas regarding appropriate lifestyles. It is, of course, possible that Syam, the head of the PKI's Special Bureau, the task of which was to infiltrate the military and 'manage' key military sympathisers, was a double agent (that is, an agent of the Army when apparently acting in the interests of the PKI), but no clear evidence has emerged to strengthen that notion.

There is the possibility that Latief simply concocted his story of a conversation with Suharto at the hospital. Suharto, certainly, has gone out of his way to make clear that he only saw Latief at the hospital and has never acknowledged a conversation having taken place.[61] In this account, Latief's allegation that Suharto knew of the conspiracy was a later construction arising out of resentment at Suharto's unexpectedly resolute opposition to and stunning victory over the conspiracy. This conclusion, itself, however, has its difficulties, chief amongst them Suharto's apparent discomfort and evasiveness about Latief's visit to the hospital. As May noted, 'there seems to have been an attempt to conceal Suharto's meeting with Latief. Even the fact that he had been to the hospital did not emerge for a considerable time'.[62] Moreover, Suharto has offered different explanations of Latief's presence at the hospital. In his interview with Brackman, he opined that Latief had come to check on him; two years later, in an interview with the German magazine *Der Spiegel*, he alleged that Latief had come to the hospital to kill him. In his autobiography, he devotes a single line to Latief's presence, acknowledging only that he saw him nearby at the hospital, and makes no further comment.[63] Latief's own subsequent treatment has raised further suspicions about Suharto's involvement. Although amongst the first plotters apprehended, Latief was not permitted to appear as a witness at the Mahmillub trials until Pono's trial in January 1972 – his earlier testimony had been presented only in writing – and he was in fact not brought to trial until 1978. Even then, he was not permitted – on the basis of their alleged irrelevance to the case at hand – to call certain witnesses, notably Suharto himself, who could put forward evidence concerning Suharto's own advance knowledge of the conspirators' plans.

Suharto's clear discomfort with Latief's visit leads one to suspect that there was in fact a conversation between the two on the evening of 30 September 1965. However, the weight of evidence seems to suggest that Suharto discounted or, rather more likely, misunderstood the message conveyed to him. In other words, the most likely explanation is that he understood that a number of generals would be summoned to the President for some kind of shaming procedure, which might perhaps involve some of them in career difficulties, but nothing more than that, and certainly nothing that would fundamentally upset the prevailing political arrangements and plunge the state and nation into crisis. Suharto may have been led to reflect upon how such an action might improve his own career prospects, but he would not have imagined that the matter needed further attention.

The alternative scenario – that Suharto knew that the generals were to be the subject of violent and life-threatening attack, or even that the greater part of the General Staff, together with Nasution, would be dismissed at a single blow, and that he did nothing to avoid such actions in the pursuit of his personal advantage – seems to suggest a recklessness acutely at odds with the well-established pattern of his thoughtful caution. It seems unlikely in the extreme that he would have done nothing to prevent the political, not to mention physical, carnage to the Army that might result from a move of this sort had he realised the scale and danger of what the plotters proposed. Nothing in his prior record as army officer – a career of thirty years of service which had brought him much by way of status and rewards – suggests that he would have stood idly by while his fellow-officers, and the reputation and effective political influence of the Army he loved, were brought down. That someone of Suharto's typically cautious outlook would consider taking such a risk – especially given that he would have realised how hastily and sloppily planned and liable for failure the conspiracy was – for such an uncertain outcome seems to beggar credibility.

The view that would implicate Suharto in the affair also faces another major difficulty: his success in rallying the Army on the morning of 1 October and keeping it under his control thereafter. On the face of it, it seems improbable that a commander like Sarwo Edhie, a very close associate of Yani, would have thrown in his lot with Suharto had he suspected Suharto, then or thereafter, of being involved in the plot. It is, of course, equally improbable that Nasution, who lost his daughter (and his adjutant) in the attack on his home, would have remained mute had he believed that Suharto either had prior knowledge about or was involved in the coup attempt.

THE ROAD AHEAD

The events of 1 October 1965 were the most crucial in Suharto's life. The manner in which he reacted to them showed a presence of mind and an extraordinary tactical capacity which had hitherto not been revealed on so public a scale, and which provided the means for his later political ascendancy. In the absence of the calamitous events set in motion by the crude efforts of the 30 September Movement, Suharto might have served out his days in efficiently executed but mundane obscurity. Now, however, the limits of what seemed possible had been breached, and the actors in what was clearly a dangerously escalating political drama began to gird themselves to contest the radically different future that lay ahead. In just a few days, the landscape of the nation's politics had been utterly transformed. Sukarno's charismatic dominance of the scene had been seriously, perhaps fatally, wounded. The PKI had been incriminated in the planning and conduct of the 30 September Movement. The Army had been seriously weakened in its leadership and the thin fabric of its unity torn apart.

Only one key person – Suharto – emerged from the tumult with his reputation enhanced. His visibility magnified by his victories over the preceding days, Suharto could no longer remain the obscure and reclusive figure of the past. He was now at the fulcrum of politics, but no one in the political public knew much of him, much less how he might cope with his newly won legitimacy and the rich range of opportunities which now presented themselves.

6 The move to power, 1965–1968

THE POWERFUL LENS of hindsight tends to focus on Suharto as a man of power and destiny, moving irresistibly towards the apex of power. The real story is both more complex and more fascinating. At the end of the first week of October 1965, Suharto stood on very dangerous ground. He had, on his own initiative and without the express support of his president, interrupted and quickly defeated an armed intervention designed to change the balance of forces within the country. In the course of his actions, he had expressly disobeyed his commander-in-chief. He had no clear sense of the support he enjoyed for anything beyond his defensive actions, and no firm strategy on how to proceed, nor towards what goal. What was clear to him was that, notwithstanding the failure of the 30 September Movement, its shocking introduction of force into the brittle Indonesian power equation had brought a fundamental change to the political terrain. It was, however, quite another and more difficult problem to explore and exploit the newly exposed ground.

Suharto's own cautious instincts, and his visceral grasp of the style of Jakarta politics, impelled him to proceed cautiously, carefully and sensitively, and with 'surprising delicacy', as one enthusiastic foreign supporter put it.[1] Mackie has described the dramatic and tense processes of the next two-and-a-half years, whereby Sukarno was diminished and Suharto elevated, as 'strangely tentative'.[2] But, given Suharto's personal unpreparedness for what had taken place, his relative obscurity (he was little known amongst the mass of Indonesians, and almost a cipher to the Americans – a matter of considerable concern to them), the chaotic and uncertain disposition of power in Jakarta after the events of early October, and the unpredictability of Sukarno's response, he had little choice but to move in carefully considered, short-term phases. He had no thought of his ultimate fate (though perhaps – as 'a leader who was created by the situation rather than one who had prepared himself for the job'[3] – he mused as he was always wont to do about the role of destiny in his life), only that the circumstances of the coup attempt had left him at the top of the military tree and had also presented him with an unlooked-for chance – and responsibility – to place a significant stamp on the course of events.

His temperament and training made him eschew the grand gesture which raises hopes but condemns results. He decided, characteristically, to adopt the tactic of the cautious military man, testing levels of support, probing for weaknesses, picking his targets only when and where he could be assured of overcoming them, never overextending himself by taking on more than one central opponent at a time, taking ground as it came to him. There was no grand vision or utopian scheming; politics and political success were a process of pragmatic manoeuvring. Those about him must have been surprised by what they found: the man reputed to be a dull but effective field commander began to manifest strengths of political strategy of which there had previously been no sign. Indeed, Suharto 'proved to be a far more wily and effective political manipulator than most commentators during the heady October days of 1965 had been willing to give him credit for'.[4]

SUKARNO AND SUHARTO

It is fascinating to speculate about Suharto's mind-set in those first days after 1 October. According to Crouch, he 'personally, had scant respect for the president', an assertion which needs more careful analysis.[5] While he held no brief for the personality and behaviour of Sukarno, he was immensely respectful of the office he held and, at the same time, acutely aware of just how popular Sukarno was amongst many members of the Armed Forces. Nonetheless, he knew that the events of 1 October had fundamentally reshaped the forces at play and provided him with a new-found wellspring of legitimacy in his relations with the President. For the first time, the shackles of restraint imposed by the previous order and Sukarno's magnetic personal authority were loosened.

Suharto was seriously piqued by Sukarno's continuing refusal to recognise the enormity of what had happened. On 6 October, Sukarno had called a cabinet meeting at his Bogor Palace, to which Suharto was invited to present a report on the situation following the failure of the 30 September Movement. Amongst those present were the communist cabinet members Lukman and Nyoto, 'who acted as if nothing had happened'.[6] Moreover, on Suharto's account, the mood was 'far from melancholy or sad ... I felt uneasy in an atmosphere of hearty laughter. I was annoyed to see the PKI people there, since I had become convinced that they were certainly connected with the kidnapping and murder of my friends'. Nyoto, for his part, denied any communist complicity in the events of 1 October, although, according to Suharto, Sukarno chided Nyoto and the PKI for having 'incited that accursed affair'.[7] The meeting was the frankest manifestation yet of Sukarno's blustering determination to minimise the political and moral impact of the coup attempt, to retake the initiative, and to carry on as before. On the same day came news of the death of Nasution's daughter in hospital as a result of the gunshot wound she had suffered on that fateful morning.

The clearest formal sign of Suharto's new-found ascendancy was Sukarno's capitulation on the question of Pranoto. Notwithstanding the President's feeble effort to retain Pranoto as the 'day-to-day' army commander, Suharto made it clear that with the army high command dismembered by the 30 September Movement he, and no one else, effectively commanded the support of the Army – notwithstanding the influence Nasution still enjoyed. Accordingly, Sukarno was forced to bow to the inevitable and appoint Suharto as 'definitive' army commander on 14 October. Neither Nasution nor Suharto had been close to Sukarno, and both, as we have seen, had been critical of Yani's inclusionist style of politics which, they thought, had suffered the PKI and its rapid upward political momentum rather too much. On 16 October, at the formal Merdeka Palace ceremony inducting Suharto as army commander and chief of staff of Koti (Supreme Operations Command) and raising him in rank to lieutenant general, Sukarno's antagonism towards Suharto was clear and 'the atmosphere ... was icy'.[8] Sukarno continued his tack of minimising the significance of 1 October; it was 'something ordinary and normal in a revolution' and 'a ripple in the ocean of revolution'.[9] At the same time he scorned those who thought that his power was on the ebb. Suharto's elevation, however, was the subject of some public enthusiasm, especially amongst Muslim groups.

Through this nervy, anxious period which saw the fall of such key figures of the old regime as First Deputy Prime Minister and Foreign Minister Subandrio and Omar Dhani, there was no talk of the coup attempt having affected the Sukarno presidency, so deeply entrenched remained his prestige and the loyalty he enjoyed amongst different cross-sections of the population. In an Order of the Day of 17 October, which contained a stipulation to 'continue to exterminate (*basmi*) the remnants of the counter-revolutionary G-30-S/PKI adventurers', Suharto reminded soldiers to 'remain submissive, obedient and loyal to the leadership of the President/Supreme Commander of the Armed Forces/Great Leader of the Revolution Bung Karno'.[10] A week later he proclaimed that 'we must be able to keep safe the Great Leader of the Revolution and apply all the orders and teachings of the Great Leader of the Revolution'.[11] On 27 October, together with Sukarno, he signed a curious document which purported to be a statement of their agreement about the left-oriented, socialist nature of the continuing Indonesian revolution, an action which can be regarded as a clear sign that he remained most unsure of his position relative to Sukarno.[12] At the end of the month he announced that 'we will be obedient without reserve to all the orders of the President/Supreme Commander/Great Leader of the Revolution Bung Karno'.[13] 'During all that time', Suharto later remarked, 'I had no thought at all of bringing down Bung Karno. To my mind he remained a dedicated leader, although he had a different view of what had happened on 1 October 1965. But I did not think it necessary continually to make public my opinion of him, except at appropriate moments'. No shadow of self-doubt seemed to cross Sukarno's mind as he embarked on a calculated attempt to minimise the political impact of the events of early October. His attitude, to Suharto's eyes, 'was totally contrary to the actions and steps I had taken'.[14]

The weeks that followed were characterised by strained and starchy relations between the President and Suharto and other senior army officers, notably Nasution, as the combatants in this uncertain new setting felt each other out for weaknesses. It was, perhaps, a sign of Suharto's hesitancy that he sought, unsuccessfully, a reconciliation between Sukarno and Nasution, perhaps as a means of restraining Nasution from courses of action for which he himself was unprepared and for which he had made no calculation. Suharto was, nonetheless, already clearly of the view that 1 October and its aftermath had seriously undermined Sukarno's power and autonomy, and he refused to buckle under to Sukarno's frequent gambits to restore his pristine authority. According to US Ambassador Marshall Green, for example, in response to Sukarno's request in December 1965 for a formal declaration of the Army's obedience to his wishes, Suharto's response was cagily qualified: he would obey those orders 'consistent with the Army's mission of maintaining national security'.[15] Increasingly, Suharto came to understand, this meant a process of pragmatically worked-out political reform that would curb Sukarno's arbitrariness, cleanse the government of corrupt and radical politicians, and begin the process of addressing the seriously sagging economy.

TARGETING THE PKI

In contrast to his ambiguity towards Sukarno, Suharto's attitude to the PKI was clear. At last freed from the artificial obsequiousness towards the party which had characterised the Old Order, as it was now termed, his most urgent need was to establish security. For him, this primarily meant moving quickly to excise the PKI from the nation's life. Already within a few days of the coup attempt, the local organisation of the PKI in Jakarta had been smashed, and the offices of the party and affiliated organisations closed. On 10 October Suharto established Kopkamtib (Operations Command for the Restoration of Order and Security). He also 'issued instructions containing basic policies to curb and get rid of G.30.S./PKI people in departments, institutions and other bodies within the government service'.[16]

Even while the coup drama was playing itself out, Suharto and other army leaders had begun to foment a mood of accusation against and retribution towards the PKI. The canny chief of Koti's political section (Koti G-V), Brig.-Gen. Sucipto, brought together younger anti-communist parties and groups on 2 October; with army encouragement, they established, under the leadership of Subchan Z. E. and Harry Can Silalahi, an 'Action Command to Crush the 30 September Movement' (KAP G.30.S), which held its first modest demonstration on 4 October. A second demonstration, attended this time by a huge throng as the anti-communist fever grew, was held four days later; it was followed by attacks on the homes of PKI leaders and ended with the burning of the PKI headquarters, with no sign of the Army to protect PKI property. Hughes reported that 'three fire trucks were in attendance, but waited carefully till only the ashes were left before they went into action. Army units were nearby, having cordoned off the streets leading to Communist headquarters. They made no attempt to interfere'.[17]

At the same time, probably at the inspiration of Ali Murtopo, Suharto began a skilful campaign of unforgiving propaganda against the PKI, aimed at both domestic and international audiences. The 30 September Movement was now identified as 'Gestapu', a maladroit but highly effective acronym for the Movement. More viciously, to legitimise their actions, Suharto and his supporters made much capital of the sadistic tortures and mutilations allegedly visited upon the dead or dying generals at Lubang Buaya by PKI members or affiliates, including graphic details of sexual depravity reportedly carried out by members of the PKI women's movement, Gerwani.[18] Whether Suharto really believed at this point that the PKI was ultimately responsible for Gestapu is difficult to decide; what is certain is that he saw the opportunity wholly to destroy the enemy and he took it avidly.

Thus armed, the Army began to hunt out and round up PKI members and associates; by 16 October 1,334 people had been arrested in the Jakarta area on the grounds of their involvement in the 30 September Movement. In moving so rapidly against the PKI, Suharto had two motives. The first, a recognition that the rules of the game had changed fundamentally since 1 October, was simply to dispose of a dangerous enemy whose ideology and ever-ascending influence had long irked him, but which now lay confused, uncertain, badly weakened and exposed. The second was a more strategic concern: the need to create solidarity and enhance legitimacy, to capitalise on the momentum of the moment to unite the anti-communist community of the nation (including the Army, its own internal fabric badly torn) behind him by focusing on a convenient scapegoat.

Suharto was, at the same time, uncertain about how to act and where to move, apart from the general principle that the PKI had to be crushed. His characteristic caution here served him well. Rather than conveying formal orders, he appears to have given local army commanders a clear sense that the PKI needed to be dealt with – pictures of the putrefying bodies reclaimed from the Lubang Buaya well were sent to units across the country – and left it to their judgement how that might best be achieved in the context of local circumstances. In the capital, he could be more forthright, for there he was indisputably in command, and within a few weeks more than 2,000 people had been arrested. Partly because of the latitude left to local commanders, partly because of the relative speed with which the military moved in different places, and partly because of the differences in local strength of PKI followings, levels of violence against the party differed greatly.

In places like West Java where the military moved swiftly to disable the party by numerous arrests, where many branches decided 'voluntarily' to dissolve themselves, where party members admitted the error of their ways and where, in any case, the PKI enjoyed only relatively weak support, there was comparatively little violence. Similarly, in North Sumatra, Kemal Idris moved almost immediately to outlaw the PKI and destroy its local organisation, although large-scale violence subsequently broke out with numerous killings. In Aceh, by contrast, Muslim civilians, in the face of army efforts to rein in the carnage, began massacring PKI members and followers, and even their families, around mid-October. In similar vein, in East Java, a period of uneasy calm and army indecisiveness following the coup attempt was overtaken around the end of the second week of October by a rising crescendo of killing by members of Ansor, the Nahdlatul Ulama youth organisation, a kind of fifth force, 'who killed with fanatical relish'.[19] Sumitro later recalled that 'I can still see, how the Brantas River was so full of bodies floating along, with others caught in the branches of trees that had fallen in at the river's edge'.[20]

In Central Java, what might have remained a relatively small-scale venture into violent retribution was immeasurably magnified by events towards the end of the third week in October. There, Diponegoro commander Suryosumpeno – with many of his reliable troops away on Confrontation duty in Sumatra, and faced with very considerable local army support for the 30 September Movement – had managed to assert a tense and tenuous control over affairs, assisted by the fact that the PKI had deliberately adopted a low-posture attitude aligned with Sukarno's strategy of minimising the impact of the coup attempt. To settle the matter, Suharto determined that he 'had to organise actions which were quick and sure. I had to organise pursuit, cleansing, and crushing'.[21] On 17 October, perhaps at Sarwo Edhie's bidding, he dispatched Sarwo's RPKAD troops on a demonstrative procession to Central Java to assist Suryosumpeno to restore order; there they moved through the cities of Semarang, Magelang and then Solo. Their presence, however, excited the ferment they had been sent to restrain. Sarwo, not confident of his ability to subdue the countryside in the face of developing PKI resistance, sought and received permission to train and arm local youths to assist in clearing the countryside; under the lead of RPKAD troops, and invigorated by their release from restraints on the expression of class and religious hatreds, they arrested and killed PKI members and suspects in the thousands.

Across the countryside, the tensions that had been steadily rising in the country for a decade or more, and upon which the PKI had built its advance, now spilled over in a horrifying spate of vengefulness. The pattern now set, a period of extraordinary violence was ushered in, especially where the Army was slow to move against the communists, or where it encouraged civilian opponents of the party to take out their anger, or where the party enjoyed widespread support. In Bali, the outrage was delayed a little, but when it took place in December, mostly the work of civilians as in East Java, it was unusually bloody even by the standards of the time. Suharto dispatched Sarwo there to rescue the place from anarchy, although 'the execution of Communists was to go on in an "orderly" fashion'.[22] Before the violence tapered off in the first months of 1966, perhaps half a million people had been killed. It was, as a CIA report later acknowledged, 'one of the worst mass murders of the 20th century'.[23] But the aim had been achieved: the PKI had been almost completely destroyed.

Suharto must bear central responsibility for the massacres, having conspired to create a mood of violent retribution, and having encouraged and approved the root-and-branch 'cleansing' of the PKI in late 1965 and early 1966 both by the Army and by army-sponsored civilians. In a speech at the end of October, Suharto spoke of 'crushing and eliminating the counter-revolutionary movement to its very roots'.[24] While the scale of the brutality that emerged was neither intended nor expected by Suharto – indeed, in mid-November he made a rapid visit to Yogya and other Central Java towns, apparently to direct local military officers to crack down on the killing spree in order to restore some measure of order to the countryside – and while he had no interest in advancing the political agendas of Muslim activists, he appears to have had no remorse, not even to have engaged in any considered reflection upon the enormity perpetrated against so many Indonesians by rampaging soldiers and civilians hell-bent on the destruction of their mortal enemy. In an eerie manifestation of his fear that the PKI threatened social and national disruption and destruction, Suharto noted that

> that movement was not a movement that erupted spontaneously on 30 September, but only came to its culmination as a result of a series of happenings which had been prepared long before. An atmosphere of slander, of fomenting the bad feelings of one group against another, and a gloomy social–economic climate which had previously been created, gave rise to a prior atmosphere and climate which was very easily seized upon by them to ignite the counter-revolutionary movement ... in any drama there are always the main performers, assistants and the mastermind [*dalangnja*]. It was just the same with the counter-revolutionary movement which called itself the 30 September Movement. There were major actors, there were also bit-players, and there was also the mastermind, the brainstrust. The main actors, whose roles amongst others were played by the Untung group and some other members of ABRI, the bit-players, whose roles were played by members of Pemuda Rakyat and Gerwani and the mastermind which, based on facts, the results of interrogation and important documents which fell into our hands, points to the involvement of the PKI as the brainstrust of the counter-revolutionary movement.[25]

As the massacres gained intensity in the countryside, the purge of the instruments of government continued. On 29 October, Brig.-Gen. Syarif Thayeb, minister for higher education, suspended administrative and academic members of his department involved with the PKI or its affiliated organisations. In mid-November, Suharto issued an instruction to purge all government departments and bureaux of any civil personnel who could be construed as having been associated with the 30 September Movement.[26] All the while, the fusillade of propaganda against the Movement was maintained and refined; on 1 December, Suharto asserted that the coup had in fact been the first stage of a planned three-stage process, which included the murder of senior figures opposed to its plans, and climaxing in the formation of a new cabinet.

Numerous observers have asserted that the United States gave close support to Suharto at this crucial time. Marshall Green, having later asserted that 'the events of October 1, 1965, came as a complete surprise to us', admitted that 'the United States stood to gain much by these momentous changes'. But, he maintained, 'it had no hand in bringing them about. This was entirely an Indonesian accomplishment. Nevertheless, the sensible U.S. policies of restraint and quiet support were helpful to the new leadership in Indonesia when it began reconstructing a nation left destitute by years of Sukarno's profligate ambitions'.[27] Evidence was to emerge, however, of much closer American assistance, including the covert provision by members of the US Embassy in Jakarta of detailed lists of PKI members to the Army, anti-PKI propaganda and the supply of medicines, radios, rice, and transport equipment, and even money and small arms.[28]

COMMANDING THE ARMED FORCES

The channelling of pent-up tensions against the PKI was a useful mechanism to legitimise his own position, but Suharto also had the task of consolidating his control of the long-factionalised and deeply divided Army. It would be wrong to think that, ensconced in his Kostrad headquarters until December, he moved smoothly into a position of undisputed authority in the army structure. Rather, he had to engage in a prolonged and difficult series of negotiations which resulted in the gradual enhancement of his power. Not only did he need to respect pro-Sukarno nationalist sentiments amongst army officers and redress excessive localism, but he also had to accommodate the fear that many felt that their own position might be prejudiced by his enhanced standing. There was, as well, the problem of inter-service rivalry, complicated not only by the events of 1 October but also by fears that the other services, much strengthened by Sukarno and consequently more strongly attached to his leadership, would suffer seriously should the Army pretend to its old ascendancy.

Suharto was, in one sense, no more than a *primus inter pares*, who had to take infinite pains to win the trust and support of his fellows. To this end, he established a consultative group within the Army, the so-called *Team Politik*, to provide a broadly based discussion forum of General Staff members, local commanders and senior holders of functional positions for the discussion of policy and decisions and to give him, as army commander, advice. A parallel strategy was to commence a purge of those members considered to be sympathetic to the PKI. Wanjakti was employed to remove or reassign high-placed officers who were suspect, although Suharto had to be careful not to alienate its members who had their own local constituencies to service. He sought, as well, to increase the Army's local capacity to secure order. At the end of 1965, he created a military command structure at sub-district level, Koramil (Military Sub-district Command), and a military presence at village level (*Badesa*), in both Central and East Java – the seats of strongest communist support.

The essence of Suharto's strategy was to convince his fellows and his troops that their security and interests, both military and otherwise, were best served by electing to throw their support behind him. One sign of this attitude was the enormous wage increases he provided for all members of the Armed Forces. He took care to ensure that regional sentiments were accommodated within the army high command; there was a place, and advancement, for Siliwangi men like Umar, who assumed control of Kostrad from Suharto in early December 1965, Maj.-Gen. Amirmachmud, who replaced Umar as Jakarta garrison commander, and H. R. Dharsono, who assumed Pranoto's place as assistant III (personnel) on Suharto's staff. Brawijaya officers, men like Basuki Rachmat and Sumitro, were similarly accommodated. Close supporters, of course, were also rewarded; the

Christian Toba Batak Maradean Panggabean was appointed deputy II, and Suharto's old Diponegoro subordinate Munadi sent as acting governor to the highly sensitive post of Central Java governor.

In all of this, Suharto was assisted by the fact that the army high command came from a generally narrow sociological base: most of its members were Javanese, and most not devoutly Muslim. He also began the process of removing local commanders whose loyalty was suspect, such as the leftist commander of the West Sumatra Kodam, Brig.-Gen. Panuju, replaced in February 1966. Nonetheless, his authority remained insecure and the subject of continuing negotiation.

EARLY 1966: THE TURNING-POINT

By early 1966, one matter had been resolved: the physical destruction of the PKI. With it went a crucial element of Sukarno's hold on power, his ability to manipulate the competition between the PKI and the Army to his own advantage. But the way forward for the country remained indeterminate. Suharto himself was in control, albeit insecurely, of the Army which, Sukarno apart, was itself the single most important focus of power, but he was timid in pushing forward further than he had already done. Apart from the significant support enjoyed by Sukarno, amongst not just the sectors of the Armed Forces but also the older party leaders who feared that a Suharto leadership would circumscribe their ambit of influence, the major reason for his hesitancy was that he was himself unclear about his longer-term goals, or even the role that he should play. There was no developed sense of a decisive new guiding ideology, and already clear indication that his political ideas remained narrow and resistant to sophistication; thus his warning to the press on 5 November about liberalism in the press media ('We only know a Pancasila press'),[29] and a later warning to the press about printing inaccurate news reports.[30] Those themes he attempted to develop were well known and well worn: the notion of the Army's solidarity with the people ('Without water, fish cannot live; thus it is with ABRI, which cannot live without the people'), and the special place of Pancasila (which was, he remarked, the key to Indonesia's survival as one nation).[31] What was required, he explained on another occasion, was 'to return to the restoration of the authority of our constitution'.[32] On 17 September 1966, he dedicated 1 October as, literally, 'the Day of the Supernatural Power of Pancasila'. There was to be no place for racism nor, indeed, for 'Western liberalism' within what was being increasingly described as the 'New Order'.[33]

Accordingly, at the beginning of 1966 Suharto restricted his attention to immediate agendas, revolving around the attempt to force the President to take those steps necessary to return the country to some kind of normality. They included banning the PKI, getting rid of ministers deemed to be either implicated with the coup or otherwise corrupt, and taking a shaping role in domestic economic and foreign political policy. There was at this stage no thought of removing or even chastising the President. What Suharto and the army leaders supporting him wanted was a secure and predictable future, but one subject, at least in broad terms, to their bidding. Domesticating Sukarno was the key to these goals. Against this background of tense negotiation and violence, what was to become a decisive new political force was in the process of being born. Late in October 1965, with the encouragement of Syarif Thayeb, students, the majority from Muslim groups, organised themselves into an Indonesian Student Action Front (KAMI).

The major problem with Suharto's limited strategy was that Sukarno refused to accommodate it. The President, despite many efforts by Suharto in private to persuade him otherwise, remained obstinate in his refusal to ban the PKI, not just because of his general identification with its ideological temper and its centrality to his Nasakom formulations, but also because he recognised the importance of the position played by the party, institutionally, in the shape of the regime he had constructed, and what its banning might signal to the nation about his own prestige and position. While he strove to keep the PKI alive as an institution, he also explored the possibility of creating another body of a similar disposition to fulfil the same institutional role. The Army's response to this stubbornness was an increasing tendency to ignore Sukarno's wishes, of which an early manifestation was West Java Commander Ajie's unilateral dissolution of the already-suspended West Java PKI on 17 November.

Suharto's problem, apart from his political naivety in comparison to the masterful Sukarno, was that he was unable to push Sukarno hard in the absence of strong and united army support. He could not be assured of backing in East Java, where Sukarnoist support remained strong, and even less so in recently mutinous Central Java. Even the fiercely anti-communist Ajie in West Java, in close proximity to the capital, could not be relied upon to support Suharto over the President if it came to a showdown. Moreover, the parties remained strongly supportive of Sukarno. It appeared by mid-February that Sukarno had won the battle of wills with the Army, and especially with Suharto; there seemed to be no effective way of dealing with the President's intransigence. Assistant Alamsyah Prawiranegara later recounted his pressing Suharto to pursue Sukarno more vigorously and Suharto replying: 'I understand what you mean. But you don't understand the guiding principles of the Javanese. For example, there is a saying: "Sabtu Pandito Ratu", which means, more or less, that you must not oppose the king'.[34] Such a response was no more than a cover for Suharto's own confusion about how he might manage what lay ahead.

Having calculated that the question of the continuing legality of the PKI was to be his central pillar, Sukarno strove with increasing vigour – and success – to achieve a psychological ascendancy over his opponents. It was, however, a strategy which carried great risks of alienating supporters. A speech in December, for example, praised the communists as bearing the greatest sacrifices during the revolution, a deliberate slight to the Army, which enraged them and alienated many civilian supporters.[35] Suharto, however, did not take the opportunity to capitalise on such errors of judgement. He remained cautious, waiting to see how things might develop. In the end, he was fortunate that other events took the running and pushed him in directions, and at a speed, which he cannot have anticipated.

The catalyst in breaking through the political entrenchment came in December and early January when, in a desperate bid to rebuild the shattered economy, the government took a number of hastily prepared but nonetheless swingeing economic measures, including devaluing the rupiah by an order of 1,000 on 13 December and raising fuel prices. The combination of savage price rises and the constant, warm, even intimate, encouragement of strategically important members of the Army, including Kemal Idris, Sarwo Edhie, members of the Jakarta regional command and Suharto's intelligence men Ali Murtopo and Yoga, stirred the students into significant action in the early weeks of 1966. The price rises sent bus fares skyrocketing, something 'the students could not tolerate'.[36] On 10 January, a KAMI meeting at the University of Indonesia's Medical School in the Jakarta district of Salemba, attended by Sarwo Edhie and his staff, formulated the 'Three Demands of the People' (*Tri Tuntutan Rakyat* – Tritura): to ban the PKI, to cleanse the cabinet of 'G-30-S/PKI elements', and to reduce prices. At the same time, KAMI sponsored a seminar, attended by Nasution, and to which Suharto sent a message of general support for the students who, he said, 'stand in the midst of the people, are aware of the people's difficulties and understand the wishes of the people'.[37]

The student movement, originally energised in Bandung but increasingly centred around the Medical Faculty in Salemba, was a crucial element in broadening the public debate beyond the 1 October events and the role of the PKI to one of the Sukarno government's management of state affairs. Thereafter it became the focus and vehicle for political change; without it, it is difficult to see how Suharto might have manoeuvred his way around an increasingly aggressive president. January, for example, saw Suharto quite unable to declare himself unequivocally for the students' demands and against Sukarno. During massive student demonstrations outside the Bogor Palace on 15 January (large numbers of students were trucked in by the Army), where Sukarno had invited student delegates to meet with him, Suharto, standing on a fence pillar in front of a huge student assembly shouting 'Dissolve the PKI', could only respond: 'The PKI has been dissolved; go home calmly'. Four days later at a meeting in Jakarta, Suharto warned the students against precipitate actions which might 'make things more difficult for me', adding that they should 'take care, there are certain groups who are on the lookout for mistakes by KAMI in order to destroy you'.[38]

It seems clear that Suharto had no other strategy at this time than to play a patient, hopeful, waiting game, including amongst his tactics that of simply ignoring Sukarno's decisions. He was highly conscious not only of the need to keep some kind of social order, but also of the opportunity presented by the student movement to achieve some much-needed change. The problem was to find a way to balance these needs. 'Time and time again I made contact with the students. I listened to their ideas, their wishes and their longings. I felt I needed to be close to them because they were the ones who would be able to help me prevent the outbreak of disorder and excesses. There must be no *chaos*.'[39]

Emboldened by the apparent success of his offensive against the political neophyte Suharto, Sukarno issued a stentorian call on 15 January to 'form your brigades, gather your forces';[40] his populist appeal was taken up by his supporters of various stripes and soon became a campaign for a 'Sukarno Brigade'. Though Suharto later reflected that he had acted decisively in the face of Sukarno's challenge ('I saw the potential danger and quickly intervened. I did not agree with it, therefore preventing a physical clash which might have produced many victims'),[41] in fact he was caught off guard; the Army, he said, stood behind the President and 'awaits his further commands'.[42] Such a lack of qualification indicated his lack of experience in political combat: when apparently cornered, all he could muster was feigned submission, while he awaited a later opportunity. Nasution, much his senior in the Byzantine ways of Jakarta politics, was not impressed; he brought together army leaders, including Suharto, and the meeting produced a much more vaguely worded statement of support for the President.

The way out of a potentially difficult situation into which Sukarno had manoeuvred the Army was provided by Ajie. While strongly supportive of the President and not sympathetic towards the students, he was also cynical about attempts by the civilians around Sukarno to clothe themselves in his prestige for their own welfare. Three days after Sukarno's speech, he issued a statement which trumped the move towards the formation of a Sukarno Brigade by stating that 'all state bodies, citizens, political parties, and mass organizations ... are in fact followers and supporters of Panca Sila and the Teachings of the Great Leader of the Indonesian Revolution ... and therefore automatically make up *barisans* [brigades] standing behind Bung Karno'.[43] Accordingly, Ajie banned any body purporting to represent itself as a *barisan* Sukarno. Suharto's response was much less sophisticated: a crude effort to assert military supervision over the Sukarno Brigade by requiring groups and persons interested in it to register with the military.

Around mid-February, Suharto met with Sukarno, aggressively on the front foot, at the Merdeka Palace in Jakarta. Suharto was increasingly disillusioned with Sukarno's stubborn refusal to acknowledge the seriousness of the events of 1 October. Sukarno's major weapon – an appeal to Suharto's loyalty – was already beginning to wear thin. Thus, while Suharto could tell Sukarno (in Javanese) that 'I always respect you as I respected my parents', he could also add that 'I want to hold you in high respect and regard but unfortunately the one who wants to be respected and his faults hidden does not want this'. What Suharto meant was that he wanted Sukarno to cut his ties to the PKI and reverse the general direction of his government. Sukarno, fully aware, in a way that Suharto was probably not at this stage, of the implications of such a move – a death blow to his legitimacy, the end of Nasakom, the demise of his long-term vision of politics – rejected Suharto's demand that he ban the PKI and ordered him to quell the student unrest. His loyalty to Sukarno increasingly shaken, Suharto was in something of a quandary: 'I could not be loyal without any reservation, because if I had followed what he asked of me, that would have meant me doing wrong'.[44] From about this time onwards, and especially as Sukarno, despite Suharto's best efforts, remained intransigent, Suharto decided that Sukarno would have to be replaced or somehow neutralised.

Sukarno moved to take further advantage of the space provided him by an uncertain and divided army, and a politically unpractised, cautious and indecisive Suharto, fearful of moving too precipitately against the President and inciting a pro-Sukarno backlash amongst senior army officers. Early in February, Sukarno restructured Koti; its focus was henceforth to be on the conduct of confrontation against Malaysia, thus limiting Suharto's ability to use his position of chief of staff for domestic political purposes. Indeed, Suharto, much on the back foot by this stage, found himself welcoming the idea 'on the grounds that it would dispel "slanders" about military dictatorship'. Sukarno raised the pressure further, praising the PKI's sacrifices in the cause of Indonesia's independence struggle in a mid-February speech in which he also renewed his call for a Sukarno Brigade, and beginning arrangements for the release of those arrested as PKI supporters.[45] Carefully modulating his actions and noting that Suharto seemed almost mesmerised, Sukarno finally and decisively raised the stakes when he reshuffled his cabinet on 21 February and produced a 'reformed Dwikora Cabinet', from which Nasution and a number of anti-communist civilians were sacked but which retained ministers thought close to the PKI, notably Subandrio and Omar Dhani, and in which the military ministers, with the exception of Suharto, were regarded as supporters of the President. Nasution's dismissal – 'an unambiguous challenge by Sukarno to his opponents'[46] – had come 'as lightning from a clear day';[47] his position as Armed Forces chief of staff was also dispensed with. The following day, Sukarno recast Koti as Kogam ('the Command to Crush Malaysia'), with himself as commander and Suharto as chief of staff; its functions were to be limited to the Malaysian confrontation. A few days later, on 26 February, Sukarno banned KAMI, a move with which Suharto found himself forced to comply. Student demonstrations were banned again, and students forbidden to collect even in small groups. Sukarno continued to speak enthusiastically about Marxism.

Suharto himself had been consulted by Sukarno about the shape of the new cabinet, although he later noted that 'when the new Cabinet was appointed not many people were happy with it because there were still many old faces'.[48] Sukarno was determined to rid himself of Nasution and offered Suharto the job of minister coordinating defence and security. Suharto refused – a sign, perhaps, of his awe of Nasution, a sensitivity to the divisions and jealousies such a move might arouse amongst his colleagues and, as well, an unwillingness to be too closely identified with the President; indeed, according to one report, he threatened to resign when he heard of Nasution's fate.[49] But, as Crouch suggests, 'Nasution's dismissal may not have been altogether unwelcome to Suharto, whose grip on the Army leadership tightened as a consequence'.[50] The night before the cabinet was announced, Suharto, aware of the impending changes, had visited Nasution with a proposal that he accept the post of deputy commander-in-chief. Nasution's in-principle acceptance marked a turning-point in their tense relationship. Nasution's influence had been waning ever since his 1962 'promotion'. Rumours had abounded in Jakarta about his imminent demise in the months before the coup; afterwards, badly affected by the loss of his daughter, sensitive to the delicate state of army unity, perhaps crippled by an enduring indecisiveness and lack of resolution to fight the battles that needed winning, he had demonstrated little political effectiveness, though his prestige remained high. He would never respond to the hopes of some of his army colleagues to 'move forward to replace Bung Karno'.[51]

The events of mid- and late February demonstrated how little progress Suharto's patient diplomacy had made, and the need for a more determined stance against Sukarno. According to one contemporary account, 'the generals seem to have lost their initiative and resolution; Sukarno on the other hand has regained a good deal of the strength and energy he seemed to have lost after September 30'.[52] The expectations aroused for political reform were gradually washing away as Suharto's civilian supporters chafed at his apparent refusal to confront Sukarno. Finally, he moved decisively to change the trajectory of politics. On the one hand, he exploited emerging evidence that suggested Sukarno's involvement in, or at least prior knowledge of, the coup attempt, in order to stiffen the resolve of senior army officers. More crucially, he also lent encouragement to anti-Sukarno officers to stimulate heightened student activism and raise tensions to such an extent that Sukarno would have no choice but to take refuge in Suharto's capacity to ensure order. Notwithstanding Suharto's claim to have controlled the student movement,[53] it enjoyed something of a life of its own, even if it relished his barely disguised support. Kostrad, operationally commanded by Kemal Idris, who came to an agreement with Amirmachmud to assume effective command of Jakarta's troops, became the intelligence centre of the student movement. Suharto was kept closely informed of these moves via his former Kostrad intelligence officers, notably Yoga Sugama and Ali Murtopo;[54] Ali himself played an active role by deploying troops at strategic points to protect the demonstrating students.

Thus encouraged, student groups, notwithstanding the ban on their activities by Amirmachmud (himself thought to be sympathetic to the President as a result of a previous posting in Bogor, and keen not to see Jakarta become a battleground of pro- and anti-Sukarno forces), began an escalating series of demonstrations from 23 February. The following day, on the occasion of the installation of the new cabinet, notable at first for student efforts to deter the new ministers from attending the ceremony by blocking traffic, demonstrations spilled onto the palace grounds and brought fire from the Cakrabirawa guards, killing a university student, Arif Rachman Hakim, and a high school girl. Suharto sent flowers to Hakim's vast funeral service, held the following day after an emotional service at the University of Indonesia at Salemba and a long procession through crowded streets. The result of Hakim's death was a further escalation of student activity. Suharto counselled the students to be patient, at the same time instructing Kemal Idris to protect them from the Cakrabirawa.[55] A subsidiary tactic was to target Sukarno's closest confidants, notably his closest and most trusted associate, Subandrio, in the hope that, if they could be separated from Sukarno, his resilience might begin to fail.

It was clear to Suharto that the continuing actions by the students were beginning to wear away at Sukarno's patience and nerve. The struggle now moved to a decisive new phase. To protect the students, Kemal Idris arranged for them to shift their base from the university to a Kostrad battle command headquarters on Jalan Kebon Sirih, where Ali Murtopo's special operations unit was situated. Under the encouragement of Kemal, Sarwo and Ali Murtopo, demonstrations began yet again, reaching new heights of fury. Sarwo Edhie even enrolled as a student at the university as a sign of his solidarity with the student cause. Suharto, for his part, continued to press for the dissolution of the PKI, but still Sukarno refused to budge. On 4 March, Suharto prevailed on Sukarno to allow him to arrest ministers thought to have been involved in the coup attempt, and again Sukarno refused to act. In order to resolve the gridlock, Suharto had to find a means to force the President's hand, but to do it in a manner that would not arouse serious opposition from military factions loyal to the President. 'ABRI', he proclaimed, 'as a tool of the revolution has no other choice than to prepare itself to face the challenges'.[56]

Early in March, Suharto held a meeting of the General Staff in the office of Sugih Arto (assistant I). After some consultation, he concluded that he should arrest the problematic members of the cabinet at the cabinet session scheduled for 11 March at Merdeka Palace. Orders were written to have the RPKAD assume that role, although Suharto is reported later to have drawn back from that plan because of a risk to the President's safety. It appears that the plan then became one of presenting an unmistakable show of force, in the context of student unrest verging on the anarchic, in the hope of pushing Sukarno into acting along the lines that Suharto had been suggesting to him. Whether Suharto was privy to the detailed planning is difficult to say; certainly Sarwo and Kemal later denied that he was.[57] However, he was probably kept closely informed about developments by his intelligence officers, and did nothing to rein in the army radicals. Sukarno needed to be convinced that the political unrest fomented by the students and the radical officers was spiralling out of control, and that only Suharto could save the day. The Kostrad history is unusually frank on this point; it reports that at the 6 March meeting with his officers, Suharto rehearsed an earlier threat to Sukarno that 'the mood within the rank of the TNI was so nasty that I could not be responsible if from among them there were those who left troops and broke discipline to join with the people's actions. That if there was a situation so nasty, I was willing to strip off my rank and leave my position to join with them'.[58]

Indeed, the plan worked better than any of the conspirators could have wished, probably because Sukarno got wind of the general drift of what had originally been decided. In the very early morning of 10 March, Suharto called a meeting at Kostrad headquarters with student leaders, already busy with attacks on the premises of various Chinese government organisations around the city, presumably to inform them of what he was about to do. While he later denied any thought of conspiracy, what took place the following day can only be explained in those terms. It was carefully crafted to achieve its desired end. 'Pak Harto took no rash steps', Sumitro later reflected; 'he never did anything in a hurry, without careful consideration'.[59] This is not to say that the conspiracy was pursued in anything more than broad detail, nor that Suharto had absolute control of all the actors in the Army. Rather, it was a plan to place pressure on the President in a way that had not been attempted before, and to seize the chance of any weakness or lack of resolve that he might show.

SUPERSEMAR

On 11 March 1966, Sukarno began the cabinet meeting sometime after 9 a.m., having received assurances from Jakarta commander Amirmachmud that there were no security problems. Suharto was absent, complaining of a throat infection. Ten minutes into the meeting, Brig.-Gen. Amirmachmud, who had been invited into the meeting (notwithstanding his protestations) by Sukarno, received a note from Brig.-Gen. Sabur, Sukarno's adjutant, requesting him to leave the meeting for a moment because there were unidentified troops outside. They were 'Sarwo Edhy's para-commandos, but, as Sarwo Edhy told me drily many months later, "We didn't advertise the fact. We weren't wearing our red berets"'.[60] Amirmachmud, not wishing to disturb the meeting, signalled to Sabur that it was nothing to worry about (*'tidak akan terjadi apa-apa'*). Sukarno continued to speak through all this. Five minutes later, Sabur sent Amirmachmud another note, with a more emphatic request for him to go outside. At the same time, Sabur sent a note to Sukarno with the same message. According to Amirmachmud, Sukarno's hands trembled as he read it; he then passed it to Subandrio. After some further discussion with Subandrio, Sukarno, perhaps alarmed at what all this meant, and probably noting Suharto's absence, suspended proceedings, passed the chair to Leimena, and left the meeting. Amirmachmud accompanied him, assuring him that he would be safe. He escorted him, after some discussion about where he might go, to his helicopter in the area in front of the palace. Sukarno was accompanied by a shoeless Subandrio, as well as by Chaerul Saleh. The helicopter took off for the presidential palace in Bogor.

Directly after the meeting had been reopened and immediately closed by Leimena, Amirmachmud was joined on the steps of the palace by Maj.-Gen. Basuki Rachmat and Brig.-Gen. Moh. Yusuf, who had been attending the meeting in their capacities as ministers for, respectively, veterans' affairs and industry. According to Amirmachmud's account, Yusuf suggested that the three travel to Bogor to join in discussion with Sukarno, 'so that Bung Karno would not feel that he had been abandoned by the Army'.[61] Before leaving, they reported to Suharto at his home at Jl. Haji Agus Salim, where he was resting. They told him of the sudden discontinuance of the cabinet meeting, sought his permission to go to Bogor, and asked if there were orders to be carried to Sukarno. According to Amirmachmud, Suharto replied: 'First convey my greetings to Bung Karno, and second tell him that there is nothing to be concerned about. We are prepared to safeguard the Pancasila and the Constitution, to safeguard the Indonesian revolution and ensure security. Our belief in those things is our motive'.[62] Suharto later stated that he 'delegated' the three officers to convey to Sukarno his readiness to 'overcome the situation if President Sukarno gave me the task and his full confidence'.[63] There was, according to Amirmachmud, no mention of a letter of authority.

Returning to the palace, the three took Sukarno's stand-by helicopter for the journey to Bogor. During the trip, they prayed. The extraordinary tension of the drama which then took place is reflected in Amirmachmud's detailed (if suitably tailored to enlarge his role) account:[64]

> We arrived at Bogor between 12 and 1 o'clock. At that time Bung Karno was asleep. We were received by Brig.-Gen. Sabur. We waited until Bung Karno woke up. Once Bung Karno had woken up he sat in the pavilion, wearing only a pair of white knee-length trousers with a singlet. Then he asked us why we had come to Bogor to meet with him. Pak Basuki Rachmat answered that we had come to be with him, so that he would not be affected [*dipengaruhi*] by the situation or what had happened at the meeting that morning, and not feel alienated, and so on and so on. So that Bapak [Sukarno] would be calm and ready to overcome the problem. Then he asked each of us what the real situation was. I answered that the situation was secure. Then he snarled at me, as follows: 'You say secure, secure, but the demonstrations keep going on'.
>
> After that we joined in discussion along with the exchange of ideas. Finally, Bung Karno raised the question of how to get on top of all this. At that time, the atmosphere was silent for a short time. Pak Basuki Rachmat, the most senior officer present, did not answer Bung Karno's question. Nor did Pak Yusuf answer. In this situation, I spontaneously interjected as follows: 'Give in easily, Pak. Bapak just governs with Pak Harto. Don't trouble yourself with it. So, Pancasila is secure, the 1945 Constitution is secure, the Revolution is carried on, development is carried on, and the safety of Bapak's family is guaranteed'. I was astonished at my courage in interjecting in this way because, in the way of oriental custom I, as the most junior officer, ought not to have given a view before those more senior than myself.
>
> Then, at this suggestion of mine, Bung Karno came back at me: 'How might this be arrived at?' I answered as follows: 'Form a team. I suggest that Pak Basuki Rachmat head the team, with Pak Yusuf as a member, and Brig.-Gen. Sabur as secretary. I myself don't need to sit on the team, because I am a commander [*panglima*]'. Bung Karno evidently agreed with my suggestion. Even though I did not sit on the team, nonetheless, in the formulation that emerged I was included in the discussion. After the formulation was finished by the team, Bung Karno called the members of the Presidium who were also present at that time at the Bogor palace. The draft formulation which had been written by hand with a fountain pen was then read by Bung Karno. Then it was read by Leimena and the others. When it came to Subandrio's turn to read it, he proposed some minor corrections, but only of an editorial kind.
>
> After being corrected by Subandrio, the draft was returned to Bung Karno. After he read it, he ordered Brig.-Gen. Sabur to type it up. I need to clarify that all of this happened in the central space of the pavilion at the Bogor palace, that is where the dining table is, so that while the typing was done, we three gathered at the open part of the pavilion. Then, after Magrib prayers, we gathered again. By then Bung Karno was wearing bright blue pyjamas, and Ibu Hartini was with him. The members of the Presidium were also all present. Then, Brig.-Gen. Sabur came bringing the draft which had just been typed.

> Then Sabur informed Bung Karno of the administrative difficulty that a Letter of Authority of this kind was not valid because from page one to page two there were no connecting words at the bottom of the page. The view of Brig.-Gen. Sabur was indeed correct; nonetheless, because I was afraid that if this matter were discussed any more, new problems would arise, I then answered spontaneously as follows: 'Dear me, in a time of revolution we are still thinking of administrative details. Just give it to Bung Karno'. Then Bung Karno read the text in a serious and calm way. Then he asked: 'So. Do I sign or not?' Repeatedly he asked with the same kind of sentence. He also asked the members of the Presidium. Remembering that, with Bung Karno's uncertainty, the thing might disappear into thin air or be undone again, I interjected: 'Do it, Pak, in the name of Allah'. My expression 'In the name of Allah' was repeated by all members of the Presidium, first by Pak Leimena who, mark you, is a Christian, followed by all present. Then, after Bung Karno had said 'In the name of Allah' as well, which was repeated together by all present, Bung Karno signed the text. After signing the document, Bung Karno gave it directly to Pak Basuki Rachmat …
>
> Then the three of us left to return to Jakarta again by car. On the Bogor Satu Duit bridge, I borrowed the text. I had to read with a torch because it was getting dark [*'waktunya shalat Isya'*]. After studying it I cried out 'Well, well. This hands over power'. We were all really surprised because at that time, really, at the time we did not think or imagine a situation of handing over power. After arriving in Jakarta, we went straight to Jalan [Haji] Agus Salim [Suharto's residence] to report to Pak Harto, but Pak Harto was at that time at Kostrad to receive commanders who had come from the regions. Because of this we three went straight to Kostrad and the document was handed over directly to Pak Harto by Pak Basuki Rachmat.

Notwithstanding the self-serving nature of this account, it accords well with the generality of other accounts, including Suharto's. It seems highly unlikely that Suharto had given explicit instructions to the three generals before they left for Bogor, and even less that they carried with them some kind of draft for Sukarno's signature. They were, however, commissioned to press him to take action to overcome what was fast becoming a chaotic situation, and to bring him to agree that his only immediate salvation lay in Suharto. There can be no doubt that the three generals harassed a seriously concerned, frightened, and probably psychologically cowed Sukarno into signing the 11 March Letter of Authority (Supersemar). This, under the circumstances, was the least dangerous course to follow, given Sukarno's view that he could always master Suharto in rugged capital-city politics. Suharto, for the first time, was to prove him wrong. He had set his course, and was determined that Sukarno would no longer deflect him from it.

That night at Kostrad, Suharto, dressed in his camouflage fatigues and with a yellow choker around his neck, called a staff meeting, attended as well by supportive civilian groups. It was clear that the authority granted to him, at least on paper, far exceeded anything he might have expected or hoped for, although when he first received the letter he had displayed no outward emotion. About 10 p.m. he emerged, together with Basuki Rachmat, to address the assembled group, and outlined the substance of the President's order. He immediately sought to give effect to a very broad interpretation of the authority granted him by dissolving and banning the PKI and its affiliated bodies. Shortly before midnight, orders were relayed to Col. Sudharmono, assisted by Lt. Murdiono, to draft the necessary decree. Suharto signed it in the early hours of 12 March. Significantly, it was in the form of a presidential decree, made in the name of the President, not Suharto himself. Its contents were broadcast at 6 a.m. by RRI.

AFTER SUPERSEMAR

The immediate aftermath of the announcement of Supersemar was an enhancement of the general tension gripping the capital. Rumour abounded of imminent clashes between the Army and the Air Force. On 12 March, Sarwo Edhie led his troops on a kind of impromptu victory parade, albeit a threatening one, through the streets of Jakarta, enthusiastically greeted by large crowds. Troops, presumably at Suharto's instigation, also burst violently into the Menteng headquarters of Subandrio's BPI (Central Intelligence Agency), apparently searching for Subandrio, and seized numerous documents.

Notwithstanding the fact that the dissolution of the PKI had been one of Suharto's main objectives since 1 October, Sukarno was shocked and angered by his rapid and decisive action. According to Amirmachmud, 'after Suharto had dissolved the PKI, Sukarno sent Leimena to Suharto's house, carrying a reprimand to Suharto from Sukarno, because Suharto had dissolved the PKI. [According to Subandrio, Suharto's response was terse: 'Pak Leimena, don't intervene. I am now the one in power'.][65] He also carried an instruction that Suharto make the three of us, that is Pak Basuki Rachmat, Pak Yusuf and myself, appear before Sukarno at Bogor'.[66] When the three did appear at Bogor, with Suharto's agreement, Sukarno abused them, saying that there was no mention in his instruction about dissolving the PKI. But he made no effort to rescind or disown the order, and he was seen later that day talking in a relaxed fashion with Suharto. Within a few days, both Air Force and Navy had issued statements of support for Suharto, the holder of Supersemar; given that the letter was from the hand of Sukarno, they had little choice in the matter.

There was, indeed, considerable debate about the nature and extent of the power transferred to Suharto by virtue of Supersemar, that 'masterly stroke of political salesmanship'.[67] Suharto appeared to hold no such doubts: 'in my view, that order was issued at a moment when the state was in a critical situation, where the integrity of the President, the Armed Forces and the people was endangered, while security, order and governance were in disarray'.[68] He seems never to have doubted that, once the authority had been given, he could exploit it ruthlessly as a means of bringing down the targets he had earlier set himself but which had been denied him by the President. Indeed, the authority of the Supersemar was fundamentally enhanced because of the way in which Suharto put it to work and the style with which he operated. It was a shock weapon – 'less as an instrument of power than as a wedge with which to attain it'[69] – to be used in a limited way for specific goals and within specific contexts. Moreover, it was a limited authority for action. The supreme power of the state still lay in the hands of the President, as Sukarno took pains to assert in an announcement of 17 March,[70] and as Suharto was careful to appreciate. As yet, Suharto had no long-range plans to usurp that power.

It is difficult to overestimate the importance, both psychological and legal, of the Supersemar – or, rather, of the generous interpretation which Suharto accorded it. Supersemar, as Ibu Tien's biographer remarked rather grandiosely, 'evolved into the historical milestone of a reborn nation'. According to Sumitro, 'what is important is what Pak Harto did in the wake of its issuance'.[71] It became, in the words of a DPR-GR memorandum of 9 June, 'the key to a new page in the history of the Indonesian Revolution, and constitutes the point of return to the true and pure basic objectives of the Revolution as sought by the Proclamation of Independence of 17th August and laid down in the Preamble and the Body of the 1945 Constitution'.[72] Rather disingenuously, Suharto later remarked that 'I have never thought of Supersemar as a means to obtain power. The Letter of Instruction of March 11 was also not a tool for staging a veiled coup'.[73] His own behaviour subsequent to the receipt of the letter gives the lie to that assertion. It was, as he later acknowledged, 'a historical milestone of the utmost importance for the safety [*keselamatan*] of the people, the country and the nation'.[74] It was, he claimed, 'the beginning of the struggle of the New Order'.[75]

Suharto's action in invoking his new authority to ban the PKI had the effect of breaking the political logjam. At last he had succeeded in moving the President decisively, and, since Supersemar was from the President's hand, he had done it in a way that could not be construed as attacking or toppling Sukarno; a few days after the Supersemar episode he told reporters that 'President Sukarno … remains in his functions as chief of state. Everything remains as usual'.[76] Heartened by the reception his banning of the Communist Party received – manifested in the widespread support of Sarwo's demonstration in Jakarta on 12 March – Suharto moved with previously unknown speed to extend his influence elsewhere. He issued information bulletins, exhorted government and business to take up their responsibilities again, and prohibited political parties from accepting into their ranks ex-PKI members. The man not much given to speechmaking now made speeches and announcements virtually every day ('his manner is wooden and his speeches are dull', opined one foreigner);[77] now he rapidly discarded the revolutionary rhetoric which had dominated political discourse in the years of Sukarno's ascendancy.

Bolder than any of this, however, was Suharto's move on 18 March, under pressure from students and radical army elements, to arrest fifteen members of the so-called reformed Dwikora cabinet, on the basis of their being suspected of playing a role in the coup attempt or on the grounds of corruption. Sukarno had strongly resisted army attempts to reshape his cabinet, but the dramatic arrests showed how quickly his real authority was ebbing in the wake of Supersemar. Nonetheless, Suharto was careful not to push 'to behead the man who once had been his "king"',[78] and probably did not judge it a realistic or even desirable option at that time.

SUHARTO IN EXECUTIVE POWER

The veiled coup successfully accomplished, Suharto could now begin to put his own stamp on Indonesia's governance. His first step was to help Sukarno fashion a new cabinet (the 'more perfected Dwikora cabinet') at the end of March to replace that which he had dismembered by arrest two weeks before. In the new cabinet, Suharto was one of six deputy premiers (the others were Adam Malik, the Sultan of Yogyakarta, Leimena, Ruslan Abdulgani, and Idham Chalid) who formed a presidium, and he himself held the post of defence minister, chief of staff of the Army, and chief of staff of Koti. In terms of personnel, however, the cabinet was a statement of continuity rather than radical change, even though the Armed Forces formed a majority. Suharto acknowledged that it 'represents the maximum possible progress in the first stage'.[79]

Nonetheless, his confidence in directing affairs appeared to be enhanced, and he became more disposed to making broad exhortatory comments about the nature of Indonesian society and its proper direction; a few days afterwards he remarked that 'Indonesia is not contented with Western democracy and other foreign democracies, with a liberal or totalitarian economy'. Those things based on liberalism or materialism 'don't bring satisfaction to the spirit of the Indonesian nation'. On the occasion of May Day 1966, he remarked that 'the Indonesian people do not know about class, and the struggle of the Indonesian working group is not a class struggle'. In August, he noted that, while ABRI was not expert in politics or economics, it had 'sufficient knowledge and consciousness of the national and international problems which had to be faced, how to solve them and those people who are able to get them done'.[80] The style he manifested on such occasions was one which invoked the trust, confidence and support of the people, as though the actions he was taking were no more than responses to their hopes and urgings.

The new cabinet was effectively a triumvirate of Suharto himself, Adam Malik as foreign minister, and the sultan, placed in charge of economic affairs. These were astute and attractive choices; both civilians, they had strong revolutionary credentials and had avoided being soiled by the disrepute into which civilian politics had fallen in the 1950s. They provided Suharto with a credible face for the new regime he was in the process of constructing. Malik's task was to resuscitate political relations with Indonesia's neighbours and especially with the Western world. The sultan had the onerous task of rebuilding the confidence of foreign investors and creating a new paradigm for Indonesia's development. Together, the three formed something of a collective leadership, in which Suharto himself was by no means supreme.

While it seems clear that Suharto had a firm sense of the general policy directions he wished to take, he was much less clear about the scope and shape of the government he wished to build, and its relation to the President. He was, of course, still far from certain of the loyalty of senior officers, even less so of regional units in other services and of the Army in East Java, where officers remained strongly supportive of Sukarno, and extremely keen to avoid any move which might have brought a probably apocalyptic showdown. But, from about this time onwards, he began to show a more definite yet finely graduated assertiveness, as he manoeuvred to tighten his grip on the Armed Forces and the state apparatus. A number of ministers were arrested, officials within the bureaucracy began to suffer renewed purges (and a greening of their senior ranks with the injection of military functionaries), a large number of officers in the Air Force were arrested, and Sukarno's palace guard, the Cakrabirawa, was dissolved. A cleansing of the membership of parliament, already under way, was intensified in March with the removal of a further sixty-three PKI members. Political cleansing also extended to the PNI in April 1966. At the party's Bandung congress, the Army, joining forces with anti-communist PNI dissidents like Suharto's old Central Java colleague Hadisubeno and Hardi, replaced its Sukarnoist leadership with one more amenable to the new situation. Opening that congress, Suharto remarked that the views of the party 'must always be in accord with the wishes of the people', otherwise 'it will be corrected by the people; it will even be put to death by the people themselves'.[81] The police force was also the subject of small-scale cleansing in mid-1966, a process that gained momentum in 1967.

The senior echelons of the Army itself also came in for attention. In May 1966, Suharto sent Ajie, Umar, and the Diponegoro commander, Suryosumpeno, to a special course at Seskoad; Ajie accepted appointment as Indonesian ambassador in London in July, while in the same month Rukman, former commander of Brawijaya and inter-regional commander for East Indonesia (and a former classmate of Suharto at SSKAD/Seskoad), was appointed to the staff at army headquarters. Suryosumpeno became Sukarno's military secretary and later accepted a high appointment in the Home Affairs department. He was replaced by a Suharto man and former Diponegoro colleague, Maj.-Gen. Surono, in July, and the Division itself was purged of about 2,500 men. Around the same time, Sumitro took over as commander of the Brawijaya in East Java, where he 'put down attempts among his officers and division veterans to rally support for Sukarno late in 1966'.[82] By mid-1967, Mursyid and the Sukarnoist inter-regional commander for Sumatra, Lt. Gen. Mokaginta, whose power pretensions apparently irritated Suharto, had been shunted off to ambassadorships. One by one, those officers whom Suharto deemed unreliable, disruptive or potential competitors were given the opportunity to absent themselves gracefully and profitably from the scene. Regional commanders were given a similar shake-up, so that by early 1967 Suharto had placed his supporters in all of the regional and inter-regional commands. Those officers still enamoured of Sukarno had no choice, however disinclined they might have been, other than to make their peace with the new realities.

Nasution's position set Suharto a different set of problems. He was the Army's senior general, and a man of very high reputation, but he had fallen in with Suharto's leadership on 1 October. His lack of assertiveness was at least partly due to the injury, shock and emotional turmoil of his own circumstances, and perhaps a realisation that, with his vexed relationship with Sukarno, it was preferable to adopt a low profile. There were, as well, many army leaders who would not have preferred the puritanical Nasution back in charge, even though, according to

Sumitro, 'the senior officers of the time had hoped that General Nasution would move forward to replace Bung Karno'.[83] There was, moreover, a clear sense that Nasution was not willing to take the chance offered him, through lack of confidence or lack of courage or both, mingled, perhaps, with a deep desire to do the right thing by the nation at this time of great trial. Suharto, for his part, was no friend of Nasution and made little effort to persuade or force Sukarno to change his mind about not appointing him as army commander in October 1965 and refusing to have him in his February 1966 cabinet. In the end, despite a desultory attempt to gain appointment to the long-vacant vice-presidency, Nasution saw that his politico-military future was limited, and he accepted Suharto's offer of appointment as chairman of the Provisional People's Consultative Assembly (MPRS).

In all these delicate manoeuvrings, Suharto and his supporters were careful to emphasise the credentials of the Armed Forces for the task that lay ahead of them, and their essential unity of spirit and interests with the people, as well as his care that constitutional fundamentals must always be preserved above naked power. The Indonesian nation, he remarked on 4 April, was based on law, not absolutism. On 13 April, he rehearsed the well-worn theme that the TNI/ABRI had been born of the people's struggle for independence.[84] In November he remarked that the TNI was the 'kernel and the vanguard in struggling for the demands that come from the heart of the people',[85] and rejected any notion that the Armed Forces should assume dictatorial power. He was, moreover, in a quite radical departure from his normal practice, constantly available for interview and even organised social events with the foreign media to explain to them the situation in Indonesia.[86]

THE MPRS SESSION

Notwithstanding Suharto's developing authority, he remained dangerously exposed by Sukarno's constitutional position, the fact that Supersemar could be withdrawn at any time, and Sukarno's legendary political astuteness. In order to provide himself with the necessary institutional ballast, he sought to convene a session of the MPRS, the Consultative Assembly and ultimate source of authority in the Indonesian state, to endorse his position.

Sukarno's well-developed political nostrils smelled the danger, and he precipitated a further stand-off with army leaders. In late April, he recast the membership of the Supreme Advisory Council in his favour; Suharto's response was to prevent it meeting and to continue the work of 'cleansing' the membership of the DPR (People's Representative Council) and the MPRS of PKI taint. Sukarno's riposte was a threat to dissolve the MPRS and call for elections, ruling in the meantime in collaboration with a National Committee in the style of the period of the revolution. The Army, however, with strong support from the students, refused to buckle under to his efforts to regain the initiative – Sukarno was, as Suharto reminded his listeners, subject to the MPRS[87] – and Suharto postponed the MPRS meeting to early June.

Managing this, the fourth general session of the MPRS, was tricky. Suharto's careful demeanour was manifest: 'I reported at the opening of the MPRS session on the actual state of affairs, trying to avoid the emergence of emotions which we did not want. I spoke as carefully as I could. I did not want a bigger shock to happen to our country'. However, notwithstanding his claim that he 'did not intend to unseat Bung Karno from his position as President',[88] the tenor of the MPRS decision-making was clearly of a kind that entertained the notion that a period of transition was in train. Indeed, by mid-1966 Suharto had finally decided that Sukarno had to be replaced, perhaps by himself, but that the process had to be managed slowly, carefully, and systematically, and in a legal and constitutional way.

The MPRS, then numbering 532 members, met from 20 June until 5 July against a background of continuing student and popular unrest increasingly focused on the person of Sukarno; 'the hall echoed to the revolutionary accents of the students and the Action Fronts'.[89] On 21 June, noting that the letter of authority of 11 March was a 'special effort to overcome the danger threatening the safe running of the government and the course of the revolution, the authority of the leadership of the revolution and also the integrity of Nation and State' which had been accepted by both the people and the DPR-GR, the MPRS decided to 'adopt and confirm the policy of the President … that is laid down in the Order dated 11th March 1966 addressed to Lieutenant General Suharto'.[90] Passage of this decree was the most basic task of the MPRS, since it raised the status of Supersemar from an authorisation of the President which, naturally, he could revoke at any time, to a decision of the highest body of the state, which the President could not overrule.

The following day, 22 June, the MPRS received Sukarno's report of accountability, the so-called 'Nawaksara' address. Sukarno took the opportunity to emphasise the leadership role granted to him by the Assembly ('I expect from the whole people, including the Members of M.P.R.S., always to follow, to execute, to put into deeds all that I am going to give in that leadership!'),[91] and to restate – yet again – his guiding principles, dressed up in their usual acronymic raiment. This was an exercise in defiance; in his relatively short statement there was no semblance of apology, and not the slightest attempt to justify his position in relation to the events of 1 October 1965. The MPRS was not impressed with what it heard; 'it falls short of fulfilling the hopes of the people, especially the members of the Provisional M.P.R., since it does not clearly contain an account for responsibility as to the policy of the President … with regard to the contra-revolutionary "30th September Movement"/Indonesian Communist Party affair and its epilogue'. The Assembly required him 'to complete the report of his responsibility to the Provisional M.P.R., in particular with regard to the causes for the occurrence of the "30th September Movement"/Indonesian Communist Party affair together with its epilogue and the economic as well as the moral decline'.[92]

On 5 July, mindful of its obligation 'to stop deviations from the 1945 Constitution', the MPRS decreed that 'all institutions of the State at both central and regional level shall be restored to the positions and functions in keeping with what is stipulated in the 1945 Constitution'.[93] On the same day, it passed a further ten decrees, which, amongst other things, called for general elections to be held by 5 July 1968; reaffirmed Indonesia's 'independent and active' foreign policy; called for the establishment of a new ('Ampera') cabinet, under Suharto, to replace the Dwikora cabinet by 17 August 1966; decided that 'should the President be prevented from performing his duties, the holder of the 11th March 1966 Order shall hold the position of Acting President'; repealed its own appointment of Sukarno as 'President for Life'; charged the government and the DPR-GR with reviewing presidential directives and regulations issued since the reintroduction of the 1945 Constitution in 1959 and with revising laws and government regulations not in accord with the 1945 Constitution; accepted and confirmed Suharto's 12 March decision to dissolve and ban the PKI; and banned the propagation of communist ideas.[94]

On the same date, the MPRS sent a note to the DPR-GR informing that body of its views on various foreign policy matters. At the top of the list was the Confrontation of Malaysia; the Assembly stated its wish for 'the peaceful settlement of this issue' and sought 'to end the policy of confrontation'. In his speech opening the final sitting of the MPRS, Nasution was notably muted in mentioning Suharto; thus, even though Supersemar had 'provided the opportunity of channelling all these wishes ... ultimately it is implementation of the 1945 Constitution consistently and in all its purity that will be the best way to achieve these ends. If that road is not taken, all these movements might head for anarchy, military dictatorship, liberalism and other dangerous phenomena'. He was at pains to point out that Suharto's authority was inextricably linked to that of the President: 'the Executor of the 11th March order cannot be separated from the person conferring the task, that is, the President, and in executing that task they should work in a cooperative spirit discussing matters and seeking agreement between them'.[95]

The result of this process was that Sukarno remained in office, but it was to be an office of a largely ceremonial kind. His sense of aggrievement and exasperation at the Assembly's handiwork was clear; nonetheless, his rambling remarks, as smoothly digestible – and as accommodating to apparently contradictory views – as ever, carried an air of resignation. He would, he said, 'accept being made Mandatory of the Provisional M.P.R.'.[96] A special target for his dismay was the fact that the new cabinet was to be the work of Suharto, not himself, a measure he described as unconstitutional. Sukarno had, however, suffered a mortal defeat. Suharto, at last, was in charge of the government. In a speech coinciding with the end of the MPRS sitting, he warned that 'anyone who repudiates the decisions of the Fourth General Sitting of the MPRS in any way whatsoever is actually going against the structural basis of the 1945 Constitution'.[97] Shortly thereafter he congratulated Sukarno on his 'largeness of spirit' in accepting the decisions of the Assembly.[98]

The new 27-member Ampera cabinet announced on 25 July after a lengthy series of consultations between Suharto and the parties, student groups and other social groups, was in some senses, as Suharto himself noted, a 'compromise between old and new ways of thinking'.[99] Its major task was to stabilise politics and the economy. Twelve ministers, six of them army men, came from the Armed Forces, but it was not a military regime. The parties were thinly represented (two PNI, two Nahdlatul Ulama), and the remaining civilians were for the most part non-party technocrats, an indication of Suharto's preference for a functionalist approach to government. Suharto himself was appointed chairman of the five-member cabinet presidium and remained minister for defence and security. The triumvirate already established emerged more clearly within the presidium, a 'compact and harmonious team'.[100] The cabinet, Suharto explained, was responsive to the people, and it was very necessary to have 'healthy and constructive opposition, criticism which leads to development, either through the forums of popular representation or the mass media'.[101] Three days later, Sukarno promoted Suharto to the rank of full general.

Suharto, at least publicly, retained his view that Sukarno merited continued respect as President. But in other areas he moved rapidly to strip away the institutions and policies of the Old Order, a move that he must have calculated would tear at Sukarno's legitimacy. He abolished many of the old state bodies which had no constitutional basis but which had served to embellish Sukarno's grip on power, including 'the National Front, Koti (the Supreme Operations Command), as well as Kogam, Kotrar (the Supreme Command for Retooling the Revolutionary State Apparatus), Kolognas (the National Logistics Command) and others'.[102]

SUHARTO'S TEAM

The virtual destruction of Yani's group on 1 October 1965 had allowed Suharto unusual freedom to choose a new staff. True to his custom, he selected a group of men for the most part well known and trusted by him, and with whom he had worked in earlier postings. Of Yani's old staff, only Mursyid and Alamsyah, himself a former junior colleague of Suharto, were made staff officers, respectively as deputy I (operations) and assistant VII (finance). On 3 November, Sugih Arto, Sumitro and Daryatmo were appointed, respectively, assistants I, II and VI. Of more immediate and crucial importance than his military staff was the network of personal assistants which he developed. This small team of army officers, which was formalised around August 1966 as Spri (Personal Staff), provided both intelligence and advice to Suharto. Each member was given a specific brief to cover, such as finance, the economy or intelligence. It was an organisational style closely attuned to Suharto's long experiences of military life, when he had surrounded himself with a small and constant group of close associates, most of whom shared his Central Java heritage.

The leader of Suharto's personal staff was Alamsyah Prawiranegara, intelligence activities came into the purview of Ali Murtopo, once he returned to Jakarta from his travels in Asia (seeking both legitimacy and much-needed funds from Chinese business sources in places like Singapore, Hong Kong and Taiwan) and in Central Java (straightening out the Diponegoro's political problems) in 1966, together with Yoga Sugama, while financial matters, loosely conceived, were in the hands of Sujono Humardani, notwithstanding his lack of formal economics credentials. Murtopo refined and expanded the Opsus (Special Operations) apparatus developed during the Kostrad days, showing special skill in recruiting a network of informal civilian intelligence gatherers. To give it intellectual energy and rigour, he brought in a number of Chinese-Catholic intellectuals, who combined passionate anti-communism and vigorous opposition to any threat of Muslim political ascendancy with the fierce personal discipline and unflinching corporatist ideas imparted to them by their mentor, the Jesuit priest Fr Jopie Beek. Murtopo also received appointment as deputy head of a new state intelligence body, Bakin (State Intelligence Coordinating Body), which replaced Subandrio's BPI. Sujono's earlier experience as Suharto's business agent in Central Java was undoubtedly crucial for his new appointment, as was his unshakeable belief in Suharto himself ('he believed that President Suharto had a mission, a divine calling [*wahyu*] to raise Indonesia to an enhanced order').[103] As Suharto's personal adviser on economics and finance, he was given the task of finding and developing off-budget sources of income for the new regime. Spri comprised six army members at its formal establishment in August 1966, and twelve by 1968.

The consolidation of Suharto's advisers was another manifestation of his growing confidence and control. In the early days after the coup attempt, he had sought advice from a very broad circle of colleagues, a tactic probably associated with his need to keep in touch with different groups and interests as much as with his need for good answers. The increasing tightness of his team of personal assistants – especially after the fading of his early political team with the co-option of its key members, Basuki Rachmat and Sucipto, into the Ampera cabinet, and the considerable latitude he afforded them in the carrying out of their loosely defined tasks – became a source of tension amongst senior officers who found themselves outside the favoured circle. According to Nasution, it insulated Suharto from receiving advice from those supporting a progressive or reformist paradigm of politics for the new regime, notably himself, Kemal and Dharsono.[104]

More remote from his close advisers but of crucial importance in the early New Order was Kopkamtib, which 'emerged as the most feared and oppressive agency of the regime, interfering in the activities of every organization and arresting people at will'.[105] Its special powers authorised local army commanders to arrest without warrant, question, and hold indefinitely those suspected of actions prejudicial to security; Kopkamtib became, in effect, the extra-legal security force of the new regime and was employed constantly in intelligence and security swoops. Local commanders, designated as Kopkamtib operatives (*pelaksana*), continued to carry out security operations under the Kopkamtib banner, even with the removal in 1967 of the Pepelrada (Regional Authority to Implement Dwikora) emergency arrangements.

This combination of an intimate and trusted circle of acquaintances and a tightly controlled but wide-ranging and active internal security force was characteristic of the early New Order. There was, to Suharto's mind, no alternative than to move in this way, given the social and political turbulence and the prevailing uncertainties over political allegiance and control, and his understandable reluctance to use the institutional machinery of the Old Order. The essence of Spri on the one hand, and the upper echelons of Kopkamtib on the other, was a vertically shaped structure of patronage networks. It would be too restrictive, however, to see these developments in purely personal terms. They represented not just the emerging power of Suharto, but also the developing political ascendancy of the Army.

ENDING CONFRONTATION, REJOINING THE WORLD

I have earlier noted that the Army had soft-pedalled the operational aspects of the Malaysian Confrontation since around early October 1964. In the aftermath of the coup, it had restricted its activities in Kalimantan. From the time of the formation of the new cabinet at the end of March 1966, Suharto, employing carefully guarded rhetoric, began to move publicly to bring the conflict to a close and restore normal relations with Malaysia, announcing that Indonesia could accommodate the concept of Malaysia if the peoples of North Borneo really favoured it. The Confrontation policy, in Suharto's view, 'was only a PKI tactic to involve us in as many confrontations as possible so that the PKI could accumulate strength and finally revolt and seize power'.[106] Confrontation had always been a dangerous military strategy for Indonesia, given the strength enjoyed in the air and at sea by the coalition of interests defending Malaysia. In the new context, in Suharto's view, it was essential that Confrontation be put to rest if negotiations for financial assistance from the West were to be successfully mounted.

From around the end of 1965, Suharto charged Ali Murtopo – highly intelligent, persuasive, and with a knack for finding solutions to tricky problems – with putting things to right. Ali, in turn, used the contacts previously established by his Bangkok team, notably with the Indonesian expatriates Des Alwi, Sumitro Joyohadikusumo, and Daan Mogot, to establish formal talks with senior Malaysian figures. At the end of May 1966, secret talks were held in Bangkok between Adam Malik and Tun Abdul Razak, Malaysia's deputy prime minister, which resulted in an agreement to provide Sabah and Sarawak with an opportunity to confirm their participation in Malaysia through elections, to cease hostilities immediately and to resume diplomatic relations. Angry opposition to the deal from Nasution – his view was shared by many other officers in the Armed Forces – who was disturbed that principle had been sacrificed in the negotiations, led to further discussions in which Suharto (anxious that the deal not provide room for Sukarno to manoeuvre or an opportunity for Nasution to resurrect his fortunes) played a prominent role through his proposal of a secret annex appended to the agreement signed on 11 August 1966 to normalise relations. In the end, partly because of Ali Murtopo's propaganda offensive, the rapid winding-down of Confrontation was 'accepted with surprisingly little protest by the politicians and public who had been enthusiastically applauding the slogans of confrontation only a short time before'.[107] Kogam was disbanded on 22 August 1966.

If further indication were needed of Suharto's accelerating confidence in taking issue with Sukarno, it was provided by his decision that Indonesia should rejoin the United Nations 'if the UN has corrected its weaknesses'.[108] According to Sujono, Suharto's answer to his question about Indonesia's attitude to the world body was answered with a single word: 'masuk' (enter). Indonesia was readmitted on 28 September 1966.

THE ARMY SEMINAR, BANDUNG, 1966

The second army seminar held in Bandung in late August 1966 was meant to provide a forum for army leaders to discuss goals and strategies for the new era of Indonesian politics. Suharto, in his opening speech, gave the seminar two tasks: to provide a strategy for stability and to develop methods for economic development.[109] The seminar was to prove of crucial importance to the intellectual content and program of what was to become the New Order; indeed, Suharto later remarked, it 'formulated the "New Order", based on the 1945 Constitution and Pancasila'.[110] According to Sumitro, 'that particular seminar was the main source, if not the only source, of inspiration for the New Order ... The New Order originated in Bandung'.[111]

The seminar, chaired by Panggabean, recently appointed as deputy commander of the Army and promoted to lieutenant general, was strongly influenced by the highly pragmatic and rationalist PSI cast of thinking of Suwarto, who had been a source of constant strategic advice to Suharto since the coup. Also attending the seminar were Western-trained economists such as the 35-year-old dean of the Faculty of Economics at the University of Indonesia, Wijoyo Nitisastro, Mohammad Sadli, Sarbini Sumawinata, Subroto and Emil Salim, together with other Western-trained academics like Selo Sumarjan, who provided the strategic political and economic framework for the early New Order. The seminar itself was organised around three syndicates, dealing with economic, political and military affairs. Thinking within these frames was something new to many members of the military in attendance; according to Sumitro, 'most of us in the Armed Forces, except for those who had affiliated themselves with a political party, knew very little about politics ... ABRI was, in fact, dominantly made up of people like me that had no political breeding'.[112]

Apart from questions of economic policy, politics, and particularly the crucial question of elections, took centre stage. Suharto himself was not enthusiastic about holding early elections, although he conceded the need for them for practical and sociological reasons. Their management, however, raised serious problems: the immediate context of insecurity and volatility was not conducive to the proper exercise of people's democratic rights; and elections might well provide the occasion for the re-emergence of the party politics – and politicians – of the 1950s. However, New Order elections would, he concluded, be very different creatures from those of the 1950s.

First, they would not be 'ideological' in nature. In mid-1966, he noted to a journalist that 'the PKI as a party has been crushed, but perhaps the PKI as an idea lives on. I well know that an idea can't be crushed except with a counter-idea. It is fortunate that the counter-idea which opposes the PKI idea is sufficiently strong in Indonesia, because indeed the PKI idea is foreign for Indonesia which is religious and attached to Pancasila'.[113] Further, 'the sequence of events which made up the whole national crisis which had arisen before 1966 had its origins in deviations from Pancasila and the 1945 Constitution, both in spirit and in practice'.[114] Elections, then, needed to be conducted not only in an atmosphere of security, but also under the ideological umbrella of Pancasila which would assist in ensuring that elections were not themselves the occasion of further instability. Second, measures needed to be taken to hamstring the existing party system; Sarbini Sumawinata, close to Suwarto and a former PSI leader, put forward a mechanism at the army seminar which aimed at breaking, or at least significantly limiting, the power of the Jakarta-based parties. Mindful of the seminar's view that 'the Panca Sila forces must be victorious in the General Elections',[115] he proposed changing the basis of election from the existing proportional system to a single-member district system with a residency provision. Third, the role of the Armed Forces in politics needed to be recognised.

Suharto's own ideas on the function of the military were clear enough by 1966. In that year he told a journalist that

> the situation of members of the military in Indonesia is very different from the situation of the military in Western countries. In Indonesia, the military have two functions, as an armed tool of the state and as a functional group for achieving the purposes of the revolution … thus ABRI takes an active part in political life in the framework of the gotong-royong [mutual help] system customary with our forefathers for thousands of years.[116]

On another occasion, he remarked that it was 'the task of the Armed Forces, especially the Army, to safeguard the state and nation from calamity', and, in his 1966 Armed Forces Day address, that the people placed their 'hopes and belief' in ABRI.[117]

THE TECHNOCRATS, ECONOMIC REFORM, AND ARMY BUSINESS

Perhaps the greatest legacy of the army seminar, however, was that it served as a policy platform for the University of Indonesia economists, most of whom were then teaching at Seskoad. Under Suwarto's guidance, they refined their ideas on the problems of economic stabilisation and presented them to the seminar. This was, for most of them, their first personal meeting with Suharto. Almost completely ignorant of the realm of economic theory, he was deeply impressed with the clarity of their ideas, the unanimity with which they were presented, and their pragmatic sense. He set them to work to develop a program for economic rehabilitation, which resulted in a raft of economic reform measures drafted in consultation with an IMF mission to Jakarta and proclaimed on 3 October 1966. It aimed to balance the budget through raising prices and cutting subsidies, to rein in debt, to reform exchange rate mechanisms, to restrict credit, to re-establish infrastructure and to promote agricultural productivity.[118]

The economists, dubbed 'technocrats', formed a special expert advisory group to Suharto which played a key role in the development of economic policy in the early years of the New Order.[119] Under the skilled convenorship of Wijoyo, their collaborative genius, unity of purpose, international focus, and general orientation to the market provided a stark contrast to the state-centred, enclosed and self-regarding regime of the late Sukarno years, while their political naivety and lack of political ambition suited them perfectly for their role. By contrast, a similarly modelled team of political advisers, headed by Sarbini and containing figures like Deliar Noer and Fuad Hasan, was unable to provide a similarly pragmatic plan for the political realm and soon fell into disuse. The influence of the technocrats' vision was further enhanced when Ali Murtopo, almost certainly at Suharto's prompting, engineered the return in mid-1967 of their mentor, former minister, PSI figure and PRRI rebel Sumitro Joyohadikusumo, from his long period of exile. Indeed, the pragmatic and disciplined cast of mind which characterised the technocrats' economic thinking echoed earlier PSI-type thinking and clearly appealed to the similarly pragmatic and orderly mind of Suharto.

Suharto himself was no economist. But he had seen the social disaffection and shattered morale arising out of Sukarno's continuing neglect of the economy, and had long been convinced of the need for economic development and, as well, the crucial role that such development might play in political pacification; 'all the deteriorations that we experienced [before 1966] had their origins in the neglect of economic development'.[120] On another occasion he noted that 'political stability requires economic development'.[121] He was, however, starting from a very low base. In both 1964 and 1965, essentially for reasons of a political nature, deficit spending had been greater than total government revenue. Massive inflation (600 per cent in 1965), escalating deficits, a collapsing banking and currency system, and huge foreign debt problems – export revenues in 1965 were only a little above the amount scheduled for debt repayment in 1966 – confronted the reformers. In comparison with Sukarno, Suharto had a reasoned, if as yet unsophisticated, response: 'it is necessary that we overcome the problem of stopping inflation, raise production and multiply the means of raising the living standards of the people'. He saw the most important question as 'balancing national income and expenditure'.[122] There was, however, little capacity, either economic or political, for utilising domestic resources and restructuring the domestic economy in the cause of economic development; quite apart from the poverty of the domestic economy, Suharto could not risk alienating either important groups or the general populace by demanding budget sacrifice or wholesale economic mobilisation. His only avenue, then, was to look abroad for the necessary resources.

The main problem was to create a domestic situation which would appear favourable to international investors. To this end, the major focus of attraction was Indonesia's resources, particularly in mining and oil. Adam Malik recalled that 'I was instructed by president Soeharto to tackle the problem of overseas assistance for Indonesian economic development … I traversed the whole outside world …

The results of these lightning trips were followed up and implemented by a team of experts'.[123] Together with the sultan, Malik's reassuring work, especially in Japan and in a United States keen to re-assert its influence in Indonesia, brought quick rewards: foreign aid started to flow, especially after the establishment of the Inter-Governmental Group on Indonesia (IGGI); efforts to renegotiate Indonesia's crippling debt schedule began; and foreign investment – openness to which was 'one of the hallmarks of the economic policies of the new regime'[124] – enticed by the generous conditions enshrined in the Foreign Investment Law introduced early in 1967, began to appear.

It would, however, be gravely mistaken to emphasise the strict observance of a rational economic policy without acknowledging the distorted economic behaviour practised by key figures of the New Order from its earliest inception. Many of the generals who provided the political backbone of the Suharto regime were long accustomed to arbitrary rent-seeking behaviour in their business dealings, often employing the mediating skills of Sino-Indonesian businessmen like 'Bob' Hasan, former golfing partner of the murdered Yani. The Army's political ascendancy now provided unlimited opportunity to enhance the reach and depth of their endeavours, providing a buttress to the developing notion of 'dual function' (*dwi fungsi*); Suharto's old Kostrad command proved an especially effective player. More to the point, Suharto's own track record demonstrated an enthusiasm for the military to embed themselves in business activity, and a proclivity to allow close associates who demonstrated energy and entrepreneurial flair to have their heads. Thus, when in 1966 Ibnu Sutowo, head of the state-owned Permina (from 1968, Pertamina) oil company and director-general for oil and gas, disregarded the authority of Minister for Mining Slamet Bratanata, who had overruled Ibnu's development of production-sharing contracts – 'Indonesia's contribution to the oil world'[125] – with foreign oil companies, Slamet found early in 1967 that Suharto had transferred his ministerial responsibilities over oil to Suharto's personal sphere of responsibility and allowed Ibnu to continue with his activities. Suharto even felt the need to defend Ibnu from charges of corruption ('according to General Harto up to now no one has found any evidence that Ibnu Sutowo has acted corruptly'[126]).

In simple terms, Suharto needed the unscrutinised, off-budget sources of income – amounting perhaps to one-half of actual government expenditures in the New Order's early years – provided by people like Ibnu to gather and cement political support in the Armed Forces and elsewhere. Notwithstanding the formation in 1967 of a Technical Team for Foreign Investment, headed by Sadli, to examine investment applications, that team had no policing powers and was frequently unable to rein in the foreign investment projects with which senior army figures were associated (and which often competed directly with domestic industry). Ibnu Sutowo disdained the technical team altogether. Army smuggling, as well as the well-worn capacity to exploit loopholes in the formal structure of the national economy, exacerbated the problem of reform.

The emergence of such contradictory patterns was not unintended by Suharto. While he clearly grasped the importance of national policy reform on the economic front, he had a shrewd grasp of the dynamics of army politics, and of the need not to alienate important bases of support within the Armed Forces and elsewhere by an overweening economic strictness. In 1967 he was said 'to have admitted privately that he cannot risk alienating the military while the very survival of the government rests largely on their loyalty'.[127] Patronage of this kind found expression, for example, in the granting of a 100 per cent pay rise to public servants and members of the Army in December 1966.

More abstractly, Suharto's own views on the interface of politics and economics were distant from the liberal, market-driven ideas of his economics advisers. Notwithstanding his blessing for the technocrats to carry out their market-oriented reforms, he himself retained a deeply felt corporate vision of Indonesia. 'Our country is a socialist country based on Pancasila', he remarked to a Portuguese journalist in 1966. The freedom of people 'is not an absolute freedom, but limited by societal interests'.[128] Freedom did not include the freedom to harm the happiness of others in the pursuit of one's own happiness. Indonesian socialism was a combination of the individuality loved in the West and the community-driven thinking of the East. Within that corporate context, the unorthodox business activities of his colleagues were, he thought, an efficient means of providing goods and services and, more generally, a higher standard of living, for the common people in whose interests he served.

The result, inevitably, was the emergence of public corruption on a scale heretofore unknown. While Suharto's early legitimacy and, its corollary, the decline of Sukarno's authority, was based at least to some extent on the curious public repute he had attained for honesty, and more particularly for his actions in revealing and punishing the grand corruption of Old Order figures like Yusuf Muda Dalam (see below), questions about the purity of New Order officials and leaders soon began to raise their heads. In response, Suharto, having agreed that the press and the government should cooperate to uncover corruption, in April 1967 revitalised the body he had established early in 1966 to inquire into the corrupt practices of Old Order officials: Pekuneg (Team to Regularise State Finances), under the headship of General Suryo, former chief of finances in Koti and another of Suharto's close associates.

In all this, Suharto moved cautiously, highly sensitive to the potentially devastating capacity of corruption as a political issue. He later remarked that 'corruption as a very potent political issue is easily believed by the public ... We must be careful in facing it, without lessening the effort to prevent and stamp out corruption itself'.[129] Corruption was not and never became a matter over which he agonised or which he made any systematic and convinced effort to address, much to the chagrin of some who championed his 'brilliant leadership'.[130] There was, as well, an enduring suspicion that those who brought charges of corruption were sometimes masking disruptive agendas under the guise of their concern.

TOWARDS VIRTUAL PRESIDENCY

To try those surviving leaders charged with involvement in the coup attempt, Suharto decided to employ the machinery of the special military tribunal

(Mahmillub) which had been established by presidential decree no. 370 of 24 December 1963. On 4 December 1965, Sukarno issued a presidential decision that the leaders of the 30 September Movement should be tried by this court; Suharto was given the power to determine who, on the basis of a preliminary investigation, should be brought before it, as well as its composition. Less than three weeks later, on 21 December, Suharto issued a decision appointing a group of seven generals to determine those members of the Army and those civilians who were to be brought before the tribunal; he reserved for himself the decision in the cases of members of the Air Force, the Police and the Navy. Already on 13 October, he had instructed local Kodam commanders to establish investigating teams to gather evidence on those involved in the 30 September Movement. These teams were formally established on 29 October.[131]

The PKI leader Nyono was the first to face trial on 14 February 1966, enduring day and night sessions in a court convened in the Bappenas building in Menteng. His trial was closely followed by that of Untung. Both men were found guilty and executed, as was Suparjo after his capture and trial in 1967. In these cases, Suharto allowed no mercy, an indication, perhaps, of his vindictiveness against both communist and military participants in the coup attempt, and perhaps, as well, an attempt to make clear to Sukarno his seriousness of purpose. The decision to bring to trial the senior ministers arrested in March was a further means to bring pressure on the President, both by revealing unsavoury aspects of his behaviour and providing a demonstration of his weakening power in that he was unable to constrain such damaging action. The trials were, in fact, a crucial turning-point in the resolution of the political crisis. The first of the ministers arrested earlier in the year, Yusuf Muda Dalam, was sent to trial and, in September 1966, found guilty of corruption and subversion and sentenced to death; he died before the sentence could be carried out. Shortly after, Subandrio was tried; he was found guilty of taking part in the coup attempt of 1 October 1965 and similarly sentenced to death. Omar Dhani's trial provided a platform for the case that Sukarno was involved in, or at least knew about, the coup attempt. The evidence from these trials made widely known the undisciplined behaviour of Sukarno's government and its members, and inevitably reflected unflatteringly upon the President himself.

The trials themselves became a scene of disputation between opposing camps; in one fracas, a student reporter, Zainal Zakse, was shot; he later died in Holland while receiving medical attention for his wounds. Egged on by Kemal Idris and Sarwo Edhie, the students raised the political temperature again, this time demanding that the President be removed and put on trial. Other bodies, including national groups for lawyers and judges, followed their lead. Suharto's refusal to accommodate their wishes saw the first major sign of collapse of the fruitful alliance between Suharto and the students – their former solidarity now rapidly giving way to bitter self-interested factionalism once the butt of their anger, Sukarno, had been pulled down – with Kostrad troops using violent methods to disperse a student demonstration in October 1966. Indeed, in the last part of 1967 and early 1968 there was increasing social disaffection with the direction of the

New Order, caused, amongst other things, by the rising prices of basic essentials (the price of rice tripled between January and November 1967), a sense that the Army was exceeding its proper authority, and the failure to deal with Sukarno. Suharto received a cohort of students early in 1968 to hear their views; 'I agreed with them that fundamental changes must be made, but it had to be done in a constitutional way'.[132]

Now Sukarno's political master, Suharto faced the problem of what to do with his president. No longer, as colleagues like Malik had reportedly been telling him,[133] could he tolerate the continuing rancour and divisiveness that Sukarno generated from his lofty formal position. Despite the political damage suffered by him at the MPRS session, he continued to defy army leaders and to take issue with the new directions of government. Notwithstanding the continuing opposition amongst key army officers to decisive action against the President, and the consequent fear of the outbreak of unrest amongst sectors of the Armed Forces, the pressure upon Suharto to make a determination increased significantly towards the end of 1966 when evidence from both the Yusuf Muda Dalam and Omar Dhani trials – mounted, as we have seen, for just this purpose – suggested Sukarno's failings in duty and perhaps his involvement in the coup attempt.[134]

The trial evidence was yet another blow to Sukarno's now seriously ailing rule. Nonetheless, he continued with his revolutionary rhetoric; the result was a fissuring of society between those who supported him and the forces of the New Order. Suharto clearly understood the sharpening tensions; 'I tried hard to curb things once again so that there would not be a collision between one group of troops and another. Armed conflict would utterly destroy us'. He himself was under increasing pressure from Siliwangi elements, strongly opposed to Sukarno, to take a firmer line with him. Sukarno, for his part, remained steadfast against the increasingly shrill calls to deal with him. In his struggle, he found support amongst army officers in East Java, where a plot was hatched to take him into protective detention during a planned visit to Surabaya to commemorate Heroes' Day (10 November 1966) and build a resistance around his leadership. Sukarno rejected these efforts on his behalf, and Suharto, no doubt apprised of what was afoot, intervened and forbade him to make the journey; 'I saw danger if he flew there. I had to guard the safety and unity of the nation'.[135]

In spite of these pressures, Suharto seemed reticent to act decisively against the badly wounded President. Indeed, according to one commentator, 'if Sukarno had been able to make the conciliatory gestures of the mea culpa that might well have saved his position, Suharto would not have stood in his way'.[136] Suharto's reluctance was, of course, partly a result of his natural caution, but he was also loath to engage in any activity that might give the aggressive Siliwangi group ideas above their station and result in a serious outbreak of fighting between troops opposed to and supportive of Sukarno. As well as the inevitable political calculation so characteristic of Suharto – including the desire not to set a precedent of bringing his predecessor to trial – it seems likely that there remained a substantial residual respect for the person of Sukarno. According to Sumitro, 'Pak Harto was deeply concerned at the situation with Bung Karno … Pak Harto did not want to see Bung Karno hurt in any way. He wanted to do no wrong toward Bung Karno'.[137] Even though Suharto knew that Sukarno had to go, he must have agonised about the enormity of what he was about to do, and the loyalty that had to be usurped to do it.

In the last months of 1966, political tensions magnified with the economic hardships endured by Indonesians and the stubborn refusal of Sukarno to recognise that he must adapt to new circumstances. Voices became louder, suggesting that Sukarno needed to be replaced and that Suharto was the right person for the position. Nasution, for example, called for Sukarno to take responsibility for the 'national tragedies' which had resulted from his policies. Amirmachmud claimed that Sukarno bore responsibility for the deaths of the generals, and raised the question as to whether he should continue as president.[138] Suharto's public position remained unchanged: Sukarno was the legitimate president who deserved respect, no matter what the circumstances. In November he explained that, having studied Sukarno's 17 August 1966 speech and other speeches, he had come to the conclusion that Sukarno had in fact 'condemned G-30-S, although using the term Gestok and ... had not hindered the dissolution of the PKI'.[139] As for himself, he had no ambition for the presidency, and serious doubts about his ability to carry out the task; 'I had never prepared myself for that. I was not educated for that. In fact, I had never dreamed of that. At that time I acknowledged that I lacked the ability to take on that exalted position'.[140]

This was a rather disingenuous stance. Whether he was consciously aware of it or not, all his actions since mid-1966 had been an effective de-legitimation of the President, which could have no other path than his removal. By December, with the conclusion of the Omar Dhani trial, this view was gaining more and more strength: student action groups accused Sukarno of involvement in G.30.S; newspapers published unflattering accounts from the trial of his behaviour at Halim on 1 October 1965; and Mashuri asserted that Sukarno was 'clearly involved' in the coup attempt, accusing him as well of cowardice at the time of the Dutch attack on Yogya.[141] A statement issued by ABRI on 21 December and signed by Suharto and the other service chiefs – promising action against anyone, no matter his position, who did not follow the decisions of the MPRS and the Constitution – was a thinly veiled threat against Sukarno, and was the catalyst for a series of meetings between him and Suharto, at which Suharto clearly placed pressure upon the President to reassess his situation. After tense discussion with cabinet and military leaders, Sukarno finally agreed to supplement his Nawaksara report, which he did in written form to the MPRS on 10 January 1967. It added little to his previous statements, opened up no possibilities to resolving the increasing tension and, indeed, served to raise it to new heights. Around the same time, Suharto appointed 108 new members to the DPR-GR, bringing its membership to 350. The Siliwangi radicals began to make military preparation for what they saw as a final and inevitable showdown between anti- and pro-Sukarno supporters; Nasution himself called for Sukarno to be put on trial,[142] and in West Java, the regional parliament suggested to MPRS leaders that Sukarno be stood down and replaced by Suharto, a step shortly after emulated by the DPR-GR.

Large and well-reported student demonstrations – in one of which Suharto's jeep was caught up – called for Sukarno to be put on trial. Adam Malik called for the use of Supersemar 'to end the political dualism'.[143]

The President, however, still enjoyed strong Armed Forces sympathy, especially amongst the marines (KKO), within the Navy and the Police (including the respective service commanders) and amongst troops in East and Central Java, East Kalimantan, and parts of Sumatra. Should Sukarno be dealt with roughly, the threat of internal army and inter-service conflict was substantial. Suharto, ever mindful of the potential for instability should Sukarno be provided with an opportunity for martyrdom, responded by effusing smiling charm and preaching the need for unity, while at the same time threatening swift retribution to those who would move against him. He ordered a slow-paced investigation into Sukarno's alleged involvement to continue its work; it was never brought to a conclusion.

The breakthrough came from East Java. On 3 February, a group of former Brawijaya officers, members of the 'great Brawijaya family', led by current commander Sumitro, went to see Sukarno and expressed a vague solidarity with him. Sarbini, a former Brawijaya panglima, who had not attended that meeting, sought and received permission from Suharto to speak with Sukarno on 5 February. It may be that the impetus for Sarbini's approach came from Suharto himself. It seems clear, notwithstanding a probably mischievous piece of press reporting, that Sukarno was told by these officers that his support in East Java was waning, and that he had to come to a resolution of the difficulties surrounding his position. Their move signified that pro-Sukarno forces within the Armed Forces had reluctantly concluded that Sukarno could no longer be saved, and that their own position would be at risk if they continued in their obstinate support for him. At a University of Indonesia graduation ceremony in February 1967, Suharto's message was clear: 'As the commander of the Armed Forces, at this opportunity I want to make it clear that ABRI has clearly expressed that it stands resolutely on the side of the New Order. This stance of ABRI is not just an expression, but it will be carried out with effect'.[144] Kostrad commander Umar himself warned on 6 February that the Army's 'patience is reaching its limits'.[145]

On 7 February, through the PNI figure Hardi, Sukarno sent two letters to Suharto.[146] The more important one was an offer to allow Suharto to take over the day-to-day activities of the government but, in doing so, to keep in a close consultative relationship with the President, who would remain as state leader and continue to determine the general thrust of policy. Suharto, now confident that his quarry was within his sights and could be dealt with more or less on his own terms – and in the context of the parliament's 9 February call for a special MPRS session to dismiss the President – rejected Sukarno's proposal on 10 February. Over the next nine days, a series of meetings between Sukarno, army leaders, and the other service commanders seemed to have ended in deadlock. On the twentieth, Suharto finally managed to persuade Sukarno and his service supporters that he was finished. His successful negotiation, which involved staring down Sukarno's last-ditch attempt to preserve something by requiring him to consult Sukarno over the exercise of his authority, probably involved Suharto's ensuring that the President's going would be handled as gently as possible and would not be followed by judicial proceedings against him. On the same day, Sukarno agreed to transfer his powers to Suharto.

With the public announcement on 22 February of Sukarno's decision to transfer his powers to Suharto, there remained only the formalities. The following day, the DPR-GR passed the resolution introduced on 15 February, requesting a special session of the MPRS to appoint Suharto as acting president. Suharto, ever alert to the possibility of division and disruption, called a meeting of 500 senior officers 'to explain to them what had actually happened. That night I gave a speech to the far reaches of the country. I maintained peace and quiet'.[147] The speech, an exhortatory mix of satisfaction with what had been achieved and a reminder of the challenges still to be surmounted, was short and unembellished. The mild queries raised about the constitutionality of what had been arranged were drowned in a general wave of support.[148]

On the cusp of his triumph, Suharto was already busy creating his legacy. In a manner unknown in previous years, celebrations were held to mark the anniversary of the 1 March 1949 attack on Yogyakarta. The sultan attended the Yogya celebration, and Suharto himself donated large quantities of tools and cloth to guerrilla veterans who took part in the remembrance celebrations in Yogya. The commemoration of 1 March 1949 was held 'throughout the region of Central Java and centred in Yogyakarta where tens of generals and other officers attended'.[149]

With intense pressure, emanating from Suharto himself, the Army and the government, now placed upon the special session of the MPRS, there was no question but that it would eject Sukarno. What was at issue was the mode of his dismissal. When the session opened on 7 March, Suharto, anxious to avoid Sukarno's prosecution, sought to minimise Sukarno's connection with G.30.S, framing the President's actions as matters of political and moral misjudgement. He sought a compromise resolution which had the effect of retaining for Sukarno the title of president, but which removed from him any capacity to exercise the powers constitutionally tied to the post and removed him from political life. It conferred on Suharto the title of 'acting President' – he was sworn in by MPRS Speaker Nasution – until such time as an MPR (People's Consultative Assembly) resulting from general elections should appoint a president, and it left him with the task of deciding whether further action should be taken against Sukarno.

This solution, agreed to on 12 March, was exquisitely ambiguous in legal terms, but in reality a simple one. As Suharto remarked in a clarificatory speech on 13 March, 'for the time being we will treat him as a president who no longer has power, as a president who has no authority of any kind in the fields of politics, the state, and government'.[150] Starkly aware of the dangers of serious unrest that still lurked, Suharto was content with what he had achieved, and manifested no interest in stripping the President of his formal title at this time or sending him off for trial. He had, no doubt, provided assurances that those who had supported Sukarno would not suffer maltreatment. He and his supporters knew that Sukarno was finished. Indeed, General Sumitro had begun hanging pictures of Suharto in public offices even before the March 1967 MPRS meeting. As if playing out a surreal fiction, in the immediate aftermath of the special session, Suharto stuck scrupulously to the legal form – and its consequent protocol – that Sukarno remained president.

The moment was notable for a curious lack of triumph and celebration. Before the MPRS session, Suharto made much at this time of his lack of ambition, his weakness, his inability to shoulder the heavy burdens of the office. According to Sumitro, 'Pak Harto was reluctant to become President'.[151] Such pretended modesty reflected, perhaps, a certain lack of confidence in his acceptability at this time as a replacement for Sukarno and, as well, a desire to mask what was clearly a gathering sense of ambition and of destiny. Underneath, however, he knew as keenly as anyone else that there was no other serious candidate for the office, and sought simply to secure a general supportive consensus before taking the final step. He held all the trump cards in his hand, and he knew it. Self-absorbedly, he was later to remark that 'eventually they were able to convince me that they really couldn't find anyone else. They didn't trust anyone else as much as me'. It was, as he saw it, a challenge to assist the people at a time of dire need, to rise to the occasion and sacrifice himself in their name. To do otherwise would have been an act of cowardice. He would proceed, on condition that he enjoyed the trust of the people as voiced by their various leaders: 'they trusted me. Finally, that trust became the key that opened the door of my heart to say "yes"'. In the end, Suharto claims, he accepted the task, but on condition only that it be as acting president for one year; 'we would use that period for mutual evaluation: whether I was capable, whether half way through there would be a change of mind, or another choice'.[152]

His insistence on accepting the post of acting president for a specified period was in one sense a measure of his patience. But providing himself with the option of withdrawing gracefully should the task prove too much or his authority ebb also revealed his own lack of self-assuredness. As well, there was a sense of strategic caution. It was, as he had always thought, 'better to go slowly but with the certainty of achieving results, rather than too quickly and achieve nothing'. His attitude also inaugurated what was to become a recurrent theme of his presidency: a claim that should he lose the people's confidence, he would gladly step aside – 'I would not defend my position, let alone do so by armed force. I would never do such a thing'.[153]

It would be wrong to see Suharto's accession to the acting presidency as the result of naked ambition. It is probably true that he would have been content, in other circumstances, to serve out his military career as a good, efficient, responsible, if somewhat dour, senior officer. But when the circumstances changed so radically on 1 October 1965, and when he found himself thrust into the central role, he enjoyed it, indeed thrived on the challenge and the excitement and respect that came his way. He found he liked being in control, while never at this stage forgetting that it might all come crashing down. So he came to the position with a fierce but ambivalent ambition. He would do it, even if he did not want to, out of duty and provided he had the support of his fellows. He was not prepared to fight for power in a competition with others, nor was he willing to throw himself into the dangers and uncertainties of seizing power through illegal and probably violent means. He would do it on his own terms, in his own style, at his own pace, and in a way that respected constitutional and procedural niceties. But he would do it. In coming to this decision, no doubt, as he claims, he sought the advice and comfort of his wife.[154] She was, undoubtedly, at least as keen as he to take up the challenge.

CHARTING THE NEW ORDER

Once Suharto was formally ensconced in the highest function of the state, his political style began to show a new edge; as he later put it, his 'fighting spirit emerged'. He saw his task as transforming society in such a way as to end the period of tumult and division, and restoring order and certainty to the political and social domains. He was no doubt assisted in this by an enormous release of the tensions which had gripped political and social life uninterruptedly since mid-1965; indeed, the traumas of the post-coup period were themselves pivotal in creating a polity that was ideologically much flatter and immensely more numbed and inert. The charade of Sukarno's pretended position rapidly began to slip away, and it soon became evident that he was under a form of house arrest ('political quarantine', as Suharto later called it) at the Bogor Palace.[155] The right to use his presidential and associated titles was stripped away by Suharto in May; his photographs soon after began to disappear from government offices. Suharto forbade him to use the state palace in Jakarta to celebrate his sixty-sixth birthday. On 29 June, the government issued a clarification that Sukarno was no longer president and was not permitted to use his titles of Head of State and President of the Republic.

In his characteristic manner, Suharto began to devote himself single-mindedly to learning the knowledge and skills the presidency demanded. The revolutionary rhetoric which he had often used to defend his actions on 1 October had now completely disappeared, replaced by other ideological incantations, notably Pancasila and modernisation/development, and which emphasised mental toughness and attitudinal correctness in overcoming difficulties.[156] The momentum for political reform of an emancipatory kind was beginning to be revealed for the illusion it was. At the same time, he began occasionally to wear civilian apparel rather than his military uniform. In a further concession to his emerging status, he had in March 1966 moved house from Jl. Haji Agus Salim 98 to a modest bungalow in a narrow street nearby, Jalan Cendana, which offered much better security, and where alterations, additions and expansion provided space for official functions. He continued to work out of the office of the presidium building on Medan Merdeka Barat 15. Unlike Sukarno, he refused to live at the Merdeka Palace because, he remarked, he wanted his family to enjoy a certain amount of freedom and not to forgo their home life. His deep attachment to his children was genuine enough, as were his efforts to impart his own values to them. His new responsibilities, however, meant that he could not give his children the attention they needed; Sumitro later remarked that 'it was only after he became President that I noticed he was losing control of his family … He had no more time to devote to his family'.[157]

Ironically, as Suharto emerged from the confusion of the previous year and a half, his longer-term position was by no means assured. His administration was perceived as indecisive and ineffective. Numerous senior officers had merely tolerated his rapid rise, in the absence of any alternative, and were keen to gauge how he handled his new authority. The PKI showed signs of a militant resurgence, establishing a resistance base in the south-central region of East Java, around Blitar, and expanding its activities amongst Chinese communities in West Kalimantan. His economic tasks seemed clear enough, as he suggested in a speech to a Bogor economic seminar shortly after his appointment as acting president: stabilising the economy, curbing inflation, and ironing out pricing problems.[158] In April 1967, the work began in earnest for the development of a new five-year economic plan. But prices continued their rise, and many Indonesians increasingly felt the pinch; rice prices, in particular, rose precipitately towards the end of 1967, causing Suharto to stage a visit to Jakarta rice markets to enquire about the source of price hikes. The lowering of interest rates in April 1967 was, indeed, an attempt to come to grips with the deflationary effects of the October 1966 credit policy. Professor Sumitro Joyohadikusumo noted that 'conditions have not improved during the nine months since the [October] reforms were introduced. As time passes, criticism of the basic economic policies of the Suharto Government is mounting'.[159] Rebellion was still in the air, evidenced by an apparent plot in July 1967 to restore Sukarno to power, and reports the following year of a foiled 'communist plot to assassinate Suharto, members of his cabinet and army leaders'.[160] Moreover, the New Order seemed to be falling prey to the same sins of corruption as the Old, while its military backbone was spreading its members and its influence inexorably across the apparatuses of the state.

These circumstances probably left Suharto little alternative but to adopt a more direct and in some ways less accommodating approach, which emphasised a return to social and military discipline, the importance of social harmony, and a continued striving for economic reform. Indeed, his frequent, hectoring speeches on these themes were couched in terms of continuing struggle and sacrifice, of the need for social solidarity in pursuit of the general good, of accomplishments which, though solid, were not sufficient for the need. In mid-1967, the four Java commanders, together with the commanders of Kostrad and the RPKAD, swore an oath in Yogyakarta to take action against anyone defying Pancasila or the 1945 Constitution. The following month, Suharto characterised the Army as the tool of the state to defend and protect the revolution. The Army crushed the East Java-based revival in 1968 and moved at the same time against the PKI resurgence within Chinese communities in West Kalimantan. Notwithstanding the ease of the Army's victories, the strongly propagated notion – no doubt fanned by Suharto – that the PKI remained a long-term threat to the nation's political stability provided the authorities with the capacity to tar centres of opposition with the PKI brush, to remind the people of the terrors of the post-coup period, and to portray itself as a continuing and vigilant guarantee against a possible return to disorder.

However, a more fundamental – and, indeed, longstanding – reason for Suharto's virulent opposition to the PKI was that it could not be accommodated within the kind of society he envisaged for Indonesia. That society, as he began to rehearse in numerous speeches, was to be one based on Pancasila, in which the nation's citizens would live in harmony and tolerance with one another by ignoring those things that divided them; 'the New Order is an order of Pancasila Democracy which puts the people's interest first and not group or private interests'. Indeed, he said upon another occasion, the New Order 'pursues institutionalisation and rejects individualisation', which meant that the press should relate 'political news which prioritised the interests of the people, the country and the state above the private interests of leaders, such as we experienced in the period of the Old Order'.[161] He called, as well, for a 'national conception of education' which 'can guarantee the realisation of Pancasila' amongst pupils. Those with an inappropriate attitude towards the 1945 Constitution and Pancasila would find themselves opposed by ABRI. 'We must', he noted in May 1967, 'defend Pancasila and the 1945 Constitution'.[162] At his inaugural Independence Day speech in 1967 – at which he broke with tradition by delivering a staid and lengthy 'state of the nation' address to the DPR-GR on 16 August rather than a colourful Sukarno-style exhortation speech on 17 August – he established the framework of the New Order, employing the word 'Pancasila' no less than sixty-four times.[163] The Old Order had deviated from Pancasila and the 1945 Constitution.

Suharto had, however, no radical vision for his New Order; it was a very conservative view in which the status quo had been altered to reflect the realities of power after 1 October. Change was something to be avoided, a path to be proceeded upon only as required and with great caution. It was a peculiarly self-centred, even smug, rendition of politics. In a speech on 23 October, he noted that there was no need any longer to discuss the issue of ideology, 'because we already have one ideology, Pancasila'.[164] In early 1968, a ban on demonstrations in Jakarta was imposed; demonstrations against high rice prices, Suharto suggested, were essentially political, not economic.[165]

The obverse of his violent anti-communism, however, was the need to minimise social difference and strive for social harmony amongst the myriad groups of Indonesian society. In the case of the 'Chinese problem', this policy required Indonesians of Chinese descent to forsake a separate identity and assimilate into the larger population. In a 1967 speech (partly a reaction to a large demonstration by alien Chinese in Jakarta in April, and a violent Indonesian response) on the 'Chinese problem', Suharto reminded his listeners that

> we must draw a clear line between foreign Chinese citizens and Indonesian citizens of Chinese descent. Notwithstanding their foreign descent, Indonesian citizens of foreign descent are Indonesian citizens, who have the same status, rights and duties as indigenous Indonesian citizens. We appealed to Indonesian citizens of Chinese descent not to keep on delaying their integration and assimilation into indigenous

> Indonesian society. With regard to foreign Chinese citizens, they would be treated in the same way as other foreigners, in accordance with prevailing international customs, but without our lessening our vigilance against the possibilities of subversion and infiltration.[166]

In December of the same year he took up the theme of religious tolerance: 'we all have a duty to practise religious tolerance, because religion takes its starting point in the conviction which adheres in one's innermost being. Therefore, religious conviction should not be forced, particularly not from the outside'.[167] In March 1968, he extended the period during which Indonesian citizens using Chinese names could change them into 'Indonesian' names. What these policies meant, in effect, was that, while Indonesians of Chinese descent enjoyed the same rights as indigenous Indonesians, they had to practise their religion and celebrate their Chinese heritage in private, they were pressured to change their names to Indonesian-sounding names, their access to Chinese-language newspapers was virtually removed, and the use of Chinese characters in public forbidden.

These contradictory tendencies expressed themselves in other ways as well. In October 1967, Suharto reshuffled his Ampera cabinet, removing the presidium and decreasing the cabinet's size to twenty-three members, and dropping the unfortunate Slamet Bratanata as well as Harjasudurja, both of whom had made the fatal mistake of attempting to restrain army business interference in state affairs. About the same time, Suharto began a long-lasting formal involvement with the Sino-Indonesian Liem Siu Liong, until then a 'moderately successful Jakarta businessman'.[168] Bank Windu Kencana, long Liem's financing vehicle, underwent a large-scale restructure; as a result, two members of Suharto's personal staff, Sujono Humardani and Suryo Wiryohadiputro, were appointed to the bank's board, entitling them to shares from the bank's profits. Suharto's patronage of Liem – continuing his earlier practice of seeking strategic business partnerships with a small and select circle of Sino-Indonesian businessmen – is probably best explained by his general personal preference for dealing in important matters with only a very small circle of highly trusted colleagues with whom he enjoyed strong personal links. That preference also became more strongly manifest in the sphere of politics through 1967, with the developing influence of the Spri group on policy, and the tightening of the circle of advisers around Suharto, of whom the most prominent were Panggabean, Basuki Rachmat and Ibnu Sutowo. By the early months of 1967, complaints were beginning to emerge that Suharto was being cordoned off and isolated from visitors and guests by scheming advisers.[169]

The discordances of domestic politics were also reflected in Suharto's probably distracted efforts at foreign policy, an arena which, he himself admitted, was not as important as that of the primary task of economic stabilisation and rehabilitation.[170] The severely strained relations with China ('caused by provocation on the part of the People's Republic of China')[171] which had emerged after the coup attempt did not, thanks to the pleadings of Adam Malik, lead to a formal break in diplomatic ties, although relations were effectively frozen in 1967, and Suharto dismissed the dual-nationality treaty with China. However, Suharto was at the same time keen to build relations with the states within Indonesia's immediate area of influence, ties that were to be based, he said, on mutual interest and not differences in ideology and domestic political practice. Indonesia would staunchly refuse to enter military pacts, and would not align itself with any particular country in opposition to another.[172] The result was the construction of the Association of South East Asian Nations (ASEAN) in August 1967. Indonesia, he stressed, had no territorial ambitions 'because this would contravene Pancasila and the 1945 Constitution'.[173]

PARTIES AND ELECTIONS

In order to fulfil the order of the 1966 session of the MPRS regarding elections, three bills, drawn up after the conclusion of the army seminar in Bandung, were eventually submitted to the DPR-GR early in 1967. They sought to establish the basic rules regarding the political parties, the mechanisms to be followed in holding elections, and the composition of the MPR, the DPR and the regional assemblies. Already this schedule lagged far behind that proposed by the MPRS, because the political realm was both so flexible and open-ended and so fragile. Moreover, the proposals immediately ran into a hail of opposition within the DPR-GR, well stocked with party politicians, because they were a barely veiled attack on the parties and, indeed, the old political party system. This should have come as no surprise, since army leaders, including Suharto, were deeply suspicious of parties and party politicians, and they were not about to hand over the fruits of victory to civilian politicians. The parties, for their part, were angry not just because of the implications of the proposed laws – based on the single-member constituency district system, they would favour locally popular candidates with no attachment to parties rather than party-sponsored candidates – but also because some of them, notably Nahdlatul Ulama, were conscious of their contribution in destroying the PKI and inaugurating the New Order, and expected a suitably generous political reward.

In general terms, there were three approaches to election matters. In the first place, the so-called New Order radicals, headed by H. R. Dharsono and including Kemal Idris, Sarwo Edhie, Juarsa, Witono and Solihin, as well as a PSI-inspired group of secular civilian intellectuals, wanted to see the complete destruction of civilian-dominated party politics. They sought, successfully in some cases, to dissolve local PNI bodies, notwithstanding Suharto's view that the PNI should not be demolished.[174] In their view, politics should be non-ideological, a narrowly constricted contest between different forces in society, assembled according to their role in society and committed to the development and modernisation of society; indeed, Dharsono took the step of enforcing the emergence of 'non-ideological' programmatic groups in West Java in 1967.[175] A second group, headed by the students of the 1966 generation and their older liberal colleagues, sought a return to the 'free-fight' liberal system of the early and mid-1950s. From the debates between these forces, a third grouping emerged, which wanted to contain the social mobilisation and dissension of the parliamentary democracy period, and to give a voice to functional groups in society, but also saw the real dangers in uprooting and dissolving the existing political parties based, at least in part, on modern renderings of primordial sentiments, and with broad and deep constituencies amongst the people. This group was also concerned, as Suharto himself noted, that the elections 'must be won by the New Order by means of an honest democratic procedure [*melalui suatu demokrasi yang jujur*]'.[176]

After considerable debate the third group, which included Suharto, triumphed. There would be no fundamental change to the political order, notwithstanding the considerable pressure for change from students and army reformers. Change, such as it was, would be limited, and carefully managed to maintain stability. In a speech of 4 July 1967, Suharto had expressed the view that political parties were an important tool of Pancasila democracy. Towards the end of 1967 he allowed greater freedom for the PNI in those areas where its activities had been limited and instructed local commanders to assist PNI efforts to reform itself and, after some prevarication around his refusal to permit new Muslim parties, agreed to the formation of a new modernist Islamic party, Parmusi, early in 1968. The function of parties, however, needed to be circumscribed, not just for the sake of economic development but also in the interests of appropriate and stable politics. Pancasila democracy, according to Suharto, was a democracy which mirrored and represented the interests of the people as a whole; it was not to be thought of as a field for competition between political parties in which sectionally based majorities would rule. In July 1967, a compromise was reached which manifested the defeat of the New Order radicals; it retained proportional representation, removed residency requirements, and at the same time allowed the government to appoint significant proportions of the MPR and DPR. Further delays came with the necessity of redrafting the laws on the basis of the July compromise, and with the inevitable political debate which accompanied it. On 10 January 1968, Suharto reported to the MPRS that the elections could not be held at the time stipulated by the 1966 MPRS session.[177]

But the elements were now in place for the holding of elections which might serve to provide some popular legitimacy to the Suharto government. Some more perspicacious civilians, however, remained suspicious: 'Was it possible for a military man [Suharto] to be more democratic than a man like Sukarno, who had thought about freedom and its problems for a long time while fighting to free the nation from colonialism?'[178]

FULL PRESIDENT

Early in 1968, the final steps in the long-drawn-out drama which brought Suharto to power were played out. In February and March, he sought to place his stamp indelibly on the fluid political situation by reorganising the parliament and the MPRS, replacing members alleged to be connected in some way to the 30 September Movement, reallocating empty seats to party members, giving seats to the action fronts, and increasing the representation of military men and 'functional groups'.[179] Such treatment exemplified the narrow understanding of participatory politics held by Suharto and his supporters; real power was held and exercised outside the representative chambers.

Notwithstanding his earlier modesty on the matter, Suharto's ascension to the fullness of the presidency was, by now, no more than a formality. He had worked ruthlessly and unremittingly to overcome 'the problem of the unity of ABRI [which] always influences my thinking' and cement his control.[180] No serious political competitor had emerged; indeed, apart from a few allegedly communist-inspired anti-government posters which appeared in Surabaya in January, and student action front demonstrations against high rice prices, there was scarcely a whiff of opposition to his continuing rule. Accordingly, at the fifth MPRS session in March 1968 – brought forward by the reconfigured DPR at his request, and secured by Jakarta commander Amirmachmud's efficient quashing of civilian protest – Suharto was elected President of the Republic for a full five-year term, and commissioned to continue his work of stabilising the nation's politics and raising its economic performance by means of a Five-Year Plan. Speaking immediately after his swearing-in on 27 March, Suharto, dressed in civilian clothes and with a *peci* (black brimless cap) on his head, emphasised the twin notions of development with freedom and constitutionality with democracy.[181] So much was the ceremony a formality that he left early the next morning for visits to Japan and Cambodia, the first time he had travelled abroad since 1961.

The MPRS session was not, however, an undiluted triumph. Held behind closed doors for the most part, the Assembly insisted on defining Suharto's emergency powers more tightly, notwithstanding the persuasive efforts of his political operatives, led by Ali Murtopo. The session was unable to agree on the broad guidelines of state policy, because of the deep-seated division between secular delegates and Muslim representatives who sought to insert key guarantees for Muslims. Disputes also sank a proposal to define and protect the rights and duties of citizens, while Suharto's Supersemar powers were clarified and restricted. Elections, postponed for three years instead of the planned five years, were scheduled to be held before July 1971. Outside the chamber, a strong military presence – thirty battalions under the command of Amirmachmud – before and during the sitting, and their vigorously efficient handling of student protesters, made a curious contrast with Suharto's protestations about democratic process.[182] It marked the final, bitter and ignominious defeat of those civilian groups which had originally aligned themselves with him in the hope of creating a more open political system. The coercion employed at the MPRS session marked the end of the civilian–military coalition which had helped him to power, and revealed a more coercive edge to New Order power. Sukarno, old, ill, dying, and denied freedom of movement, wrote to Suharto to congratulate him on his election as president.[183]

CONCLUSION

It took many of the Jakarta elite some time to realise that the cool, restrained, taciturn, and ever-smiling Suharto had grown into a devastating, ruthless, manipulative politician who had managed by shrewd calculations of timing, bluff and threat to dethrone the father of Indonesian nationhood and himself attain the highest office in the nation within thirty months of the 1 October affair.

This extraordinary rise to power by one whose career, before 1965, had been marked by workmanlike competence, little sign of political ambition or preference for political involvement, a sensitivity to publicity, a stolid, unattractive public face and a demeanour which contrasted sharply with the charismatic Sukarno, cries out for explanation. It is partly to be explained by the absence of any serious competition, especially when Sukarno was brought down by his overreaching refusal to accommodate himself to the new realities of the political situation after 1 October. Nasution, alone amongst the senior generals after the coup attempt had devastated their numbers, had the legitimacy to challenge him, but not the stomach for the fight nor the active support of the Army's senior echelons, especially once Suharto made it clear that he would not interfere with, and would indeed enhance with bounteous patronage, army business interests. The skilful manipulation of the political arena by Suharto and his close supporters made the emergence of a significant civilian opponent impossible. Most of all, however, it was his skill and patience in exploiting the appropriate political moments that told in his favour. He was careful to do so in a manner that could be defended as being in accord with formal constitutional procedures, nursing (or, as required, forcing) his cause through three sessions of the MPRS, the only body with the power to make and unmake presidents. He was careful not to act in such a way that his individual weight in the scale of politics was unduly magnified.

Patience, stubbornness and calculation were Suharto's watchwords – pushing forward when he saw openings, holding ground when opportunities closed, orchestrating the isolation and departure of potential obstacles or troublemakers. Sometimes this attitude brought upon him the criticism that he was too reticent, modest or indecisive; his response was that certain tasks needed to be done softly. As a senior technocrat later remarked, 'This is one thing I have learned during my years working with the President: to stick to my main objectives while manoeuvring to get things done'.[184] In the doing, Suharto had managed to carve out a reputation as an achiever, one who would, in the end, deliver the necessary results.

7 Legitimation and consolidation, 1968–1973

WE SAW THAT NO sooner had he been sworn in than, in company with his wife, President Suharto left for an official visit to Japan, leaving the sultan in charge of the day-to-day affairs of the government. In two rounds of official talks with Prime Minister Sato and elsewhere, Suharto was at pains to seek enhanced economic assistance from Japan for the task of economic development. The attempt, however, was a rather embarrassing failure. Suharto, on the advice of Alamsyah, who had organised the venture, had been expecting the Japanese to commit a large sum, more than US$100 million, in aid to Indonesia, but the best that he could extract from them was an undertaking to consider increasing their aid, without specifying any amounts, in the current year; no final communiqué was signed. Notwithstanding his disappointment with the Japanese response, the trip gave Suharto a first chance to press internationally his ideas about Indonesia's foreign policy and its place in the world. In Cambodia, for example, which he visited after Japan, Suharto made clear his view that 'the nations of Southeast Asia should remain free to choose their values consonant with their own interests and desires'.[1]

THE FIRST DEVELOPMENT CABINET

Suharto was now president of one of the largest and most complex nations on earth; it was just two-and-a-half years since he had been catapulted from obscurity. Now he was charged and authorised to guide his massive and unwieldy country. With his long-polished sense of orderliness, he began increasingly to dress in civilian clothes, eschewing the uniform with which he had become so closely associated in the public eye over the previous thirty months.

Amongst his first tasks as president was to name a new cabinet, termed the First Development Cabinet to set it apart from previous ones which had emphasised various aspects of ideologically inspired social engineering. It was 'a combination of experts from university circles and members of the Armed Forces',[2] and the result of a long period of discussion and negotiation with military leaders and party and non-party civilians. The new cabinet, comprising eighteen portfolio ministers and five ministers of state, was announced on 6 June 1968, Sukarno's sixty-seventh birthday. Its military membership was reduced from nine to six, and many of the civilian members were noted for their expertise and academic distinction. As a general rule, the military men were placed in positions where security was a sensitive issue; where the economy needed attention, Suharto appointed his technocratic advisers. Sumitro Joyohadikusumo – shocked at the magnitude of Indonesia's economic decline during his long absence – was appointed minister for trade, to a mixture of applause and some hints of opposition to his elevation, and Ali Wardhana as minister for finance. Frans Seda, previously finance minister, was transferred to the Communications portfolio after pressure from Muslim commercial interests was brought to bear upon him.[3]

In Suharto's mind, the early New Order faced three major challenges: economic improvement, the development of a political system based upon the principles of the 1945 Constitution (which included 'a healthy democracy, the rule of law [*negara hukum*], and a constitutional system', and combating the continuing threat of communism.[4] Suharto was firmly attached to the notion that the people of Indonesia had suffered unduly because of his predecessor's predilection for playing politics. For him, as he told members of action fronts in March 1968, 'the most important problem in this period is development'.[5] His own reign would be characterised by an unrelenting search for means to increase the wealth and prosperity of the mass of Indonesians, and thus he entrusted the technocrats, under Wijoyo, with developing the first of a rolling series of five-year plans to rebuild and enhance Indonesia's ruined economy. Suharto always envisaged that his concept of staged development, leading towards industrialisation, would take at least a generation to achieve. The MPRS had provided his new government with no broad guidelines, leaving the new president a free hand to move as he wished. In his view, there were five key goals: 'political stability, including the conduct of foreign policy; general elections; the restoration of order and security; reform and cleansing of the state apparatus and economic stability with the first five-year development plan'.[6]

The cabinet itself was not designed to provide the impetus to drive the simple Suharto formula of security and development. It took the form, rather, of a meeting of ministers, assembled much as it had been during the Sukarno regime, although more regularly (on a monthly basis), to hear the directions of its chairman, to receive ministerial reports (which Suharto encouraged to be short and to the point), and to gain a general sense of the government's agenda. The rambling monologues of his predecessor were replaced by a businesslike purpose, which the astute, disciplined and hardworking cabinet secretary, the military lawyer Sudharmono ('very adept at taking advantage of opportunities when they presented themselves') did much to foster,[7] and where Suharto's grasp of detail and insistence on clear and firm outcomes were in evidence. Sometimes Suharto invited non-cabinet members to attend, especially where their expertise was thought necessary for the purposes of advice or to clinch an issue. The decisions that cabinet made were nearly always prefaced by wide-ranging discussion, subsequently neatly summarised by Suharto, and were of the nature of generalised endorsements of broad parameters of action. Suharto, true to his suspicious and secretive nature, as well as his long-ingrained habits of staff work, preferred problematic discussions to take place in smaller groups at more subterranean levels of government.

Suharto had taken the opportunity in June 1968 to apply cosmetic surgery to his personal staff arrangements in the face of growing student and press criticism that they exercised excessive influence upon policy matters. He disbanded his close advisory group, Spri; the three most important and influential of his advisers, all members of the Army, were thereafter designated as 'personal assistants' (Aspri). Amongst them were Sujono Humardani (already promoted to brigadier-general the previous year), who provided a sounding-board for Suharto on issues of finance and politics generally as well as serving as his personal messenger, and Ali Murtopo, head of Opsus. Other key former members of Spri were placed in influential advisory and administrative positions close to the centre of things. Suharto trusted these men deeply; they were made to feel that they held special personal responsibility for the tasks he allotted them. They repaid him with unwavering loyalty and devotion, and their preponderant influence over his decisions seemed to become increasingly great. Alamsyah, however, had made the mistake of misleading Suharto on the preparedness of the Japanese to provide financial assistance to Indonesia, or so Suharto perceived it. While he remained state secretary, a post to which he had been appointed early in 1968, his influence had already begun to wane, and he failed to secure appointment as an Aspri. Sujono Humardani quickly replaced him as Suharto's Japan adviser and bridge-builder. Spri and, to a lesser extent, Aspri were manifestations not just of the institutional weakness and divisions within Indonesian politics, but also of Suharto's desire to be surrounded by close and trusted colleagues who could ensure that his wishes would be implemented.

Aspri was a highly personalised mechanism of government in which interpersonal dynamics and sensitivities played a crucial role. Notwithstanding the delegation of formal duties to his personal assistants, Suharto expected them to understand and accommodate his modes of thinking. Sujono, for example, later explained that 'he could not wait for Suharto to come to him for advice, but that he had to anticipate the questions which he would be asked and prepare for them'.[8] Policy-making and personality were often fused – and confused:

> When I [Suharto] was about to take a decision to increase the price of fuel from Rp 4 to Rp 16 per litre in 1967 or 1968, Ali Murtopo was panicky. He even cried in front of me while he pleaded with me not to make that decision. 'If you make a decision like this,' he said, 'the people will revolt and the government could fall. We want to keep you, Pak Harto,' he said. 'If you insist on taking this decision to raise the fuel price, it will destroy the New Order government.' … I told him, 'I have calculated everything.' And indeed in my preparations I had calculated from every angle.[9]

As well, a considerable part of the government's work was to be found in the agencies and bodies established by Suharto for specific tasks. Thus, Ibnu Sutowo was personally responsible for the oil industry, former Kostrad officer Brig.-Gen. Achmad Tirtosudiro was placed in control of a new body, Bulog (National Logistics Command, from 1967 National Logistics Board), a state-sponsored rice-trading organ, while Suhardiman took charge of PT Berdikari, an army-controlled trading company. Suharto sought, as well, to secure more orderly administrative procedures across the range of government departments, hitherto marked by an addiction to administrative chaos.

ECONOMIC REHABILITATION

The major problem facing Suharto's new government was the state of the economy. The reform measures of 3 October 1966, though welcomed by foreign markets, had not yet delivered their promised fruit. Indeed, soon after Suharto's election, a violent KAPPI-led demonstration at Tanjung Priok against rising prices had left one student dead and a number wounded.[10] The cabinet meeting of 1 May 1968 reiterated the need for drastic economising measures. One result of the government's budget discipline was a huge increase in fuel prices, a stratagem to compensate for unexpected expenditures in other parts of the budget. Suharto took to the task of marketing hardship with relish: 'It is better that we suffer now, but later things will get better. We will certainly feel happy in the days to come after we have experienced the bitter situation we do now'.[11]

In mid-June 1968, World Bank President Robert McNamara's first journey overseas was to Jakarta, where he offered a small amount of development credit and technical expertise on economic issues. A few days later, Trade Minister Sumitro Joyohadikusumo introduced a series of steps to curtail non-necessary imports. These were initial steps in the construction of a trade-off between international capital and the Indonesian government, the former providing the much-needed funds for Indonesia's economic stabilisation, the latter conditions of investment favourable for mobile international capital. The team of advisers appointed by Suharto to guide economic policy-making comprised Wijoyo (leader), Sumitro Joyohadikusumo, Ali Wardhana, Sadli, Emil Salim, Subroto, Frans Seda, and Radius Prawiro. They established the macro settings; Wijoyo, in particular, as head of Bappenas (National Development Planning Board) was responsible for drafting the first Five-Year Development Plan (Repelita) of the New Order, introduced in April 1969. The government, led by Suharto, sold the technocrat package to the international financial community. In September 1968, for example, Suharto received a group of forty businessmen, involved in a roundtable with government officials and local businesspeople, to preach on the investment opportunities which Indonesia presented.

The major targets for foreign investment were in capital-intensive extractive industries. The policies adopted in pursuit of that aim did not endear themselves to domestic businesspeople, who carried meagre influence in the new political configuration. Little attention was paid during these early phases of stabilisation to the development of manufacturing. Not only did the new policies facilitate the entry of foreign companies to compete with local ones, they also saw an enhanced inflow of imported consumer goods which damaged the interests of local manufacturers. 'The circumstances', Crouch noted, 'were certainly not propitious for the emergence of a "national bourgeoisie"' and indeed served to weaken Muslim entrepreneurs still further; the Domestic Investment Law, in force in November 1968, was designed to provide them with some solace.[12]

A significant component of foreign capital inflows was the aid which assisted the rehabilitation of the economy. Notwithstanding his earlier problems with the Japanese, Suharto, through the tireless brokerage activities of Sujono Humardani, eventually established a good working relationship which appears to have begun in April 1969 with the visit to Jakarta of Japanese Finance Minister Takeo Fukuda, and which flourished in the early 1970s. Suharto's May 1972 trip to Japan was well planned; he had been preceded by two weeks by Radius Prawiro, governor of Bank Indonesia, who had paved the way for his arrival; his meetings with the Japanese brought a promise from them to assist with soft loans in return for Indonesian supplies of low-sulphur oil.

The adoption of an apparently insensitive economic orthodoxy to rein in inflation, stabilise the currency and enhance investment had two important ramifications. The first was that there developed, almost immediately, a vision of economic reform and development which stood in contradiction to the technocrats' US-oriented approach. It was centred in those closest to Suharto, notably Sujono and Ali Murtopo, who shared notions of state-led bureaucratic/economic nationalism modelled on the experiences of late nineteenth-century Japan and modern Singapore, and who preferred an approach to development which could protect Indonesia from the rapacity of foreign capital and would take greater account of Indonesia's own capacities.[13] Suharto himself had considerable sympathy with this approach; he remarked in November 1968 that the Indonesian economy 'would under no circumstances slide in the direction of liberalism'.[14]

The second was the creation, in tandem with the technocrats' free-market approach, of a secret economy which was essentially inimical to the concept of markets, and which valued privilege and contacts above competition. The champion of this method was, of course, Ibnu Sutowo. There emerged, then, a curious dualism in the economy. On the surface, it was smooth, open, regular, a work of art by rationally driven, US-trained economists. At more subterranean depths, however, it worked by different methods and sleights of hand. The technocrats themselves could devise a budget, but it was never the real budget – in the New Order's early phase, at least, Crouch doubts 'whether the official budget raised more than half the revenues actually utilized by the government apparatus'[15] – nor could they control the movement of resources at the subterranean level which had their sources in Pertamina (increasingly awash with funds from 1968 onwards as foreign oil companies increasingly surrendered to Ibnu's concept of production-sharing contracts, and as Pertamina diversified into insurance, transport, petrochemicals and steel), in the military-backed foundations which began to emerge, and from other forms of army business. Notwithstanding their frustrations, however, the technocrats did what they could within these structural limitations. They were themselves, as a result of their long contacts with the Army, well aware of the style of army business and apparently thankful that army political dominance at least gave them a stable context. Wijoyo himself noted that 'the army at least has an organization and regulations governing procedures clearly spelled out. This is something political parties and civilians have never been able to do'.[16]

The competition between formal and informal economies gave rise to a tension, sometimes creative, sometimes destructive, between champions of different models of development upon which Suharto himself thrived, and for which he was well prepared from his days with Diponegoro and Kostrad. It served his purposes perfectly to be able to point to rising levels of international investment and the benefits they brought in their wake; at the same time it was much more in keeping with his style to have at his disposal the means to satisfy the needs of potential political opponents and to grease the wheels of politics. At this stage of his early presidential career, he was keenly aware of the need to secure consensus and not adopt stances which might destabilise his still-tenuous grip on power.

In the formal sphere of the economy, the greatest attention was placed upon agricultural development; as the first five-year plan asserted, 'the chosen field of battle is the agricultural field'.[17] The plan, carried out under the rubric of the Bimas (mass guidance) program, called for an increase in rice production of almost 50 per cent, to be achieved through the employment of new high-yielding seed varieties, improved irrigation, and the application of fertilisers and pesticides. Suharto himself proclaimed the aim that, by 1973, Indonesia would have achieved self-sufficiency in rice. Notwithstanding impressive improvements in rice production, the scheme was beset by problems, ranging from the use of force to compel peasants to participate, inflexibility in the input packages provided farmers, farmers' inability to repay agricultural credits advanced them, and commercial arrangements with foreign suppliers of agricultural inputs, notably chemicals, in one of which General Suryo, one of Suharto's personal staffers, was shown to have a significant if indirect interest. Suharto himself, in an attempt to gauge public reaction to the Bimas campaign, undertook a purportedly low-key tour of villages in West and Central Java in April 1970. 'He was dressed in the same way he appears in the palace, a green or grey suit, but had a hat on and held a walking stick',[18] and his discussions with farmers revealed the depths of their disillusionment with the scheme, which he discontinued a month later as a prelude to a fundamental recasting of it to remove foreign participation. A second key aspect of agricultural development was a much-enhanced focus on transmigration. Suharto emphasised its 'importance in the implementation of Repelita'; transmigration was not, he noted, just 'moving people from densely populated regions to less densely populated regions', but rather a means of increasing prosperity by allowing farmers access to better fields and increased production.[19]

Such close contact with the peasantry – his frequent tours around the regions to check on all manner of development projects were now an entrenched part of his presidential routine – was indicative of Suharto's close concern with agricultural matters, a product not only of his upbringing but also of his attention during his stint as Diponegoro commander. It was a card he played consistently and well, reaping the maximum publicity from his efforts to identify himself with the day-to-day problems of the common people. In addition to visits to farming communities, he also made a practice of symbolic private donations of agricultural equipment to villages. Early in 1969, for example, he donated five water pumps to the village of Wuryantoro, in Wonogiri, Central Java, 'so that the people there can increase food production with these pumps';[20] in September 1971, he donated rice mills, sprayers and motors to village chiefs in Riau, and in the same month, to celebrate Farmers' Day, he received almost 500 farmers in the state palace. From 1969, each village received a payment of Rp100,000 for local development projects.

Together with agricultural intensification, Suharto sought a fundamental realignment of Indonesia's attitude towards birth control, a 'sensitive and difficult problem';[21] Sukarno had looked askance at any suggestion that Indonesia should not continue to grow as rapidly as possible. Suharto's views on birth control appear to have developed from the advice of his technocrats, who impressed upon him the connections between unchecked population growth, agricultural development, employment and prosperity. By 1967, Indonesia was a signatory to the UN Declaration on Population. In September 1968, Suharto, having the previous year established an ad hoc advisory body on family planning, instructed Welfare Minister Idham Chalid to establish ('immediately') a national Family Planning Institute, which in 1970 Suharto developed into an enhanced National Coordinating Body for Family Planning, responsible to himself. Family planning proved spectacularly successful, with a remarkably rapid take-up of contraceptives through the early 1980s. In promoting family planning, Suharto later acknowledged the difficulty of a president with six children telling his people that two children were enough, and acknowledged a sour smile when a newspaper published a photo of him opening a condom factory. He refused, however, to have anything to do with abortion as a method of family planning; 'abortion runs contrary to religion'.[22]

Suharto also attempted to grapple with the problem of a bloated and inefficient state bureaucracy. In an ingenious move, he sought to have excess staff removed – or, rather, encouraged not to attend the office – while keeping them on the payroll, but the move stalled in the face of public criticism. He also banned new hirings and effected considerable increases in salaries, but without any notable improvement in performance. His efforts even went as far as to issue a presidential instruction in 1972 which specified the differing kinds of uniforms to be worn by civil service officials. These strategies were not as central to reform as the insinuation of military figures into the civilian bureaucracy, but, taken together, they had the effect of radically depoliticising it and furthering the process of recreating it as a tool of the regime.

In the midst of this welter of big-picture economic policy-making and implementation, Suharto retained his long-held affinity for cooperatives. In a speech in mid-1968 commemorating the twenty-first anniversary of Cooperatives Day, he talked up their economic prospects, rebuking those who proclaimed that 'cooperatives can survive only with the help of the government', and extolled the role they might play in development.[23]

Slowly, gradually, and notwithstanding the critics and doomsayers, the economy began to improve, with the rate of inflation in hand, greatly enhanced price stability already evident towards the end of 1967, an exceptional rice harvest in 1968, and taxation returns sufficient to cover routine outgoings in 1968. In his 1968 end-of-year speech, Suharto felt sufficiently confident to proclaim that 'we have achieved the bases which made possible the implementation of development'. His determination to succeed could not be denied: 'development will not fail, and will not be allowed to fail'.[24] By 1970 an observer noted that 'the army has set the country on the right road. An admirable rescue operation has achieved economic stabilisation. This has since been matched by an even more astonishing political stabilisation, which promises to keep Indonesia along the pragmatic road towards sensible development for some time'.[25] As economic difficulties emerged, they could generally be addressed by adjustments, such as Suharto's decision to devalue the currency by 10 per cent in August 1971, the first devaluation of the New Order period. Economic success had immediate political rewards; those whose employment prospects had grown, whose salaries had risen, whose business opportunities had multiplied, and whose general sense of security was markedly enhanced compared with the agitated uncertainties and economic frailty of the later Old Order found much to admire in Suharto's work.

IDEOLOGY

In addition to laying down prescriptions for economic recovery, Suharto was at pains to emphasise the ideological basis of his government, drawing upon, reinforcing and extending core ideas which he had developed in the 1950s. The centrepiece of his thinking was the ideology of Pancasila (the five principles). Shortly after his assumption of the full presidency, he made it clear that his sense of Pancasila was a narrowly constructed one. In a speech on 15 April 1968 he asserted that 'efforts to employ a basis for the state other than Pancasila or deviations in implementing it will bring only catastrophe to the whole nation, as the bitter experience of the past demonstrates'. On 18 April, he standardised the formulation of Pancasila and forbade its abbreviation. Later in the year, he asserted that 'the one and only ideology of ABRI [the Armed Forces] is Pancasila ... ABRI will not permit Pancasila to be changed in any way at all, or by anyone at all, because changing Pancasila means treason against the purity of the struggle of ABRI itself'.[26] It was crucial, he noted in 1972, that the spirit of 1945 be handed down to succeeding generations to provide them with the proper bearings for developing national unity.[27]

Amidst growing public concerns regarding the Army's role in politics, Suharto repeatedly asserted that there was no desire amongst the military for the seizure of power or the establishment of a military dictatorship; although it had a genuine and necessary interest, by virtue of its dual function, in both social and political spheres, *dwi fungsi* 'will not be used to monopolise power'. 'ABRI has become the pioneer of the New Order, and now we must become the pioneer of the order of development', he remarked at a ceremony commemorating the seventeenth anniversary of the founding of the RPKAD in 1969.[28] What Suharto wanted, of course, was the political stability which he saw as a precondition to economic performance; ABRI was the key to that stability; 'history', he proclaimed in April 1969, 'has placed the Indonesian Armed Forces as a stabiliser in realising the national struggle',[29] a remark that seemed to forebode a permanent role of this kind. Indeed, the following year, he asserted that 'the dual function of ABRI is one part of the implementation of democracy based on Pancasila and the national state system of Indonesia'.[30]

On a visit to Lampung, in June 1968, Suharto urged the people 'to leave behind political and religious controversies in the interests of achieving national stability which is an absolute condition for carrying out development'.[31] In a wide-ranging speech to the parliament on the eve of 1968 Independence Day – his first as full President of the Republic – he emphasised that development ('the struggle to free the people from poverty')[32] was premised on stability, and that stability was to be based upon unswerving observation of the spirit of the 1945 Constitution which he construed as being above change. Successful development, he reminded the 200,000 people who greeted him in Medan on 1 September, was premised on the prior securing of political stability. The ideological battles and sloganising so characteristic of the Old Order needed to be left in the past; 'they were of no use and only caused confusion'; indeed, 'the problem of ideology is not an issue and can no longer be questioned because our ideology is clear, Pancasila'. Narrow ideologies, he noted, had 'become a source of tension and contention in earlier periods'.[33]

Suharto's ideology had, indeed, become that of development, with security its necessary condition and expected result. Development, in its various aspects, was a numbingly recurring theme in the multitude of speeches he delivered, day in and day out, through these early years of his presidency; in fact, it is difficult to find a speech in which it escapes mention. In his hands, the task of development assumed heroic proportions. His speech on the occasion of the Heroes' Day celebration in 1968 was built around the theme that heroes were needed 'not only at the time of the independence war, but also in the sphere of development'. The struggle for development, he proclaimed, was 'a struggle to provide content' to the independence that had been achieved so long ago. Development, however, was dependent upon a number of factors:

> 1) a more and more powerful political stability, 2) an increasingly solid economic situation and development which is increasingly extensive, 3) an increasingly secure state apparatus with an enhanced capacity to perform routine tasks as well as development, 4) an increasing internal cohesiveness in the Armed Forces which can constantly protect and guarantee security, 5) a people who are increasingly infatuated [*gandrung*] with development, and 6) a growing confidence [in Indonesia] on the part of foreign countries.[34]

The past could never be forgotten, and Suharto moved quickly to ensure that, moulded in the appropriate way, it could itself perform an ideological function. The 1968 remembrance of the coup attempt held at Lubang Buaya was attended by all the nation's highest leaders, who 'gathered there to remember it'. After the ceremony, which included a reading of the Pancasila by Nasution, Suharto dedicated the first stages of the vast monument being erected there to the 'seven heroes of the revolution' who had lost their lives in the coup attempt. He also sought to represent, and enhance, other pasts in which he had played a role; on 1 March 1973, he inaugurated a monument constructed in the heart of the city of Yogyakarta and dedicated to the attack of 1 March 1949.[35]

ANTI-COMMUNISM

The corollary of Suharto's concern with orthodoxy was the maintenance of the regime's bitter opposition to communism, exacerbated by evidence of a resurgence of PKI militancy. Early in 1967, Suharto had asserted that the remnants of the PKI were still intending to mount a coup, and that the communists 'would always take every opportunity ... to achieve their goal', including infiltrating anti-communist organisations.[36] Such warnings of the dangers of a communist resurgence resurfaced from time to time. There were, in Suharto's mind, three ways to attack the PKI: physical destruction of PKI remnants, national unity of purpose, and raising the standard of living. Reports of PKI remnants intent on causing mischief emerged at more or less regular intervals.[37] As I have noted, the resurgence in south Blitar in mid-1968 was rapidly crushed by the Army, while the guerrilla activity in West Kalimantan was controlled by the end of that year. The purge of the administrative apparatus continued; in East Java alone, almost 9,000 officials were dismissed between March and early June because of alleged involvement in the September 30 Movement. At the same time, the Armed Forces were scoured of those thought to be sympathetic to the PKI or the old regime. Reports also emerged of mass killings of prisoners housed in detention camps.[38] It was, perhaps, not coincidental that PKI leaders Nyono, Sudisman and Wiryomartono were executed in October 1968.

Although the communist movement was effectively destroyed by the end of 1968, communist scaremongering thereafter remained a stock-in-trade of the New Order regime. On 11 March 1969, for example, Suharto, reflecting on the dissolution of the PKI three years previously, remarked that 'if you study the doctrine and tactics of the PKI ... [you realise that] that party will keep on launching *illegal* movements to try to come back to life'. At the end of 1969 and early 1970, he spoke of the continuing need to take action against clandestine 30 September Movement remnants still in the midst of society.[39] The aim of the PKI in 1965 had been the same as in 1948, he remarked on the fifth anniversary of Supersemar in 1971: 'to change Pancasila and the 1945 Constitution in order to replace them with another system'.[40] In August 1971, he warned that, while the PKI's physical power may have been destroyed, 'they constantly try to mount sabotage, subversive activities and similar actions'. Upon his return from state visits to Australia and New Zealand early in 1972, he observed that the small demonstrations he had encountered were evidence of the attempt by international communism to revive the PKI.[41] The constant reiteration of the PKI 'threat' served, above all, to justify the increasingly aggressive and authoritarian tactics of elements of the government, restricting freedoms, pressuring politicians, reshaping politics according to its will.

The Suharto government's treatment of those who had suffered arrest after the defeat of the 30 September Movement was of a piece with this thinking. Those who had stood for the forces behind the 1965 coup could be shown no mercy. Brian May reported a discussion with Suharto on the fate of the noted author Pramudya Ananta Tur:

> During an interview in November 1972 I asked Suharto if he really thought that Pramoedya knew of the conspiracy. 'No', he said with a smile; but Pramoedya, he went on, was a member of Lekra, which the PKI had established as part of its plan to 'consolidate its forces and overthrow the government'. If the coup had succeeded, people like Pramoedya would have ratified it, he said. Suharto made no further comment; apparently he considered he had said enough to justify the destruction of artists and academics on Buru Island.[42]

SECURING THE STATE

The general pattern of Suharto's political tactics was clear. On the one hand, he was acutely aware of the need to compromise and seek consensus to ensure that he did not unnecessarily provide grounds which might fracture his untested rule, which was, after all, based on an uncertain coalition of army supporters. On the other hand, he was, by character and experience, suspicious of the potential for local unrest and disunity to brew, and from the very beginning of his tenure he attached enormous importance to the development of a security/intelligence approach to state control.

Ali Murtopo's Opsus (Special Operations) formed one branch of this approach, but its major manifestation came in the development of Kopkamtib (Operations Command for the Restoration of Order and Security). Originally established with a mandate to secure the nation against the communist threat, Kopkamtib, no doubt at Suharto's instigation, and perhaps in concert with his centralising of Armed Forces power, increasingly asserted itself as a weapon of repression against assumed threats to the state emanating from any quarter. In 1969, its ambit of authority had been extended to cover all varieties of extremism and subversive behaviour and to ensure the safety and integrity of the government apparatus. Suharto, having divested himself of direct operational supervision of the Armed Forces by the creation of the post of deputy commander, filled by Panggabean, similarly transferred operational control of Kopkamtib to the deputy commander, Sumitro.

Kopkamtib was not, as I have already noted, an independent force. Rather, it was a new set of powers granted to army commanders at various levels of the military hierarchy to take actions against perceived threats to security. Under the guiding hand and organisational talents of Sumitro, Kopkamtib's fearful reputation intensified. The powers available were extensive and arbitrary; they included the capacity to suspend or ban newspapers and to arrest demonstrators;

Kopkamtib, accordingly, became 'a key instrument in maintaining the government's authority'.[43] Kopkamtib was assisted in its work by Bakin (State Intelligence Coordinating Body), headed from January 1970 by Sutopo Yuwono and responsible for extra-military intelligence. One scholar writing in the early 1970s was moved to remark that 'the passionate and unswerving attention to problems of security since 1965 has been extraordinarily intense'.[44]

Outside the centre, military domination of regional administration proceeded apace. By 1969, military officers comprised more than half of the nation's *bupatis* and mayors; early in 1971 more than 70 per cent of Indonesia's twenty-six governors had military backgrounds, and the proportion increased thereafter. This was not just a matter of security and control, but also a means of granting the military access to a wide variety of perquisites within the administration, including appointments, licences and contracts. The greening of the regions was enhanced by a strengthening of the old 'civic action' activities; in early 1969, the Army announced that one-third of its troops would be dispatched to rural areas to help farming communities. Local autonomy, though occasionally discussed, was to have little substance: 'the giving of regional autonomy', Suharto remarked, 'will be proportionate to the capacity of the respective regions, and for regions which do not have the capacity to look after their own affairs in a technical manner, it is difficult for them to be given autonomy'.[45]

WEST IRIAN: THE 'ACT OF FREE CHOICE'

Securing the state also meant completing the formality of integrating West Irian into the Indonesian nation. The provisions of the 1962 agreement had required that Indonesia implement a plebiscite before the end of 1969 to determine popular sentiment regarding integration. Given that, without exception, the Indonesian political elite believed that West Irian was an integral part of the nation proclaimed on 17 August 1945, and given the lack of international concern for the territory's status, the question was not so much what the Irianese might think but, rather, how to ensure that they responded in the appropriate way. Indeed, Sukarno had come close in 1965 to threatening not to bother with any consultative process at all because, he said, the Irianese were clearly in favour of integration.

Suharto, mindful of his need for favour from the West, did not have that option – he had confirmed in 1967 that the Irianese would be afforded a plebiscite – but, as Mandala commander in 1962, he had held even more strongly than most of his fellows to the notion that West Irian was an inseparable component of the Indonesian Republic and that any suggestion of independence would simply not be entertained. A vote for separation would, in any case, have been politically disastrous for him. Having rebuffed a plea for enlarged autonomy from a West Irian delegation in 1966 – he blamed their situation on the neglect of the Dutch administration – and having spoken in 1968 of the plebiscite as a mere formality, in 1969 he even went so far as to assert that a decision in favour of separation would be treasonous.[46] He therefore commissioned Ali Murtopo to take the necessary measures to ensure that the Irianese produced a vote confirming their integration into the Republic. Ali's methods were similar to those he was to employ in the 1971 election: a judicious mixture of browbeating and intimidation (including by Suharto himself in meeting with Irianese tribal chiefs in Jakarta), and persuasion and bribery. The latter saw vast quantities of consumer goods and gifts flown into the territory and dispensed to local chiefs and popular representatives, as well as efforts at political conversion by cadres trained by Fr Beek; the former was evidenced by a strong presence of military force, under the redoubtable and reliable Sarwo Edhie, which allowed no expression of any independence sentiment and freely arrested those who dared to give vent to such ideas.

In the end, Indonesia decided that the 'act of free choice' would be exercised by special consultative assemblies which would represent the genuine aspirations of the people. Ali Murtopo ensured that these assemblies were well peopled with pro-integrationist Irianese. In August, the assemblies provided the expected assent, and Suharto officially established West Irian as an 'autonomous province' of Indonesia on 16 September 1969. Notwithstanding the protests of the UN representative, F. Ortiz Sanz, about restrictions placed on the exercise of the population's rights, notably to free speech, the United Nations on 19 November 'noted' the result, without dissent, an action which effectively endorsed the 'plebiscite' and extended formal recognition of Indonesian sovereignty over the territory. For his part, Suharto announced in October 1969 a plan to assist Irian's development by placing 200,000 Irianese children with Indonesian families.[47]

INCREASING RIGIDITY

Suharto's ascension to the presidency, the high-pressure politics which had preceded it, and the subsequent efforts to assert far-reaching political control effectively ended the last vestiges of enthusiastic student and reformist civilian support for the newly consolidated regime. Suharto himself made it clear that the students had to adjust to the new realities. As well, there was a sense that the fissuring student movement, held together for a short time only by its desire to rid the country of Sukarno and his supporters, had increasingly run out of steam and was casting about for a new agenda to sustain its flagging momentum. Some of its major figures as well had thrown in their lot with the regime, adopting a 'functional' role within state institutions like the DPR (the Representative Council).

Those who refused such domestication, however, began to direct their criticisms towards the regime they had helped to create, targeting in particular senior figures within the New Order whom they saw as corrupt. Suharto's response was in keeping with the heightened sensitivity to criticism and the gathering authoritarianism of his regime, notwithstanding his occasional declarations of the receptiveness of his government to 'constructive' criticism. In a meeting with KAPPI leaders in January 1969, he remarked that 'demonstrations no longer accord with the current situation because, in the era of development, activities of that kind disturb peace and calm as well as the efforts which have been made to stabilise politics'.[48] When, in August, a magazine asserted that Suharto had ordered a 'de-Siliwangi-isation' of the Armed Forces, he labelled the report a 'slander', adding that he intended to order the office of the attorney-general to begin an investigation of the weekly.[49]

Similarly symptomatic of his increasing rigidity, and of his political confidence, was his gathering disinclination to entertain the questions of journalists. There were exceptions, of course – in February 1969 he received fifty-five American pressmen, visiting under the auspices of the information ministry, and took their questions – but his direct involvement with the press now tended to be much more tightly circumscribed and limited to those occasions when he perceived clear political advantage in accommodating the media. Thus, on 1 April, the day of Repelita's launch, he adopted a *'personal approach'*, entertaining Jakarta journalists at the Bogor Palace the better to involve the media in the task of making Repelita a success.[50] In August 1970 in West Germany, his meeting with journalists seems to have been intended to break down their image of him as a military strongman.

THE END OF SUKARNO

Meanwhile, Sukarno was ailing. In May 1968 he was briefly allowed to leave his residence at Bogor to attend the wedding of his daughter, Megawati, in Jakarta. He had moved, with Suharto's permission, early in 1968 from the pavilion of the Bogor Palace to a house in Batutulis, near Bogor, for reasons of his health. Then, early in 1969 he was moved to Jakarta, to the Wisma Yaso on Jalan Gatot Subroto. During his time under effective house arrest, Sukarno had been forced – apparently at Suharto's order, with an eye to a possible future trial of the former president – to endure interrogation by operatives from Kopkamtib about his relations with the PKI, but when Suharto learned of the seriousness of his illness he had such questioning stopped. On 15 June 1970 Sukarno was admitted to Gatot Subroto hospital, where he died at 7 a.m. on 21 June. Upon hearing the news, Suharto 'rushed to the hospital'.[51] His thoughts, however, were probably already focused on the political implications of the former president's passing.

Sukarno's death once more illustrated Suharto's ambivalent feelings towards his former president. He accorded Sukarno a state funeral, but refused to accede to his request, and that of his family, to 'rest under a leafy tree, surrounded by beautiful landscape, beside a river with fresh air and a lovely view … I wish my final home to be the cool, mountainous, fertile Priangan area of Bandung'.[52] That was altogether too close to the capital, and might too easily in the future allow too many sympathetic visitors and perhaps even the development of a shrine of resistance to the New Order. Suharto accordingly ignored the pleas of relatives and ordered him buried in the small East Java town of Blitar, near his mother's grave. Suharto himself did not attend the burial ceremony on 22 June.

FOREIGN POLICY

The most significant aspect of Suharto's attitude towards foreign policy once he had assumed the presidency was his relative inattention to it. Unlike his predecessor, he was focused on domestic problems and the national weakness they had wrought. He did only what was required in the foreign policy arena to secure regional cooperation and security, although from the start he pointed to the economic gulf between rich and poor nations. More detailed initiatives he left to Adam Malik, who successfully managed to deflect the wishes of Ali's Opsus people, as well as other generals, to forge a tighter defence-related association with the United States and to bring weight to bear for ASEAN to assume the character of a military pact. Notwithstanding such tensions as arose in 1968 from Singapore's insistence, in the face of a personal plea for clemency by Suharto (conveyed to Singapore by his special emissary, Cokropranolo), on hanging two Indonesian marines captured during Confrontation, Suharto saw a more strongly developed ASEAN solidarity as a means of disabling outside efforts to intervene in the region itself.

Suharto made his second presidential trip overseas in March 1970, a week-long visit to Malaysia, the first such visit by an Indonesian president. He remained unenthusiastic about the resumption of normal relations with China. 'Indonesia will not easily forget, and will always take in the lesson, of Peking's assistance to the PKI in advancing a coup against the lawful government', he remarked in October 1972, although he admitted some months later that he had not put the idea aside altogether.[53] Relations with the other great communist power, the Soviet Union, which had seriously sagged in the wake of the coup, revived to such an extent that an agreement on Indonesia's debt repayment was eventually finalised in 1970.

Nonetheless, Suharto was increasingly enjoying the praise of the West for his domestic efforts at economic development and political stability. The greatest endorsement yet of his policies was the visit of President Nixon to Jakarta in July 1969, the first time a US president had visited Indonesia. Suharto's rhetoric mirrored his real interests, focused solidly on the local: 'In order to make an effective contribution to the efforts at world peace, the Republic of Indonesia must be strong internally'. Less than two weeks later he related that in answer to Nixon's query about Indonesia's greatest enemy, he had replied that 'Indonesia's greatest enemy is the failure of Pelita [the five-year development plan] ... because if Pelita fails, the people will then no longer believe in the government and all its development plans and no longer believe in themselves'. It was a similar attitude of attending to what he perceived to be Indonesia's real priorities that led to his decision not to attend the twenty-fifth anniversary celebrations of the United Nations; he was preoccupied 'with the many different domestic activities of the president'. Suharto was, however, happy to accept high-ranking visitors; it gladdened him especially if their presence indicated a form of approval of his government; thus in March 1970 he received Prince Bernhard, 'the first member of the Dutch royal family to visit Indonesia in the twenty-five years of our independence'.[54]

Suharto's disposition to look inwards rather than outwards can only have been strengthened by his first experience of the Non-Aligned Movement in Lusaka in September 1970, a meeting that left him sour and unimpressed. It seemed to him that, rather than embodying the 'free and active' principles which had originally characterised the conduct of Indonesian foreign policy, most members of the movement were in fact strongly anti-Western and effectively aligned with one or other of the communist blocs. Because of his destruction of the communist party at home, 'they did not like me being there'.[55] As a consequence of this unhappy experience – nicely captured in a photograph of a bored and glum Suharto at one of the conference sessions – it was to be many years before he again took an active interest in the Non-Aligned Movement. When he did travel abroad, what appeared to excite him most was the opportunity to explore various exemplary models of economic development and to gauge their applicability to the Indonesian case. In this context, even in the early 1970s he manifested a strong interest in technology. In Switzerland in 1972, the Swiss combination of industrial technology and modern management 'motivated him to see that country as a source of inspiration for ideals of peace and development'.[56]

RESHAPING THE ARMED FORCES

By 1969, Suharto was in unchallenged control of the Army, a result both of his political performance and of the clinical moves he had made with command and non-military appointments over the previous couple of years. The Air Force had been thoroughly purged after the coup attempt, but the Navy and the Police still enjoyed the considerable autonomy with which they had been provided during the Sukarno years, notwithstanding the abolition of the separate service ministries in August 1967. The Police endured a gradual process of purging which culminated in 1968 with the replacement of the police commander, Sucipto Yudodiharjo, by his first deputy, Hugeng Imam Santoso, a reform-minded character generally thought to be attuned to PSI-type thinking. The Navy proved a tougher nut to crack, because it had its marine force at its disposal and had resisted earlier efforts at purging, but again Suharto prevailed in reordering the command structure by offering ambassadorial perquisites and placing intransigent officers under house arrest. His old comrade from West Irian days, Admiral Sudomo, was placed in command of the Navy at the end of 1969. Like his patron, Sudomo was a middle-aged paracommando trainee, and he did the job Suharto required of him: 'by his own account, Sudomo purged more than 1500 officers from the Navy between 1969 and 1973'.[57]

In October and November 1969, apparently after more than two years of weighing and planning, Suharto then proceeded to unify the previously operationally independent commands, reducing service commanders to the status of chiefs of staff under his overall control as commander of the Armed Forces. Six regional defence commands (Kowilhan) were created to integrate armed service activities from the command staff level downwards, and the non-military (that is, political) authority and range of activities previously enjoyed by service and Kodam commanders were removed and apportioned to the Ministry of Defence, under Suharto himself. The effect of these measures was a thoroughgoing centralisation of command structures in the hand of the President, rather than the service or territorial commanders, and a corresponding diminution of the independent power of the Army; 'he is no longer in a position to control it closely', one commentator remarked, 'and he must therefore prevent its being too potent a weapon in the hands of another'.[58] Once the process of centralisation was completed, 'no effective opposition in the armed forces remained';[59] they were, at last, effectively subjugated to the regime, and 'warlordism [had] thus arrived at its final conclusion'.[60]

RESHAPING THE PARTIES

Suharto's decision to allow the political parties to contest the elections foreshadowed for 1971 was a recognition of the deep roots they enjoyed in society, and his fear that their abnegation would cause serious social unrest. But his decision created a new set of problems which he worked through patiently and systematically, sensitive to the thinking of other actors and what their limits might be, ever ready to talk things through but clinical once he had weighed matters and decided to act.

Suharto was keenly aware, as we have seen, of the dangers presented by a radical reformation of the basis of society. Accordingly, he had opposed the ideas of the New Order radicals, notwithstanding a certain intellectual affinity with their goals. When Dharsono forcibly introduced a modification of his ideas, in which parties were moulded into two programmatic groups, into several West Java legislatures, Suharto finally moved to cripple the radical movement, exploiting its inability to build a larger and more popular front. Kemal Idris was moved to East Indonesia, while Dharsono's exit from the political scene was made by way of a holding position in the foreign ministry and then appointment as ambassador to Thailand. Easing them out was made more straightforward for Suharto by the fact that the pair's forthright attacks on the 'financial' generals so close to Suharto, notably Ibnu Sutowo, as well as the uncompromisingly robust style of their politicking, had not enamoured them to other army leaders who otherwise were broadly sympathetic with their ideals.

He then took the decision – apparently concerned that further delays might weaken his authority and legitimacy, as well as ABRI's dwi fungsi (dual function) claims, and against the advice of his counsellors – to proceed to elections within the timeframe specified by the MPRS. Calling a series of meetings with party leaders in October 1969, he affirmed his determination to keep to the MPRS deadline, a neat piece of positive politics which undermined the parties' efforts to seek their advantage over points of the proposed laws, notably Suharto's rights of appointment to legislatures; party leaders soon dropped their demands for adaptations of the electoral laws. The finally agreed draft of the law on the composition of the new DPR provided that 100 of the 460 seats be set aside for members of the Armed Forces. On 22 November, the laws passed parliament and the government announced that elections would be held on 5 July 1971.

Suharto himself had no brief for the parties, whose record under both liberal and guided democracy had, in his view, been characterised by self-interest and narrow horizons, in contrast to the guardianship of the national interest that he and his supporters now provided. Nonetheless, he stated, the government 'always guarantees the right of existence of political parties simply because they are but vital evidence of the existence of democracy'. The trick was 'to discover how political parties as instruments of democracy can discharge their function effectively',[61] New Order code for the task of creating a series of mechanisms which would prevent, or at least significantly block, party influence – especially that with Old Order roots – in both parliament and MPR. Suharto already had a clear vision of what elections should produce: 'The strategic objectives which must be achieved by means of the general election are fixed: the defence of Pancasila and the 1945 Constitution, strengthening political stability, increasing the fervour of society in carrying out development, and implementing the dual function of ABRI more effectively in accord with the needs of the national struggle'.[62]

The first mechanism was to attempt to shape the parties in acceptable ways from within. I have already noted the tack taken by Suharto in April 1966, when the Hardi/Hadisubeno group seized power from the PNI leadership of Ali Sastroamijoyo. Even though some of his commanders, notably Sarwo Edhie and Juarsa, were excessively enthusiastic in cutting down the PNI in their local areas, Suharto managed to rein them in to preserve his policy of retaining a purified PNI as a component of the New Order. When his plans were complicated by the sudden death of Osa Maliki, the army-supported leader of the PNI, in September 1969, Suharto made it clear through Ali Murtopo's Opsus that he wished Osa to be succeeded by Hadisubeno, his old friend from his Diponegoro days in Semarang, rather than Hardi, urbane, moderate, inclusivist by disposition, and suspected of harbouring anti-military sentiments and perhaps too close to PSI shades of thinking. Suharto's calculus, and that of Ali Murtopo, seems to have been that Hadisubeno, notwithstanding his pro-Sukarno views, was best positioned to construct an arrangement of understanding between the PNI and Suharto's regime. In these efforts, Suharto was assisted by the fact that Opsus provided the PNI with significant financial support. To this planning was added considerable and quite openly exercised pressure on delegates, transmitted through local military commanders before the PNI conference in Semarang in April 1970, and by Opsus operatives themselves while the conference was in session. They were clearly made to understand that the future of their party rested on their making the correct choice of leader, and they did as they had been directed. The choice at once returned the PNI to its distinctively Javanist and Sukarnoist cast.[63]

Efforts of a similar kind were set in motion to shape Islamic politics. In the first instance, there was the need to provide a political platform for supporters of the Masyumi party, banned in 1960. In its place was established Parmusi (Indonesian Muslim Party), to serve as a vehicle for this sentiment which had shown increasing signs of disaffection with the New Order's secularist approach to politics; it was, of course, to be a means for containment and control, not free expression.

This move was a significant concession by Suharto, whose intense opposition to the regional rebellions of 1958 was well known. Indeed, early in 1967 he had turned back efforts to re-establish Masyumi, which, he said, 'did not officially condemn the deeds of its members' in supporting the PRRI (the counter-government movement). Thus, 'legal, political and psychological factors have led the armed forces to the opinion that the armed forces cannot accept the rehabilitation of the former political party, Masyumi'.[64] Shortly thereafter, however, Suharto – attempting to balance deep-seated opposition amongst the military and Java-based parties to a Masyumi resurgence with the need to create a vehicle to incorporate and channel Masyumi-type political sentiment rather than cut it adrift – opened the way for the formation of a new party. He took steps, of course, to ensure that the new party should not adopt the ideological legacy of Masyumi; at a meeting with Parmusi delegates in August 1968, he called for the new party to eschew old ideology for program-oriented politics, based on Pancasila and the 1945 Constitution. He was careful, however, not to allow it to begin operation until he was satisfied that its leadership would be appropriately accommodating to the New Order; as a result, it was not until February 1968 that the new party received official sanction. After the party exhibited some rebelliousness in regard to the election of a new leadership with close ties to the old Masyumi in late 1968 – the government refused to acknowledge the new board – Ali Murtopo's Opsus engineered a coup through which a new leadership was installed in October 1970. The predictable backlash against this chicanery invited government intervention; in November Suharto placed one of his ministers, Mintareja, an Islamic accommodationist by disposition, into the post of party chairman 'to overcome the discord which had taken place in this party',[65] a decision which brought the party into 'utter disarray'.[66] Parmusi had become the property of the New Order, 'founded by presidential decision, leadership changes blocked by presidential opposition, executive reorganization effected by presidential decree'.[67]

The third major party, Nahdlatul Ulama (NU), was not seen as a potential danger to the New Order, since its habit had always been to shape itself to accommodate prevailing winds. Accordingly, the government found no need to intervene in the party's internal affairs, at least not until early 1972 when the independently minded NU leader and former student activist Subchan found himself the victim of an Opsus move that dumped him from his NU leadership role.

Shaping and domesticating the parties was Suharto's first task; the second and altogether more difficult job was to frame the electoral terrain in such a way as to prevent the parties, notwithstanding the moulding they had already endured, from gathering the lion's share of the vote in the forthcoming elections. 'The conducting of general elections', Suharto later noted, 'must be able to secure the benefits and aims of those elections … to achieve political stability … we must be able to carry out general elections in such a way as to guarantee the defence of Pancasila and the 1945 Constitution, not disturb the smooth implementation of Repelita and at the same time to reinforce political stability'.[68] Elections which provided simply for a return to the selfish partisanship of the Old Order, and the attendant problems, would serve no benefit. But how to achieve the desired end? General Sumitro later remarked that 'because the economy was the main concern, in particular the development of the national economy, we hoped to reduce the number of politicians, who had graduated from socio-political faculties, in the legislature. We wanted to see their seats filled with technocrats, experts in economy and finance, as well as in other related fields'.[69] The key to the radical restructuring of the electoral terrain was Golkar.

GOLKAR AND THE ELECTION STRATEGY

Suharto had numerous reasons, both domestic and international, for wanting to hold general elections. On the domestic front, he was keen that the political forces could exercise themselves in an election contest to provide some sense of solidarity with his New Order; there was also a sense that, having decided to use the device of dwi fungsi in a context of civil institutions rather than pursue outright military rule, he had no choice but to pursue an electoral contest. Internationally, elections offered the attractive target of legitimacy and stability. In all this, however, it was of the utmost importance that the ruling hand of the government not be compromised. Given the early expectation that the political parties would dominate the electoral outcome, it had been necessary for Suharto to shape party leaderships so that they would be appropriately docile in the parliament.

The government also wanted to have its own voice in the parliament, in the shape of Sekber Golkar (Joint Secretariat of Functional Groups), an entity established in 1964 by the Army to coordinate anti-communist groupings; in fact, the government had begun appointing its civilian supporters as Golkar representatives to the parliament in 1967 and 1968. It was expected that Golkar could win no more than about 30 per cent or so of the vote in any election – a major reason for Ali Murtopo's wanting to delay the elections as long as decently possible. However, once Suharto had determined to hold the elections in July 1971, he gave Ali Murtopo the job of attempting to draw as much electoral support as possible to Golkar.

The origins of Suharto's decision to adopt Golkar and engineer it in the way he did are difficult to disentangle. Indeed, there was some suggestion that he was initially attracted to the idea of forming some kind of partnership with the PNI. Ali Murtopo, by one account, was originally unattracted by the Golkar concept, both because of its uninspiring reputation and because of the conservative (that is, Sukarnoist) bent of some of its leaders. Suharto himself had had little involvement in the beginnings of Sekber Golkar, although, as with other institutions, he had cleansed and domesticated its leadership in the first years of the New Order. But he was probably intuitively attracted to the notion of finding a special place in Indonesian politics for functional groups, a quite different space from that occupied by the old political party system and with a capacity to stabilise the political system against the possibility of party dominance. Perhaps, too, he was influenced by men like his old military colleague Daryatmo, who had had some political experience of Golkar in its earlier manifestation. The greatest attraction of Golkar, however, was that it provided the structure of a state party without party politicians. Once the strategy of mobilising it was accepted, Suharto commissioned Ali Murtopo and Sujono Humardani to ensure its success.

Time was short. Golkar had no political roots at all in society – one seasoned observer commented that 'despite [Suharto's] obvious popularity with the people, he has not yet established a party base from which to make his bid for a second term'[70] – and it faced electoral opponents who had every prospect of making gains through calling for support based on primordial loyalties, even if a large number (almost 22 million) of electors had never before enjoyed the privilege of voting in a general election. The strategy employed by Suharto and his electoral manager, Ali Murtopo – once Ali had 'hijacked' Sekber Golkar for its new mission – had three aspects. First, the effort would be made to construct an ideology which sharply separated it from the existing parties. It was to be ideology based on non-ideological themes: development, stability, order, unity. The idea of a functional grouping which did not take refuge in partisan and ideologically tinged politics but which presented itself as purveying a strong vision of a developing Indonesia set it starkly apart from the parties. This non-ideological, pragmatic and programmatic aspect of the Golkar program proved highly attractive to many secular urban intellectuals, particularly those from PSI and Catholic backgrounds, who despised and feared the ideological politics and self-interested parties of the Sukarno period and who now sought a more 'modern' and enlightened approach to politics. The second aspect was less elevated, but bound to be more effective: Golkar would simply use its access to government largesse to buy itself position by establishing itself as a patronage-dispensing apparatus. Third, it would use its access to political power to turn matters to its advantage.

Ali's keen but unscrupulous mind took to the task with relish. He and his Opsus men, including those like former Catholic student labour leader and activist, Harry Can Silalahi, devised numerous strategies designed to cripple the electoral support of the parties and embellish that of Golkar. Amongst them was the ability to disbar candidates from contesting the election. More indirect were Ali's efforts to domesticate the Indonesian Journalists Association (PWI); when his attempt to secure the election of B. M. Diah as its head failed to defeat the group around Rosihan Anwar, the government simply recognised the Diah group as the valid representative of the PWI. In any case, Ali already enjoyed control of two newspapers to spread the Golkar word: *Berita Yudha* and *Suara Karya.*

Golkar's government sponsorship allowed it to make significant inroads into party support without much difficulty. Even though 1970 regulations permitted the great bulk of civil servants to join political groups and did not require them to resign until they had actually accepted a seat in the parliament, the minister for home affairs, the tough, thick-skinned and unscrupulous Amirmachmud, 'was determined that his department would become the backbone of the Golkar'.[71] He introduced regulations in 1969, the famous Permen 12, which prevented Golkar representatives in regional and local assemblies from having any party affiliation. Further regulations early in 1970 disallowed ABRI personnel and civilian Defence Department employees, as well as judges and public prosecutors, from membership of parties. Compared with 1955, his department enjoyed greatly enhanced powers to manage the electoral process; through the concept of monoloyalty, he exerted heavy pressure on Home Affairs employees, previously with strong attachments to the PNI, to support Golkar. Indeed, as one scholar who monitored the electoral process closely in East Java noted, 'the government identification with

Golkar, if slightly disguised at the province level, became closer and closer as one descended to the lower reaches of administration'.[72] The campaigning rules that Amirmachmud framed prevented any questioning of Pancasila or the 1945 Constitution, or criticism of religion, or of the government or its agents, or efforts to deride other organisations involved in the election; political prisoners labelled A, B or C were disallowed from voting. His efforts were materially assisted by workplace voting, so that 'the civil servant who dares to vote against Golkar risks exposure'.[73] Kopkamtib was employed to scour lists of electoral candidates and remove the names of those deemed unsuitable, as well as employing its uncircumscribed powers to maintain 'security' during the campaign.

Ali Murtopo, for his part, placed heavy pressure upon local administrators to secure specified quotas of the vote in the regions. His role as chief of the Election Commission's Logistics and Supply Board provided him with a wonderful source of patronage. Thus, Crouch remarks, 'by pulling to its own side those who had once formed the backbone of the PNI, the Golkar was able to destroy much of the PNI's electoral influence'.[74] The same tactic of playing on patrimonial ties was evident in the government's approach to Muslim leaders, where the promise of funding for trips to Mecca, for religious buildings and for plum jobs on government organisations was held out to try to ensure that leaders delivered the votes of their constituencies to Golkar. Ali Murtopo, revivifying the Association for Improving Islamic Education (GUPPI), sought to draw influential Muslim leaders into the fold. Suharto himself took three NU *kiyayi* (Islamic scholars) with him on a European visit in 1970, and made a well-publicised tour of Central and East Java in mid-1970 where the generosity of his gifts to local Islamic boarding schools (*pesantren*) could only have reinforced the notion that Golkar would provide well for those that supported it. The close Golkar identification with both the Armed Forces and the government also facilitated election fund-raising. Golkar election safaris infused a sense of entertainment as well as a promise of munificence, and helped to establish strong identifications: 'Golkar is Pantja Sila, so don't be anti-Golkar; Golkar is the government, devoted to construction, such as that beautiful mosque, that splendid regency office, the best in Asia; Golkar is ABRI, so don't criticise Golkar or ABRI will take action'.[75] Army strong-arm tactics were also in evidence to secure the result, especially by 'persuading' former PKI members and associates to vote for Golkar. Sukarno's eldest son, Guntur Sukarnoputra, was not allowed to stand for the PNI (though he took part vigorously in the campaign), and plans to utilise Sukarno's gravesite to commemorate his death were rebuffed. For his part, Suharto attempted to keep a statesmanlike distance from the electoral fray, portraying himself as an avuncular patron and dispensing funding and vehicles to all electoral groups; on those occasions when he could not resist exhibiting his partisanship, however, he made it clear that he strongly supported a vote for Golkar.

The only unambiguous sign of energetic opposition came from the *Golongan Putih* (Golput – White Group), led by disaffected members of the Generation of '66 like Arief Budiman, who urged electors to vote informally because the choices offered – a vote for the parties or for Golkar – were not worthy of support and deserved only protest. The government's response was to refuse permission for Golput's discussion meetings and to ban Golput itself in mid-June 1971.[76]

Notwithstanding the enormous and authoritative support it received, Golkar's prospects were thought to be relatively modest because of the short time for preparation at its disposal. However, the election result was surprisingly decisive; Golkar won 62.8 per cent of the vote and 236 seats in the DPR. Of the nine parties allowed by Suharto to contest the election, only NU emerged from the unequal contest unscathed – indeed, its vote improved slightly over its 1955 showing – simply because from the outset it had decided not to fight. The PNI, devastated by the effects of monoloyalty, was crushed, while Parmusi did even worse. The singular significance of the 1971 elections for Suharto, however, was not in the dimensions of the victory itself, but in what it both represented and portended for Indonesian politics and society. The manufacture of electoral success had demonstrated his determination to succeed with his vision of social engineering. The people themselves were not to be trusted to deliver a mandate; rather, the decision, such as it was, was the result of cleverly cynical artifice. Moreover, a site had now been cleared for the erection of the political superstructure of the Suharto regime, one in which, despite his protestation that Golkar would not simply nod its head in accord with the wishes of the government,[77] alternative visions of politics and the future would have no place.

Almost immediately, Suharto began his construction, suggesting – not for the first time – that the number of fractions in the new parliament be reduced from thirteen to four; the parties agreed to his proposals on the new architecture of parties and fractions (described as 'material-spiritual, spiritual-material, Golkar and ABRI').[78] As Suharto later explained, 'with the one and only road already there, why must we have so many cars, as many as nine? Why must we have wild speeding and collisions? . . . It is not necessary to have so many vehicles. But it is not necessary to have only one. Two or three is fine'.[79] When the new parliamentarians were installed at the end of October, he communicated his conviction that only two party 'groupings', together with Golkar, would present themselves for the elections planned for 1976. He also made it clear that, in line with the spirit of the 1945 Constitution, there would be no formal opposition within the newly elected parliament, which did not, he hastened to add, imply that the government would rule without control. A year later, at the swearing-in of MPR members, Suharto emphasised that 'defending and implementing Pancasila is a task which we must carry out without the slightest hesitation'.[80]

The staggering success of this exercise in political engineering inevitably raises questions about Suharto's understanding of democracy. It was not a democracy of the Western liberal kind, already tried, found wanting, and abandoned, as he had pointed out in his 1969 Independence Day speech.[81] Rather, he viewed it as a uniquely Indonesian creation, built upon indigenous culture and national identity, subservient to and embodied in Pancasila, and responsible. This version of democracy, 'Pancasila democracy' as it came to be called, would be 'healthy and responsible, based on morality and healthy thinking, grounded in a single ideology, that is, Pancasila'.[82] While he had earlier boasted of the freedom of expression and the press which his regime had installed as evidence of the regrowth of democracy, democracy of the Indonesian kind, Suharto proclaimed in his end-of-year speech of 1970, 'integrates freedom and responsibility in relation to common interests, and the nation and state' and 'supports and stimulates the implementation of development'.[83] Already in mid-1969 he had proclaimed that 'in our democracy based on Pancasila, there can be differences of opinion. What is not allowed is a sharpening of opinions which can result in dissension'. Nor did he think democracy had to wait until development had been achieved; 'development and democracy are two issues which can be implemented at the same time'. At the end of 1971, Suharto took satisfaction in the results of the elections, which were 'important steps in our effort to develop a healthy democracy'; at the same time he warned that 'we cannot allow a misuse of these democratic rights which have only a destructive purpose and which provoke unrest and disappointments in society'.[84]

THE CORPORATE POLITICAL STRUCTURE

There had already been premonitions of the shape of the new political terrain of the New Order. As we have seen, as early as February 1970 Suharto had suggested that the nation's needs would best be served by a simplification of the existing nine parties and Golkar into three groups – 'national', 'spiritual' and 'functional' – that would represent, rather than parties of contestation, three different aspects of the New Order developmentalist agenda.[85] What he wanted was programmatic parties which were united on the ideological basis of Pancasila; there could be no return to the eras of liberalism or Guided Democracy. The parties, by now badly demoralised, could only signal their 'consensus' with the suggestion. The same logic drove the second major development – the idea of the 'floating mass' – 'to distract the people's attention from political problems and ideological exclusiveness',[86] the better to devote themselves to the task of development, and to adopt the political docility that notion presupposed. The idea, originally suggested by the Muslim student leader Nurcholish Majid, soon thereafter was endorsed and embellished by the Diponegoro panglima Maj.-Gen. Widodo, and then by Ali Murtopo.[87]

Inevitably and inexorably, these processes took their predetermined path. In January 1973, the nine parties which had contested the 1971 elections were reduced to just two non-partisan and programmatic parties: the Development Unity Party (PPP), a merger of the four existing Islamic parties (NU, Parmusi, PSII, and Perti); and the Indonesian Democratic Party (PDI), into which were collapsed the five non-Islamic parties (the Catholic and Protestant parties, together with PNI, IPKI and Murba). The 'floating mass' concept took deep root after the elections. Thus, noted Ali Murtopo, ended the period of 'an excessive number of political parties, each with its own particular ideology' and inaugurated 'the waging of political competition on the basis of the merits of the respective party programmes, rather than ideologies'.[88]

Corporatisation also began to spread beyond the specifically political arena. At the end of 1971, the government announced the creation of a single organisation to cater for all government employees: Korpri (Civil Servants Professional Association). Similar sentiments led to the development of a single trade union organisation to embrace the needs of all workers: FBSI (All Indonesian Workers' Federation), established in February 1973 under the hand of Manpower Minister Mohammad Sadli, quickly followed by the establishment of the Cooperative Farmers Association in April and the All-Indonesia Fishers' Association in July. The abiding concern here was the notion of partnership, rather than antagonism, between employers and owners and their workers; all were to work together for the greater good of the whole society.

A further crucial feature of Suharto's developing political corporation was its attitude to law. Notwithstanding his frequent claims regarding the respect the law enjoyed under the New Order ('an important target of the New Order is to uphold the law once more and to revere justice', to be achieved by 'restoring judicial power as free power, liberated from the influence of government power'),[89] he never understood Western conceptions of the separation of powers.

SUHARTO AND BUSINESS

Suharto's business career had been temporarily sidelined in 1959 with his dismissal from the command of the Diponegoro Division as a result of unconventional fund-raising activities. He was, in some sense, unfortunate, since such activities were common in efforts to provide the means to make good shortfalls in budgeted funding. With the establishment and consolidation of the New Order, as we have already seen, such methods of finding funds gathered more strength as the Army's control over the polity deepened.

In general, this development meant that army officers were permitted, even encouraged, to establish or extend businesses to provide new sources of funds for their operations and, indeed, for the private gain of the officers concerned. The regime would provide the necessary conditions, and support as needed, to allow these kinds of activities to continue, and it expected to receive an appropriate proportion of the funds thus generated. Indeed, Suharto's office building, Bina Graha, adjacent to the Merdeka Palace, was constructed wholly from Pertamina funds, and in the early years of his presidency, Pertamina was the single greatest non-government contributor to the Armed Forces, without being bothered about such niceties as first siphoning resources through government coffers. The business autonomy accorded military officers like Ibnu Sutowo was in no danger of restriction, so long as the necessary funds kept flowing. One example of the pleasing flexibility it gave Suharto was provided at the end of 1971 when he presented 110 jeeps to Java military commands from his own resources 'because Hankam [the Ministry of Defence and Security] is not able to provide it'.[90]

Pertamina was the outstanding example of an army enterprise. Under Ibnu Sutowo, it developed from unpromising beginnings to dominate the Indonesian oil industry. Ibnu enjoyed a special relationship with Suharto, such that he was allowed virtually total autonomy in the running of Pertamina. As we have noted, efforts in 1966 by the mining minister, Slamet Bratanata, to make Ibnu accountable were answered by Suharto's transferring the oil and gas directorate to his own office and sacking the minister the following year. Bulog was another cash cow of the highest order for the New Order regime, as well as for the army staff who managed it, and a continuing irritant to the technocrats. Established in 1966 as an agency to purchase rice (the majority on international markets, for which it held a monopoly) for government officials and Armed Forces members, in 1970 it became the government mechanism to control rice price fluctuations by creating a buffer rice stock. It had access to cheap loans from the central bank and was able to make large profits from its rice sales and from re-investing its cheap credit with private banks at much higher rates. Bulog's concern with making money, however, at times left it badly positioned to achieve its major aim of achieving rice price stability. PT Berdikari, the huge army-run state trading company also set up in 1966, was less successful in the longer term than its fellows and fell into financial difficulties when its bank collapsed in 1968. In 1969, the Army consolidated many of its foundations as private companies under the umbrella of the army enterprise PT Tri Usaha Bhakti.[91]

The regime also sponsored other forms of 'private' business, in particular in association with a small number of Sino-Indonesian businessmen. The general modus operandi was that the government provided credit facilities or privileged access to a certain market, in the expectation that members of the government (often sleeping partners in the arrangements) would be suitably paid for their cooperation. Amongst the key businessmen of the early New Order was Liem Siu Liong, long a broker for army business schemes but now catapulted to new heights by the Army's political dominance. Having already formed a business partnership in the early period of the New Order with Suharto's cousin Sudwikatmono, together with Juhar Sutanto and Ibrahim Risyad, in the CV Waringin company which prospered on government credit and officials' favour, in 1969 Liem established, in association with his business partners, PT Bogasari, a flour-milling concern which Suharto himself officially opened in 1971. Part of the profits of Bogasari were directed to foundations associated with the military. In 1968, with the assistance of Sumitro Joyohadikusumo, Liem acquired a part share in a clove import monopoly with his company PT Mega; a further share was provided to Mercu Buana, a company owned by Probosutejo, Suharto's half-brother. In 1970, Liem's PT Tarumatex textile company was reportedly favoured with a lucrative contract to provide military uniforms for the Army.[92]

A similar story of rapid economic ascendancy occurred with William Suryajaya (Cia Kian Liong), the owner of Astra. His political connections, including, amongst others, Sujono Humardani – together with a large investment in the state-owned General Motors assembly plant – paid off. He moved quickly to establish himself as a broker for foreign companies wishing to export to Indonesia, becoming the sole agent for large Japanese and US manufacturers like Toyota, Xerox and Kodak, as well as the dominant figure in vehicle manufacture in Indonesia. Amongst other prominent Sino-Indonesian businessmen involved in army business were Nyoo Han Siang, Yap Swie Kie and 'Bob' Hasan. Sino-Indonesian–Army cooperation was also exemplified in the operations of the Kostrad foundation (established by Suharto in 1964 and managed by Brig.-Gen. Sofyar), which developed rapidly in this context, assisted by Suharto's close relationship with Liem Siu Liong. Together, Sofyar and Liem reshaped Bank Windu Kencana, and the bank (flush with deposits as a result of its impeccable political connections) financed further business development into air transport, building and processing. Another army-sponsored enterprise, Inkopad, completed the construction of the up-market Kartika Plaza in association with a Hong Kong company. Tri Usaha Bhakti, grouping a score of ABRI-sponsored companies, was a similar site for the military's favoured brokerage role in business. Local commanders were equally as enthusiastic about fund-raising as their Jakarta counterparts; like them, their role was to smooth the political road (gaining permissions, licences, monopolies) for their partner Chinese or foreign business associates who took on the task of actually running the enterprises, and to provide them with 'protection' against unwanted opposition and the threat of prosecution should their activities encompass illegality.[93]

It was inevitable, especially in a context in which foreign capital was coming more frequently under jaundiced nationalist notice, that such fruitful association with Sino-Indonesian businessmen should have political repercussions and raise social tensions; 'the Chinese are accused of being the favourites of the military and of getting contracts and credits denied indigenous operators', remarked one journalist in 1971.[94] To address growing unrest about Chinese dominance of Indonesian business, Suharto in March 1972 announced a proposal that the government purchase 50 per cent of the shares of these concerns and sell them to *pribumi* (indigenous) businesspeople at favourable rates of interest. In the following days, first Sudharmono and then Suharto himself watered down the proposal; it was, said Sudharmono, only a suggestion, while Suharto said that compulsion on the Chinese would be counterproductive and would not be invoked to realise his idea.[95] The problem, however, refused to go away; it was characterised by unproductive proposals and debates about how best to promote the interests of pribumi entrepreneurs, with no noticeable slippage in the business connections between military officers and Chinese businessmen. Suharto's public line on business investment remained firm, however. Addressing a meeting in Bengkulu in June 1972, he remarked that 'we obtained our foreign debts with very light conditions, and all of it is used for development'.[96]

An associated aspect of these business activities was the vigour with which Suharto's wife, Tien, took to fund-raising activities for purportedly philanthropic purposes. As early as 1966 she had formed an association of the wives of cabinet members to carry out social development work to raise people's living standards. The most well-known of her business creations – the 'Our Hope' Foundation, established with Ibnu Sutowo's wife – built its success on the shameless solicitation of 'donations' from businesses that could not afford to endure the regime's displeasure, and on arrangements which provided it with a specified cut from operations like PT Bogasari. Another foundation, Yayasan Mangadek, devoted to the upkeep of the cultural legacy of the Solo royal house of Mangkunegaran (to which Ibu Tien was very distantly related), and managed by the wealthy Solo businessman and associate of Ibu Tien, Sukamdani, involved itself in a range of joint ventures, including timber exporting.

Ibu Tien's business activities were, of course, part of a larger round of duties which were mostly focused on the family. Her eldest children were now attaining adulthood. Notwithstanding her efforts, there were signs of indiscipline, perhaps attributable to their father's preoccupations, and the glare of publicity which surrounded his movements and intruded into even such private moments as the celebration of his fiftieth birthday at the house of Ibu Tien's parents at Kalitan in Solo. In July 1968, for example, Sigit was fined for speeding after a traffic accident. Tutut, the eldest daughter, had enrolled at the Technology Faculty of Trisakti University, a private institution popular amongst the Jakarta elite for their children's higher education, where she began studies (never completed) in technology, with a special interest in space aviation; she married Indra Rukmana Kuwara in February 1972. All of Suharto's children had attended a private junior high school in Cikini before moving for their senior high school years to a private school on Jalan Budi Utomo. Suharto's pride in his maturing family was counterbalanced by a loss that must have affected him deeply: the death in 1971 of his stepmother, Ibu Prawirowiharjo, the woman who had nurtured him through to his own maturity. His characteristic animosity to what he saw as tampering with his own family history was already evident; a member of a trade delegation to Taiwan allegedly passed himself off as Suharto's younger brother, prompting an immediate investigation by the public prosecutor.

SCANDALS, CORRUPTION AND CRITICISM

Suharto had assumed the presidency on a wave of goodwill and popular support. The heavy-handedness of the election process, increasing cynicism about dwi fungsi and, more directly, the increasing evidence of corruption and collusion within his administration, however, combined around the beginning of 1970 to arouse the first consistent and wide-ranging disillusionment with the tenor of his rule. For the next few years, criticism of the corruption of the New Order was to be the staple of dissident voices, and the major targets of those protests were the generals closest to Suharto: Ibnu Sutowo, Sujono, Achmad Tirtosudiro, Alamsyah, Suhardiman, and Suryo. Strangely, Suharto himself remained free from personal criticism on this score.[97]

The immediate occasion for the first major outbreak of disaffection with Suharto's regime came in January 1970, when price rises for kerosene, petrol and staple goods put into stark relief the luxurious style of life which those around him were increasingly seen to enjoy. The demonstrations, led by student activists like Arief Budiman, Marsillam Simanjuntak, and Syahrir, were labelled by one commentator as 'the strongest anti-corruption outburst in the 25-year history of the

Republic'.[98] Demonstrations on a similar scale took place six months later. Stunned and probably puzzled by this reaction, on 31 January 1970 Suharto, irritated at the readiness of the press to report on matters relating to corruption, and emphasising his previous record and his willingness to combat corruption 'in a fundamental way',[99] appointed a four-man commission, headed by esteemed former prime minister Wilopo and assisted by Mohammad Hatta, to investigate and report on corruption. Suharto remarked in early February:

> Corruption and deviant actions in the economic field in general not only conflict with the law and with security, but are clearly incompatible with morals, and puncture the feeling of justice. Corruption blocks the implementation of the state's programs, damages the principles and reduces the authority of the government apparatus, if it is not curbed, lessened and suppressed as much as possible.[100]

His testiness about the rising tide of criticism was apparent from his reaction to the 'Kita Ingin Tahu' ('We Want to Know') Group; no longer would the government accommodate their wishes, and Achmad Tirtosudiro, scheduled to participate in a 'We Want to Know' forum in February, was instructed not to speak.

Over the next few months, the Commission of Four took to its work with gusto, engaging in long meetings with Suharto himself and with key figures in the corruption investigations, such as the Bulog chief, Achmad Tirtosudiro. It provided a stream of highly critical reports to Suharto, laying bare a series of financial improprieties, lax practices and irregular modes of operation in such state instrumentalities as Pertamina, Bulog and Perhutani, the state forestry company, as well as questionable connections between state enterprises and private individuals. In mid-year, student criticism of corruption again began to make itself heard. Apparently chastened by what he knew of the Commission of Four's findings thus far, Suharto adopted a variant of the mode he had adopted in facing the Bimas problems. Meeting face-to-face with a fifteen-member student delegation on 14 July, he pointed out the difficulties of proceeding with corruption charges without clear and sufficient proof of wrongdoing, and he agreed to make himself available at a regular time (Saturdays, between 9 a.m. and 12 noon) to receive students who could provide him with that evidence. Four days later, four students, including Arief Budiman and Mar'ie Muhammad, appeared with evidence that Suharto's close associate, General Suryo, had opened a large account in Dutch guilders. Suharto, adopting a calm, friendly and reasonable mien, nevertheless refused to take action on the grounds that there was nothing wrong with the procedure employed by Suryo, and that it was unclear that Suryo himself had pocketed the amount in question. According to Arief Budiman's account, the President 'told them they were being used as tools by the politicians'.[101] Suharto continued the practice of making himself available to student complainants about corruption for a few more weeks before discontinuing the practice 'because those who came … did not bring concrete information'.[102] Arief, as he later recounted, 'was disappointed to see that the group who served Suharto obediently became stronger, while those who supported Suharto critically were slowly thrown out of the circle'.[103]

In the meantime, the commission had completed its investigation, deprecating the practice of non-budgetary funds, especially those at the President's disposal, and recommending structural reform to the attorney-general's office and, in addition, that action be taken in respect of cases involving figures including General Suryo and Suharto's cousin, Sudwikatmono. The affair was highly embarrassing to Suharto because the commission report was leaked to the press and published by *Sinar Harapan* in late July, clearly a move with a political motive.[104] His embarrassment, however, did not lead to the desired reforms, since he was not about to sacrifice those closest to him to assuage public disgruntlement. He insisted, in the course of his annual Independence Day address, that 'there should no longer be any doubts about it. I myself will lead the fight against corruption',[105] but resulting actions led only to the punishment of a few minor officials, a requirement that officials disclose their private assets, a new law on corruption and another which sought to control Pertamina's activities more closely.

Suharto had been, it needs to be emphasised, a public man throughout his life, always close to the state and its work, always emphasising that his own work was the state's work. Critics should not have been surprised at his passivity and apparent lack of commitment in his anti-corruption efforts. He himself was the product of a culture and life experience that drew no sharp division between public and private spheres and public and private property, something reflected in his own definition of corruption as 'taking something to which you have no right for your own benefit'. To his mind, the state's wealth could be turned to purposes that benefited society as a whole. It was this that had motivated his earlier efforts in Semarang in the late 1950s to tax the people in the interest of the welfare of his soldiers. The same logic could easily be turned to favour the business interests of those who he knew could deliver results. If they could progress his beloved development, then they should be allowed to do so and be paid adequately for their efforts.

Accordingly, Suharto appears to have had significant, and genuine, difficulty in appreciating just what the fuss was about. On the one hand, he chastised those who, by force of economic circumstance, had availed themselves of public goods, while seeking on the other to exonerate them by his 'conviction' that 'corruption in our country comes about not because of a corrupt mentality, but results rather from economic pressures'.[106] He had nothing to say, however, about those who were already wealthy seeking to enlarge themselves at the public expense or through private kickbacks and commissions – provided that they continued to perform their duties well and did not embarrass the government – and his silence can only be taken to mean that he saw no moral problem in social leaders disposing of public goods for their own benefit if the generality of their activities led to the greater good of the whole community, that is, the process of development. His own behaviour, of course, had long been governed by such thinking. Accordingly, the actions that he took at this time, such as tinkering with his 'Team to Combat Corruption', and his August 1970 decree specifying the duties and powers of Aspri and denying them any executive power, were designed not to solve the problem of corruption as such but, rather, to contain the political damage which revelations of high-level corruption brought.

His frequent criticisms of corrupt behaviour carried a similar stamp. He cavilled against those who purchased foreign imports purely as a matter of extravagance. At the height of the corruption uproar in early 1970, Suharto angrily appealed at an ABRI commanders' meeting for members of the Armed Forces and their families not to live extravagantly, to control their children ('in matters like *ngebut* ['playing chicken'], the use of service cars, carrying firearms, wearing their hair long'), and for ABRI wives not to wear mini-skirts. Early in 1972, he issued an instruction against the private use of government telephones, and again warned members of ABRI about the dangers of their children damaging the good name of the Armed Forces.[107] It should not be thought that Suharto was being deliberately duplicitous here, as though he was simply voicing these sentiments for general public consumption without meaning what he said. He was genuinely concerned about corruption, but his sense of corruption was of a curiously limited and warped kind. The point of his criticism was not that the individual private use of public goods was in itself morally wrong – Suharto's moral calculus did not deal in such categories – but rather that such behaviour might soil the good repute of the government and the Armed Forces and thus damage the fabric of the regime.

The intricacies of Suharto's personal behaviour, though initially puzzling, provide us with some further clarificatory clues. While he was by now personally wealthy, and while he lived comfortably, his style of life (like his personal communicative style) was muted and unostentatious and bore traces of unforgiving puritanism. His house in Menteng was modest (unlike those of many of his army and business contemporaries, who competed to outdo each other in crude and tasteless extravagance), his cultural tastes unelaborate. Notwithstanding claims to the contrary ('It is tempting to suggest that personal greed was also important in his calculations from the very start'),[108] he was never personally rapacious nor avaricious, never one to use what wealth he had as a means of personal material gratification. He used his wealth – or rather, his access to funds – in ways that accorded with and advanced his general goals for the nation, and for him, therefore, the question of corruption simply never arose. In accord with his fundamentally corporatist ideas, the private use of the public good was unacceptable only if the public interest, as he defined it, was thereby harmed.

Finally, there was another important reason for Suharto's unwillingness to take strong steps against high-level corruption. Inexperienced in governance, facing a multitude of problems and, notwithstanding his public popularity, with only a tenuous grip on power, he was constrained to govern through a kind of consensus of his generals. He understood that to annoy seriously, much less jettison, a military supporter of the stature, power and resources of Ibnu Sutowo or a staunch henchman like Alamsyah in the face of public criticism could well have disastrous consequences for his regime and all it represented. Indeed, rumours of an officers' plot to restore Sukarno's rule had provided grounds for the arrest of Maj.-Gen. Mursyid in late 1969 and, soon after, that of Maj.-Gen. Suadi, head of the

National Defence Institute, apparently because of their close contacts with Sukarno. One commentator opined that 'at the lieutenant-general level some officers still regard Suharto as a "peasant boy", "an uneducated follower of mysticism", with "no good family background". They feel there could be better leaders'.[109] Given these circumstances, and given that there was no guarantee that replacements would be any more pure than those already in place, and probably much less reliable, it made little sense to disturb things unnecessarily. To this explanation one might also add the fact that those closest to the corruption scandal were integral parts of Suharto's personal group, to whom he felt strong loyalty and upon whom he depended so closely for advice and support.

If Suharto was looking for some relief from domestic political pressure through state visits in early September 1970, he was not to find it. Indeed, he was forced to delay leaving for the Netherlands, West Germany and Zambia for forty-eight hours because of violent anti-New Order demonstrations in Holland, and himself encountered further demonstrations both there and in Germany. His experience at the subsequent Lusaka meeting of the Non-Aligned Movement made for an altogether unhappy foreign excursion. On his return, Suharto faced an emerging mood of public disgruntlement with the direction of the New Order, a stunning turnaround from his triumphant rise to the presidency eighteen months before. Towards the end of the year, he was forced to deny emphatically the accusation that he no longer listened to the students.[110] A year later, a commentator wrote that

> the voices of the students and other dissenting civilian elements will not be easily stilled. For the most part, the students remain especially restless and sceptical about the future. They do not like the way the Suharto government chooses to rule. They find too much vagueness about its aims and purpose, too much that is temporary and 'stop-gap' about its planning, and too much mystery about the way it often acts.[111]

The much smaller demonstrations during Suharto's visits to Australia and New Zealand early in 1972 he put down, as we saw, to the work of communists.

Suharto's failure to appreciate the real dimensions of the corruption problem was exemplified in two later scandals. The first resulted from the action of Police Commissioner-General Hugeng Imam Santoso in September 1971 in making public his success in breaking a smuggling operation at the Tanjung Priok port in which luxury cars were imported, with army protection (and the reported active involvement of Ibu Tien), for profitable local resale. Hugeng's reward was to be sacked a few days later and replaced by an official with a more seasoned understanding of the problem.

The second was the development of Ibu Tien's dream, *Taman Mini Indonesia Indah* (Beautiful Indonesia-in-Miniature Park), the theme park she developed to the south-east of Jakarta on the model of Disneyland and Thailand's cultural park, Timland. To finance her dream, conceived in 1971, Ibu Tien made it clear to business leaders and local government officials that it would be in their best interest to make substantial donations to fund Taman Mini's development, for which her Yayasan Harapan Kita was responsible. The project raised the ire of students and other civilian dissidents, not only because of Ibu Tien's fund-raising methods and the belief that people had been forced to sell their land for the proposed site, but also because they saw it as an extravagance – the first phase alone cost 4.5 billion rupiah – which their impoverished nation could ill afford, a crucial diversion of much-needed funds for a spurious purpose. The task of fending off student protesters fell to long-time presidential aide Cokropranolo and to Sukamdani, himself deeply involved in the construction of Taman Mini. Armed toughs bashed student protesters, both to defend Ibu Tien's name and 'to give a warning to "people behind" the protest movement'.[112] In the face of these protests, Ibu Tien remained fiercely determined that the project proceed.

The fracas drew Suharto's ire in a way that people had not witnessed since the dark days of early October 1965. Manifesting his inability to comprehend the objections to Taman Mini, he chose as the site of his attack the opening of the luxurious Pertamina hospital in January 1972, itself a 'lighthouse' project grounded in the same notion of prestige that had given birth to Taman Mini. Speaking without notes, Suharto lashed Ibu Tien's critics. He categorised them as bent upon disrupting national stability and opposed to the national interest, and he threatened to employ his Supersemar powers to deal with them. 'I will pummel anyone who tries to violate the constitution, and I will get support from ABRI', he raged; moreover, 'if there are lawyers who say that the President is not able to take action against people who do not understand and who do not wish to understand, I can use Supersemar as a basis because they are disturbing general security'. Warming to his task, he rejected the view that the Taman Mini project was a wasteful burden upon the people, and claimed that the issue was merely a facade for a campaign to discredit his regime, remove ABRI from the political scene, and force his own removal. 'I want to make clear that I am not going to dissolve the dwifungsi of ABRI', he continued, much less accede to demands for his eviction. He had been appointed by the MPR and could only be dismissed by it, and any attempt to change matters in an unconstitutional way would be answered with force. 'I will again take up the attitude I took on 1 October 1965, when facing the PKI. At the time only my wife supported me, while the Front Pancasila and the Angkatan '66 had not yet been born'.[113] Amongst those arrested soon afterwards were Arief Budiman, Aristides Katoppo, managing editor of *Sinar Harapan*, and the iconoclastic Dutch-born activist and chair of the Human Rights Foundation, Haji Johannes Prinsen. Suharto's show of public anger was probably strongly influenced by the deep sense of solidarity he felt towards his wife. Privately, however, he directed that the project proceed slowly and unostentatiously.

Concerns about naked corruption and the diversion of public resources in socially unhelpful projects slowly coalesced into more serious criticisms about the structure and nature of the New Order, which combined around the theme of foreign, especially Japanese, capital and its increasing dominance over the economy and society.[114] Opposition to such trends was not limited to civilians. Increasingly, military officers, some of them younger and professionally trained graduates of the Magelang Academy, established in 1957, and now moving into senior positions, saw these developments as a corrupting influence amongst senior echelons of the military, the so-called 1945 generation, tempting them to betray the ideals of the revolution. Moreover, they became increasingly uneasy about the excesses of corruption and the related management failures of the generals clustered closely around Suharto, and the effects these might have on the political legitimacy and durability of the New Order. Occasionally miffed as well by the Suharto group's political activities, which caused problems on the ground for local commands, they sought to create more regular and professional patterns of military behaviour.

Accordingly, a critique emerged amongst both civilians and these 'professionally minded' officers which focused on the baleful social effects of foreign, particularly Japanese, capital, and the loss of national independence and élan which it was alleged to occasion. This mood found a natural target in the men closely associated with Suharto, who were seen as the architects of the current problems and those who had most benefited from its implementation. Its military manifestation increasingly centred around the persons of Sumitro and Sutopo Yuwono, a long-term competitor with Ali Murtopo in intelligence affairs, and to a lesser extent the younger Magelang graduate Sayidiman Suryohadiprojo, deputy chief of staff of the Army, who were informal leaders of the 'professionalisers', popularly dubbed the 'Hankam group'. The official response to this increasing sense of disjointedness was frequently to suggest that the unrest was somehow related to efforts at communist-inspired subversion. Suharto, however, was himself conscious of the effects on youthful identity of the impact of foreign cultural influences and the increasing distance from the country's central foundational experiences of the revolution; he asserted that 'society must be able to feel the results of development', and even raised the spectre of 'social revolution ... if national development could not raise the standard of living of the people'.[115]

By late 1973, criticism of the New Order was gathering increasing steam as students centred in Jakarta and Bandung adopted a tone of persistent questioning of its basis and fundamental direction. At a deeper level, these criticisms were concerned with what was seen to be a characteristic soullessness and pragmatism at the centre of the New Order. In 1969, Nasution had told a visiting Australian academic that 'we can't go on ignoring ideological issues'.[116] What he meant was that the New Order had attempted to remove divisions not by a process of reasoned debate and compromise but simply by fiat, replacing ideological concerns with dry pragmatism; there was, he noted on another occasion, no 'new vision', only 'the old strategy, that is, stabilisation and economic development'.[117] While this style of politics had a certain appeal after the high theatre of Sukarno's rule, by 1970 it was becoming boring, irksome and deeply unsatisfying to those groups whose original faith in Suharto, they began to feel, had been seriously misplaced. Suharto, for his part, increasingly began to distance himself from the public; already by the early 1970s the characteristic mode of his interactions with the press was becoming evident: ministers, aides, senior officials and generals would join in discussions with him, usually at Cendana. Upon their appearance, they would brief the press about the content of their discussions, becoming the conduit of Suharto's views on political, social and economic problems. Increasingly, the mode of direct contact which he had employed so successfully in the mid- and late 1960s began to ebb away.

THE ROAD TO RE-ELECTION

The critics, both civilians and 'professional' groups in the military, remained, however, relatively small in both size and influence. With the elections successfully completed, Suharto set to serving out the remainder of his presidential term, and to preparing the ground for a succeeding term. His first step was a cabinet reshuffle in September 1971 which reduced Armed Forces representation in the cabinet to only five, masking the fact of military dominance of the government. The cabinet appointments were a triumph for the technocrats, with the introduction of Sadli, Wijoyo and Emil Salim in charge, respectively, of manpower, planning and development, and state apparatus. Seven of the President's economic advisers were now in cabinet, and the eighth, Radius Prawiro, was named governor of the central bank. Two other notable changes were made, the one involving the appointment of Professor H. A. Mukti Ali as minister for religious affairs – the first time in eighteen years that the ministry had not been in the charge of an NU leader, and an indication of Suharto's prevailing secular attitude to Islam in politics – and Panggabean as state minister assisting the President in matters of defence and security, with the title of deputy commander of ABRI. Suharto's second step, long foreshadowed, was the division of the parliament into the four fractions, an arrangement formalised early in 1973 with the creation of two new parties to subsume the roles played by the existing nine. The old party system was dead; now it was buried.

In March 1973, against a background of heavy military security, the MPR convened for the first time since 1968 to perform its constitutional tasks. Nasution no longer chaired the body; no longer needing to be mollified, he had been eliminated from his erstwhile role through the simple mechanism of not being appointed. For the first time, the MPR heard an address of accountability delivered by Suharto, an explanation of his carriage of the mandate entrusted to him in 1968. In a three-hour speech, he extolled the achievements of his first term, especially in the fields of economic progress and political stabilisation, as well as rehearsing some well-worn themes: a cautious and unapologetic approach to the issue of reviving relations with China, the continuing threat of communism, the need to receive Indonesian Chinese as Indonesian citizens.

Having endorsed the President's performance, the Assembly proceeded clinically – the process took just eight minutes – to his unopposed re-nomination and re-election for another five-year term and – the first time it had ever performed this task – to the election of a vice-president. Suharto's choice, the Sultan of Yogyakarta, a person of immense popular stature, was unproblematic. To complete its work, the MPR prolonged Suharto's Supersemar powers, provided a mechanism for the succession in the event of the incapacity of both president and vice-president to perform their duties, and produced a document – already supplied by the administration (and to which, Suharto remarks, he contributed by 'gathering material from a broad cross-section of society in a democratic way')[118] – which set out the broad guidelines of state policy.

CONCLUSION

Notwithstanding the difficulties which had gradually gathered about him, Suharto now appeared impregnable, buttressed on the one hand by military power and, on the other, by general civilian acquiescence to his regime. 'After all the tiring turmoil', remarked one commentator, 'firm government going somewhere is what the mass of Indonesians, as distinct from some intellectuals perhaps, definitely want'.[119] His Second Development Cabinet, announced on the evening of 27 March 1973, was a matter of fine tuning. Professor Sumitro Joyohadikusumo, 'rather too much a prima donna',[120] and his old PSI connections a source of antagonism at that moment, was demoted from his Trade post to the much less important Research portfolio, but the technocrats' hold on the development agencies remained strong. As well as Sumitro Joyohadikusumo, the cabinet numbered amongst its members Ali Wardhana (minister for finance), Radius Prawiro, Sadli, Emil Salim, and Subroto, with Wijoyo taking office in the new role as coordinating minister for economics, finance and industry, as well as the headship of Bappenas. The new cabinet had a strongly conservative tack, with an emphasis on stability and on continuing and intensifying the directions taken by the first cabinet. As well, it had the task of carrying out the second New Order elections by 1977 at the latest.

Suharto's first term of office had been a period of portentous political creativity. Contradicting charges that he was a dourly reactive and excessively pragmatic leader, he had gradually, purposefully and systematically crafted a wholly new political system which both manifested and effected his special understanding of the proper structure of Indonesia and the real needs of its people. The economic policies over which he had presided, including 'the success story of Repelita I',[121] had delivered impressive growth rates, greatly enhanced flows of foreign capital, a huge expansion in exports, mostly timber and oil, and an extraordinary boom in rice production (notwithstanding a monumental rice harvest failure in 1972) which promised self-sufficiency by the middle of the decade.

Suharto's New Order was, of course, to be an enduring construction but, as we shall see, it was built upon a series of contradictions both in structure and implication which would, in the end, bring it tumbling down. The first signs of its inherent problems began to appear by the end of the 1960s. Suharto, however, did nothing positive to protect himself from the gathering clouds of criticism and attack. Indeed, he and his ruling group, now tightly bound and increasingly isolated from the society they ruled, either tried to demean or simply ignored or deflected the criticisms of the style and substance of his rule, and to repress those who held these ideas. Notwithstanding his pre-eminence and the apparent durability of his rule, he was facing a long decade of struggle and turmoil to keep his place and his vision for Indonesia intact.

8 Negotiating the problems of the New Order, 1973–1983

THE BEGINNING OF Suharto's second presidential term ushered in a long period of bitter domestic political strife, different in kind from that which he had encountered either during the tense stand-off with Sukarno following Gestapu, or the rather more cushioned period which had seen him fundamentally reshape the structure of Indonesian politics. The characteristic feature of this phase – except for the period of his downfall, the most critical, difficult and dangerous stage of his long reign – was that it represented the bitter implementation of the logic of the consolidated New Order and the effective crushing of all those who sought a different dispensation in Indonesian politics. Suharto was not to know that his greatest battles would come against those who had once supported him in the attainment of power; indeed, as one crisis mounted upon another, he evinced an attitude of incredulity, together with a mounting anger and parallel repressiveness, that his subjects and erstwhile supporters should choose to threaten, oppose, even betray, his vision for Indonesia.

THE ROAD TO MALARI

As the New Order moved into its early maturity, the signs of emerging corporatism were unmistakable. They were manifested, as we have already seen, by the development of a single umbrella body for all trade unions in Indonesia, the All-Indonesia Workers' Federation (FBSI), a task brought to its summit by Subroto in his capacity as minister for manpower, and lauded by Suharto. By mid-1974, Subroto was able to report to Suharto the establishment of FBSI management boards in twenty-three provinces. 'Labour and industry', Suharto remarked in 1975, 'are not forces which must stand in mutual opposition, rather they must be brothers in arms, working together for the development of Indonesia'. Strikes, therefore, were not only unnecessary but not in accord with labour relations based on Pancasila. Education was also a target: 'without education which has Pancasila as its foundation and direction', Suharto noted, 'we cannot develop a society based on Pancasila'. The whole people of Indonesia, he noted a little later, 'must socialise [*memasyarakatkan*] Pancasila and Pancasila-ise [*mempancasilakan*] society'.[1]

Emerging corporatism was similarly evident in Golkar's post-election development. At the group's first national conference in Surabaya, Suharto, accompanied by a clutch of senior ministers and Aspri and ABRI figures, opened the proceedings and placed his stamp on the organisation; as its senior figure, he received the power to determine the membership of its central board. ABRI's partnership with Golkar was affirmed with a previously unwitnessed clarity. However, Golkar's role remained, purposely, vague and unclear; Suharto clearly viewed it as little more than an institutional vehicle to deliver the periodic election vote, and had no serious thought that it should begin the process of expanding its roots and developing options for input into the policy process.

At the same time, however, as we have noted, signs of emerging elite competition were in evidence, notable most clearly in the efforts of the reformist Hankam group gradually coalescing around Kopkamtib Commander Sumitro. It was strongly influenced by PSI values, keen to preserve and foster the professionalism of the Army (and now with more readily available formal funding to do it) and gathering support from the younger, more broadly based and academically trained officers. It sought especially to contain the freedom of movement afforded by Suharto to the Murtopo/Sujono group in particular, and the 'political' and 'financial' officers in general, who were bent on broadening the Army's sway in politics, in business and in society more generally, and who had benefited substantially from Suharto's politically motivated patronage strategies. The group achieved its first success at the Golkar conference with the election of Gen. Amir Murtono as Golkar's first chairman, a move designed to undercut Ali Murtopo's efforts to make the organisation his own. Suharto, however, would not let them advance too far and upset his balance; he rebuffed Sumitro's attempt to have his favoured candidate, Charis Suhud, become deputy commander of Kopkamtib and appointed his long-time colleague, Admiral Sudomo, himself close to Murtopo, instead.

These steps manifested Suharto's maturing confidence in his position and stature, as well as a liking for the centrality it afforded him. Jakarta was rapidly becoming a beacon for world leaders, either from the developed world (eager to present aid and to invest in the new Indonesia) or the developing one (keen to find out for themselves how a ramshackle economy could be rejuvenated so spectacularly). Suharto's centrality, as we have seen, was also reflected in the consolidation of an enduring style of communicating with his people. After meetings of the cabinet or other forums, or after discussions with ministers or other assembled personages, the details of the matters discussed would be disbursed to the waiting throng of the media corps by the person with whom Suharto had spoken or a delegated spokesman; Suharto himself, notwithstanding his frequent public appearances, was becoming ever more reluctant to face the press himself.

Suharto's more private face went hand in hand with the growing sense of disenchantment with the policies and directions of his government, and particularly that the system of army patronage, together with the rising tide of foreign investment in manufacturing, particularly from Japan, was harming the economic prospects of indigenous entrepreneurs and workers. Emerging civil unease was most spectacularly manifested in a serious anti-Chinese riot which broke out in Bandung on 5 August 1973, occasioned by an insignificant traffic accident. Gangs went on a wild rampage, targeting Chinese shops and houses, damaging more than a thousand, as well as burning cars, reportedly causing almost US$3 million in damage.[2] The apparent lack of enthusiasm of local Siliwangi troops to restore order – their task took almost nine hours – appeared to indicate some sympathy with the actions of the mobs and, more generally and seriously, significant disaffection with what were perceived to be government policies helpful to the interests of Chinese and foreign enterprises. Suharto was not slow to grasp the significance of what had occurred and to move firmly to control the damage; 'the government will act resolutely against all those involved in that disturbance', he remarked.[3] He summoned Sumitro to brief the cabinet on the incident, and took pains to emphasise the need for national integration. He also hauled the governor of West Java, Solihin, over the coals, extracting from him a guarantee that future incidents of this kind would not take place.

A contemporaneous manifestation of political division was the furore that descended upon the government's effort to install a new uniform marriage law in the last half of the year. The revised draft law, which, amongst other things, placed new restrictions on divorce and polygamy, was essentially the work of Ali Murtopo and his think-tank (the Centre for Strategic and International Studies, established in the early 1970s), and drafted without reference to or advice from Muslim teachers. Part of Murtopo's broader strategy of depoliticising society and enhancing its 'rational' secularity, the marriage bill evoked a storm of protest from Muslim politicians and leaders who perceived it as an affront to Muslim values and a general threat to social stability, notwithstanding Suharto's emphatic denial that the bill offended Islamic beliefs.[4]

Both incidents crystallised the escalating sense of unease and criticism at the bearings of the government. Students became more vociferous in attacking what they saw as the loss both of a sense of national morality (evidenced in the appearance of casinos and massage parlours in Jakarta) and of sovereignty over the nation's wealth. They used such occasions as the framing of a 'Petition of 24 October' by University of Indonesia students and the mid-November visit of the young Dutch minister for development cooperation, Dr J. P. Pronk, to maximise the political impact of their views about corruption and foreign investment.[5] As well as demanding a greater voice in national affairs, the students targeted bodies like Aspri which they perceived as barriers to the impact of popular sentiment upon policy. For his part, Suharto vigorously defended his development policies, linking them closely to religion:

> Development and religion are two sides of the same coin [*senafas*] … religion without development will not make progress, while development without religion will go in the wrong direction … development brings with it changes which, if we are not careful, can cause human values to decline. In this context, the moral

and ethical teachings provided by religion can form a sturdy fortress which can help us avoid the nasty side effects of development.[6]

The emerging mood of disenchantment provided an opportunity for Sumitro's Hankam group, perhaps alarmed by the events in Thailand in October 1973 which had seen the collapse of Thanom Kittikachorn's military-dominated government, to position themselves for popular favour. Sumitro, notwithstanding his Kopkamtib role, did not take effective steps to bring the growing protests under control; indeed, he became something of a regular feature on campuses in November where he spoke in terms of a 'new pattern of leadership', a government more receptive to public opinion and of the need for 'two-way' communication between people and government, sentiments which inevitably invited an escalation of student activity.[7] Sumitro's reception contrasted starkly with that received by the technocrats as they sought to hose down student alarm at the direction of economic policy; so robustly was Sumitro Joyohadikusumo challenged at a meeting at the Bandung Institute of Technology that he was forced to leave. Furthermore, together with Bakin chief Sutopo Yuwono, General Sumitro took on the role of broker on the question of the proposed marriage law, and hammered out a compromise solution with Muslim groups that formed the basis of the new law which passed parliament in December. (Somewhat ironically, given the circumstances, Suharto was later to claim credit for the bill's passage.)[8]

Sumitro's stance was the first clear challenge to Suharto's supremacy since the beginnings of the New Order. It was a combination of not-so-subtle distancing from the regime, attacks on (and encouraging others to criticise) those close to Suharto, notably the Aspri group and, especially, Ali Murtopo (to whose corrupt and interfering behaviour and anti-technocrat development ideas was attributed the social and moral damage suffered under New Order economic policies), and open courting of important dissident social groups, student activists, Muslim groups, and a newly vigorous press. He publicly endorsed a play by W. S. Rendra which was critical of the government and even stage-managed a press visit to the political prisoner camp at Buru. For their part, Ali Murtopo and Sujono responded by launching attacks against the technocratic vision of Indonesian development, most strongly embodied in Bappenas. Suharto's apparently sharp and summary efforts to call Sumitro to heel and restore a working relationship with Murtopo, begun in November and climaxing on the first days of January 1974, were ineffective; Sumitro persisted in his efforts at garnering further support amongst such alienated military figures as Nasution and Sarwo Edhie over the following two weeks.[9] The political drama that ensued reached its denouement in the serious disturbances of the so-called Malari affair of mid-January 1974.

The immediate occasion for the unrest was the visit by Japanese Prime Minister Kakuei Tanaka. The iconic significance of the visit – the Japanese economic penetration into urban Indonesia in such spheres as electrical appliances and vehicles was by now overwhelmingly evident – in the context of the political competition between Sumitro and Ali Murtopo, and Sumitro's miscalculation of the security implications of his decision to allow free rein for student protests against corruption, government economic policy and what they saw as the inappropriate political influence exercised by senior figures like Ali and Sujono, resulted in vast demonstrations. Quickly they turned into open riots (effectively taken over by Jakarta's large class of poor and underprivileged), leaving 11 dead, almost 200 seriously injured, over 800 people arrested, and extensive vehicle and property damage (including the firing of the Astra Motor Company's Toyota showrooms in downtown Jakarta and the Senen shopping centre the following day). Suharto was forced to employ a helicopter to transfer his prime ministerial guest to the airport for his departure on the morning of 17 January.

Sumitro's gamble at embarrassing Ali and Sujono had turned disastrously wrong once the rioting got out of control. His motives remain unclear, but perhaps included using the demonstrations as a pretext for arresting Ali and Sujono and terminating their political lives, securing undisputed status as the second most powerful man in the regime, and perhaps even using the situation as a stepping-stone in a larger plan to unseat Suharto himself (something which Sumitro vehemently denied). What he had hoped to be a manifestation of popular disaffection with Ali and Sujono had turned into a serious security scare and might have escalated into something more ominous had he persisted with his gamble.

Suharto's reaction to the embarrassing mayhem of 15–16 January, which he later admitted was the result of a power struggle between sections of the Army and Ali and Sujono, in which both sides were to blame, was swift; he chaired a meeting of his inner cabinet to discuss the crisis immediately upon his return from the task of farewelling Tanaka. Sumitro was effectively dismissed as Kopkamtib commander in late January, and in March forced to resign from his post as deputy commander of ABRI. In a departure from the normal pattern of officers who had overstepped the mark and been removed, he refused Suharto's offer of the ambassadorship to Washington. Those close to him in the Hankam group, notably Sutopo Yuwono, Charis Suhud and Sayidiman, were also removed from positions of influence and shunted off to ambassadorships and similarly powerless sinecures. The gentle retribution visited upon them, as well as his decision to replace Sumitro with Surono as Armed Forces deputy commander, indicated Suharto's fears that the mood they represented enjoyed broad support within the Army which he would be ill advised to confront too strongly. Suharto took the opportunity of a meeting with senior journalists to deny vigorously reports that he or his family, especially Ibu Tien, had connections with certain large businesses.[10]

Suharto also took speedy steps to repair the institutional damage. Sudomo assumed operational control of Kopkamtib, which Suharto, having re-appointed himself its commander, now monitored with an eagle eye to ensure that it would no longer maintain the independence it had enjoyed under Sumitro. Ali Murtopo's apparently unrestrained exercise of power was restricted, at least in the sense that his credibility and reliability in the eyes of his boss were reduced, although he and others of similar stripe like Sujono and Suryo remained close to the President. Suharto, shocked at the results of this first serious elite contestation, sought also to purge the security and intelligence ranks to shore up his grip on power, and to integrate their activities more tightly under his control. Benny Murdani, resigned and apparently comfortable in a diplomatic posting in South Korea, was hastily recalled. Meeting briefly with the President, he was informed by him that there was 'a leadership problem', and ordered to a posting as deputy head G-1 in Hankam to sort out its intelligence aspects.[11] Yoga Sugama, left languishing as Indonesia's representative at the United Nations since 1971 after a minor scandal which led to a falling-out with Suharto, was similarly recalled to take over Bakin from Sutopo. To distract attention from the inter-elite, military squabbling, the blame for the unrest was levelled at supporters of the old PSI and Masyumi parties. A number of alleged civilian agitators were arrested on subversion charges, including PSI-associated figures like Sarbini Sumawinata and Subadio Sastrosatomo; some of them, including student leaders Hariman Siregar and Syahrir, were sentenced to long jail sentences and others held in detention without trial for more than two years. Rounding things off, Suharto issued a presidential direction banning members of the Armed Forces and civil servants from entering gambling places, nightclubs and steambath houses, and placing limits on their official privileges.[12]

More generally, Suharto set to introducing new measures of an economic nationalist kind, designed to blunt the force of the criticisms made of the actions of his assistants and the thrust of economic policy. Just a week after the riots, apparently at his direct instruction, changes were introduced to stiffen the requirements for foreign investment, and the spheres and modes in which it operated, and to assist indigenous businesspeople in business participation and ownership. He sought, as well, to rein in the lifestyles of officers and limit imports of items of conspicuous consumption, and to enhance the living conditions of the ordinary soldiery 'whose friendliness towards student demonstrators had caused concern'.[13] In May 1975, for example, Suharto placed restrictions on the registration of imported luxury cars in order to promote 'a modest way of life' and so that wealthy people 'no longer show off their wealth'.[14] More specifically, in late January he abolished the four-member Aspri, the symbol in the eyes of many middle-class Indonesians of the arrogant isolation of the government. Panggabean and Yoga were detailed to undertake foreign trips designed to reassure investors about the security of their commitments.

Most of all, Suharto recognised the acute dangers presented by allowing elite rivalry to simmer uninterruptedly and, more important, of allowing those close to him a base of power for the exercise of public politics even vaguely independent of his own favour and from which he might be challenged. He never made the same mistake again.[15] Whereas his previous style of rule had been characterised by a tendency towards passivity and drift while things were proceeding normally, now he began to understand that he must be politically and managerially vigilant, always and for always. The result was a much more tightly narrowed structure of power at the apex of the New Order, in which Suharto asserted himself as the central manager. His coterie of advisers were made plainly aware of the fact that their position was wholly dependent on the President's goodwill; they had no base of political or military power, no resources of influence other than those he had granted them. While they competed, like isolated atoms around a nucleus, for his attention and favour – Suharto sometimes encouraged competition amongst them to test ideas and policies and to ensure a certain creative tension within their ranks – they were left under no illusion about the source of their status, position and influence. They realised that, once their usefulness as his agents evaporated or, even more important, once his confidence in them had dissipated, they had no political future.

Moreover, the Malari incident provided a further incentive for Suharto, if he needed one, to continue the construction of his corporatist New Order. The dangers of allowing the grievances of society-based participatory forces, whether manipulated or not, to influence the political dispensation at the apex of the New Order, were clear. They would not be allowed to emerge again. In the aftermath of the affair, Suharto created a Council for Political Stabilisation and National Security; one of its earliest decisions was to provide generous subsidies to the two parties and to Golkar, as well as funding for their congresses. The incident completed the movement of the New Order from its early populist flavour towards a regime in which repression and force would be the key tools in containing any pluralist tendencies which might emerge, and in which the corporatist manufacturing of a 'Pancasila society' would be a central concern.[16] The role of the parties and Golkar, Suharto explained, was to be 'vehicles to channel the aspirations of the people'.[17] Equally, the episode confirmed the regime's character as exclusionary, and guaranteed the emergence of a sullen and frustrated quasi-opposition made up both of civilians (including the now-cowed student movement) and Armed Forces members. One important manifestation of the gathering mood was the 1974 bill on regional autonomy, which enjoyed a rapid and successful course through the DPR and which was, in fact, the means to intensify centralised rule, providing a uniform vertical administrative system across the archipelago, handing very wide discretionary powers to the minister for home affairs and presenting Suharto with the personal right to appoint provincial governors.

Suharto's increasing distance from his people was paralleled by an increasing sensitivity to matters that touched on his personal life. His Pertamina hospital outburst in 1972 had been an early example. Late in 1974, the pattern re-emerged with the publication, mentioned earlier, of a Suharto family tree in the magazine *POP*, alleging that he was descended from Yogyakarta royalty. Such allegations flew in the face of his long-polished image of himself as the doughty and determined son of a peasant farmer, succeeding in life against all the odds; it also raised, as we have seen, the issue of the legitimacy of his parentage. Ironically, it appears that the article was a ham-fisted attempt by Ali Murtopo (whose senior Opsus operative, Col. Aloysius Sugianto, owned the magazine) to refurbish his relations with Suharto, bruised by Malari. Suharto's response, as we earlier noted, was as caustic as it was deliberate. In a stage-managed press conference, he delivered a passionate defence of his peasant origins, complete with the assembling of a variety of alleged relatives to provide further credibility. Interestingly, and notwithstanding this impressive show of family solidarity, Suharto himself did not make a habit of visiting his family village, even when he was close by on extended official business in the Yogyakarta region.

A distancing of a different kind, but with similar rustic resonances ('I very much feel at home in the environment of agriculture and animal husbandry; it's in my bones. My great interest in the problems of agriculture and animal husbandry comes from my experience as a child')[18] came with the development in 1974 of Suharto's ranch, Tapos. Originally part of a Dutch plantation taken over by the Indonesian state, the 700-odd hectare ranch was provided for his use by the governor of West Java, Solihin G. P., and managed by a corporate body, PT Rejo Sari Bumi – Unit Tapos, the shares of which were owned by Suharto's children. Suharto immediately began to develop Tapos as a kind of exemplary agricultural experimental station; in August 1975, for example, he presented six West Java bupati each with ten specimens of Australian sheep to be used as rearing stock in their various regions. He was excessively proud of the ranch, and few things gave him greater pleasure than to lecture his assembled guests, probably as perplexed as they were bored, on the intricacies of cattle-raising or other agricultural pursuits. Tapos provided Suharto with a much-loved respite from the gruelling demands of office, which were themselves expanding to take in a never-ending schedule of official openings and dedications of new projects – chemical plants, cement works, plastics factories, and even golf courses – as the country's industrial infrastructure rapidly expanded.

A key element in Suharto's capacity to overcome the political crisis of 1973–74 was the rapidly expanding flow of oil receipts, which provided the state budget and less public sources of funding with an undreamt-of capacity for expenditure on a huge variety of projects. Not only did oil give members of the New Order elite greatly enhanced opportunities for private business dealings, but it also pulsed money throughout the economy, providing infrastructure and employment on a much greater scale, especially amongst the urban middle classes. Firms with high-level access to the centre of power prospered: Ibu Tien's brother, for example, was awarded a large reafforestation contract in South Sulawesi in 1976; Amirmachmud's son won a large contract in 1978 to develop a new market in Ujung Pandang, funded under the Inpres (Presidential Instruction) program. Private business conglomerates, especially those with favourable political links, grew swiftly.

Oil helped Suharto to achieve what was later called 'performance legitimacy'. Its absence may have been calamitous for the soul and structure of his regime. At the same time, however, the bonanza mood critically weakened the capacity of the technocrats to influence the directions of economic policy; there was little to be said for, and no political advantage in, the undiluted market disciplines close to the technocrats' hearts. The strength of the technocrats had been their capacity to put in place policies friendly to the interests of international capital as a means of dragging Indonesia out of its 1965 financial chaos. As oil money washed into Indonesia, their erstwhile centrality in the sphere of economic policy-making receded sharply.

As he presided over the intensification and elaboration of his regime's patrimonial style, Suharto retained his almost childlike attachment to the idea of cooperatives. Cooperatives, he remarked in mid-1973, 'have a great role in the development of Indonesia'. A few years later he remarked that 'the form of the cooperative is the best economic form for Indonesia'.[19] In 1981 he asserted that 'in the long term, cooperatives must become the central pillar of our economy'.[20] Hand in hand with the cooperative rhetoric – and, in an important sense, integrally associated with that idea – came Suharto's development of foundations. 'It was clear to me', he later noted, 'that not every problem can be handled by the government ... we need to look for funds from non-governmental sources. [Such funds] could be of great benefit for material development'.[21] Yayasan Beasiswa Supersemar, a fund intended to assist needy and deserving students with the costs of their education, was established in 1974. The following year, Dharmais was born. Established 'with the intention of gathering funds which were needed by all orphanages', one of its later purposes was to provide assistance to the widows and orphans of soldiers killed in East Timor, as well as for disabled veterans of that conflict.[22]

EAST TIMOR

The heat of the Malari friction had scarcely abated when a problem, as unexpected as it was troubling, emerged for Suharto. The Portuguese revolution of April 1974 suddenly raised the prospect of the rapid decolonisation of Portugal in circumstances which can only have raised the anxiety of Suharto and his advisers – amongst whom at that time the most influential came from intelligence and security rather than operational backgrounds – for its implications for Indonesia's regional and domestic security and integrity.

The rapid development in Portuguese Timor of indigenous political parties, loosely organised around the political options for the colony – association with Portugal, integration with Indonesia, or independence – in a context in which the independence-leaning Portuguese authorities were keen to quit their hold as soon as possible, raised acute fears that a leftist, independent East Timor would emerge in the centre of the Indonesian archipelago.[23] 'We are ... vitally concerned', remarked Ali Murtopo to a journalist in October 1975, 'that developments in Portuguese Timor do not disturb our security and stability', and particularly concerned that Portugal would support a unilateral declaration of independence by Fretilin.[24] These fears were boosted by the continuing friction and instability between the East Timor party groupings, and underlined by the outbreak of civil discord which had come with the attempt of UDT (Timorese Democratic Union) to stage a coup on 10 August 1975 and which resulted in a virtually complete victory by Fretilin (Revolutionary Front of Independent East Timor) forces by early September.

Suharto's approach to the emerging East Timor problem was shaped by his characteristic caution. Already in mid-1974 Adam Malik had assured Timorese emissary Jose Ramos Horta that Indonesia had no intention of involving itself in the situation. In October, Suharto appeared to endorse that position by assuring the Portuguese inter-territorial coordinating minister, Almeida Santos, that Indonesia had no intention of colonising or expanding into the territory of

Portuguese Timor, although he did not dismiss the possibility of its integration with Indonesia.[25] In Townsville, North Queensland, in April 1975, he assured Australian Prime Minister Gough Whitlam that Indonesia had no designs on the territory and denied any intention of seeking a military solution to the problem,[26] although by early July, returning from a visit to the United States, he affirmed publicly that East Timorese independence was not a practical option. In August, he instructed his security and intelligence officers to keep a watching brief on developments in the hope that matters would be solved directly by the people of Portuguese Timor themselves. A few days later, in his state speech commemorating Independence Day, he again emphasised that Indonesia had no territorial ambitions in regard to Portuguese Timor, but that Indonesia was open to the prospect of the territory's integration with the Republic should its people so wish.[27] Notwithstanding his fears of the emergence of a left-inclined, independent – and probably mendicant – East Timor, he did not want to risk the favour of his foreign backers (especially in the context of the Pertamina collapse, of which more later), or unnerve his regional allies, by attempting to solve the problem by the application of military power.

Suharto's view, however, was hotly contested in the upper reaches of the military ('most top military leaders … feel that a battalion or two of regular troops could solve the problem in a matter of days if not hours').[28] He preferred, instead, to play a waiting game. He hoped first that, especially through the secret 'diplomatic' strategy – international in orientation but not averse, under the guise of the Bakin-inspired 'Operation Komodo', to aggressive efforts to mould popular thinking and invigorate pro-Indonesian sentiment in Timor itself – he had entrusted to Ali Murtopo and his associates (including such figures as Col. Aloysius Sugianto and Harry Can Silalahi) in late 1974, Portugal would remain in Timor until such time as Timor's integration with Indonesia became locally acceptable. When that hope collapsed, he trusted that the Indonesian blockade of the territory, the support he enjoyed from regional powers, most of whom preferred the colony's integration into Indonesia in the longer-term interest of regional security, and the lack of international support for Fretilin, would cause the independence movement to collapse.

Apparently supported by the confidence he had placed in Ali Murtopo's capacity to engineer a covert and satisfactory outcome to the crisis, and the cautious advice of Sujono Humardani, Suharto moved only with great reluctance. Even following the Fretilin 'counter coup' of 11 August, he refused to countenance the proposal for a short, sharp campaign in late August to occupy Dili and invite the Portuguese back to resume authority, preferring the option of introducing Indonesian 'volunteers' to assist the pro-Jakarta forces arraigned on the western border of the territory. On 15 September, he received a request from the UDT, Trabalhista and Kota parties expressing the 'wish of the people' of Portuguese Timor to integrate with Indonesia, but he remained unmoved. According to the Australian ambassador, Richard Woolcott, Murdani remarked in late September that 'the old man … is still standing firm' and that Suharto did 'not want to carry the blame for the rest of his life' of an overt military intervention.[29] Even in late

November, Murdani remarked to Woolcott that 'the President continued to believe that Indonesia's objectives could be secured by steady pressure'.[30] Only following Fretilin's declaration of a 'Democratic Republic of East Timor' on 28 November, and after receiving the highest-level American imprimatur,[31] did he 'authorise' a full-scale military invasion on 7 December 1975. Even then, according to Yusuf Wanandi, 'at no stage did the President ever issue a clear instruction to go in. He simply indicated in a Javanese way that the job should be done, but that he didn't wish to know about it'.[32]

In the end, Suharto could not accommodate the risks to national unity which he and his circle judged a new, left-leaning and independent state presented, a potential source of domestic subversion moored in the heart of the Indonesian archipelago. As well, he succumbed to the promptings of his military advisers that, in the context of the communist success in Vietnam, an independent East Timor might present dangers to the external security and freedom of action of Indonesia. Further, his weakened domestic position, post-Malari, probably left him, in the end, no choice but to follow the hard-line military strategy once all other options had been exhausted.

Once the invasion had been completed (notwithstanding the lamentable performance of the invading troops), East Timor was incorporated into the Republic of Indonesia: 'For hundreds of years', said Suharto, 'we have been separated by the walls erected by colonial governments ... The people of East Timor will unite with their blood brothers in the unitary state of the Republic of Indonesia'. He had then to face the resultant international opprobrium, which he did with a vigorous stoicism: 'Indonesia could not do nothing', he remarked in his end-of-year address, 'when faced with the crisis which had occurred in the former Portuguese colony directly bordering on Indonesia, because the situation there has disturbed and can endanger the integrity of the region of the Republic of Indonesia'.[33] He was particularly incensed by the notion that his actions in authorising the invasion had stemmed from an expansionist vision; 'I was elected to develop Indonesia', he reportedly told a guest, 'not to get into a war. Indonesia could have taken Timor any time. We didn't want it. In Repelita I and II there was no money earmarked for Timor'.[34] Notwithstanding the bloody intervention, things at first seemed to go as well as circumstances could permit. Suharto, having earlier agreed to accept the title of 'Father of Peasants' for East Timor, made his first visit to the new province in mid-1978 to celebrate the second anniversary of its integration into the Republic. The welcome he received, whether orchestrated or not, clearly impressed him, and he delivered an impromptu speech on the two themes closest to his heart: development and unity.[35] Fretilin was a small and bedraggled force, no more than 3,000 in number, apparently fighting for a hopeless cause.

The East Timor problem was one aspect of the larger, continuing battle between Adam Malik, a champion of the non-interventionist 'free-and-active' line of foreign policy, and the heavily security-minded generals in Suharto's inner circle, notably Panggabean. Malik, accordingly, continued to oppose the notion that ASEAN develop a security aspect, as well as efforts to have Indonesian troops committed to the Vietnam and Cambodian wars in support of the Americans.

He was, as well, inclined to hold a softer line against China than the generals. Suharto supported Malik on this issue; for him, the essence of ASEAN should be economic, not military, cooperation, although his leadership at its heads of government summit in Bali in February 1976 led to an ASEAN diplomatic offensive aimed at minimising Vietnamese (and Soviet) sway within the region. His concerns for peace and security in the region had other outcomes as well; through his intelligence people (notably Yoga Sugama and Benny Murdani), he sought a productive intervention in Malaysia's dispute with the Philippines over Sabah, and to mediate in the Philippines' Moro 'problem' in the south. Suharto himself even met the Moro leader, Nur Misuari, and conveyed the contents of his discussion to President Marcos; the mediation, however, came to nothing. Papua New Guinea Prime Minister Michael Somare was prevailed upon to prevent his territory being employed as both a base and a refuge by groups associated with the 'Free Papua Movement' (OPM), which sought the independence of Irian Jaya from Indonesian rule. As well, Suharto instructed his justice minister, the noted lawyer Mochtar Kusumaatmaja, to work for the international recognition of the concept of Indonesia's archipelagic authority within the developing discussions of the Law of the Sea. More broadly he was beginning to develop a keener understanding of what was later to take shape as the North–South Dialogue; 'developed countries', he remarked in 1976, 'have a responsibility to help developing countries'.[36]

Generally, however, Suharto's interests were fixedly domestic. Following his unhappy experience at the Non-Aligned Movement conference in Lusaka, for example, he decided that Indonesia's participation in that movement should be formal rather than engaged and enthusiastic. He sent no representative to its foreign ministers' conference at Georgetown in 1972 and pleaded pressure of work to avoid the conference in Algeria in September 1973, sending Adam Malik in his place. It was to be many years before Suharto again took himself to Non-Aligned Movement conferences.

THE PERTAMINA SCANDAL

To the raft of problems facing the thickening New Order came the startling economic collapse of its milch-cow, Pertamina, in February 1975. The reasons for the crisis were simple enough, and mostly to be found in Ibnu Sutowo's indefatigable and carefree expansion and diversification of the oil company's activities into such arenas as steel (notably the long-troubled Krakatau steel mill project in West Java), natural gas, property, insurance, agriculture, shipping, tourism, construction and petrochemicals, funded by short-term credit which, at the crunch, could not be rolled over. To these liquidity problems were later added inflated and financially ruinous commitments on the purchase of oil-tankers, all of which delivered a US$10 billion sea of debt to be serviced and renegotiated by Bank Indonesia.

Suharto was initially, and understandably, reluctant to dispense with Ibnu, a man with whom he was on close and familiar terms. Ibnu had revelled in the confidence placed in him by Suharto; he was the man who had single-handedly built up Indonesia's oil industry with an extraordinary entrepreneurial flair, and who had powerful and many-stranded international connections, a vision for Indonesia's industrial development, and unmatched technical competence. His strategic financial largesse had been crucial to the development and maintenance of the New Order, and his business success, encouraged by Suharto, was an icon of New Order economic performance. He was, one commentator later remarked, 'living proof to many Indonesians that the tables could be turned on the foreign mortgagers, and that boldness could achieve short-cuts in the laborious task of developing this impoverished country'.[37] Pertamina had come, indeed, to resemble 'an institution of national development'.[38]

Suharto had learned of Pertamina's looming problems at least as early as October 1974, but had taken no serious action to rein things in, presumably confident that Ibnu could sort matters out. While Ibnu had his business and borrowing independence severely circumscribed immediately following the debacle, and a committee under Lt. Gen. Hasnan Habib was charged in June with reforming and reorganising the company's affairs and lines of authority and responsibility, Suharto did not move to replace him. Indeed, he sought to deflect attention from Ibnu's performance in his 16 August Independence Day speech by arguing that 'what we must evaluate is our collective experience, not the mistakes or services of individuals'.[39] The strong support offered Ibnu by Ali Murtopo, himself no friend of the technocrats, was also influential; he reportedly had advised Suharto that Ibnu was irreplaceable, while Suharto himself, conscious of the enormous debt he owed Ibnu, and the fact that his own encouragement and demands for funding for various projects had helped Ibnu to overreach himself, reportedly requested Ali to defend Ibnu from attacks.

Only in late 1975, when the oil-tanker revelations surfaced (a matter apparently not reported by Ibnu to Suharto), together with reports of spectacular excesses – what one journalist called 'productive corruption'[40] – and extraordinarily prodigal mismanagement, Ibnu's arrogantly obstinate, unrepentant and aggressive attitude towards the investigations of his tenure, and the damage the crisis had done to the proposed budget became clear, was Suharto (recovering from a December gall-bladder operation) forced to move against his old friend. He summoned him for his 'honourable discharging' on 3 March 1976, following Ibnu's return from medical treatment in the United States via the ASEAN leaders summit in Bali on 23 February (where Ibnu's intrusive and imperious behaviour at a gathering which Suharto wished to dominate probably inflamed Suharto's ire), and replaced him as president-director with the army technocrat Maj.-Gen. Piet Haryono.[41] Ibnu was pensioned off and never proceeded against, notwithstanding a period of informal house detention in 1977–78, apparently to protect Indonesia's legal interests in continuing court battles over payment obligations on Ibnu's oil-tankers, and an occasional veiled hint to the contrary. Apparently having been enjoined by Suharto to keep a low public profile, Ibnu left to enjoy a prosperous and busy retirement as a successful businessman. He felt, he later said, 'no personal responsibility for the difficulties experienced by Pertamina or Indonesia'.[42]

The circumstances of Ibnu's dismissal reveal Suharto's cautious patience in handling the affair ('I kept quiet until the boiling water had cooled down sufficiently for me to drink it'), his capacity, paradoxically, to strike suddenly and mortally against those who had exceeded the bounds allotted them and whom he perceived as having betrayed his trust, and his fear for independently minded centres of power outside his immediate control. It was, he later remarked, 'a bitter experience and a lesson for us all'.[43] His uncharacteristically direct references to the Pertamina affair and the managerial inadequacies which had caused it signalled that Ibnu's tenure was in danger; it was by this time clear that the financial catastrophe that Pertamina had visited upon the Indonesian economy had both depressed and angered Suharto, who had set such store on his performance in that realm. It seems likely that Ibnu had resisted Suharto's efforts to remove him in a more gradual and dignified way, leaving Suharto no option but to excise him, however galling Suharto might have found the exercise. Moreover, Ibnu was dismissed along with seven other Pertamina directors, six of whom were later reappointed, clear in the knowledge that their renewed positions were at the favour of Suharto himself, not Ibnu; 'the point of loyalty [had] been made'.[44]

Ibnu was the second New Order giant to be toppled within two years, signalling a gathering desire on the part of Suharto further to tighten and narrow the power structure of the regime. The collegiality that had characterised the early years of the New Order had now completely evaporated; Suharto was now unquestionably the single and final arbiter of politics. If a further indication was needed of his desire for tightened control, it came with the mid-1977 appointment as mayor of Jakarta of his long-time friend and loyal assistant, Lt. Gen. Cokropranolo, to replace the charismatic, populist, flamboyant and unpredictable Ali Sadikin, whose eleven-year tenure had transformed the city, and who had been increasingly disposed to distance himself from the policies and demeanour of the New Order regime and provide a focus for alternative political views. Cokropranolo, who had worked with Suharto in Kostrad in the early 1960s, and more recently served as one of his Aspri group and as his personal secretary for military affairs, was just the kind of agent Suharto wanted and needed for this sensitive post: loyal, dependable, predictable and politically unthreatening.

The regularisation visited upon Pertamina had broken Ibnu's power, since the revenues that it had previously had access to were now directed to Bank Indonesia. It also saw a re-assertion of the influence of the technocrats, for some years in retreat in the face of Ibnu's developmental brilliance, with their 'planning and economic orderliness'[45] approach which contrasted so strongly with Ibnu's 'can-do' dynamism. It brought, as well, a decline in the influence of Ali Murtopo, whose activities had been generously funded by Ibnu.

Ironically, the very nature and dimensions of the Pertamina disaster brought into relief the positive economic achievements of the government, which had managed, between 1967 and 1976, an annual growth rate of around 7 per cent, a massive increase in industrial and food production, a huge lift in imports, and progress on social fronts like population control. The oil crisis, of course, added much weight to these figures, but the trend had been set before the explosion in oil prices. Equally, Pertamina's collapse raised serious questions about the managerial competence of Suharto, who had allowed things to come to such a pass.

The Pertamina crisis, as well as this pattern of growth in the real economy, served to strengthen the hand both of the civilian technocrats and the military professionals, because it made available resources for enhancing the budget in orthodox ways and, equally, reduced the government reliance on off-budget sources of income and those who managed them. At least for the time being, the technocrats, whose unity of purpose and influence on central policy had been diluted since the early 1970s by their recruitment to specific ministerial duties, were back in united ascendancy in the continuing factional battle with the economic nationalist camp which numbered amongst its adherents Ibnu, Ali Murtopo and Ali Sadikin. Their ascendancy, however, was not to last long, beaten down by the excitement of the second oil boom in 1979.[46]

Ironically, the readiness of the international financial community to come to Indonesia's aid to overcome the Pertamina crisis was an important manifestation of its trust in the Suharto regime, and more particularly a vote of confidence in his ability to manage the difficulties in a rational and systematic way. Such confidence further enhanced his domestic standing. There was, equally, some irony that Ibnu's forced retirement from government was closely followed by Suharto's own retirement from the Armed Forces. When he turned 55 on 8 June 1976, Suharto formally ended his active service career of almost thirty-one years. His retirement came a little over a month after the death of his much-loved foster-father, Prawirowiharjo.

DEVELOPING DEVELOPMENT

These domestic problems seem not to have distracted and, indeed, to have intensified Suharto's belief in the need for the country's development. The second Five-Year Development Plan, hurriedly assembled, and inaugurated in April 1974, sought to build on the stabilisation of the economy established under the first plan, accelerate agricultural development and strike higher growth rates. Suharto's 1975 tour to the Middle East, Eastern Europe, North America and Japan was aimed at securing credits for development projects and equipment, of which the most spectacular was the vast, US$2 billion Asahan hydroelectric/aluminium project in Sumatra, a project in which Sujono Humardani had played a key developmental role. A mission to the Middle East in October 1977 was similarly designed to bring in substantial quantities of fresh investment. In all these arrangements, a crucial consideration was Indonesia's new status as a major oil exporter. By late 1975, it had 'projects or investment programmes, government and private "either in early stages of implementation, ready to go, seeking financing or in advanced planning stages" which add up to a total roughly equivalent to Indonesia's GNP'.[47] In the 1976–77 budget, the development side of the budget was, for the first time, greater than the amount projected to be spent on routine matters. By 1978, notably in Sumatra, huge development projects like the Arun gas fields and huge fertiliser, oil, cement, aluminium and coal projects, mostly financed with Japanese money, with associated infrastructure, aimed at exploiting and harnessing Indonesia's natural resources, were in full swing. At a smaller scale, estate and smallholder rubber, pepper, coffee and fisheries industries enjoyed new levels of investment.

Development, of course, had its other side. On 20 April 1975, Suharto had officiated at the opening ceremony of his wife's pet project, the Taman Mini cultural theme park. Notwithstanding the furore over its construction, Suharto noted in his speech that the park was 'an addition to the national wealth and a component of national development, because it accords with the basic pattern of development laid down in the Broad Outlines of State Policy'.[48]

The oil boom was crucial in providing funds for labour-absorbing programs in rural areas, of which the most important were the *kabupaten* (district) program (established in 1970 to develop local transport and irrigation infrastructure) and the Inpres program. At the same time, foreign borrowing remained important, if less crucial than in the regime's earlier years. Sensitive to the potential for political debilitation deriving from economic nationalist concerns about the levels of foreign aid, and the political damage caused by the Pertamina crisis, Suharto was at pains to explain in his 1976 Independence Day speech that foreign borrowing did not diminish the nation's sovereignty and independence of action, and argued for its importance in development. Throughout, he laboured the point that development was a long hard slog, an enduring battle against the odds, but one which had as its goal the deliverance of his people. Thus, in a 1977 speech, he remarked that

> the development currently under way aims at making people into human beings ... great ideals are not dreams, but must be struggled for so that they gradually become reality. That struggle will certainly be long, perhaps very long, and perhaps onerous as well ... development will succeed only if all levels of society, all groups and the whole power of the Indonesian nation plays a role in it.[49]

THE SAWITO AFFAIR

The sub-surface tensions and resentments into which the New Order regime – on which Suharto's personal authority had been stamped so strongly by the recent crises – had sunk by 1976 were starkly manifested in the curious affair of Sawito Kartowibowo, a non-active employee of the Department of Agriculture and a devotee of the Javanese mystical arts. Convinced by his meditations and mystical practices that he had been divinely chosen to rule Java, in July 1976 he began publishing documents highly critical personally of Suharto's performance as president and of the state of moral decay which the New Order had delivered to the nation. Indeed, one such document called upon Suharto to transfer the presidency to former vice-president Mohammad Hatta as the head of a four-man ruling group. Sawito also wrote a document, entitled 'Towards Salvation', pointing to the moral decay and cultural alienation consequent upon the New Order's program of development and – a sign of the surreal flavour of politics at the time – managed to convince a number of important national figures, the most prominent of whom was Hatta himself, to endorse it.[50]

Appointed president, March 1968. (Department of Information, Indonesia)

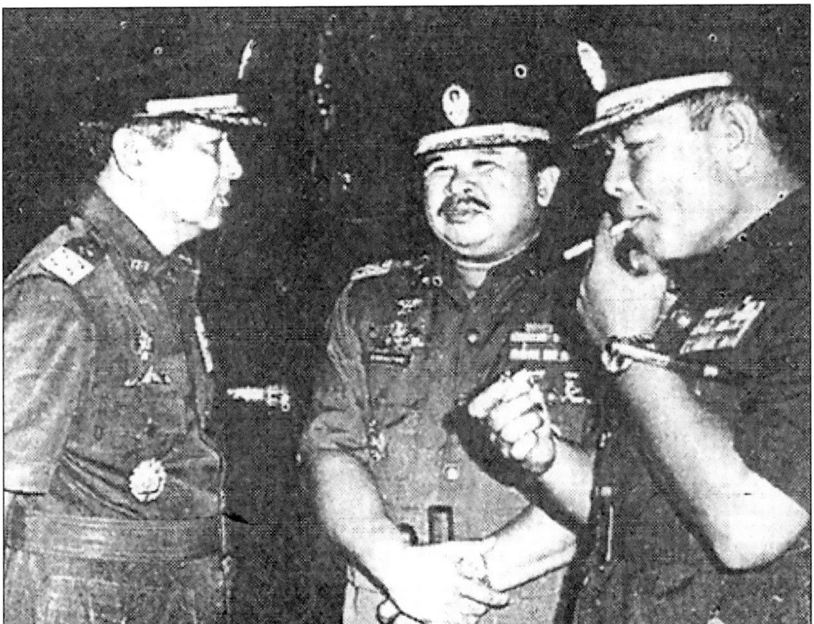

Suharto, Sumitro and Panggabean. (Tempo)

Suharto at the Non-Aligned Movement meeting in Lusaka, 1970. (State Secretariat, Indonesia)

Attending Ali Murtopo's body, May 1984. (Kompas)

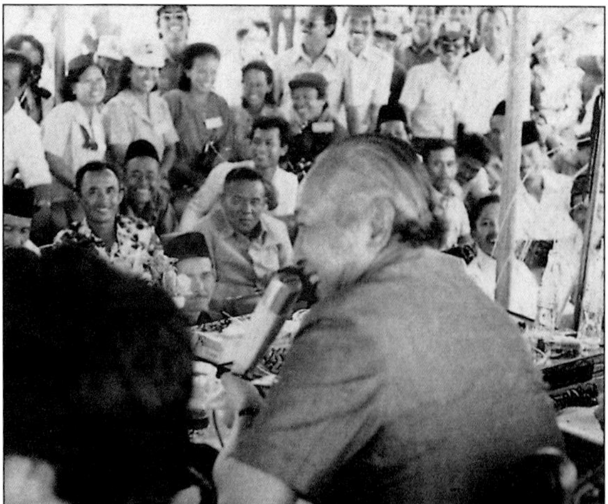

Talking with farmers in West Java. (State Secretariat, Indonesia)

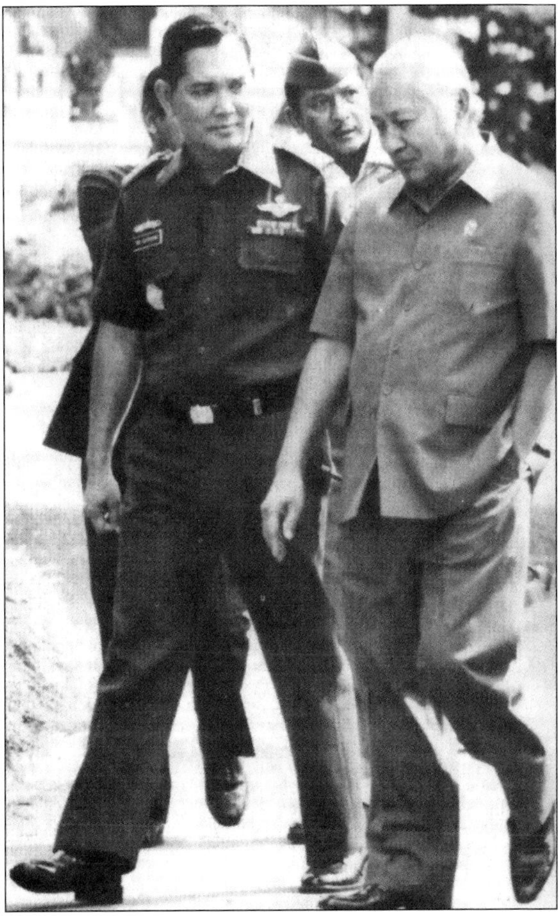

Suharto and Try Sutrisno. (State Secretariat, Indonesia)

Affection for Ibu Tien. (State Secretariat, Indonesia)

Suharto meeting Arafat, 1984. (Kompas)

With Sudharmono. (State Secretariat, Indonesia)

Playing tennis. (State Secretariat, Indonesia)

This bizarre episode is most worthy of note because Suharto reacted so bitterly when he learned of Sawito's activities in September 1976. His reaction may have been partly due to the fact that eminent figures had been drafted in support of Sawito's cause, thus adding weight and credibility to the attack upon the moral direction of the New Order, and suggesting that their views were more broadly held amongst Jakarta's elite. As well, the method employed by Sawito – notwithstanding Suharto's prim assertions about the necessity of constitutional propriety in the matter of replacing presidents – was uncomfortably close to the Supersemar model employed with such success by Suharto ten years before (a point made pointedly and repeatedly at Sawito's trial by his defence attorney, Yap Thiam Hien). There was also, perhaps, a sense in Suharto's mind that larger and more shadowy forces lay behind Sawito's venture, which had to be confronted directly and sharply.

Most of all, perhaps, was the fact that Sawito had made an intensely personal attack upon the President, as well as impugning his family. That brought a bitter response from Suharto; Sawito, he said, had made 'a very cruel evaluation' of the achievements of the New Order and had 'attacked an innocent man'.[51] Suharto's belligerence manifested the insecurity he felt both in the performance of his regime and his more proprietorial attitude towards his own role and power. None of his own family, he asserted, had benefited from his position, and a stylised press conference held by his half-brother, Probosutejo, and eldest son, Sigit, parroted these same sentiments.[52] Sudharmono released a long document which hinted at Sawito's involvement in an 'illegal' movement. Such cantankerousness had its own reward; in its 8 November 1976 issue, the international journal *Newsweek* carried a cover story highly critical of Suharto's leadership and particularly of the corruption in which his family was allegedly involved.[53] Suharto's response, and that of those close to him who sought to press their loyalty, was predictable and sharp; the attack on the President was construed as an attack on the integrity of the nation, and the journal (and its journalists) summarily banned.[54]

Once the matter was out in the open, the security forces pounced on Sawito and members of his group, and Suharto made great efforts to persuade the signatories to withdraw the support they had proffered Sawito's cause. All of them promptly did, most of them professing to having been duped into signing it under false or misleading pretences. Nonetheless, the fact that so wild a conspiracy should attract the attentions of senior figures and, in its planning and conceptualisation, gather the support of others, such as Gen. Ishak Juarsa, indicated the depth of alienated dissatisfaction which part of the Jakarta elite were suffering as Suharto further consolidated his position. Sawito's trial, running from late 1977 to mid-1978 before a packed courtroom, was replete with allegations as bizarre and performances as theatrical as the events that had preceded it. Sawito was convicted – according to Suharto, his movement was 'a refined attempt to bring down the government'[55] – and sentenced to eight years jail.

In mid-November 1976, jaded or jolted by the series of mishaps that had plagued his recent life, Suharto sought refuge and a space for reflection by undertaking an unannounced and incognito five-day safari through East and Central

Java, 'talking with peasants, small traders and teachers in rural areas',[56] in order to discover something of their conditions and problems for himself. This was an activity he hugely enjoyed; that he undertook it perhaps reflected his sense that in his troubles he needed to touch again what he imagined as the real Indonesia. As he noted in his New Year address of 1977, the year ahead was to be 'full of challenges and tests'.[57]

ELECTIONS, STUDENTS AND SOCIAL FERMENT

In ensuring the 'success' of the 1977 parliamentary elections, the major problem facing Golkar was 'not so much that Golkar will not get enough votes but that it will get too many'.[58] Ali Murtopo himself remarked in 1976 that 'it may be anticipated that Golkar will obtain approximately the same proportion of votes as in the 1971 election, or perhaps even a little more due to the great improvements that have been made in terms of internal consolidation and cadre training since 1971'.[59] The government's quandary related particularly to the possibility that the weak and divided rabble comprising the PDI – whose first congress in April 1976 had been notable for its intense infighting, and even a fist-fight – might fail so utterly that politics thereafter might become an uncomfortable competition between the government and the Muslim PPP. Mindful of the Muslim threat, Suharto made it clear that he would not countenance the use of Muslim sermons as vehicles for politicking or criticising the regime. He probably failed to see the irony that his government's repressiveness had helped to invigorate Muslim political life, especially amongst young people; 'nowhere is Muslim activity more pronounced than on campuses'.[60]

The regime's efforts to constrain the emergence of a critical Muslim political entity – 'only the PPP has the communications to challenge Golkar's grip on Government channels', remarked one foreign observer in 1976[61] – climaxed in the curious saga of the Komando Jihad (Holy War Command). Komando Jihad first came to public notice in April 1977 with the arrest by Kopkamtib of 700 people, most of them from areas noted for strong attachment to Islam, accused of terrorist activity on the part of the movement. The mood of threat created by the 'discovery' of Komando Jihad, allegedly a resurgence of the old Darul Islam movement, allowed the government to move with unusual freedom to cripple the activities of Muslim politicians and to portray PPP as dangerously linked to Islamic fundamentalism. Komando Jihad's emergence was, however, so conveniently timed that it raised many suspicions amongst Muslims and others about its real nature and source, particularly when some of those arrested allegedly attested that they were working to a script drawn up by army intelligence. While it seems likely that Komando Jihad, in the sense of a militant Muslim force, had its own existence, it appears that it may have been infiltrated by Ali Murtopo's agents who incited its members to acts which were guaranteed to draw attention to the group's existence and its alleged threat to the nation's security. Whatever the case, the affair provided a handy lightning rod for the government on the eve of the elections, scheduled for 2 May 1977.

The election campaign bore, if not so crudely as in 1971, the marks of government restriction on substantive or sensitive political debate, and of intimidation and pressure on voters, exercised both by the military and by local government officials, to support Golkar. Complaints and protests about Golkar-friendly election irregularities were dismissed by Suharto's threat against those who sought to impugn the results of the people's choice. Golkar, under the leadership of Murtono, was the party of development, which had provided Indonesia with so much; it was the party of patronage; it was the heart of the government. The identifications made a deep impact but, notwithstanding the government's efficient management of the election, Golkar's result fell a little below its 1971 achievement, and PPP, after a boisterously enthusiastic campaign, recorded some notable local victories, including a famous plurality in the New Order heartland of Jakarta. PDI's poor performance reflected the vexed condition of its party organisation and leadership. The election result confirmed the political potency of resurgent Islam. Personally for Suharto, this election – the first since his military retirement – was the only occasion he had voted since 1957.

While Suharto may not have been directly involved in efforts to constrict the rise of Islamic political fervour, he was no doubt conscious of the problem and kept aware of the measures put in train to limit the PPP's electoral success. His attitude to political expressions of Islam bore strong similarities to that earlier espoused by the Dutch colonial government. He assisted and promoted Islam's purely religious activities and worked strenuously to build tolerance of other beliefs amongst Muslims ('National concord and unity can be realised only if there is concord and unity between the groups within the big family of the Indonesian nation'),[62] but took severe action against what he construed as narrowly conceived expressions of political Islam which endangered national unity and stability by working towards some version of an Islamic state. 'I strongly oppose religious conflicts which can cause trouble. The first principle of Panca Sila is belief in the One Almighty God, and it is not exclusive to any one religious belief.'[63] Early in 1978 he noted that 'we always feel concerned to see the emergence of symptoms which indicate group fanaticism and fail to see the broader interest, which is the integrity and unity of the nation'.[64] Privately, he was said to have greeted a visiting group of prominent Catholics around the time of the 1977 elections with the words: 'Our common enemy is Islam!'.[65]

With the exception of the Muslim political threat, perhaps the most notable aspect of the campaign was that it provided the context for a resurgence of student political activism – notwithstanding Suharto's injunction to rectors early in 1977 to 'develop a special campus life with Indonesian characteristics, so that our campuses do not develop into campuses which just imitate foreign patterns'[66] – emerging from the quietism and passivity engendered by the fierce crackdown following the Malari affair of early 1974. The reactivation of student political concerns was a response to the prevailing political mood of 1975–77, one in which there was a general sense that Suharto's New Order had not delivered the promised fruits of development throughout society, was mired in high-level corruption and moral vacuity, and was becoming increasingly repressive and unresponsive.

Moreover, for the first time in the history of the New Order, the target of the students' ire was Suharto himself. One New Order response in mid-1977 came in the form of the prison sentences handed out to four university students on charges of insulting the President and his family. Apart from symbolic gestures, such as the 'nomination' of Ali Sadikin for the presidency by a former chair of the University of Indonesia's Student Council, the renewed movement sought to develop a dialogue with the government. In response, Suharto, on the advice of Prof. Sumitro Joyohadikusumo, agreed to the notion that the technocrats should attempt to educate the students about the nature of the New Order's economic policies. The effort, undertaken in August–September 1977, proved a public relations disaster for the government and provided further fuel to the students. Sumitro's ministerial delegation's tour through campuses was met with derision and accompanied by pointed questions on matters relating to corruption, the Armed Forces' dual function, and the domestic security machinery, as well as attempts to press reforms. Finally, in Bandung, Sumitro's team walked out of a meeting at Pajajaran University and the schedule of further visits was cancelled.

A similar public relations exercise was that mounted by Kopkamtib chief Sudomo from mid-1977, at Suharto's request. Named Opstib (*Operasi Tertib* – Operation Order), Sudomo's well-publicised campaign had as its proclaimed aim to search out and punish those involved in corruption. Targeted particularly at illegal transport levies and other illegal payments (*pungli*), it claimed significant success, yet, characteristically, did little to rein in systematic corruption at higher levels in society or to bring those conducting it to account. Like similar earlier (and later) campaigns, it produced some politically unimportant high officials, some lower or medium-level victims, price rises, and a significant degree of public cynicism.

The sureness of Suharto's political grip, following his injudicious response to the Sawito allegations the previous year, was further put under question when news emerged about the planned construction of a family mausoleum in the hills of south-central Java, near Solo, allegedly at a cost of nearly US$10 million. It was not surprising, therefore, that the student movement gathered strength as the New Order's morale sagged under the weight of critics' attacks and its own mismanagement of events. As was his wont at times of crisis, Suharto warned in his 1977 Independence Day speech of the dangers threatened by 30 September Movement/communist remnants; the following year he urged the rapid publication of a 'White Book' (*Buku putih*) giving the 'true' version of events on and around 1 October 1965.[67] Further, in a new twist that was probably not without domestic political rationale, he and Ibu Tien left for a visit to the Middle East in October which, together with efforts to promote investment, included Suharto's performance of the *umrah* in Mecca.[68] Upon his return, Suharto made available subsidies for the construction of mosques and other religious edifices.

Such activities had little impact in quelling restiveness. Large student demonstrations in Jakarta, Bandung, Surabaya and elsewhere in early November derided the foibles of Suharto and his leadership group; 'the people are hungry and the boss prepares his grave', proclaimed one Jakarta poster. The Bandung students infuriated Suharto with the charge that he had violated the Constitution. The student criticisms were given added weight by the mid-November comments of Alamsyah, deputy head of the Supreme Advisory Council and speaking in its name, which pointed to the failures of Indonesia's development plans to secure their goals, to gathering crime and corruption, and to the widening gap between rich and poor. In November, Bung Tomo, hero of the Battle of Surabaya in 1945, was detained following a series of critical speeches. The mood of disenchantment was more broadly reflected in popular culture which satirised official corruption; it was not difficult to equate 'Tante Sun' (Aunty Sun), the Jakarta businesswoman parodied in a rock song created by a Bandung group, with Ibu Tien.[69]

Suharto's reaction to the ever-bolder student criticisms of himself and his family – not only of Ibu Tien, but also of Sigit, his eldest son, allegedly involved in the purchase of a mansion in Jakarta from one of Suharto's business (and fishing) associates, Hasyim Ning – was not long in coming. He was clearly deeply hurt and angered by the personal nature of the attacks now regularly descending upon him. His responses ranged from efforts to defend his record (including a call to TVRI to increase its coverage of the benefits flowing from development), calls to the security forces to increase their vigilance, and even a lecture to university rectors to educate their students about the truth of his mausoleum project. Finally, a two-day closed meeting of top Armed Forces leaders in Jakarta in December, assembled by Panggabean but clearly called by Suharto in the atmosphere of mounting crisis, vigorously asserted that the Army would act strongly and decisively against any opposition to the nation's leadership. Suharto reportedly rehearsed the familiar theme that, while he had never sought the presidency, he would shoulder its burdens as best he could, but that he feared that a continuation of the critical sniping would seriously erode the power of the office in the future. The military's closing of ranks behind him was a clear sign that the limits of openness had been exceeded, and signalled the initiation of a tougher and more repressive political mode. More important, perhaps, it demonstrated that Suharto had no serious political competitor and that the military – its control over the state apparatus unthreatened – had effectively granted him a gilt-edged security for the nation's highest office.

The reasons for the military's backing of Suharto was simple enough. He had been the linchpin in the construction of a system of rule which suited military interests perfectly. As one who himself had had a long history of business dealings, and a strongly held view about the necessity of the Armed Forces' political role, he understood the 'necessity' for military figures to develop their political and financial interests for the sake of the welfare of the Armed Forces and the nation as a whole. No one else had the measured, broad understanding of the realities of power that he enjoyed, no one else was as skilled at handling the patronage aspects of political power, no one else was as predictable as Suharto. The generals' statement was thus an effective surrender of their independent power to the person of Suharto. By 1978, he had begun his final move to the apex of politics. The three men who might have served to challenge, or at least to provide an alternative channel of political power – Gen. Sumitro, Ibnu Sutowo and Ali Murtopo (his influence on the wane, and troubled by health problems through 1977) – had seen their power either snapped or remorselessly ground away.

It was, then, no surprise that, when the students tested the authorities' political will by a series of demonstrations and anti-Suharto declarations in the first part of January 1978, climaxing in the issuing of a 'White Book', a Bandung student manifesto calling for fundamental political change in the country, the security forces acted with little patience. The government moved on 20 January to ban four major newspapers, including the leading dailies *Kompas* and *Sinar Harapan.* Suharto later explained that he had been forced to take this action because, 'towards the end of last January, the freedom of the press had developed with virtually no restriction, bringing into danger the firm basis of dynamic national stability. If it had been allowed to go a little further, it would have come close to endangering the safety of the Nation and State'.[70] Simultaneously, authorities began rounding up student activists across Java. About the same time, the decision was also announced that the ASEAN secretary-general, Lt. Gen. H. R. Dharsono, was to be dismissed from his position, presumably because of a highly critical assessment of the New Order regime he had delivered in Bandung on 13 January. On 9 February, student hold-outs at Bandung Institute of Technology were rounded up and the campus occupied by units of the Siliwangi Division, presaging a rash of similar confrontations between troops and students across the country which had the effect of virtually closing down leading universities in the run-up to the presidential election. Suharto later put it like this: 'Syarif Thayeb, the Minister of Education and Culture, settled the campus problem with the rectors'.[71] Syarif's work was enthusiastically continued by the incoming minister for education and culture, French-educated Daud Yusuf, who sought to depoliticise the campuses and redirect the attention of students towards their studies. His so-called 'normalisation of campus life' abolished independent student councils, made university rectors responsible for their students' activities, and drew universities more tightly under state control.[72]

RE-ELECTED AS PRESIDENT

The mood of political challenge, notwithstanding the gathering repression, endured into the meeting of the MPR, which assembled on 11 March 1978 to receive Suharto's address of accountability, to elect a president and vice-president and to issue the Broad Outlines of State Policy, the loose blueprint intended to govern the general directions of government policy for the succeeding five-year period. Having already rebuffed a suggestion that he should deliver his accountability speech to the old MPR which had elected him rather than the one resulting from the 1977 elections (360 members) and the subsequent appointments of another 560 members, Suharto proceeded, through a 93-page text which took three-and-a-half hours to deliver, to account for his five-year tenure as president.[73]

Even before the MPR met, Suharto and his men had set in train efforts to combat and confound the Muslim political groups which they saw as fundamental to the growth of opposition sentiment to the New Order since the early 1970s.

For the first time, what was to become the recurring theme of the presidential succession was seriously raised. As Suharto later admitted, 'It is true that at that time there was a certain group that did not want my renomination as president. But I just went along with the people's wishes'.[74] The state policy outlines contained references to *kepercayaan* (belief), which many (including the esteemed Muslim elder statesman Mohammed Natsir) interpreted as supportive of Javanese meditative practices, as the first step to having kepercayaan accepted as one of the officially received religions in the nation, and as an implicit effort to diminish the Muslim community.

The only dissident voice in reply to Suharto's accountability speech came from the PPP leader, Chalid Mawardi; in a wide-ranging address he attacked the military crackdown on students, raised concerns about the propriety of the 1977 electoral procedures, questioned the direction and achievements of Suharto's economic policies, and accused the government of harassing Muslims and Muslim organisations.[75] Debate on the Broad Outlines of State Policy evoked further PPP opposition; the PPP was particularly incensed about the inclusion of 'beliefs' (kepercayaan) and at the broader policy on Pancasila. Having forced a vote on amendments – something unprecedented in the history of the New Order MPR – a large bloc of PPP members walked out of the chamber when the vote on these sections was taken. Such action was, in the end, symbolic. Suharto's election was not in doubt; he had already been nominated by three of the four MPR fractions, and there was no other credible candidate; indeed, the possibility of his not standing again, something which he occasionally vaguely mentioned, was 'seen by New Order leaders as a major national disaster'.[76] On 22 March, Suharto was elected, unopposed and by acclamation, for his third five-year term, avoiding the contested election which troublesome Muslim politicians had seemed to threaten.

His election, however, was clouded by the last-minute decision of the Sultan of Yogyakarta not to stand for another term as vice-president. The sultan had been an unobtrusively loyal deputy, but it appears he had become thoroughly dissatisfied with the manner in which he had been marginalised on policy issues by Suharto and his advisers during his tenure, and reportedly angered at high-level corruption and the harshness of government repression of the renascent student movement and others critical of the regime. He chafed, as well, at the security restrictions on his freedom of movement. While he had determined long before the end of his term not to seek re-election, he delayed informing Suharto, a measure clearly intended to embarrass the President. Suharto was genuinely surprised and dismayed to learn of the sultan's decision, so much so that it took three formal letters from the sultan before Suharto would agree, with great reluctance, to his not continuing.[77] Suharto was then forced into an embarrassing search for a vice-presidential candidate at very short notice – it is highly likely that the sultan's late withdrawal was intended to cause Suharto this trouble – and finally managed, after an attempt to recruit NU leader Idham Chalid to the post failed, to persuade former foreign minister and current parliamentary Speaker Adam Malik to accept the post. Malik, despite a propensity to speak with a refreshingly critical bluntness about the failings of the New Order and a certain tendency to run ahead of the government's foreign policy line, especially in relation to the matter of resuming connections with China – a cast of mind which irritated the controlled and disciplined Suharto – proved an able and loyal deputy, and his frankness provided a nice contrast to Suharto's dour purposefulness. In the end, notwithstanding the difficulty caused by the sultan's late withdrawal, the symbolic protests by Muslim politicians, and an explosion at the MPR building on 19 March, allegedly the work of young activists, the MPR session ran smoothly enough.

In designing the Third Development Cabinet, Suharto made it clear where the new disposition of power lay. In his speech of 29 March announcing the composition of the cabinet, he emphasised, calling upon the authority of the Elucidation of the Constitution, that cabinet members were not responsible to the parliament but were, indeed, assistants of the President: 'to establish the policy of the government and coordination in the governance of the state, ministers must all work together as solidly as possible under the leadership of the President'.[78] He went on to outline what he described as the seven targets of his new cabinet, emphasising social justice, economic growth, stability, a clean and authoritative state apparatus, unity based on Pancasila, the successful conduct of elections, and a foreign policy in the service of the national interest.

In addition to the seventeen portfolio ministers and six junior ministers with specific tasks, such as in the areas of transmigration, youth, cooperatives and housing, Suharto created three coordinating ministries: Panggabean was appointed to the Political and Security 'superministry', Surono to that governing social welfare and religious and cultural affairs, and Wijoyo to that governing economics, finance, industry, trade, agriculture, mining and communications. This itself was a further manifestation of Suharto's confidence in his more certain control of the political scene; those given coordinating roles were the essence of hard-working, unquestioning loyalty, men who owed their careers to his favour. In the cases of Panggabean and Surono, their new posts were in reality no more than gentle ways of retiring them from serious politics. It was further manifest by the fact that no political party leader enjoyed a cabinet position, and in the fate of Ali Murtopo. Ali Murtopo, long thirsting for a substantial formal role, strove to be appointed to the powerful and prestigious Home Affairs ministry, or perhaps to Foreign Affairs. Suharto, however, trumped his hopes, first by elevating him to the ministry, and then consigning him to the relative unimportance of the Ministry of Information. The devoutly Muslim Bugis aristocrat, Gen. Mohammad Yusuf, installed as defence minister, immediately began to put some teeth into the widespread demand for military officers to adopt more reserved styles of living, and sought to bridge the gap between the military and society and to bring a greater degree of professionalism and military skill to the forces. Sudharmono was named state secretary, recognition of the complete trust placed in him by Suharto, and his rapidly increasing authority within the realm of elite politics where he had taken on and much embellished the role of cabinet manager and, more important in the highly personalised style of Jakarta politics, the task of gatekeeper for Suharto, coordinating and controlling access to the President for all but the small circle of Suharto's closest confidants and advisers. Suharto appointed a little-known newcomer, Prof. Dr Ir B. J. Habibie, as minister for research and technology.

Habibie was, however, already well known to Suharto, who had kept an eye on his progress since their first meeting in Makasar in 1950. Sent to Germany in the mid-1950s to further his engineering studies at the behest of Mohammad Yamin, Habibie completed a doctorate in aeronautical engineering at the Technische Hochschule in Aachen in 1965, and by 1974 had developed a distinguished reputation in his field and risen to become a vice-president at Messerschmitt-Bolköw-Blohm. Upon his return in 1974, at Suharto's request (a matter apparently organised during a visit by Ibnu Sutowo to West Germany in December 1973), Habibie had been appointed presidential adviser on technology and assigned to Pertamina's technology division to develop an aircraft industry in Bandung: PT Industri Pesawat Terbang Nurtanio, established in April 1976.[79] Habibie was a key component in the President's plans for the future. As Suharto later noted, 'For the development of strong industries in general and advanced industries in particular, since the beginning of the second stage of the long-term development plan there was a great need for a high-level central agency to stand alongside Bappenas ... entrusted with the task of investigating and applying technology and with the capacity to prepare detailed plans for industries which needed to be established'.[80]

Suharto, his re-election achieved, faced a plethora of political difficulties which were the occasion of some reassessment of the regime's direction. The by-now customary repressiveness was not abandoned; such notables as Mahbub Junaidi, deputy secretary-general of the PPP, the noted constitutional lawyer Ismail Suny and, once more, Bung Tomo, were arrested in April 1978, apparently in an effort to silence their criticisms. But there was also evidence of a more strategically motivated inclusiveness. An immediate challenge was the need to contain newly vigorous Muslim political strength; Suharto's characteristically pragmatic response was to enliven the almost moribund PDI by promoting its attachment to Sukarno and reshaping it in the image, though not the substance, of the old PNI. As early as the PDI's fifth birthday celebration in January 1978, Ali Murtopo had announced a project to refurbish Sukarno's nondescript gravesite at Blitar, and the project took shape in earnest on the occasion of the eighth anniversary of Sukarno's death in June 1978, when the plans to erect a marble memorial to Sukarno were announced at a special ceremony at the gravesite.

More broadly, there remained the difficulty of calming what had become a turbulent and restless civil society, clamouring for reform and a new direction. Suharto's response was to attempt to connect his policies more closely with the perceived needs of the people. Opstib, for example, took on a more genuinely aggressive stance towards corruption. The sense that Suharto was becoming more attentive to the structural ills which had caused the rain of criticism through the mid-1970s was also reflected in the policy discussions leading to the development of the Third Five-Year Plan, due for implementation in April 1979. Conscious of the reproach that the much-vaunted development had delivered little real improvement for the mass of the people – according to one contemporary observer, 'a large proportion of village people seem to have gained little of the overall rise in prosperity, and some may have seen their welfare actually decline'[81] – Suharto took steps to change the emphasis of development. In contrast to the two previous plans, as he hinted in his 1978 Independence Day speech, which had emphasised stabilisation and subsequently aggregate growth, the new plan sought to concentrate on the 'basic needs' of the people and a better distribution of the gains of development.[82] As well, he sought to still Muslim criticism with a stipulation, introduced by Minister for Religion Alamsyah, forbidding religious proselytisation and requiring foreign assistance for religion to be channelled and directed through the Department of Religion. A similar mood saw an acceleration in the release of prisoners arrested in the aftermath of the coup attempt of 1965; all category B prisoners not required to stand trial were freed by the end of 1979.[83]

THE REFINEMENT OF AUTHORITARIAN CORPORATISM

That such measures were not meant to signal a diminution of Suharto's ever more enveloping dominance of Indonesian politics was indicated by his appointment as chair of the newly initiated Golkar Advisory Board (*Dewan Pembina*), with powers of appointment to the board, at the second Golkar congress in October 1978 in Bali. Suharto also took with renewed vigour to the continuing project of Indonesia's political corporatisation. It was now the appropriate time to implement his long-held vision that 'the application of Pancasila and the 1945 Constitution to every part of the life of our nation will be a guarantee of the continual growth and welfare of our nation'.[84] As he later related:

> I was conscious that, on the basis of our own experience, the political system and multi-party system of the previous era had failed to carry our nation forward to achieve progress by means of development. In developing political life, we could not go backwards. We could not return to Parliamentary Democracy or Guided Democracy which had failed to support national development. On the contrary, we were looking ahead to improve the application of Pancasila Democracy in parallel with achieving a more developed stage from our development in general.[85]

Accordingly, in 1978 Suharto's effort to 'Pancasila-ise our society' reached its take-off point. In November he remarked that

> as a country which has experienced various crises and political turbulence in past times, we must prevent the repeat of destructive events which bring only suffering to many people. Such saddening events can arise if we are forgetful or neglectful in comprehending and applying the basic ideas which we have received and which we possess together. And those basic ideas … are no other than those contained in Pancasila and the 1945 Constitution.[86]

Already he had set in train a vast program of education to develop the 'full comprehension and implementation' (*penghayatan dan pengamalan*) of Pancasila. The program, known as P-4, was 'a new stage in the efforts of all of us to realise and perpetuate Pancasila'.[87] It involved the creation of an array of management bodies for the development and conduct of the program; these bodies in turn spawned a continuing series of courses, initially directed at civil servants and members of the Armed Forces; 'only those civil servants who understand Pancasila, the 1945 Constitution and the Broad Outlines of State Policy will be able to carry out properly their task as servants of the state and servants of the people'.[88] The P-4 program was guided by a presidential advisory committee, which became known as P-7. Another team compiled instructional propaganda and trained the indoctrination instructors. A third team, BP-7 (Supervisory Body for the Implementation of Guidance for the Comprehension and Practice of Pancasila), oversaw the whole massive indoctrination program.

This policy was all of a piece with Suharto's jaundiced view of liberal ideas. Freedom of the press, for example, was construed to mean freedom 'with responsibility': 'a press that is free and responsible will strengthen the development of dynamic national stability, allow creativity to sprout and a healthy democracy blossom'. While differences of view were acceptable, even with the government itself, they must 'be accompanied by a good solution, while efforts to create different ideas must be done in democratic ways based on the Pancasila and the 1945 Constitution'. Equally, the concept of the rule of law needed careful understanding in the Indonesian context. 'As a nation based on law, Indonesia must defend the rule of law, but this principle must also be interpreted in a positive and dynamic way. This means that, in its implementation, the rule of law must always be promoted in accordance with the development of the interests and aspirations within society.' Rights and freedoms brought with them 'responsibilities and obligation … freedom is not absolute'. More broadly, democracy did not mean licence: 'democracy must know discipline and responsibility, because without both those things democracy means only confusion'. Pancasila underlay everything: 'Pancasila is the source of all our ideas concerning what we think of as the right kind of society, which guarantees the tranquillity of us all, which is able to bring material and spiritual prosperity to us all'.[89]

FOSKO AND THE PETITION OF 50

Suharto's formal retirement from active service in 1976 signalled the onset of a generational change within the Army. Those who had served with him in the 1950s and 1960s, and even in the revolutionary days, were moving into retirement. For a small group of these officers, however, retirement meant not just the time and ease for greater involvement in business or golf, but the opportunity, free from the shackles of army discipline, to express their long-building dissatisfaction with the tenor and direction of the New Order.

The first serious manifestation of veteran dissatisfaction came in 1977; senior retired officers of the Diponegoro, Brawijaya and Siliwangi 'divisions' sought to establish a study and discussion club to bring together those who shared similar dissonant views on the New Order. Officially sanctioned by Army Chief of Staff Widodo in April 1978 under the name of Fosko (Army Study and

Communication Forum), the group was soon directing a stream of increasingly elaborate and critical ideas to army headquarters about the need to reduce the heaviness of the military's dual function and to enhance democratic procedures. The following year, in June, Nasution – who had been very critical of the democratic shortcomings of the 1977 elections and later had spoken of a crisis of leadership[90] – with the cooperation of other senior retired military figures such as Ali Sadikin and Hugeng, and others including the eminent Mohammad Hatta, established another body: the Institute for Constitutional Awareness Foundation (LKB).

The reaction of the government, shaken by the outpouring of civil dissent accompanying the 1977 election campaign and the lead-up to the presidential election, was predictable. An LKB seminar scheduled for January 1979 was not permitted to take place, on the orders of Sudomo. Undeterred, the group successfully managed to persuade members of the parliament, including those attached to the ABRI fraction, to take part in discussions in the months after August. In the longer term, however, the diversity of views within LKB doomed its effectiveness; it was, in Jenkins's words, 'a brittle and essentially temporary alliance'.[91] Fosko itself, a cause of particular displeasure to Suharto, was dissolved in May 1979 by order of Widodo and replaced by a purportedly limp substitute which was to keep its views private, a consequence of Fosko's invasion of the sensitive territory of the dual function of the Armed Forces. When Fosko proved unable to endure this passivity, the Army ended its association with the group in mid-1980.

The gist of the disquiet was a strongly felt sense that the Armed Forces had departed from their proper role as independent guarantors of the values of Indonesian nationhood and associated themselves too closely with Suharto's regime and policies, and Golkar in particular – 'the "contradiction" between Abri's claim to be above all groups in society and the reality of its continuing support for Golkar'.[92] A particular concern was the depth and intensity of the insertion of military figures into functional roles in society which, in the past, had been mostly the preserve of civilians. By the mid-1970s, more than 20,000 members of the military were serving in non-military roles, ranging from ambassadors and provincial governors to university rectors and departmental civil servants. Their prime function was to provide a disciplined and responsive backbone to essentially civilian service structures. There was a strong sense, both amongst these veterans groups and even in the higher reaches of ABRI, including staff at the Army Staff and Command School (Seskoad) in Bandung, that there needed to be a significant reduction of this *kekaryaan* (functional) role exercised by the military, that such activity was eating away at the purity of purpose of the Armed Forces. Some staff members at Seskoad produced a paper in mid-1977 strongly arguing that ABRI withdraw from the kinds of political collusion with Golkar that had marked the 1977 election campaign; in October the following year, recently appointed Army Chief of Staff Widodo issued a paper that mirrored the sentiments of the Seskoad paper.[93]

Suharto was enraged at these developments, and apparently bemused that anyone should want to contradict the notion of the essential unity of purpose of

Golkar and ABRI, apparently the subject of an order by Suharto to Sudomo in October 1979.[94] He was, as well, miffed at the parliamentary walkout staged by NU elements within the PPP during discussion of the electoral bill in parliament in February 1980. Speaking without a text at an Armed Forces Commanders' Call (*Rapim ABRI*) at Pekanbaru on 27 March,[95] Suharto spoke in terms reminiscent of his famous defence of Ibu Tien at the Pertamina hospital nearly a decade before. ABRI, he stated, must choose as its partners those who defended Pancasila and the 1945 Constitution – leaving listeners to draw the conclusion that the champion of Pancasila was Golkar and its enemy those Muslim political forces, especially in NU, who allegedly refused to accept Pancasila's centrality, and contradicting assurances given by Defence Minister Yusuf that ABRI would not champion any particular cause but stand above all political players. Nearly three weeks later, in another fierce impromptu speech at a Kopassandha anniversary function in Cijantung, West Java, Suharto attacked alleged opponents of Pancasila and publicly raised allegations made about the supposedly corrupt activities of his wife and even stories about his own supposed fling with a film star.[96]

In response, a group of retired generals, including Nasution, Mokaginta, Yasin, Hugeng and Ali Sadikin, generally referred to as *sakit hati* (sick at heart) – together with disaffected prominent civilians, amongst whom were numbered former prime ministers Mohammed Natsir and Burhanuddin Harahap, and the leader of the emergency government in Sumatra during the latter stages of the revolution, Syafruddin Prawiranegara – composed a petition and delivered it to the parliament on 13 May. The Petisi 50 (Petition of 50), as it came to be called, was highly critical of Suharto for adopting a narrowly self-serving interpretation of Pancasila, and of promoting the collaboration of ABRI with Golkar, when ABRI should stand above all social forces. Yasin, the wiry little former Brawijaya commander and deputy army chief of staff, added his own seven-page critique of the Suharto regime as well, criticising, amongst other things, Suharto's acquisition and equipping of his cattle ranch, Tapos, and accusing him of hypocrisy.[97]

The Petition of 50 enraged Suharto: 'I didn't like what they did. I didn't like their methods'. What seemed to irk him most was the notion of an enduring and powerful opposition which might threaten a continuing instability. 'We do not recognise the Western style of opposition here, opposition for opposition's sake, just to be different.'[98] In classic, crude backlash, Sudomo and Yoga produced an obviously invented document to a meeting of newspaper and magazine editors, which Yoga claimed originated from the sakit hati generals and which called for the overthrow of the regime. Later, according to Ali Sadikin, when nineteen DPR members raised queries in July with the government about Suharto's comments, Sudharmono was deputed by Suharto to respond to them; he attached transcripts of the speeches to Suharto's reply, which included the message that the parliamentarians should study them. If they were not satisfied, they should take things further through the vehicle of their parliamentary fraction. Nothing eventuated from that corner.

Notwithstanding the fact that the Petition of 50 caused a large, if short-lived, public furore, its political impact was small. The issue at stake was too abstruse and removed from the immediate concerns of most Indonesians, and the debate conducted within such lofty echelons of the elite that it was never likely to ignite any serious community outrage. Suharto himself quickly determined that his best weapon against the petition was simply to ignore it; the press was instructed to act in similar vein. The signatories of the petition were subsequently saddled with annoying and inconveniencing restrictions (some petty, some more damaging) on their activities, including closing off their credit, denial of government contracts for their businesses, arbitrary harassment, the loss of the right to travel abroad – and, at Suharto's express instruction, being struck from the list of invitees to the Independence Day celebrations at the palace – which reeked of spite rather than real fear of political danger. By April 1981, the restoration of orthodoxy was signified by the production by a selected team of authors, headed by Dr Nugroho Notosusanto, director of the Centre for the History of the Armed Forces, of a long report, known as the Hankam paper, which endorsed the essence of the presidential view of the dual function of the Armed Forces.[99]

ELECTIONS AND RE-ELECTION

The effective destruction of the reform movement – notwithstanding occasional surfacings of dissident petitions by disaffected members of the elite – centred around the members of the Petition of 50 left Indonesian politics in a strangely quiescent mood. Indeed, government efforts to limit opposition had even resulted in the effective expulsion of Australian journalists Warwick Beutler (apparently because of Radio Australia's broadcasts of corruption allegations made against Suharto in a courtroom in Singapore)[100] and Peter Rodgers (for reporting on famine conditions in East Timor) in June 1980 and February 1981, respectively.[101] Muslim politicians were also chastened early in 1981 by the hijacking of a domestic Garuda DC9 jetliner, allegedly by Muslim extremists connected to Komando Jihad, and the rescue of its hostages by Indonesian special forces at Bangkok airport. A lacklustre – 'the opposition parties were in even worse shape than they were in 1977'[102] – though occasionally violent parliamentary election campaign, including a huge riot at a Golkar rally in Banteng Square in Jakarta and an election-related death toll of about sixty people, culminated on 4 May 1982 with another easy Golkar win. This time, the by-now ritualised victory at this 'festival of democracy' had been achieved by enhanced political organisation and with less overt support from ABRI, instructed by Yusuf to adopt a more neutral line in the campaign. The following month, Suharto entered hospital for an operation on his prostate gland.

In preparing for the presidential election of 1983, Suharto, chastened by his experience in 1978, was keen to avoid the embarrassment provided him by the sudden news of the sultan's withdrawal from vice-presidential candidature. In order to be better equipped, he consulted with members of Golkar and ABRI, and appointed a five-member panel to assess potential vice-presidential candidates. Notwithstanding these consultations, it is certain that Suharto himself had the determining say in the final decision: the Sundanese Umar Wirahadikusumah, a

Siliwangi veteran, best known as the commander of the Jakarta garrison at the time of G.30.S, and more recently chief of the National Audit Agency.

Other potential problems remained, amongst them social restlessness about apparently declining standards of rural welfare, reflected perhaps in the anti-Chinese rioting which broke out in Solo and Semarang in 1980. In response to these difficulties, Suharto, no doubt sensitised by the recent furore over the dual function and the need to draw back on the functional role of ABRI in the management of the country, began to appreciate that he must fashion a new kind of vehicle for his political ambitions. From the late 1970s onwards, he moved gradually more closely towards his trusted assistant, Sudharmono, a champion of state-sponsored economic management (relieving, equally, the technocrats of the power they had enjoyed before the second oil boom), setting in train a strategy to develop a more disparate civilian base of support, while at the same time he narrowed the ideological thrust of his regime. In his 1981 Independence Day speech, he underlined that the basis of his regime was the Pancasila and the 1945 Constitution, and he explained that his appointment of a segment of the MPR membership was explicitly designed to prevent amendments to the Constitution – but not to enthrone him as a permanent president. The proper Indonesian economy, he suggested, was one based on state control and ultimately focusing on cooperatives. In his 1982 address, he noted that the violence of the election campaign had resulted from the failure of some groups to accept Pancasila as their foundation, and signalled a forthcoming period of ideological cleansing.[103]

CONCLUSION

The period from the mid-1970s to the early 1980s was the low point in Suharto's presidential career. Relentlessly, his administration was plagued by crisis, almost without exception the legacy of the structural infelicities of the New Order. Notwithstanding the strength of his own position, an increasingly defensive president, frayed by constant criticism, especially from erstwhile colleagues and supporters in the military, realised that the broad coalition of support which had brought him to power in the late 1960s had narrowed to a dangerous degree; 'every five years Suharto's circle is becoming smaller', remarked Nasution.[104]

Despite these dangers and difficulties – characteristically, he warned in 1982 of the need to redouble vigilance against the latent threat of communism – Suharto had made some key advances in regime-building during this period. On the infrastructural side, he presided over a state which now possessed instrumental and human capital and capacities across numerous sectors, both in the public and private spheres, which his predecessor could only have dreamt of and which were rapidly changing the nature of his society. One sign of heightened state capacity was a two-thirds growth in the bureaucracy in the decade from 1974, another the steadily increasing proportion of GDP attributable to state activity. On the ideological front, he had positioned the essential building blocks for his corporatisation of Indonesia. By the turn of the 1980s, the renewed surge in oil prices and a series of excellent rice harvests had helped to re-establish what some had dared to perceive as his waning legitimacy. Indeed, in 1981, Suharto had expressed the confident wish to do nothing else with what remained of his life than 'to serve the interests of the people'.[105]

These social and economic developments in turn laid the groundwork for a new kind of Indonesia, one in which military power of itself was neither so necessary nor appropriate. It was, in hindsight, entirely appropriate that the early 1980s would see the emergence of bureaucratic and legal expertise-as-power as a force in its own right. Its chief protagonist was Sudharmono, at Suharto's right hand as he had been since the late 1960s, backed by a highly effective network of senior civil and legal administrators of an economic nationalist bent. Symptomatic of Sudharmono's emerging power, and the social and institutional realities which prompted it, was presidential decision 10 of 1980, ceding to him and his 'Team 10' (named for the decision), based in his stronghold of the State Secretariat, gatekeeping rights for all government purchases greater than Rp500 million.[106] The new Indonesia which had given Sudharmono his opportunity for pre-eminence was, as well, to provide the means for Suharto to distance himself from his aging military colleagues like Ali Murtopo and his tiresome military critics and to begin to unravel his dependence upon the military itself. This program was to be Suharto's means of achieving his ascendancy.

9 Ascendancy

SUHARTO'S INVITATION TO address the fortieth anniversary commemoration of the UN Food and Agriculture Organisation (FAO) in Rome in November 1985 was a source of intense pride – indeed, so much so that he later chose the event to begin his autobiography. His evident joy at the honour – a recognition of Indonesia's success in doubling rice production in the fifteen years after 1969 and in arriving at the long-sought goal of rice self-sufficiency in 1984 – provides a sharp insight into the self-image of the man who had always prided himself on being the simple son of a Javanese villager, and thus close to the heart and soul of what it meant to be truly Indonesian. The many problems the program of rice self-sufficiency encountered, he recalled, were solved by 'sheer determination'. 'You can imagine', he related, 'what it was like for a man who, more than sixty years before was just a small boy playing in the mud amidst the farmers of the village of Kemusuk, when he took the platform and spoke before so many experts and world statesmen'.[1] To press home the point, Suharto ended his speech by announcing his country's donation of 100,000 tonnes of unmilled rice for distribution to famine victims in Ethiopia. In July 1986 in Jakarta, to commemorate the achievement of rice self-sufficiency, the director-general of the FAO presented a beaming Suharto with two gold medals, bearing his image and inscribed with his name.

This success was a crowning achievement of what Suharto liked to see as a gradual and increasingly successful program of development under his guidance. 'I see and feel – and because of that I am happy and thank God – that the level of general welfare and intellectual life of our country have undergone significant improvements.' Not only had the focus on agricultural development and intensification brought enormous production improvements for farming families – 'the largest segment of our population' – but the general developmental thrust had also brought with it success in family planning ('Today around six in ten couples of childbearing age consciously follow our family planning program, with almost 16 million people active in the program'), in the enhancement of educational opportunity for all children, and in the construction of social and economic infrastructure across the countryside, in both urban and rural areas. Needless to say, the stress on agricultural production and its success had laid the groundwork for stability both in the rural sectors, where prosperity was generally in evidence, and in the cities, where cheap food, the price of which was carefully controlled to balance the interests of consumers and producers, underpinned political satisfaction. Economic progress was not without its shortcomings, of course; 'there are still those who are poor, while there are also those who have become wealthy. But that is what happens in the development process. Had we not brought these policies to bear, for example by directly implementing equitable distribution, where are the people with capital who would work themselves to death without the prospect of profit?'[2] Suharto's triumphalism reflected the fact that the mid-1980s were the apex of his power and influence in Indonesia, a time of virtually unalloyed political triumph.

Suharto's international acclaim came a year after his unanimous election for a fourth five-year term as president and the MPR's granting him the title of 'Father of Development' (*Bapak Pembangunan*). As before, a vital component of his dominance of the now supine MPR – no votes were taken and no repeat of the 1978 walkout occurred during its eleven-day session in March 1983 – was the enhanced success of Golkar in the 1982 parliamentary elections, notwithstanding his boast that, 'even if Golkar had not won, evidently the demand for me to return for the next term would not have changed, because it was not just Golkar which had asked me to take on another term as president but the other parties as well'.[3] Suharto's Fourth Development Cabinet was cast in similar style as his choice for vice-president: low-key, professional, experienced, safe, despite the departure of several long-serving strongmen like Amirmachmud. Notwithstanding Wijoyo's going, technocratic influence remained strong, with Ali Wardhana replacing him as coordinating minister; Ali Murtopo, in poor health and his influence evaporated, was finally pushed aside to a sinecure on the Supreme Advisory Council; he was replaced by Harmoko, an influential former journalist. Sudharmono's influence deepened as well.

SECURING THE NEW ORDER: CORPORATE INTEGRITY

Economic and political triumph did not of itself, however, guarantee the security so dear to Suharto's heart. To achieve it, he worked on two fronts. The first was to continue and, indeed, intensify the unforgivingly punitive approach against those whom he saw disturbing the flaccid tranquillity for which he yearned. The second was to bring to new heights his efforts to corporatise the Indonesian state and its subjects.

There were two key examples of Suharto's intolerance of any shades of non-compliant opposition towards the elaborating construction of his passive society. The first came in the form of a long-running series of murders of alleged criminal underworld figures and ex-convicts in the early and mid-1980s. Beginning in Yogyakarta in March 1983, the bodies of murdered criminal figures were found in prominent places; soon the phenomenon, popularly labelled Petrus ('mysterious shootings'), spread to Jakarta and other cities in Java and beyond. Newly appointed Armed Forces Commander Benny Murdani repeatedly denied that the security forces were involved in the killings, attributing the events to warfare between criminal gangs, although it was popularly believed that they were taking the law into their own hands in an effort to reduce the skyrocketing rates of crime which had come hot on the heels of economic development and dislocation in the swelling cities of Indonesia.[4]

It was not until the publication of Suharto's autobiography in 1989 that he acknowledged publicly for the first time the extent of official involvement:

> There was nothing mysterious about these events. The real problem was that the events had been preceded by a terror felt by the people. Threats had come from criminals, robbers, murderers, and so on. The peace had been disturbed. It was as if there was no longer peace in the country, only a feeling of fear. What the criminals did went well beyond the realm of the humane. They not only broke the law, but they acted inhumanely. For example, an old man was robbed of all he had, and then just killed. That is inhumane. If you want to take it, then take it, but don't kill in cold blood. There was a woman who was robbed of her possessions and then also raped by the criminal in front of her husband. That is far too much! Do we just ignore this? Obviously we had to apply a treatment, drastic action. But how drastic? Well, we had to use force. But this did not mean that we just shot them, bang, bang, just like that. No! Those who resisted, yes, they had to be shot willy-nilly. Because they resisted, they were shot. Some of the bodies were just left there. This was for shock therapy so that people would understand that criminal actions would still be combatted and overcome. Those actions were employed in order to stamp out all crimes which exceeded the bounds of humanity. Thus these loathsome crimes abated.[5]

The Petrus campaign was, as one scholar put it, 'the classic case of an intelligence-based state terror campaign'.[6] Petrus apparently began on the initiative of a single military officer in Yogyakarta, but it quickly caught on in other areas as an efficient method of containing the crime wave sweeping Indonesia, which normal policing and court procedures could not inhibit, and it endured because there was no move to contain it. While Suharto himself did not instigate the idea, he knew about it and did nothing to rein it in. Indeed, apart from the minor qualification that only those who 'resisted' were shot, he expressed no remorse and considerable satisfaction in his autobiography at what had been achieved.

There have been some suggestions that the real targets of the Petrus campaign were petty criminals and thugs who had previously been agents of Ali Murtopo for various security-related activities, but who were either potentially embarrassing for the state or had outlived their usefulness, or had not proved tractable for Murdani's emerging purposes.[7] There is, however, no clear evidence on that score, and the notion of the need for the New Order regime to impose its own kind of tranquillity makes perfect sense, and is all of a piece with the ruling ethos that the individual was essentially subservient to the needs of the community. There can be no doubt that the security forces were integrally involved in the operation, which claimed between 5,000 and 10,000 victims before the Petrus campaign ceased in early 1985. In a 1998 interview, Murdani explained that the courts were simply incapable of dealing with the crime wave. Accordingly, the intelligence forces put a tail on a suspected criminal in order to verify that he was indeed what he seemed to be. Once that was established, the criminal was simply dispatched.[8]

The same ruling mentality was at work in the style of state opposition to incipient political unrest. As we have seen, the major source of such disquiet since the late 1970s had been disaffected Islamic elements. The New Order's response had been unswervingly hostile to any suggestion that Muslim political and social ideas should be entertained; that hostility was deepened because of regime suspicion that Muslim forces would resist more strongly than others the integralist intentions of the government. Suharto repeatedly emphasised that Indonesia was not a religious state, that it was based on freedom of religion, and that he valued highly the religious life. Matters climaxed in September 1984, when an incident in Jakarta's port area of Tanjung Priok in which soldiers were alleged to have desecrated a mosque resulted in a full-scale anti-government riot, which was put down ferociously by the Jakarta garrison at the cost of dozens, perhaps even hundreds, of lives. Subsequently, security forces arrested a number of political and religious leaders, who were charged with conspiracy in relation to bomb attacks on two Jakarta branches of Bank Central Asia early in October. Amongst them was Lt. Gen. (ret.) H. R. Dharsono who, together with twenty-two others, most of them members of the Petition of 50 group, had signed a statement which contested the account of the Tanjung Priok incident provided by Murdani and called for an independent investigation of the matter. Dharsono had attended anti-government meetings held at the house of the well-known Islamic leader and preacher (and former assistant for religious affairs to Ali Sadikin) A. M. Fatwa, himself arrested by Kopkamtib in September. Sanusi Harjadinata, a former Sukarno-era home affairs minister (1957–59) and member of the Ampera cabinet (1967–68), was also arrested in early October.[9]

The disaffection exhibited by Islamic elements and by members of the Petition of 50 group such as Sanusi, Nasution and Natsir, and manifested in the Tanjung Priok riots, had been inflamed by the government's intention to legislate to make the Pancasila the 'sole foundation' (*azas tunggal*) of all mass organisations in Indonesia.[10] The result was a series of further acts, and threats, of violence, including the huge explosion of an ammunition dump at a marine base in Cilandak, south Jakarta, on 29 October. Suharto himself, 'who has kept completely silent about the recent political unrest',[11] made an unpublicised trip to inspect the area and to talk to people whose homes had been wrecked by the blast; he went in the company of Murdani, who discounted the incident as just a fire. In January 1985, a bomb destroyed some stupas atop the glorious ninth-century Buddhist monument of Borobudur, near Magelang in Central Java.

Like all who hold uncompromisingly simplistic philosophies, Suharto found such disturbances difficult to comprehend:

> Clearly what was behind this [the Tanjung Priok incident] related to Pancasila. The person involved opposed the establishment of Pancasila as the sole principle of our political arrangements. He didn't understand the real issue. He thought that with our consensus Pancasila would replace religion and so on. So he incited the people to rebel … It seems, like Dharsono, he had calculated that the government would not dare to take action because he was a former military commander. He thought he had great influence.

Of the explosion at Borobudur, Suharto remarked: 'Nine stupas were blown up by these uncivilised people. The explosion is an example of the attitude of people who have no national pride … Truly, the people who did this were narrow-minded. Worse still, it was done on the basis of religion. It is clear they did not understand the true teachings of their religion'.[12] His strategy, as before, was to diminish the political potency of Islam by linking it with the threat of political instability and of terror; the problems made it all the more clear to him how centrally important was the need to embed his corporate vision of political orthodoxy throughout Indonesian society.

One commentator has argued that 'it is hard in the final analysis to detect any meaningful social concepts behind [Suharto's policies]', and that 'Suharto's chief political skill was as a tactician, not a long-term strategist'.[13] But such a view misses the central and supreme importance to Suharto of his efforts to corporatise Indonesian society. He envisaged the introduction of Pancasila as the 'sole foundation' as the keystone of his New Order edifice:

> This is an extremely important and fundamental decision for us. We made this decision in order to lay the groundwork in both ideological and political spheres as a preparation for the coming take-off stage … Our objective is nothing more than the integration (*memanunggalkan*) of all layers, groups, forces and generations of our nation with the basis, ideology and ideals of our country and state. In this way we can preserve all layers, groups, and forces of our country from both inner conflicts and tensions which become the source of division and national wounds.[14]

To put it another way, through implementation of Pancasila 'all demands which appear mutually incompatible, all differences within an extremely complex society can be prevented from developing into sources of disagreement and conflict'. What he was attempting to do was to legislate his own integralist political and philosophical convictions. He had come to realise ever more strongly that, 'based on our own experience, the multi-party political system of the past had failed to conduct our nation towards achieving progress through development'. Pancasila democracy, by contrast, 'originates in an understanding of the family principle and *gotong-royong* [mutual assistance]. Pancasila democracy is not established by pressure or force, but by unanimity which emerges as a result of wise consideration'. 'In Pancasila democracy', he later remarked, 'there is no place for a Western style opposition. In the realm of Pancasila democracy we recognise *musyawarah* [deliberation] to reach the *mufakat* [consensus] of the people … We do not recognise opposition as in the West. Here we do not recognise opposition based on conflict, opposition which is just trying to be different'. The community, he asserted, must always take precedence over the individual. The Constitution itself laid down that 'the prosperity of society is the priority, not the prosperity of individuals'. This view was grounded in the fact that 'the greater part of our lives depends on other people; thus, community life is truly more basic, although individuality should not be discounted'. Further, he noted, 'in carrying out the development we have taken up, we must be completely convinced of the truth of Pancasila. A society which is not convinced of the truth of Pancasila will not build a Pancasila society'. Thus, 'I call on us to be wary of extreme ideas, both from the left as well as the right. Be wary of foreign influences. We want nothing else but Pancasila and the 1945 Constitution'. The fixing and inculcation of these principles provided a firm basis for the recognition and celebration of regional difference: 'At a time when national unity is as sturdy and strong as it is now, the rediscovery of regional cultures no longer presents a danger of dividing the nation'.[15]

Pancasila was the New Order manifestation of the integralist or organicist stream of thought; it provided 'the theoretical basis of the government's rejection of "Western" notions of human rights and plural democracy'. Allegedly drawing upon traditional indigenous conceptions of the right order of society, notably village society, it conveniently married New Order political intentions with notions of national authenticity. It was 'an ideology which rejects the very idea of opposition, depicting it as un-Indonesian'.[16] It found its highest expression in the law on mass organisations, generally known as Ormas, which was passed in mid-1985 and which, in addition to assaulting pluralism by enforcing the adoption of Pancasila as the sole foundation of mass organisations, imposed impossible legal constraints on the feasibility of changing the Constitution. Less central, but nonetheless important, was another law passed in 1985 which raised the number of parliamentarians from 470 to 500 (increasing thereby the number of appointed representatives) and ensuring Golkar dominance.

Ormas was, to many Muslims, a profound rebuff for the values they held most dear. While many recognised the political primacy of Pancasila, they sought to infuse it with Islamic sentiments and values and were deeply disturbed that its installation as the sole foundation was understood as an abnegation of Islam's centrality to the nation's spiritual and civil life. A clear manifestation of this direction was the 1985 legislation which required parties to use Pancasila symbols, thus disallowing the PPP's employment of the image of the Kaaba as its party symbol; another, less remarked upon, was the program under which religious teachers were dispatched for their further education to Western universities (notably McGill University in Canada), rather than to venerable Islamic institutions in the Middle East.

The bow wave of the Ormas legislation was the Pancasila ideology courses, a consequence of the 1978 MPR decrees which, amongst other things, as Suharto claimed, 'gave me a specific mandate concerning the Guidance for the Comprehension and Practice of Pancasila'. The resultant P-4 program was, as we have seen, a massive, highly bureaucratised, disruptive and hugely expensive ideological training program, directed most intensely at members of the state apparatus and the Armed Forces; 'only public servants and members of the Armed Forces who understand Pancasila, the 1945 Constitution and the Broad Guidelines of State Policy will be able to carry out their duties properly as servants of the state and servants of society'. More generally, Suharto expected, the P-4 program would play 'an important part in developing the national ideology, especially the consolidation of Pancasila as the basis of the state and our national philosophy of life', and would 'raise our citizens' consciousness of their rights and duties, and thereby all our citizenry will participate actively in the life of the state and in development'. 'I place very great significance to these upgrading courses', he remarked, noting with some satisfaction that 'by March 1983 no less than 1.8 million public servants and almost 150,000 members of ABRI had taken the courses'. More generally, 'our national education system does not only seek to develop the intellectual life of the nation but must also develop people permeated with Pancasila'. P-4 was nothing less than Suharto's supreme effort at building a new and comprehensive sense of what it meant to be Indonesian, which included the rejection of sectional interests based on religion (read: Islam) and ethnicity, the annihilation of leftist and liberal thinking ('liberal thinking is not rooted in our own identity'), a familist understanding of the 1945 Constitution which gave no ground to notions of individual human rights, and the embracing of an enforced collegiality to overturn the old culture of conflict and disharmony.[17]

Since Pancasila was to be implemented 'in every facet of the life of our nation and state',[18] the thrust of the Pancasila avalanche was directed, predictably and consistently, into other fields, such as the press. There was no such thing as the pure freedom of the press; free expression had to be modulated with concern for the general social good. 'Our experience has shown that freedom alone without responsibility can clearly be destructive', Suharto later reflected. Thus, 'the national press ... must continue to improve its role of constructive social control as well as accommodating and channeling public sentiments which arise'.[19] But, with the striking logic of integralism, he could at the same time proclaim that 'there is no need to worry that with Pancasila as the single foundation freedom of association, of assembly, and of the expressions of views will suffer limitation'.[20]

In April 1986, however, the government – piqued by a Sydney newspaper article penned by the highly regarded David Jenkins, the headline of which suggested a comparison between Suharto and the vastly corrupt and recently fallen Marcos – sent a plane-load of Bali-bound Australian tourists back home, refused to allow Australian journalists to cover US President Reagan's visit to Bali shortly thereafter, and refused to renew the visa of Australian journalist Michael Byrnes, while Bakin placed a complete ban on the issue of visas to Australian journalists. (American newspaper reports critical of Suharto around this time were ignored.)[21] Early in October, the highly esteemed daily, *Sinar Harapan*, still beset with liberal intellectual pretensions, was also banned – probably at Suharto's personal initiative – apparently because it dared to speculate (in ways that stimulated attention on the President's family and business friends) about his plans to revise the system of import monopolies (NTB) which had allowed a clutch of businessmen close to the palace to dominate the importation of important commodities. It appears that Suharto succumbed to the suggestion that the banning had unnecessarily damaged Indonesia's international reputation, and he allowed it to resume publication under another identity.

Similarly, organised labour needed to ground itself in the nation's needs. 'In fact we do not need to forbid strikes, but strikes are not necessary if both sides can work well together. We do not forbid strikes in themselves ... Three forces must be united – workers, employers, and government. Then it is not necessary to have strikes.'[22] It was, accordingly, no coincidence, especially in the context of the economic difficulties of the mid-1980s, and the subsequent drive for export-led recovery, that former Kopkamtib chief and long-time Suharto associate Sudomo was appointed minister for manpower in 1983, in association with Sutopo Yuwono. Under Sudomo and Sutopo, the notion of Pancasila labour relations – entailing the view that the production of useful industrial labour outcomes flowed from the tripartite collaboration of government, employers and labour – reached its apogee in the construction of a single, centrally controlled labour union, SPSI (All-Indonesia Association of Workers), in 1985. In this context, there was no capacity – and, indeed, no need, according to New Order ideologues – for labour to adopt a singular, oppositionist or confrontationist position in relation to the issues it faced. Should it have designs of any such kind, intelligence and intervention teams were put in place to disabuse it of any hopes of a successful outcome. A creature of a similar kind, of course, was HKTI (Harmony Association of Indonesian Peasants); according to Suharto, 'HKTI needs to make itself into a movement to advance the peasant group [*kaum tani*] especially, and the development of agriculture generally'.[23]

The imposition of strong integralist thinking, together with the enforcement muscle provided by the Army (itself much attracted by the integralist agenda so consonant with its favourite notions of kekaryaan and dwi fungsi), led to a degree of social control labelled by one foreign scholar as 'phenomenal, considering the past divisiveness of its population and Indonesia's former economic difficulties'.[24] Suharto claimed that he was doing nothing other than returning the country to the purity of its origins: 'the total correction and renewal carried out by the New Order is for no other purpose than to rectify the deviations and correct the errors made in the implementation of Pancasila and the 1945 Constitution'.[25] These failings had not only weakened the Republic's unity following the achievement of independence, but Pancasila itself had also become marginalised during the periods of liberal and guided democracy.

What Suharto sought, however, was a society free of any dissonance, so that the real work of development could reach its climax; 'for as long as ideological and political conflicts persist, development directed towards improving the people's living standards can certainly not be realised', and again, 'national stability must not be obstructed, because it is a prerequisite for carrying out development'.[26] Despite his assertions that his program was not intended as an exercise in (further) depoliticisation, and his declarations that people might still have legitimate differences in society,[27] the reality of the all-encompassing flatness of the Pancasila 'consensus' was clear. By the late 1980s, Suharto was satisfied that the task of creating an integral society had more or less been achieved; 'the legal basis to develop the political foundation to carry out the take-off stage is complete'. 'Thanks be to God', he noted in the last pages of his autobiography, 'we have arrived at a system which can guarantee the continuation of our state and nation. It took up twenty years of struggle and discussion to reach the point of accepting Pancasila as the one and only foundation. But no matter what, we reached it'.[28]

The success of Suharto's efforts, and those of the ever-growing band of New Order ideologues, in creating a mood in which opposition was seen not only to be difficult but also subversive and anti-Indonesian was evidenced in the sullen and cynical mood of political quiescence and passivity which descended over the country. The student movement, with the odd exception such as the violent November 1987 student unrest in Ujung Pandang (Makasar), directed against local government restrictiveness (its policing a new regulation requiring motor cyclists to wear helmets) and declining economic conditions, and the subsequent protests and demonstrations by Bandung students, was quite unequal to and unprepared for the task of opposing the ideological behemoth of New Order orthodoxy and its NKK regulations which, as we have noted, effectively forbade student political activity on campus.

A grim manifestation of the Suharto supremacy was the execution of prisoners long ago found guilty of involvement in the 30 September Movement and sentenced to death, but whose sentences had not been carried out. In May 1985, PKI Politburo member Mohammed Munir was executed without fanfare or publicity. Soon thereafter, another three men sentenced in 1975 were executed. In September 1986 another nine men who, between 1966 and 1972, had been sentenced to death as a consequence of their convictions for involvement in the 1965 events, were brought to a similar fate. Chief amongst them, it was reported, was Syam, the alleged mastermind of the coup plot.[29]

Since Suharto alone had the power to order the executions, we must speculate on the reasons why these elderly men were done to death at this time, when the long passage of time since their sentences had been passed – and since the late 1960s when others allegedly involved in the coup attempt had been executed – must have given them hope that they had been permanently reprieved. Commentators wondered whether the executions were meant to serve as a warning against incipient radicalism at a time of severe economic downturn and the collapse of the Marcos dictatorship, or whether they were meant to hose down Muslim sentiment so recently bruised by the Tanjung Priok and Ormas debacles, and the recent execution of a Komando Jihad leader or, again, whether they were meant as a signal to China not to expect too much politically from closer economic relations, or perhaps even a means of improving relations by removing the embarrassment of incarcerated Indonesian communists. Some even suggested that the executions had been delayed in some cases so as not to cause anxiety amongst wives or kin,[30] whose passing now permitted the sentences to be carried out. There was even the view that the government needed to be satisfied that it had drained the prisoners of every last dreg of information before carrying out their executions.

While some or all of these motives may have played in Suharto's mind, it is difficult to avoid the conclusion that the executions were a kind of symbol of what he took to be the final triumph of the New Order. This action was the conclusive sign that, even if victory could never be taken for granted, his political program was ascendant and its future assured. Thus he noted towards the end of the 1980s, 'in a general sense, Pancasila has taken root more broadly; society has become more conscious, more honest and more convinced in comparison with the situation in the past'.[31]

NEW ALIGNMENTS

Suharto's increasing satisfaction through the early 1980s with his ideological and economic handiwork provided the background for a generational and, much more important, attitudinal and strategic change in his relations with the military. As we have seen, Ali Murtopo's star, for so long in the ascendant, had begun to wane following his heart attack in 1978 (he died in May 1984), while Sujono Humardani's influence faded in the early 1980s with the arrival of more professional and technically skilled bureaucrats. Suharto, accordingly, cast about for a new style of military leadership.

He found it in the person of Murtopo's intelligence protégé, the rugged, combative and bluntly spoken Benny Murdani, who was rapidly promoted from his formal position as assistant for intelligence at army headquarters (during which tenure he had also acted as a well-travelled 'odd-jobs' man for Suharto) to the position of ABRI commander in March 1983. Murdani, long experienced in carrying out special duties for Suharto – though with no experience of commanding any unit larger than a battalion – represented a tougher and more professional face to the Army's relationship with the regime. His appointment, significantly, was a harbinger of a new approach by Suharto to position and promotion, which was to dog the unity of ABRI thereafter. No longer surrounded by old, close and trusted associates who had emerged from the ranks with him, Suharto took to appointing men below the topmost ranks of seniority, progressing them rapidly, and thereby binding them to him personally. It spoke volumes that he himself pinned on Murdani's fourth star upon his promotion to full general.

Murdani's position was formally strengthened by the provisions of the 1982 Law on 'Basic Provisions for the Defence and Security of the Republic of Indonesia' which finally gave legal force to the dual function of ABRI. He also took to refurbishing the Armed Forces intelligence capacity with the construction of Bais (Strategic Intelligence Body) ABRI, formed in 1983 from the smaller body, Pusintelstrat (Strategic Intelligence Centre), and connecting the senior echelons of the Army with the various layers of intelligence officers through the territorial command and, as necessary, the Kopkamtib capacities of local commanders, down to villages and hamlets.

Murdani's appointment, as I have remarked, was to set a pattern for future Armed Forces appointments. Previously, Suharto had always felt most comfortable with those who had served with him from the early days. They, however, were fading away; the early and mid-1980s were marked by the deaths of many of his generation: Murtopo, Adam Malik, Sujono Humardani.[32] What Suharto wanted was someone with a record of previous service and loyalty who also shared his own steely determination to get the job done. It was, of course, no hindrance to Murdani's fortunes that he was a Catholic and thus barred, to all intents and purposes, from any chance of using his position as a stepping-stone to the presidency. His appointment continued the tradition that no ABRI commander had been both Javanese and Muslim. In this appointment, as in all the others he had ever made, Suharto did not want to spark any sense of vaulting ambition amongst those he chose. He went outside the normal table of seniority to pick his own man: Murdani, who leapfrogged many others who might have felt themselves better qualified and who doubtless felt a certain resentment at being passed over.

The sense of enhanced professionalism within ABRI was manifested in Murdani's efforts to move away from the old idea of a society-based guerrilla force towards a structure which combined the capacity for domestic political policing with a more sophisticated conventional defence capacity against external threat. The new structure, made public in 1985, enhanced Murdani's direct control over his forces by disbanding the four Kowilhan regional commands, reorganising the 16 Kodams into 10, all responsible to the centre, and beefing up the social–political role at Kodam and Korem level. Its emphasis was on a further development of highly trained mobile elite forces and on the acquisition of new weapons systems. Equally, there was no longer room for the shadowy operations of an Opsus; with Ali's departure, it simply ceased to exist, replaced by Murdani's more all-encompassing control of a more formalised and bureaucratised domestic security apparatus which took a fierce and unforgiving approach – later styled the 'security approach' – to what it took to be threats to internal security. The top echelon of the military became heavily populated with officers from intelligence and security backgrounds.

Suharto, however, had more elaborate plans. Side by side with his enhancing the professionalism of the Armed Forces and tying its members more closely to his favour came the first real inklings of his desire to distance himself politically from dependence on the military and to craft a new political framework for his New Order. As I have already suggested, the most overt and significant manifestation of this desire was his gradual moves to strengthen the hand of his faithful state secretary, Sudharmono. Allied to this development came the emergence of the notion that Golkar should attempt to develop itself as a genuine political party, which involved both the provision that individuals might become members (previously only groups could aspire to membership) and an endeavour to expand its size significantly through a process of cadre-isation and civilianisation. Sudharmono's stunning achievement in securing the Golkar chairmanship from 1983 had the effect of weakening ABRI control of Golkar and enhancing bureaucratic/civilian influence in the organisation, within which vigorous and intelligent civilian progressives like Sarwono Kusumaatmaja, general secretary from 1983, were making their impact felt. Suharto himself became the first individual member of Golkar at a ceremony at his home in January 1984.[33] He was, as we will see, laying the groundwork for a new kind of political architecture, one more responsive, within the framework of his totalising Pancasila ideology, to the new Indonesia that he had created.

THE OIL CRISIS AND A NEW ECONOMIC PARADIGM

As Suharto strove, with real success, to consolidate his political mastery, his New Order faced a sudden challenge to the economic growth which had always underpinned its political success. By the early 1980s, the oil boom which had fuelled Indonesia's economic growth and secured its political stability began to dissipate. Earnings from oil and gas exports, having peaked at almost US$19 billion in 1981–82, fell to US$14.7 in 1982–83 – a fall that brought in its wake a 27.6 per cent devaluation of the rupiah in March 1983 – and to US$12.4 billion in 1985–86. In 1986, the bottom fell out of oil prices altogether. Oil and gas earnings in 1986–87 were a miserly US$6.9 billion; in 1986, the economy grew by only 1.9 per cent. The problems were exacerbated by a weak US dollar and a significant fall in the value of Indonesia's non-oil/gas commodity exports.

This was a crisis of unforeseen dimensions and gravity for Suharto ('in front of us lies a difficult and onerous battlefield'),[34] whose proclivity for state-sponsored economic activity and patrimonialist behaviour to his favoured lieutenants was profound (notwithstanding his remark that 'now in the period of the New Order, we must use each [foreign] loan for development, never for consumption, and even less for prestige projects').[35] His enduring confidence that the oil (and aid) money which had sloshed through the system would continue indefinitely had greatly strengthened his capacity to accommodate the political drive of economic nationalism and, indeed, to bring it to new heights under Sudharmono. Sudharmono (together with his lieutenants, notably Ginanjar, who made up the famous Team 10) had proceeded to expand their control over the government's procurements empire, at the same time massively enhancing their powers of patronage as they promoted the interests of *pribumi* (indigenous) businesses as well as those of Golkar.

Suharto's confidence in himself and in the New Order project – 'there is no difficulty which we cannot overcome'[36] – was sufficient for him, once the technocrats had finally persuaded him of the need, to embark upon the wholly new and potentially dangerous development of a new economic paradigm. In one clear sense, he had no choice, because he realised how dependent his regime – and his own personal political security, based so singly on patronage – were on the re-establishment of economic health. His 1984 Independence Day speech was a call to 'put aside the destructive attitude, as though the development which is half-way completed will experience total failure and that tomorrow Indonesia will be enveloped in darkness'.[37] Reinstalling the technocrats he had effectively cast down from the heights of policy since the early 1980s – though he was careful not to allow them to wander into the broader pastures of legal or bureaucratic/governmental reform – he gave them significant rein to begin to develop a more efficient, deregulated and market-oriented economy, a radical departure from the introspective import-substitution regime that oil and aid had allowed to prevail for so long but which was no longer sustainable. They in turn began the economically orthodox but, in the Indonesian context, long and politically dangerous task of demolishing the state-dominated import-substitution orientation of government policy and replacing it with a paradigm of economic growth through deregulation and a new orientation towards exports, employing Indonesia's wealth of cheap urban labour.

In September 1986, Suharto made the 'very difficult and troubling decision' to devalue the currency – the fourth time he had so acted during the New Order – by 31 per cent.[38] Major reform packages were announced in May and October 1986 and in January and December 1987. Integral to this strategy were efforts to promote the inflow of foreign capital by deregulating the banking sector (the old 1967 bank law had prohibited the establishment of new banks), slice through the maze of regulations governing licensing – in the early 1980s, for instance, 'to acquire all the licences and permits necessary to establish a hotel ... more than 20 signatures were needed' – and reduce tariffs on a wide range of goods.[39] Symptomatic of the new push – and of Suharto's confidence in his capacity to manage it effectively with minimal domestic opposition – was his startling decision in 1985 to employ a Swiss firm (Société Générale de Surveillance) to handle the inspection and collection of duty on goods at the waterfront. Equally significant was his withdrawal in 1988 of the powers previously enjoyed by Team 10.

By the late 1980s, the Indonesian economy was well on the way to recovery. It was a leaner looking and more efficient animal, perked up by the significant shift in economic activity from the government (which had previously always dominated economic activity) to the private sphere, and dragged from its old dependence on primary production and state direction. According to a later commentator, 'Indonesia has never been as close to becoming a market economy as it was in the reform period of 1983–92'.[40] It would be wrong, however, to suggest that Suharto had completely left his moorings; the deregulation was never allowed to run completely unmonitored, notwithstanding the huge growth in the private sector, and, even if 'the state's monopolization and insulation of the policy process [was] no longer so complete',[41] he was sufficiently shrewd to maintain key elements of the old state/patrimonial system. In one commentator's words, 'he allowed his ministers to liberalize just enough to guarantee annual infusions of foreign aid and investment'. What emerged was a curious dualism in the economy. On the one hand, deregulation looked for clear rules, certainty, transparency. At the same time, Suharto insisted on retaining key patrimonialist features which he saw as crucial to his continued political supremacy. Thus, 'the technocrats made enormous efforts to shape a new economic landscape, but were unable to alter fundamentally the socio-political context governing the environment ... What they created was an impressive façade'.[42]

A similar dualism appeared in relation to Suharto's efforts to achieve greater equity. Repelita IV, begun in 1984, was premised around the notion of greater equity across the regions, with resources distributed throughout the archipelago by means of a gigantic and highly centralised bureaucracy in Jakarta. At the same time, however, he sought to extinguish any sense that income differentials between individuals should be a cause of disaffection or conflict. 'People with limited means should always look for contentedness within their means. And those who are better off should not let loose their appetite for indulgence and ignore the plight of less fortunate people.'[43]

Thus, even though 'the old hostility to capitalism and market forces [had begun] to dissipate in the 1980s',[44] Suharto's move to a new economic paradigm was only partial, and heavily impeded not just by his own brand of patrimonialist financing and nervousness about the private direction of the economy but also by a stubborn economic nationalism and caution about the perils of Western financial hegemony. In his autobiography, he commented critically on the economic policies of the West:

> Look at the way in which the idea of the North–South dialogue has progressed. This has not been smooth, if not completely stalled. Then there is the trade protection measures imposed by developed countries. This all indicates that they are not much concerned for the interests of developing countries ... I am convinced that we must develop on the basis of our own strength just like we did when we struggled to achieve our independence.[45]

THE CHILDREN AND THEIR COMMERCE

Perhaps the most obvious manifestation of the dualism of Suharto's politico-economic thinking was to be found in his attitude to the business interests of his own offspring. From the early 1980s, his children began to move into serious adulthood. Although some of them advanced to university study, none was especially brilliant academically. Siti Hediyati Haryadi (Titiek) graduated from the Faculty of Economics at the University of Indonesia and married the rising military son of Sumitro Joyohadikusumo, Major Prabowo Subianto, in a grand ceremony at Taman Mini. Siti Hutami Endang Adiningsih (Mamiek) graduated from the Faculty of Mathematics at Bogor Agricultural Institute in 1987, boarding at Bogor during her studies, and had had intentions of becoming an agricultural statistician before marriage intervened. But it was the world of business, rather than that of the mind or (at this time) of politics, which beckoned them.

Tommy, the youngest son, having finished junior high school, continued his studies at the Civil Aviation Academy before proceeding to the United States to study agriculture, returning with those studies uncompleted. He then began a meteoric rise in the realm of business, matched only by the speed of the sports cars and power boats he raced for a hobby, ever more buoyed by his capacity to land rich government-sponsored contracts. With his older brother, Sigit Haryoyudanto, he established the Humpuss group in 1984, himself holding 60 per cent of the equity. While Sigit, a serious recreational gambler, took a low profile and appeared content with the role of investor rather than active manager, Tommy proved an energetic and highly flamboyant business operator, relentlessly parlaying his impeccable connections into new ventures which were characterised by his shameless capacity to appropriate for private gain business activities which already existed in the state domain. First grounded in Tommy's acquisition of some Pertamina-related distribution rights, Humpuss diversified rapidly through the 1980s.[46]

In 1982, Suharto's second son, Bambang Trihatmojo combined with three student friends to create Bimantara. His earliest venture, a monopoly licence to import and export goods by air, was followed in 1984 by a successful tender by the company to buy, renovate and then resell the Palapa B-2R satellite, an integral part of Indonesia's telecommunications network. To this were added land ventures, including the construction of the luxury Grand Hyatt hotel on cheaply acquired land on the Hotel Indonesia circle in central Jakarta. Exploiting its connections, and under the savvy of its executive director, Peter Gontha, Bimantara soon found itself a share of monopoly rights to import plastics and permission to export a part of Pertamina's oil. Bambang also moved into communications, establishing the station RCTI (*Rajawali Citra Televisi Indonesia*) in 1988; a ban on commercial television, imposed by the government as being not in the best interests of development, was overturned in 1988, allowing RCTI to broadcast in Jakarta.[47]

Tutut proved as resourceful in business as her brothers; with her husband and sisters she established her own business group, Citra Lamtoro Gung, in 1983. To the stake in Liem Siu Liong's Bank Central Asia which she shared with Sigit, she added a raft of businesses from the late 1980s, notably toll-road development and the acquisition of an educational television channel which employed TVRI's facilities without cost. As well, she partnered Titiek in founding another business group, Daya Tata Matra (Datam), in the early 1980s.[48]

Suharto not only encouraged state enterprises to assist his children, but also – even as he talked up the values of deregulation and economic discipline – quietly nudged private businesspeople in the same direction. One prominent political commentator noted in the early 1990s 'the burgeoning business empires of his [Suharto's] children who seem to have first option on all big government contracts and many small ones as well',[49] a matter of some concern to military businesses which had suffered the depredations of Sudharmono's Team 10.

Suharto's relentless indulgence of his children, despite the growing political risk it occasioned him, requires explanation. General Sumitro's psychological assessment was that Suharto was 'weak in relation to his family and those to whom he feels he owes something'.[50] He also suggested that Suharto's own lack of attention to his family because of his pressing military and political obligations – notwithstanding reports of him dutifully helping the young Tommy and Mamiek with their arithmetic[51] – may have aroused a sense of guilt that could only be assuaged by indulging them. The children themselves, Sumitro adds, were an irresistible target for businesspeople who wanted to enjoy the prestige and guaranteed success which came from proximity to the Suharto family.[52] Others have suggested that Suharto's own modest origins, and the difficulties of identity and belonging that he encountered in his early and emotionally tumultuous life, led him to the conviction that his children should never have to endure the same sufferings.[53] There was, as well, the view that the undiluted intensity of the children's move into business was intended as a form of insurance to maintain their influence once their father had left politics.[54] Certainly, Suharto could point to their achievements to contradict criticisms that he excessively promoted Sino-Indonesian business concerns.

Perhaps the best explanation lies in Suharto's characteristic blindness to the distinction between public and private benefit. When queried on the children's activities, his customary response, delivered in an angered tone, was that their success was due to their skill as businesspeople. It was as though he refused to recognise, as many powerful people do, the extent to which his own political dominance permeated other sectors of activity. Whatever the case, it is clear that the dramatic success of the children lay in securing positions of privilege and monopoly – notwithstanding Suharto's startling assertion that 'monopolies for individuals are not allowed in Indonesia'[55] – in both state and private business sectors, usually as importers of specific items or as tenderers for large and lucrative projects.

THICKENING PATRIMONIALISM, FATTENING CORRUPTION

Suharto's treatment of his children was all of a piece with his distinctively styled business dealings with those close to him. I have already discussed his key relationship with Sino-Indonesian businessmen in the early years of the New Order. In the heated days of deregulation of the mid-1980s, these relationships became, for those favoured by them, even more crucial for commercial success. The age of the giant conglomerate, embryonically emerging since oil-boom revenues had worked to deepen and broaden the national economy, had arrived with a vengeance in Indonesia.

The most well-known of Suharto's favoured businessmen remained Liem Siu Liong. His business interests had developed spectacularly over the years. Amongst the strongest of his diversified activities was Bank Central Asia, which, under the management of Mochtar Riady (Lee Mo Sing), grew from two branches in early 1975 to forty-nine by mid-1988 and to the status of Indonesia's largest private bank. By the mid-1980s, as a result of canny acquisitions, Liem's empire extended to cement, steel, real estate and property development, shipping, textiles, mining, insurance, foodstuffs, motor vehicles and, of course, flour milling; by 1988, the group was estimated to have assets of US$3.5 billion.[56] Its proximity to the regime, especially manifested in the presence in the Liem group of Suharto's half-brother Sudwikatmono, made it an especially attractive target for foreign investors, but it was also good at what it did. Its political importance meant, as well, that it could call in support from government at times of need, as in the decision to take up a 35 per cent share in Liem's Indocement company in 1985 at a time of economic downturn and significant surplus capacity. By 1990, the annual revenue of the Salim Group was approaching US$10 billion. Other well-known stars in the gathering firmament of Indonesian conglomerate chiefs included William Suryajaya, Prayogo Pangestu (Phang Jun Phen), and Sofyan Wanandi.

It was probably partly to deflect domestic criticism of the soaring success (especially as deregulation proceeded) of his business friends, particularly those with Chinese roots, that Suharto began again in the late 1980s to emphasise the spiritual importance of cooperatives for the Indonesian economy.[57] There were, of course, more distant historical routes to his fascination with the concept (if not the practice) of cooperativisation. I have already noted his development of co-operatives in the early 1950s; to this must be added the fact that the integralism/familism so strongly promoted for political and social purposes in the 1980s drew from the same well of ideas as did his cooperative thinking. While recognising that much remained to be done to develop the concept – he spoke vaguely about cooperatives assuming greater importance in a 'following stage', once private capital had been permitted to maximise wealth – Suharto proclaimed that 'co-operatives must become the backbone of our economic life', a stage to which the Indonesian economy would advance subsequent to the era of private investment, when 'cooperatives must share in the ownership of private enterprises'.[58]

Equally, he liked to de-emphasise the role of private capital in the economy, suggesting, for example, that even though in theory the sale of shares would distribute ownership more evenly throughout society, it was 'not yet possible' to take that step in Indonesia; a public share market would result in inequities in society, because 'at this time [1987] ... going public would actually result in shares falling into the hands of wealthy individuals'. 'Equitable distribution', he noted, was one of the trilogy of development (the others were national stability and economic growth).[59] Various efforts were made to defend the policies on monopolies, usually by the claim that they were not meant to benefit a few members of the elite but, rather, to fulfil important social purposes such as domestic price stabilisation.[60] Suharto himself mounted a similar defence when he noted that 'what must be the rule is that everything should be carried out for the greatest possible prosperity of the people'. At the same time, however, he was keen to recognise the contribution of Sino-Indonesian capitalists to the nation's development; their assets were part of the 'national potential ... We must call upon (*himpun*) their capital and experience, as well as their expertise, all the more so if one realises that their potential is greater than that owned by the mass of our people'.[61]

Throughout the economic crisis of the 1980s, economic reforms did not seriously erode Suharto's capacity to funnel moneys to those whose support he needed. Pertamina, for example, remained a source of significant off-budget funding for ABRI's weapons purchases, and its significance – together with that of other ABRI business operations, on one estimate, yielding up to 35 per cent of the official budget for ABRI – increased in the context of serious relative declines in the official military budget. Allegations of corruption were easily dismissed as irrelevant to his actions and policies. 'Certainly', Suharto remarked, 'the government will not permit corruption. The government will take firm action in accordance with the law in force against corruption and all other forms of irregularity.

All of these things are in conflict with the law and stand in the way of development'.[62] The problem, was, however, that of actually finding proof that people had acted in this improper way.

THE EXPANDING FOUNDATIONS

A major key to the maintenance of Suharto's personal financial power was found in the ever-expanding reach of his foundations, long a favourite method of providing 'extra funding' for needed purposes which the state itself could not provide directly. One such foundation established under his aegis in 1982, the Yayasan Amal Bhakti Muslim Pancasila, purportedly raised funds for the construction of mosques and other Islamic facilities. Public servants were 'encouraged' to donate small sums from their pay each month; from this income, Suharto said, 'we can build three mosques each month'. Thus, 'I draw funds from public servants to build mosques to serve as a service for Pancasila Muslims. I know that not all civil servants are Muslims, so charitable donations collected from Christians and other non-Muslims are set aside, and I channel them through the Dharmais Foundation to orphanages'.[63]

Closer to the bone, the Yayasan Dana Abadi Karya Bakti (Dakab) was intended to finance the activities of the 'Great Golkar family' – 'a money printing machine', according to one commentator[64] – and the foundation donated Rp200 million per month to the various levels of the organisation. By 1985, Suharto boasted, its assets amounted to Rp43 billion.[65] The other parties received help from a general presidential assistance fund (Banpres), sourced from profits from income from the clove monopoly granted to companies owned by Liem Siu Liong and Probosutejo, and which also provided assistance for small-scale agriculture and other needy causes. This personalised dispensing of funds remained wholly outside the state budget and otherwise unaccounted for; according to one scholar, 'there is a sense in which the secret of Suharto's grip on power is less the power of the gun and more that of the purse'.[66]

Notwithstanding the fabulous riches of the foundations, and the accelerating business success of his children, Suharto angrily disputed that he shared in the benefits in any personal way. 'There are people who say that I am rich; indeed I am rich, but only as the chairman of the foundations.' He himself was, he claimed, simply the manager of the funds; he also enrolled his children to assist, without payment, in their operation. Thus, 'Sigit and Indra [Tutut's husband] are in the Yayasan Dharmais; then I put Tommy and Bambang into the Yayasan Dakab. Thus they can begin to train themselves to think about and make a contribution to social activities'.[67] His wife's long interest in foundations remained strong; in addition to her longstanding Yayasan Harapan Kita, which amongst other things provided funds for the construction of a new National Library building in Jakarta, opened in 1989, she established a family foundation, Yayasan Purna Bhakti Pertiwi, and the Yayasan Dana Gotong Royong Kemanusiaan, to assist the victims of earthquakes; the latter was the target of generous donations by leading

Indonesian businessmen. The yayasans were big business, so big that they received their own splendid new building in 1990 to carry out their work.

AT THE APEX OF POWER

In the late 1980s, Suharto stood at the height of his powers and his power was immense; no decision of any consequence was taken without his assent. The threat of economic collapse engendered by the oil price collapse had receded, and his legitimacy as the provider of economic development was further embellished. His ideological campaign to narrow the focus of politics and political thinking had been received without significant disturbance. He was the master of the political system he had created. Having subdued or domesticated all civilian opposition, he was unchallengeable in his position as paramount power in the state. He enjoyed that status, increasingly, in his own right, quite independently of the power of the Armed Forces which had buttressed his progress since 1965. 'Soeharto', remarked two noted scholars, 'has ... imposed the stamp of his personality and political style upon the New Order so strongly ... that we simply cannot disregard the personal factor in any analysis of the political, social and structural dynamics of the regime'.[68] He had developed for his country a new concept of nation, built upon the foundations of growth and stability and expressed personally in the obvious delight he took – generally accompanied by a squad of ministers and senior officials – in opening yet another power station or dedicating yet another factory.

His achievement was considerable. Indonesia's history as an independent state had been marked by upheaval, fissiparousness and frequent violence. Suharto, finally, had wrought a sense of stability and purpose in Indonesian politics; he had won the battle for food self-sufficiency, made great inroads into ridding the country of the persistent and abject poverty that had been its byword, ended the apparently perennial expressions of discord over religions and ethnicity, and made his country the object of international esteem. There were no challengers to his throne, and no serious independent sources of political power; indeed, an aura of indispensability was gathering about him. He was the linchpin of what one commentator called 'a powerful and self-confident political centre'.[69] The New Order, refined and consolidated, worked as the state in Indonesia had never worked since the period of high Dutch colonialism in the 1920s. Suharto himself increasingly became the personal exemplar of the system he had built. More and more he was required to make public statements of the values and goals which the New Order espoused. Photos appeared in newspapers with him as model New Order citizen: visiting the tax office to present his tax returns, exercising to promote physical fitness, promoting child immunisation campaigns.[70]

Suharto's sense of security, political confidence and achievement saw him move with growing assurance and purposefulness on the world stage that he had always regarded as marginal to his real interests (indeed, in the early 1980s, one foreign commentator had noted that, although Indonesia 'belongs to every major Third-World forum, it has simply refused to stand out in any of them').[71] Suharto's unambitious and solid leadership of and support for ASEAN had brought an unaccustomed sense of security and stability to the region as a whole. His recipe for successful regionalism was a simple one:

> If national stability is achieved in the respective member countries [of ASEAN], regional stability will be realised. Based on this thinking ... I still consider it necessary to have members of ABRI as ambassadors in the region of Southeast Asia and in other neighbouring countries, so that the members of ASEAN will really be able to adapt themselves to the effort of developing their own national resilience.[72]

He also encouraged the development of inter-ASEAN cooperation in trade and investment, as one of the ways to achieving the 'national resilience' which he saw as the keystone for successful regional cooperation. Now, however, his horizons were broadening. Having made just twelve overseas trips in the years 1980–87, he began to take more readily to travelling, not, as he had done in the 1970s, to seek credits and contracts but in order to parade his talents as statesman. In 1989, at the behest of Foreign Minister Ali Alatas, he made a triumphant personal return to the Non-Aligned Movement's forum for the first time since his unhappy experience at Lusaka nearly twenty years before. In August 1990, having finally been persuaded that he could never hope for an apology for the events of 1965, he presided over the long-gestating restoration of relations with the People's Republic of China.

Now Suharto was a leader of stature, perhaps even a world figure. Leaders wanted to know how he managed things, and he was happy to indulge them. He liked this treatment very much indeed.[73] Such experiences generated a heightened interest in problems of world poverty, and particularly the North–South divide, which he came to see at least partly as a function of the selfishness of the West. His relations with the Americans had cooled as the result of the developing pressure placed on him by President George Bush (with whom he enjoyed a poor rapport), Vice-President Dan Quayle and Paul Wolfowitz regarding his economic management and, particularly, the size of Indonesia's debt. Indeed, Suharto remarked rather testily in his autobiography that 'it is not true that Indonesia is under the shadow of America'.[74] By contrast, his visit to the Soviet Union in September 1989 saw him feted by Mikhail Gorbachev, found him lauding the Soviet role in the campaign to liberate West Irian in the 1960s, and brought an immediate strengthening of Soviet–Indonesian relations.

Suharto's new-found attention to the world stage had some important domestic consequences. One of them was the 1988 decision – made in response to a request from East Timor Governor Mario Carrascalao as a means of enhancing the economic and social integration of the province – to open East Timor from the beginning of 1989, a response to Suharto's felt need to embellish Indonesia's international image as he sought a larger role in world affairs, and in particular within the Non-Aligned Movement, the leadership of which he increasingly coveted and campaigned for in the late 1980s. An almost immediate consequence was the movement to East Timor of large numbers of people from other parts of Indonesia, seeking a livelihood from trade or work; by the end of 1991, the number of arrivals was estimated at 70,000. The East Timor decision angered Murdani, who thought the province still in need of strict security attention and who sought to absolve ABRI of blame for what might take place there in the wake of the decision.[75] Sensitivity to world opinion, however, did not relieve those championing Irian Jaya's independence from government harshness; while a fierce army reaction to incipient rebelliousness sent more than 10,000 Irianese fleeing over the Papua New Guinea border in 1984, Suharto's transmigration schemes continued to ferry in new settlers, perhaps 100,000 of them through the 1980s.

Suharto himself was developing his own sense of political destiny (and a corresponding concern about his place in Indonesian history), a project which reached its apotheosis in the publication of his ghosted and intensely self-centred autobiography (*Pikiran*) in 1989. Again and again in this work, he turned to his role in the major task of modern Indonesia, its development, and his central task of mapping and guiding its progress. It was a destiny shaped by long and continuing struggle, resoluteness and effort: 'the road of development along which we travel is still a long road, and it is not free of trials. It requires a high level of determination, strong resilience, firmness in keeping our direction and hard work which does not recognise fatigue'.[76] By the mid- and late 1980s, he could take some satisfaction from the fact that he was well on the way to solving the problems he had identified as the key causes of Indonesia's previous discontent: 'deviations from Pancasila and the 1945 Constitution, both in spirit and in implementation' and 'the neglect of economic development'. But the task had been a thankless and unforgiving one; 'sometimes I feel tired … But I may not complain, much less give up. Development is a fierce struggle'. He recalled 'sweat pouring out of my whole body and my black hair quickly turning white because all the effort demanded unlimited energy and thought'.[77] The massive task required a disciplined order of life:

> I always make an effort not to let work pile up or accumulate or to put it off. As far as possible I finish it immediately. I don't want to postpone it with the excuse 'I'm tired, I'll leave it till later', and so on … My motto is 'get things done immediately, finish them off' … My routine thus far, which I think is a good one, is that I wake at 5.00 a.m., immediately say my prayers, and then I read and finish correspondence until about 7.30 or 8.00. That means that I have already worked for three hours in the morning. I bring all the documents to my adjutant for immediate distribution. Only then do I have a cup of coffee … Then I bathe and have breakfast, and then leave for the office to receive reports personally, something which usually begins at 9.00 a.m. … Now and then I finish correspondence in the evening so that I don't get tired. Usually, after watching the world news, I finish them no later than 12 midnight, so that I will feel refreshed the next morning. I go to bed no later than twelve o'clock. So I sleep for only five hours, because I'm up again at 5.00 a.m. Only if I'm extremely tired do I sometimes need a short nap in the afternoon, and then it's back to work.[78]

Suharto's ascendancy, however, was not to endure, at least not in the shape it had in the mid- and later 1980s. Just at the moment when he had reached the heights, the dynamics at work within Indonesian politics and society – and the very logic of the political system which he had created and refined – began to nibble at the foundation of his rule.

THE 1987 ELECTIONS

The 1987 election campaign was amongst the least cantankerous in New Order history. Its relative tranquillity reflected the subdued mood of the PPP, severely weakened by the decision of Nahdlatul Ulama at its December 1984 congress – with a new progressive leadership which included as head of its executive board Abdurrahman Wahid, the East Javanese grandson of the movement's founder – to withdraw from party politics to devote itself exclusively and single-mindedly to social and educational pursuits, and to free itself from the limitations imposed by its formal political role.

It reflected, too, Suharto's determination to domesticate the PDI more fully to his will, and perhaps add to its appeal. In a characteristically strategic move, he had sought in the previous year to appropriate for himself the legitimacy of Sukarno, whose reputation, enhanced by romantic nostalgia and the passing of time, was such that his gravesite in Blitar drew as many as a thousand people a day. In November 1986, Suharto formally acknowledged Sukarno and Hatta as proclaimers of Indonesian independence, in a ceremony held at Merdeka Palace and attended by Sukarno's children, including Megawati who, together with her brother, was a PDI candidate in the coming elections. Suharto was rewarded for his efforts when a compliant PDI, now led by Suryadi, endorsed the existing political system during a meek election campaign, in which the only boisterousness came from the PDI's espousing the memory of Sukarno.[79] Indeed, so little was there deemed worth discussing that the campaign period was shortened from the usual forty-five days to a mere twenty-five.

Perhaps most of all, it reflected the political dominance of the New Order and its ideological success in crushing or cowing any small sign of opposition. By mid-1986, there was already a loud clamour of support for Suharto to accept another term as president. He himself was moved to beat off rumours of a lifetime presidency; 'according to our constitution, the president is chosen to carry out the GBHN [Broad Outlines of State Policy], and the GBHN is valid for five years'.[80] But it came as no surprise when, as early as October 1986, Suharto (who, according to one reporter, 'continues to impress visitors with his intelligence and lucid memory')[81] announced to a Golkar twenty-second anniversary gathering his thinly veiled intention to make himself available for a fifth successive presidential term. It came with the usual carefully constructed modesty ('each time I hear statements like that [seeking his candidature] … I feel horrified, the hairs on my neck stand up … the question arises as to whether I am still capable of carrying out this task'). There was, however, a new refrain: 'if in the middle of carrying out the coming five-year task I am no longer judged to be capable, I should be replaced immediately'.[82]

The results of the elections for a parliament which had been increased in size from 460 to 500 members (of which 100, rather than 75, were now allocated to

ABRI) were as predictable as they were crushing for the non-Golkar groups. The PPP, sadly lacerated by the absence of NU, saw its vote collapse from 27.9 per cent to only 16 per cent. Golkar's share, almost solely the pickings from the departed NU, rose from 64.3 per cent to 73.2 per cent, well above its 70 per cent target, and included a first-time win in Aceh. Desultory ABRI efforts to promote the cause of PDI helped to give that party significant gains, but changed nothing in the larger scheme of things.[83]

THE 1988 ELECTION, SUDHARMONO AND THE MILITARY

The parliamentary elections completed, Suharto's election for a fifth time on 10 March 1988 was the most formal of formalities. Most living Indonesians had never known any other leader. It was perhaps symptomatic of his dominance of the political system – the belief that the presidency was, in a special sense, his property by right – that, for the first time, his family appeared to witness his swearing-in at the concluding session of the MPR, on 11 March (he had picked the day carefully).

Their attendance excited comment that Suharto expected that this might be his final term, a view which seems to receive confirmation from his 1989 autobiography:

> When one of my children said that this appointment (1988) would be my final one as President, I could well understand it. Indeed, it is common sense that at my age of 67 it is only reasonable that this will be the last appointment for me. When I will have reached the end of my period of service as president (1988–1993) I will be 72 and will stop being president. Given that the average lifespan of Indonesians is 56, if I'm not mistaken, the age of 72 is well over the average and can be considered rather old. So, it is no exaggeration to say that my appointment on 11 March 1988 is my final appointment as President/Mandatory of the MPR.[84]

While most observers have given little credibility to this notion – one commentator remarked that 'it would be naive to assume he intended the power structure to change, or become any less focussed on himself'[85] – there are grounds for thinking that Suharto seriously considered in 1988 that he would not continue upon completion of the coming term of office, notwithstanding Nasution's comment that 'he will stay there as long as he can'.[86] There was even the question of whether he might stand down during that term. Whatever his thinking on the matter, however, as we shall see, the internal bickering it stimulated must have gone a considerable way to convincing him finally that Indonesia could not continue its upward path without his stabilising and guiding hand at the tiller.

The major problem Suharto encountered at the 1988 MPR session revolved around the vice-presidency. For one whose previous choices for the position had had the virtue of never being serious aspirants to the presidency, he startled everyone with his choice this time: Sudharmono. Given his closeness to the inner workings of the New Order, his faithful and devoted service as its legal architect, his patronage and management skills, and his vigorously active involvement in politics, Sudharmono was not cut from the usual template of New Order vice-presidents.

Suharto's choice of Sudharmono reflected his extraordinary capacity to catch the currents of the times, and represented the culmination of a key strategic direction since the late 1970s. He had realised that the economic achievements of his New Order, most recently exemplified in the radical economic reforms which had wrenched Indonesia from the looming precipice of the early 1980s, had changed his country in fundamental ways. As the economy moved into a more mature phase, the result of a combination of longer-term development in concert with the 1980s reforms, social modernity was emerging in Indonesia. The growth of investment opportunities and the promoted and diversified role of private capital in the economy, together with the focus on export-oriented production, had brought forth a new group of businesspeople and enhanced the size and political potency of the emerging educated middle class, as well as a young and sometimes querulous urban working class. Many of these rising groups sought their salvation not in the arms of state-sponsored companies but in private business; they required not privileged patronage but transparency, objectivity and lack of arbitrariness in the rules under which they operated. Side by side with these developments came imaginings that politics in Indonesia was seriously under-developed and might better emulate such business values of initiative, shared responsibility and consultation.

In this context, there is good reason to believe that Suharto had reached the final stage of grooming Sudharmono to take the ultimate prize of the presidency. Here was someone who had many of his master's political and bureaucratic sensitivities, vast experience in the bureaucracy and a mastery of the arts of patronage. Sudharmono shared with his mentor, as well, a sensitivity to the changing social order of the country, and the means to accommodate those changes through enhancing the civilianising and participatory trends already evident in the post-1983 Golkar, within, of course, the Pancasila framework. Suharto himself, for some long time, had been moving towards the conviction that he could never expect ABRI to demonstrate a similar kind of strategic flexibility, notwithstanding Murdani's occasional cautious statements in favour of a more open and responsive political system. It was no accident, accordingly, that Suharto had stipulated before the MPR session that the necessary attribute of a vice-president was 'to be acceptable to all layers of society, manifested by the support of the large and dominant socio-political force'.[87]

Accordingly, he began to lay the groundwork for Sudharmono. On 10 February 1988, a month before the presidential election and two months after he had granted Murdani a twelve-month extension of service, Suharto struck his most telling blow, relieving Murdani of his post as ABRI commander and replacing him with army chief of staff and former presidential adjutant (1974–78) Try Sutrisno, the first officer to hold that position who had not served during the revolution. According to one observer, 'Murdani was visibly shocked by the news' as he emerged from his meeting with Suharto.[88] In retrospect, the break between the leader and one of his most steadfast and long-serving lieutenants had been gestating for some time (although Suharto may have calculated its timing so that Murdani was not in command of troops when he learned of Suharto's choice of Sudharmono as vice-president). Murdani's apparent incapacity to appreciate the fresh socio-political currents in Indonesia's new society, his obsession with developing intelligence networks, and his unblinking firm-mindedness and his lack of political suppleness had inevitably set him against the President. Notwithstanding the common view that the break was a result of Murdani's temerity in criticising Suharto's favouritism towards his children's business interests and his refusal to favour them with lucrative military procurements, this could only have been the trigger, and not the underlying reason, for the alienation.

Ironically, as Suharto strove to create a broadly based and inclusive style of politics – the actualisation of the Pancasila state – he became personally more reclusive. In 1986 he ended his custom of holding open house over the Ramadhan greeting season. His gathering reclusiveness should not surprise. His physical and political longevity meant that he was one of the few remaining figures of his generation; most of his former colleagues had left the scene or been pushed from it. He was, in ways he had never before experienced, alone in his weighty responsibilities, denied the familiar teamwork of long-cherished colleagues of past years. His governing style began to take on a new and distant imperiousness; while the flashing, disarming smile could still be employed with devastating effect, the face he often presented to the world was one of efficient, if sometimes careworn, dutifulness and responsibility. As if to compensate for his earlier neglect, his attentions turned more and more to his close family, especially as it expanded with the arrival of more grandchildren; Ibu Tien found herself the recipient of various honours from the presidential hand.

Suharto's speeches often returned to the theme that this was a time of generational change:

> The 1945 generation is in the process of completing its historic task of bringing the country to the stage of having a strong foundation for the take-off towards a just and prosperous society based on Pancasila. At the same time, the coming generation within ABRI in particular and the nation as a whole has begun to take up a larger share of responsibility.[89]

The great majority of those with whom he worked – his inner council by the late 1980s consisted of newer, younger representatives of the emerging generation, men like the civilian state secretary and Golkar men Murdiono, Sarwono, Cosmas, Ginanjar, and Akbar, and the younger professional military types (like Try, Edi Sudrajat, Sugiarto and Siswono Yudoyono, the products of Magelang and other military academies) – were better educated and more outwardly sophisticated than the old generals. Suharto had little to share with them by way of common experience; for their part, they treated him with awe and reverence and kept their emotional distance. Increasingly, he tended to ensure loyalty not by affection but by creating division and competition.

His unmistakable supremacy was reflected in his relation with his ministers. He gave the impression that they came to him to seek wisdom and advice, not to proffer it; those who did best were sufficiently experienced and cagey to know how to present their ideas in non-proprietorial ways and without a hint of hectoring. 'When [ministers] come to me', he remarked, 'they need my instructions [*petunjuk*], what my thoughts are on this or that. They certainly have their own thoughts and ideas. But they need to check so that there is no error or lack of coordination. To ensure they are not acting on their own, I give them my instructions. That's how things work'.[90]

In all these circumstances, Sudharmono was not, nor could have been expected to be, a popular choice as vice-president in the eyes of the Army. Apart from the scant respect the Army accorded his essentially 'civilian' military background (Sudharmono had never commanded troops), senior officers were highly conscious of his efforts as state secretary to distance them from the lucrative contracts upon which they had prospered, and which increasingly found their way into the hands of Suharto's children and business friends. His hostile competition with Murdani for favour within the upper echelons of the New Order was also well known. Indeed, the ferocity of the military's campaign against Sudharmono – 'seldom has the ABRI leadership made a point more forcefully'[91] – adds weight to the notion that Suharto was serious about Sudharmono's eventual accession to the presidency.

In an unprecedentedly public display of political animus, Murdani launched a campaign amongst ABRI representatives in the MPR to deny Sudharmono the vice-presidential post. The result was the nomination by the PPP faction of Naro, withdrawn only at the last moment under intense pressure from Suharto himself.[92] In another demonstration of anger, Brig.-Gen. Ibrahim Saleh took it upon himself to stage a protest at the MPR session, briefly mounting the platform and beginning a verbal attack upon Sudharmono before being cut short by a group including Murdani and Try.

The unseemly ruckus concluded, Sudharmono's 'unanimous' election as vice-president proceeded. But ABRI had made its point: Sudharmono was not acceptable to the Armed Forces as a future president. To underline the opposition, Sarwo Edhie, long-time supporter of Suharto and head of BP-7 in 1984–87, resigned from parliament in protest at Sudharmono's election. Suharto's refusal to resile from his choice in the face of the military's earnest pleadings brought a crunching realisation to the army leadership that their capacity to exercise a serious influence on the course of events had been seriously eroded – 'Senior officers were said to be startled by their failure to persuade the president to heed their objections to his vice-presidential choice, Sudharmono'[93] – and that their much-vaunted dual function was dangerously minimalised.

In the aftermath of the embarrassing fracas, the Army, fearful that Sudharmono would continue as Golkar chairperson as well as holding the vice-presidency – especially given the emerging uncertainty about the presidential succession – campaigned vigorously to secure sufficient regional votes to remove him from the Golkar post at the fourth Golkar congress in October 1988. At the same time, damaging allegations that Sudharmono and some of his followers were somehow linked with the PKI were circulated.[94] Such tendencies – the re-assertion of ABRI influence in Golkar, the tired and old-fashioned resort to the dangers of communism – clashed with the views of younger civilian Golkar leaders, reinforced by the unnerving examples of political instability in Burma, the Philippines and South Korea, that the party needed to move further down the road of embracing a greater degree of political openness and popular participation within the Pancasila framework. The result at the congress, however, was an unqualified victory for the Army. Sudharmono declined, in the circumstances, to stand again, citing the pressure of his vice-presidential duties; the Army re-asserted its control of the organisation, casting a stain on purported leftists within Golkar – presumably the supporters of Sudharmono – and seriously damaged Sudharmono's independent power. Wahono, old colleague of the President (he was Suharto's deputy chief of staff at Kostrad on 1 October 1965 and later himself Kostrad commander) but neither politically astute nor ambitious, was recruited by Suharto to lead the organisation.

Suharto, however, was not one to cave in to this resurgent demonstration of army resoluteness, manifested, amongst other things, in a bout of student agitation in the middle of 1989 apparently sponsored, or at least tolerated, by ABRI. His new cabinet, developed on the advice of a nine-man team, of whom only three were Armed Forces members, was clearly transitional in nature, combining some old and trusted faces in positions where their toughness could be utilised (Cosmas Batubara in public housing), together with a bevy of new and untried ministers. However, it bore some unmistakable political messages. In the first place, the Armed Forces role was considerably diminished, with the number of ABRI members in the forty-person cabinet dropping to just ten. This was a further sign of the declining role of ABRI within the political apparatus. Sudomo, Suharto's long-serving and ever-faithful lieutenant, took office as coordinating minister for politics and security, presumably with a mandate to keep an eye on variant thinking within military circles. The Sudharmono camp received a significant boost with the elevation of Ginanjar, Sudharmono's close associate and acolyte for economic nationalism, and a manifestation both of the Golkar civilianising tendency and the proportionate contraction of the position of the technocrats. Ali Wardhana was replaced by the more pragmatic Radius Prawiro, and Subroto, after a long tenure of the Mining and Energy portfolio, dropped from cabinet. Former army chief of staff Rudini, distanced from Murdani, was appointed to the politically crucial portfolio of Home Affairs; it was not long before he began issuing statements denying any obligations upon public servants to vote for Golkar and endorsing their freedom of association.[95] In an unexpected nod towards increasing international concern about environmental matters, and a sign of his developing sense of Indonesia's global context, Suharto established a specific Ministry of the Environment and appointed the technocrat Emil Salim as minister. In another move, out of the blue – Murdani, now holding appointment as defence minister in the new cabinet, had no premonition or advance warning of the decision – and calculated to weaken Murdani's power and his capacity to damage Sudharmono, Suharto dismantled Kopkamtib, headed by Murdani, in September

1988. Kopkamtib's notorious and well-travelled capacity for independent and arbitrary repressive action was removed; a new body, Bakorstanas (National Stability Coordinating Board), under the leadership of Try Sutrisno and including civilian membership, was in future to coordinate such activities, which could proceed only with presidential assent.[96]

Numerous reasons have been advanced to explain the demise of Kopkamtib, but the most obvious one was Suharto's desire to curtail and damage the intricate intelligence networks upon which Murdani had based his rise to prominence. No doubt, too, he was sensitive, given his desire to play a more prominent international role, that Kopkamtib's fearsome reputation harmed his international prestige. Perhaps, too, he recognised (as Sumitro claimed to have done during his tenure as commander)[97] that Indonesia's new social configuration was no longer an appropriate site for an operation in the style of Kopkamtib.

Suharto's cogitations about his future, together with the overt conflict which had arisen as a result of the Murdani and Sudharmono affairs of 1988, raised speculation about the succession to a new height. 'We are discussing openly a topic that has never happened in the past', remarked Sudomo. Sudomo himself had the previous year reported a Suharto statement that a contest for the presidency was acceptable provided only one name eventually went forward for the MPR vote. Suharto, apparently caught on the back foot by the accelerating discussion of his future, angrily told economic ministers at a May 1989 cabinet meeting to desist from making statements championing this or that successor to the presidency.[98]

ABRI's efforts at re-assertion, however, persisted. Matters which had previously remained taboo subjects were now increasingly brought into the open for discussion, so that Try Sutrisno found it necessary to reassure Suharto at an August 1989 commanders' meeting that ABRI would 'focus its efforts on ensuring the continuity of the national leadership of the New Order'.[99] In December, army chief of staff Edi Sudrajat publicly proclaimed the view that the authoritarian bent of the New Order needed to be reined in, comments given added force and poignancy with the publication early in 1990 of deathbed comments of revolutionary hero and former Armed Forces chief of staff T. B. Simatupang on the need for the regime to undertake renewal and correction.[100] But Suharto had so decisively outplayed the military politically, capitalising on the rampant disunity and suspicion which had long characterised its upper echelons, and had played his own card of personal loyalty so skilfully, that ABRI's response to its blatant diminution through the 1980s could never have amounted to a systematic attempt to oust him.

Suharto, however, needed to respond to the damage that had been done and his response was characteristically strategic. From about the middle of 1989, he began espousing a style of tolerance and reasonableness in an attempt to defuse the sting of the ABRI counter-attack which, incidentally, civil reformers also delighted in taking up. It would be a mistake, however, to see his actions in this regard purely as those of a man driven only by pragmatic political expediency. As I have argued, he had become increasingly conscious since the end of the 1970s of the fact that his Indonesia was changing rapidly, and that new agendas to contain and control these changes were presenting themselves. His encouragement of Sudharmono's Golkar civilianisation push was also evidence that he sought a larger, reconstructed political vehicle, the better to articulate the interests of ruler and ruled. As early as his Independence Day address in August 1987, he spoke in favour of a more open political atmosphere, even if he coupled this remark with the observation that national stability must not be disturbed.[101] At the same time, because of the furore over the Sudharmono election, it seems that Suharto was turning away from the possibility of voluntarily vacating the presidency, even if Sudharmono, a busy regional tourer, was continuing to work hard to develop and broaden his political visibility and his own bases of political support. While he spoke of Pancasila as an 'open ideology', one receptive to new ideas, at his 1989 Independence Day speech, a few weeks later he repeated the warning, already made that year: he would react with severity ('I will pummel (*gebuk*) them. Whoever they are, I will pummel them') in the face of any attempt to replace him unconstitutionally.[102]

Suharto's efforts to maintain the high ground involved a recognition that the new forces in Indonesian society needed to be accommodated as a condition of their eventual domestication. Broader discussion of political issues could be entertained, but only within the limited compass of prevailing New Order orthodoxy. His response to emerging civil unrest, manifested in protests at the forced resumption of peasant land for the Kedung Ombo dam project in Central Java, was perfectly consistent with this attitude. Those who were encouraging peasants to press their case (from a region, Suharto noted, which 'used to be a stronghold of the PKI') were doing them a disservice and 'actually pushing them down and causing them trouble'.[103] ABRI did not, however, rush to side with him on this point.

An emerging theme in his discourse, apparently intended to mollify rising fears of economic polarisation within society, was a renewed emphasis on the need to more fully implement Article 33 of the Constitution, dealing with cooperative economic endeavour, in order to ensure a more equitable distribution of the fruits of development. At an April 1989 cabinet meeting, he was reported to have given voice to fears about gathering 'social envy', and around the same time he began to espouse the theme that the wealthier segments of society should contribute a portion of their wealth to the establishment of cooperatives.[104]

Related to the notion that private capital needed to play a stronger hand were Suharto's efforts to refine, and redefine, the meaning of the dual function of the Armed Forces, in ways that did significant damage to ABRI's central location in politics and the economy:

> [While the dual function] will always remain inseparable from ABRI as an element in the dynamic implementation of Pancasila democracy, the functional task of ABRI definitely does not mean the channeling of ABRI's energy into social and government life. The functionality [*kekaryaan*] of ABRI takes the form of a contribution which ABRI can make through the best of its members to the nation and state outside the core task as a force of defence and security.[105]

This kind of statement mirrored the views of people like Rudini. It also reflected the fact that ABRI's resources had been seriously squeezed by the plummeting price of oil and the economic reforms of the mid-1980s, which militated against state enterprises and promoted the growth of private investment.

Another emerging strand, first clearly visible in 1989 but perhaps originating before then, was Suharto's wholly revised attitude towards Islam. His victory in entrenching Pancasila as the sole foundation meant that his speeches no longer resounded with fears and threats associated with the political dangers of Islamic fundamentalism. In September 1989, twenty-one senior Muslim leaders and teachers, under the leading hand of former Suharto aide and minister Alamsyah, made public their wish that Suharto serve another term. His presence at NU's congress in November was noted for the warmth with which he greeted delegates; he used the occasion to acknowledge that NU had led the way in accepting Pancasila as its sole foundation.[106]

HABIBIE AND TECHNOLOGY

A final strand of Suharto's new strategy was to provide significant embellishment to Indonesia's drive towards technological advancement. In this context, Suharto began a vigorous campaign to raise the power and profile of the energetic, ambitious and missionary Dr B. J. Habibie. Habibie's views on economic development differed radically from those so long entrenched by the technocrats. He offered a new vision, not one based upon the exploitation of Indonesia's abundant supplies of labour and low-wage regime which would inevitably be the victim of its own success. Rather, he sought a state-sponsored technological revolution: the accelerated development of technologically advanced industries, strategically chosen, and the highly trained and skilled workers to operate them, whose expertise would have innumerable multiplier effects across the economy and prevent the decline which, in the long term, would inevitably ruin the technocrats' vision.

It was a perception of things that – notwithstanding recurring, withering criticism of Habibie's curious economic ideas, such as his 'balloon' theory of development[107] – found warm acceptance by Suharto who, having apparently mastered the routines of textbook development, was searching for the best route forward towards Indonesia's 'take-off'. 'I am especially conscious', he noted, 'of just how important it is to master science and technology for the progress of our nation in the future. To be able to achieve take-off, in the coming years we need to make greater progress in the fields of science and technology'.[108] His fascination with technology, and his infatuation with the notion that Indonesia's capacity to master it was a signal to the world of his country's progress – 'we can master modern technology'[109] – and maturity, had first led him to back Habibie's plans to develop an indigenous aircraft industry (IPTN) in the late 1970s, and to continue that backing in the face of opposition and envy from other ministers who resented Habibie's privileged relationship with the President and his capacity to carry off large chunks of funding from the state budget and other off-budget sources like Pertamina at the expense of their own projects. By the early 1980s, the Habibie-run PT Nurtanio was assembling helicopters and small passenger planes under licence from foreign firms.

Suharto was clearly satisfied at what Habibie had managed to achieve by the mid-1980s, as profiled in the first Indonesian air show held in 1986; 'Our success in developing high technology as in the aircraft industry has reinforced our feeling of self-belief that in using every opportunity available our people can master and develop even the most advanced technology', he remarked.[110] By this time, Habibie already managed a vast technology empire, building aircraft, ships, and even weapons. In August 1989, Suharto enlarged the reach of Habibie's portfolio of strategic industries to embrace steel and container production, and Habibie increasingly leveraged his business through privileged access to army and navy procurement. He now enjoyed a cleverly engineered familiar access to Suharto that few could match, adopting the attitude of the high-performing but always obedient and respectful son, seeking always greater illumination and wisdom from his father.

Suharto's attraction to Habibie had a personal element as well, reflecting not just Suharto's own small role in his youth in Makasar but also certain qualities in Habibie that endeared him to Suharto. Habibie, like Suharto himself, was a 'can-do' man. Suharto also admired his willingness to forgo his own profitable career in Germany to serve his country. Most of all, perhaps, he succumbed to Habibie's willingness to flatter and accommodate him:

> Each time he reports to me, for hours at a time he stays with me because he wants to grasp my thinking, my philosophy. And after he has understood my standpoint, my philosophy, he develops it in accordance with his expertise as an engineer ... He always asks my advice on the principles of living ... He always thinks of me as his own parent.[111]

CONCLUSION

By the end of the 1980s, the ascendancy which Suharto had crafted by the middle of the decade was showing some signs of vulnerability. He ruled a society which was rapidly changing as a result of the revolutionary social and economic changes which had emerged under his leadership. A nascent civil society was emerging which clamoured for a more direct and transparent participation in politics, and the moulding of newer kinds of institutions to accommodate that yearning. His erstwhile and generally unwavering support from the Armed Forces was evaporating, as senior officers began to realise with a previously unimagined horror that their role and centrality had been whittled away, and that they had become increasingly marginalised in the cockpit of power. In one commentator's view, 'the demilitarization of Suharto's New Order has gone so far it is barely recognized as a military-led government'.[112] Suharto, as he had done so often in the past, had realised the strategic importance of the moment before anyone else, and had seized it.

While civil society and the serving military were on vastly divergent courses, their leaders and spokespeople, including amongst others numerous senior and retired generals such as Sumitro and Rudini, could agree that the kind of society they wanted no longer necessarily included Suharto in the top job. Such a notion had been unthinkable even half a decade before. The Army began a period of reflection on just what its role might be in the new constellation of forces, and how that might relate to Suharto's rule. There was as yet no sense that he had to go, but a much keener, sharper realisation that his replacement must be an appropriate one, and minds turned to the mechanism that might deliver that desired result.

10 Decline, fall, accounting

Everyone in this game will have to go, sooner or later.
(Adam Malik, In the service of the Republic, *p. 20)*

BY THE EARLY 1990s, Suharto was an old, tired man. 'I'm weary, I'm tired', he told Alamsyah in mid-1993. His physique, once slim, rangy and powerful, had become shrunken, squat and rotund.[1] In 1991, he turned 70, much exceeding the average Javanese male age at death. His age notwithstanding, Suharto's decision to remain at the helm meant that he had to force his aging body, tired mind and fraying emotions to keep working to fulfil Indonesia's destiny, a task for which, he had now decided, he was indispensable. But he could still exhibit the self-deprecating sense of humour that is the privilege of those in power. Meeting the Indonesian National Youth Committee early in 1991, he responded to calls for him to stand again for the presidency in 1993:

> It is obvious that the older I am the more I am on top. Top not meaning the highest, but top with two letter P's: TOPP. T is short for *tua* [old], because as time goes by I'm getting older, and so I become *ompong* [toothless] and then *peot* [lame]. And once you're lame you automatically become *pikun* [senile]. So the MPR will be choosing a TOPP man.[2]

THE MEANING OF OPENNESS

Suharto had been battling since the mid-1980s, with mixed success, to come to terms politically with the new social forces which his policies had created in Indonesia. Indicative of the quasi-revolutionary changes which had been wrought was the fact that in 1991, for the first time, manufacturing's share of GDP exceeded that of agriculture. In the same year, for the first time ever, private banks held larger sums in deposit than state banks, although they still tailed the state institutions in loans outstanding. Such developments were aspects of Western-initiated globalising tendencies, and led some civilian reformists in Indonesia to hope that Western liberal values might accompany them.[3]

But the openness espoused by Suharto did not have that intention, although it had the effect of eliciting the circulation of muted criticisms and calls for substantial reforms (including significant modifications to the dual function of ABRI) and limitations on the executive, and even calls for the President to stand down at the end of his current term.[4] Such calls emanated from senior civilian intellectuals such as former minister and close colleague Mashuri and Golkar figure Marzuki Darusman, as well as retired generals such as Sumitro, Sayidiman Suryohadiprojo and Nasution, and the Petition of 50 group of which Nasution was a member (which was, to Suharto's apparent annoyance, invited to discussions at the parliament in mid-1991). None of this, however, amounted to serious opposition; Suharto, for example, dismissed the notion of ABRI retiring from its social–political role. 'If you pull the guts out, the thing will die', he remarked in February 1992, referring to ABRI's visceral position within the state.[5] In retrospect, it may well be that the relative weakness and clear disunity of expressions of discontent – 'the new middle class has a strong stake in the evolution of a stable and orderly political system'[6] – emboldened Suharto to press forward into the future, both relieved at the thinness of dissent and scornful of the quality and viability of the alternatives presented.

He sought to do this not only by the deliberate policy of attempting to broaden and civilianise his regime, but also in efforts to extend the basis of his popular support. His Independence Day speech of 1990 embraced the idea of greater freedom of expression, a sentiment echoed a little later by Sudomo, while Suharto himself appeared to call for a lessening of the emphasis on his executive leadership.[7] Home Affairs Minister Rudini made a name for himself by espousing a rhetoric of civil reform and responsibility which contrasted sharply with the hardline security approach brandished by Murdani and his supporters, something especially evident in the aftermath of the massacre of East Timorese at Santa Cruz cemetery in Dili on 12 November 1991. As Suharto went about the business of recasting himself in pursuit of what he believed to be the realisation of his Pancasila society, he was careful to portray an image of the serious and diligent statesman, the tireless, wise and responsive leader, consumed by, yet handily coping with, the complexity and difficulties with which his post confronted him.

An inkling of this mood came in March 1990 when Suharto summoned the heads of leading business conglomerates to Tapos for discussions. All but a couple of them were Sino-Indonesian businessmen, many of them now enjoying an unlooked-for prominence (and disfavour) as a result of their well-profiled and highly successful engagement in the deregulated economy of the mid- and late 1980s. Suharto aimed to use the meeting to reduce sensitivity about the role and influence of Sino-Indonesian commerce, and to portray himself – again – as the champion of the 'little people'. He had earlier, both in his autobiography and in statements made early in 1990, raised the prospect of private business assisting in the development of the always-limping cooperative movement, and even of cooperatives being 'able to buy shares in [private] companies'.[8] On national television, he used the Tapos meeting to suggest to the assembled businessmen that they transfer as much as a quarter of their assets to cooperatives as a means of closing the gap between rich and poor. The theatre – for theatre it was, given that his wish was not translated into reality – had its effect. The notion of a more equal sharing of the nation's wealth emerged as an important theme in Suharto's rhetoric through the 1990s.[9]

The second effort was the construction of ICMI (Association of Indonesian Muslim Intellectuals), which held its founding symposium – opened by Suharto, and with no Armed Forces officers in attendance – in Malang, East Java, in December 1990. ICMI was more than just a grouping of intellectuals, although it was never intended to be politically activist; it represented a gathering (but never fully united) mood in the political landscape of the New Order, with its own newspaper, its own think-tank (CIDES), and its push to develop Muslim commercial interests, notably in the form of an Islamic bank. Its formation was Suharto's attempt to claim the support of key intellectual Muslim leaders, as well as to stake out new and broader grounds for political support amongst the Muslim community which he had previously sought to browbeat and shackle. After a six-hour meeting with Habibie, during which he demonstrated his knowledge of the finer points of Islamic doctrine, Suharto decreed that Habibie should assume the chair of ICMI, a move designed to provide the organisation with some political and intellectual ballast, to enhance Habibie's political fortunes, and also, perhaps, to ensure that it did not develop into a dangerous Muslim 'ginger' group. Suharto's ICMI venture also had the virtue of distancing him from his Sino-Indonesian cronies and propelling a new pribumi business thrust. According to one close observer, 'with this new strategic alliance, President Suharto casts himself as pro-pribumi, pro-Islam, and pro-modern technology'.[10] Such strong official support was guaranteed to fertilise ICMI's growth; by mid-1994 it already enjoyed a formal membership of 20,000 and embraced Muslims of different religious and political complexions, as well as a good number of others who did not wish to be seen to be missing the mood of the times.

Although ICMI managed to attract many important Muslims to its fold, such as the inclusivist Nurcholish Majid and the more narrowly constructed and aggressive Amien Rais, as well as longstanding and respected political figures like Emil Salim, it also evoked a reaction from key Muslim figures who saw its development as antithetical to their own and the country's interests. The major non-participant was the NU leader Abdurrahman Wahid, who was deeply concerned at what he viewed as emerging sectarianism – some Muslim intellectuals like Amien Rais were soon to raise the idea of an 'Islamic society'[11] – and at the same time profoundly sceptical about Suharto's intentions; 'for Soeharto, ICMI is a short-term marriage of convenience. He thinks he can control [ICMI modernists] if they go too far. I'm afraid the strategy will backfire'.[12] As well, the highly respected Muslim modernist intellectual, Deliar Noer, refused to have any truck with the organisation, a combination of his scorn for Habibie's Islamic credentials and his distrust of Suharto's motives.

These ploys had something in common and marked a further development in Suharto's political strategy. In both cases, ethnic and cultural divisions which had earlier been closed over were revealed and prodded in a painful way, so that he could be seen to be reaching out to new constituencies. In the case of the Tapos meeting, 'in one fell swoop, Soeharto had undone a great deal of New Order effort to sweep ethnic divisions under the carpet',[13] and, indeed, had strengthened the general perception that the activities of Sino-Indonesian businesspeople were somehow inimical to broad national prosperity. The ICMI move had a more mainstream character about it, especially given the fact that submission to the *azas tunggal* (sole foundation) regulation of the 1980s had – ironically, in view of the furore it caused at the time – served to assist Muslims to assume a respectability that had previously been denied Islam under the New Order. The origins of Suharto's move to constitute an Islamic identity were to be found in the late 1980s; they involved such measures as a greater empowerment of Islamic courts, the removal of petty school restrictions on the wearing of the Islamic head covering, the *jilbab*, an enhanced focus on Islam in school education, and the severity of the state's reaction to the publication by a magazine, *Monitor*, of a popularity poll in which the Prophet Mohammed was ranked only eleventh (Suharto came first). They climaxed in June 1991 when Suharto and his family, together with a large accompanying party, made a heavily publicised pilgrimage to perform the *hajj* in Mecca.[14]

The pressures moving Suharto in these new directions were becoming increasingly complex. It would have been natural for him, with a lifelong predisposition towards spirituality and in the last phases of a long and crowded life, to gravitate towards a more formal personal affiliation with Islam. It is likely, too, that he was deeply influenced by the recent experience of the Soviet Union, which he had visited in 1989, and from which he drew lessons about the extraordinary difficulties of keeping imperiums intact in an era of growing neo-nationalism and waves of democratisation. Perhaps the most important emerging influence, however, was the ending of the Cold War, which meant that he could no longer depend upon the support of the West and no longer be shielded from the attacks of human rights activists and, more broadly, the criticisms of the international community, in the name of the fight against communism. These insights were added to his prevailing perception of the necessity, as his nation's gathering prosperity created a more subtle and sophisticated society, to lead and manage social change with political acuity rather than relying on outmoded forms of trenchant authoritarianism.

For all these reasons, there was for a brief time, from about 1989 until at least the end of 1991, an extraordinary period of political openness, during which wide-ranging debate was allowed to proceed virtually unhindered and a new sense of the importance of human rights appeared to emerge (Indonesia was admitted as a member of the UN Human Rights Commission early in 1991). Suharto himself spoke of Pancasila as an 'open ideology' and appeared to praise the increasing diversity of Indonesian intellectual life. (By contrast, noted poet and editor Gunawan Mohamad thought that 'universities are dead, ideas are dead. The government's obsession with security is like a black hole swallowing all independent thought'.)[15] In the wake of the 1991 Santa Cruz massacre, Suharto expressed his regret, his sorrow at the loss suffered by the families of those killed, and came close to apologising for the incident. He took the unusual steps of establishing an interim investigation under Jaelani to establish what exactly had taken place, dismissed commanders, and ordered a military tribunal to investigate whether charges should be laid. Privately he took out his rage on the defence and foreign affairs departments, as well as the military and civil administration officials, reportedly demanding of subordinates to 'make sure what happened in Dili doesn't happen again'.[16]

Within society in general, there appeared to be a strongly developing sense that the deregulation of the economy had to be accompanied both by the systematic construction of more predictable and transparent channels of economic policy and by a similar deregulation and decentering of political thinking and modes of political expression, a stark contrast to the avalanche of integralist propaganda that dominated the first half of the 1980s. One way in which that mood was expressed was through a growing tendency for political outsiders – peasants and workers in particular, but also urban-based environmental and human rights activists as well – to protest against their failure to receive a hearing within the New Order's corporatist framework. The demonstrations against the land evictions consequent upon the construction of the Kedung Ombo dam were perhaps the most notable expression of this swelling tide. But there were other manifestations as well, including a tendency for non-corporatist bodies, such as Muchtar Pakpahan's SBSI (Indonesian Prosperous Workers' Union) (May 1992) and, later, the Alliance of Independent Journalists (AJI), to emerge in an effort to secure some representation. One close participant in political life was even moved to the view that 'a consistent but extremely graduated process of democratization is under way'.[17]

Wahid's opposition to ICMI and what he alleged it stood for crystallised in the formation in April 1991 of Forum Demokrasi (Democracy Forum), a vaguely organised association of forty-odd Indonesian intellectuals, clearly established in response to ICMI and designed to provide some intellectual leadership and ballast (but not of itself activism) in the struggle for a more open, tolerant and inclusive society. Wahid's agenda found further expression in a massive NU rally he organised in Jakarta in March 1992 (despite efforts by security forces to diminish the attendance), meant both to boost his own credentials as NU leader and to profile his understanding, appropriately expressed in the vocabulary of New Order Pancasila-ism, of the secular tolerance of Islam. Wahid himself was unwilling to add his endorsement to the candidacy of Suharto for a sixth term in 1993. That, of course, made no difference to Suharto, whose annoyance with Wahid was manifest in efforts to oppose the forum's public activities and Wahid's plans for the provision of rural banking services in association with Bank Summa, and in his omission of Wahid from 1993–98 MPR membership. Suharto proceeded serenely, and in the fashion of one long accustomed to the deference which comes with unalloyed success, to election in 1993 for a sixth term as president.[18]

In retrospect, however, Suharto's choice for yet another term was a crucial step in his undoing. Notwithstanding views to the contrary – Wahid, for example, had earlier expressed the belief that 'the presidential succession will take place in maybe 1995, but if not in 1995 then in 1998'[19] – his decision signalled to all that, his health to one side, he would never willingly stand down, that he had come finally to a perfect identification of his own political paramountcy with the health and salvation of the Indonesian nation. That decision, or more correctly the new political paths he had trodden to achieve it, opened the first cracks in the edifice of unanimity he had so painstakingly constructed about him, and gave some small opponents the courage to stamp their opposition to his eternal rule. His task, having abandoned the strategy of army-sponsored integralist repression to sustain himself, was to forge a new consensus. His downfall resulted from his failure to pursue that path with conviction, because he himself might not necessarily have the dominant role in it. Equally, he shied back from the precipice of market-driven economic deregulation, which would have denied him the means of sustaining and expanding his characteristic role as dispenser of patronage.

PLUNGING

The first deeply serious signs of terminal decay in Suharto's regime probably became evident with his re-election – accompanied, significantly, by a set of MPR state policy guidelines which reinforced integralist thinking – and the formation of his 1993 cabinet, following the disappointing electoral success of Golkar the previous year, when Suryadi's PDI had campaigned robustly on a platform of political reform. It was a cabinet that, despite the retention in technocrat hands of the key jobs of finance minister and Bank Indonesia governor, turned its back firmly on the technocrats who had saved Suharto's political life in the mid- and late 1980s and presented the rewards of office to economic nationalists, of whom the most senior and influential was Habibie.[20] Ginanjar was appointed as the new head of Bappenas. No ICMI activists – those with an overtly Muslim political program – were included, a demonstration of Suharto's enduring suspicion of Islam's political potency.

The most striking event at this time, however, was the manner in which the Armed Forces outmanoeuvred Suharto over the choice of his vice-president. It seems likely that he wanted Habibie to take that post. ABRI, however, sought successfully to limit his freedom of choice by backing the candidacy of ABRI commander Try Sutrisno in February 1993, before Suharto had declared his own intentions, and Suharto found himself angrily unable to oppose the move. Try, under the tutelage of Murdani (himself of the view that Suharto should properly stand aside), had become increasingly disenchanted with Suharto's treatment of the military. According to Murdani, 'We took the decision five years ago. We decided after Sudharmono was elected vice president in 1988 that ABRI must decide the next vice president. So we decided on Try'.[21] At the subsequent MPR session to elect the president and vice-president, an outwardly smooth process saw Try accede to the vice-presidency, with the only sign of unrest an effort by the PDI, reined in by MPR Chair Wahono, to seek reforms of the electoral process. ABRI's reward was a significant erosion in its cabinet influence; Try was to endure five idle years of being ignored by Suharto.

Both in his cabinet appointments and at the later Habibie-managed Golkar congress in October 1993, Suharto turned firmly away from ABRI, much to the chagrin, even anger, of the generals. He embraced not just civilians but civilians close to him, such as Habibie and the new Golkar chair, Harmoko – the first civilian to hold this position, his success due to Suharto's personal bidding in the face of army branch control and angry army opposition – as well as encouraging the budding political ambitions of his children (Bambang acceded to the post of Golkar treasurer, while Tutut claimed one of eight vice-chair positions; both already held appointed seats in the MPR).[22] These moves, and the obstinacy they represented, seemed to signal a certain freezing in Suharto's legendary political adaptability. At the Golkar congress, notwithstanding the strong ABRI influence amongst delegates, Golkar head Wahono, old colleague of Suharto, was passed over for a new term, apparently in retribution for Golkar's disappointing electoral performance for which Suharto held him personally responsible. According to one report, Suharto was critical of Wahono's performance because 'Golkar failed to meet public demands for greater democracy, better respect for human rights, social justice and protection of the environment … [It] lacks the initiative to disseminate the government's programmes in the areas of administrative reform and the improvement of public services'.[23] Wahono was amongst the last of the Suharto clique to lose the favour of his master.

Suharto had determined that Indonesia's political future was a function not of ABRI support – he was by now dismissive of ABRI's political substance and its contribution to his power and, in addition, suspicious of its real loyalties – but, rather, through the political vehicle of Golkar, not a reformed and open Golkar but a Golkar controlled by those close to him and who offered him unquestioning loyalty. Suharto had thus cut the opportunity which he had seemed to be striving for in the late 1980s to build a new and more populist vehicle for his political aspirations. Thereafter, any vague sense of social inclusiveness was gone, along with any faint hopes that had existed for an attenuation of the focus on presidential power in favour of a more pluralistic system.

Suharto's efforts to maintain control of ABRI now took the form of an increasingly scrupulous personal interest in the minutiae of promotions and placements, of whittling back further the *karyawan* placements of officers in governorships and ambassadorships,[24] and especially of appointing those who had been close to him to accelerated promotion and high position. Chief amongst the winners in this process was his son-in law, the highly ambitious Prabowo Subianto, who rose from an East Timor Kostrad battalion command in the late 1980s to a strategically important position in Kopassus and the rank of full colonel by 1992, which he used, amongst other things, to press for a hard-line military approach to the East Timorese independence movement.

In response to these developments, in a brief and temporary re-emergence of the openness policy in the last half of 1993, signs of civil rebelliousness, of a kind not seen for over a decade, began to appear. A wave of protests by students and Muslim groups towards the end of 1993 had the result of forcing the government to abandon its support for a state-run lottery. Their success raised the limits of the possible, and there were even voices calling for a special session of the MPR to demand an account of Suharto's stewardship – an unlikely prospect, given that the MPR had unanimously elected him in March. Around the same time, efforts to seat a new, tame leader for the PDI – Suryadi had seemingly overstepped the mark and incurred Suharto's ire by criticising the government's performance and calling for limitations on presidential terms in the run-up to the 1992 parliamentary elections – ran into difficulties at the Surabaya PDI congress in late 1993, a function of military support for Megawati, allegedly by Murdani's affiliates miffed at Harmoko's election as Golkar chair (notably Jakarta commander and former intelligence operative Hendropriyono), which allowed Megawati to gain the chair. Voters in Central Kalimantan refused to accept the new governor foisted on them from on high, and the Indonesian Chamber of Commerce failed to choose Suharto's favoured candidate as its new chair. Early in 1994, *Primadosa*, an irreverent book highly critical of what it called the 'Suharto empire', appeared and, after drawing criticism from Suharto himself, was almost immediately banned by Attorney-General Singgih because of its potential to 'disconcert the people'.[25] And ABRI members of the DPR, notably Maj.-Gen. Sembiring, who dared to show their displeasure at Suharto's apparent indifference to ABRI's importance, found themselves removed from their parliamentary seats early in 1994.

These signs were embarrassing manifestations of a still-inchoate sense that the country was in need of a fundamental change of direction to accommodate the social imperatives of a new society, and that Suharto's leadership could not be expected to provide a realistic platform for change. According to one commentator, 'the upper reaches of Indonesian society are growing weary of the state's paternalistic manner', and again, 'after reaching a certain level of development and social stability, many Indonesians thirsted for political stimulation'.[26] There was, however, no sense that Suharto should be hurried from the scene – that was, in any case, practically impossible, and likely to unleash all kinds of unforeseen instabilities – but it did mean that the timing of the succession, and the identity of the person who might succeed, were becoming matters of ever more urgent debate, and even that a more delegated exercise of his authority might be expected. Early in 1994, Suharto himself made a rare positive comment to a visiting American university president, Donald W. Wilson: 'People say that I don't like talking about the issue of succession. That's not true. I am not president for life. The people have chosen me, and it is they who must decide how long I must stay in this job'.[27] This statement seemed to clarify that Suharto had no intention of standing down before the expiration of his five-year term in 1998.

The increasing nervousness of the government towards the vaguely emerging opposition focused on efforts in 1994 to prevent Wahid securing another term of his influential leadership position in Nahdlatul Ulama, and the more vital efforts to cripple the growing capacity of Megawati Sukarnoputri – increasingly viewed by Suharto as constituting a real political threat to a tired Golkar – to attract votes from the more youthful reaches of the constituency.

LOSING HIS TOUCH

Suharto was struggling to come to terms with these new forces. One attempt to do so was his decision in 1993 to establish a National Human Rights Commission.

It was, however, a defensive decision, guided not by any sense on his part that the protection of human rights was an important priority of the government, but purely, acceding to pressure from his foreign affairs ministry, to use the institution of the new body to deflect growing international criticism of Indonesia's human rights record, especially in the wake of the massacre at Santa Cruz cemetery in Dili.

The period of so-called 'openness' – already under threat in late 1993 by Suharto's comparison of the tactics of pro-democracy reformers with those of the long-banned PKI and by a wave of arrests of students and Muslim activists (some of them charged with the crime of insulting the person of the President) – formally ended in mid-1994 with the banning of three magazines, the most notable being the highly regarded *Tempo*, over their reporting of Habibie's purchase, albeit with the backing of Suharto and the opposition of the military, of thirty-nine old frigates from the now-defunct East German navy (plus huge associated costs for refurbishing and shipyard development). What angered the President was the liberal manner in which the press commented upon (and allegedly incited, according to him)[28] elite disagreements over the ships' purchase, notably between Habibie and the candidly righteous Finance Minister Mar'ie Muhammad, who was unwilling to approve the required funds. This was a public laundering of dirty linen which Suharto could not abide.

Habibie's power was now solidly entrenched, much to the hostility of the military who saw not just their territory under encroachment but also their access to lucrative defence-related income streams under serious threat from his escalating efforts to create business for the raft of 'strategic industries' entrusted to him by Suharto. His growing political influence was further evidenced by such incidents as Suharto's intervention to protect PT PAL, Habibie's state-owned shipbuilding enterprise, from paying due tax in 1991, and Suharto's decision to rebuff Mar'ie Muhammad's efforts to limit the finance made available to Habibie late in 1994 by shifting US$185 million in state funds, set aside for reforestation, into Habibie's aircraft projects.[29]

The end of 'openness' was a key turning-point in the history of the late New Order. It was not, as has been claimed, proof that 'Soeharto's earlier promises of a freer public discourse were merely empty rhetoric'.[30] Rather, it signalled that Suharto, notwithstanding his prescience in appreciating how his Indonesia had changed and grown and attempting to accommodate himself to the new realities, no longer had the patience and vision, nor, indeed, the unalloyed political supremacy, to manage the forces of change without letting them overwhelm him. Thereafter, containment and angry repression became ever more the watchwords of his regime's decaying days.

Suharto now ruled alone. The colleagues who had joined him on the journey to power more than three decades earlier – and whose powerful personalities had been allowed significant expression – had all passed from the scene, their like (and independent influence) not to be seen again. Those now close to him enjoyed their position because they could be trusted not to object to – nor even debate with any seriousness – contentious new policies and approaches. He was, perhaps as never before, the centre of decision-making; he made all the important ones, and nothing significant moved without his knowledge and permission. He was held in extraordinary reverence and awe, and fear, even by those who worked closely with him. Few dared report to him criticisms or news that might provoke the flashes of impatience and anger to which he was becoming increasingly prone. Those close to him, equally, were probably enthusiastic in suggesting to him his continuing indispensability to the safety, security, development and reputation of his country. Such a situation was virtually guaranteed to fill him with an overweening confidence that he, and he alone, had the answers to Indonesia's problems, and that any opposition to his wishes was, by definition, against the interests of the Indonesian state and nation. The institutional narrowing of his regime resulting from his distancing of ABRI from the portals of power had not been compensated for by a proportionate empowerment of civilian political institutions. Suharto's rule was now resting on tenuous foundations, buttressed only by his personal authority. He knew what he was doing; he was aware, as Schwarz noted with great prescience in 1994, 'that once loyalty to him begins to slip, it could evaporate quickly'.[31]

But Suharto's acuity in managing and balancing the swirl of competitive politics was growing less sure. Whereas in the past he had succeeded in bringing out the best in his subordinates by placing them in active competition one with another, his tendency now was to demand unquestioning loyalty from underlings whose prominence was a function of his own choice and making. Feisal Tanjung, long close to Habibie and installed as commander of the Armed Forces in May 1993, was an example of a Suharto creation who sought to please his leader – and advance and prolong his career – rather than promote the interests of the institution which he led, which was increasingly impoverished by failing access to off-budget funding and minimal government contributions. More and more, the Army became factionalised between an older nationalist group, gathered loosely about Murdani (now ensconced in the vast office at CSIS formerly occupied by Ali Murtopo, and enjoying close relations with Wahid), and a new 'green' faction, loosely under Prabowo's influence and brought to power by Suharto, so named because of its close affiliation with modernist Islam. With a rapid officer rotation through regional and central commands, ABRI lost further ground politically.

Many of those in Suharto's inner circle – men like Suyono, Wiranto and Subagyo Hadi Siswoyo – had learned their place and proven their loyalty from earlier stints as presidential adjutant or bodyguard. The professional trust he had previously bestowed on, and the responsibilities he had previously invested in, those close to him like Murtopo and Murdani were also rapidly ebbing; he required, for example, that even quite junior Armed Forces promotions and appointments be subject to his personal approval. Those who failed to read the signs of the times, like Ridwan Fataruddin, head of the domestic airline company Merpati (who failed to respond to the suggestion that he lease sixteen IPTN-produced aircraft from a leasing firm owned by Tommy), lost their positions. The remnants of Murdani's power, notably the once-powerful intelligence body Bais, which had sniped at Suharto by manipulating information and had sought to damage Sudharmono by enlivening anti-PKI sensitivities, was downgraded to the humdrum BIA (Armed Forces Intelligence Body). More and more, the political capacities of the Armed Forces were eroded.

Suharto's daughter Tutut boosted the thinning membership of the inner circle, becoming something of a protector and mouthpiece. His growing irascibility and impatience and the ebbing of his gifted capacity as a listener, as well as an imperious style, was not calculated, as his famous smile had been, to subdue by personal charm; former environment minister Sarwono Kusumaatmaja complained that 'you can't even hold a conversation with Soeharto anymore. He just gives lectures on everything under the sun. He knows everything'.[32] His sensitivity to personal criticism had also reached new heights. Facing a demonstration in Dresden (whose numbers included parliamentary critic Sri Bintang Pamungkas), he labelled the participants as 'insane and no longer rational'.[33]

The atrophying political calculus in the centre can have done nothing to dissuade the Armed Forces from continuing and even embellishing their 'security' approach to problems of internal dissent. Thus it was that festering problems in East Timor, in Irian Jaya, a rich province with impoverished inhabitants, and in Aceh – notwithstanding emerging reports of large-scale, systematic army violations, including mass executions – were all met with an intensification of the same obdurate physical response. The problems in East Timor were made all the worse, in Suharto's eyes, by the award of the Nobel Peace Prize in 1996 to Bishop Carlos Filipe Ximenes Belo, head of East Timor's Catholic Church, and Jose Ramos Horta, fluent, engaging and an untiring opponent of Indonesian occupation, and later by the efforts of Nelson Mandela to secure the release of Xanana Gusmao.

The response to political exception-taking closer to home bore a similar stamp. Journalists were jailed (under the 'sowing hatred' regulations introduced by the Dutch to contain the early nationalist movement) in response to their efforts to consolidate an independent professional association. Union organiser Muchtar Pakpahan, head of the extra-legal SBSI, received a three-year prison term on charges of inciting worker riots in Medan in 1994; the previous year in Sidoarjo, East Java, a young female labour activist named Marsinah had been murdered in circumstances that strongly suggested the involvement of security forces. The nervousness and uncertainty thus displayed saw the first inklings around 1995 of the movement of Sino-Indonesian capital out of the country to the more secure environment of Singapore.

50 YEARS OF INDONESIAN INDEPENDENCE

The frozen state of Indonesian politics was exemplified by Suharto's address in 1995 on the occasion of the fiftieth anniversary of Indonesia's independence. Notwithstanding his country's extraordinary economic progress, to which he referred at great length, his speech still reeked of struggles ahead:

> Let us strengthen everything that is good, let us improve what is not good, let us correct what is in error … whether we wish it or not, whether we like it or not,

> whether we are ready or not, we will be part of the new era of humankind. We have no choice, we must prepare ourselves as well as we can from now on. If we are not ready we will be left further and further behind by the progress of this era.

As far as political stimulus was concerned, he could find only the firm corporatism he had established in the 1980s. 'Finally', he noted, 'we have agreed that Pancasila is the one and only foundation for the life of society, the nation and the state'. Retracing familiar criticisms of the pre-1966 order, he found that the parliamentary period was inherently unstable and 'did not support a climate of development for the progress of the nation and the prosperity of the people', while 'the era of "revolutionary competition" which was indeed pushed by the PKI clearly brought an atmosphere of mutual suspicion and dissension, tension and lack of stability, a declining economy and distanced the people from prosperity'.[34]

This recycling of stale ideas and claims offered Indonesians no new vision and no solace. Perhaps as a sop to public opinion and to his opponents, Suharto in 1995 gave the government-funded Indonesian Institute of Sciences (LIPI) the task of investigating alternative systems of holding general elections and also of researching the socio-political role of ABRI. He ignored the completed reports.

FAMILY INTERESTS

The narrowing of the base of the regime coincided with the thickening of family favouritism and cronyism. The proliferation of rent-seeking on a massive scale which characterised the last decade or so of the New Order was a function of the same kind of thinking that had allowed Suharto to dismiss the criticism of men like Suryo in the early 1970s. According to one reporter, 'Suharto genuinely seems to see his children as opportune instruments of his development policy'.[35] This for him was not corruption but, in the literal sense, the business of development. 'There is no problem', he remarked early in 1998, 'if the enterprises [of his children] are useful to the Indonesian people'.[36] There was also a personal element involved. Suharto wanted to ensure, in the event of his sudden passing from the scene, that his children would be so well provisioned that they could not be disentangled from their role at the heights of Indonesia's economy. A commentator suggested that one particularly spectacular exercise in rent-seeking was 'intended as little more than a lucrative superannuation scheme for Tommy'.[37]

Amongst the more notorious of the schemes hatched by his children and endorsed by their father was Tommy's clove business. Put in its simplest terms, Tommy – who bore a striking resemblance to his father at the same age – was permitted, with the help of a hefty injection of state funds, to insert himself as the monopoly middleman between clove producers and cigarette manufacturers in Indonesia's lucrative clove production business, the key element in the kretek cigarette industry. Tommy promised to deliver higher prices to clove producers, but his intervention brought only chaos to the industry. These activities were but a part of his larger Humpuss empire, involved in sea and air transport, petrochemicals, oil, toll-roads, banking, property, communications, and luxury car production – Tommy purchased the Italian Lamborghini car firm in November 1993 – all of it lubricated by special deals, often in partnership with Suharto cronies like 'Bob' Hasan, which provided him with unearned monopoly rights to resources and services.

In 1994, Bambang's Bimantara received, without payment of any kind, a licence to share the provision of international telephone calls with the state provider, PT Indosat. He then invited bids for a stake in Bimantara's telcom arm, Satelindo, for a quarter-share of which the German company Deutsche Telekom reputedly paid more than half a billion dollars. At Suharto's behest, the government also provided privileged tariff treatment for the troubled petrochemical project, Chandra Asri, in which Bambang was involved with logging concessionaire Prayogo Pangestu and Henry Pribadi (Lin Yunhao) (related to Liem Siu Liong's long-time business partner, Juhar Sutanto/Liem Un Kian); the project also enjoyed easy access to huge loans. Suharto's grandson, Ari Sigit, managed to leverage for himself a deal in which he was farmed out the monopoly right to collect a local tax, to which he added his own generous levy, on beer sold in Bali (Suharto later dropped the monopoly after a clamour of protest), as well as hatching a scheme to force schoolchildren to buy a certain (expensive) brand of shoe of which one of his companies was the sole supplier.[38]

Perhaps the most infamous example of the pervading rottenness was the saga – for that it was – of the Timor national car. Suharto's desire for a national car industry was all of a piece with his abiding preference for state-sponsored development; Indonesia would demonstrate its social and industrial maturity by developing its own car. One key problem, however, was the identity of the company which would pursue the project. A bitter battle ensued between prospective business partnerships led, respectively, by Tommy and Bambang; eventually Suharto decided, early in 1996, that the Timor car contract would go to Tommy, his last and favourite son. (There were rumours that Ibu Tien had supported this decision, and even that the family furore over the contract had caused such stress as to result in her fatal heart attack.) It was, in the largest sense, a licence to make money. In mid-year, Suharto decreed that, under the terms of an agreement with Korea's Kia Car Co., the Timor cars would be assembled in Korea and imported without payment of duties or luxury tax, enabling the national car to undercut competitors' prices. Tommy was permitted to delay his promised completion of assembly facilities in Indonesia. Suharto seemed unmoved by the furore created by his decision, although his battle to secure much state financing for the project reportedly drew the ire of Mar'ie Muhammad and resulted in an angry cabinet exchange in which Suharto, thumping the table, ordered Mar'ie to find the necessary funding. The objections raised by Minister for Trade S. B. Yudono, that the arrangements were in breach of Indonesia's World Trade Organisation (WTO) obligations, resulted only in his sacking – the first example of a mid-term ministerial ejection in the history of the New Order.

Such schemes were part of the general picture of the children's extraordinary economic advance through the 1990s. Almost never risking their own venture capital – state banks could be relied upon to provide cheap or free loans to those in political favour – and exploiting unmercifully and unrelentingly their unsurpassed proximity to the centre of power, the children carried rent-seeking behaviour to new heights, taking especial advantage of Indonesia's trend towards 'privatisation' of state companies, through which undreamt-of riches came their way. Suharto remained outwardly unperturbed by these developments, and characteristically hostile at attacks and grumblings, both within civilian circles and the Armed Forces, on his favouritism. That the children's business success depended squarely on their father was clearly manifested in mid-1996 when clumsily managed news emerged that Suharto was travelling to Germany for a series of medical tests at a clinic near Hanover (which revealed kidney stones, but generally indicated a man in good health for his age); the share price of Bambang's now-listed Bimantara sagged nearly 9 per cent within the space of two days, while Tutut's toll-road company, CMNP, fell 3.5 per cent.

Suharto's close business mates also enjoyed the largesse of his patrimonialism, much to the chagrin of pribumi businessmen (including his half-brother, Probosutejo) who populated Kadin, the Chamber of Commerce and Industry, and who sought to rein in the rapid growth of huge Sino-Indonesian conglomerates and the technocrat influence which they thought promoted it. In 1991, for example, the collapse and liquidation of Astra's Bank Summa, under the hand of William Suryajaya's son, Edward, saw the Astra group – long regarded as amongst the best-run businesses in the country, and not especially close to the palace – restructured and large portions falling into the hands of Prayogo Pangestu, Liem Siu Liong and Eka Cipta Wijaya (Ui Ek Chong). Liem's Bogasari now completely dominated the domestic flour industry; 'Bob' Hasan and Prayogo Pangestu became timber kings, paying minimal rent for their control over national forest resources. There was, of course, a price to be paid. The problems of Bank Duta, three-quarters owned by Suharto-chaired foundations and found to be suffering losses from imprudent foreign currency trading of US$420 million late in 1990, were solved by cash injections of US$200 million each from Prayogo Pangestu and Liem Siu Liong. Their reward was a share each in a number of large projects originally conceived by Ginanjar to assist pribumi business, as well as other forms of business assistance.[39]

The heights of ludicrousness were still to be scaled. In 1996, news emerged of a monumental gold discovery at Busang in Kalimantan. The succeeding months saw an unseemly scramble for a share of the gold rush by Suharto's family, foundations and cronies, notably 'Bob' Hasan, until the 'find' was finally revealed in 1997 as a gigantic scam. Efforts by economic advisers and officials to promote deregulatory policies increasingly fell on Suharto's deliberately deaf ears.

Notwithstanding the accelerating rent-seeking by family and cronies, particularly after 1993 when the technocrats were in retreat before the advance of the 'technologists', the economy seemed to be powering on through the mid-1990s. By 1993, clothing and textile exports were more than forty times the 1980 figure. Demand for electricity to power the production of non-oil exports grew by 17 per cent a year. A radical deregulation package, highly favourable for foreign investment, was introduced in mid-1994 and was responsible for a flood of new overseas investment, with the total approved in the period mid-June to the end of July greater than the total for the whole of 1993. An upward shift in oil prices and a strong flow of domestic investment added to the picture, clouded only by the increasingly worrisome (to the technocrats, anyway) banking regulation and external debt problems, a banking industry, both state and private, beginning to sag under a proliferation of bad, sometimes crony-linked, loans and, of course, ever more rampant cronyism, subject to control only when its perpetrators – such as Eddy Tansil (Tan Cu Fuan), jailed in 1994 for twenty years after siphoning for his private benefit a US$420 million loan meant for a petrochemical plant – went beyond the bounds of the politically permissible.

Any discussion of the corruption of Suharto's children and cronies would be incomplete without addressing the question of Suharto's own fortune. Some commentators made much of his alleged wealth: 'Suharto is not merely rich; he can claim to be among the world's super-rich'.[40] Whatever the truth of these assertions – and they generally overestimated the true value of the family fortune, much of which was based around politically organised rent-seeking – they often disregarded the fact that Suharto was not personally a greedy man, and to paint him in these terms was to miss the key point of his undoubted massive corruption.[41] He was not interested in money for its own sake, nor for what it might bring him in a material sense. He lived a comfortable life, but not an especially ostentatious one; indeed, the houses he had gradually accumulated on Jalan Cendana were somewhat dowdy and dated in their appointments. He was interested in money because it was central to his capacity to maintain power and to move Indonesia in the directions he desired.

The key to Suharto's fund-raising strategies was the time-honoured tool of the foundation, which, despite occasional efforts to subject it to greater scrutiny, continued to expand.[42] In 1996, he revealed yet another foundation-based scheme, in which wealthier taxpayers were 'encouraged' to donate 2 per cent of their after-tax income to the new Prosperous Self-Reliant Fund, designed to promote entrepreneurial activity amongst poor people.[43] The foundation, chaired by Suharto himself, had Liem Siu Liong and Sudwikatmono (often thought to be a proxy for Suharto in such arrangements) as deputy chairs, and Bambang as treasurer, and soon managed to win a promise from the finance minister that state-owned companies would provide 2 per cent of profits for the foundation's use. Suharto claimed in his autobiography that he 'never touched' the vast sums he controlled through his foundations, not even by way of an honorarium.[44]

THE DEATH OF IBU TIEN

The unravelling of Suharto's hitherto unbreakable political fibre was accelerated by the unexpected death of Ibu Tien on 28 April 1996. While she had played an active, enthusiastic and energetic role in business, in charity work, in social life and as the indefatigable companion of the President on scores of tours and trips, Ibu Tien had more recently slipped somewhat into the background, as had the reputation she had earlier earned as a vigorous collector of commissions on state-sponsored projects. She had had, it seems, a strong preference that her husband stand down from office in the late 1980s and was thought to have been unhappy in the extreme that he chose re-nomination again in 1992, a view not widely held amongst the couple's children. She had sought, more than anything, a peaceful, family-centred retirement.

While Ibu Tien had been troubled in recent times by diabetes and sundry ailments, her fatal heart attack – she died only an hour or so after being admitted to hospital – left Suharto shocked and shattered. She had been for him a dream partner and deep friend, intensely loyal, intelligent, patient, resourceful, unendingly cooperative in acceding to his military and political ambitions, and a reliable source of commonsense and somewhat prudish advice, on people rather than policy. Ibu Tien fitted perfectly (and probably profoundly shaped) Suharto's notion of the ideal woman: one who 'must realise that she is both a housewife and someone who wants to progress. She may take up a career, but she should not sacrifice her duty as a housewife ... A woman who can truly function in both these spheres is the ideal woman'.[45] Now, suddenly, his pillar was gone.

Tien's death meant that any effective control on Suharto's abiding predisposition to champion his children's business interests was lost. Thereafter, family corruption thickened, so that in 1997 Indonesia achieved the title of being the most corrupt country in Asia. Her death also allowed Tutut, already a vice-chair of Golkar, to emerge more clearly both as Suharto's manager and as a political actor in her own right, which in turn saw the promotion of the political interests of the rising Madurese army officer, Raden Hartono, with whom Tutut was very close. Hurrying home from Europe for the Solo funeral, Tutut took her place at her father's side and read a special message of farewell to her mother.

The death of his wife seems, if anything, to have hardened Suharto's political resolve. He now had little to strive for except to maintain his hold on power, which he ever more deeply believed was essential for his country's future. By mid-decade, his health was still good, despite his kidney stone episode in 1996. One journalist reported that, 'during a recent visit to Kazakhstan, the president ... startled even his aides by climbing on a stocky local horse and going for a quick canter'.[46] It had become clear that he had no intention of standing aside. He reportedly assured a visiting US scholar early in 1994 that 'I'll let you know at the earliest convenience when I'll step down. One thing is for sure – I will step down right on time. I'm Javanese and I'm sure you know what that means'.[47] Such displays of confident competence quickly led to an abatement of discussion about his immediate future, and talk then turned to his possible next-term vice-president. Sudomo, now chair of the Supreme Advisory Council, remarked in May 1995 that Suharto's preference was for a civilian, while Golkar's deputy chair, Ali Mursalam, suggested Tutut and Harmoko as possible nominees for the post.

INTERNATIONAL LEADER

Ironically, as Suharto's domestic problems thickened, his reputation as an international statesman enlarged dramatically as his conviction grew that Indonesia's

Suharto Golfing. (Tempo)

With conglomerate heads at Tapos, March 1990. (State Secretariat, Indonesia)

Making the hajj, June 1991. (State Secretariat, Indonesia)

With Habibie.
(State Secretariat, Indonesia)

Fishing with Prayogo Pangestu.
(State Secretariat, Indonesia)

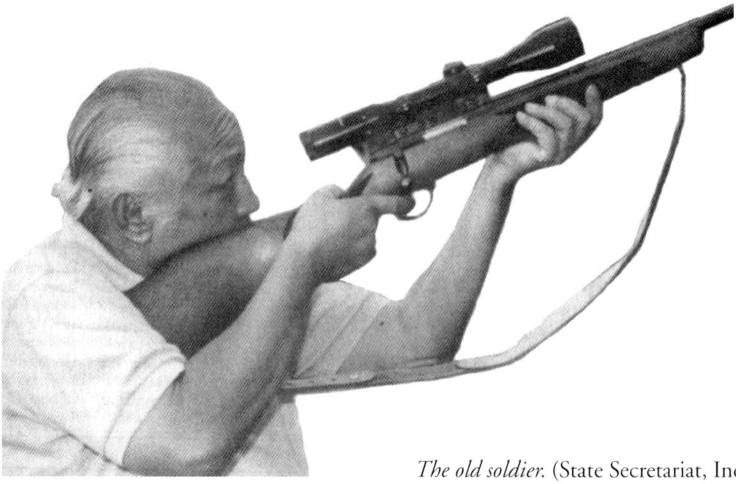

The old soldier. (State Secretariat, Indonesia)

Facing the future. (State Secretariat, Indonesia)

Ibnu Sutowo. (Kompas)

Probosutejo. (Kompas)

Wijoyo. (State Secretariat, Indonesia)

Sumitro Joyohadikusumo.
(State Secretariat, Indonesia)

Ali Murtopo. (Tempo)

Yoga Sugama. (Tempo)

Sudwikatmono. (Tempo)

Liem Siu Liong. (Tempo)

Tutut. (Tempo)

Bambang. (Tempo)

Tommy. (Tempo)

developmental success both allowed and entitled it to play a larger role in international affairs. His key achievement was winning the chair of the 108-nation Non-Aligned Movement in 1992, where he made a sound impression with his continuing push for greater recognition of the problems of the developing world and, in particular, his efforts to secure deeper and more useful South–South development collaboration. His long-term economist advisers, for example, were requested 'to explore ways of assisting African countries'.[48] Within ASEAN, Suharto cooperated with the development of the Regional Forum in 1993, which sought to develop multilateral discussions on security matters. Indonesia also played the key role in securing the 1993 agreement of Cambodia's deeply antagonistic factions to UN-sponsored and managed elections, in promoting a peaceful intermission (as it proved) to the Muslim rebellion in the southern Philippines, and in efforts to solve the enduringly contentious issue of the Spratly islands. Indonesia enjoyed a term of membership of the UN Security Council, sent peace-keeping troops to Bosnia – which Suharto visited in March 1995, offering Indonesian assistance in resolving the conflict – and Cambodia, and entered a security agreement with Australia in December 1995 aimed, Suharto reportedly noted, at ending Australian suspicion at the potential for Indonesian aggression.[49]

After some hesitation, Suharto also embraced the APEC (Asia Pacific Economic Cooperation) concept, and the meeting he hosted at Bogor in 1994 (the famous batik shirts donned by the assembled leaders were Ibu Tien's idea) was a key turning-point in the forum's road to vitality and relevance. According to Emil Salim, 'this was his own decision, and was based simply on commonsense',[50] in that Indonesia's strategic position, in a context of accelerating globalisation, required a positive adoption and management of the challenge of the open economy. Suharto's attendance at the Asia–Europe Meeting (ASEM) in Thailand in March 1996 tickled his sense of irony; half a century after decolonisation, Europe's leaders were now trooping to Bangkok to exchange ideas on an equal footing with their former colonial subjects.[51]

Suharto's international mission also included the defence of what he took to be slurs on his country. In March 1992, for example, he disbanded the Inter-Governmental Group on Indonesia because of his unhappiness about Dutch suspension of aid following the Dili massacre, thereby garnering significant popularity at home. Doubtless, too, he took great satisfaction in the fact that its successor body, the CGI (Consultative Group on Indonesia), subsequently increased its contributions, which seemed to belie the notion that it was serious about using aid as a campaigning weapon in the cause of improving human rights in Indonesia. At the 1994 APEC meeting, in the wake of an occupation of the US Embassy by East Timor protesters, he reportedly took pains to deflect President Clinton's suggestions for a special degree of autonomy for East Timor.[52] In 1997, Suharto cancelled a planned purchase of nine F-16 fighters from the United States as a result of Congressional criticism of Indonesia's human rights record. His intense irritation at Western criticisms of Indonesia was fuelled not only by his corporatist ideas but also by what he saw as the hypocrisy of the Western stance and the refusal of Western countries to take account of cultural difference and relative levels of economic development. Dutch criticism was a special thorn in the flesh when he remembered Dutch behaviour during Indonesia's colonial and revolutionary periods.[53]

DEVELOPING UNREST

Suharto's increasing contempt for any signs of opposition were most obviously manifest in his efforts to destroy the political aspirations of Megawati Sukarnoputri. The aristocratic Megawati, slightly gifted personally but the inheritor of the growing nostalgia for her father's personality, had enjoyed a modest career within the PDI until she was pitchforked, by popular election by its membership, into the leadership following the regime's success in removing Suryadi. The government, alarmed that so popular a figure and potential political nuisance as Megawati had fallen into the top job, refused to accede to her election, supported the continuation of an anti-Megawati PDI structure, and sponsored a rebel PDI congress (meeting in Medan in June 1996 and closed to Megawati and her followers) to unseat her – and replace her with Suryadi.

Megawati, stubborn and undeterred by such efforts to be rid of her, insisted on the reality of her leadership, symbolised by her holding the official PDI office on Jl. Diponegoro in central Jakarta. Late in July 1996, an attack on the office by hired thugs and troops disguised as civilians, weakly dressed up as an effort by the government-supported wing of the party to reclaim its rightful territory, left five people dead and over twenty others unaccounted for, the office in ruins, and Megawati's reputation enhanced. Her supporters' dismay at the government's action precipitated a round of looting and burning in the streets of Jakarta not witnessed since the Malari riots more than twenty years before and estimated by the city governor to have caused damage of Rp100 billion. The government, for its part, blamed the disarray on the incitement caused by an emerging illegal leftist group, the People's Democracy Party (PRD), led by the young activist Budiman Sujatmiko, and created the conditions, including a comparison of PRD's activities with the banned PKI, for a swoop on PRD activists. Suharto himself remarked that 'the riot was caused by a group of people who refused to abide by the constitution. We arrested the leaders and this problem is now ready to be resolved'.[54]

Evidence, however, rapidly accumulated about Suharto's own involvement in the mayhem. The most revealing aspect was that no one appeared to claim that he had given any kind of direct order; the security forces who planned the violence seem simply to have assumed that he would countenance such action, since the kind of opposition that Megawati threatened was so thoroughly incongruent with the society that he had erected.[55] Suharto's curiously warped understanding of the affair was expressed in his annual Independence Day speech:

> Forcing one's own desires or forcing change by means of violence, destruction and burning of buildings and public facilities is the action of anarchy; it is not democratic and it is not responsible. Any government bears the responsibility to protect society from anarchy, wherever it comes from and whatever it is based upon. That is why the security tools of the state acted strongly in overcoming the recent disturbance of

> 27 July in the capital. That disturbance was not closely connected with democracy. Those who incited and carried out the disturbance must bear responsibility for their actions before the law.[56]

He concluded by congratulating ABRI on its handling of the disturbance.

The enveloping political tension found other expression as well. Within the Armed Forces, Suyono found himself dismissed, apparently held responsible for the rioting consequent on the attack on PDI headquarters; just two years earlier, Agum Gumelar and Hendropriyono had suffered the ignominy of dismissal, apparently for being seen to be too friendly with Megawati and her PDI group. Those close to Suharto, notably Prabowo and Wiranto, found their rise accelerated. Prabowo was placed in command of Kopassus in December 1995, with a brief to expand its strength to 5,000 men, and promoted to major-general in August 1996, less than a year after earning his first star, while Wiranto was placed in charge of Kostrad, a position not without historical significance in dangerous times.

Within civilian politics, discontent began to take more obvious forms. Some small voices of criticism, perhaps encouraged by Speaker Wahono's occasional irritated failure to toe the Golkar line, began to be heard in the parliament, and ICMI notable and critical PPP parliamentarian Sri Bintang Pamungkas eventually found himself sentenced to almost three years jail for insulting the President during a lecture at a Berlin university in April 1995, and pushed out of the parliament and off ICMI's board. His subsequent pleas to boycott the 1997 parliamentary elections led to another trial for 'unconstitutional activities'.[57] His response to such treatment was the formation in May 1996 of a new party, PUDI (United Indonesian Democracy Party). Labour groups and non-government organisations (NGOs) became more adventuresome in their expressions of dissent. Amien Rais, American-educated university lecturer, intellectual, prominent ICMI member and, since 1995, leader of the modernist Muhammadiyah, was also proving irksome to Suharto by criticising development policy, particularly in relation to mining ventures, supporting the suggestion that presidents should serve no more than two terms, and denouncing family and crony corruption. Suharto saw to his expulsion from ICMI late in 1997.

More broadly, there were signs of serious social strain and impending breakdown, expressed particularly in ethnic tensions. In October 1996, a blasphemy trial in Situbondo led to the burning of more than twenty Christian churches. At the end of the year, rioters in Tasikmalaya torched another ten churches, as well as Chinese shops and houses, upon hearing that police had beaten up some Muslim teachers. In late 1996 and early 1997, large-scale ethnic unrest broke out in West Kalimantan, as indigenous Dayaks wreaked gruesome vengeance on Madurese settlers who had usurped their rights to land and employment, leaving perhaps a thousand dead. The smoke haze caused by numerous uncontrollable forest fires – many of them lit to assist tree and tree-crop plantations with their clearing – and which contributed to Indonesia's greatest air disaster near Medan in September 1997, added an eeriness and sense of menace to the scene.

Suharto remained unmoved, however, apparently unconscious of the serious fraying of the social consensus he had sought to build. The month after the July 1996 riots, he confirmed that there would be no fundamental changes to the shape of the New Order, but an intensification of the implementation of a Pancasila society. Any effort to deviate from this, he remarked, would simply encourage extremism as the champions of new social principles brought them to the fore; 'This will easily instigate the narrow fanaticism of a group, that may be manipulated by extreme groups within or outside the group concerned. Group fanaticism will not benefit anybody, in fact, it may become the seed of discord and unrest that is hard to contain'.[58]

The election campaign in 1997 – interrupted in late April for the celebration of Tommy Suharto's wedding at Taman Mini to a minor descendant of Solo's Mangkunegoro royal line – was conducted in a surreal atmosphere, made all the more so by rumours that Suharto would soon marry the younger sister of 'Bob' Hasan's wife. Perhaps to compensate for the political tension, Golkar supporters and fellow-travellers were exhorted to demonstrate their support for the New Order by literally painting their houses, fences and shops yellow, the colour of Golkar. In November 1996, the characteristically erratic Wahid had effectively abandoned his Forum Demokrasi and sought to re-mend his fences with Suharto, in the process labelling Tutut as a 'figure of the future'.[59] Suharto had smiled and accepted his hand, aware of his political dominance over the fickle Muslim leader.

With political opposition at a height unknown since the late 1970s, bans on campaign street processions, heavy injections of fear and foreboding, and extensive campaign violence, Golkar romped to its greatest-ever victory, claiming 74.3 per cent of the vote (and 322 DPR seats, of which four were allocated to Suharto's children) as against PPP's 22.6 per cent and the emasculated PDI (Megawati and her supporters were disbarred from campaigning and candidacy) with just over 3 per cent. The sense of unreality endured after the election; Harmoko, the victory's architect, was cut from his post as information minister and demoted to a meaningless state ministry, apparently because of his arrogance at the magnitude of his success. The military still enjoyed its privileged seats in the parliament, although that number had been cut from 100 to 75, seemingly in recognition of the declining role of the military in karyawan postings and, perhaps too, another signal by Suharto – who had obliquely suggested the change when addressing parliament in 1992 – of its marginalised political influence. A few weeks later, Suharto had his seventy-sixth birthday, an event 'almost not celebrated' because of his desire to avoid festivity for a period of a thousand days following the death of his wife.[60]

TOWARDS CRISIS

In his 1989 autobiography, Suharto had remarked that 'the values and élan of the struggle will remain important in the years of development which lie before our country, since the coming years will be full of trials and weighty challenges, especially because various developments in the world economy will not be favourable for our development'.[61] 1997 saw his prediction realised. Tremors and forebodings about the economic health of some of the 'miracle' economies of Asia, manifest in such incidents as the collapse of the Hanbo Iron and Steel Co. in South Korea in January 1997, began their swift realisation in July. Thailand, unable any longer to support the baht's exchange rate, floated the currency. It tumbled rapidly, followed by the currencies of its capitalist neighbours. Indonesia stood up reasonably well to the onslaught; in the views of many commentators, its economic fundamentals were sound and Suharto's capacity as an economic manager was not to be underestimated.

When Indonesia freed the rupiah to float in mid-August, its value fell but settled at just under Rp3,000 to the US dollar. Apparently satisfied at the situation (in his Independence Day speech on 16 August, he remarked that 'the fundamental condition of the Indonesian economy at this time is very stable'),[62] Suharto rejected efforts by his economic ministers to engage the crisis actively through a package of broad economic reform measures. He permitted some adjustments, notably a reining in of expensive public infrastructure projects, but still the rupiah fell. By early October Suharto, recently elevated to the status of Honorary Great General, a five-star rank, found himself – to the surprise of many – forced to call in the assistance of the IMF for what eventuated as a US$43 billion bailout facility. The initial IMF reforms, notably a clampdown on subsidies and the closure of sixteen private banks, did nothing to stem the problems. The failure to deal with the more extreme examples of cronyism, not to mention the fact that Bambang was easily able to reopen his Bank Andromeda (one of those closed) under another name, was symptomatic of the lack of seriousness with which Suharto and those aligned with him reacted to the crisis, and caused a further damaging loss of confidence.

In December, at the order of his doctors, Suharto took an unprecedented ten days rest following a gruelling overseas tour in the last half of November; rumours abounded that he was dead.[63] His cancelling on 12 December of a planned trip to Kuala Lumpur for an ASEAN informal summit meeting gave rise to rumours that he had had a stroke, setting in motion a new and more disastrous run on the currency. The predominant view, of course, was that Suharto was the key to finding the answer to Indonesia's financial problems and, as a result, news of his illness sent the rupiah tumbling close to Rp6,000 to the US dollar.[64]

Within weeks, however, the same Suharto who had been seen as the necessary condition to Indonesia's stabilisation was seen as the major obstacle to national salvation. Two key events secured this astounding turnaround. The first was his extraordinarily optimistic budget statement of 6 January 1998. So unrealistic was it that financial commentators for the first time realised with a compelling clarity how remote the President had become from political and economic realities. The rupiah dived to almost Rp10,000 to the US dollar, and middle-class shoppers invaded supermarkets and cleared the shelves of food items. The second was Suharto's clear indication from mid-January that he intended to secure the election of Habibie, whose curious and extravagant policies had been for so long the target of merciless criticism from orthodox economists, as his vice-president. By

22 January, the rupiah had plunged to the depths of almost 17,000 to the dollar; six months before, it had stood at around 2,400 to the dollar.

Unreality was the leitmotif of succeeding months. Successive efforts by the IMF to provide rescue packages, based on Indonesian undertakings to introduce a swag of economic and socio-political reforms, stalled on Suharto's incapacity to deliver what he had promised. Every effort to cut into the patterns of crony- and family-inspired special interests, such as Tommy's Timor car project, foundered. At the most famous of the series of IMF agreement signings, that on 15 January which cut the tax privileges on Tommy's car project and wound back many of Habibie's projects, IMF Managing Director Michel Camdessus stood towering above Suharto, arms folded in an unintended gesture of scornful superiority and dismissiveness, as the aged, portly ruler bent to sign the document, a move interpreted by many Indonesians who watched the theatre on television as a belittling, humiliating capitulation and a forced abnegation of the nation's proudly held sovereignty.[65]

It was rapidly becoming clear that Suharto was politically and personally unable to make the reforms being forced on him. He himself recognised the acute danger, and it was this that governed his behaviour. President Clinton sent former vice-president Walter Mondale to Jakarta in March to counsel Suharto on the need to adopt the bitter IMF medicine, with the softener that things would improve within six months. 'I don't have six months', Suharto is alleged to have replied; 'there will be a revolution'.[66] He had by now clearly lost any lingering faith in the capacity of his technocratic advisers to solve the country's economic problems. To the chagrin of his economic and finance ministers, pacing up and down outside meetings, Suharto insisted on negotiating reform packages on his own with IMF representatives; he was simply unable, it seems, to appreciate that the IMF was a qualitatively different and superior kind of creature to his domestic political opponents and would not roll over meekly under the force of his personality. He also turned to unorthodox measures, such as his brief flirtation with the currency board theories of the American economist Steve Hanke, flown in by the family to stabilise the currency.

As the crisis deepened and darkened, social breakdown appeared closer. Through the first months of 1998, in a number of towns, anti-Chinese rioting broke out, apparently arising out of deeply held suspicions that Chinese shop-owners and traders were manipulating the crisis to their benefit. Anti-Chinese feeling was manifest in elite circles as well, exemplified in the questioning – perhaps at Suharto's order – of Sofyan Wanandi (who had recently expressed the wish that Try Sutrisno should continue as vice-president) in relation to an alleged PRD bomb plot to disrupt the coming MPR session. A clutch of anti-Suharto activists disappeared in mysterious circumstances, apparently victims of Prabowo's special forces.

In January, Amien Rais had stated his willingness to become a candidate for the office of president and had unsuccessfully sought a form of political cooperation with Wahid and Megawati. His challenge had some significance, since it was the first sign that a senior political figure intended overtly to challenge Suharto, but it went no further than that. Suharto had asked Harmoko to investigate whether he still enjoyed popular support for another term as president; Harmoko, research not done, had dutifully reported back that indeed all the people were behind him. On 20 January, Suharto formally accepted Golkar's nomination for him to serve another term. On 10 March, therefore, notwithstanding his comment in 1996 that 'there is a need to prepare a new leader',[67] what observers early in the decade could not have imagined in fact took place: the thousand members of the MPR (which included four of his six children), surrounded by intense military security, acclaimed Suharto as president for his seventh five-year term. In accounting for his previous term, Suharto made little mention of the economic crisis, although, according to Tutut, his indispensability to the nation at this time of crisis had spurred him to accept despite his age and weariness. Moreover, he succeeded in drawing from the MPR a broad power to take action in an emergency. He made it clear that he would remain in office, God willing, for the entire five years.[68]

The cabinet announced by Suharto on 14 March – apparently Tutut was heavily involved in its architecture – served only to deepen the mood of unreality and to heighten incredulity. Amongst the tired band assembled, which included such loyal warriors as Ali Alatas, were two startling new faces. One of them was 'Bob' Hasan, the timber tycoon whose monopolies had been a prime target of the IMF, and who had been associated with Suharto in business ventures (the most recent substantial one involving the partnership of three large Suharto foundations with Hasan's PT Nusantara Ampera Bakti (Nusamba)) going back more than forty years. His naming to the Trade portfolio was a deliberate response to IMF criticism and policy. The other was Tutut herself, parading as minister for social welfare. The other matter of significance was that Wiranto, recently appointed ABRI commander and identified with the red-and-white faction of the Army, was named minister of defence, balancing off the recent appointment of Prabowo as Kostrad commander and that of his 'green' associate Subagyo Hadi Siswoyo as army commander. Suharto was not about to commit his future solely to his erratic son-in-law.

The cabinet captured, as nothing else might have done, the mixture of tired, faded hopes and arrogant cronyism which had beset Suharto's regime in the final years. In one sense, the cabinet was a rejection of all the IMF wanted. Such an interpretation, however, might grant Suharto more perceptiveness than he in fact enjoyed at that time. It was more, perhaps, a desperate attempt by Suharto, now close to panic at his inability to influence the larger forces circling him, which he could neither understand nor control, to surround himself with the few he thought he could trust.

CONFLAGRATION AND FALL

The effort to understand Suharto's attitude in the last few months and weeks of his presidency may be enlightened by his professed attitude to the post in 1966–67. Then, he was adamant that he would do the job only if he enjoyed the broad support and, more important, the trust of the Indonesian people. Reflecting on his elevation to the political heights in 1967, Suharto in his autobiography remarked that, 'if at a certain time, in a proper and legitimate way, they [the people] withdraw their trust in me, then I would accede with a glad heart. I would not defend my position, much less defend it by employing armed force. I would absolutely never act like that!' Following his 1973 election, he had expressed the desire to be just a simple villager once more.[69]

Within weeks of Suharto's re-election, as the Indonesian economy plumbed the depths, long-contained forces of opposition began to emerge. What provided a focus for the ascent of anti-Suharto criticism was the emergence of a student movement early in 1998, which became more emboldened following his re-election. Large-scale student demonstrations across the country, for the most part contained to campuses and in which faculty staff and senior officers took part, preceded and followed the March MPR meeting; students, linked by their mobile phones and Internet access, began to push to take their wishes to the streets. By April, Amien Rais had courageously moved to the informal leadership of the growing movement to unseat Suharto and was openly calling on popular support for his cause. By May, the protests were beginning to spill out of the campuses and onto the roadways.

Suharto's only response to the heightening tension was to make some vague promises of reform through constitutional means, maintaining, however, that no significant reform could be undertaken until at least 2003. But he was sufficiently confident of his position, and his support, to order an IMF-directed reduction in petroleum subsidies on 4 May, which immediately and severely pushed up pump prices and occasioned rises in bus fares. The immediate reaction was a savage anti-Chinese riot in Medan, and the first serious signs that students would no longer be contained to campus-based protest. Suharto was still unable to grasp the significance of the mounting movement against him. He elected, apparently from his deeply entrenched sense of duty, to fly to Egypt on 9 May to take part in a G-15 economic conference in Cairo, advising his opponents as he left that the security forces would deal ruthlessly with disruptions.

In his absence, four students from the conservative private university, Trisakti, located alongside the airport toll-road west of the city's central area, were shot dead as they re-entered the campus towards the end of a day-long demonstration on the late afternoon of 12 May. The deaths of the students, and their funerals the following day, unleashed a torrent of pent-up frustration, in which Jakarta's poor – reportedly incited and directed by mysterious figures in different places across the city – proceeded to lay waste to large parts of Jakarta on 13 and 14 May.[70] Particular targets of the animosity were Sino-Indonesian shops, which were looted and fired, and Sino-Indonesian women, a large number of whom were raped. Similar violent rioting and destruction broke out in other cities, notably in Solo. Liem Siu Liong's north Jakarta house was burnt out by a mob. Suharto, watching the televised mayhem from Cairo, must have been devastated. He proclaimed that he was unwilling to employ force for the purpose of securing his rule; he also made vague claims that he proposed to stand aside (*lengser keprabon*) and provide the nation with a kind of distanced moral guidance. When, having cut short his trip, he arrived back in his capital early on the Friday morning of 15 May, large parts of the city, particularly those inhabited by Sino-Indonesians, were smoking ruins. More than a thousand people were dead, most killed in huge shopping mall fires. Sino-Indonesians and foreigners sought as best they could to escape the country, enduring spasmodic violence from mobs along the open freeway to Jakarta's Sukarno-Hatta International Airport. Some sold their vehicles at the airport before they fled.

Many observers attributed the ferocity of the destruction visited on Jakarta to the crudely wily Prabowo, since early in 1998 promoted to his third star and appointed as Kostrad commander, and the Jakarta garrison commander Syafrie Syamsuddin, former bodyguard of Suharto during his overseas trips and closely identified with Prabowo.[71] Certainly, the garrison made few effective efforts to curb the 13 May outburst, despite orders from Wiranto to that effect, and many suspected that Prabowo was attempting to engineer a situation to damage Wiranto's credibility so that Suharto would invest him with emergency powers to bring the situation under control.

Upon his return from Cairo, Suharto's immediate response was to cancel the fuel price rises and to order the forcible restoration of order, as well as to announce plans for a cabinet reshuffle. It was all too late. In the end, his 'hold on power … unravelled with astonishing speed'.[72] In the days that followed, calls for him to stand down came thick and fast, notably from his former favourite and now DPR/MPR Speaker Harmoko who, flanked by Syarwan Hamid, head of the parliamentary ABRI fraction, and other fraction leaders, on the afternoon of 18 May made an astonishing call for Suharto to resign and gave him until the following Friday to stand down, under threat that impeachment proceedings would be commenced against him. The day before, Tourism Minister Abdul Latief had submitted his own resignation for 'family reasons'.[73] On the morning of 18 May, the students had occupied the hump-roofed parliamentary building, where they were supervised by a sympathetic marine force, apparently placed there by Wiranto; the symbolism of them squatting on the building's roof was clear to everyone.

Suharto made desperate attempts to cling to power, at least for a little longer, and he received some sign of support from Wiranto who, for his own reasons, dismissed Harmoko's call for an immediate resignation, labelling it an 'individual view'.[74] That evening, Suharto met with the leading Islamic figure Nurcholish Majid to discuss the latter's ideas about how best to proceed; at that meeting, Suharto indicated that he was prepared to stand down. The following morning, he met with nine senior Muslim leaders and revealed his plan for a reform committee and a new cabinet; he himself wished to lead the reform process. 'I'm fed up with being president', he remarked to the group; 'the trouble is if I resign, is that a guarantee the trouble will stop?'[75] He used the opportunity to disparage the idea that Habibie would succeed him; 'there is a question of whether he is capable'.[76] Thereafter, in a national address, he formally announced his chief trump card, as he thought: his undertaking to dispense with the two-month-old cabinet, form a new one, to be named the Reform Cabinet (*Kabinet Reformasi*), establish a committee charged with taking forward the reform process by preparing new laws, and arrange elections ('as soon as possible'); he himself would not be a candidate for another term as president once the new MPR was assembled.[77] That evening, commenting to his speechwriter Yusril Izra Mahendra on student demands for a special session of the MPR to dismiss him, Suharto declared that 'they do not understand. If the special session can be drawn up, that will just add to the confusion. If that happens, ABRI will take over the reins, right?'[78]

In the midst of these desperate efforts, Amien Rais was coordinating student protests and threatening to assemble a million demonstrators in Jakarta on 20 May to call for Suharto's resignation; Suharto's address made no impact on him or others who suspected that the President was merely planning another scheme to delay his going. For his part, Habibie was floored and deeply hurt by Suharto's ungenerous remarks about his capacities, and quickly relayed to Suharto the view that Suharto's best chances for the future lay with a Habibie presidency.

Suharto had finally lost the faith even of those he had so closely nurtured. While Rais's march did not go ahead – derailed by the threat of military violence against the demonstrators – other forces were on the move. On the morning of 20 May, Suharto met with three of his former vice-presidents (Umar, Sudharmono and Try), presumably to discuss the situation and his options; meanwhile, State Secretary Saadillah Mursyid announced that Suharto would name the members of his Reform Committee the following morning. Suharto, however, was unable to find suitable persons to serve on his proposed 45-person committee and new cabinet; by evening there were only three takers. That evening also, news emerged that his financial ministers, led by the man he had brought to the summit, Co-ordinating Minister Ginanjar Kartasasmita, had met and composed a statement that they were not prepared to serve in the new cabinet, and urging Suharto to stand down. The statement, delivered to Cendana around 8 p.m., shook Suharto severely. It is, however, not clear whether he had already received it when he began a meeting with Habibie at around the same time, apparently to canvass a handover to him on 23 May, once Suharto himself had named the new cabinet. Habibie, realising the direction in which politics was going, quickly refused. At a meeting on the same evening, Wiranto, on the advice of a group of constitutional lawyers and political scientists, had come to a similar conclusion: that, for the sake of the nation, the best solution was a constitutional transfer of power from president to vice-president. Wiranto conveyed his views to Suharto that night.[79]

Suharto now realised, with the arrival of Ginanjar's letter and with what must have been a stunning, shocking finality, that his career as leader of his nation was over – 'Well, that's it, then [*terserahlah*]', Probosutejo reported him as saying – and that he must hand over power immediately to Habibie.[80] Habibie, having returned to his home in Kuningan, assembled a meeting with the four coordinating ministers. Around 11 p.m., not clear about what was transpiring, he called the President's home, only to be informed by Saadillah that Suharto would formally resign in the morning and hand power to the vice-president. Any international support for Suharto to stay on had evaporated; just before midnight, US Secretary of State Madeleine Albright broadcast a statement calling for him to step aside in the interests of a transition to democracy.

At 9 a.m. the following day, 21 May 1998, Suharto, dressed in a dark-grey short-sleeved safari jacket, entered a grand room in the Istana Merdeka, followed by his vice-president, B. J. Habibie, senior military officers, and a trail of members of the Supreme Court. His face was puffy and colourless but his demeanour remarkably composed as he cleared his throat and began reading a short statement in which he announced that his efforts to constitute a new cabinet had failed and that he would resign, effective from the moment he finished reading his statement. He thanked the nation, apologising for his 'mistakes and shortcomings'.[81] His statement concluded, he remained while a nervy, wild-eyed Habibie was sworn in as Indonesia's third president by the Chief Justice of the Supreme Court. Then Suharto shook Habibie's hand, wordlessly, and those of a number of the assembled judges, turned on his heel and was gone, halting briefly on the arm of Tutut to deliver a weakly resigned smile and wave to the photographers waiting outside, before returning in a private car to his heavily guarded home on Jalan Cendana. Inside, Wiranto addressed the throng, promising loyalty to Habibie and protection of the person and family of Suharto.

Suharto's resignation, broadcast to an enthralled nation and beyond, was the occasion of an immediate uproar of celebration amongst the students entrenched in the parliament buildings. Incredible as it had seemed only a week or so earlier, Suharto was gone, forever.

WHAT BROUGHT SUHARTO DOWN?

One commentator has opined that, 'towards the end of Suharto's reign, his scattered opponents, once or still within the New Order's framework, had begun to unite in a common cause'.[82] In fact, little cohesive oppositional unity was discernible at any stage in the process of dethroning Suharto. Equally, the view that he was felled by the Asian currency crisis is misleading; he had survived crises before and emerged stronger as a result. The crisis was, rather, the catalyst which allowed a broad constellation of factors, many of them the products of long gestation, to come together and build so much pressure that Suharto found himself with no option but to stand down.

Corruption, of course, played its part. In the mid-1970s, one experienced journalist had commented that 'corruption is the Achilles heel of the Indonesian government'. Another commentator reasoned that 'the anger at the wealth accumulated by [the Suharto family] that finally proved his undoing arose more because many Indonesians felt that the Soeharto family had gone too far, rather than because the Soehartos had commenced the journey down the road of corruption in the first place'. The same writer estimated that 'at the time of Soeharto's resignation, there were at least 1251 separate, active companies in Indonesia alone in which members of the Soeharto family had significant shares'.[83]

Of enormous importance, too, is the fact that Suharto's guiding style of management was comprehensively unequipped to deal with the rapidly spiralling danger to his rule. As his biographer had commented nearly three decades before, 'it has been [Suharto's] practice, ever since the communist putsch of September, 1965, to wait and see, to gauge the most important forces in society, to let ideas develop and to discuss problems, and then to act'.[84] In the context of May 1998, there was simply no time to allow this leisured strategy to have effect, even if Suharto had been in a position to muster the support needed to carry forward his wishes. Moreover, that style had itself become corrupt under the arrogant confidence which his long period of ascendancy had inspired. He boasted in his autobiography that 'I always ask "what do you think?", and always listen carefully to the answer to my question. If the idea is good, then OK'.[85] By May 1998, an increasingly erratic Suharto had long dispensed with the inclusiveness engendered by asking and acting upon others' views.

More generally, in the end, it was the incapacity of Suharto's New Order to accommodate the social progress that he himself had engineered that brought him low. Nearly thirty years earlier, the veteran foreign commentator Derek Davies had opined that 'prosperity is the greatest liberalising force. A modern industrialised Indonesia would not long tolerate a military oligarchy'. Suharto had for some long time been aware of that danger, but he had proved unable to develop a political architecture to accommodate it; stripped of its characteristically incorporatist logic, and with its legitimacy as the guarantor of prosperity in tatters, his ever more narrowly constructed regime could not last.[86]

JUST WAITING

In the period immediately after his resignation, Suharto lived in almost complete isolation from the rest of the world. On 22 May he coldly disabused the desperate Prabowo, effectively sidelined by Habibie and Wiranto, of any hopes that he might secure his resurrection. He had no contact with Habibie at all in the early days of the latter's presidency. He granted few interviews and was seldom seen in public; his half-brother reported that he was 'gathering material to answer his critics'.[87] Wahid made some desultory and unsuccessful efforts late in 1998 to draw Suharto back into the political process, apparently because he believed that Suharto was orchestrating outbreaks of violence aimed at destabilising society. Notwithstanding continuing allegations that groups associated with him were making systematic efforts to undermine successor leaders and government,[88] he seems simply to have absented himself from the world of politics – apart from rare forays such as his resignedly bitter comments in April 1999 about the coming general elections, the East Timor problems, and IMF policies[89] – which he had dominated for so long. For the most part he lived, as he had since 1966, at Jalan Cendana, although sometimes he was reported to be residing at a recently constructed house close by Taman Mini in east Jakarta. Occasionally he was sighted attending religious ceremonies; to celebrate Idul Fitri in January 2000, for example, Suharto and his family performed their ritual prayers at the At-Tin mosque inside the Taman Mini complex. That he still enjoyed significant popular support was clear from the large number of people who sought to greet him; they were perhaps part of those people who 'still remember that real economic development for them began only after

Repelita I, the first five-year plan, was instituted in 1969'.[90] According to Wahid, Suharto remained convinced that he had done nothing wrong, nothing for which he should apologise or seek forgiveness.[91]

It is difficult to know what Suharto made of the seismic changes that descended on Indonesia after his fall: the freeing of the press, the release of political prisoners, the emergence of democratic practice and the birth of a multitude of new parties, the reverberating calls for secession and greater degrees of regional autonomy, the release of East Timor – and, of course, the continuing economic crisis. Perhaps, he mused, this was simply fate exercising its freedom.

THE PURSUIT OF SUHARTO

The special session of the MPR convened in November 1998 saw Habibie's continuing survival. It also formally called for an investigation into corruption and the private amassing of public wealth, specifically that related to Suharto. The last day of the session witnessed the deaths of around fifteen students, shot dead by security forces as they swarmed about the parliamentary building and the Semanggi area. Suharto's comment that the violence had been caused by the failure of the government to give ear to the hopes and aspirations of the students was sadly ironic.[92]

Habibie had no strong interest in pursuing the claims about Suharto's corruption, both out of respect for the former president and because he realised that such an investigation might open a Pandora's box of retribution for New Order schemes, including his own. In order to keep control of any inquiry, he had already dispensed with Attorney-General Sujono Atmonegoro and replaced him with Andi Muhammad Ghalib, a serving military officer of unquestioned loyalty to Habibie.

As more and more stories emerged about the greed of his children at the public trough, Suharto attempted to defend himself. Appearing on his daughter's TV station in September 1998, he denied that he held a single cent in any foreign bank account and dared his critics to prove otherwise. In November, he handed over to the government the control of seven of the foundations he chaired, with total assets of more than half a billion dollars.

Habibie's response to the gathering demands to investigate Suharto's wealth was to establish a special commission. An attempt to recruit noted human rights lawyer Adnan Buyung Nasution to the commission failed when Habibie refused to grant the commission the powers Nasution sought. In the end, Ghalib headed the panel and was ordered to report to Habibie once the investigation was complete. Suharto was questioned for three hours on 9 December 1998. A tape of a phone conversation the following day, allegedly between Habibie and Ghalib, seemed to indicate that the government was not serious about the investigation, and that Suharto had encouraged it to avoid the prospect of others taking the law into their own hands. Not surprisingly, Ghalib's investigations turned up no evidence that Suharto had acquired wealth through improper means.[93]

With the election of Abdurrahman Wahid as president in October 1999, following Indonesia's first free parliamentary elections since 1955, public pressure for a reopening of Suharto's case became too great to ignore, despite Wahid's undertaking that he would pardon the former president if he were found guilty. Attorney-General Marzuki Darusman began the long, slow process of assembling evidence against Suharto and finally succeeded early in August 2000 in presenting charges in relation to his allegedly corrupt management of his foundations. The nature of the charge laid, and the slowness with which the case had been assembled, suggested to some that Marzuki and the government he represented were not enthusiastic about genuinely pursuing the former president. The tactics of Suharto's lawyers were to prevent their client, under city arrest since April, from facing trial on the grounds of his failing health.

CONCLUSION

Suharto was, indeed, failing. Successive strokes, the most recent on 19 July 1999, had left him with badly slurred speech, poor memory, and unable to express or understand anything more than simple ideas. He filled empty days watching cartoons and documentaries on television, sleeping, and praying; his children often called on him.

The efforts by the attorney-general's office to have Suharto undergo medical examination to judge his fitness for investigation reached comical proportions when he received a visit at his home from Wahid on 8 March 2000, the latter unaware of the fact that Suharto had been summoned to Cipto Mangunkusumo hospital for an examination that same day. A group of parliamentarians who had visited his house in February to question him about his allegedly improper channelling of bank loans had been turned away by Tutut and Suharto's lawyer, Juan Felix Tampubolon, because Suharto, according to Tampubolon, was 'unfit to undergo any clarification process or questioning'.[94] Shortly thereafter, he failed to respond to summonses to appear at the attorney-general's office to answer questions. Two efforts by a prosecution team to interview him in April were concluded prematurely when his blood pressure began to rise dangerously. On three separate occasions, he failed to respond to summonses to appear in court. Eventually, on 28 September, the chief judge of the south Jakarta district court, Lalu Mariyun, leading a five-member panel, dismissed the case against Suharto on the grounds that a panel of independent doctors had found him permanently too ill to face trial, and released him from city arrest. His health appeared to fail further in late 2000 and early 2001.

Notwithstanding the attorney-general's attempt to appeal to the Supreme Court to override the ruling, it appeared that Suharto would never face a formal accounting. Early in February 2001, the court ruled that he should not face trial until he was sufficiently healthy to do so, relieved him of the city arrest which it had imposed the previous November, and required the state to provide him with medical treatment. The ruling effectively ended any prospect that legal humiliation would be added to Suharto's political death.

11 The man and his legacy

IN 1996, SUHARTO was thought by the influential magazine *Asiaweek* to be the most powerful man in Asia.[1] In 1999, that same man, ill, weak, sunken and sallow of face, was wheeled into a Jakarta hospital, no longer the most powerful man in the region, his political achievements destroyed, his economic triumphs maligned, and the object of hatred and derision by his own people. Towards the end of 1997, he was thought – and believed himself[2] – to be the indispensable key to reviving Indonesia's economy, battered by the Asian currency crisis; two months later he was seen as the source of the problem, and his going indispensable to Indonesia's return to health. For most of his life he seemed unattracted by and indifferent to high politics, but he became the region's master politician. He was born into a poor peasant family, but he presided over his country's industrial transformation and is thought by many to control a family fortune worth billions of dollars.[3] Such paradox is a key motif of his life; together with his public mask – 'the smiles mask his emotions, for Suharto is not a man to betray what he thinks'[4] – and evasive, undemonstrative manner, it makes the task of attempting to understand the man elusive in the extreme.

Suharto was always strongly affected by his roots in the small but densely populated Central Java village of Kemusuk. The beauty of the surrounding countryside, with its shimmering flooded rice-fields, intensely green foliage, and the backdrop of the smoking, cloud-shrouded volcano of Mt Merapi, belied the reality of the crowded, weathered and poverty-ridden lives of its inhabitants. From the very beginning Suharto found life poor, troubled and difficult. That suffering developed in him a toughness and resilience and, perhaps, an inner guardedness about depending on others for anything, and a preference for a small number of close relationships in which he was the dominant figure. He was, by dint of circumstances, his own man from very early on.

Suharto was both an extraordinarily complex and extraordinarily simple man. Intellectually, he was narrow and simple, a reflection of his limited schooling, his curious failure to be selected, as were most of his peers, like Yani, for officer training in the United States in the 1950s, and the fact that he was 40 before his first trip overseas. Through circumstance and, perhaps, predilection, he was never much given to reading, or to reflection about abstract ideas, or to theorising. He has left us no body of writings as did Mao or Ho Chi Minh or even Mahathir, no evidence of his wrestling with intellectual problems, no abiding sense of horizons broader than those of Indonesia itself, nor longer than the short to medium term. His reading was mostly restricted to the newspapers and the briefing books prepared by his staff, although he also liked listening to the radio and watching television. One of his most senior colleagues told me in an interview of his efforts to broaden Suharto's range of intellectual interests and his sense of the world around him. He recounted how he arranged to leave with Suharto a pile of English-language magazines like *Time*, through which he might browse and which contained issues which he hoped might capture the President's attention. It did no good. Each week, when he visited Suharto for his routine discussion of matters of state, the magazines remained where he had placed them, untouched and unread. In the end, he gave up trying to educate Suharto.

Suharto's efforts at broader thinking went no further than a firm, even childlike, trust in and internalisation of ethical aphorisms of Javanese mystical thought, or variations on them, like loyalty to friends, duty to nation, trust in God. To mark his fortieth wedding anniversary, his eldest child, Tutut, had published an elaborate collection of sayings from Javanese ethical lore, which Suharto himself had apparently compiled.[5] They included such sayings as 'Virtue requires a firm mind', 'Prudence results from keen observation of one's experience' and 'Silence is an asset. Whoever has a sharp tongue will suffer. Whoever is silent will accumulate wealth. One who is silent is like a lighthouse' and, again, 'A glorious country has the Lord's blessing in the form of a state system and a spiritual system that provide well-being to the nation, a strong army, and a people who are faithful', 'Wealth indicates one's ability to put worldly situations under one's control', and 'You shall not fear difficulties, as life in this world is difficult'. This collection was published for the edification of the general public under the title *Butir butir budaya Jawa: mencapai kesempurnaan hidup berjiwa besar mengusahakan kebaikan sejati* (*Kernels of Javanese culture: attaining perfection in life with a great spirit striving for real goodness*).[6] The centrality of aphorism to Suharto's mental universe is of great interest. It indicates a mind uncluttered by the problematic or the unresolved, one based on inner reflection on life's personal experiences rather than the ideas of others, and underpinned by a very strongly felt sense of fate, duty and destiny.

These limitations on Suharto's intellectual horizons were also reflected in his language. He was, of course, born and bred to Javanese, and later learned Indonesian simply because he had to, speaking it always with that distinctively rounded and thick Javanese accent and peppering it with Javanese words and sayings. Unlike Sukarno, who had spattered his public pronouncements with borrowings from German philosophy and French literature, and who had customarily spoken Dutch to his colleagues, Suharto was only reluctantly multi-lingual. Having never enjoyed a Dutch-language education, he knew little of that language, although he occasionally used a Dutch phrase in his reports and speeches in the early 1950s.

He did learn English, presumably from his Australian house guest, Clive Williams, but while he read it reasonably well he spoke without fluency. He preferred always to speak Javanese to his close colleagues if they were also Javanese speakers; Indonesian was much his second language.

His intelligence was not an academic intelligence; it was of a different, more flinty, more instrumentalist and more strategic kind. He was a passive, patient, but voracious learner, one who recognised strategic deficiencies in his knowledge and sought out the expert who could fill the void in his understanding. He was not one to puzzle things out for himself. If he needed to know something, he went to the people who knew and simply listened to them until he had absorbed what he judged to be sufficient knowledge to carry out the required task. Having interviewed a number of those economists/technocrats who provided the economic programs to rehabilitate the Indonesian economy in the early years of Suharto's New Order, I discovered that they all told the same story about his quest for understanding economics at the beginning of his long rule. He simply sat, patiently, and industriously devoured and digested what they told him about currency rates, inflation, balances of payments, surpluses and deficits, and agricultural and industrial production. One told me that for the first couple of years when they met with Suharto, he would sit and listen; with a fat Parker pen he would make notes on a pad while they talked on and on. But, this technocrat told me, after a couple of years, once he had sufficiently conquered what he needed to know, it was he who did the talking and they who pulled out their pens to note down what he wanted done.[7]

He could seize upon a detailed brief or a complex problem,[8] master it, dissect it, map out appropriate strategies and, only when the time was right, act ruthlessly and obdurately to achieve a satisfactory solution. Political calculation was his great strength. All his contemporaries were constantly amazed at his capacity to master an enormous wealth of detail, often of a statistical kind, and then produce it at an appropriate time, sometimes months later, with unerring accuracy. Ministers were at times cowed by the fact that the facts and figures they mounted to secure their arguments could be later used against them if things did not turn out as they had predicted. He had an unerring ability to map out and keep to a strategy, often in the face of criticism, biding his time until the moment was right to move. This strategic genius was driven by a set of uncomplicated, unqualified, and probably uncontested ideas, which were similar in kind to his beloved Javanese aphorisms. They included an all-embracing attachment and devotion to the enduring integrity and development of the Indonesian nation, the continuing importance of the guiding and nurturing role of the Armed Forces in politics and society, a deep distrust and fear of the potentially disintegrative effects of materialism, liberalism and, of course, communism, an unqualified sense that his people should enjoy a better standard of living (and be thankful to him for providing it) and a view, more deeply entrenched with every passing year, that the nation needed his guiding and controlling presence and could not be trusted to finding its proper path without him.

Suharto was a man of abstemious and homely habits, rather colourless, cautious, diligent, reliable, loyal – again, a significant contrast to his predecessor,

Sukarno. Having married a plumpish, plain, modestly aristocratic and upwardly ambitious girl, Siti Hartinah, in 1947, he remained married to her until her death in 1996. There is every reason to believe that he also remained faithful to her, notwithstanding the odd rumour of flings with film stars ('I think "free love" is not good. I myself have been able to curb myself in that regard').[9] He did not like the high life of womanising, drinking and partying which was the staple of many of his peers who occupied the elite suburb of Menteng south-east of the centre of Jakarta. His only nod towards vanity was the pencil moustache he sometimes affected in the late 1940s and 1950s; but it never appeared thereafter. He drank hardly at all, only to fulfil his social obligations and put his guests at ease. He occasionally smoked, cigarettes in his earlier days but later usually cigars or pipes. Characteristically, the sports he most enjoyed, fishing and golf – he often played golf three times a week – were individual rather than team pursuits, which took their point from the ability to shape and discipline oneself in contest with the environment.

Suharto was not naturally a convivial person, much preferring his own company and that of his wife and close family. He had six children by Ibu Tien and was devoted to all of them; indeed, he tended to spoil and indulge them more and more as he grew older and busier, and as he saw less and less of them. They remained devoted to him, although not necessarily purely as a way of reciprocating his affection for them. Although he had a very wide circle of acquaintances, he preferred small and very tight groups of close colleagues, who in turn repaid him with great devotion and loyalty, at least until he no longer had need for them or if they betrayed his faith in them. This was a characteristic of him from the very beginning. A number of those who served under him during the revolutionary years of the late 1940s were members of his staff during his period as Diponegoro commander in the late 1950s, and a good number of them were still with him in the mid-1960s. His two closest and most notorious acquaintances, Ali Murtopo and Sujono Humardani, joined him in the mid-1950s and served him devotedly until the 1970s, when political ambition on the one hand and poor judgement on the other caused them to be cast aside.

To those he met he was invariably polite and often charming; he rarely gave any indication of his mood or intention by facial expression and body signals, presenting shuttered eyes and a wide smile which was so characteristic that his authorised biography was entitled *The smiling general*.[10] He took special pleasure in engaging with villagers about the things close to them; 'his eyes light up, he laughs readily and often, and he loves to ask teasing questions'.[11] Few people, except in the last years, ever saw him express anger openly. But he was also stubborn and obdurate. While he often did not make up his mind quickly, repeatedly calculating the costs and benefits of one course of action over another, he was not easily moved once his mind was made up. While in army service, he made his displeasure felt when he was overruled, either by absenting himself from proceedings (as when his military tactics were changed by a superior officer in Makasar in 1950) or by finding subtle ways of ignoring or subverting his commander's wishes. Sukarno was not wrong when he characterised him 'stubborn'. And he could be cruelly vindictive to those who he thought had betrayed him or his purpose.

Much has been made of Suharto's Javaneseness. During the height of his power, we were often regaled in the popular press, and even in more scholarly sites, with the notion that he was above all Javanese. There were, it seems, two dominant strands of this discourse. The first was that he was something of an atavistic throwback to the era of the old Javanese kings, imbued with old-fashioned feudal concepts and, indeed, consciously attempting to reconfigure modern Indonesia as a Javanese kingdom, in both form and substance.[12] The second was that he was somehow entrapped in Javanese mysticism, refusing to move until the signs were right, attributing arcane significance to apparently mundane or natural events, constantly consulting soothsayers and gurus about what the future might portend, or seeking periods of meditation and asceticism in the mist-shrouded upland caves of Central Java.[13]

An interesting aspect of this way of thinking about Suharto – labelled 'essentialised cultural accounting' by one scholar[14] – is that so many Indonesians seem to adopt it uncritically themselves. 'You must understand', they would say to me, 'that Suharto is *orang Jawa*', which appeared to be an invitation to interpret him by systems of significance wholly foreign to me and, it seems, to those who advised me in this way. This kind of assertion has sometimes sent Western analysts into something approaching panic; one remarked that, 'for the analyst trying to understand Suharto, the need to shuttle between universal concepts of power politics and those which are specifically Javanese is a constant and baffling concern'.[15]

I find this concentration on the exotic to be fundamentally misleading and obfuscatory, almost wholly unhelpful, and to raise as many problems as it purports to solve. Suharto was indubitably Javanese, if by that is meant a certain style of thinking characterised by inner reflectiveness, calculation and control ('bringing the inner self close to our creator'),[16] which manifested itself in certain moral and practical rules. The structure of his personality and emotions, the architecture of his mental framework, and his sense of historical meaning and trajectory were strongly influenced by the customs and beliefs of Java.[17] He claimed to be an adept in Javanese religion, and his style can be characterised as typically and centrally Javanese. His earnest and fundamental attachment to his roots was exemplified in 1985, when the Solo palace was badly damaged by fire; Suharto donated half his official salary for five months to the restoration fund and later had Sujono Humardani inaugurate the new construction. In the end, however, the category of Javaneseness itself does not provide us with a code for actions and behaviour which might otherwise be inexplicable, and I have found no strong evidence that his 'being Javanese' fundamentally affected his decisions in ways that make them otherwise incomprehensible.

Suharto himself was sceptical about suggestions like these. In his own mind, 'the essential nature of humankind is universal, indeed, it is shared by all countries wherever they are, in Europe, Asia, America or Russia'. When it was suggested that he was unduly influenced by the mystical Javanist ideas of his close adviser, Sujono Humardani, Suharto responded:

> It is indeed true that [Sujono] liked to come to me bringing a book of his notes. He was a believer. And he liked to give me suggestions. I listened to his suggestions in order to make him feel good. But I didn't just swallow those suggestions. I analysed and weighed up what was rational and what was not. If it was rational, if it made sense, I would accept it. If it did not, then certainly I would not use it.[18]

The advice he often sought from mystical teachers was probably subject to the same kinds of interrogation. Again, he remarked that

> we should use all our natural capacities which have been given us by God. Then we sift all the information and ideas which come from outside. Then we settle on some alternatives before making a decision. We choose the best from amongst the available alternatives. With all this it doesn't mean that we must indulge in meditation or burning incense or anything like that. We use our powers of reason, our brains, our feelings, our five senses. If we were in a war and we have to look for a *dukun* [traditional adviser], we would be shot dead first.[19]

Suharto had a curiously historicist sense of the past – all of a piece with his understanding of fate and destiny – of which he was, quite naturally, the terminus. His view of Indonesian history, and of its people, was a relatively simple and unproblematic one. Indonesia had been born into its freedom because of the united struggles of its peoples; 'the history of the War of Independence', he remarked, 'clearly demonstrates that the strength of the Republic lies in its People. The People are the source of our strength. The People are the real capital in the struggle of our nation'.[20] The Army itself had come from the people. But the people were erratic; they could be led astray by false and seductive views of the world and led along by ambitious civilian leaders. Because of the weakness and fractiousness of the civilian leaders of the revolution, who had surrendered to the Dutch at the Republic's greatest time of trial, it was the Army which had ultimately won the victory against the Dutch. This victory had given the Army a special status and duty in the affairs of the independent Republic; securing the triumph of the revolution, it also became the guarantor of what that victory had promised: a united and prosperous Indonesia.

The post-revolutionary history of Indonesia was at first a story of wasted opportunities, as civilians, back in control, spent their energies in squabbling and self-interestedness, which had brought the country close to economic ruin and physical disintegration by the late 1950s, and as the people, shiftless and impressionable, were drawn in different and divisive directions. Only in 1965 could the Army re-assert its proper role to save the people from their erstwhile leaders and from themselves, a project concretised in the construction of the New Order. That role was twofold: to ensure the unity and stability of the Republic, come what may, and to act as the agent of the nation's move towards prosperity. The Army, then, though born of the people, had become the tool for the realisation of the people's real aspirations; it had to show the people what unity meant, to achieve that unity, and to adopt a paternalist role in uplifting the people's material and spiritual fortunes. Suharto was, in his own mind, the personification of this idea, as evidenced by his extraordinarily self-centred biography and the six volumes of his published diaries which equate the proclaimed success of his personal presidential career with that of the Indonesian state.

This was both an arrogant and a highly conservative view of Indonesia's history. It was arrogant because, while it was purportedly based in the people's aspirations, it did not trust those people; the people were like children, they became an objectified category upon which Suharto had to work to give them what they really needed in the interests of the total society. Those who were committed to shaping Indonesian society in new and threatening ways, for example that section of 'the people' who made up the PKI in 1965–66, were denied their very humanity. They could not be negotiated back into the political realm because they were unable to accept the fundamentals of the conservative order that Suharto wanted to preserve and intensify. They could only be destroyed or otherwise removed from the scene by remorseless violence. That segment of 'the people' who were not in some way part of the PKI conspiracy were, however, also the object of his mistrust and fear, because of their erratic ways. Some years later, Suharto attributed the massacres to the 'very sharp conflict between the national leadership and the people. The situation became very strained and uncertain. Thousands of victims fell in the regions because the people acted on their own, also because of nasty prejudices between groups which for many years were cultivated by narrow political practices'.[21] A similar manifestation of this attitude emerged when Suharto attempted, many years later, to defend his Supersemar-based decision to ban the PKI, claiming that his action was necessary as a means of asserting government authority and reining in the violence. 'I had to dissolve the PKI ... The increasingly sharp conflict of opinion between President Sukarno and the people has brought into decline the authority of the supreme leadership of the government of the state.' Because of this, only with the dissolution of the PKI 'can general security be restored, the feeling of justice fulfilled, and the unity of the people restored'.[22]

Suharto's mistrust of the people, of course, endured. Thus, the engineering of Golkar's win in the 1971 elections both represented and portended the future for Indonesians and their politics and society. The people themselves were not to be trusted to deliver a mandate; rather, the decision, such as it was, was the result of cleverly cynical artifice. Equally, he justified his repression of student groups in the lead-up to the 1978 presidential elections by noting that 'ABRI would not let a small group of people set off spot-fires in an irresponsible way which could end up in incinerating the whole body of the people'.[23] 'The people', then, were like a shiftless mob; they could attain their true humanity only if they were brought into a state of malleable passivity by strong and focused leadership – the kind that he himself provided.

Suharto's view of history was highly conservative because it was based upon an unchanging notion of Indonesian society. Already in 1945 the basis had been laid – the corporatist and paternalist vision of the 1945 Constitution and the state ideology of Pancasila. Indonesian society, then, was not to change in any structural sense; those who were destined to rule had the task of improving people where they stood, not changing the essential structures of the society; to do that would risk unleashing the many demons in society which could tear it all apart.

How, then, did Suharto succeed in his purpose? It must be said at the outset that we need to pay due attention to that joker in the historian's pack: the notion of good luck. In 1945, Suharto was a nobody, a low-ranking soldier in what might be called a Japanese-created Home Guard. Twenty-three years later he was president of the fifth largest nation on earth, and he remained in that position for another thirty years. He was fortunate that he came to maturity at a time of extraordinary social flux and mobility, the end of the Pacific War and the beginning of what Indonesians at one time quaintly called their 'physical revolution'. Moreover, he was fortunate to be in and around Yogyakarta, the seat of revolutionary struggle, and to come in close contact and familiarity with the nation's political and military leaders: Sukarno, Syahrir, Hatta, Sudirman, Nasution, and others. In the 1950s he was fortunate that his period as Diponegoro commander in Central Java coincided with the declaration of a state of war and siege, which enabled him to begin to practise the arts of politico-military command. He was fortunate that American intervention in the West Irian crisis came just at the moment when he was about to commit large-scale forces to an attack on the Dutch, which would surely have been a military and possibly political disaster. He was fortunate that he happened to be in Jakarta as the senior serving officer in direct command of troops on the morning of 1 October 1965, at the outbreak of the coup attempt. He was fortunate that his early rise to power came just at the iciest time of the Cold War, in the same year that the United States committed ground troops to Vietnam, and when his emergence was welcomed and supported by the United States as its best news in Asia for years, and where the grisly massacres his regime visited upon the communists and others could be safely ignored by the world community as an unfortunate but necessary exercise. He was fortunate that the shakiest period of his rule, the early 1970s, coincided with the astounding ballooning of oil prices, providing him with a massive windfall not just for the purposes of political patronage but also for consolidating and accelerating the process of domestic economic development which eventually provided him with what came to be called performance legitimacy. He was lucky, too, that when oil prices sank again in the mid-1980s, he was able to jump onto the bandwagon of the Asian economic miracle.

Luck, of course, is important. But so is skill. What role did that play in Suharto's extraordinary longevity? And what were those skills that he used to such advantage for so long? First, he had the capacity to attract to himself people of significant talent. These, generally, were of two kinds. There were those who were able to cut through political and bureaucratic red tape to get things done without worrying too much about the ethics of the means chosen. Chief amongst these, of course, was Ali Murtopo, his brilliant, charming 'special operations' man, who counted amongst his triumphs the ending of Confrontation, the direction of the student protests that were so crucial in bringing Sukarno down, and the fashioning of the political system and Golkar, the election-winning vehicle, which saw Suharto assume the presidency unopposed in 1973, 1978, 1983, 1988, 1993 and

1998. Then there were those who were the civilian experts, of whom the most influential were the technocrats like Wijoyo, Sadli, Subroto, Emil Salim and Sumitro, who provided the policy settings which first allowed the ravaged Indonesian economy to be rehabilitated, and then rescued it from potential disaster in the mid-1980s. The characteristic of both those groups of supporters was their extraordinary devotion to Suharto as an individual. He was the most uncharismatic of leaders in a popular sense, but, until the later stages of his rule, he clearly had the capacity to attract the best brains and wills and to inculcate into them an almost mesmeric, reverential subjugation to his dominance.

Second, we must look at Suharto's remarkable skill in establishing and maintaining an elaborate patronage machine which ensured that virtually all the actors in the New Order were so thoroughly compromised and in his debt that they had no room for effective political manoeuvre. This was achieved by the adroit distribution of oil money, managed by his oil czar, Ibnu Sutowo, and by the sophisticated allocation of business opportunities. When those dissatisfied with his policies and leadership became problems, they were gently moved out into areas which provided them with status and business opportunities which they found hard to reject.

Third, and closely associated with his patronage strategy, was his extraordinary ruthlessness. His political opponents knew that if they could not be bought off gently, they would suffer unrelenting punishment. The fate of those few hardy souls who chose this path, like the Siliwangi officer H. R. Dharsono, was a sign to others not to make the same choice. 'Suharto is vindictive', remarked Ali Sadikin; 'those who know him say he is a vindictive person'.[24] His ruthlessness with those who dared to disturb the tranquillity of New Order Indonesia was exemplified in the so-called Petrus killings of the early 1980s. His capacity to strike real fear into those about him was a characteristic of his method of rule and illustrative of the power of his personality. One senior military figure, for example, who had determined to raise with Suharto his misgivings about the directions of the New Order, found once he sat down face to face with Suharto that he was so frozen by fear that he could only discuss routine matters with his President before beating a hasty retreat from Cendana. Another Suharto cabinet minister, Yuwono Sudarsono, spoke evocatively of 'the density of [Suharto's] silence'; 'he would stare you in the face and create a sense of awe … It was his presence and his stare. He looked right through you. Every five years, 1,000 people met in a congress and there was not one who was brave enough to stand up and say, "Enough"'.[25]

Fourth, we need to recognise the success of his strategy for corporatising Indonesia. Suharto never read the business or political science literature of corporatism, but he was a master at its exercise. His corporatism policy, while fleshed out by New Order ideologues, came essentially from within, fuelled by those narrowly constructed ideas about Indonesian society to which I have already referred. What he wanted was a polity in which power flowed from on high; there was never room for significant contestation amongst political actors. Thus, political parties of the Western, liberal kind were quashed; in their place Suharto engineered political organisations whose role was to advance the national interest as already conceived, not to contest it. The intellectual roots of these ideas are not entirely clear; some ascribe them to the influence of fascist ideas transmitted to the Indies in the 1920s and 1930s, others see them as part of Javanese organicist ideas about governance. Whatever the case, the New Order state constructed on this basis – backed by the Army and tied together by patronage networks, and ideologically hamstrung by very narrow conceptions of the state ideology of Pancasila, which made criticism of the New Order state synonymous with treason – rendered the task of effective opposition almost impossible.

Fifth, we need to recognise Suharto's extraordinary political and strategic skills. He was a master of the detailed calculation. He never crushed an opponent if he saw the opportunity of winning him over first. In combating his enemies, he was always careful to isolate them first so that they could never find support in numbers. He was incurably patient, testing the waters, feeling out strengths and weaknesses, probing for the advantage. Once he had adopted a course of action, he struck unexpectedly and in a deadly fashion. No one ever resurrected his fortunes or rehabilitated himself once Suharto had dealt with him. Where he was uncertain, he often sent different supporters in deliberately contradictory circles, assessing the impact their missions had, bringing his opponents to the surface, testing out the feasibility of a certain strategy, and then taking advantage of circumstances as they developed in his favour.

In his last years, these capacities began to desert him one by one, and sometimes even to betray him. His love of those close to him and his unremitting homeliness led him to protect and enhance the extraordinary business privileges he extended to his children – licences for toll-roads, special import rights for consumer goods, the disastrous Timor car fiasco – notwithstanding the enormous cost to him politically. The loss of his wife, Ibu Tien, networker, strategist, sounding-board, and discipliner of his children, probably affected him more deeply and crucially than has been recognised. His political longevity meant that he outgrew the tight band of supporters who had nurtured him during the earlier phases of his rule, and his inability to communicate so effectively with the emerging generations meant that he became increasingly isolated from the deeper currents of politics. His very eminence and stature, not to mention the remoteness that had come with his complete ascendancy in the realm of Indonesian politics, left him more and more irritated by criticism, real or unintended. Coolness, control and composure were replaced by an increasing irascibility and sensitivity. The patronage networks which had insured his earlier years began to fray, unable to accommodate the greedy reach of his children. The calculus was still there – witness his placing Habibie on the vice-presidential seat in the belief that no one would contemplate dethroning him if Habibie was the alternative – but it was failing, especially when the economy began its grand collapse in late 1997. The irony of it all was that his resignation was forced by the loss of support from the twin pillars of his long-lived regime: the Army, which reluctantly agreed that his time had come, and his economic ministers, the modern representatives of the technocrats upon whom he had relied for wisdom for so long.

What did he achieve? There can, I think, be no question that Suharto's abiding legacy will be the extraordinary economic growth that his rule brought. No more and no less, his clear-sighted policies and the disciplines he imposed (despite occasional blurrings in their implementation) brought Indonesia, from being a 'poor and stagnant country',[26] into the modern world. His achievement is all the more startling given the chequered history of economic growth in Indonesia; his period of office represented probably the greatest enduring period of growth and prosperity in that country's history, and brought hitherto only imagined levels of prosperity and hope to millions of Indonesians.[27] Moreover, whatever the damage caused by corruption, much of that growth was channelled into productive investment, into the elaboration of physical infrastructure and communications, into education, into family planning, into agricultural and industrial development. So great was his achievement that the damage caused by the 1997–98 financial meltdown – itself ascribed by Suharto to Indonesia's dearth of appropriate systems and 'talented men' to handle the rapid economic growth of the late 1980s and early 1990s[28] – made little impact on his overall record.

On the political front, his record is much more mixed. When he came to power, Indonesia was in political ruin, racked by turbulent difference and disharmony; when he left the scene, the chaos into which the country descended made it virtually ungovernable. It is a tribute to his political skills that, in between, he created a long-lived phase of political order and relative tranquillity such as the country had not known since the high days of Dutch colonialism. But that order came at great cost. It was created by the imposition of an artificial and repressive set of ideas that abolished pluralism and by the engineering of a paternalistic political framework that could not accommodate change. That regime reached its apogee in the Pancasila corporatism of the 1980s. It is, perhaps, true that Indonesia needed some measure of blunt authoritarianism if it were to emerge intact from the cataclysms of 1965–66. But the soul of New Order polity remained forever determinedly suspicious of the people it claimed to serve, relentlessly compressing their lives into the pattern it judged best promoted their real (as distinct from imagined) best interests. It was not coincidental that, to achieve that goal, the state had to be violent with its people, periodically and systematically.

This kind of polity had three essential flaws, which not only brought down its creator but, more important, also doomed Indonesia to a long and painful period of reorientation once he had gone. The first was its fixedness; once the goal of a Pancasila state and society had been more or less achieved by the mid-1980s, all that remained was the work of technical adjustment to new challenges which, it was assumed, could be managed within the existing order of things. Such a view, as it turns out, was blind to the magnitude of the New Order's success in moulding a wholly new Indonesia, and simply incapable of responding to the range of new pressures which emerged from that success: workers seeking freedoms of association and a more humane life, middle classes mounting claims for greater transparency and accountability to guarantee their new material gains, students seeking vaguely defined ideas of *reformasi*, Muslims wanting their religious aspirations taken seriously by the state, other nations and international bodies wanting Indonesia to toe the line on issues of human rights. The frozen boundaries of New Order corporatism simply could not accommodate the clamour of this emerging diversity forever. In this sense, Suharto's New Order represented the refusal to countenance change, and a systematic failure to confront the political challenges which were the inevitable consequence of the social and economic developments it secured.

Second, Suharto's dominance of the New Order, and his particular style of rule, ensured that the political and bureaucratic machinery of the New Order never achieved independent institutional solidity and permanence, nor any capacities to check his personal exercise of power. With the final collapse of his mandate, the fragile texture of the state machine almost immediately began to fray; Suharto, in important senses, had been the state, and a frightening task of institution-building awaited his successors, themselves unpractised in leadership because of his overweening dominance.

Third, the very artificiality of New Order thinking, and the totalistic rigour with which that thinking was pursued, left Indonesia a wasteland of political ideas and with its identity seriously underdeveloped. 'I think that it is Soeharto's worst crime', opined Buyung Nasution, 'that he has made Indonesians afraid to think, afraid to express themselves'.[29] Suharto was not wholly to blame for this development; indeed, it was his predecessor who set in motion the wheels of ideological vacuity. But in creating, and imposing, so persistently and rigidly, his frozen vision of Pancasila society, a vision that had little moral content and provided no credible bearings for the road ahead, and that sought little more than political containment, Suharto did his country a grave disservice. The fundamentally important questions about the identity and trajectory of the Indonesian nation were not addressed in any meaningful way; they were simply ignored out of fear of what the consequences of addressing them might bring. The result, now that the New Order has evaporated, is that Indonesia is today a nation adrift, without foundations, without a clear sense of what unites it or what its role and purpose might be, without an uncontradicted vision of where it wants to travel and how it might best make that journey. It is no wonder, in this context, that a defensive, exaggerated and easily outraged sense of sovereignty is so dominant in Indonesia today.

The paradoxical legacy of Suharto's rule is that the transformations he tried to contain were a direct if unintended consequence of his efforts at social and economic modernisation. The most serious problem for Indonesia is that there is no leader in sight who might combine Suharto's political and strategic skills with a broader and more humane understanding of the world and Indonesia's proper place in it.

Glossary and abbreviations

AACMI Algemeen-Archief van de Centrale Militaire Inlichtingendienst (NEFIS)
ABRI *Angkatan Bersenjata Republik Indonesia* – Armed Forces of the Republic of Indonesia
ADC aide-de-camp
AJI *Aliansi Jurnalis Independen* – Alliance of Independent Journalists
Akabri *Akademi Angkatan Bersenjata Republik Indonesia* – Indonesian Armed Forces Academy
All-Indonesia Fishers' Association *Himpunan Nelayan Seluruh Indonesia*
alun-alun square
Ampera *Amanat Penderitaan Rakyat* – Message of the People's Suffering
anak buah close, son-like, subordinate
Ansor Nahdlatul Ulama (NU) youth organisation
APEC Asia Pacific Economic Cooperation
APRA *Angkatan Perang Ratu Adil* – Army of the Just Ruler
APRIS *Angkatan Perang Republik Indonesia Serikat* – Armed Forces of the Republic of the United States of Indonesia
ASEAN Association of South East Asian Nations
ASEM Asia–Europe Meeting
Aspri *Asisten Pribadi* – personal assistant (to Suharto)
azas tunggal sole foundation
Babinsa *Bintara Bina Desa* – Village Guidance NCOs
Badesa Village Development NCOs
Bais *Badan Intelijen Strategis* – Strategic Intelligence Body
Bakin *Badan Koordinasi Intelijens Negara* – State Intelligence Coordinating Body
Bakorstanas *Badan Koordinasi Stabilitas Nasional* – National Stability Coordinating Board
Banpres *Bantuan Presiden* – presidential assistance
Bappenas *Badan Perencanaan Pembangunan Nasional* – National Development Planning Board
barisan brigade
Barisan Penjagaan Umum General Guard Unit
BFO *Bijeenkomst voor Federale Overleg* – Federal Consultative Assembly
BIA *Badan Intelijen ABRI* – Armed Forces Intelligence Body

Bimas *Bimbingan Massal* – mass guidance
BKR *Badan Keamanan Rakyat* – People's Security Body
BP-7 *Badan Pembinaan Pelaksanaan Pedoman Penghayatan dan Pengamalan Pancasila* – Supervisory Body for Implementation of Guidance for Comprehension and Practice of Pancasila
BPI *Badan Pusat Intelijen* – Central Intelligence Agency
Buku Putih White Book
Bulog *Badan Urusan Logistik* – National Logistics Board
bundan military squad of about ten men (Japanese)
bundancho leader of bundan
bupati head of a kabupaten
CAD *Centraal Archievendepot* – Central Archive Depot
Caduad *Cadangan Umum Angkatan Darat* – Army General Reserve
CGI Consultative Group on Indonesia
chudancho company commander (Japanese)
CIDES Center for Information and Development Studies
Cooperative Farmers Association *Kerukunan Tani Indonesia*
CPI Communist Party of Indonesia
CSIS Centre for Strategic and International Studies
daidan battalion (Japanese)
daidancho battalion commander
Dakab *Yayasan Dana Abadi Karya Bakti* – Eternal Fund for Noble Service Foundation
Dharmais *Yayasan Dharma Bhakti Sosial* – Duty of Social Service Foundation
DI/TII *Darul Islam/Tentara Islam Indonesia* – Darul Islam/Islamic Army of Indonesia
DPR *Dewan Perwakilan Rakyat* – People's Representative Council
DPR-GR *Dewan Perwakilan Rakyat – Gotong Royong* – People's Representative Council – Mutual Assistance
dukun traditional (rural) adviser/healer
dwi fungsi dual function
Dwikora *Dwi Komando Rakyat* – People's Double Command
FBSI *Federasi Buruh Seluruh Indonesia* – All Indonesia Workers' Federation
Finek Diponegoro Division's finance and economic planning division
Fosko *Forum Studi dan Komunikasi TNI-AD* – Army Study and Communication Forum
Fretilin *Frente Revolucionária do Timor-Leste Independente* – Revolutionary Front of Independent East Timor
GBHN *Garis-garis Besar Haluan Negara* – Broad Outlines of State Policy
GBN *Gerakan Banteng* – Buffalo Operation
Gerwani *Gerakan Wanita Indonesia* – Indonesian Women's Movement
Gestapu *Gerakan September Tiga Puluh* – 30 September Movement
GMNI *Gerakan Mahasiswa Nasional Indonesia* – National Students Movement of Indonesia
Golkar *Golongan Karya* – Functional Groups
Golput *Golongan Putih* – White Group
gotong-royong mutual assistance
GUPPI *Gabungan Usaha-usaha Perbaikan Pendidikan Islam* – Association for Improving Islamic Education
Hankam *Departemen Pertahanan Keamanan* – Department of Defence and Security
Hizbullah Army of God
HKGS Archive of the Hoofdkwartier van de Generale Staf van het Leger in Indonesië

HKTI *Himpunan Kerukunan Tani Indonesia* – Harmony Association of Indonesian Peasants
HMI *Himpunan Mahasiswa Indonesia* – Indonesian Students Association
HMI *Himpunan Mahasiswa Islam* – Islamic Students Association
ICMI *Ikatan Cendekiawan Muslim se-Indonesia* – Association of Indonesian Muslim Intellectuals
IGGI Inter-Governmental Group on Indonesia
IMF International Monetary Fund
Inkopad *Induk Koperasi Angkatan Darat* – Central Board of Army Cooperatives
Inpres *Instruksi Presiden* – Presidential Instruction
IPKI *Ikatan Pendukung Kemerdekaan Indonesia* – League of Upholders of Indonesian Freedom
IPTN indigenous aircraft industry
kabupaten district (largest administrative region below province)
Kadin Chamber of Commerce and Industry
KAMI *Kesatuan Aksi Mahasiswa Indonesia* – Indonesian Student Action Front
kampung (urban) village
KAP G.30.S *Komando Aksi Pengganyangan G.30.S* – Action Command to Crush the 30 September Movement
KAPI *Kesatuan Aksi Pelajar Indonesia* – Indonesian Student Action Front
KAPPI *Kesatuan Aksi Pemuda dan Pelajar Indonesia* – Indonesian Youth and Student Action Front
kekaryaan (functional) role exercised by the military
kepercayaan belief
KGSS *Kesatuan Gerilya Sulawesi Selatan* – Union of South Sulawesi Guerrillas
kiyayi Islamic scholar
KKO *Korps Komando Operasi* – Marine Corps
KL *Koninklijk Landmacht* – Dutch Army
KNI *Komite Nasional Indonesia* – Indonesian National Committee
KNIL *Koninklijk Nederlandsch-Indisch Leger* – Royal Netherlands Indies Army
KNIP *Komite Nasional Indonesia Pusat* – Central Indonesian National Committee
KNPI *Komite Nasional Pemuda Indonesia* – Indonesian National Youth Committee
Kodam *Komando Daerah Militer* – military region
Kodamar *Komando Daerah Maritim* – Maritime Regional Command
Kodim *Komando Distrik Militer* – district military region
Koga *Komando Siaga* – Vigilance Command
Kogam *Komando Ganyang Malaysia* – Crush Malaysia Command
Kohanudad *Komando Pertahanan Udara Angkatan Darat* – Air Defence Command
Kolaga *Komando Mandala Siaga* – Alert Theatre Command
Kolognas National Logistics Command
Kopassandha *Komando Pasukan Sandhi Yudha* – Army Paracommandos
Kopassus *Komando Pasukan Khusus* – Special Forces Command
Kopkamtib *Komando Operasi Pemulihan Keamanan dan Ketertiban* – Operations Command for the Restoration of Order and Security
Kopur *Komando Tempur* – Battle Command
Koramil *Komando Rayon Militer* – Military Sub-district Command
Korem *Komando Resort Militer* – Resort Military Command
Korpri *Korps Pegawai Republik Indonesia* – Civil Servants Professional Association
Korra I *Korps Tentara I* – First Army Corps

Korud *Komando Regional Udara* – Regional Air Command
Kosgoro *Koperasi Serba Guna Gotongroyong* – Cooperative of Mutual Assistance
Kostrad *Komando Cadangan Strategis Angkatan Darat* – Army Strategic Reserve Command
Kostrad Dharma Putra *Yayasan Kesejahteraan Sosial Dharma Putra Kostrad* – Kostrad Social Welfare Foundation
Koti *Komando Operasi Tertinggi* – Supreme Operations Command
Kotrar *Komando Tertinggi Retooling Aparatur Revolusi* – Supreme Command for Retooling the Revolutionary State Apparatus
Kowilhan *Komando Wilayah Pertahanan* – Regional Defence Command
kraton palace
kretek clove-scented cigarette
KRIS *Kebaktian Rakyat Indonesia Sulawesi* – Devotion of the Indonesian People of Sulawesi
KSHKGS *Krijgsgechiedkundige Sectie van het Hoofdkwartier Generale Staf in Indonesië* – War History Section of the General Staff Headquarters in Indonesia
lasykar rakyat popular militias
LIPI *Lembaga Ilmu Pengetahuan Indonesia* – Indonesian Institute of Sciences
LKB *Yayasan Lembaga Kesadaran Berkonstitusi* – Institute for Constitutional Awareness Foundation
Mahmillub *Mahkamah Militer Luar Biasa* – Extraordinary Military Tribunal
Malari *Malapetaka Limabelas Januari* – Calamity of 15 January
Masyumi *Majelis Syuro Muslimin Indonesia* – Council of Indonesian Muslim Associations
MBR Mobile Brigade Ratulangi
MPP *Markas Pimpinan Pertempuran* – Battle Leadership Headquarters
MPR *Majelis Permusyawaratan Rakyat* – People's Consultative Assembly
MPRS *Majelis Permusyawaratan Rakyat Sementara* – Provisional People's Consultative Assembly
Muhammadiyah modernist Islamic association
Munas *Musyawarah Nasional* – National Conference
Murba *Partai Murba* – Proletarian Party
MvD *Ministerie van Defensie* – Ministry of Defence
Nahdlatul Ulama traditionalist Islamic association (NU)
Nasakom *Nasionalisme, Agama, Kommunisme* – Nationalism, Islam, Communism
National Coordinating Body for Family Planning *Badan Koordinasi Keluarga Berencana Nasional*
NEFIS Netherlands Forces Intelligence Service
negara hukum rule of law
Negara Islam Indonesia Islamic State of Indonesia
NGO non-government organisation
NICA Netherlands Indies Civil Administration
NIT *Negara Indonesia Timur* – State of East Indonesia
NKK *Normalisasi Kehidupan Kampus* – Normalisation of Campus Life
NU see *Nahdlatul Ulama*
OPM *Organisasi Papua Merdeka* – Free Papua Movement
Opstib *Operasi Tertib* – Operation Order
Opsus *Operasi Khusus* – Special Operations group
Ormas the law on mass organisations
'Our Hope' Foundation *Yayasan Harapan Kita*

P-4 *Pedoman Penghayatan dan Pengamalan Pancasila* – Guide to the Comprehension and Practice of Pancasila
P-7 *Panitia Penasehat Presiden mengenai Pedoman Penhayatan dan Pengamalan Pancasila* – Presidential Advisory Committee for P-4
Pakualam minor traditional ruler in Yogyakarta
pamong praja civilian territorial officials, especially in Java
Pancasila the five principles of Indonesia's state ideology: belief in one God, a just and civilised humanity, Indonesian unity, democracy through representative deliberation, and social justice
Panglima Besar High Commander
panglima commander
Parmusi *Partai Muslimin Indonesia* – Indonesian Muslim Party
PDI *Partai Demokrasi Indonesia* – Indonesian Democratic Party
Pekuneg *Pengatur Keuangan Negara* – The Team to Regularise State Finances
pemuda young people
Pepelrada *Penguasa Pelaksanaan Dwikora Daerah* – Regional Authority to Implement Dwikora
Peperda *Penguasa Perang Daerah* – Regional War Authority
Permesta *Piagam Perjuangan Semesta* – Charter of Total Struggle
Pertamina *Pertambangan Minyak dan Gas Bumi Nasional* – National Oil and Gas Mining
Perti *Persatuan Tarbiyah Islamiyah* – Islamic Education Association
pesantren rural Islamic boarding school
Pesindo *Pemuda Sosialis Indonesia* – Indonesian Socialist Youth
Peta *Pembela Tanah Air* – Defenders of the Fatherland
Petisi 50 Petition of 50
Petrus *penembakan misterius* – mysterious shootings
PKI *Partai Komunis Indonesia* – Indonesian Communist Party
PNI *Partai Nasional Indonesia* – Indonesian National Party
PPP *Partai Persatuan Pembangunan* – Development Unity Party
PRD *Partai Rakyat Demokrasi* – People's Democracy Party
pribumi indigenous
priyayi nobility
Prosperous Self-Reliant Fund *Dana Sejahtera Mandiri*
PRRI *Pemerintah Revolusioner Republik Indonesia* – Revolutionary Government of the Republic of Indonesia
PSI *Partai Sosialis Indonesia* – Indonesian Socialist Party
PSII *Partai Sarekat Islam Indonesia* – Indonesian Islamic Association Party
PUDI *Partai Uni Demokrasi Indonesia* – United Indonesian Democracy Party
Pusintelstrat *Pusat Intelijen Strategis* – Strategic Intelligence Centre
PWI *Persatuan Wartawan Indonesia* – Indonesian Journalists Association
Repelita *Rencana Pembangunan Lima Tahun* – Five-Year Development Plan
RIS *Republik Indonesia Serikat* – Republic of the United States of Indonesia
RMS *Republik Maluku Selatan* – Republic of the South Moluccas
Rp rupiah
RPKAD *Resimen Pasukan Komando Angkatan Darat* – Army Commando Regiment (later Kopassandha and later again Kopassus)
RRI *Radio Republik Indonesia* – Republic of Indonesia Radio
RTP *Resimen Tempur* – Battle Regiment

Rukun Istri Ampera Pembangunan an association of cabinet members' wives formed by Ibu Tien in 1966

sawah wet rice-fields

SBSI *Serikat Buruh Sejahtera Indonesia* – Indonesian Prosperous Workers' Union

Sekber Golkar *Sekretariat Bersama Golongan Karya* – Joint Secretariat of Functional Groups

Seskoad *Sekolah Staf dan Komando Angkatan Darat* – Army Staff and Command School (SSKAD before 1961)

shodancho platoon commander (Japanese)

SOB *Staat van Oorlog en van Beleg* – State of War and Siege

SOBSI *Sentral Organisasi Buruh Seluruh Indonesia* – All-Indonesia Centre of Labour Organisations

SOKSI *Sentral Organisasi Karyawan Socialis Indonesia* – Central Organisation of Indonesian Socialist Employees

Spri *Staf Pribadi* – Personal Staff

SPSI *Serikat Pekerja Seluruh Indonesia* – All-Indonesia Association of Workers

SSKAD *Sekolah Staf dan Komando Angkatan Darat* – Army Staff and Command School (Seskoad from 1961)

SUAD General Staff

Supersemar *Surat Perintah Sebelas Maret* – Letter of Authority of 11 March

SWK sub-Wehrkreise

Taman Mini *Taman Mini Indonesia Indah* – Beautiful Indonesia-in-Miniature Park

Team to Combat Corruption *Team Pemberantasan Korupsi*

TII *Tentara Islam Indonesia* – Islamic Army of Indonesia

TKR *Tentara Keamanan Rakyat* – People's Defence Army (later *Tentara Keselamatan Rakyat* – People's Welfare Army)

TNI *Tentara Nasional Indonesia* – Indonesian National Army

TRI *Tentara Republik Indonesia* – Army of the Republic of Indonesia

Trikora *Tri Komando Rakyat* – Triple Command of the People

Trikora Orphan Foundation *Yayasan Yatim Piatu Trikora*

Tritura *Tri Tuntutan Rakyat* – Three Demands of the People

TT *Tentara dan Territorium* – military territorial region

TVRI national television broadcaster of the Republic of Indonesia

UDT *União Democrática Timorense* – Timorese Democratic Union

Wanjakti *Dewan Pertimbangan Jabatan dan Kepangkatan AD Tingkat Tinggi* – Advisory Council for Assignments and Ranks for the Senior Level of the Army

Wehrkreise independent military, political and economic defence area during the guerrilla struggle

WTO World Trade Organisation

yayasan charity foundation

YPTE *Yayasan Pembangunan Territorium Empat* – Fourth Territory Development Foundation

YTE *Yayasan Territorium Empat* – Fourth Territory Foundation

Notes

PREFACE

1 Vatikiotis, *Indonesian politics under Suharto,* 1993, p. 100.
2 Vatikiotis, 'Setting the scene for succession', *Far Eastern Economic Review* [hereafter *FEER*], 3 March 1988, p. 24.
3 McIntyre, 'Foreign biographical studies of Indonesian subjects', p. 294.
4 Tanter, 'Intelligence agencies and Third World militarization', p. 7.
5 Kingsbury, *The politics of Indonesia,* p. 3. See also Lyon, 'Mystical biography', p. 213.
6 Rae, 'Liberating and conciliating', p. 240.
7 Jackson, 'Bureaucratic polity', p. 5.
8 Ramage, *Politics in Indonesia,* p. 4.
9 These reports were empirically sound, even if they suggested a greater sense of order amongst the Indonesian fighting groups than actually existed.
10 Soeharto, *Pikiran.*
11 *Jejak langkah Pak Harto,* edited by Dwipayana and Nazaruddin and, after Dwipayana, by Nazaruddin alone.
12 Sundhaussen, *The road to power,* p. 195. Such characteristics are not, of course, found only in Indonesia.

1 BEGINNINGS AND YOUTH

1 This account, except where otherwise noted, is based upon Soeharto, *Pikiran,* pp. ix–x, 5–15; Roeder, *The smiling general,* pp. 81–8; Anon., 'Mengenal kehidupan Presiden Soeharto', pp. 47–8; 'Kata pendahuluan: uraian Bapak Probosutejo' and 'Penjelasan Presiden Soeharto tentang silsilah keturunan beliau di depan pers bertempat di Binagraha tanggal 28 Oktober 1974 jam 11.20 – 13.15 WIB', both in Suryohadi (ed.), *Silsilah Presiden Soeharto anak petani.* (The revamped version of Roeder's *The smiling general,* published as *Anak desa,* incorporates much of the material about Suharto's early life from Suryohadi's *Silsilah.*)
2 Soeharto, *Pikiran,* p. x.
3 Soeharto, *Pikiran,* p. x.
4 McDonald, *Suharto's Indonesia,* p. 9; Soeharto, *Pikiran,* p. 7.

5 *Ngebleng* involves deprivational practices aimed at the erasure of social identity and 'total self-abnegation before God' (Keeler, *Javanese shadow plays*, p. 45). See also Keeler, *Symbolic dimensions of the Javanese house.*
6 'Penjelasan', p. 29.
7 Soeharto, *Pikiran*, p. 231.
8 Vol. 2, no. 17.
9 McDonald (*Suharto's Indonesia*, p. 9) relates rumours that Suharto was 'a lost or unacknowledged son' of Hamengkubuwono VIII, father of the then Sultan of Yogyakarta. He also reports stories that Suharto was the offspring of a senior military officer at the court. Vatikiotis (*Indonesian politics*, 1993, p. 10) reported rumours that Sultan Hamengkubuwono IX had confirmed that Suharto was the son of a court retainer. Similar tales often emerged in my own interviews, including one that he was the son of a courtly servant entrusted with wielding the yellow parasol above the head of Sultan Hamengkubuwono VIII (interview with Sumiskum, Jakarta, 12 July 1997). See also Roeder, *Anak desa*, p. 140n. For a concise collection of gossip about Suharto's origins, see Wimandjaja K. Liotohe, *Primadosa*, pp. 26–7.
10 'Penjelasan', pp. 14, 34, 37.
11 Roeder, *The smiling general*, pp. 83–90; 'Penjelasan', pp. 21–9; Anon., 'Mengenal kehidupan Presiden Soeharto', p. 47; Soeharto, *Pikiran*, p. 6; 'Kata pendahuluan', p. 6; Anon., *Soeharto, President of the Republic of Indonesia*, p. 2; Suharto, 'Watashi no rirekisho' ['My personal history'], *Nihon Keizai Shimbun*, part 3, 4 January 1998, p. 40.
12 Soeharto, *Pikiran*, p. 7.
13 Anon., 'Isu Soeharto Cina, siapa bapaknya?', wysiwyg://47/ http://www.geocities.com/CapitolHill/4120/soeharto.html, accessed 26 January 2000.
14 'Suharto lived in the village until the age of 19' (*Kompas*, 23 March 1973).
15 Soeharto, *Pikiran*, p. 13.
16 Suharto, 'Watashi', part 3, 4 January 1998, p. 40.
17 Roeder, *The smiling general*, p. 93.
18 *Kompas*, 23 March 1973.
19 Penders, *Milestones on my journey*, p. 50. See also O'Malley, 'Indonesia in the Great Depression', pp. 185–6.
20 Soeharto, *Pikiran*, p. 16.
21 Soeharto, *Pikiran*, p. 16.
22 Soeharto, *Pikiran*, pp. 230–1.
23 Soeharto, *Pikiran*, pp. 235–6.
24 Cited in Toriq Hadad, 'Mengayunkan langkah keenam', *Tempo*, 13 March 1993, p. 16.
25 Soeharto, *Pikiran*, p. 297.
26 Syahrir, cited in Mrazek, *Sjahrir*, p. 26.
27 Sukarno, *An autobiography as told to Cindy Adams*, p. 39.
28 McIntyre, *Soeharto's composure*, p. 16; Soeharto, *Pikiran*, p. 231.
29 Soeharto, *Pikiran*, p. 17; Suharto, 'Watashi', part 4, 5 January 1998, p. 40.
30 Two-thirds of KNIL personnel were Indonesians, although only a very small number of them were officers. There were almost 13,000 Javanese in service in 1937 (Zwitser and Heshusius, *Het Koninklijk*, p. 10).
31 Soeharto, *Pikiran*, p. 20; Suharto, 'Watashi', part 4, 5 January 1998, p. 40.
32 Soeminto (ed.), *Presiden dan wakil Presiden*, p. 281; Roeder, *The smiling general*, p. 97; *Kompas*, 15 October 1965.

33 Soeharto, *Pikiran*, p. 22.
34 Soeharto, *Pikiran*, pp. 22, 23. He seems to have paid only cursory attention to the requirement of learning Japanese (Suharto, 'Watashi', part 5, 6 January 1998, p. 40).
35 Oudang, *Perkembangan kepolisian*, p. 36.
36 Soeharto, *Pikiran*, p. 23; Suharto, 'Watashi', part 5, 6 January 1998, p. 40.
37 Nugroho, *The PETA-army in Indonesia*, p. 17.
38 Suharto, 'Watashi', part 5, 6 January 1998, p. 40.
39 Nugroho, *The PETA-army*, p. 3.
40 Soeharto, *Pikiran*, p. 24. See also Nugroho, *The Peta army during the Japanese occupation*, p. 116.
41 *Kompas*, 28 March 1968.
42 Soeharto, *Pikiran*, p. 25; Suharto, 'Watashi', part 5, 6 January 1998, p. 40.
43 Nugroho, *The PETA-army*, p. 20.
44 George Kahin, *Nationalism and revolution in Indonesia*, p. 109; Benedict Anderson, *Java in a time of revolution*, p. 24.
45 The bundan (squad) usually consisted of about ten men, commanded by a bundancho; there were usually four bundan in one platoon (shodan) (Nugroho, *The Peta army*, p. 131).
46 Anderson, *Java*, p. 15.
47 Soeharto, *Pikiran*, p. 27.
48 Kahin, *Nationalism and revolution*, p. 130.
49 B. R. O'G. Anderson, 'Japan: "The light of Asia"', p. 21.

2 SOLDIER IN THE REVOLUTION

1 Indeed, in George Kahin's classic analysis of the struggle (*Nationalism and revolution in Indonesia*), Suharto is not once mentioned.
2 Feith, *The decline of constitutional democracy in Indonesia*, p. 18.
3 Interview with Dayno, in Widadi, 'Kata Bung Karno kamu harus sadarkan Soeharto', *De Tak*, 29 September–5 October 1998, p. 11; Anon., 'Kolonel (Purn.) Marsudi: "Saya sudah mengingatkan Pak Harto"', *Forum Keadilan*, 26 December 1999, p. 82; Anon., 'Kampung politik bernama Pathuk', *Adil*, 30 September–6 October 1998, p. 6; interview with Sumarsono, Sydney, 30 June 1999. According to Marsudi, a military subordinate of Suharto, this group had no particular political affiliations or leanings. Others have later seen Suharto's involvement with the Pathuk group in more sinister terms. According to Wertheim ('Whose plot?', p. 203), Syam was working as a cadre for the Indonesian Socialist Party, and often hosted Suharto at his house. Another source describes the Pathuk group as a leftist group which included Suharto, Syam and Untung Samsuri, another key figure in the 1965 'coup', amongst its members, and long-time communist Alimin as one of its intellectual leaders/propagandists (*pembina*) (Anon., 'Agen RI-CIA-KGB bicara keterlibatan Soeharto', *De Tak*, 29 September–5 October 1998). Some claim that Suharto himself had nationalist communist (Murba) leanings at this time (interview with Anton, in Anon., 'Saat itulah, Soeharto mulai didekati CIA', *De Tak*, 29 September–5 October 1998). Syam, according to a recent source, took part in the battles of Magelang, Semarang and Ambarawa in 1945 and early 1946, and led a leftist fighting group based in Yogya (Anon., *Gerakan 30 September antara fakta dan rekayasa*, p. 15). According to other reports (*Sinar Harapan*, 13 March 1967; Saur Hutabarat, 'Eksekusi bulan September',

Tempo, 11 October 1986, p. 15), Syam was a member of Suharto's Battalion X in Yogyakarta in 1945.

4 A. H. Nasution, *Sekitar perang kemerdekaan Indonesia*, vol. 1, pp. 357–8.
5 The TKR's name was changed to People's Welfare Army on 7 January 1946, to TRI (Army of the Republic of Indonesia) on 25 January 1946, and finally to TNI (Indonesian National Army) on 3 June 1947.
6 Kahin, *Nationalism and revolution*, p. 164.
7 Benedict Anderson, *Java in a time of revolution*, p. 106.
8 Soeharto, *Pikiran*, p. 28.
9 Tuti Indra Malaon and Drigo L. Tobing, 'Say tak mau jadi godfather' (interview with Y. B. Mangunwijaya), *Matra*, 21 April 1988, p. 22.
10 'Report by Wing Commander T. S. Tull OBE on Operation Salex Mastiff, Mid-Java, 10th September to 15th December 1945', part I, p. 7, Indische Collectie no. 007414-007453, Nederlands Instituut voor Oorlogsdocumentatie.
11 'Report by ... Tull', part III, p. 15.
12 Anderson, *Java*, p. 151.
13 Soeharto, *Pikiran*, p. 36.
14 'Penjelasan Presiden Soeharto tentang silsilah keturunan beliau di depan pers bertempat di Binagraha tanggal 28 Oktober 1974 jam 11.20 – 13.15 WIB', in Suryohadi (ed.), *Silsilah Presiden Soeharto anak petani*, p. 30.
15 Soeharto, *Pikiran*, p. 36.
16 Malik, *In the service of the Republic*, p. 15.
17 Salim Said, *Genesis of power*, p. 84.
18 This account is based upon Anon., *Putusan*, pp. 88–9.
19 Soeharto, *Pikiran*, p. 38.
20 The text of these draft proclamations can be found in Nasution, *Sekitar*, vol. 3, pp. 346–8.
21 Anon., *Putusan*, p. 89.
22 Nasution, *Sekitar*, vol. 4, p. 479.
23 Netherlands Forces Intelligence Service [hereafter NEFIS]. Afdeeling Militaire Intelligence [hereafter AMI]. Wekelijks Militair Overzicht [hereafter MO] [21 February 1947], Hoofdkwartier van de Generale Staf van het Leger in Indonesië [hereafter HKGS], GG5, no. 101a, Ministerie van Defensie, Centraal Archievendepot, Rijswijk [hereafter MvD].
24 'Wekelijks Territoriaal Inlichtingen Rapport' [hereafter WTIR], no. 27 [27 September 1949], HKGS, GG61, no. 7646a, MvD.
25 NEFIS. AMI. MO [17 and 31 October 1947], HKGS, GG5, no. 101e, MvD.
26 Suharto, 'Watashi', part 7, 8 January 1998, p. 40.
27 Roeder, *The smiling general*, p. 116.
28 Gafur, *Siti Hartinah*, pp. 47, 121.
29 Soeharto, *Pikiran*, p. 45.
30 Suharto, 'Watashi', part 7, 8 January 1998, pp. 38, 40.
31 NEFIS. AMI. MO no. 48/3 [24 January 1948], HKGS, GG31, no. 438, MvD.
32 NEFIS. AMI. MO no. 48/5 [7 February 1948], HKGS, GG37, no. 4382, MvD.
33 McVey, 'The post-revolutionary transformation', part I, p. 137.
34 NEFIS. AMI. MO no. 48/14 [10 April 1948], HKGS, GG31, no. 438, MvD.
35 NEFIS. AMI. MO no. 48/16 [14 June 1948], HKGS, GG37, no. 4382, MvD.
36 NEFIS. AMI. MO no. 48/19 [17 July 1948], HKGS, GG31, no. 438, MvD.

37 Overzicht en Ontwikkeling van de Toestand [hereafter OOT] [9 August 1948], KSHKGS, AA19, no. 1, MvD.
38 OOT [4 February 1949], KSHKGS, AA21, no. 1, MvD.
39 NEFIS. AMI. MO [14 March 1947], HKGS, GG5, no. 101b, MvD.
40 Kahin, *Nationalism and revolution*, p. 251; David Anderson, 'The military aspects', p. 1.
41 'A. Traject Salatiga-Bojolali-Klaten-Djocja. (gegevens t/m Augustus 1948)', Algemeen-Archief van de Centrale Militaire Inlichtingendienst (NEFIS) [hereafter AACMI], AA15, MvD.
42 Nasution, *Sekitar*, vol. 8, p. 222.
43 Soeharto, *Pikiran*, p. 50.
44 Soeharto, *Pikiran*, pp. 44–5. Anderson's account ('The military aspects', p. 27n) accords with Suharto's.
45 Salim Said, *Genesis*, p. 77.
46 According to Sumarsono (interview, Sydney, 30 June 1999), Suharto signed a statement (prepared by Sumarsono) to that effect, published in the local newspaper within a day or two. Sumarsono claimed that Suharto stayed in Madiun for three days.
47 Salim Said, *Genesis*, p. 77.
48 'Centrale Militaire Inlichtingendienst (CMI). Signalement No. 26' [8 October 1948], NEFIS, no. 1017, Ministerie van Buitenlandse Zaken [hereafter MBZ].
49 NEFIS. AMI. Order of Battle TRI (Java, Bali) [hereafter OB] [15 November 1948], KSHKGS, AA10, no. 22, MvD.
50 Suharto himself speaks of the continuing and fruitless discussions between the Dutch and the Republic 'bringing on a sense of weariness in me' (Soeharto, *Pikiran*, p. 56).
51 Nasution, *Fundamentals of guerrilla warfare*, p. 116.
52 Sukarno, *An autobiography*, p. 252.
53 'Verslag No 5 van de R.V.D.-agent H. Leopold, "Indrukken Djokja"' [24 December 1948], Archief van de Algemene Secretarie van de Nederlands–Indische Regering en de daarbij gedeponeerde archieven, 1942–50, no. 5538, Algemeen Rijksarchief, The Hague [hereafter ARA]. Emphasis in original.
54 Interview with Michael Vatikiotis, 26 July 1990, cited in Vatikiotis, *Indonesian politics*, p. 21.
55 Soeharto, *Pikiran*, p. 57.
56 Quoted in *Kompas*, 2 March 1973.
57 Nasution, *Sekitar*, vol. 10, p. 34.
58 Simatupang, *Report from Banaran*, p. 664.
59 Nasution, *Fundamentals*, p. 137.
60 'Desaverdediging' [accompanying letter of 29 December 1949], Notebook of 2nd Lt. K. Meijer (Archief NI 45–50, 0101/1A), Archives Sectie Militaire Geschiedenis, Koninklijk Landmacht, The Hague.
61 Simatupang, *Report from Banaran*, p. 63.
62 'Penjelasan', p. 30.
63 'Reorganisatie/Dislocatie Divisie III MA 19 December 1948' [11 March 1949], HKGS, GG51, no. 631, MvD.
64 Except where otherwise noted, this paragraph is based upon Soeharto, *Pikiran*, pp. 56–64; *Kompas*, 2 March 1973.

65 OOT [13 January, and 3 February 1949 to 10 February 1949], HKGS, GG51, nos 629 and 631, MvD.
66 OOT [13 January 1949], HKGS, GG51, no. 631, MvD.
67 *Merdeka*, 25 February 1949.
68 OOT [13 January 1949], HKGS, GG51, no. 631, MvD.
69 Reid, *Indonesian national revolution*, p. 155.
70 Nasution, *Fundamentals*, p. 199.
71 Kahin, *Nationalism and revolution*, p. 395 and note; see also Kahin's 'Some recollections and reflections', p. 13 and note.
72 OOT [13 January 1949], HKGS, GG51, no. 631, MvD (the *Tentara Pelajar* was a generally pro-government student armed force; it may well have been at Suharto's direction); OOT [25 February 1949] KSHKGS, AA21, no. 1, MvD.
73 Soeharto, *Pikiran*, p. 61.
74 'Analyse van de situatie in het stadsgebied Djocja' [8 February 1949], HKGS, GG55, no. 4859, MvD.
75 Roeder, *The smiling general*, p. 124; note the passive voice.
76 Nasution, *Sekitar*, vol. 10, p. 585 (see also Nasution interview with Vatikiotis, 11 November 1989, in Vatikiotis, *Indonesian politics*, p. 13); Simatupang, *Report from Banaran*, p. 65.
77 Salim Said, *Genesis*, p. 126; see also Salim Said, 'Seorang raja di garis depan', *Tempo*, 23 August 1986, p. 18. Selo Sumarjan (interview, Jakarta, 15 June 1998) was of the view that the strategic thinking behind the idea was fundamentally the sultan's, although Suharto may have formulated the operational plan.
78 Although Suharto later claimed that 'supporting the diplomatic struggle' was one of the major aims of this and other attacks (*Kompas*, 2 March 1973), and that the idea of the general attack came to him while listening to broadcast reports of Dutch claims about the success of their 'police action' (*Pikiran*, p. 60).
79 Anon., 'Republic under siege', p. 186. See also Nanang Junaedi et al., 'Serangan Oemoem 1 Maret 1949: Soeharto cuma pelaksana lapangan', *Tajuk*, 4–17 March 1999, via apakabar@saltmine.radix.net; Budiman S. Hartoyo et al., 'Lebih besar dari tahtanya', *Tempo*, 8 October 1988, p. 30.
80 'Rapport volgno. 718 van T.I.G. Djocja dd. 6 Mei 1949 volgno. 12159', NEFIS, no. 2871, MBZ. Jatikusumo was the uncle of the Susuhunan of Solo.
81 Nasution, *Sekitar*, vol. 10, p. 94.
82 Anon., 'Kolonel (Purn.) Marsudi', p. 82.
83 OOT [25 February 1949], KSHKGS, MvD, AA21, no. 1, MvD.
84 Lapré, *Het Andjing NICA Bataljon*, n.p.
85 *Kompas*, 2 March 1973.
86 Sedjarah Militer Kodam VII/Diponegoro, *Sedjarah TNI-AD Kodam VII*, p. 191.
87 Soeharto, *Pikiran*, p. 62.
88 Regerings Voorlichtingsdienst. Indonesische Pers en Radio [5 March 1949 and 7 March 1949], Rapportage Indonesië, no. 74, ARA.
89 Roeder, *The smiling general*, p. 125.
90 Sedjarah Militer Kodam VII/Diponegoro, p. 192.
91 Anon., *Serangan Umum 1 Maret 1949*, p. 248.
92 Salim Said, *Genesis*, p. 109; Gafur, *Siti Hartinah*, p. 154.
93 Anon., *Peranan TNI Angkatan Darat*, p. 160; Anon., *Soeharto*, pp. 1, 6.
94 Kahin, *Nationalism and revolution*, p. 411; Reid, *Indonesian national revolution*, p. 153.

95 'Overzicht Nr. 30 van de plaats gehad hebbende acties in Indonesië' [2 March 1949], HKGS GG69, no. C, MvD.
96 'Verslag van de bespreking ten huize van Kolonel van Langen te Djokjakarta op Dinsdag 2 Maart 12.00', Collectie Spoor, no. 93, ARA.
97 Telegram from PXTT, 2 March 1949, HKGS, ZGZG 5, no. 29, MvD.
98 Report of Military Observers Capitaine de Corvette Brasseur-Kermadec (French Navy) and Lt. A. G. Thalhamer (US Navy), attached to letter Acting Chairman Netherlands Delegation to Minister of Foreign Territories, 12 March 1949, Archief Indonesische Kwestie: Indonesië in de Veiligheidsraad [hereafter IKVN], no. 999, MBZ.
99 Soeharto, *Pikiran*, p. 62.
100 According to the sultan, the Playen broadcast was made to the republican receiver in Bukittinggi, and then relayed to India for further distribution (Anon., 'Republic under siege', p. 186). See also *Kompas Online*, 16 March 1997, via indonesia-p@indopubs.com.
101 Soeharto, *Pikiran*, p. 62.
102 Soeharto, *Pikiran*, p. 62.
103 Nasution, *Sekitar*, vol. 11, p. 264.
104 WTIR no. 4 [2 April 1949], HKGS, GG62, no. 7788, MvD.
105 'Report no. 7 Team 7 Jogja Java', Milobs rapporten September 1948–August 1949, IKVN, no. 999, MBZ.
106 *Merdeka*, 21 March 1949.
107 WTIR no. 6 [15 April 1949], HKGS, GG62, no. 7788, MvD.
108 Nasution, *Sekitar*, vol. 10, p. 95.
109 Anon., *Peranan*, p. 160 (see also pp. 161–2).
110 Soeharto, *Pikiran*, p. 65.
111 Anon., 'Several Indonesian views of the struggle', p. 208.
112 Kahin, *Nationalism and revolution*, p. 411.
113 Report of Military Observers.
114 A. H. Nasution, *Memenuhi panggilan tugas*, vol. 2, p. 135.
115 Nasution, *Sekitar*, vol. 10, pp. 103, 590.
116 WTIR no. 13 [3 June 1949], KSHKGS, AA22, no. 6, MvD.
117 Nasution, *Sekitar*, vol. 10, pp. 557–8.
118 'Vertaling 4A: "Een beschouwing van de activiteiten der partijen vanaf de aanval der Nederlanders op Jogja tot de sluiting der overeenkomst op 7 Me"' [23 June 1949], AACMI, AA16, MvD.
119 Letter J. B. van Oerthal and V. W. Gontha to Director CMI Batavia, 17 May 1949, NEFIS, no. 2741, MBZ.
120 'Volg. No. 5843 – dd. 8 Mrt '49 – OOT – HKGS 10X', NEFIS, no. 2871, MBZ.
121 WTIR no. 13 [3 June 1949], HKGS, GG62, no. 7788, MvD.
122 WTIR no. 10 [13 May 1949], HKGS, GG62, no. 7788, MvD.
123 Soeharto, *Pikiran*, p. 65; see also *Kompas*, 23 March 1973.
124 WTIR no. 13 [3 June 1949], HKGS, GG62, no. 7788, MvD.
125 Soeharto, *Pikiran*, p. 67; *Merdeka*, 2 July 1949.
126 What follows is based entirely on sometimes garbled and often alarmist and misleading Dutch intelligence reports; the problems of interpreting them are heightened by the fact that the timing and sequence of events are far from clear in the documentation.
127 WTIR no. 17 [1 July 1949], HKGS, GG62, no. 7788a, MvD.

128 Soeharto, *Pikiran*, p. 67.
129 WTIR no. 18 [8 July 1949], KSHKGS, AA22, no. 6, MvD.
130 Reid, *Indonesian national revolution*, p. 155.
131 Marsudi remembers him as 'resolute. Brave ... calm and hard' (Anon., 'Kolonel (Purn.) Marsudi', p. 82). Abdul Latief, with reason to be unkind to Suharto, later remarked that 'as a military man [Suharto's] disposition was tough [*stroef*], rigid and rather taciturn. Those below him rarely dared to come to meet with him' (Interview in Mindo, 'Mereka melaksanakan perintah Sjam', *De Tak*, 29 September–5 October 1998, p. 21).
132 McVey, 'The post-revolutionary transformation', part I, p. 142.
133 Tjokropranolo, *Panglima Besar TNI Jenderal Soedirman*, pp. 181–3; Nasution, *Memenuhi panggilan tugas*, vol. 2, p. 174.
134 Soeharto, *Pikiran*, pp. 72–3.
135 This conviction was shared by nearly all the Indonesian elite (Cribb and Brown, *Modern Indonesia*, p. 32).
136 It is, perhaps, noteworthy that Sukarno makes no mention of the general attack of 1 March in his autobiography.

3 CENTRAL JAVA COMMANDS

1 This paragraph is based on Van Dijk, *Rebellion under the banner of Islam*, pp. 163–4; Sundhaussen, *The road to power*, pp. 55–6; Feith, *The decline of constitutional democracy*, pp. 67–9.
2 What follows is based upon Bardosono, *Peristiwa Sulawesi Selatan*, pp. 92–4.
3 Roeder, *The smiling general*, pp. 130–1.
4 Roeder, *The smiling general*, p. 131. See also Soeharto, *Pikiran*, pp. 80–1.
5 Soeharto, *Pikiran*, p. 78.
6 Sedjarah Militer Kodam VI Siliwangi, *Siliwangi dari masa ke masa*, p. 414.
7 Van Dijk, *Rebellion*, pp. 165–6.
8 Suharto claims (*Pikiran*, p. 80) that this stipulation was made at his insistence.
9 For a description of the process, see Harvey, 'Tradition, Islam and rebellion', pp. 214–17.
10 Penders and Sundhaussen, *Abdul Haris Nasution*, p. 55.
11 Suharto, 'Watashi', part 8, 9 January 1998, p. 40.
12 Gafur, *Siti Hartinah*, p. 181.
13 McDonald, *Suharto's Indonesia*, p. 29.
14 Gafur, *Siti Hartinah*, pp. 181–2.
15 Soeharto, *Pikiran*, p. 83.
16 Soeharto, *Pikiran*, p. 83. See Van Dijk, *Rebellion*, for the most complete treatment of the Darul Islam rebellion. Hizbullah was the general name given to Muslim fighting bands in the revolutionary period.
17 Sedjarah Militer Kodam VII/Diponegoro, *Sedjarah Tentara Nasional*, p. 392; Van Dijk, *Rebellion*, p. 150.
18 Feith, *Decline*, pp. 207–8.
19 Sewaka, *Tjoret-tjaret*, p. 309.
20 'Merdeka' was the name commonly given to government military operations established to overcome recalcitrant irregular fighting elements.
21 Van Dijk, *Rebellion*, p. 153; Anon., '"Pembersihan" dan pembersihan', *Siasat*, 17 February 1952, p. 6.

22 Van Dijk, *Rebellion*, p. 410n.
23 Anon., 'Bataljon 426', *Siasat*, 3 February 1952, p. 6.
24 A. H. Nasution, *Fundamentals of guerrilla warfare*, pp. 77–8. See also Nasution, *Memenuhi panggilan tugas*, vol. 2, pp. 320, 321, for a more oblique criticism of Suharto.
25 Soeharto, *Pikiran*, p. 85.
26 The GBN (Buffalo Operation) area took in the north-western part of Central Java, especially the regions of Pekalongan and Tegal.
27 'Kata pendahuluan: uraian Bapak Probosutejo', in Suryohadi (ed.), *Silsilah Presiden Soeharto anak petani*, p. 7; Gafur, *Siti Hartinah*, pp. 183–4. Kertosudiro was buried in the plot of the Kepoh family, near the place of Suharto's birth ('Penjelasan', p. 33).
28 'Penjelasan Presiden Soeharto tentang silsilah keturunan beliau di depan pers bertempat di Binagraha tanggal 28 Oktober 1974 jam 11.20 – 13.15 WIB', in Suryohadi (ed.), *Silsilah Presiden Soeharto anak petani*, p. 30.
29 See Crouch, *The army and politics in Indonesia*, pp. 29–31; Sundhaussen, 'The military', p. 46.
30 Soeharto, *Pikiran*, p. 87.
31 McVey, 'The post-revolutionary transformation', part I, p. 150n. See also Nugroho Notosusanto (ed.), *Pejuang dan prajurit*, p. 71; Simatupang, *The fallacy of a myth*, p. 134.
32 Soeharto, *Pikiran*, p. 86. See also Gafur, *Siti Hartinah*, p. 185.
33 Roeder, *The smiling general*, p. 132.
34 Soeharto, *Pikiran*, p. 92; Roeder, *The smiling general*, p. 132.
35 Crouch, *The army and politics*, p. 31.
36 Feith, *Decline*, p. 379.
37 *Kedaulatan Rakyat*, 22 February 1955.
38 Soeharto, *Pikiran*, p. 88.
39 Roeder, *The smiling general*, p. 133.
40 Mossman, *Rebels in paradise*, p. 245.
41 McVey, 'The post-revolutionary transformation', part II, p. 168.
42 Feith, *Decline*, p. 403.
43 Lev, *The transition*, pp. 12, 15, 68.
44 Editorial, *Kedaulatan Rakyat*, 4 September 1956.
45 *Suara Merdeka*, 5 and 7 September, 5 October, 10 November, 3 December 1956.
46 Mody, *Indonesia under Suharto*, p. 51.
47 Wiwoho and Bandjar, *Memori Jenderal Yoga*, p. 80. Yoga's position meant that he was in regular contact with all regional commanders, and in this capacity he had come to know Suharto (p. 77).
48 McDonald, *Suharto's Indonesia*, p. 30.
49 Lev, *The transition*, pp. 16, 63.
50 *Merdeka*, 22 March 1957. See also Sundhaussen, *The road to power*, p. 131.
51 Lev, *The transition*, pp. 60, 61.
52 *Duta Masyarakat*, 25 March 1957.
53 See, for example, his speeches on Independence Day 1957 (*Suara Merdeka*, 16 August 1957), National Awakening Day in 1958 (*Kedaulatan Rakyat*, 21 May), Independence Day 1958 (*Kedaulatan Rakyat*, 18 August), and Heroes' Day in 1958 (*Kedaulatan Rakyat*, 10 November).
54 *Merdeka*, 27 March 1957.
55 *Merdeka*, 5 April 1957; *Duta Masyarakat*, 5 April 1957.

56 Suharto, 'Watashi', part 9, 10 January 1998, p. 40.
57 Soeharto, *Pikiran*, p. 90.
58 Wiwoho and Bandjar, *Memori Jenderal Yoga*, p. 82.
59 See the report of Suharto's press conference, which explained the mechanism for collecting development funds and the purposes to which they would be put (*Kedaulatan Rakyat*, 23 November 1957). Suharto also discussed the problem of reducing overpopulation, 'which can be achieved by means of transmigration, family planning, reducing the number of outsiders (*orang asing*) who come in, and so on'.
60 This and the following paragraph are mostly based on Malley, 'A political biography of Major General Soedjono Hoemardani', p. 35.
61 Soeharto, *Pikiran*, pp. 90, 92; see also Gafur, *Siti Hartinah*, p. 180.
62 Quoted in Soetriyono, *Kisah sukses Liem Sioe Liong*, p. 13.
63 Soetriyono, *Kisah*, pp. 13–14.
64 McDonald, *Suharto's Indonesia*, p. 120.
65 Soetriyono, *Kisah*, pp. 16, 44–5.
66 Sujono, interview with Ann Gregory (1969), quoted in Malley, 'Soedjono Hoemardani', p. 39.
67 Lev, *The transition*, p. 71.
68 Sujono, interview with Gregory (1969), cited in Malley, 'Soedjono Hoemardani', p. 34. Hemp was another crop targeted, in order to provide clothing for the people (*Kedaulatan Rakyat*, 12 August 1959).
69 *Kedaulatan Rakyat*, 21 January 1959.
70 Soeharto, *Pikiran*, p. 92.
71 Roeder, *The smiling general*, p. 133.
72 Soeharto, *Pikiran*, pp. 91, 248. See also Roeder, *The smiling general*, p. 135.
73 Quoted in Gafur, *Pak Harto*, pp. 101–2.
74 Sundhaussen, *The road to power*, p. 103.
75 Soeharto, *Pikiran*, p. 90.
76 Hatta, interview with George Kahin, 12 December 1958, cited in Audrey Kahin and George Kahin, *Subversion as foreign policy*, p. 279.
77 Sedjarah Militer Kodam VI Siliwangi, *Siliwangi*, p. 428.
78 Lev, *The transition*, p. 29. See also Sundhaussen, *The road to power*, p. 106.
79 *Kedaulatan Rakyat*, 31 December 1957.
80 Kahin and Kahin, *Subversion*, p. 280 (see also p. 198).
81 Lev, *The transition*, p. 148.
82 *Kedaulatan Rakyat*, 10 April 1958.
83 *Antara News Bulletin*, 3 and 4 September 1959; see also Wiwoho and Bandjar, *Memori Jenderal Yoga*, p. 104.
84 Lev, *The transition*, pp. 134–5.
85 Mossman, *Rebels*, p. 247.
86 Lev, *The transition*, p. 191.
87 The SSKAD abbreviation was changed to Seskoad in early 1961.
88 *Kedaulatan Rakyat*, 5 October 1959.
89 *Duta Masyarakat*, 17 July 1957.
90 Aidit, *Indonesian society and the Indonesian revolution*, p. 43 (see also p. 66).
91 Lev, *The transition*, p. 9.
92 Aidit, *Indonesian society*, p. 52.
93 Lev, *The transition*, p. 10.
94 Lev, *The transition*, p. 92.

95 Sundhaussen, *The road to power*, p. 132.
96 *Antara News Bulletin*, 6 and 7 August, 5 September 1959; *Duta Masyarakat*, 8 August 1959; *Merdeka*, 8 August 1959.
97 *Antara News Bulletin*, 20 July 1959.
98 *Duta Masyarakat*, 16 October 1959. The remainder of this paragraph is based upon this source.
99 Gafur, *Siti Hartinah*, pp. 180–1.
100 Mossman, *Rebels*, p. 247.
101 Ramadhan, *Soemitro*, p. 265. A report in *Duta Masyarakat*, 11 May 1959, mentions the construction of infantry barracks at Mujen, near Magelang. The construction of a channel to provide the barracks with water was alone estimated to cost Rp1 million.
102 Anon., 'Kolonel (Purn.) Marsudi: "Saya sudah mengingatkan Pak Harto"', p. 82.
103 McVey, 'A preliminary excursion', p. 80.
104 Wiwoho and Bandjar, *Memori Jenderal Yoga*, p. 119.
105 Nasution, *Memenuhi*, vol. 5, p. 24.
106 Sundhaussen, *The road to power*, p. 64.
107 Soeharto, *Pikiran*, p. 92.
108 Roeder, *The smiling general*, p. 135.
109 Wiwoho and Bandjar, *Memori Jenderal Yoga*, p. 119.
110 Ali Moertopo, 'Pak Harto', p. 36.
111 Sujono, interview with Ruth McVey (1981), quoted in Malley, 'Soedjono Hoemardani', p. 36.
112 *Duta Masyarakat*, 19 October 1959.
113 Soeharto, *Pikiran*, pp. 93, 94.
114 Roeder, *The smiling general*, p. 134.
115 McVey, 'A preliminary excursion', p. 7.

4 HIGH OFFICE

1 Cited in Roeder, *The smiling general*, p. 135. (The abbreviation SSKAD was changed in 1961 to Seskoad.)
2 Suharto, 'Watashi', part 10, 11 January 1998, p. 32.
3 Soeharto, *Pikiran*, p. 94.
4 McDonald, *Suharto's Indonesia*, p. 33. See also Reeve, *Golkar of Indonesia*, pp. 185–97.
5 Suwarto, 'Suatu "approach"', p. 33.
6 Suwarto and Kartomo, 'Bantuan Angkatan Perang', pp. 309–10.
7 *Merdeka*, 19 December 1960. See also *Merdeka*, 15 January 1962; *Suluh Indonesia*, 20 July 1963.
8 Suharto et al., 'Perang wilayah sebagai konsepsi pertahan Indonesia', pp. 9–27.
9 Suharto et al., 'Perang', pp. 12, 15, 20, 27.
10 Anon., 'Kesimpulan dan hasil pembahasan persoalan kedua', pp. 62–6.
11 Anon., 'Pembahasan dan pendapat kelompok^2 seminar terhadap hasil telaahan militer kelompok III jang disimpulkan', p. 67.
12 McDonald, *Suharto's Indonesia*, p. 34. Interviews with Subroto, Jakarta, 20 June 1998, 4 February 1999; Sadli, 'Recollections of my career', p. 39. Suharto fails to mention them in his autobiographical treatment of his SSKAD days.
13 Soeharto, *Pikiran*, p. 94.
14 Roeder, *The smiling general*, p. 135.

15 McVey, 'A preliminary excursion', p. 6. Benedict Anderson ('Old state, new society', p. 111) suggests that Sukarno may have agreed to Suharto's appointment because Suharto had not had officer training in the United States.
16 Soeharto, *Pikiran*, p. 95.
17 McVey, 'The post-revolutionary transformation', part II, p. 177.
18 Soeharto, *Pikiran*, p. 102.
19 *Merdeka*, 20 December 1961.
20 *Duta Masyarakat*, 10 January 1962; *Merdeka*, 10 January 1962. Soeharto (*Pikiran*, p. 103) dates his appointment as Mandala commander from 23 January, the date of Sukarno's letter of appointment.
21 Soeharto, *Pikiran*, p. 103. (Sapta Marga is the Soldier's Oath.)
22 *Merdeka*, 10 and 15 January 1962.
23 *Duta Masyarakat*, 1 January 1962.
24 *Duta Masyarakat*, 16 January 1962.
25 *Duta Masyarakat*, 24 January 1962.
26 *Merdeka*, 26 January 1962.
27 McDonald, *Suharto's Indonesia*, p. 35.
28 Cited in Cholil, *Sedjarah*, p. 51.
29 *Suluh Indonesia*, 21 April 1962.
30 Pour, *Laksamana Sudomo*, pp. 122–3.
31 Soeharto, *Pikiran*, p. 104. See also Anon., *Tri Komando Rakyat*, p. 93, based on an interview with Suharto in 1987.
32 Mackie, *Konfrontasi*, p. 100.
33 Gafur, *Pak Harto*, p. 9. See also Panitia Penyusun Sejarah Kostrad, *Kostrad dharma putra*, p. 36; Soeharto, *Pikiran*, p. 107.
34 *Suluh Indonesia*, 24 July 1962.
35 Soeharto, *Pikiran*, p. 106.
36 De Geus, *De Nieuw-Guinea kwestie*, p. 186. It appears that both Yamin and Subandrio thought Suharto's plan for an amphibious assault on Biak too adventurous (Anon., *Tri Komando Rakyat*, p. 263).
37 Quoted in Roeder, *The smiling general*, p. 132.
38 Soeharto, *Pikiran*, p. 108.
39 Quoted in Roeder, *The smiling general*, p. 137.
40 Soeharto, *Pikiran*, p. 109. See also Anon., *Tri Komando Rakyat*, p. 269.
41 *Suluh Indonesia*, 26 September 1962.
42 Soeharto, *Pikiran*, pp. 109–10.
43 *Suluh Indonesia*, 20 May 1963.
44 *Suluh Indonesia*, 24 May 1963; *Harian Rakyat*, 23 May 1963; *Merdeka*, 23 May 1963.
45 McVey, 'The post-revolutionary transformation', II, p. 177.
46 This paragraph is based on Panitia Penyusun Sejarah Kostrad, *Kostrad dharma putra*, pp. 83–6.
47 Soeharto, *Pikiran*, p. 111.
48 Roeder, *The smiling general*, pp. 8–9. This view, however, seems to be at odds with Suharto's earlier claimed scepticism about the Nasakom idea, related in chapter 3.
49 Soeharto, *Pikiran*, p. 112. See also Suharto, 'Watashi', part 10, 11 January 1998, p. 32.
50 Mackie, *Konfrontasi*, p. 110.

51 The specific story is most persuasively and elegantly told in Mackie, *Konfrontasi.* For penetrating analyses of domestic political alignments, see Feith's 'Dynamics of Guided Democracy', and his 'President Sukarno, the army and the communists', pp. 969–80.
52 Mackie, *Konfrontasi*, pp. 84, 134, 178. See also Sundhaussen, *The road to power*, p. 166.
53 Crouch, *The army and politics*, p. 70 (see also p. 61).
54 Mackie, *Konfrontasi*, p. 214.
55 Crouch, *The army and politics*, p. 204.
56 Roeder, *The smiling general*, p. 139.
57 *Suluh Indonesia*, 11 July 1964.
58 Crouch, *The army and politics*, p. 72.
59 Soeharto, *Pikiran*, p. 115.
60 Mackie, *Konfrontasi*, p. 213.
61 Mackie, *Konfrontasi*, p. 216.
62 *Suluh Indonesia*, 18 and 19 August 1965.
63 Kahin and Kahin, *Subversion as foreign policy*, p. 223.
64 In an interview in 1997, Murdani told me that great confusion surrounded the military aspects of the Confrontation. No one knew what should be done, or why. The response of the Army was to look busy, but to make sure that no long-term or serious damage was done.
65 Soeharto, *Pikiran*, p. 115.
66 Panitia Penyusun Sejarah Kostrad, *Kostrad dharma putra*, p. 51.
67 McDonald, *Suharto's Indonesia*, p. 39.
68 Crouch, *The army and politics*, p. 21.
69 Crouch, *The army and politics*, pp. 87–8.
70 Polomka, *Indonesia since Sukarno*, p. 70. See also Mackie, *Konfrontasi*, pp. 93–4; Legge, *Sukarno*; Hauswedell, 'Sukarno', pp. 108–43.
71 Crouch, *The army and politics*, p. 82.
72 Roeder, *The smiling general*, p. 139.
73 Crouch, *The army and politics*, pp. 24–5, 81–2; Dewi Fortuna Anwar, *Indonesia's strategic culture*, p. 24.
74 Soebandrio, 'Kesaksianku', p. 8.
75 Yani, *Ahmad Yani*, p. 280; Brackman, *The communist collapse*, p. 50, based on an interview with Umar Wirahadikusumah.
76 Roeder, *The smiling general*, pp. 138–9.
77 Reeve, *Golkar*, pp. 243–4.
78 Mody, *Indonesia under Suharto*, p. 4.
79 Crouch, *The army and politics*, pp. 94, 121.
80 Sundhaussen, *The road to power*, p. 200. Sukendro, fortunately for himself, was in China on 1 October 1965.
81 Hughes, *Indonesian upheaval*, p. 103.

5 THE COUP ATTEMPT

1 Gafur, *Siti Hartinah*, pp. 201–2; Suharto interview with Brackman, cited in Brackman, *The communist collapse*, p. 100. See also Crouch, *The army and politics*, p. 124n.
2 Gafur, *Siti Hartinah*, p. 202; Soeharto, *Pikiran*, p. 118.

3 Soeharto, *Pikiran*, p. 118. See also Brackman, *The communist collapse*, p. 97; Soeharto, 'Pidato sambutan Men/Pangad Mayor Jenderal TNI Soeharto di depan PB. Front Nasional (15 Oktober 1965)', in Alex Dinuth (ed.), *Dokumen terpilih sekitar G.30.S/PKI* (Jakarta: Intermas, 1997), pp. 105–18.
4 Soeharto, *Pikiran*, p. 118.
5 Suharto interview with Brackman, quoted in Brackman, *The communist collapse*, p. 98.
6 An English translation of the text of this radio address can be found in Anderson and McVey, *A preliminary analysis*, pp. 121–2.
7 Soeharto, *Pikiran*, p. 119. The following material is based upon Soeharto, *Pikiran*, pp. 119–20. The reference to Alimin is curious, presumably a reference to his alleged propaganda role amongst Suharto's troops in Solo in the 1950s. Its mention in this context is presumably to demonstrate the alleged role of the PKI in masterminding the 'coup attempt', as well as Suharto's own sharp-mindedness in realising the 'fact' so early.
8 Quoted in Brackman, *The communist collapse*, p. 98.
9 Crouch, *The army and politics*, p. 97.
10 Soeharto, *Pikiran*, pp. 120–1.
11 Nugroho and Ismael, *The coup attempt*, p. 67.
12 Soeharto, *Pikiran*, p. 122 (see also pp. 123–4); Crouch, *The army and politics*, p. 130.
13 Soeharto, *Pikiran*, p. 122; Nugroho (ed.), *Pejuang dan prajurit*, p. 118; Hughes, *Indonesian upheaval*, p. 64.
14 Gafur, *Siti Hartinah*, p. 205; Sekretariat Agitasi-Propaganda CCPKI, *Buku putih*, p. 141; Nugroho and Ismael, *The coup attempt*, p. 35; USCIA, *Indonesia – 1965*, p. 17; Hughes, *Indonesian upheaval*, pp. 53–4; Oey, 'Sukarno and the pseudo-coup', pp. 121–2.
15 An English translation of this 'Decree No. 1' can be found in Anderson and McVey, *A preliminary analysis*, pp. 123–4.
16 USCIA, *Indonesia – 1965*, p. 47n.
17 Crouch, *The army and politics*, p. 128, citing Omar Dhani's trial evidence.
18 Gafur, *Siti Hartinah*, pp. 209–11.
19 Soeharto, *Pikiran*, p. 125; Dwipayana and Nazaruddin (eds), *Jejak langkah Pak Harto 1 Oktober 1965–27 Maret 1968*, p. 6; Anon, 'Kisah-kisah Oktober, 1965', *Tempo*, 6 October 1984, p. 14 (interview with Bambang Wijanarko).
20 Crouch, *The army and politics*, p. 131; Oey, 'Sukarno and the pseudo-coup', p. 126. See also McVey, 'A preliminary excursion', p. 102.
21 Crouch, *The army and politics*, p. 132.
22 Crouch, *The army and politics*, p. 98. See also Dwipayana and Nazaruddin (eds), *Jejak langkah Pak Harto*, p. 5; Sekretariat Agitasi-Propaganda CCPKI, *Buku putih*, p. 132.
23 Soeharto, *Pikiran*, p. 126.
24 Soeharto, *Pikiran*, p. 124.
25 The text of Suharto's address is presented in Soeharto, *Pikiran*, pp. 127–8.
26 USCIA, *Indonesia – 1965*, p. 55.
27 Soeharto, *Pikiran*, p. 129; Dwipayana and Nazaruddin (eds), *Jejak langkah Pak Harto*, p. 7. It appears that Senayan remained Kostrad headquarters for a few days after 1 October (Yani, *Profile*, p. 135), with Suharto and Nasution 'working and sleeping' there (Hughes, *Indonesian upheaval*, p. 121).
28 Crouch, *The army and politics*, p. 101.
29 Nugroho and Ismael, *The coup attempt*, p. 57.

30 McDonald, *Suharto's Indonesia*, p. 49.
31 Soeharto, *Pikiran*, p. 130; Dwipayana and Nazaruddin (eds), *Jejak langkah Pak Harto*, p. 7.
32 Crouch, *The army and politics*, p. 138.
33 Soeharto, *Pikiran*, pp. 134, 136.
34 Hughes, *Indonesian upheaval*, p. 125.
35 Oey, 'Sukarno and the pseudo-coup', p. 129. Sukarno had, however, taken the step of declaring the murdered seven 'heroes of the revolution' and posthumously raising them each one rank (*Kompas*, 6 October 1965).
36 Ramadhan, *Soemitro*, pp. 308–9.
37 Amongst the latter might be included the recently minted notion that the PKI intended to kill Sukarno at the planned Armed Forces parade on 5 October in the style of the assassination of Anwar Sadat of Egypt (Rangga et al., 'Konspirasi Soeharto–PKI dalam G30S', *Adil* 52, 1998, p. 4).
38 This view is argued most strongly in Nugroho and Ismael, *The coup attempt*, and in USCIA, *Indonesia – 1965*.
39 Anderson and McVey, *A preliminary analysis*, p. 63.
40 Crouch's work best represents this view (*The army and politics*, pp. 105, 109, 115). See also Mody, *Indonesia under Suharto*, p. 21.
41 Interview with Abdul Latief, in Mindo, 'Mereka melaksanakan perintah Sjam', *De Tak*, 29 September–5 October 1998, p. 21; Anon., 'Wawancara Kolonel A. Latief: ternyata Pak Harto diam saja', *Tajuk* 1, 15 (1998), p. 16.
42 Roeder, *The smiling general*, p. 9. A variant of this view, in which Sukarno is strongly suspected of prior knowledge of and an accommodative attitude towards the coup, is USCIA, *Indonesia – 1965*.
43 Brackman, *Indonesia: the Gestapu affair*, pp. 19–20.
44 Budiardjo, 'Did Suharto mastermind the 1965 "coup attempt"?', p. 12.
45 For a vigorous, if not especially rigorous, analysis of these issues, see Wimandjaja, *Primadosa*, pp. 32–41. Suharto remarked of *Primadosa* that 'they have distorted the facts' (Idrus F. Shahab, 'Setelah promosi Prima Dosa', *Editor*, 3 February 1994, p. 53).
46 See, for example, Patrick Walters, 'Suharto's secret role in coup'; 'Jail walls hold coup secrets', *Australian*, 25 May 1998; Anon, 'Wawancara Kolonel A. Latief', p. 15; Bina Bektiati and Ardi Bramantyo, 'Kolonel A. Latief: "Saya ingin meluruskan sejarah"', *Tempo*, 16 April 2000, pp. 59–61.
47 See Tabah, *Dua jenderal besar bicara tentang Gestapu/PKI*, pp. 21, 23.
48 Soeharto, 'Sambutan', in Tabah, *Dua jenderal*, p. xv.
49 Anderson and McVey, *A preliminary analysis*, p. 6.
50 Interview with Abdul Latief, in Mindo, 'Mereka melaksanakan perintah Sjam', p. 21.
51 Interview with Anton in Anon., 'Saat itulah, Soeharto mulai didekati CIA', *De Tak*, 29 September–5 October 1998, p. 8. See also Anon., 'Agen RI-CIA-KGB bicara keterlibatan Soeharto', *De Tak*, 29 September–5 October 1998, p. 1.
52 Latief, *Pledoi*, pp. 93–7; Latief, 'Laporan', in Latief, *Pledoi*, pp. 279–80, 282; Latief, 'Daftar riwayat hidup singkat Abdul Latief', in Latief, *Pledoi*, pp. xii–xiii.
53 Latief, 'Laporan', p. 280. Subandrio makes the same claim (Soebandrio, 'Kesaksianku', pp. 42–3).
54 Oey, 'Sukarno and the pseudo-coup', p. 124.
55 Mackie *Konfrontasi*, p. 311. Umar 'was generally known as "safe", being by reputation cautious, unambitious, and impartial' (McVey, 'A preliminary excursion', p. 78).
56 McVey, 'A preliminary excursion', p. 31.

57 Wertheim, 'Whose plot?', p. 208.
58 Anon., 'Wawancara Kolonel A. Latief', p. 15. In his trial evidence, Latief noted that he took moral support from the fact that Suharto did not react to his news (Latief, *Pledoi*, p. 129).
59 Anon., 'Wawancara Kolonel A. Latief', p. 15; Latief, 'Laporan', p. 279.
60 Latief, *Pledoi*, pp. 13, 30, 31, 41, and so on. Wertheim, in similar vein, remarked that 'Suharto should at the very least be held co-responsible because of his failure to report the putsch plans immediately to his superiors' ('Whose plot?', p. 208).
61 See, for example, Soeharto, *Pikiran*, p. 118.
62 May, *The Indonesian tragedy*, p. 118. See also Hughes, *Indonesian upheaval*, p. 59; Wertheim, 'Whose plot?', p. 208.
63 Soeharto, *Pikiran*, p. 118. In his most recent autobiographical account, Suharto made no mention of Latief's visit to the hospital in his recounting of the events of 30 September – 1 October ('Watashi', part 11, 12 January 1998, p. 40).

6 THE MOVE TO POWER

1 Pauker, *Indonesia in 1966*, p. 7.
2 Mackie, *Konfrontasi*, p. 309.
3 Budiman, 'Portrait of a young Indonesian', p. 78.
4 Penders and Sundhaussen, *Abdul Haris Nasution*, p. 184.
5 Crouch, *The army and politics*, p. 141.
6 Ruslan Abdulgani, interview with Brackman, quoted in Brackman, *The communist collapse*, p. 106.
7 Soeharto, *Pikiran*, p. 138. See also Crouch, *The army and politics*, p. 162.
8 O. G. Roeder, 'Aidit in trouble', *FEER*, 28 October 1965, p. 150.
9 Quoted in Crouch, *The army and politics*, p. 162.
10 Paraphrased in Dwipayana and Nazaruddin (eds), *Jejak langkah Pak Harto 1 Oktober 1965–27 Maret 1968*, pp. 11, 12.
11 'Pidato Mayor Jenderal TNI Soeharto di hadapan Panca Tunggal di Istana Negara (tanggal 23-10-1965)', in Dinuth (ed.), *Dokumen terpilih sekitar G.30.S/PKI*, p. 122.
12 A copy of this document, entitled 'Revolusi Indonesia' and bearing the signatures of both men, was published in *Pedoman Rakyat* on 11 December 1965. I am grateful to Harry Can Silalahi and Henk Schulte-Nordholt for bringing this document and its publication to my notice.
13 *Kompas*, 1 November 1965.
14 Soeharto, *Pikiran*, pp. 137, 139.
15 Green, *Indonesia*, p. 77.
16 Soeharto, *Pikiran*, p. 140. See also Dwipayana and Nazaruddin (eds), *Jejak langkah Pak Harto 1 Oktober 1965–27 Maret 1968*, pp. 21–2; Roeder, 'Aidit in trouble', p. 150.
17 Hughes, *Indonesian upheaval*, pp. 132–3.
18 In fact, as the autopsies personally ordered by Suharto himself showed, there was no evidence of bodily mutilation apart from that possibly caused by the application of rifle butts or stones (Ben Anderson, 'How did the generals die?').
19 Hughes, *Indonesian upheaval*, p. 154. See also Anon., 'Terror in review', *FEER*, 12 May 1966, p. 282; Jean Contenay, 'Another bloodbath?', *FEER*, 23 November 1967, pp. 357–8, 361–7; Seymour Topping, 'Slaughter of Reds gives Indonesia a grim

legacy', *New York Times*, 24 August 1966; Hermawan Sulistyo, 'The forgotten years', pp. 181–207.
20 Ramadhan, *Soemitro*, p. 114.
21 Soeharto, *Pikiran*, p. 137.
22 Hughes, *Indonesian upheaval*, p. 181.
23 USCIA, *Indonesia – 1965*, p. 71n.
24 *Kompas*, 1 November 1965.
25 *Kompas*, 1 November 1965.
26 Instruction no. 22/Koti/1965; see Dwipayana and Nazaruddin (eds), *Jejak langkah Pak Harto 1 Oktober 1965–27 Maret 1968*, p. 24.
27 Green, *Indonesia*, pp. 2, 63 (see also p. 64). See also Anon., 'Kesaksian bekas Dubes', *Tempo*, 20 February 1988, p. 85 [interview with Green]; William P. Bundy, 'Foreword', in Green, *Indonesia*, pp. xii–xiii; Anon. (ed.), *Foreign relations of the United States, 1964–68, vol. XXVI, Indonesia; Malaysia–Singapore; Philippines* (2001), http://www.gwu.edu/~nsarchiv/ NSAEBB/NSAEBB52/, p. 301n.
28 Kadane, 'The CIA supplied Suharto with death lists in 1965', pp. 12–13; Bunnell, 'American "low posture" policy', pp. 52, 59; Bambang Harymurti, 'Kami cuma beri walkie-talkie', *Tempo*, 4 August 1990, p. 26; Anon. (ed.), *Foreign relations of the United States, 1964–68, vol. XXVI*, pp. 308, 323, 337n, 343–53, 357–66, 368–71, 373–5, 379–87, 390–5, 401–9, 422–6.
29 Quoted in Dwipayana and Nazaruddin (eds), *Jejak langkah Pak Harto 1 Oktober 1965–27 Maret 1968*, p. 22.
30 *Kompas*, 30 December 1966.
31 Addresses on 8 November 1965 and 3 June 1966, paraphrased in Dwipayana and Nazaruddin (eds), *Jejak langkah Pak Harto 1 Oktober 1965–27 Maret 1968*, pp. 22, 83.
32 *Kompas*, 26 May 1966.
33 Dwipayana and Nazaruddin (eds), *Jejak langkah Pak Harto 1 Oktober 1965–27 Maret 1968*, pp. 112–13.
34 Quoted in Anon., 'Sekarang calon itu sudah ada', *Tempo*, 5 March 1994, p. 32.
35 Legge, *Sukarno*, p. 400.
36 Soeharto, *Pikiran*, p. 161.
37 Crouch, *The army and politics*, pp. 166–7.
38 Quoted in Gafur, *Pak Harto*, pp. 21, 22.
39 Soeharto, *Pikiran*, p. 162.
40 Quoted in Crouch, *The army and politics*, p. 167.
41 Soeharto, *Pikiran*, p. 163.
42 Quoted in Crouch, *The army and politics*, p. 168.
43 Quoted in Crouch, *The army and politics*, p. 169.
44 Soeharto, *Pikiran*, pp. 166, 167.
45 Crouch, *The army and politics*, pp. 172–5 (see also p. 225). See also Ramadhan, *Soemitro*, p. 356.
46 Legge, *Sukarno*, p. 401.
47 Harald Munthe-Kaas, 'Konfrontasi 2', *FEER*, 3 March 1966, p. 393.
48 Soeharto, *Pikiran*, p. 163.
49 Munthe-Kaas, 'Konfrontasi 2', p. 394.
50 Crouch, *The army and politics*, p. 177.
51 Ramadhan, *Soemitro*, p. 167. Kemal Idris shared Sumitro's view that the generals wanted Nasution to replace Sukarno (interview, Jakarta, 18 June 1998). See also Penders and Sundhaussen, *Nasution*, p. 258.

52 Munthe-Kaas, 'Konfrontasi 2', p. 393.

53 Soeharto, *Pikiran*, p. 139.

54 It appears that these connections gave rise to the later involvement of student leader Sofyan Wanandi (Liem Bian Khun) in Kostrad's business activities.

55 Soeharto, *Pikiran*, pp. 163–4; Rahmayanti and Aribowo Suprayogi, 'Saya sangat kecewa' (interview with Kemal Idris), *Editor*, 19 September 1992, p. 85. See also Panitia Penyusun Sejarah Kostrad, *Kostrad dharma putra*, p. 6; Susanto Pudjomartono, 'Setelah tiga jenderal kembali dari Bogor', *Tempo*, 15 March 1986, p. 15.

56 *Kompas*, 8 March 1966.

57 Ramadhan, *Soemitro*, pp. 90–2. See also Kemal, *Bertarung dalam revolusi*, pp. 186–7; Crouch, *The army and politics*, pp. 189–90n.

58 Panitia Penyusun Sejarah Kostrad, *Kostrad dharma putra*, pp. 74–5; see also interview with Kemal Idris, *Kompas*, 16 August 1968.

59 Ramadhan, *Soemitro*, p. 89.

60 Hughes, *Indonesian upheaval*, p. 233. See also Anon., 'Saksi-saksi sebelas Maret', *Tempo*, 15 March 1986, p. 17.

61 Amirmachmud, *H. Amirmachmud menjawab*, p. 54. See also Tony Hasyim and Santoso, 'Jenderal (Purn.) Amirmachmud: "Supersemar itu suatu mukjizat"', *Forum Keadilan*, 31 March 1994, p. 75; Susanto Pudjomartono, 'Setelah tiga jenderal kembali dari Bogor', *Tempo*, 15 March 1986, p. 16.

62 Amirmachmud, *H. Amirmachmud menjawab*, p. 55. See also Panda Nababan, Tony Hasyim and Sudarsono, 'Jenderal (Purn.) Amirmachmud: "Surat Perintah 11 Maret yang asli dua lembar"', *Forum Keadilan*, 14 October 1993, p. 72; Soeharto, *Pikiran*, pp. 170–1; *Kompas*, 10 April 1966; Gafur, *Pak Harto*, p. 128; Sekretariat Agitasi-Propaganda CCPKI, *Buku putih*, p. 138.

63 *Kompas*, 12 March 1971.

64 Amirmachmud, *H. Amirmachmud menjawab*, pp. 56–7, 59. He provides essentially the same account in *Kompas*, 15 March 1971. Subandrio's account (Soebandrio, 'Kesaksianku', pp. 98–101) does not contradict Amirmachmud's account in any significant way.

65 Soebandrio, 'Kesaksianku', p. 102.

66 Amirmachmud, *H. Amirmachmud menjawab*, p. 59. See also interview with Sri Mulyono Herlambang, former air force commander, in Agustono, 'Dendamnya kepada Pranoto bukan main', *De Tak*, 20 September–5 October 1998, p. 12; Soebandrio, 'Kesaksianku', p. 102.

67 McDonald, *Suharto's Indonesia*, p. 2.

68 Soeharto, *Pikiran*, p. 173.

69 May, *The Indonesian tragedy*, p. 139.

70 Dwipayana and Nazaruddin (eds), *Jejak langkah Pak Harto 1 Oktober 1965–27 Maret 1968*, p. 57.

71 Gafur, *Siti Hartinah*, p. 220; Ramadhan, *Soemitro*, p. 92.

72 Memorandum of the DPR-GR (People's Representative Council – Mutual Assistance), 9 June 1966, in Anon., *Decisions of the fourth plenary session*, p. 43. See also *Kompas*, 10 June 1966. Suharto's autobiography (Soeharto, *Pikiran*, p. 174) mirrors these words closely. (The 'GR', in DPR-GR, was added by Sukarno but gradually dropped from usage in the early years of the New Order.)

73 Soeharto, *Pikiran*, p. 174. See also Dwipayana and Nazaruddin (eds), *Jejak langkah Pak Harto 1 Oktober 1965–27 Maret 1968*, p. 68 [24 April 1966]; *Kompas*, 12 March 1971.

74 Paraphrased in Dwipayana and Nazaruddin (eds), *Jejak langkah Pak Harto 28 Maret 1968–23 Maret 1973*, p. 105 [11 March 1969].
75 Soeharto, *Pikiran*, p. 174.
76 *Kompas*, 17 March 1966.
77 Hanna, 'The magical–mystical syndrome in the Indonesian mentality', p. 7.
78 Roeder, *The smiling general*, p. 188.
79 Quoted in O. G. Roeder, 'Land of smiles', *FEER*, 7 April 1966, p. 6. See also Penders and Sundhaussen, *Nasution*, p. 198.
80 *Kompas*, 5 April, 2 May, 5 September 1966.
81 Quoted in Crouch, *The army and politics*, p. 255.
82 McDonald, *Suharto's Indonesia*, p. 59.
83 Ramadhan, *Soemitro*, pp. 176–7.
84 *Kompas*, 5 and 20 April 1966.
85 Paraphrased in Dwipayana and Nazaruddin (eds), *Jejak langkah Pak Harto 1 Oktober 1965–27 Maret 1968*, p. 124. See also *Kompas*, 14 November 1966.
86 See, for example, Dwipayana and Nazaruddin (eds), *Jejak langkah Pak Harto 1 Oktober 1965–27 Maret 1968*, pp. 78, 84; McDonald, *Suharto's Indonesia*, p. 113; *Kompas*, 11 April 1966.
87 Anon., 'Far Eastern roundup', *FEER*, 14 April 1966, p. 44.
88 Soeharto, *Pikiran*, pp. 176, 177. Suharto had publicly identified himself with the stance taken in an ABRI statement of 5 May that Sukarno would be retained and his authority respected ('Waperdam a.i. Bidang Hankam Let. Djen. Soeharto dalam tanja-djawab dengan wartawan Ichiro Iwatate … tgl. 6 Djuni 1966', in Achmad (ed.), *Wawantjara*, p. 12; *Kompas*, 18 June 1966.
89 O. G. Roeder, 'Statesmanship', *FEER*, 16 March 1967, p. 482.
90 Decree no. IX/MPRS/1966, in Anon., *Decisions*, p. 7. The decree was to be 'valid until the Madjelis Permusjawaratan Rakjat has been formed on the basis of general elections' (p. 8).
91 Nawaksara address, in Anon., *Decisions*, p. 163.
92 Decision no. V/MPRS/1966, in Anon., *Decisions*, pp. 131–2.
93 Decree no. X/MPRS/1966, in Anon., *Decisions*, pp. 10, 11. See also Dwipayana and Nazaruddin (eds), *Jejak langkah Pak Harto 1 Oktober 1965–27 Maret 1968*, p. 203 [23 August 1967].
94 Anon., *Decisions*, pp. 13–14, 15–18, 19–23, 28–9, 34–6, 37–9, 95–8.
95 Anon., *Decisions*, pp. 135, 136, 143, 145.
96 Sukarno's speech to MPRS, 6 July 1996, in Anon., *Decisions*, p. 158.
97 *Kompas*, 7 July 1966.
98 Cited in Nasution, *Memenuhi panggilan tugas*, vol. 7, p. 53.
99 Soeharto, *Pikiran*, p. 179.
100 Malik, *In the service of the Republic*, p. 252.
101 *Kompas*, 28 July 1966.
102 Soeharto, *Pikiran*, p. 180.
103 Silalahi, 'Kata sebuah riwayat', pp. 5–6.
104 Nasution, *Memenuhi panggilan tugas*, vol. 8, p. 154; Penders and Sundhaussen, *Nasution*, p. 209; Vatikiotis, *Indonesian politics*, 1993, p. 69.
105 Sundhaussen, 'The military', p. 64 (Sundhaussen is referring here especially to the period from 1969).
106 Soeharto, *Pikiran*, p. 180.
107 Mackie, *Konfrontasi*, p. 1.

108 'Tanja djawab wartawan "Diario Popular" (Lisboa) Dr. Franciscoi Balsemao dengan Waperdam Bid. Hankam', in Achmad (ed.), *Wawantjara*, p. 11.

109 Dwipayana and Nazaruddin (eds), *Jejak langkah Pak Harto 1 Oktober 1965–27 Maret 1968*, p. 105.

110 Soeharto, *Pikiran*, p. 181.

111 Ramadhan, *Soemitro*, p. 143. The formal results of the seminar are contained in Anon., *Sumbangan fikiran TNI-AD kepada Kabinet Ampera.*

112 Ramadhan, *Soemitro*, p. 145. See also Sarbini Sumawinata, 'Recollections of my career', p. 50.

113 'Wawantjara Pak Harto dengan "The Statesman"' (14 June 1966), in Achmad (ed.), *Wawantjara*, p. 19.

114 Soeharto, *Pikiran*, p. 232.

115 Quoted in Crouch, *The army and politics*, p. 248.

116 'Tanja djawab wartawan "Diario Popular"', p. 6.

117 *Kompas*, 19 September, 5 October 1966.

118 *Kompas*, 5 October 1966; Dwipayana and Nazaruddin (eds), *Jejak langkah Pak Harto 1 Oktober 1965–27 Maret 1968*, p. 117; Anon., 'The Bung at bay', *FEER*, 23 February 1967, p. 263; O. G. Roeder, 'Indonesia without Sukarno', *FEER*, 13 April 1967, p. 61.

119 The major figures were Wijoyo (PhD, UC Berkeley, 1961); Ali Wardhana (PhD, UC Berkeley, 1962); Emil Salim (PhD, UC Berkeley, 1964), J. B. Sumarlin (MA, UC Berkeley, 1960), Subroto (MA, McGill; PhD, University of Indonesia), and Mohammad Sadli (MSc, MIT; PhD, University of Indonesia).

120 Soeharto, *Pikiran*, p. 232.

121 Dwipayana and Nazaruddin (eds), *Jejak langkah Pak Harto 1 Oktober 1965–27 Maret 1968*, p. 126.

122 'Tanja djawab wartawan "Diario Popular"', p. 8.

123 Malik, *In the service of the Republic*, p. 256.

124 White, 'Problems and prospects of the Indonesian foreign exchange system', p. 152.

125 Anthony Goldstone, 'Following the Indonesian lead', *FEER*, 9 August 1974, pp. 51–3.

126 *Kompas*, 21 July 1967.

127 O. G. Roeder, 'Spring cleaning', *FEER*, 1 June 1967, p. 480.

128 'Tanja djawab wartawan "Diario Popular"', p. 6. One commentator noted in 1965 that 'rejection of capitalism and espousal of socialism as the preferred pattern of economic organisation has been an almost universal element in Indonesian political ideology since independence' (L. C., 'Socialism and private business: the latest phase', *Bulletin of Indonesian Economic Studies* 2 (1965), p. 13).

129 Soeharto, *Pikiran*, p. 252.

130 Roeder, *The smiling general*, p. 196.

131 Nugroho and Ismael, *The coup attempt*, pp. 85, 88n, 92, 190–2, 193–7, 199–201, 228–46.

132 Soeharto, *Pikiran*, p. 225.

133 Hughes, *Indonesian upheaval*, pp. 274–5.

134 Crouch, *The army and politics*, p. 118; Mody, *Indonesia under Suharto*, p. 22; Dwipayana and Nazaruddin (eds), *Jejak langkah Pak Harto 1 Oktober 1965–27 Maret 1968*, pp. 112, 117, 136, 147–8; O. G. Roeder, 'Trial by proxy', *FEER*, 22 December 1966, pp. 587–8.

135 Soeharto, *Pikiran*, pp. 182, 184.

136 Van der Kroef, *Indonesia after Sukarno*, p. 44.
137 Ramadhan, *Soemitro*, pp. 75, 76–7.
138 *Kompas*, 8 November, 14 December 1966.
139 *Kompas*, 11 November 1966.
140 Soeharto, *Pikiran*, p. 184.
141 *Kompas*, 21, 22, 24 December 1966.
142 See the report of the 'order of battle' meeting between Kemal Idris (Kostrad), Sarwo Edhie (RPKAD), and Dharsono (Siliwangi) on 24 January, in *Kompas*, 25 January 1967. See also Penders and Sundhaussen, *Nasution*, pp. 203–4; Vatikiotis, *Indonesian politics*, 1993, p. 68; USCIA, *Indonesia – 1965*, p. 258.
143 *Kompas*, 1 February 1967.
144 Quoted in Gafur, *Pak Harto*, p. 25.
145 *Kompas*, 7 February 1967. See also Alamsyah's statement on behalf of Suharto, reported in the same issue.
146 This paragraph is based upon *Kompas*, 24 February 1967; Soeharto, *Pikiran*, pp. 187–8; Dwipayana and Nazaruddin (eds), *Jejak langkah Pak Harto 1 Oktober 1965–27 Maret 1968*, pp. 155–6, 299; Roeder, 'Statesmanship', p. 484; Crouch, *The army and politics*, p. 216.
147 Soeharto, *Pikiran*, p. 190; Dwipayana and Nazaruddin (eds), *Jejak langkah Pak Harto 1 Oktober 1965–27 Maret 1968*, pp. 159–60. The radio address was delivered on 23 February; the text can be found in *Kompas*, 24 February 1967.
148 *Kompas*, 25 and 27 February 1967.
149 *Kompas*, 2 March 1967.
150 'Pidato penjelasan pelaksanaan pengamanan Ketetapan MPRS no. XXXIII/MPRS/1967 oleh Jenderal Soeharto selaku pengemban Ketetapan MPRS no. IX/MPRS/1966', in Dwipayana and Nazaruddin (eds), *Jejak langkah Pak Harto 1 Oktober 1965–27 Maret 1968*, p. 307. See also *Kompas*, 13 March 1967; Suharto 'Watashi', part 15, 16 January 1998, p. 36.
151 Ramadhan, *Soemitro*, p. 168. See also Anon., 'Sekarang calon itu sudah ada', *Tempo*, 5 March 1994, p. 32.
152 Soeharto, *Pikiran*, pp. 189, 190.
153 Soeharto, *Pikiran*, p. 191.
154 Soeharto, *Pikiran*, pp. 191–2.
155 Soeharto, *Pikiran*, pp. 191, 244.
156 *Kompas*, 22 May 1967.
157 Ramadhan, *Soemitro*, pp. 265–6. See also Soeharto, *Pikiran*, pp. 228–9; Suharto, 'Watashi', part 16, 17 January 1998, p. 40; O. G. Roeder, 'Tense harmony', *FEER*, 24 November 1966, p. 423; Roeder, *Anak desa*, p. 263; Johan Budi S. P., 'Jalan Cendana Soeharto punya', *Tempo*, 17 September 1966, p. 26.
158 Dwipayana and Nazaruddin (eds), *Jejak langkah Pak Harto 1 Oktober 1965–27 Maret 1968*, pp. 167–8 [26 March 1967]. See also Anon., 'A stony road', *FEER*, 13 February 1969, p. 282.
159 Cited in O. G. Roeder, 'Sumitro speaks', *FEER*, 10 August 1967, pp. 287–8.
160 Van der Kroef, 'Indonesian communism since the 1965 coup', p. 44.
161 Speeches on 3 April and 2 June 1967; see Dwipayana and Nazaruddin (eds), *Jejak langkah Pak Harto 1 Oktober 1965–27 Maret 1968*, pp. 171, 185.
162 *Kompas*, 22 March, 13 April, 3 and 16 May 1967.
163 Dwipayana and Nazaruddin (eds), *Jejak langkah Pak Harto 1 Oktober 1965–27 Maret 1968*, pp. 201–2; Mody, *Indonesia under Suharto*, p. 172.

164 Speech to Ansor Congress, 23 October 1967, paraphrased in Dwipayana and Nazaruddin (eds), *Jejak langkah Pak Harto 1 Oktober 1965–27 Maret 1968*, p. 217.
165 Dwipayana and Nazaruddin (eds), *Jejak langkah Pak Harto 1 Oktober 1965–27 Maret 1968*, p. 246.
166 Soeharto, *Pikiran*, p. 279. On 7 September 1966, the government had closed ten Chinese-language daily newspapers; only a single such paper, *Harian Indonesia*, was allowed to continue operation (Dwipayana and Nazaruddin, eds, *Jejak langkah Pak Harto 1 Oktober 1965–27 Maret 1968*, p. 111).
167 Soeharto, *Pikiran*, p. 259. See also *Kompas*, 1 December 1967, which presents a less elaborated version of the speech.
168 Mackie, 'Towkays and tycoons', p. 94.
169 *Kompas*, 31 May 1967.
170 *Kompas*, 20 May 1967; Dwipayana and Nazaruddin (eds), *Jejak langkah Pak Harto 1 Oktober 1965–27 Maret 1968*, p. 265 [2 March 1968].
171 'Tanja djawab Letdjen Soeharto dengan wartawan Pilipina', p. 27.
172 Dwipayana and Nazaruddin (eds), *Jejak langkah Pak Harto 1 Oktober 1965–27 Maret 1968*, p. 177 [5 May 1967]; 'Waperdam a.i. Bidang Hankam Let. Djen. Soeharto', pp. 13–14; 'Wawantjara Pak Harto', p. 18; 'Tanja djawab Letdjen Soeharto', p. 26. See also the statement by Adam Malik in *Kompas*, 5 April 1966.
173 *Kompas*, 17 February 1968.
174 Crouch, *The army and politics*, pp. 234–5.
175 Crouch, 'The army, the parties and elections', p. 177; Crouch, *The army and politics*, p. 252. See also *Kompas*, 26 January 1968.
176 *Kompas*, 12 May 1967.
177 Dwipayana and Nazaruddin (eds), *Jejak langkah Pak Harto 1 Oktober 1965–27 Maret 1968*, pp. 193, 239.
178 Budiman, 'Portrait of a young Indonesian', p. 77.
179 The size of the parliament rose from 347 to 414 members. See *Kompas*, 10 February, 15 March 1968; Mody, *Indonesia under Suharto*, p. 163; Polomka, *Indonesia since Sukarno*, p. 142; Penders and Sundhaussen, *Nasution*, pp. 214–15; Feith, 'Suharto's search for a political format', p. 98. Bourchier notes that 'many of the pro-democracy intellectuals appointed to the MPRS from the ranks of the New Order coalition in 1966 lost their seats in the shakedown' ('Lineages', p. 177).
180 *Kompas*, 29 November 1967.
181 *Kompas*, 29 March 1968. Interestingly, the speech as reported in *Kompas* differs significantly in content from the account of it provided in Soeharto, *Pikiran*, pp. 226–8.
182 Polomka, *Indonesia since Sukarno*, p. 142; McDonald, *Suharto's Indonesia*, pp. 98–9; Feith, 'Suharto's search', pp. 101, 102; Roeder, *The smiling general*, p. 154. See also *Kompas*, 18 June 1966, 19 and 28 March, 16 April 1968.
183 *Kompas*, 13 April 1968.
184 Salim, 'Recollections of my career', p. 62.

7 LEGITIMATION AND CONSOLIDATION

1 Paraphrased in Dwipayana and Nazaruddin (eds), *Jejak langkah Pak Harto 28 Maret 1968–23 Maret 1973*, p. 9 [1 April 1968].
2 Soeharto, *Pikiran*, p. 238.

3 O. G. Roeder, 'Little rice – and no circuses', *FEER*, 20 June 1968, p. 606; Budiman, 'Portrait of a young Indonesian', p. 78; *Kompas*, 10 June 1968; Polomka, *Indonesia since Sukarno*, p. 107; McDonald, *Suharto's Indonesia*, pp. 77–8.
4 Paraphrased in Dwipayana and Nazaruddin (eds), *Jejak langkah Pak Harto*, p. 18 [19 May 1968].
5 *Kompas*, 21 March 1968.
6 Soeharto, *Pikiran*, p. 238.
7 Pangaribuan, *The Indonesian state secretariat*, p. 24.
8 Malley, 'A political biography of Soedjono Hoemardani', p. 49.
9 Soeharto, *Pikiran*, p. 441. Suharto may here be referring to the fuel price rise of early 1970.
10 KAPPI was a youth and high school student organisation formed in February 1966.
11 *Kompas*, 7 May 1968.
12 Crouch, *The army and politics*, p. 300; Ward, *The 1971 election in Indonesia*, p. 125; White, 'Problems and prospects of the Indonesian foreign exchange system', p. 153; Robison, *Indonesia: the rise of capital*, pp. 138–9.
13 In 1971, Ali established a private think-tank, the Centre for Strategic and International Studies (CSIS), to develop policy around these ideas. CSIS was thought by many to exercise great influence on government policy, something Suharto strongly denied (see Soemitro, *Pangkopkamtib Jenderal Soemitro*, p. 41).
14 Paraphrased in Dwipayana and Nazaruddin (eds), *Jejak langkah Pak Harto*, p. 62.
15 Crouch, *The army and politics*, p. 323.
16 Interview with Polomka, reported in Polomka, *Indonesia since Sukarno*, p. 109. See also Crouch, *The army and politics*, pp. 242, 276, 300, 322.
17 Cited in Glassburner, 'Indonesia's new economic policy and its sociopolitical implications', p. 143. See also Subroto, 'Recollections of my career', pp. 79–80.
18 *Selecta*, 11 May 1970, quoted in Britton, 'The Indonesian army', pp. 150–51n.
19 Paraphrased in Dwipayana and Nazaruddin (eds), *Jejak langkah Pak Harto*, p. 114 [21 April 1969], p. 476 [14 October 1972]; *Kompas*, 6 March 1968.
20 Paraphrased in Dwipayana and Nazaruddin (eds), *Jejak langkah Pak Harto*, p. 95 [4 February 1969].
21 Soeharto, *Pikiran*, p. 241.
22 Soeharto, *Pikiran*, p. 243 (see also p. 240). See also Dwipayana and Nazaruddin (eds), *Jejak langkah Pak Harto*, p. 49; McDonald, *Suharto's Indonesia*, p. 183; Suharto, 'Watashi', part 19, 20 January 1998, p. 40.
23 Dwipayana and Nazaruddin (eds), *Jejak langkah Pak Harto*, p. 28 [12 July 1968].
24 *Kompas*, 2 January, 5 March 1969.
25 Derek Davies, 'The army's double duty', *FEER*, 31 October 1970, p. 23.
26 *Kompas*, 16 April, 18 December 1968.
27 Dwipayana and Nazaruddin (eds), *Jejak langkah Pak Harto*, p. 423 [4 March 1972]; see also pp. 425–6, and Benedict Anderson, 'Notes on contemporary political communication', pp. 72–3.
28 *Kompas*, 23 February 1971, 17 April 1969. See also *Kompas*, 7 October 1968, 3 June 1969; Anon., 'Kompensasi', *FEER*, 24 October 1968, p. 191; Dwipayana and Nazaruddin (eds), *Jejak langkah Pak Harto*, p. 95 [5 February 1969]; Anon., *The Armed Forces/Army civic mission is not militarism.*
29 Quoted in O. G. Roeder., 'Progress before politics', *FEER*, 24 April 1969, p. 249. See also Roeder, 'A thousand Bungs', *FEER*, 16 January 1971, p. 44.
30 *Kompas*, 6 October 1970.

31 Paraphrased in Dwipayana and Nazaruddin (eds), *Jejak langkah Pak Harto*, p. 28 [15 July 1968].
32 *Kompas*, 19 August 1968.
33 Paraphrased in Dwipayana and Nazaruddin (eds), *Jejak langkah Pak Harto*, p. 301 [27 January 1971], p. 354 [16 August 1971].
34 Paraphrased in Dwipayana and Nazaruddin (eds), *Jejak langkah Pak Harto*, p. 61 [10 November 1968], p. 353 [10 August 1971], p. 354 [16 August 1971].
35 *Kompas*, 2 October 1968, 2 March 1973. The latter monument cost Rp20,870,000, of which Suharto himself contributed Rp5,000,000.
36 *Kompas*, 1 March 1967.
37 See, for example, *Kompas*, 15 May 1968.
38 O. G. Roeder, '"New Order" on trial', *FEER*, 13 March 1969, p. 439; Van der Kroef, 'Indonesian communism since the 1965 coup', pp. 51–2. See also Martin Ennals, 'What happened in Indonesia? An exchange', *New York Review of Books* 25, 1 (1978), pp. 44–5, for a discussion of the rubbery quality of Indonesian government figures on the number of detainees.
39 Paraphrased in Dwipayana and Nazaruddin (eds), *Jejak langkah Pak Harto*, p. 106 (see also pp. 179, 190).
40 *Kompas*, 12 March 1971.
41 Paraphrased in Dwipayana and Nazaruddin (eds), *Jejak langkah Pak Harto*, p. 354 [16 August 1971], p. 419 [22 February 1972].
42 May, *The Indonesian tragedy*, p. 38.
43 Crouch, *The army and politics*, p. 223.
44 Ward, *The 1971 election*, p. 5.
45 *Kompas*, 23 July 1968.
46 *Kompas*, 20 August 1968; Bob Hawkins, 'Stoney faces', *FEER*, 29 August 1968, p. 386; Van der Kroef, *Indonesia after Sukarno*, pp. 135–6.
47 Van der Kroef, *Indonesia after Sukarno*, p. 154. See also Saltford, 'United Nations involvement'.
48 Paraphrased in Dwipayana and Nazaruddin (eds), *Jejak langkah Pak Harto*, pp. 91–2, 111. See also *Kompas*, 15 April 1968.
49 *Kompas*, 25 August 1969.
50 Dwipayana and Nazaruddin (eds), *Jejak langkah Pak Harto*, p. 111. Emphasis, and English, in original.
51 Soeharto, *Pikiran*, p. 245; see also *Kompas*, 23 June 1970.
52 Sukarno, *An autobiography*, p. 312.
53 Paraphrased in Dwipayana and Nazaruddin (eds), *Jejak langkah Pak Harto*, pp. 476–7 [16 October 1972], p. 516 [12 March 1973]. Malik's influence was probably important in softening Suharto's mood against China.
54 Paraphrased in Dwipayana and Nazaruddin (eds), *Jejak langkah Pak Harto*, p. 142 [27 July 1969], p. 148 [7 August 1969], pp. 265–6 [13 October 1970], p. 208 [12 March 1970].
55 Suharto, 'Watashi', part 14, 15 January 1998, p. 36.
56 Paraphrased in Dwipayana and Nazaruddin (eds), *Jejak langkah Pak Harto*, p. 484 [20 November 1972].
57 Tanter, 'Intelligence agencies and Third World militarization', p. 472.
58 McVey, 'The post-revolutionary transformation of the Indonesian army', II, p. 180.
59 Crouch, *The army and politics*, p. 241.
60 Sundhaussen, 'The military', p. 61.

61 Quoted in O. G. Roeder, 'Reprieve for politics', *FEER*, 20 March 1969, p. 521.
62 *Kompas*, 23 February 1971.
63 McDonald, *Suharto's Indonesia*, p. 103; Polomka, *Indonesia since Sukarno*, pp. 134, 137; Crouch, 'The army, the parties and elections', p. 186; Malley, 'Soedjono Hoemardani', pp. 54–6. See also Crouch, *The army and politics*, pp. 257–9; Van der Kroef, *Indonesia after Sukarno*, p. 50; Ward, *The 1971 election*, pp. 16, 144; Ichlasul, *Regional and central government in Indonesian politics*, p. 126.
64 Quoted in Crouch, *The army and politics*, p. 260.
65 Dwipayana and Nazaruddin (eds), *Jejak langkah Pak Harto*, p. 272 [14 November 1970]. See also McDonald, *Suharto's Indonesia*, p. 103; Crouch, 'The army, the parties and elections', p. 188; Ward, *The 1971 election*, pp. 17, 115.
66 Ward, 'Indonesia's modernisation', p. 70.
67 Ward, *The 1971 election*, p. 129.
68 Soeharto, *Pikiran*, pp. 260–1.
69 Ramadhan, *Soemitro*, p. 274.
70 O. G. Roeder, 'Pemilu pemalu', *FEER*, 6 November 1969, p. 294. Golkar gained support from such people as Cosmas Batubara, A. B. Nasution, Mochtar Lubis and Rosihan Anwar.
71 Crouch, *The army and politics*, p. 267; see also Ward, *The 1971 election*, p. 49.
72 Ward, *The 1971 election*, p. 78.
73 O. G. Roeder, 'Between the acts', *FEER*, 3 July 1971, p. 6.
74 Crouch, *The army and politics*, p. 268.
75 Ward, *The 1971 election*, pp. 85–6.
76 Roeder, 'Between the acts', p. 6; Ward, *The 1971 election*, p. 50; Budiman, 'Portrait of a young Indonesian', p. 81n; *Kompas*, 10 June 1971.
77 Paraphrased in Dwipayana and Nazaruddin (eds), *Jejak langkah Pak Harto*, p. 365 [7 September 1971].
78 Dwipayana and Nazaruddin (eds), *Jejak langkah Pak Harto*, pp. 374–5.
79 Soeharto, *Pikiran*, p. 266.
80 Paraphrased in Dwipayana and Nazaruddin (eds), *Jejak langkah Pak Harto*, p. 475 [1 October 1972]; see also p. 378 [28 October 1971].
81 O. G. Roeder, 'The lady grows up', *FEER*, 28 August 1969, p. 526. See also Soeharto, *Pikiran*, p. 228.
82 Paraphrased in Dwipayana and Nazaruddin (eds), *Jejak langkah Pak Harto*, p. 273 [20 November 1970].
83 Paraphrased in Dwipayana and Nazaruddin (eds), *Jejak langkah Pak Harto*, p. 282 [31 December 1970]. See also *Kompas*, 2 January 1969.
84 *Kompas*, 18 August 1969, 20 June 1968, 3 January 1972.
85 Polomka, *Indonesia since Sukarno*, p. 210; Dwipayana and Nazaruddin (eds), *Jejak langkah Pak Harto*, pp. 197–8 [7 February 1970], p. 204 [27 February 1970]; O. G. Roeder, 'Indonesia: the limits of democracy', *FEER*, 19 March 1970, p. 17.
86 Ali Moertopo, 'Some basic considerations in 25-year development', p. 20.
87 Mody, *Indonesia under Suharto*, p. 312; Ward, *The 1971 election*, pp. 188–9; *Kompas*, 30 September 1971. See also Crouch, *The army and politics*, p. 272.
88 Ali Murtopo, quoted in Hamish McDonald, 'We're now much more mature', *FEER*, 14 May 1976, p. 27.
89 Paraphrased in Dwipayana and Nazaruddin (eds), *Jejak langkah Pak Harto*, pp. 365–6 [8 September 1971].

90 Dwipayana and Nazaruddin (eds), *Jejak langkah Pak Harto*, p. 382 [6 November 1971].
91 Crouch, *The army and politics*, pp. 277–8, 280–1, 283, 324–5.
92 Soetriyono, *Kisah sukses Liem Sioe Liong*, pp. 15–17, 20; Manggi Habir and Anthony Rowley, 'The extended (corporate) family of Liem Sioe Liong', *FEER*, 7 April 1983, pp. 52–3. Crouch, *The army and politics*, pp. 285–7; Robison, *Indonesia: the rise of capital*, pp. 232–3.
93 Schwarz, *A nation in waiting*, 1994, p. 108; Jonathan Friedland, 'An engine of growth', *FEER*, 17 November 1988, p. 100; Robison, *Indonesia: the rise of capital*, pp. 277, 289–96; S. Iskandar, 'Friends on high', *FEER*, 27 August 1973, p. 23; David Jenkins, 'The military in business', *FEER*, 13 January 1978, p. 24; Crouch, *The army and politics*, pp. 283–4.
94 O. G. Roeder, 'Chinese beware', *FEER*, 13 March 1971, p. 24.
95 Dwipayana and Nazaruddin (eds), *Jejak langkah Pak Harto*, p. 428 [27 March 1972]; S. Iskandar, 'Suharto stirs a hornet's nest', *FEER*, 15 April 1972, p. 50; Anon., 'Division of wealth', *FEER*, 20 August 1973, p. 17.
96 Paraphrased in Dwipayana and Nazaruddin (eds), *Jejak langkah Pak Harto*, p. 445 [14 June 1972].
97 Crouch, *The army and politics*, p. 294. See also Van der Kroef, *Indonesia after Sukarno*, pp. 230–1; Ward, *The 1971 election*, p. 29. According to Arief Budiman (interview, Melbourne, 5 July 2000), Suharto was at that time thought not to be corrupt, but it was considered necessary by Arief and others to make him aware of the corruption of his close advisers.
98 Smith, 'Corruption, tradition and change', p. 21. See also *Kompas*, 26 January 1970; Budiman, 'Portrait of a young Indonesian', p. 79.
99 Dwipayana and Nazaruddin (eds), *Jejak langkah Pak Harto*, p. 193. See also *Kompas*, 2 February 1970.
100 *Kompas*, 2 February 1970.
101 Budiman, 'Portrait of a young Indonesian', pp. 79–80. See also *Kompas*, 20 June 1970.
102 *Sinar Harapan*, 20 July 1970; Dwipayana and Nazaruddin (eds), *Jejak langkah Pak Harto*, pp. 248, 249.
103 Budiman, 'Portrait of a young Indonesian', p. 79.
104 J. A. C. Mackie, 'The Commission of Four report on corruption', pp. 96–101; McDonald, *Suharto's Indonesia*, p. 124; *Sinar Harapan*, 18, 20, 21, 22, 23, 24 July 1970. See also Crouch, *The army and politics*, p. 297.
105 *Kompas*, 18 August 1970; see also Dwipayana and Nazaruddin (eds), *Jejak langkah Pak Harto*, pp. 248–9.
106 Soeharto, *Pikiran*, p. 252.
107 Dwipayana and Nazaruddin (eds), *Jejak langkah Pak Harto*, p. 391 [11 December 1971], p. 203 [25 February 1970], p. 403 [10 January 1972], pp. 404–5 [21 January 1972]. See also *Kompas*, 4 March 1970.
108 Winters, *Power in motion*, p. 50n.
109 O. G. Roeder, 'A general sort-out', *FEER*, 22 January 1970, p. 41.
110 *Kompas*, 21 December 1970.
111 Polomka, *Indonesia since Sukarno*, pp. 211–12.
112 O. G. Roeder, 'Beautiful authority', *FEER*, 15 January 1972, p. 16.
113 Dwipayana and Nazaruddin (eds), *Jejak langkah Pak Harto*, pp. 401–2 [6 January 1972].
114 S. Iskandar, 'Japan's Indonesian inroads', *FEER*, 27 May 1972, p. 33. Suharto himself later commented that the great visibility of Japanese economic penetration had

contributed to the growth of anti-Japanese feeling amongst Indonesians (Suharto, 'Watashi', part 18, 19 January 1998, p. 40).

115 *Kompas*, 11 April 1972.

116 Quoted in Polomka, *Indonesia since Sukarno*, p. 156.

117 *Kompas*, 20 November 1972.

118 Soeharto, *Pikiran*, p. 276.

119 Harvey Stockwin, 'An ability to lead', *FEER*, 2 April 1973, p. 26.

120 Stockwin, 'Winners and losers', *FEER*, 2 April 1973, p. 16.

121 Philip Bowring, 'Dilemma of Repelita II', *FEER*, 29 October 1973, p. 52.

8 NEGOTIATING THE PROBLEMS OF THE NEW ORDER

1 Paraphrased in Nazaruddin (ed.), *Jejak langkah Pak Harto 27 Maret 1973–23 Maret 1978*, pp. 268, 311, 386 [22 July, 16 December 1975, 16 August 1976].

2 Anon., 'Division of wealth', *FEER*, 20 August 1973, p. 17.

3 *Kompas*, 8 August 1973. See also Soeharto, *Pikiran*, p. 278.

4 *Kompas*, 27 August 1973.

5 *Kompas*, 26 October 1973; Rosihan Anwar, 'The students and the technocrats', *FEER*, 10 December 1973, p. 19; O. G. Roeder, 'A campus call for harmony', *FEER*, 10 December 1973, pp. 17–18; Crouch, *The army and politics*, p. 311; Soeharto, *Pikiran*, p. 250.

6 Paraphrased in Nazaruddin (ed.), *Jejak langkah Pak Harto 27 Maret 1973–23 Maret 1978*, pp. 58–9 [14 October 1973].

7 Ramadhan, *Soemitro*, p. 377 (see also p. 351). See also *Kompas*, 19 November 1973; Anon., 'The importance of security', *FEER*, 10 December 1973, p. 18; Soemitro, *Pangkopkamtib*, p. 115.

8 Soeharto, *Pikiran*, p. 298.

9 Sundhaussen, 'The military', pp. 6, 70, 78; Guy Sacerdoti, 'Freedom – to a degree', *FEER*, 26 June 1981, p. 34; Crouch, *The army and politics*, p. 314; *Kompas*, 9, 20 November 1973 and 2, 3, 7, 8 January 1974; Nazaruddin (ed.), *Jejak langkah Pak Harto 27 Maret 1973–23 Maret 1978*, pp. 72, 74–5, 90, 91; Anon., 'Killing a rumour', *FEER*, 14 January 1974, p. 35.

10 *Kompas*, 22 January 1974. The businesses mentioned were Astra, Bogasari, Batik Keris and Sahid.

11 Interview with Gen. (ret.) L. B. Murdani, Jakarta, 7 July 1997. Yoga claims that he proposed this action to Suharto (Wiwoho and Bandjar, *Memori Jenderal Yoga*, p. 278).

12 *Kompas*, 9 and 12 March 1974.

13 McDonald, *Suharto's Indonesia*, p. 140. See also Crouch, *The army and politics*, p. 317; Susumu Awanohara, 'A change of tack', *FEER*, 23 May 1975, p. 31; Dan Coggin, 'Uncertainty prevails', *FEER*, 18 July 1975, pp. 34–6; David Jenkins, 'End of the Klondike', *FEER*, 30 July 1976, p. 76.

14 Paraphrased in Nazaruddin (ed.), *Jejak langkah Pak Harto 27 Maret 1973–23 Maret 1978*, p. 246 [20 May 1975].

15 Suharto, 'Watashi', part 18, 19 January 1998, p. 40. See also Soeharto, *Pikiran*, pp. 440–1.

16 See, for example, Suharto's speech on the occasion of Armed Forces Day 1973, and also the *Kompas* editorial (*Kompas*, 6 October 1973). See also Nazaruddin (ed.), *Jejak langkah Pak Harto 27 Maret 1973–23 Maret 1978*, pp. 66, 71.

17 Paraphrased in Nazaruddin (ed.), *Jejak langkah Pak Harto 27 Maret 1973–23 Maret 1978*, p. 353 [12 April 1976].
18 Soeharto, *Pikiran*, p. 295.
19 Paraphrased in Nazaruddin (ed.), *Jejak langkah Pak Harto 27 Maret 1973–23 Maret 1978*, p. 36, and p. 467 [13 March 1977].
20 *Kompas*, 16 August 1981.
21 Soeharto, *Pikiran*, p. 283. See also Anon., 'Presiden menjelaskan', *Tempo*, 4 February 1978, p. 8.
22 Nazaruddin (ed.), *Jejak langkah Pak Harto 27 Maret 1973–23 Maret 1978*, pp. 141, 368; *Kompas*, 20 September 1975; Soeharto, *Pikiran*, pp. 283–6; Nazaruddin (ed.), *Jejak langkah Pak Harto 29 Maret 1978–11 Maret 1983*, pp. 85, 138–9, 167, 306–7.
23 Robin Osborne, 'The Indonesian offensive', *FEER*, 14 March 1975, pp. 24–5. See also Dan Coggin, 'Timor: the waiting game', *FEER*, 17 October 1975, pp. 10–12. In 1998, Gen. (ret.) Benny Murdani emphasised the perceived fears for Indonesia's external security (interview, Jakarta, 17 June 1998). Murdani was responsible for planning and implementing the invasion, with little reference to or involvement from senior operational commanders (Tanter, 'Intelligence agencies', p. 350; Jenkins, *Suharto and his generals*, pp. 24–5n. See also Crouch, *The army and politics*, p. 341).
24 Dan Coggin, 'Indonesia's "special interest"', *FEER*, 17 October 1975, pp. 13–14.
25 Nazaruddin (ed.), *Jejak langkah Pak Harto 27 Maret 1973–23 Maret 1978*, p. 166 [18 October 1974]. But see also 'Record of meeting with Tjan' [21 August 1974], in Way (ed.), *Australia and the Indonesian incorporation of Portuguese Timor 1974–1976*, pp. 85–7.
26 'Record of conversation between Whitlam and Soeharto' [4 April 1975], in Way (ed.), *Australia and the Indonesian incorporation*, pp. 246–7 (see also p. 218, 'Cablegram to Canberra' [8 March 1975]); Nazaruddin (ed.), *Jejak langkah Pak Harto 27 Maret 1973–23 Maret 1978*, p. 235 [4 April 1975] (see also p. 222 [8 March 1975]).
27 Nazaruddin (ed.), *Jejak langkah Pak Harto 27 Maret 1973–23 Maret 1978*, pp. 276, 277 [12 and 16 August 1975].
28 Coggin, 'Timor: the waiting game', p. 10. See also 'Cablegram to Canberra' [3 September 1975], in Way (ed.), *Australia and the Indonesian incorporation*, p. 376.
29 'Cablegram to Canberra' [27 September 1975], in Way (ed.), *Australia and the Indonesian incorporation*, p. 436 (see also p. 399).
30 'Cablegram to Canberra' [27 November 1975] [Woolcott's rendering], in Way (ed.), *Australia and the Indonesian incorporation*, p. 584 (see also p. 592 [1 December 1975]).
31 McDonald, *Suharto's Indonesia*, p. 211; Nazaruddin (ed.), *Jejak langkah Pak Harto 27 Maret 1973–23 Maret 1978*, p. 310.
32 'Letter from Arriens to Fisher' [18 December 1975], rendering Yusuf Wanandi's sentiments, in Way (ed.), *Australia and the Indonesian incorporation*, p. 642.
33 Paraphrased in Nazaruddin (ed.), *Jejak langkah Pak Harto 27 Maret 1973–23 Maret 1978*, pp. 312, 367–8. On 17 July 1976, Suharto signed the bill incorporating East Timor into Indonesia as its twenty-seventh province.
34 Quoted in David Jenkins, 'Suharto: a decade of deeds and dilemmas', *FEER*, 20 August 1976, p. 21.
35 Anon., 'Developing a feeling of unity', *FEER*, 4 August 1978, pp. 24–5. See also *Kompas*, 14 April 1977.
36 Paraphrased in Nazaruddin (ed.), *Jejak langkah Pak Harto 27 Maret 1973–23 Maret 1978*, p. 355 [22 April 1976].

37 McDonald, *Suharto's Indonesia*, p. 143. See also Winters' interview with Ibnu, quoted in Winters, *Power in motion*, p. 85; Dan Coggin, 'Pertamina piling up the debts', *FEER*, 11 July 1975, p. 34.
38 Emmerson, 'The bureaucracy in political context', p. 115.
39 Quoted in Hamish McDonald, 'Now, crisis of loyalty for Suharto', *FEER*, 19 March 1976, p. 46.
40 Harvey Stockwin, 'Letter from Semarang', *FEER*, 26 March 1976, p. 70.
41 McDonald, 'Now, crisis of loyalty for Suharto', p. 47; Winters, *Power in motion*, p. 91n.; Schwarz, *A nation in waiting*, 1994, p. 324 n35; Bresnan, *Managing Indonesia*, pp. 184–6. See also Dan Coggin, 'Letter from Jakarta', *FEER*, 16 January 1976, p. 106; Harvey Stockwin, 'Why the general had to go', *FEER*, 19 March 1976, pp. 44–6.
42 *Kompas*, 16 February 1977.
43 Soeharto, *Pikiran*, pp. 305–6. It is interesting to note that there is no mention in Suharto's published 'diary' of his discussions with and determinations about Ibnu at the time of Pertamina's difficulties.
44 Stockwin, 'Why the general had to go', p. 46. See also Anon., 'Ibnu pergi. Piet akan memberesi', *Tempo*, 13 March 1976, pp. 5–6.
45 Harvey Stockwin, 'Indonesia: a depressing inertia', *FEER*, 20 February 1976, p. 44.
46 MacIntyre, 'Politics and the reorientation of economic policy', p. 143. See also Robison, *Indonesia: the rise of capital*, pp. 244–5; David Jenkins, 'Defending Indonesia's oil windfall', *FEER*, 27 July 1979, pp. 94–5.
47 Derek Davies, 'Rapture modified by reality', *FEER*, 7 November 1975, p. 3, citing a report from the US Department of Commerce.
48 Paraphrased in Nazaruddin (ed.), *Jejak langkah Pak Harto 27 Maret 1973–23 Maret 1978*, p. 239.
49 Paraphrased in Nazaruddin (ed.), *Jejak langkah Pak Harto 27 Maret 1973–23 Maret 1978*, p. 491 [26 May 1977]. See also David Jenkins, 'Suharto: borrowings justified', *FEER*, 27 August 1976, p. 93; McDonald, *Suharto's Indonesia*, p. 73.
50 McDonald, *Suharto's Indonesia*, p. 7; David Jenkins, 'The man who would be king', *FEER*, 18 November 1977, p. 38; Anon., 'The Orhiba connection', *Tempo*, 2 October 1976, p. 5.
51 Jenkins, 'The man who would be king', p. 40. See also Nazaruddin (ed.), *Jejak langkah Pak Harto 27 Maret 1973–23 Maret 1978*, pp. 395–6 [21 September 1976].
52 David Jenkins, 'Suharto battens down', *FEER*, 5 November 1976, p. 19.
53 Richard M. Smith, 'Indonesia: fading hopes', *Newsweek*, 8 November 1976, pp. 7–11.
54 Anon., 'Ramai-ramai sekitar Newsweek', *Tempo*, 20 November 1976, pp. 5–6; David Jenkins, 'Suharto slates a critic', *FEER*, 26 November 1976, p. 36; Anon., 'Sudah minta maaf?', *Tempo*, 12 February 1977, p. 16.
55 Soeharto, *Pikiran*, p. 348.
56 Nazaruddin (ed.), *Jejak langkah Pak Harto 27 Maret 1973–23 Maret 1978*, pp. 412–13.
57 *Kompas*, 3 January 1977.
58 David Jenkins, 'Pulling strings for Golkar', *FEER*, 12 November 1976, p. 34.
59 Ali Murtopo, quoted in Hamish McDonald, 'We're now much more mature', *FEER*, 14 May 1976, p. 27.
60 Anwar Nasir, 'Popularity by default', *FEER*, 2 July 1987, p. 42 (see also p. 41). See also Michael Vatikiotis, 'Faith without fanatics', *FEER*, 14 June 1990, p. 25.

61 Hamish McDonald, 'Muslims: an unknown quantity', *FEER*, 27 August 1976, p. 18.
62 Paraphrased in Nazaruddin (ed.), *Jejak langkah Pak Harto 27 Maret 1973–23 Maret 1978*, p. 268 [21 July 1975].
63 Soeharto, *Pikiran*, p. 259.
64 Paraphrased in Nazaruddin (ed.), *Jejak langkah Pak Harto 27 Maret 1973–23 Maret 1978*, p. 600 [20 February 1978].
65 Quoted in Jenkins, *Suharto*, p. 29.
66 Paraphrased in Nazaruddin (ed.), *Jejak langkah Pak Harto 27 Maret 1973–23 Maret 1978*, p. 459 [26 February 1977].
67 The 'White Book', produced by Kopkamtib and entitled *Gerakan 30 September Partai Komunis Indonesia (G.30.S/PKI)* (*The 30 September Movement of the Communist Party of Indonesia*), was published in 1978; a second and elaborated version was published in 1994 by the State Secretariat (Sekretariat Negara Republik Indonesia). See *Sinar Harapan*, 21 July 1978, for favourable editorial comment on the project. See also Anon., 'Buku putih yang pertama', *Tempo*, 5 August 1978, pp. 5–7.
68 The umrah is a ritually shortened form of pilgrimage conducted outside the *hajj* season (Nazaruddin, ed., *Jejak langkah Pak Harto 27 Maret 1973–23 Maret 1978*, pp. 557–8 [10 October 1977]; Anon., 'Memang mereka mengucapkan ahlan wa sahlan', *Tempo*, 29 October 1977, pp. 6–9; Soeharto, *Pikiran*, p. 281. Suharto and his party were permitted to enter the Kaaba during his visit.
69 McDonald, *Suharto's Indonesia*, p. 243; Jenkins, 'A chorus of critics for Suharto', *FEER*, 9 December 1977, pp. 26–7; Soeharto, *Pikiran*, p. 331; *Kompas*, 17 November 1977.
70 *Kompas*, 10 February 1978 (the date on which *Kompas* was allowed to start publishing again).
71 Soeharto, *Pikiran*, pp. 331–2.
72 David Jenkins, 'A gathering storm on campus', *FEER*, 7 March 1980, pp. 38–9, and 'What makes Daud Jusuf run?', *FEER*, 10 October 1980, pp. 36–8; Bourchier, 'Lineages', p. 220.
73 See *Kompas*, 13 March 1978.
74 Soeharto, *Pikiran*, p. 331.
75 McDonald, *Suharto's Indonesia*, pp. 247–9.
76 Sundhaussen, 'The military', p. 73.
77 Soeharto, *Pikiran*, p. 332; interview with Selo Sumarjan, Jakarta, 10 July 1997. See also David Jenkins, 'Muslim threat to Suharto', *FEER*, 10 March 1978, p. 27, and 'The sultan upstages Suharto', *FEER*, 24 March 1978, p. 18; Bresnan, *Managing Indonesia*, p. 201.
78 Soeharto, 'Penjelasan dan pengumuman tentang pembentukan Kabinet Pembangunan III, di Istana Merdeka, pada tanggal 29 Maret 1978', in Soeminto (ed.), *Presiden dan wakil Presiden*, p. 291.
79 Soeharto, *Pikiran*, p. 281; Nazaruddin (ed.), *Jejak langkah Pak Harto 27 Maret 1973–23 Maret 1978*, pp. 386–7 [23 August 1976]; Guy Sacerdoti, 'Acrobatic technocrats star in an Indonesian balancing act', *FEER*, 16 May 1980, p. 45.
80 Soeharto, *Pikiran*, pp. 280–1.
81 McDonald, *Suharto's Indonesia*, p. 166.
82 David Jenkins, 'Setting up the next five years', *FEER*, 13 October 1978, p. 61; McDonald, *Suharto's Indonesia*, pp. 251–3.
83 Anon., 'Indonesia', *Far Eastern Economic Review Asia 1980 Yearbook*, p. 188; Soeharto, *Pikiran*, p. 343; Soegih Arto, *Indonesia & I*, pp. 213–14. The government's action was probably attributable as well to the passage of the Fraser Amendment in the

United States in 1975 which linked American security-related aid to human rights performance. See also Nazaruddin (ed.), *Jejak langkah Pak Harto 27 Maret 1973–23 Maret 1978*, p. 402 [6 October 1976]; Nazaruddin (ed.), *Jejak langkah Pak Harto 29 Maret 1978–11 Maret 1983*, p. 21 [6 May 1978].

84 Paraphrased in Nazaruddin (ed.), *Jejak langkah Pak Harto 27 Maret 1973–23 Maret 1978*, p. 57 [5 October 1973].

85 Soeharto, *Pikiran*, pp. 334–5.

86 Nazaruddin (ed.), *Jejak langkah Pak Harto 27 Maret 1973–23 Maret 1978*, p. 386; Nazaruddin (ed.), *Jejak langkah Pak Harto 29 Maret 1978–11 Maret 1983*, pp. 85–6 [15 November 1978].

87 Suharto's end-of-year address in 1978, paraphrased in Nazaruddin (ed.), *Jejak langkah Pak Harto 29 Maret 1978–11 Maret 1983*, p. 99.

88 Soeharto, *Pikiran*, p. 337. See also David Jenkins, 'The tale of P4 – and how P7 irked P3', *FEER*, 24 July 1981, pp. 31–2.

89 Paraphrased in Nazaruddin (ed.), *Jejak langkah Pak Harto 27 Maret 1973–23 Maret 1978*, pp. 37, 223, 228 [16 July 1973, 8 and 26 March 1975]; Nazaruddin (ed.), *Jejak langkah Pak Harto 29 Maret 1978–11 Maret 1983*, pp. 71, 134 [1 October, 20 June 1978] (see also pp. 93, 124–5).

90 *Kompas*, 5 May, 5 November 1977.

91 Penders and Sundhaussen, *Abdul Haris Nasution*, p. 225; Jenkins, *Suharto*, p. 111.

92 Jenkins, *Suharto*, p. ix.

93 The complex story of the gestation of the Widodo paper is told in Jenkins, *Suharto*, chs 3–5.

94 For a discussion of the official push to consolidate the identity of interest between ABRI and Golkar, see David Jenkins, 'A question mark over the army', *FEER*, 11 January 1980, pp. 21–2, and 'The aging of the New Order', *FEER*, 27 June 1980, p. 24. For an intricate analysis of the debates and intrigue surrounding the issue of the twinning of ABRI and Golkar, see Jenkins, *Suharto*, ch. 7.

95 See *Berita Buana*, 28 March 1980, for a report of his impromptu address.

96 See *Berita Buana*, 17 April 1980; David Jenkins, 'Pancasila belongs to everyone', *FEER*, 30 May 1980, p. 23. See also Soeharto, *Pikiran*, pp. 534–5.

97 David Jenkins, 'A blow to the Achilles heel', *FEER*, 30 May 1980, pp. 22–3, and 'All my own work, even the typing', *FEER*, 30 May 1980, p. 23. See also Jenkins, *Suharto*, pp. 164–7; Jasin, *Saya tidak pernah*, pp. 135–55.

98 Soeharto, *Pikiran*, p. 346.

99 Jenkins, *Suharto*, pp. 191–201. The Hankam paper was later published as Nugroho Notosusanto (ed.), *Pejuang dan prajurit*.

100 These allegations related to the case of the corruptly obtained inheritance of former Pertamina official, Achmad Tahir. See Anon., 'Kartika, ia berkelit', *Tempo*, 26 July 1980, pp. 12–13.

101 David Jenkins, 'The mirror on the wall', *FEER*, 27 February 1981, pp. 19, 21. An American journalist was also expelled in late 1980.

102 Susumu Awanohara, 'Islam on the hustings', *FEER*, 23 April 1982, p. 25.

103 Guy Sacerdoti, 'Consensus conundrums', *FEER*, 21 August 1981, pp. 34–5, and 'The catch-all catchword', *FEER*, 21 August 1981, pp. 34–5; Susumu Awanohara, 'A change in the law?', *FEER*, 27 August 1982, pp. 20–1.

104 Nasution, quoted in David Jenkins, 'The distinguished dissident', *FEER*, 22 August 1980, p. 22.

105 *Kompas*, 6 November 1981.

106 Jenkins, *Suharto*, p. 21; Schwarz, *A nation in waiting*, pp. 117–18; Sudharmono, *Pengalaman*, pp. 295–307. A series of other decrees around the same time sought to give preference in government contracting to indigenous businesses (Robison, *Indonesia: the rise of capital*, pp. 185, 227). For a full discussion of Team 10 and its significance, see Winters, *Power in motion*, pp. 123ff. For a fascinating analysis of the State Secretariat and Sudharmono's use of it, see Pangaribuan, *The Indonesian State Secretariat*, especially chs 2 and 3.

9 ASCENDANCY

1 Soeharto, *Pikiran*, pp. 1, 2, 5, 392. See also *Kompas*, 15 November 1985; Bambang Bujono, 'Dari sawah naik ke Roma, swasembada jalan terus', *Tempo*, 23 November 1985, pp. 12–13.
2 Soeharto, *Pikiran*, pp. 364, 396, 399, 400.
3 Soeharto, *Pikiran*, p. 372.
4 Susumu Awanohara, 'Rough justice in Jakarta', *FEER*, 9 June 1983, pp. 17–18; Anon., 'Army killer squads spread terror in the cities', *Tapol Bulletin* 58 (1983), pp. 1–5; Anon., 'Petrus, di mata Broek', *Tempo*, 14 January 1984, p. 13; Van der Kroef, 'Petrus', pp. 750–1, 753–4; Guy Sacerdoti, 'Enter the communist bogey', *FEER*, 3 October 1980, p. 43.
5 Soeharto, *Pikiran*, pp. 389–90.
6 Tanter, 'Intelligence agencies and Third World militarization', p. 375.
7 Tanter, 'Intelligence agencies', p. 378.
8 Interview with L. B. Murdani, Jakarta, 17 June 1998. See also Tanter, 'Intelligence agencies', p. 340.
9 *Sinar Harapan*, 19 November 1984; Susumu Awanohara, 'Clampdown on the "50"', *FEER*, 22 November 1984, pp. 16–17; Cribb, 'The trials of H. R. Dharsono', pp. 3–5; Tanter, 'Intelligence agencies', p. 383. See also Dharsono, *Soeharto on trial*; Susanto Pudjomartono, '10 untuk Ton', *Tempo*, 18 January 1986, p. 14; Lincoln Kaye, 'Jail for the minister', *FEER*, 23 May 1985, p. 16, and 'Guilty as charged', *FEER*, 23 January 1986, pp. 10–11; Burns, 'The post-Priok trials', pp. 65–70.
10 See, for example, Syafruddin Prawiranegara, 'Pancasila as the sole foundation', pp. 74–83.
11 Susumu Awanohara, 'Clampdown on the "50"', p. 17.
12 Soeharto, *Pikiran*, pp. 406–7.
13 Vatikiotis, *Indonesian politics under Suharto*, 1993, pp. 54, 219.
14 Soeharto, *Pikiran*, pp. 408–9. See also *Kompas*, 3 April 1984.
15 Soeharto, *Pikiran*, pp. 227, 334, 346, 352, 370, 382, 387, 408–9, 438, 464. See also Ramage, *Politics in Indonesia*, p. 38; Ichlasul Amal, *Regional and central government*, p. 201.
16 Bourchier, 'Lineages', pp. x, 2.
17 Soeharto, *Pikiran*, pp. 334, 336, 337, 338, 405, 464.
18 Suharto's 1983 Independence Day address, paraphrased in Nazaruddin (ed.), *Jejak langkah Pak Harto 16 Maret 1983–11 Maret 1988*, p. 48 [16 August 1983].
19 Soeharto, *Pikiran*, pp. 422, 423. See also 'Atas kebebasan yang bertanggung jawab harus disadari pers sendiri' (sambutan Presiden pada pertemuan pemimpin redaksi dan PWI se Indonesia, di Istana Negara Jakarta tanggal 11 September 1981), in Anon., *Pers pembawa panji-panji demokrasi: Presiden Soeharto tentang pers Indonesia* (Jakarta: Persatuan Wartawan Indonesia (PWI) Pusat, 1983), p. 48.

20 Soeharto, *Pikiran*, p. 409. See also Schwarz, *A nation in waiting*, 1994, p. 239; Susumu Awanohara, 'An industry in better shape than ever before', *FEER*, 1 March 1984, pp. 28–30.
21 David Jenkins, 'After Marcos, now for the Soeharto billions', *Sydney Morning Herald*, 10 April 1986; Hamish McDonald, 'Press war continues', *FEER*, 24 April 1986, p. 18, and 'The price of freedom', *FEER*, 8 May 1986, pp. 44–5; Michael Byrnes, 'Jakarta's army lashes out at the threat from the south', *Australian Financial Review*, 3 June 1986; Shim Jae Hoon, 'Permission denied', *FEER*, 4 December 1986, p. 22.
22 Soeharto, *Pikiran*, p. 375.
23 *Kompas*, 28 April 1984.
24 Federspiel, 'Muslim intellectuals', p. 234.
25 Soeharto, *Pikiran*, p. 410.
26 Soeharto, *Pikiran*, pp. 418, 347.
27 See, for example, *Kompas*, 18 August 1984, 16 April 1986.
28 Soeharto, *Pikiran*, pp. 410, 566.
29 Lincoln Kaye, 'The killing time', *FEER*, 27 June 1985, pp. 34–5; Saur Hutabarat, 'Eksekusi bulan September', *Tempo*, 11 October 1986, pp. 15–16; Harold Crouch, 'Postponed executions may have political messages', *FEER*, 20 November 1986, p. 50. It remains unknown whether Syam was actually executed; Jakarta gossip has long related stories that he was in fact released and allowed to assume another identity in another country (see Benedict Anderson, 'Petrus dadi ratu', *New Left Review* 3 (second series), 2000, pp. 13–14).
30 Marzuki Darusman recounted to me his efforts to have the death sentences of PKI prisoners commuted; Suharto's response was not to commute them but at the same time not have them carried out for the sake of the families of the condemned (interview, Jakarta, 5 February 1999).
31 Soeharto, *Pikiran*, p. 337.
32 The fact that Suharto mentions the deaths of these three indicates that their rapid passing affected him significantly (Suharto, *Pikiran*, p. 440).
33 *Kompas*, 11 January 1984.
34 Quoted from Suharto's 1986–87 budget speech, *Tempo*, 11 January 1986, p. 12.
35 Soeharto, *Pikiran*, p. 256.
36 Quoted from Suharto's 1986–87 budget speech, *Tempo*, 11 January 1986, p. 12.
37 Paraphrased in *Kompas*, 18 August 1984.
38 Soeharto, *Pikiran*, p. 475. See also Anon., 'Melangkah ke mana lagi, setelah devaluasi?', *Tempo*, 27 September 1986, p. 72. On Suharto's decision, including his changes of mind, see Salim, 'Recollections of my career', p. 72.
39 Sjahrir and Brown, 'Indonesian financial and trade policy deregulation', p. 126; Michael Vatikiotis, 'The biggest market', *FEER*, 4 May 1989, p. 80. The reform initiatives are summarised in Winters, *Power in motion*, pp. 156–7.
40 Simanjuntak, 'The Indonesian economy in 1999', p. 71.
41 MacIntyre, 'Politics and the reorientation of economic policy', pp. 146, 150.
42 Vatikiotis, *Indonesian politics*, 1993, pp. 174, 176.
43 Soeharto, *Pikiran*, p. 412.
44 MacIntyre, 'Politics and the reorientation of economic policy', p. 152.
45 Soeharto, *Pikiran*, p. 417.
46 John McBeth, 'To market, to market', *FEER*, 25 August 1994, p. 47; Adam Schwarz, 'Monopoly under fire', *FEER*, 30 April 1992, p. 58; Schwarz, *A nation in waiting*, 1994, p. 143.

47 Jonathan Friedland, 'Jakarta's Rockefellers', *FEER*, 24 November 1988, pp. 80–1; *Asian Wall Street Journal*, 24, 25, 26 November 1986, 17 September 1990; Jonathan Friedland, 'The making of a cash cow', *FEER*, 24 November 1988, p. 82.
48 Paul Handley, 'Coming to the defence of the family business', *FEER*, 22 May 1986, p. 40; Adam Schwarz, 'Corporate catalyst', *FEER*, 30 April 1992, pp. 56–7; Schwarz, *A nation in waiting*, 1994, p. 142; Adam Schwarz, 'Father and children', *FEER*, 30 April 1992, p. 55.
49 Crouch, 'An ageing president, an ageing regime', p. 43.
50 Ramadhan, *Soemitro*, p. 420.
51 Anon., 'Mengenal kehidupan Presiden Soeharto', p. 50.
52 Ramadhan, *Soemitro*, pp. 265–6.
53 Interview with Arief Budiman, Melbourne, 5 July 2000.
54 Anon., 'A monopoly is forever', *FEER*, 26 February 1987, p. 57.
55 Soeharto, *Pikiran*, p. 515.
56 Mackie, 'Towkays and tycoons', p. 83.
57 See, especially, ch. 96 of Soeharto, *Pikiran*.
58 Soeharto, *Pikiran*, pp. 352, 373, 526–7.
59 Soeharto, *Pikiran*, pp. 365, 527, 413.
60 See Shim Jae Hoon, 'Minister defends Suharto family imports', *FEER*, 11 December 1986, p. 12 (comments by Cooperatives Minister Bustanil Arifin).
61 Soeharto, *Pikiran*, pp. 526, 379.
62 Soeharto, *Pikiran*, p. 538.
63 Soeharto, *Pikiran*, p. 286. See also Anwar Nasir, 'House and household', *FEER*, 2 July 1987, p. 38; Priyono B. Sumbogo and Bambang Sujatmoko, 'Ratusan masjid, seribu dai', *Tempo*, 6 July 1991, p. 29.
64 Iswandi, *Bisnis militer Orde Baru*, p. 260.
65 Soeharto, *Pikiran*, p. 288.
66 Vatikiotis, *Indonesian politics*, 1993, p. 52.
67 Soeharto, *Pikiran*, pp. 288, 293.
68 Mackie and MacIntyre, 'Politics', p. 4.
69 William Liddle, 'Of virtue and vice … of decisive action', *FEER*, 16 May 1985, p. 49.
70 Adam Schwarz, 'The indirect route', *FEER*, 30 March 1989, p. 50; Anon., 'Ia datang membayar pajak', *Tempo*, 4 February 1989, pp. 19–20.
71 Richard Nations, 'Modesty rewarded', *FEER*, 22 October 1982, p. 28.
72 Soeharto, *Pikiran*, pp. 488–9.
73 Vatikiotis, *Indonesian politics*, 1993, pp. 183, 192.
74 Soeharto, *Pikiran*, p. 480 (also p. 421). See also Suharto, 'Watashi', part 26, 27 January 1998, p. 40. (Paul Wolfowitz was US Ambassador to Indonesia 1986–89.)
75 Feith, 'East Timor', p. 64.
76 *Kompas*, 15 March 1984. See also Nazaruddin (ed.), *Jejak langkah Pak Harto 27 Maret 1973–23 Maret 1978*, p. 423 [31 December 1976].
77 Soeharto, *Pikiran*, pp. 232, 294, 364.
78 Soeharto, *Pikiran*, pp. 427–8. Suharto neglected in this passage to mention that 'almost every morning I exercise on an exercise bike' (p. 450).
79 Rodney Tasker, 'Support for Suharto from the "opposition"', *FEER*, 23 April 1987, p. 28; Shim Jae Hoon, 'Megawati power', *FEER*, 2 July 1987, pp. 20–1. See also Shim Jae Hoon, 'Minority political parties face struggle for votes', *FEER*, 20 November 1986, pp. 48–9.
80 Cited in Anon., 'Tak ada presiden seumur hidup', *Tempo*, 4 October 1986, p. 25.

81 Shim Jae Hoon, 'Searching for signs of Suharto's successor', *FEER*, 20 November 1986, p. 49.
82 Quoted in Anon., 'Pak Harto tentang calon presiden', *Tempo*, 25 October 1986, p. 12. See also Soeharto, *Pikiran*, p. 467.
83 A. Luqman, 'Sepah tak akan dibuang', *Tempo*, 6 September 1986, p. 17 (interview with Sudharmono); Shim Jae Hoon and Rodney Tasker, 'Signals for Suharto', *FEER*, 7 May 1987, pp. 32–3; Anwar Nasir, 'House and household', *FEER*, 2 July 1987, p. 38; Michael Vatikiotis, 'Reviving the red threat', *FEER*, 9 June 1988, p. 27; Vatikiotis, *Indonesian politics*, 1993, pp. 77–8.
84 Soeharto, *Pikiran*, p. 555. See also Gafur, *Siti Hartinah*, pp. 491–2. (*Mandataris* – the person holding the mandate.)
85 Vatikiotis, *Indonesian politics*, 1993, p. 195.
86 Quoted in Rodney Tasker, 'Suharto's staying power', *FEER*, 14 May 1987, p. 22.
87 Soeharto, *Pikiran*, p. 547. See also Michael Vatikiotis, 'A closer eye on young civilian leaders', *FEER*, 10 November 1988, p. 25.
88 Vatikiotis, *Indonesian politics*, 1993, p. 83.
89 Soeharto, *Pikiran*, p. 462 (see also ch. 101); Anderson and Kahin, 'Current data on the Indonesian military elite', *Indonesia* 36, 1983, pp. 99–112; *Sinar Harapan*, 5 October 1985; Michael Vatikiotis, 'The slow handover', *FEER*, 16 June 1988, p. 20.
90 Soeharto, *Pikiran*, p. 430.
91 Michael Vatikiotis, 'Siege tactics', *FEER*, 18 January 1990, p. 19.
92 Vatikiotis, *Indonesian politics*, 1993, pp. 83–4. Suharto's anger at these proceedings is clear in his extended discussion of the matter in his autobiography (Soeharto, *Pikiran*, pp. 547–52).
93 Michael Vatikiotis, 'Lines of allegiance', *FEER*, 18 January 1990, p. 24.
94 Michael Vatikiotis, 'Reviving the red threat', *FEER*, 9 June 1988, p. 27, and 'A communist comeback?', *FEER*, 16 June 1988, pp. 20–1.
95 Michael Vatikiotis, 'Outspoken official', *FEER*, 9 February 1989, p. 13.
96 Michael Vatikiotis, 'Mission completed', *FEER*, 22 September 1988, p. 18, and 'Stirrings on campus', *FEER*, 6 April 1989, p. 34; Herry Mohammad, 'Kopkamtib, sejarahnya dulu', *Gatra*, 8 February 1997, via indonesia-p@igc.apc.org; Amran Nasution et al., 'Melepas tongkat, menjelang lepas landas', *Tempo*, 17 September 1988, pp. 22–5; Rodney Tasker, 'Old soldiers never die', *FEER*, 21 April 1988, p. 16; Michael Vatikiotis, 'Intelligence influence', *FEER*, 24 November 1988, p. 16, and 'Guided by the past', *FEER*, 29 December 1988, p. 17; Tanter, 'Intelligence agencies', pp. 283, 348; Lowry, *The Armed Forces of Indonesia*, p. 61.
97 Tanter ('Intelligence agencies', p. 282n) cites his interview with Sumitro on 9 June 1988 to this effect.
98 Michael Vatikiotis, 'Suharto's staying power', *FEER*, 18 January 1990, pp. 22, 23. See also Vatikiotis, 'Succession talk', *FEER*, 27 April 1989, p. 28, and 'Spiking speculation', *FEER*, 22 June 1989, p. 25.
99 Cited in Michael Vatikiotis, 'Brass tacks', *FEER*, 7 September 1989, p. 28.
100 Michael Vatikiotis, 'Echoes from the grave', *FEER*, 18 January 1990, p. 26.
101 Michael Vatikiotis, 'Caution is the catchword for political rejuvenation', *FEER*, 3 March 1988, p. 27.
102 Nazaruddin (ed.), *Jejak langkah Pak Harto 21 Maret 1988–11 Maret 1993*, p. 197 [16 August 1989]; Amran Nasution et al., 'Harus konstitusional, kata presiden', *Tempo*, 23 September 1989, p. 14.

103 Quoted in Michael Vatikiotis, 'Stirrings on campus', *FEER*, 6 April 1989, p. 34. See also Nazaruddin (ed.), *Jejak langkah Pak Harto 21 Maret 1988–11 Maret 1993*, pp. 422–3 [18 May 1991].
104 Michael Vatikiotis, 'Directing the debate', *FEER*, 17 August 1989, p. 31.
105 Soeharto, *Pikiran*, pp. 459–60.
106 Ramage, *Politics in Indonesia*, pp. 40, 54, 84, 224n; Bambang Hatymurti, 'Halal-haramnya kebulatan tekad', *Tempo*, 26 May 1990, pp. 22–3; Alamsjah, *Perjalanan hidup*, pp. 313–18; Michael Vatikiotis, 'Call to the faithful', *FEER*, 14 December 1989, p. 34.
107 Susumu Awanohara, 'The balloon goes up on an offshore island', *FEER*, 7 February 1985, pp. 61–2.
108 Soeharto, *Pikiran*, p. 404. See also *Kompas*, 29 November 1984.
109 Paraphrased in Nazaruddin (ed.), *Jejak langkah Pak Harto 16 Maret 1983–11 Maret 1988*, p. 56 [10 September 1983].
110 Soeharto, *Pikiran*, p. 452.
111 Soeharto, *Pikiran*, pp. 455–7.
112 Vatikiotis, *Indonesian politics*, 1993, p. 61.

10 DECLINE, FALL, ACCOUNTING

1 Quoted in Anon., 'Sekarang calon itu sudah ada', *Tempo*, 5 March 1994, p. 33. Even in the mid-1970s, as he approached his mid-fifties, Suharto's 167 cm tall frame had carried only 76 kg (Roeder, *Anak desa*, p. 265).
2 Quoted in Ahmad K. Soeriawidjaja et al., 'Saya orang biasa', *Tempo*, 26 January 1991, p. 14.
3 See, for example, Mulya Lubis, 'The future of human rights in Indonesia', p. 117.
4 Anon., 'Suharto should step down in 1993', *Inside Indonesia* 24 (1990), pp. 6–7; Michael Vatikiotis, 'Wisdom of the elders', *FEER*, 30 August 1990, pp. 10–11, and 'Glasnost or 100 flowers', *FEER*, 18 October 1990, p. 24; Vatikiotis, *Indonesian politics under Suharto*, 1993, pp. 76, 144.
5 Quoted in Agus Basri et al., 'Kalau ABRI masuk kandang', *Tempo*, 29 February 1992, p. 34.
6 Harold Crouch and Hal Hill, 'Introduction', in Crouch and Hill (eds), *Indonesia Assessment 1992*, p. 2.
7 'Democracy indeed needs much deliberation, discussion, exchanging of views, and dialogue' (quoted in Diah Purnomawati and Linda Djalil, 'Isyarakat 17 Agustus 1990: kreativitas', *Tempo*, 25 August 1990, p. 25); Michael Vatikiotis, 'Glasnost or 100 flowers', *FEER*, 18 October 1990, pp. 23–4.
8 Soeharto, *Pikiran*, p. 529.
9 See Michael Richardson, 'Indonesian firms vow fresh support for plan to bridge wealth gap', *International Herald Tribune*, 27 January 1997, via indonesia-p@indopubs.com; Adam Schwarz, 'Piece of the action', *FEER*, 2 May 1991, p. 40.
10 Arief Budiman, 'Suharto's revised New Order', *FEER*, 22 December 1994, p. 21. See also Mark Clifford, 'Question of loyalty', *FEER*, 29 April 1993, p. 54; John McBeth, 'Hidden currents', *FEER*, 18 August 1994, p. 27.
11 Ramage, *Politics in Indonesia*, p. 64.
12 Quoted in Schwarz, *A nation in waiting*, 1994, p. 197. See also Michael Vatikiotis, 'The Muslim ticket', *FEER*, 20 December 1990, p. 10; Ramage, *Politics in Indonesia*, pp. 57–8.

13 Schwarz, *A nation in waiting*, 1994, p. 101. See also Vatikiotis, *Indonesian politics*, 1993, p. 173.
14 See Priyono B. Sumbogo et al., 'Kini tak bisa ditunda lagi', *Tempo*, 11 May 1991, p. 24. See also Ramage, *Politics in Indonesia*, pp. 86, 87–8; Budiman S. Hartoyo, 'Setelah panggilan Ibrahim dipenuhi', *Tempo*, 29 June 1991, pp. 14–15, and the special report in the following (6 July 1991) issue of *Tempo*; Vatikiotis, 'The Muslim ticket', p. 10; Michael Vatikiotis, 'Practical piety', *FEER*, 14 June 1990, p. 32, and 'Muffling the Monitor', *FEER*, 15 November 1990, pp. 83–4; Adam Schwarz, 'A worrying word', *FEER*, 25 April 1991, p. 23; Schwarz, *A nation in waiting*, 1994, pp. 175, 191.
15 Bourchier, 'Lineages', p. 258. See also Adam Schwarz, 'Opening gambits', *FEER*, 24 January 1991, p. 31.
16 Quoted in Schwarz, *A nation in waiting*, 1994, p. 214.
17 Marzuki Darusman, 'Indonesian political developments', p. 106.
18 Ramage, *Politics in Indonesia*, pp. 57, 67, 157ff.; Adam Schwarz, 'A worrying word', *FEER*, 25 April 1991, p. 23; Abdurrahman Wahid, 'The 1992 election', pp. 127–8; Schwarz, *A nation in waiting*, 1994, pp. 188–9, 192.
19 Wahid, 'The 1992 election', p. 126.
20 Habibie was wont to refer to Suharto in excessively reverential terms: 'Pak Harto is really like a father to me. He is my teacher' (quoted in Agus Basri et al., 'Mister Crack dari Pare-Pare', *Tempo*, 10 October 1992, via http//:www.pdat.co.id/arsiptmp71/92/nas).
21 Murdani interview with Vatikiotis, 3 May 1993, in Vatikiotis, *Indonesian politics*, 1993, p. 208. Murdani provided much the same account in 1998 (interview, Jakarta, 17 June).
22 Vatikiotis, *Indonesian politics*, 1993, p. 213; John McBeth, 'Father knows best', *FEER*, 25 November 1993, p. 25, and 'New kids on the block', *FEER*, 25 November 1993, p. 26.
23 Cited in John McBeth, 'Party patron', *FEER*, 4 November 1993, p. 14.
24 *Karyawan* (lit. 'employees in an office') refers here to the placing of military officers in positions normally filled by civilians, especially within the state bureaucracy.
25 Suharto remarked of *Primadosa* that 'they have distorted the facts [about the implications to be drawn from his relationship with Untung and Latief]' (Idrus F. Shahab, 'Setelah promosi Prima Dosa', *Editor*, 3 February 1994, p. 53); Dadi R. Sumaatmaja, 'Dia menggugat Presiden', *Editor*, 3 February 1994, p. 56.
26 Vatikiotis, *Indonesian politics*, 1993, pp. 96, 215.
27 As rendered by Wilson in Anon., 'Sekarang calon itu sudah ada', *Tempo*, 5 March 1994, p. 32.
28 John McBeth, 'Stop press', *FEER*, 23 June 1994, p. 17. See also Soeharto, *Pikiran*, p. 453.
29 Ramage, *Politics in Indonesia*, p. 142; Schwarz, *A nation in waiting*, 1994, pp. 72, 95; John McBeth, 'Techno-battles', *FEER*, 7 April 1994, p. 26; Margot Cohen, 'High anxiety', *FEER*, 29 September 1994, p. 32.
30 Schwarz, *A nation in waiting*, 1999, p. 320.
31 Schwarz, *A nation in waiting*, 1994, p. 279.
32 Interview with Adam Schwarz, 10 March 1998, quoted in Schwarz, *A nation in waiting*, 1999, p. 325.
33 Quoted in John McBeth, 'Succession talk recedes', *FEER*, 18 May 1995, p. 50.
34 Soeharto, *Pidato kenegaraan … 16 Agustus 1995*, pp. 6, 8, and *Pidato kenegaraan … 16 Agustus 1996*, pp. 7–8.

35 McBeth, 'Succession talk recedes', p. 48.
36 Suharto, 'Watashi', part 28, 29 January 1998, p. 40.
37 Kingsbury, *The politics of Indonesia*, p. 213.
38 Henny Sender, 'Bambang's challenge', *FEER*, 5 September 1996, p. 56; John McBeth, 'Middle ground', *FEER*, 19 January 1995, p. 48, and 'All in the family', *FEER*, 14 March 1996, pp. 50–1; Schwarz, *A nation in waiting*, 1994, pp. 152–3; Backman, *Asian eclipse*, pp. 278–9.
39 For a listing of Indonesia's largest conglomerates in 1993, see Anon., 'Peringkat 200 konglomerat 1993', *Warta Ekonomi*, 25 April 1994, pp. 28–35.
40 Kingsbury, *The politics of Indonesia*, p. 202.
41 For a crisp and incisive analysis of the dimensions of Suharto's corrupt behaviour, see Indonesian Corruption Watch, statement no. 051/SK/ICW/X/98, 'Proof of criminal act in the form of abuse of power by former President Soeharto' (mimeo).
42 See Kelly Bird, 'Survey of recent developments', *BIES* 32, 1 (1996), p. 18, which details Tax Department efforts to audit money-making foundations.
43 Except where noted, this paragraph is based on Margot Cohen, 'Twisting arms for alms', *FEER*, 2 May 1996, pp. 25–8; Anon., 'Tokoh kunci yayasan-yayasan raksasa', *Warta Ekonomi*, 13 July 1998, pp. 9–13; Naphtarina Mussolini et al., 'Enaknya punya yayasan raksasa', *Warta Ekonomi*, 13 July 1998, pp. 14–15.
44 Soeharto, *Pikiran*, p. 292.
45 Soeharto, *Pikiran*, p. 301. See also John McBeth, 'Ibu Tien's legacy', *FEER*, 9 May 1996, p. 20.
46 McBeth, 'Succession talk recedes', p. 48.
47 Quoted in Anon., 'In other words', *FEER*, 10 March 1994, p. 13.
48 Salim, 'Recollections of my career', p. 69.
49 *Straits Times*, 21 December 1995, in INTEL no. 313, via apakabar@clarknet.
50 Salim, 'Recollections of my career', p. 71.
51 Suharto, 'Watashi', part 27, 28 January 1998, p. 40
52 John McBeth, 'Some things linger', *FEER*, 1 December 1994, p. 16. Suharto ('Watashi', part 21, 22 January 1998, p. 40) later commented that Clinton's views were made with a view to his own re-election.
53 See, for example, Suharto, 'Watashi', part 6, 7 January 1998, p. 40; part 29, 30 January 1998, p. 40.
54 Interview in *Nihon Keizai Shimbun*, as reported in *Antara*, 15 August 1996, in INTEL no. 35, via apakabar@clark.net.
55 See, for example, 'It was Soeharto's order: Sutiyoso', *Jakarta Post*, 12 September 2000; 'Syarwan named suspect in attack on PDI office', *Indonesian Observer*, 17 October 2000; 'Zacky declared suspect in attack on PDI HQ', *Jakarta Post*, 30 October 2000; 'Feisal Tanjung points at Soeharto', *Jakarta Post*, 10 November 2000; 'July 27 attack ordered by Feisal Tanjung', *Indonesian Observer*, 15 November 2000 – all via indonesia-p@indopubs.com. See also John McBeth, 'Political encirclement', *FEER*, 21 October 1993, p. 14.
56 Soeharto, *Pidato kenegaraan … 16 Agustus 1996*, p. 13.
57 John McBeth, 'Line in the sand', *FEER*, 27 March 1997, p. 14.
58 *Antara*, 19 August 1996, INTEL no. 35, via apakabar@100-mail.clark.net.
59 McBeth, 'Line in the sand', p. 15; Patrick Walters, 'Suharto critic defends alliance', *Australian*, 15 April 1997. See also *Kompas*, 4 February, 3 April 1997.
60 *Kompas Online*, 9 June 1997, via indonesia-p@indopubs.com.
61 Soeharto, *Pikiran*, p. 559.

62 *Suara Merdeka*, 18 August 1997, via indonesia-p@indopubs.com.
63 *Kompas Online*, 6 December 1997, via indonesia-p@indopubs. He smiled when State Secretary Murdiono told him of the rumours of his death (*Kompas*, 10 December 1997, via indonesia-p@indopubs.com).
64 Hadi Soesastro and M. Chatib Basri, 'Survey of recent development', pp. 9–12, 21.
65 See Camdessus's explanation for his posture in Paul Kelly, 'Body language wrongly read', *Australian*, 9–10 May 1998.
66 Confidential interview, Jakarta, 10 June 1998.
67 Interview in *Nihon Keizai Shimbun*, as reported in *Antara*, 15 August 1996, in INTEL no. 35, via apakabar@clark.net.
68 *Kompas Online*, 12 March 1998, via indonesia-p@indopubs.
69 Soeharto, *Pikiran*, p. 191; *Kompas*, 18 June 1973.
70 See, for example, Volunteer Team for Humanity, 'Early documentation no. 1', 22 May 1998, and 'Early documentation no. 2', 9 June 1998; Patrick Walters, 'Riots engulf Jakarta', *Australian*, 14 May 1998; Patrick Walters, Don Greenlees and Robert Garran, 'Rioters control Jakarta streets', *Australian*, 15 May 1998; Patrick Walters and Don Greenlees, 'Death toll soars in riots' wake', *Australian*, 16–17 May, 1998.
71 Forrester, 'Introduction', pp. 21–2. See also Tim Tajuk, 'Teka-teki Jenderal Sjafrie', *Tajuk*, 3 September 1998, pp. 12–15.
72 Schwarz, *A nation in waiting*, 1999, p. 308.
73 *Kompas Online*, 18 May 1998, via indonesia-p@indopubs.com.
74 Cited in Sinansari, *Kronologi situasi penggulingan Soeharto*, p. 88.
75 Nurcholish Majid, interview with Michael Vatikiotis, 20 May 1998, quoted in Vatikiotis, *Indonesian politics*, 1998, p. 230.
76 Quoted in Schwarz, *A nation in waiting*, 1999, p. 361.
77 The text of Suharto's address is contained in Sinansari, *Kronologi*, pp. 102–11. See also Patrick Walters, 'I will surrender power', *Australian*, 20 May 1998.
78 Quoted in Sinansari, *Kronologi*, p. 114.
79 Interview with Ryaas Rasyid, Jakarta, 12 June 1998; Schwarz, *A nation in waiting*, 1999, p. 364. It seems clear that, notwithstanding his views on the need, for the good of the country, for Suharto to stand down, Wiranto remained loyal to him to the end (interview with Nazaruddin Syamsuddin, Jakarta, 17 June 1998), and did not make any special deal to preserve his position with Habibie.
80 Sulaeman Sakib and Hartono, 'Wawancara H. Probosutedjo: saya betul-betul jauh dari nepotisme', *Tajuk* 1, 15 (1998), p. 31. For a poignant reconstruction of those final moments, see Schwarz, *A nation in waiting*, 1999, pp. 308–9.
81 An English translation of his resignation speech can be found in Forrester and May (eds), *The fall of Soeharto*, pp. 246–7.
82 Kingsbury, *The politics of Indonesia*, p. 99.
83 David Jenkins, 'The politics of corruption', *FEER*, 20 August 1976, p. 19; Backman, *Asian eclipse*, pp. 12, 261.
84 O. G. Roeder, 'Progress before politics', *FEER*, 24 April 1969, p. 249.
85 Soeharto, *Pikiran*, p. 249.
86 Derek Davies, 'The army's double duty', *FEER*, 31 October 1970, p. 22. For a stimulating discussion based around the themes of 'circulation' and 'congestion' within the regime, see Sidel, 'Macet total'.
87 Sulaeman Sakib and Hartono, 'Wawancara H. Probosutedjo: saya betul-betul jauh dari nepotisme', *Tajuk* 1, 15 (1998), p. 32.

88 See, for example, the comments of Minister of Defence Yuwono Sudarsono (*Jakarta Post*, 14 June 2000, via indonesia-p@indopubs.com).
89 *Dow Jones Newswires*, 14 April 1999, via apakabar@saltmine.radix.net.
90 Susumu Awanohara, 'Jakarta aims to spread development's benefits throughout the nation', *FEER*, 7 February 1985, p. 43.
91 *Detikcom*, http://www.detikcom/berita/199812/981219-1/46.html (accessed 1 November 2000).
92 Cited in Schwarz, *A nation in waiting*, 1999, p. 375.
93 Jenny Grant, 'Phone tap points to Suharto cover-up', *South China Morning Post*, 19 February 1999, via Reuters Business Briefing (http://wwwf.briefing.reuters.com). Ghalib and Justice Minister Muladi travelled to Switzerland in May 1999 to investigate *Time* magazine reports of the massive riches of the Suhartos but found no trace of this alleged wealth (Johan Budi S. P. and Iwan Setiawan, 'A tortuous trail to Suharto's trial', *Tempo* (English edn), 10 September 2000, p. 18).
94 *Jakarta Post*, 19 February 2000, via indonesia-p@indopubs.com.

11 THE MAN AND HIS LEGACY

1 *Asiaweek*, 5 July 1996.
2 Suharto, 'Watashi', 31 January 1998, p. 40.
3 John Colmey and David Liebhold, 'The family firm', *Time*, 24 May 1999, pp. 36–48. Suharto's lawyers subsequently and unsuccessfully sought to sue *Time* for US$27 billion for libel (*Siar*, 6 June 2000, via apakabar@saltmine.radix.net).
4 Vatikiotis, *Indonesian politics*, 1993, p. 27.
5 Soeharto, *Pikiran*, p. 434.
6 Siti Hardiyanti Hastuti Rukmana (ed.), *Butir butir budaya Jawa.*
7 Interview with Subroto, Jakarta, 20 June 1998.
8 Interview with Frans Seda, Jakarta, 11 February 1999.
9 Soeharto, *Pikiran*, p. 300.
10 O. G. Roeder, *The smiling general.*
11 John McBeth, 'Succession talk recedes', *FEER*, 18 May 1995, p. 48. See also Schwarz, *A nation in waiting*, 1994, p. 44.
12 See, for example, Mody, *Indonesia under Suharto*, p. 132; Schwarz, *A nation in waiting*, 1994, p. 278.
13 See, for example, Hanna, 'The magical–mystical syndrome', p. 8; May, *The Indonesian tragedy*, p. 38; McDonald, *Suharto's Indonesia*, p. 1.
14 Pemberton, *On the subject of 'Java'*, p. 8.
15 Vatikiotis, *Indonesian politics*, 1993, p. 201.
16 Soeharto, *Pikiran*, p. 311.
17 A remarkable example of Suharto's thinking in Javanese categories can be found in 'Laporan stenografi amanat Presiden Soeharto pada malam ramah tamah dengan pengurus K.N.P.I. tanggal 19 Juli 1982 di Jalan Cendana no. 8 Jakarta' (kindly made available to me by Ken Ward).
18 Soeharto, *Pikiran*, pp. 382, 441–2. See also Ramadhan, *Soemitro*, p. 309; Suharto, 'Watashi', part 24, 25 January 1998, p. 36; Soemitro, *Pangkopkamtib*, p. 42.
19 Soeharto, *Pikiran*, p. 235.
20 Soeharto, 'Dalam perjuangan dibidang apapun, kekuatan andalan dan modal utama kita adalah rakyat', p. 2.

21 *Kompas*, 12 March 1971. It is interesting in this connection to note that Suharto's private secretary, Anton Tabah, responded to my assertion of Suharto's responsibility for the 1965–66 massacres by remarking that 'it was the people who destroyed the PKI' ('yang menumpas PKI adalah Rakyat') (pers. comm., 1 January 2000). Arief Budiman spoke to me of the ways in which those hunted down and killed, often in horrendous ways, were thought of as being sub-human (interview, Melbourne, 5 July 2000).
22 Quoted in SH, 'Sebuah keputusan 12 Maret', *Tempo*, 23 March 1986, p. 13.
23 Soeharto, *Pikiran*, p. 332.
24 Quoted in Anon., 'Interview with Ali Sadikin', *Inside Indonesia* 16 (1988), p. 3.
25 Quoted in Seth Mydans, 'The nutty President, a man for his times', *New York Times*, 17 June 1999.
26 Mackie and MacIntyre, 'Politics', p. 1.
27 See van der Eng's instructive and nuanced, 'Indonesia's economy and standard of living during the 20th century'; see also Booth, 'Poverty and inequality in the Soeharto era'.
28 Suharto, 'Watashi', part 30, 31 January 1998, p. 36.
29 Quoted in Schwarz, *A nation in waiting*, 1994, p. 237 (see pp. 235–6 for a broader critique of the cultural poverty of the New Order period).

Select bibliography

ARCHIVES

Ministerie van Buitenlandse Zaken, The Hague: Archief van de Netherlands Forces Intelligence Service/Centrale Militaire Inlichtingendienst (NEFIS/CMI) 1942–1949; Archief Indonesische kwestie: Indonesië in de Veiligheidsraad

Algemeen Rijksarchief, The Hague: Archief van de Algemene Secretarie van de Nederlands-Indische Regering en de daarbij gedeponeerde archievem, 1942–1950; Collectie Spoor; Rapportage Indonesië 1945–1950; Procureur-Generaal bij het Hooggerechtshof van Nederlandsch-Indië 1945–1949; Dossiersarchief van het Ministerie van Koloniën en opvolgers (1859–) 1945–63 (–1979)

Ministerie van Defensie, Centraal Archievendepot, Rijswijk: Algemeen-Archief van de Centrale Militaire Inlichtingendienst (NEFIS); Hoofdkwartier van de Generale Staf van het Leger in Indonesië; Krijgsgeschiedkundige Sectie van het Hoofdkwartier Generale Staf in Indonesië; Archief 'T' Brigade

Sectie Militaire Geschiedenis, Koninklijk Landmacht, The Hague: Notebook of 2nd Lt. K. Meijer (Archief NI 45-50, 0101/1A); Archive 'T' Brigade 216-5

Nederlands Instituut voor Oorlogsdocumentatie: Indische collectie

NEWSPAPERS AND MAGAZINES

Adil, Antara, Antara News Bulletin, Asian Wall Street Journal, Asiaweek, Associated Press, Australian, Australian Financial Review, Berita Buana, D & R, Daily Yomiuri Online, De Locomotief, De Tak, Dow Jones Newswires, Duta Masyarakat, Economist, Editor, Far Eastern Economic Review (and *Yearbook*)*, Forum Keadilan, Gatra, Guardian, Harian Rakyat, Independent Monthly, Indonesia Business Weekly, Indonesia Raya, Indonesian Herald, Indonesian Observer, Indonesian Times, Inter Press Service On-Line, International Herald Tribune, Jakarta Post, Jawa Pos, Kedaulatan Rakyat, Keng Po, Kompas, Matra, Media Indonesia, Merdeka, New York Review of Books, New York Times, Newsweek, Nihon Keizai Shimbun, Pedoman Rakyat, Republika, Reuter, Review of Indonesia, Siasat, Sinar Harapan, South China Morning Post, Straits Times, Suara Merdeka, Suara Pembaruan, Suluh Indonesia, Sydney Morning Herald, Tajuk, Tempo, Tempo Interaktif, Time, Tiras, United Press International, Warta Ekonomi*

BOOKS, DISSERTATIONS AND JOURNAL ARTICLES

Abdurrahman Wahid, 'The 1992 election: a devastating political earthquake?', in Crouch and Hill (eds), *Indonesia Assessment 1992.*

Abrar Yasra and Ramadhan K. H., *Hoegeng: polisi idaman dan kenyataan* (Jakarta: Pustaka Sinar Harapan, 1993).

Achmad D. S. (ed.), *Wawantjara djendral dengan wartawan* (Solo: Rilan, 1966).

Adian Husaini, *Soeharto 1998* (Jakarta: Gema Insoni, 1996).

Aidit, D. N., *Indonesian society and the Indonesian revolution* (Jakarta: Yayasan 'Pembaruan', 1958).

Alamsjah Ratu Prawiranegara, *Perjalanan hidup seorang anak yatim piatu* (Jakarta: Pustaka Sinar Harapan, 1995).

Ali Moertopo, 'Pak Harto, Pak Yoga and saya, terpisah tapi berjalan berhimpitan', in Wiwoho and Bandjar, *Memori Jenderal Yoga.*

—— 'Some basic considerations in 25-year development', *The Indonesian Quarterly* 1, 1 (1972), pp. 3–25.

Amirmachmud, *H. Amirmachmud menjawab* (Jakarta: CV Haji Masagung, 1987).

Amnesty International, *Power and impunity: human rights under the New Order* (London: Amnesty International Publications, 1994).

Anderson, B. R. O'G., 'Japan: "The light of Asia"', in Josef Silverstein (ed.), *Southeast Asia in World War II: four essays* (New Haven: Yale University, 1966).

Anderson, Ben, 'Current data on the Indonesian military elite', *Indonesia* 40 (1985), pp. 131–64.

—— 'Current data on the Indonesian military elite', *Indonesia* 45 (1988), pp. 137–60.

—— 'Current data on the Indonesian military elite', *Indonesia* 48 (1989), pp. 65–96.

—— 'How did the generals die?', *Indonesia* 43 (1987), pp. 109–34.

Anderson, Benedict R. and Ruth T. McVey (with the assistance of Frederick P. Bunnell), *A preliminary analysis of the October 1, 1965 coup in Indonesia* (Ithaca: Modern Indonesia Project, Cornell University, 1971).

Anderson, Benedict R. O'G., 'Cartoons and monuments: the evolution of political communication under the New Order', in Jackson and Pye (eds), *Political power and communications in Indonesia.*

—— 'Notes on contemporary political communication', *Indonesia* 16 (1973), pp. 38–80.

—— 'Old state, new society: Indonesia's New Order in comparative historical perspective', in Benedict R. O'G. Anderson, *Language and power: exploring political cultures in Indonesia* (Ithaca: Cornell University Press, 1990).

—— *Java in a time of revolution: occupation and resistance, 1944–1946* (Ithaca: Cornell University Press, 1972).

Anderson, Benedict and Audrey Kahin, 'Current data on the Indonesian military elite', *Indonesia* 29 (1980), pp. 155–75.

—— 'Current data on the Indonesian military elite', *Indonesia* 33 (1982), pp. 129–48.

—— 'Current data on the Indonesian military elite', *Indonesia* 36 (1983), pp. 99–134.

—— 'Current data on the Indonesian military elite (continued)', *Indonesia* 37 (1984), pp. 145–69.

—— 'The Fourth Development Cabinet announced March 17, 1983', *Indonesia* 35 (1983), pp. 37–52.

Anderson, Benedict and Judith Ecklund, 'Current data on the Indonesian military elite', *Indonesia* 23 (1977), pp. 175–90.

Anderson, Benedict, Judith Ecklund and Audrey Kahin, 'Current data on the Indonesian military elite', *Indonesia* 26 (1978), pp. 159–77.

Anderson, Benedict and Elizabeth Graves, 'Current data on the Indonesian military elite after the reorganization of 1969–1970', *Indonesia* 10 (1970), pp. 194–208.

Anderson, Benedict, Elizabeth Graves, Filino Harahap, Mildred Wageman and Elizabeth Witton, 'Current data on the Indonesian military elite', *Indonesia* 7 (1969), pp. 195–201.

Anderson, Benedict and Susan Hatch, 'Current data on the Indonesian military elite', *Indonesia* 15 (1973), pp. 187–97.

—— 'Current data on the Indonesian military elite', *Indonesia* 18 (1974), pp. 153–67.

Anderson, Benedict, Takashi Shiraishi and James T. Siegel, 'Current data on the Indonesian military elite', *Indonesia* 60 (1995), pp. 101–46.

—— 'Current data on the Indonesian military elite: October 1, 1995–December 31, 1997', *Indonesia* 65 (1998), pp. 179–94.

—— 'Current data on the Indonesian military elite: January 1, 1998–January 31, 1999', *Indonesia* 67 (1999), pp. 133–62.

—— 'The Indonesian military in the mid-1990s: political maneuvering or structural change?', *Indonesia* 63 (1997), pp. 91–105.

Anderson, David Charles, 'The military aspects of the Madiun affair', *Indonesia* 21 (1976), pp. 1–63.

Anhar Gonggong, *Abdul Qahhar Mudzakkar: dari patriot henggga pemberontak* (Jakarta: Grasindo, 1992).

Anon., '1.7 million ex-tapols are being re-registered', *Tapol Bulletin* 70 (1985), p. 1.

—— '18 tahun Sekolah Staf dan Komando Angkatan Darat 1950–1969', special issue of *Kata Wira Jati*, no. 31, 1969.

—— 'Anti-communist witch-hunt, 1985', *Tapol Bulletin* 72 (1985), pp. 15–16.

—— 'Army killer squads spread terror in the cities', *Tapol Bulletin* 58 (1983), pp. 1–5.

—— 'Berdirinja S.S.K.A.D.', in Anon., *Documentaria Cursus 'C'. Sekolah Staf & Komando Angkatan Darat Tentara Nasional Indonesia. Angkatan ke 1 Oktober '58/Desember '59* (n.p.: n.p., n.d.).

—— 'Buyung Nasution interviewed by Tapol', *Tapol Bulletin* 50 (1982), pp. 3–9.

—— 'A clean up for Suharto's image', *Tapol Bulletin* 72 (1985), pp. 18–19.

—— 'Colonel Latief's defence', *Tapol Bulletin* 35 (1979), pp. 8–10.

—— 'Daftar pembagian kelompok dalam pembahasan pada tgl. 12-12-'60 untuk membahas pertanjaan 1, persoalan 1', *Karya Wira Jati* 1 (1961), p. 59.

—— 'Daftar pembagian kelompok dalam pembahasan pada tgl. 13-12-'60 untuk membahas pertanjaan 2, persoalan 1', *Karya Wira Jati* 1 (1961), p. 60.

—— 'Daftar pembagian kelompok dalam pembahasan persoalan II tentang penggunaan kekuatan militer dalam penjelesaian keamanan dalam negeri pada tgl. 14-12-'60 /d tgl. 15-12-'60', *Karya Wira Jati* 1 (1961), p. 75.

—— 'Former police chief speaks out on regime' [interview with Hugeng], *Tapol Bulletin* 13 (1975), pp. 4, 7.

—— 'Hal² mengenai Seminar I SESKOAD tentang masalah² pertahanan', *Karya Wira Jati* 1 (1961), pp. 5–7.

—— 'Interview with Ali Sadikin', *Inside Indonesia* 16 (1988), pp. 2–4.

—— 'Isu Soeharto Cina, siapa bapaknya?', wysiwyg://47/http://www.geocities.com/CapitolHill/4120/soeharto.html, accessed 26 January 2000.

—— 'Kesan penindjauan Presiden Soeharto selama delapan hari ke 53 projek di desa-desa Djawa Tengah dan Djawa Timur', *Indonesia Magazine* 5 (1970), pp. 43–50, 109–23.

—— 'Kesimpulan dan hasil pembahasan persoalan kedua', *Karya Wira Jati* 1 (1961), pp. 61–6.
—— 'Kesimpulan dan hasil pembahasan persoalan pertama', *Karya Wira Jati* 1 (1961), pp. 46–9.
—— 'Mengenal kehidupan Presiden Soeharto', *Indonesia Magazine* 19 (1973), pp. 45–54.
—— 'Pembahasan dan pendapat kelompok² seminar terhadap hasil telaahan militer kelompok III jang disimpulkan', *Karya Wira Jati* 1 (1961), pp. 67–74.
—— 'Pembahasan dan pendapat² kelompok² seminar terhadap hasil telaahan militer kelompok I jang disimpulkan', *Karya Wira Jati* 1 (1961), pp. 50–8.
—— 'A profile of Ali Murtopo (1924–)', *Tapol Bulletin* 50 (1982), p. 22.
—— 'A profile of General Benny Murdani', *Tapol Bulletin* 57 (1983), pp. 16–17.
—— 'Republic under siege: an interview with Sri Sultan Hamengku Buwono IX', in Wild and Carey (eds), *Born in fire.*
—— 'The Rudy Habibie empire', *Tapol Bulletin* 127 (1995), pp. 8–9.
—— 'Sedjarah perkembangan Sekolah Staf dan Komando Angkatan Darat', in Anon., '18 tahun Sekolah Staf', pp. 8–24.
—— 'Seminar Angkatan Darat ke II di-Bandung. Tanggal 26 Agustus 1966' (typescript held in Monash University library).
—— 'Several Indonesian views of the struggle: an interview with four participants', in Wild and Carey (eds), *Born in fire.*
—— 'Soal² yang telah dipeladjarkan di C "C" I SSKAD dari bulan ke bulan', in Anon., *Documentaria cursus 'C'.*
—— 'Suharto should step down in 1993', *Inside Indonesia* 24 (1990), pp. 6–7.
—— 'White Book of the 1978 students' struggle', *Indonesia* 25 (1978), pp. 151–82.
—— *The Armed Forces/Army civic mission is not militarism* (Jakarta: Department of Information, 1967).
—— *CSIS 20 tahun* (Jakarta: n.p., 1991).
—— *Decisions of the fourth plenary session of the Madjelis Permusjawaratan Rakjat Sementara (The Provisional People's Consultative Assembly) 20th of June–5th of July 1966* (special issue 005/1966, Jakarta: Department of Information, 1966).
—— *Documentaria cursus 'C'. Sekolah Staf & Komando Angkatan Darat Tentara Nasional Indonesia. Angkatan ke 1 Oktober '58/Desember '59* (n.p.: n.p., n.d.).
—— *Foreign relations of the United States, 1964–68, vol. XXVI, Indonesia; Malaysia–Singapore; Philippines* (2001), http://www.gwu.edu/~nsarchiv/NSAEBB/NSAEBB52/.
—— *G-30-S dihadapan Mahmillub 3 di Djakarta* (Jakarta: P.T. Pembimbing Masa, 1966–67).
—— *Gerakan 30 September antara fakta dan rekayasa: berdasarkan kesaksian para pelaku sejarah* (Yogyakarta: Center for Information Analysis/Penerbit Media Pressindo, 1999).
—— *Jawa Nenkan* [Java Year Book] (Jakarta: Jawa Shinbunsha, 1944).
—— *Peranan TNI Angkatan Darat dalam perang kemerdekaan (revolusi pisik 1945–1950)* (Bandung: Pusat Sedjarah Militer Angkatan Darat, 1965).
—— *Putusan Mahkamah Tentara Agung Republik Indonesia de Djogjakarta tanggal 27 Mei 1948 dalam perkaranya: terdakwa²; Djenderal Major Sudarsono, Mr. Muhamam Yamin, Mr. Achmad Subardjo, Mr. Iwa Kusuma Sumantri c.s. Peristiwa 3 Juli 1946* (Jakarta: G.C.T. van Dorp, 1949).
—— *Serangan Umum 1 Maret 1949 di Yogyakarta: latar belakang dan pengaruhnya*, 5th printing (Jakarta: Citra Lamtoro Gung Persada, 1992 [originally published by Seskoad, Bandung, 1989]).

—— *Soeharto, President of the Republic of Indonesia* (Jakarta: Department of Information, 1988?).

—— *Sumbangan fikiran TNI-AD kepada Kabinet Ampera: hasil seminar AD ke-II tanggal 25 s/d 31 Agustus 1966 di Graha Wiyata Yudha/Seskoad Bandung* (n.p.: Seksi Penerangan Koti, 1966?).

—— *Tri Komando Rakyat: pembebasan Irian Jaya (Trikora)* (Jakarta: Pusat Sejarah dan Tradisi ABRI, 1995).

Anwar, Dewi Fortuna, *Indonesia's strategic culture: ketahanan nasional, wawasan nusantara and Hankamrata* (Brisbane: Australia–Asia Papers No. 75, Centre for the Study of Australia–Asia Relations, Griffith University, 1996).

Anwar, Rosihan, *Soebadio Sastrosatomo: pengemban misi politik* (Jakarta: Pustaka Utama Grafiti, 1995).

Ascher, William, 'From oil to timber: the political economy of off-budget development financing in Indonesia', *Indonesia* 65 (1998), pp. 37–61.

Aspinall, E., 'Students and the military: regime friction and civilian dissent in the late Suharto period', *Indonesia* 59 (1995), pp. 21–44.

Aspinall, Ed, 'Opposition and elite conflict in the fall of Soeharto', in Forrester and May (eds), *The fall of Soeharto.*

Aspinall, Edward, Herb Feith and Gerry van Klinken (eds), *The last days of President Suharto* (Clayton: Monash Asia Institute, 1999).

Backman, Michael, *Asian eclipse: exposing the dark side of business in Asia* (Singapore: John Wiley & Sons, 1999).

Bardosono, *Peristiwa Sulawesi Selatan 1950* (Jakarta: Yayasan Pustaka Militer, 1955).

Barr, Christopher M., 'Bob Hasan, the rise of Apkindo, and the shifting dynamics of control in Indonesia's timber sector', *Indonesia* 65 (1998), pp. 1–36.

Bertrand, Jacques, 'False starts, succession crises, and regime transition: flirting with openness in Indonesia', *Pacific Affairs* 69, 3 (1996), pp. 319–40.

Booth, Anne, 'Poverty and inequality in the Soeharto era: an assessment', *Bulletin of Indonesian Economic Studies* 36, 1 (2000), pp. 73–104.

Bourchier, David, 'Crime, law, and state authority in Indonesia', in Budiman (ed.), *State and civil society in Indonesia.*

—— 'Habibie's interregnum: *reformasi*, elections, regionalism and the struggle for power', in Manning and van Dierman (eds), *Indonesia in transition.*

—— 'Lineages of organicist political thought in Indonesia', PhD thesis, Monash University, 1996.

—— 'The 1950s in New Order ideology and politics', in Bourchier and Legge (eds), *Democracy in Indonesia.*

Bourchier, David and John Legge (eds), *Democracy in Indonesia: 1950s to 1990s* (Clayton: Centre of Southeast Asian Studies, Monash University, 1994).

Brackman, Arnold, *The communist collapse in Indonesia* (New York: W.W. Norton, 1969).

Brackman, Arnold C., *Indonesia: the Gestapu affair* (New York: American–Asian Educational Exchange, 1969).

Bresnan, John, *Managing Indonesia: the modern political economy* (New York: Columbia University Press, 1993).

Britton, Peter, 'The Indonesian army: "stabiliser" and "dynamiser"', in Mortimer (ed.), *Showcase state.*

Brooks, Karen, 'The rustle of ghosts: Bung Karno in the New Order', *Indonesia* 60 (1995), pp. 61–99.

Budiardjo, Carmel, 'Political imprisonment in Indonesia', in Taylor et al., *Repression and exploitation in Indonesia.*
—— 'Did Suharto mastermind the 1965 "coup attempt"?', *Tapol Bulletin* 50 (1982), pp. 12–14.
Budiman, Arief, 'A conversation with Pak Harto', in Roger M. Smith (ed.), *Southeast Asia: documents of political development and change* (Ithaca: Cornell University Press, 1974).
—— 'Indonesian politics in the 1990s', in Crouch and Hill (eds), *Indonesia Assessment 1992.*
—— 'Portrait of a young Indonesian looking at his surroundings', *Internationales Asienforum* 4 (1973), pp. 76–88.
Budiman, Arief (ed.), *State and civil society in Indonesia* (Clayton: Monash Papers on Southeast Asia No. 22, 1992).
Bunnell, Frederick, 'American "low posture" policy towards Indonesia in the months leading to the 1965 "coup"', *Indonesia* 50 (1990), pp. 29–60.
Bunnell, Frederick Philip, 'The Kennedy initiatives in Indonesia, 1962–1963', PhD thesis, Cornell University, 1969.
Burns, Peter, 'The post-Priok trials: religious principles and legal issues', *Indonesia* 47 (1989), pp. 61–88.
Cammack, Mark, 'Indonesia's 1989 Religious Judicature Act: Islamization of Indonesia or Indonesianization of Islam?', *Indonesia* 63 (1997), pp. 145–68.
Capizzi, Elaine, 'Trade unions under the New Order', in Taylor et al. (eds), *Repression and exploitation in Indonesia.*
Cholil, M., *Sedjarah operasi² pembebasan Irian-Barat* (Jakarta: Departemen Pertahanan Keamanan, Pusat Sedjarah ABRI, 1971).
Coppel, Charles A., 'Patterns of Chinese political activity in Indonesia', in J. A. C. Mackie (ed.), *The Chinese in Indonesia: five essays* (Honolulu: University Press of Hawai'i, 1976).
Cribb, Robert, 'Elections in Jakarta', *Asian Survey* 24, 6 (1984), pp. 655–64.
—— 'Heirs to the late colonial state? The Indonesian Republic, the Netherlands Indies and the revolution, 1945–1949' (unpublished paper, Netherlands Institute of Advanced Studies, n.d.).
—— 'Indonesian political development, 1989–1990', in Hal Hill and Terry Hull (eds), *Indonesia Assessment 1990* (Canberra: Political and Social Change Monograph 11, Australian National University, 1990).
—— 'Problems in the historiography of the killings in Indonesia', in Robert Cribb (ed.), *The Indonesian killings of 1965–1966: studies from Java and and Bali* (Clayton: Monash Papers on Southeast Asia No. 21, Monash University, 1990).
—— 'The trials of H. R. Dharsono', *Inside Indonesia* 7 (1986), pp. 3–5.
—— *Historical atlas of Indonesia* (London: Curzon, 2000).
—— *Historical dictionary of Indonesia* (Metuchen, NJ: Scarecrow Press, 1992).
Cribb, Robert and Colin Brown, *Modern Indonesia: a history since 1945* (London: Longman, 1995).
Crouch, Harold, 'An ageing president, an ageing regime', in Crouch and Hill (eds), *Indonesia Assessment 1992.*
—— 'Another look at the Indonesian "coup"', *Indonesia* 15 (1973), pp. 1–20.
—— 'The army, the parties and elections', *Indonesia* 11 (1971), pp. 177–92.
—— 'Introduction', in Budiman (ed.), *State and civil society in Indonesia.*
—— *The army and politics in Indonesia*, rev. edn (Ithaca: Cornell University Press, 1988).

Crouch, Harold and Hal Hill (eds), *Indonesia Assessment 1992: political perspectives on the 1990s* (Canberra: Political and Social Change Monograph 17, Australian National University, 1992).

Dasman Djamaluddin, *Jenderal TNI anumerta Basoeki Rachmat dan Supersemar* (Jakarta: Grasindo, 1998).

De Geus, P. B. R., *De Nieuw-Guinea kwestie: aspecten van buitenlands beleid en militaire macht* (Leiden: Martinus Nijhoff, 1984).

Deliar Noer, *Aku bagian ummat, aku bagian bangsa: otobiografi Deliar Noer* (Bandung: Penerbit Mizan, 1996).

Departemen Dalam Negeri, *Departemen Dalam Negeri dari masa ke masa: tentang biografi menteri-menteri 1945–1995* (Jakarta: Departemen Dalam Negeri, 1996).

Departemen Penerangan, *Susunan kabinet Republik Indonesia 1945–1970* (Jakarta: Paramita, 1970).

Dharsono, H. R., *Soeharto on trial: Gen. H. R. Dharsono's plea* (Amsterdam: Lembaga Merah Putih, 1986).

Dinas Sejarah Militer TNI-Angkatan Darat, *Cuplikan sejarah perjuangan TNI-Angkatan Darat* (Bandung/Jakarta: Dinas Sejarah Militer TNI-Angkatan Darat/Fa. Mahjuma, 1972).

Dinuth, Alex (ed.), *Dokumen terpilih sekitar G.30.S/PKI* (Jakarta: Intermas, 1997).

Djamal Marsudi, *Menjingkap-tabir fakta-fakta pemberontakan P.K.I. dalam peristiwa Madiun* (Jakarta: Merdeka Press, 1966).

Djudjuk Juyoto S. T., Lazuardi Adi Sage and S. Budhi Raharjo, *Gemuruh Kemusuk: profil desa perjuangan* (Jakarta: Tifa Proyeksi Utama, 1991).

Drooglever, P. J., 'Mars in beweging. Denkbeelden over legerhervorming in het tijdvak van de dekolonisatie', in G. Teitler and P. M. H. Groen (eds), *De politionele acties* (Amsterdam: De Bataafche Leeuw, 1987).

—— 'Sultan in oorlogstijd: Hamengkubuwono IX en de bezetting van Yogyakarta in 1948/49', inaugural professorial lecture, 15 May 1996, Katholieke Universiteit Nijmegen (n.p.: n.p., n.d.).

—— 'Uneasy encounters: Semarang, Ambarawa and Magelang during the first months of the revolution', in T. Ibrahim Alfian et al. (eds), *Dari babad dan hikayat sampai sejarah kritis: kumpulan karangan dipersembahkan kepada Prof. Dr. Sartono Kartodirdjo* (Yogyakarta: Gadjah Mada University Press, 1987).

Drooglever, P. J. and M. J. B. Schouten (eds), *Officiële bescheiden betreffende de Nederlands-Indonesiasche betrekkingen 1945–1950* vols. 16 and 17 ('s-Gravenhage: Instituut voor Nederlandse Geschiedenis, 1991–92).

Dwipayana, G. and Nazaruddin Sjamsuddin (eds), *Diantara para sahabat: Pak Harto 70 tahun* (Jakarta: Citra Lamtoro Gung Persada, 1991).

—— *Jejak langkah Pak Harto 1 Oktober 1965–27 Maret 1968* (Jakarta: Citra Lamtoro Gung Persada, 1991).

—— *Jejak langkah Pak Harto 28 Maret 1968–23 Maret 1973* (Jakarta: Citra Lamtoro Gung Persada, 1991).

Emmerson, Donald K., 'The bureaucracy in political context: weakness in strength', in Jackson and Pye (eds), *Political power and communications in Indonesia.*

—— 'Indonesia in 1990: a foreshadow play', *Asian Survey* 31, 2 (1991), pp. 179–87.

—— 'Understanding the New Order: bureaucratic pluralism in Indonesia', *Asian Survey* 23, 11 (1983), pp. 1220–41.

Evans III, Bryan, 'The influence of the United States Army on the development of the Indonesian Army (1954–1964)', *Indonesia* 47 (1989), pp. 25–48.

Fazlur Akhmad, 'The Indonesian student movement, 1920–1989: a force for radical social change?', *Prisma* 47 (1989), pp. 83–95.

Federspiel, Howard M., 'Muslim intellectuals and Indonesia's national development', *Asian Survey* 31, 3 (1991), pp. 233–46.

Feith, H., 'Dynamics of Guided Democracy', in Ruth McVey (ed.), *Indonesia* (New Haven: Human Relations Area Files Press, 1963).

—— 'President Sukarno, the army and the communists: the triangle changes shape', *Asian Survey* 4 (1964), pp. 969–80.

Feith, H. and Lance Castles (eds), *Indonesian political thinking* (Ithaca: Cornell University Press, 1970).

Feith, Herb, 'Constitutional democracy: how well did it function', in Bourchier and Legge (eds), *Democracy in Indonesia.*

—— 'East Timor: the opening up, the crackdown and the possibility of a durable settlement', in Crouch and Hill (eds), *Indonesia Assessment 1992.*

—— 'Growth and development in Asia: some criticisms of conventional approaches', Lecture to the Asian Leadership Development Centre of World Student Christian Federation, Tosanzo, Japan, October 1972.

—— 'Suharto's search for a political format', *Indonesia* 6 (1968), pp. 88–105.

Feith, Herbert, *The decline of constitutional democracy in Indonesia* (Ithaca: Cornell University Press, 1962).

—— *The Indonesian elections of 1955* (Ithaca: Modern Indonesia Project, Southeast Asia Program, Cornell University, 1957).

Feith, Herbert and Daniel S. Lev, 'The end of the Indonesian rebellion', *Pacific Affairs* 36 (1963), pp. 32–46.

Forrester, Geoffrey, 'Introduction', in Forrester and May (eds), *The fall of Soeharto.*

Forrester, Geoffrey and R. J. May (eds), *The fall of Soeharto* (Bathurst: Crawford House, 1999).

Gafur, Abdul, *Pak Harto: pandangan dan harapannya* (Jakarta: Pustaka Kartini, 1987).

—— *Siti Hartinah Soeharto: first lady of Indonesia* (Jakarta: P.T. Citra Lamtoro Gung Persada, 1992).

Gatot Mangkupradja, Raden, 'The PETA and my relations with the Japanese: a correction of Sukarno's autobiography', *Indonesia* 5 (1968), pp. 105–34.

Gellert, Paul K., 'A brief history and analysis of Indonesia's forest fire crisis', *Indonesia* 65 (1998), pp. 63–85.

Glassburner, Bruce, 'Indonesia's new economic policy and its sociopolitical implications', in Jackson and Pye (eds), *Political power and communications in Indonesia.*

Green, Marshall, *Indonesia: crisis and transformation 1965–1968* (Washington, DC: Compass Press, 1990).

Groen, P. M. H., *Marsroutes en dwaalsporen: het Nederlands militair-strategisch beleid in Indonesië 1945–1950* (Meppel: Ten Brink, 1991).

Habib, A. Hasnan, 'The role of the armed forces in Indonesia's future political development', in Crouch and Hill (eds), *Indonesia Assessment 1992.*

Hadi Soesastro and M. Chatib Basri, 'Survey of recent development', *Bulletin of Indonesian Economic Studies* 34, 1 (1998), pp. 3–54.

Hadiningrat, *Kusumah, Sejarah operasi^2 gabungan dalam rangka DWIKORA* (Jakarta: Departemen Pertahanan Keamanan Pusat Sedjarah ABRI, 1971).

Hanna, Willard A., 'The magical–mystical syndrome in the Indonesian mentality, part V. Pak Harto: the myth, the man and the mystery', *American Field Service Reports Services, Southeast Asia Series* 15, 9 (1967), pp. 1–19.

Hansen, Gary, 'Episodes in rural modernization: problems with the Bimas program', *Indonesia* 11 (1971), pp. 63–81.

Hansen, Gary E., 'Bureaucratic linkages and policy-making in Indonesia: BIMAS revisited', in Jackson and Pye (eds), *Political power and communications in Indonesia.*

Harsja W. Bachtiar, *Siapa dia? Perwira tinggi Tentara Nasional Indonesia Angkatan Darat (TNI-AD)* (Jakarta: Djambatan, 1988).

Harvey, Barbara S., *Permesta: half a rebellion* (Ithaca: Southeast Asia Program, Cornell University, 1977).

Harvey, Barbara Sillars, 'Tradition, Islam and rebellion: South Sulawesi 1950–1965', PhD dissertation, Cornell University, 1974.

Haseman, John B., 'The dynamics of change: regeneration of the Indonesian army', *Asian Survey* 26, 8 (1986), pp. 883–96.

Hauswedell, Peter Christian, 'Sukarno: radical or conservative? Indonesian politics 1964–5', *Indonesia* 15 (1973), pp. 108–44.

Hefner, Robert W., 'Islam, state and civil society: ICMI and the struggle for the Indonesian middle class', *Indonesia* 56 (1993), pp. 1–35.

—— 'Islamization and democratization in Indonesia', in Robert W. Hefner and Patricia Horvatch (eds), *Islam in an era of nation-states* (Honolulu: University of Hawai'i Press, 1997).

Hein, Gordon R., 'Indonesia in 1988: another five years for Soeharto', *Asian Survey* 29, 2 (1989), pp. 119–28.

—— 'Indonesia in 1989: a question of openness', *Asian Survey* 30, 2 (1989), pp. 221–30.

Hermawan Sulistyo, 'The forgotten years: the missing history of Indonesia's mass slaughter (Jombang-Kediri 1965–1966)', PhD dissertation, Arizona State University, 1997.

Heru Atmojo, 'Mengungkap tragedi kemanusiaan 1965' [unpublished typescript sent to Tapol in 2000 and kindly made available to me by Liem Sui Liong. Published in part as 'G30S, an army intelligence operation', *Tapol Bulletin* 160 (2000), pp. 9–12].

Hidayat, R. A. et al. (eds), *Umar Wirahadikusumah dari peristiwa ke peristiwa* (Jakarta: Yayasan Kesejahteraan Jayakarta/Badan Penerbit 'Sandaan' Jakarta, 1983).

Hill, Hal, *The Indonesian economy since 1966: Southeast Asia's emerging giant* (Cambridge: Cambridge University Press, 1996).

Hindley, Donald, 'Alirans and the fall of the Old Order', *Indonesia* 9 (1970), pp. 23–66.

—— 'Indonesia's confrontation of Malaysia: a search for motives', *Asian Survey* 4, 6 (1964), pp. 904–13.

—— 'Political power and the October 1965 coup in Indonesia', *Journal of Asian Studies* 26 (1967), pp. 237–49.

—— *The communist party of Indonesia, 1951–1963* (Berkeley: University of California Press, 1964).

Holtzappel, Coen, 'The 30 September Movement: a political movement of the armed forces or an intelligence operation?', *Journal of Contemporary Asia* 9, 2 (1979), pp. 216–40.

Hong Lan Oei, 'Implications of Indonesia's new foreign investment policy for economic development', *Indonesia* 7 (1969), pp. 33–66.

—— 'Indonesia's economic stabilisation and rehabilitation programme: an evaluation', *Indonesia* 5 (1968), pp. 135–74.

Hughes, John, *Indonesian upheaval* (New York: David McKay Co., 1967).

Ichlasul Amal, *Regional and central government in Indonesian politics: West Sumatra and South Sulawesi 1949–1979* (Yogyakarta: Gadjah Mada University Press, 1992).

Indonesian Corruption Watch, statement no. 051/SK/ICW/X/98, 'Proof of criminal act in the form of abuse of power by former President Soeharto' (mimeo).
Ismail-Mahn, Christina, *President Suharto: a profile* (Jakarta: Yayasan P. K. Lebak Bulus, 1981?).
Iswandi, *Bisnis militer Orde Baru*, rev. edn (Bandung: Remaja Rosdakarya, 2000).
Jackson, Karl D., 'Bureaucratic polity: a theoretical framework for the analysis of power and communications in Indonesia', in Jackson and Pye (eds), *Political power and communications in Indonesia.*
—— 'The political implications of structure and culture in Indonesia', in Jackson and Pye (eds), *Political power and communications in Indonesia.*
Jackson, Karl D. and Lucien Pye (eds), *Political power and communications in Indonesia* (Berkeley: University of California Press, 1978).
Jasin, M., *Saya tidak pernah minta ampun kepada Soeharto: sebuah memoar* (Jakarta: Pustaka Sinar Harapan, 1998).
Jenkins, David, *Suharto and his generals: Indonesian military politics 1975–1983* (Ithaca: Modern Indonesia Project, Cornell University, 1984).
Jones, Howard Palfrey, *Indonesia: the possible dream* (New York: Harcourt Brace Jovanovich, 1971).
Jusmar Basri, *Gerakan Operasi Militer VI (untuk menumpas 'DI/TII' di Djawa Tengah)* (Jakarta: Mega Bookstore, 1965).
Kadane, Kathy, 'The CIA supplied Suharto with death lists in 1965', *Inside Indonesia* 23 (1990), pp. 12–13.
Kahin, Audrey R. and George McT. Kahin, *Subversion as foreign policy: the secret Eisenhower and Dulles debacle in Indonesia* (New York: New Press, 1995).
Kahin, Audrey et al., 'Current data on the Indonesian military elite', *Indonesia* 53 (1992), pp. 93–136.
—— 'Current data on the Indonesian military elite', *Indonesia* 55 (1993), pp. 176–98.
—— 'Current data on the Indonesian military elite', *Indonesia* 56 (1993), pp. 119–52.
—— 'Current data on the Indonesian military elite', *Indonesia* 58 (1994), pp. 83–101.
—— 'Current data on the Indonesian military elite', *Indonesia* 59 (1995), pp. 45–63.
—— 'The Sixth Development Cabinet announced March 17, 1993', *Indonesia* 55 (1993), pp. 166–76.
Kahin, G. McT., 'The sultan and the Dutch', in Atmakusumah et al. (eds), *Tahta untuk rakyat* (Jakarta: Gramedia, 1982).
Kahin, George McT., 'A personal view of the war', in Wild and Carey (eds), *Born in fire.*
—— 'Some recollections and reflections on the Indonesian revolution', *Indonesia* 60 (1995), pp. 1–16.
Kahin, George McTurnan, *Nationalism and revolution in Indonesia* (Ithaca: Cornell University Press, 1970 [1952]).
Kawilarang, A. E., *Untuk Sang Merah Putih* (Jakarta: Pustaka Sinar Harapan, 1988).
Keefer, Edward C. (ed.), *Foreign relations of the United States, 1961–1963. Volume XXIII Southeast Asia* (Washington, DC: US Government Printing Office, 1994).
Keeler, Ward, *Javanese shadow plays, Javanese selves* (Princeton: Princeton University Press, 1987).
—— *Symbolic dimensions of the Javanese house* (Clayton: Working Paper No. 29, Centre of Southeast Asian Studies, Monash University, 1983).
Kemal Idris, *Bertarung dalam revolusi* (Jakarta: Pustaka Sinar Harapan, 1997).
Kementerian Penerangan, *Republik Indonesia. Daerah Istimewa Jogjakarta* (Jakarta: Kementerian Penerangan, 1953).

—— *Republik Indonesia. Propinsi Djawa-Tengah* (Jakarta: Kementerian Penerangan, 1953).

Kingsbury, Damien, *The politics of Indonesia* (Melbourne: Oxford University Press, 1998).

Kreutzer, R., 'Een stuk geschiedenis: het voorspel van Madioen', *Tijdschrift voor Diplomatie* 10 (June 1980), pp. 685–701.

L. C., 'Socialism and private business: the latest phase', *Bulletin of Indonesian Economic Studies* 2 (1965), pp. 13–45.

Lane, Max, '"Openness", political discontent and succession in Indonesia: political developments in Indonesia, 1989–1991' (Brisbane: Centre for the Study of Australia–Asia Relations, Griffith University, 1991).

—— 'Students on the move', *Inside Indonesia* 19 (1989), pp. 10–18.

Lapré, S. A., *Het Andjing NICA Bataljon (KNIL) in Nederlands-Indië (1945–1950)* (Ermelo: self-published, n.d.).

Latief, A., *Pledoi Kol. A. Latief: Soeharto terlibat G 30 S* (Jakarta: Institut Studi Arus Informasi, 2000).

Legge, J. D., *Central authority and regional autonomy in Indonesia: a study of local administration 1950–1960* (Ithaca: Cornell University Press, 1961).

—— *Sukarno: a political biography* (Harmondsworth: Penguin, 1973).

Lev, Daniel S., 'Becoming an *orang Indonesia sejati*: the political journey of Yap Thiam Hien', *Indonesia* (special issue on 'The role of the Indonesian Chinese in shaping modern Indonesian life'), 1991, pp. 97–112.

—— 'On the fall of the parliamentary system', in Bourchier and Legge (eds), *Democracy in Indonesia.*

—— 'The political role of the army in Indonesia', *Pacific Affairs* 36 (1963–64), pp. 349–64.

—— *The transition to Guided Democracy: Indonesian politics, 1957–59* (Ithaca: Modern Indonesia Project, Cornell University, 1966).

Liddle, R. William, 'Indonesia in 1986: contending with scarcity', *Asian Survey* 27, 2 (1987), pp. 207–18.

—— 'Indonesia in 1987: the New Order at the height of its power', *Asian Survey* 28, 2 (1987), pp. 180–91.

—— 'Indonesia's threefold crisis', in Liddle, *Leadership and culture in Indonesian politics.*

—— 'Participation and the political parties', in Jackson and Pye (eds), *Political power and communications in Indonesia.*

—— 'The relative autonomy of the Third World politician: Soeharto and Indonesian economic development in comparative perspective', in Liddle, *Leadership and culture in Indonesian politics.*

—— 'Soeharto's Indonesia: personal rule and political institutions', *Pacific Affairs* 58, 1 (1985), pp. 68–90.

—— 'The 1977 election and New Order legitimacy', in K. S. Sandhu et al. (eds), *Southeast Asian Affairs 1978* (Singapore: Heinemann, 1978).

—— *Leadership and culture in Indonesian politics* (Sydney: Allen & Unwin, 1996).

Loveard, Keith, *Suharto: Indonesia's last sultan* (Singapore: Horizon Books, 1999).

Lowry, Robert, *The Armed Forces of Indonesia* (Sydney: Allen & Unwin, 1996).

Lyon, Margot L., 'Mystical biography: Soeharto and kejawen in the political domain', in McIntyre (ed.), *Indonesian political biography.*

MacDougall, John A., 'Patterns of military control in the Indonesian higher central bureaucracy', *Indonesia* 33 (1981), pp. 89–121.

MacIntyre, Andrew J., 'Indonesia in 1992: coming to terms with the outside world', *Asian Survey* 33, 2 (1993), pp. 204–10.
—— 'Indonesia in 1993: increasing political movement?', *Asian Survey* 34, 2 (1993), pp. 111–18.
—— 'Politics and the reorientation of economic policy in Indonesia', in Andrew J. MacIntyre and Kanishka Jayasuriya (eds), *The dynamics of economic policy reform in South-east Asia and the South-west Pacific* (Singapore: Oxford University Press, 1992).
—— 'State–society relations in New Order Indonesia: the case of business', in Budiman (ed.), *State and civil society in Indonesia.*
Mackie, J. A. C., 'Anti–Chinese outbreaks in Indonesia, 1959–68', in J. A. C. Mackie (ed.), *The Chinese in Indonesia: five essays* (Honolulu: University Press of Hawai'i, 1976).
—— 'Australia's relations with Indonesia: principles and policies, I', *Australian Outlook* 28, 1 (1974), pp. 3–24.
—— 'Changing patterns of Chinese big business in Southeast Asia', in McVey (ed.), *Southeast Asian capitalists.*
—— 'Civil–military relations and the 1971 elections in Indonesia', *Australian Outlook* 24, 3 (1970), pp. 250–62.
—— 'The Commission of Four report on corruption', *Bulletin of Indonesian Economic Studies* 6, 3 (1970), pp. 87–101.
—— *Konfrontasi: the Indonesia–Malaysia dispute 1963–1966* (London: Oxford University Press, 1974).
—— *Problems of the Indonesian inflation* (Ithaca: Modern Indonesia Project, Cornell University, 1967).
Mackie, Jamie, 'Towkays and tycoons: the Chinese in Indonesian economic life in the 1920s and 1980s', *Indonesia* (special issue on 'The role of the Indonesian Chinese in shaping modern Indonesian life'), 1991, pp. 83–96.
Mackie, Jamie and Andrew MacIntyre, 'Politics', in Hal Hill (ed.), *Indonesia's New Order: the dynamics of socio-economic transformation* (Sydney: Allen & Unwin, 1994).
Maher, Michael, *Indonesia: an eyewitness account* (Melbourne: Viking, 2000).
Malik, Adam, *In the service of the Republic* (Jakarta: Gunung Agung, 1980).
Malley, Michael, 'The 7th Development Cabinet: loyal to a fault?', *Indonesia* 65 (1998), pp. 154–78.
Malley, Michael Sean, 'A political biography of Major General Soedjono Hoemardani, 1918–1986', MA dissertation, Cornell University, 1990.
Mann, Richard, *Plots and schemes that brought down Soeharto* (Jakarta: Gateway Books, 1998).
Manning, Chris, 'Structural change and industrial relations during the Soeharto period: an approaching crisis?', *Bulletin of Indonesian Economic Studies* 29, 2 (1993), pp. 59–95.
Manning, Chris and Peter van Dierman, 'Recent developments and social aspects of *reformasi* and crisis: an overview', in Manning and van Dierman (eds), *Indonesia in transition.*
Manning, Chris and Peter van Dierman (eds), *Indonesia in transition: social aspects of reformasi and crisis* (Singapore: Institute of Southeast Asian Studies, 1999).
Marjoto, 'Mengungkap lahirnja SP-11 Maret 1966', *Vidya Yudha* 6 (1969), pp. 88–104.
Marzuki Darusman, 'Indonesian political developments: problems and prospects', in Crouch and Hill (eds), *Indonesia Assessment 1992.*
May, Brian, *The Indonesian tragedy* (London: Routledge and Kegan Paul, 1978).
McDonald, Hamish, *Suharto's Indonesia* (Blackburn: Fontana/Collins, 1980).

McIntyre, Angus, 'Divisions and power in the Indonesian National Party, 1965–1966', *Indonesia* 13 (1972), pp. 183–210.

—— 'Foreign biographical studies of Indonesian subjects: obstacles and shortcomings', in McIntyre (ed.), *Indonesian political biography.*

—— 'Introduction', in McIntyre (ed.), *Indonesian political biography.*

—— *Soeharto's composure: considering the biographical and autobiographical accounts* (Clayton: Working Paper No. 97, Centre of Southeast Asian Studies, Monash University, 1996).

McIntyre, Angus (ed.), *Indonesian political biography: in search of cross-cultural understanding* (Clayton: Monash Papers on Southeast Asia No. 28, Centre of Southeast Asian Studies, Monash University, 1993).

McLeod, Ross, 'Soeharto's Indonesia: a better class of corruption', *Agenda* 7, 2 (2000), pp. 99–112.

McMahon, Robert J. (ed.), *Foreign relations of the United States, 1958–1960. Volume XVII Indonesia* (Washington, DC: US Government Printing Office, 1994).

McVey, Ruth T., 'The case of the disappearing decade', in Bourchier and Legge (eds), *Democracy in Indonesia.*

—— 'The materialization of the Southeast Asian entrepreneur', in R. McVey (ed.), *Southeast Asian capitalists* (Ithaca: Cornell University Southeast Asia Program, 1992).

—— 'Nationalism, Islam and Marxism: the management of ideological conflict in Indonesia', introduction to Sukarno, *Nationalism, Islam and Marxism* (Ithaca: Modern Indonesia Project, Cornell University, 1970).

—— 'PKI fortunes at low tide', *Problems of Communism* 20 (1971), pp. 25–36.

—— 'The post-revolutionary transformation of the Indonesian army', part I, *Indonesia* 11 (1971), pp. 131–76; part II, *Indonesia* 13 (1972), pp. 147–81.

—— 'A preliminary excursion into the small world of Lt. Col. Untung' (typescript).

—— *Redesigning the cosmos: belief systems and state power in Indonesia*, rev. edn (Copenhagen: Nordic Institute of Asian Studies, NIAS Reports No. 14, 1995).

'Memori Gubernur Yogyakarta (J. E. Jaspers), 29 September 1929', in Sartono Kartodirdjo et al. (eds), *Memori serah jabatan 1921–1930 (Jawa Timur dan Tanah Kerajaan)* (Jakarta: Arsip Nasional Republik Indonesia, 1978).

Mody, Nawaz B., *Indonesia under Suharto* (New York: Apt Books, 1987).

Mohtar Mas'oed, 'The state reorganisation of society under the New Order', *Prisma* 47 (1989), pp. 3–24.

Mortimer, Rex, 'Class, social cleavage and Indonesian communism', *Indonesia* 8 (1969), pp. 1–20.

—— 'Indonesia: growth or development?', in Mortimer (ed.), *Showcase state.*

—— *Indonesian communism under Sukarno: ideology and politics, 1959–1965* (Ithaca: Cornell University Press, 1974).

—— *Showcase state: the illusion of Indonesia's accelerated modernisation* (Sydney: Angus & Robertson, 1973).

Mossman, James, *Rebels in paradise: Indonesia's civil war* (London: Jonathan Cape, 1961).

Mrazek, Rudolf, 'Tan Malaka: a political personality's structure of experience', *Indonesia* 14 (1972), pp. 1–48.

—— *Sjahrir: politics and exile in Indonesia* (Ithaca: Southeast Asia Program, Cornell University, 1994).

Mulya Lubis, T., 'The future of human rights in Indonesia', in Crouch and Hill (eds), *Indonesia Assessment 1992.*

Nasution, Abdul Haris, *Fundamentals of guerrilla warfare*, 2nd edn (Jakarta: Seruling Masa, 1970).
—— *Memenuhi panggilan tugas*, vols 2–9 (Jakarta: Gunung Agung/Haji Masagung, 1983–93).
—— *Sekitar perang kemerdekaan Indonesia*, vols 1–11 (Bandung: Angkasa, 1976–82).
—— *Tentara Nasional Indonesia*, 3 vols (Jakarta: Seruling Masa, 1956–69).
Nasution, Adnan Buyung, *The aspiration for constitutional government in Indonesia: a socio-legal study of the Indonesian Konstituante 1956–1959* (Jakarta: Pustaka Sinar Harapan, 1992).
Nazaruddin Sjamsuddin (ed.), *Jejak langkah Pak Harto 27 Maret 1973–23 Maret 1978* (Jakarta: Citra Lamtoro Gung Persada, 1991).
—— *Jejak langkah Pak Harto 29 Maret 1978–11 Maret 1983* (Jakarta: Citra Lamtoro Gung Persada, 1992).
—— *Jejak langkah Pak Harto 16 Maret 1983–11 Maret 1988* (Jakarta: Citra Lamtoro Gung Persada, 1992).
—— *Jejak langkah Pak Harto 21 Maret 1988–11 Maret 1993* (Jakarta: Citra Lamtoro Gung Persada, 1993).
Nono Anwar Makarim, 'The Indonesian press: an editor's perspective', in Jackson and Pye (eds), *Political power and communications in Indonesia.*
Nugroho Notosusanto, *Pemberontakan tentara Peta Blitar melawan Djepang (14 Pebruari 1945)* (Jakarta: Lembaga Sedjarah Hankam, Departemen Pertahanan Keamanan, 1968).
—— *Some effects of the guerillas on armed forces and society in Indonesia, 1948–1949* (Jakarta: Centre for Armed Forces History, Department of Defence and Security, 1974).
—— *The Peta army during the Japanese occupation of Indonesia* (Tokyo: Waseda University Press, 1979).
—— *The PETA-army in Indonesia 1943–1945* (Jakarta: Centre for Armed Forces History, Department of Defence and Security, 1971).
Nugroho Notosusanto (ed.), *Pejuang dan prajurit: konsepsi dan implementasi dwifungsi ABRI*, 3rd printing (Jakarta: Sinar Harapan, 1991 [1984]) [Hankam paper].
Nugroho Notosusanto and Ismael Saleh, *The coup attempt of the 'September 30th movement' in Indonesia* (Jakarta: Pembimbing Masa, 1968).
O'Malley, William Joseph, 'Indonesia in the Great Depression: a study of East Sumatra and Jogjakarta in the 1930s', PhD dissertation, Cornell University, 1977.
Oei Hong Lan, 'Indonesia's economic stabilization and rehabilitation program: an evaluation', *Indonesia* 5 (1968), pp. 135–74.
Oey Hong Lee, 'Sukarno and the pseudo-coup of 1965: ten years later', *Journal of Southeast Asian Studies* 7, 1 (1976), pp. 119–35.
Oudang, M., *Perkembangan kepolisian di Indonesia* (Jakarta?: Mahabarata, 1952?).
Pandjaitan br. Tanbunan, Marieke, *D. I. Pandjaitan: gugur dalam seragam kebesaran* (Jakarta: Pustaka Sinar Harapan, 1997).
Pangaribuan, Robinson, *The Indonesian State Secretariat 1945–1993*, tr. Vedi Hadiz (Perth: Asia Research Centre on Political and Economic Change, 1995).
Panitia Penyusun Sejarah KOSTRAD, *KOSTRAD dharma putra* (Jakarta: Panitya Penyusun Sejarah KOSTRAD, 1972).
Pauker, G. J., *The rise and fall of the Communist Party of Indonesia* (Santa Monica: RAND Corporation, Memorandum RM-5753-PR, February 1969).
Pauker, Guy J., *Indonesia in 1966: the year of transition* (Santa Monica: RAND Corporation, Paper P-3525, February 1967).

Pemberton, John, *On the subject of 'Java'* (Ithaca: Cornell University Press, 1994).

Penders, C. L. M. (ed.), *Milestones on my journey. The memoirs of Ali Sastroamijoyo, Indonesian patriot and political leader* (St Lucia: University of Queensland Press, 1979).

Penders, C. L. M. and Ulf Sundhaussen, *Abdul Haris Nasution: a political biography* (St Lucia: University of Queensland Press, 1985).

Polomka, Peter, *Indonesia since Sukarno* (Harmondsworth: Penguin, 1971).

Pour, Julius, *Benny Moerdani: profile of a soldier statesman*, tr. Tim Scott (Jakarta: Yayasan Kejuangan Panglima Besar Sudirman, 1993).

—— *Laksamana Sudomo: mengatasi gelombang kehidupan* (Jakarta: Gramedia, 1997).

Rae, Lindsay, 'Liberating and conciliating: the work of Y. B. Mangunwijaya', in McIntyre (ed.), *Indonesian political biography*.

—— 'Sutan Sjahrir and the failure of Indonesian socialism', in McIntyre (ed.), *Indonesian political biography*.

Ramadhan K. H., *Soemitro: former commander of Indonesian security apparatus* (Jakarta: Pustaka Sinar Harapan, 1996).

Ramage, Douglas, *Politics in Indonesia: democracy, Islam and the ideology of tolerance* (London: Routledge, 1995).

Reeve, David, 'The corporatist state: the case of Golkar', in Budiman (ed.), *State and civil society in Indonesia*.

—— *Golkar of Indonesia: an alternative to the party system* (Singapore: Oxford University Press, 1985).

Reid, Anthony J. S., *Indonesian national revolution 1945–50* (Hawthorn: Longman, 1974).

Republic of Indonesia, Kementerian Penerangan, *Lukisan revolusi, 1945–1950* (Jakarta: n.p., n.d. [1954?]).

Reviv, Dan and Yossi Melman, *Every spy a prince: the complete history of Israel's intelligence community* (Boston: Houghton Mifflin, 1990).

Rieffel, Alexis, 'The Bimas program for self-sufficiency in rice production', *Indonesia* 8 (1969), pp. 103–33.

Rizal Mallarangeng and R. William Liddle, 'Indonesia in 1995: the struggle for power and policy', *Asian Survey* 36, 2 (1996), pp. 109–16.

Robison, Richard, 'Indonesia: tension in state and regime', in Kevin Hewison, Richard Robison and Garry Rodan (eds), *Southeast Asia in the 1990s: authoritarian, democracy and capitalism* (Sydney: Allen & Unwin, 1993).

—— 'Towards a class analysis of the Indonesian military bureaucratic state', *Indonesia* 25 (1978), pp. 17–39.

—— *Indonesia: the rise of capital* (Sydney: Allen & Unwin, 1986).

Rocamora, J. Eliseo, 'The Partai Nasional Indonesia 1963–1965', *Indonesia* 10 (1970), pp. 143–81.

Roeder, O. G., *Anak desa: biografi Presiden Soeharto* (Jakarta: Gunung Agung, 1976).

—— *The smiling general: President Soeharto of Indonesia*, 2nd rev. edn (Jakarta: Gunung Agung, 1969).

Sadli, Mohammad, 'Recollections of my career', *Bulletin of Indonesian Economic Studies* 29, 1 (1993), pp. 35–51.

Saleh A. Djamhari, *Markas Besar Komando Djawa, 1948–49* (Jakarta: Lembaga Sedjarah Hankam, 1967).

Salim Said, *Genesis of power: General Sudirman and the Indonesian military in politics 1945–49* (Singapore: Institute of Southeast Asian Studies, 1993).

Salim, Emil, 'Recollections of my career', *Bulletin of Indonesian Economic Studies* 33, 1 (1997), pp. 45–74.

Saltford, John, 'United Nations involvement with the act of self-determination in West Irian (Indonesian West New Guinea 1968 to 1969)', *Indonesia* 69 (2000), pp. 71–92.

Samad, Paridah Abd., *General Wiranto: the man emerging from the midst of Indonesian reformation: a political analysis* (Kuala Lumpur: Affluent Master, 1999).

Samson, Allan, 'Conceptions of politics, power and ideology in contemporary Indonesian Islam', in Jackson and Pye (eds), *Political power and communications in Indonesia.*

Sarbini Sumawinata, 'Recollections of my career', *Bulletin of Indonesian Economic Studies* 28, 2 (1992), pp. 43–53.

Sato, Shigeru, *War, nationalism and peasants: Java under the Japanese occupation 1942–1945* (Sydney: Allen & Unwin, 1994).

Sayidiman Suryohadiprojo, *Mengabdi negara sebagai prajurit TNI: sebuah otobiografi* (Jakarta: Pustaka Sinar Harapan, 1997).

Schwarz, Adam, *A nation in waiting: Indonesia in the 1990s* (Sydney: Allen & Unwin, 1994; 2nd edn, 1999).

Scott, Peter Dale, 'The United States and the overthrow of Sukarno', *Pacific Affairs* 58, 2 (1985), pp. 239–64.

Sedjarah Militer Kodam VI Siliwangi, *Siliwangi: dari masa ke masa* (Jakarta: Penerbit Fakta Mahjuma, 1968?).

Sedjarah Militer Kodam VII/Diponegoro, *Sedjarah Tentara Nasional Indonesia Komando Daerah Militer VII Diponegoro (Djawa Tengah)* (n.p.: n.p., n.d.).

—— *Sedjarah TNI-AD Kodam VII/Diponegoro* (Semarang: Yayasan Penerbit Diponegoro, 1968).

Sekretariat Agitasi-Propaganda CCPKI, *Buku putih tentang peristiwa Madiun* (n.p: n.p., n.d.).

Sekretariat Negara Republik Indonesia, *Gerakan 30 September: pemberontakan Partai Komunis Indonesia. Latar belakang, aksi, dan penumpasannya* (Jakarta: Sekretariat Negara Republik Indonesia, 1994).

Sen, Krishna, *Indonesian cinema: framing the New Order* (London: Zed Books, 1994).

Sewaka, *Tjoret-tjaret dari djaman ke djaman* (Bandung?: n.p. 1955).

Shin, Yoon Hwan, 'The role of elites in creating capitalist hegemony in post oil-boom Indonesia', *Indonesia* (special issue on 'The role of the Indonesian Chinese in shaping modern Indonesian life'), 1991, pp. 128–43.

Sidel, John T., 'Macet total: logics of circulation and accumulation in the demise of Indonesia's New Order', *Indonesia* 66 (1998), pp. 159–94.

Silalahi, Harry Tjan [Can], 'CSIS lahir dari tantangan jaman', in Anon., *CSIS 20 Tahun* (Jakarta: Centre for Strategic and International Studies, 1991).

—— 'Kata sebuah riwayat', in Anon. (ed.), *Soedjono Hoemardani: pendiri CSIS 1918–1986* (Jakarta: Centre for Strategic and International Studies, 1987).

Simanjuntak, Djisman S., 'The Indonesian economy in 1999: another year of delayed reform', in Manning and van Dierman (eds), *Indonesia in transition.*

Simatupang, T. B., *Report from Banaran: experiences during the people's war* (Ithaca: Modern Indonesia Project, Cornell University Press, 1972).

—— *The fallacy of a myth*, tr. Peter Sunarso (Jakarta: Pustaka Sinar Harapan, 1996).

Sinansari, S., *Kronologi situasi penggulingan Soeharto* (Jakarta: Mizan Pustaka, 1998).

Siti Hardiyanti Hastuti Rukmana (ed.), *Butir butir budaya Jawa: mencapai kesempurnaan hidup berjiwa besar mengusahakan kebaikan sejati* (published on occasion of Suharto's 40th wedding anniversary in 1987).

Sjafruddin Prawiranegara, 'Pancasila as the sole foundation', *Indonesia* 38 (1984), pp. 74–83.

Sjahrir and Colin Brown, 'Indonesian financial and trade policy deregulation: reform and response', in Andrew J. MacIntyre and Kanishka Jayasuriya (eds), *The dynamics of economic policy reform in South-east Asia and the South-west Pacific* (Singapore: Oxford University Press, 1992).

Sjamsuar Said, 'Beberapa tjatatan mengenai Operasi 17 Agustus', *Vidya Yudha* 6 (1969), pp. 82–7.

Smail, John R. W., 'The military politics of North Sumatra: December 1956–October 1957', *Indonesia* 6 (1968), pp. 128–87.

Smith, Theodore M., 'Corruption, tradition and change', *Indonesia* 11 (1971), pp. 21–40.

Soebandrio, H., 'Kesaksianku tentang G-30-S' [this unpublished manuscript, due to be published by Gramedia in late 2000, was suddenly withdrawn from publication].

Soedjati Djiwandono, J., 'Indonesia in 1994', *Asian Survey* 35, 2 (1995), pp. 227–33.

Soegih Arto, *Indonesia & I* (Singapore: Time Books International, 1994).

Soeharto, 'Atas kebebasan yang bertanggung jawab harus disadari pers sendiri' (sambutan Presiden pada pertemuan pemimpin redaksi dan PWI se Indonesia, di Istana Negara Jakarta tanggal 11 September 1981), in Anon., *Pers pembawa panji-panji demokrasi: Presiden Soeharto tentang pers Indonesia* (Jakarta: Persatuan Wartawan Indonesia (PWI) Pusat, 1983).

—— 'Dalam perjuangan dibidang apapun, kekuatan andalan dan modal utama kita adalah rakyat', sambutan Presiden para peringatan Empat Windu Permulaan Perang Kemerdekaan II tanggal 19 Desember 1980 di Yogyakarta, in *Mimbar Kekaryaan ABRI*, no. 121, January 1981, pp. 2–5.

—— 'Laporan stenografi amanat Presiden Soeharto pada malam ramah tamah dengan pengurus K.N.P.I. tanggal 19 Juli 1982 di Jalan Cendana no. 8 Jakarta' (mimeo).

—— *Pidato kenegaraan Presiden Republik Indonesia Soeharto di depan sidang Dewan Perwakilan Rakyat 16 Agustus 1995* (Jakarta: Republik Indonesia, 1995?).

—— *Pidato kenegaraan Presiden Republik Indonesia Soeharto di depan sidang Dewan Perwakilan Rakyat 16 Agustus 1996* (Jakarta: Republik Indonesia, 1996?).

—— *Pidato pertama Djendral Soeharto setelah dilantik sebagai Pedjabat Presiden RI* (n.p.: Doa Restu, 1967).

—— *Pikiran, ucapan dan tindakan: otobiografi seperti dipaparkan kepada G. Dwipayana dan Ramadhan K. H.* (Jakarta: Citra Lamtoro Gung Persada, 1989), in English translation as Soeharto, *My thoughts, words and deeds: an autobiography as told to G. Dwipayana and Ramadhan K. H. English translation by Sumadi; edited by Muti'ah Lestiono* (Jakarta: Citra Lamtoro Gung Persada, 1991).

Soeharto, Tien, *On the development of the project Indonesia in Miniature 'Indonesia Indah'* (Jakarta: Executive Body for the Development & Preparation for the Management of the Project Indonesia in Miniature 'Indonesia Indah', 1971).

Soeminto (ed.), *Presiden dan wakil Presiden Republik Indonesia 1978–1983* (Jakarta: Yayasan Murga Jaya, n.d. (1978?)).

Soemitro, *Pangkopkamtib Jenderal Soemitro dan peristiwa 15 Januari '74 sebagaimana dituturkan kepada Heru Cahyono* (Jakarta: Sinar Harapan, 1998).

Soetojo, 'Fungsi Kursus "C" dalam rangka pembangunan Angkatan Darat Republik Indonesia', *Karya Wira Jati* 2 (1961), pp. 129–37.

Soetriyono, Eddy, *Kisah sukses Liem Sioe Liong* (Jakarta: Indomedia, 1989).

Sofyan Wanandi and J. Soedjati Djiwandono, 'Soedjono Hoemardani dan Jepang', in Anon. (ed.), *Soedjono Hoemardani: pendiri CSIS 1918–1986* (Jakarta: Centre for Strategic and International Studies, 1987).

Sori Esa Siregar and K. T. Widya, *Liem Sioe Liong: dari Futching ke mancanegara* (Jakarta: Pustaka Merdeka, 1988).

Southwood, Julie, 'Indonesia's political trials: "legal" dimensions of a continuing tragedy', *Tapol Bulletin* 37 (1980), pp. 3–17.

Southwood, Julie and Patrick Flanagan, *Indonesia: law, propaganda and terror* (London: Zed Press, 1983).

Subroto, 'Recollections of my career', *Bulletin of Indonesian Economic Studies* 34, 2 (1998), pp. 67–92.

Sudarisman Purwokusumo, 'Yogyakarta sewaktu sebagai Ibukota RI', *Vidya Yudha* 17 (1973), pp. 66–76.

Sudharmono, *Pengalaman dalam masa pengabdian: sebuah otobiografi* (Jakarta: Grasindo, 1997).

Sudjadi, 'Sedjarah KORRA I/TJADUAD', *Vidya Yudha* 5 (1968), pp. 99–112.

Sudjarwo Tjondronegoro (ed.), *Illustrations of the revolution, 1945–1950*, 2nd edn (Jakarta: Ministry of Information, 1954).

Suharto, 'Watashi no rirekisho' ['My personal history'], *Nihon Keizai Shimbun*, 1–31 January 1998 (daily articles).

Suharto, Sahirdjan, R. O. S. Sunardi and Wahyu Hagono, 'Perang wilayah sebagai konsepsi pertahan Indonesia', *Karya Wira Jati* 1 (1961), pp. 9–27.

Sukarno, *An autobiography as told to Cindy Adams* (Hong Kong: Gunung Agung, 1966).

Sundhaussen, Ulf, 'The fashioning of unity in the Indonesian army', *Asia Quarterly* 2 (1971), pp. 181–212.

—— 'The military: structure, procedures and effects on Indonesian society', in Jackson and Pye (eds), *Political power and communications in Indonesia.*

—— *The road to power: Indonesian military politics 1945–1967* (Kuala Lumpur: Oxford University Press, 1982).

Suratmin et al., *Sejarah perlawanan terhadap imperialisme dan kolonialisme di Daerah Istimewa Jogjakarta* (Jakarta: Departemen Pendidikan dan Kebudayaan, 1982–83).

Suripto, *Ibu Tien Soeharto: Ibu Negara jang ramah tamah* (Surabaya: P.T. Pantja Pudjibangun, n.d.).

—— *Soeharto: suatu sketsa karier dan politik* (Surabaya: Grip, 1972).

—— *Surat perintah 11 Maret* (Surabaya: Grip, 1969).

Suryadinata, Leo, *Prominent Indonesian Chinese: biographical sketches* (Singapore: Institute of Southeast Asian Studies, 1995).

Suryohadi (ed.), *Silsilah Presiden Soeharto anak petani: bahan dan foto-foto dari HUMAS SEKNEG Jakarta* (Surabaya: Penerbit 'Grip', 1974).

Sutopo Juwono, 'Semester masalah pertahanan, dalam rangka kurikulum SESKOAD', *Karya Wira Jati* 6 (1962), pp. 164–71.

Suwarto, 'Perang wilayah', *Karya Wira Jati* 49–50 (1981), pp. 1–22.

—— 'Suatu "approach" mata peladjaran "masalah² pertahan" di SSKAD', in Anon., *Documentaria Cursus 'C'. Sekolah Staf & Komando Angkatan Darat Tentara Nasional Indonesia. Angkatan ke 1 Oktober '58/Desember '59* (n.p.: n.p., n.d.).

Suwarto and Kartomo, 'Bantuan Angkatan Perang dalam pembangunan suatu persiapan pembinaan wilajah', *Karya Wira Jati* 8 (1962), pp. 295–313.

Swift, Ann, *The road to Madiun: the Indonesian communist uprising of 1948* (Ithaca: Cornell Modern Indonesia Project, Cornell University, 1989).

Tabah, Anton, *Dua jenderal besar bicara tentang Gestapu/PKI* (Klaten: Sahabat, 1999).

Tan Malaka, *From jail to jail*, tr. and intro. Helen Jarvis (Athens, Ohio: Monographs in International Studies, Ohio University, 1991).

Tan, Mély G. 'The social and cultural dimensions of the role of ethnic Chinese in Indonesian society', *Indonesia* (special issue on 'The role of the Indonesian Chinese in shaping modern Indonesian life'), 1991, pp. 112–25.

Tanter, Richard, 'Intelligence agencies and Third World militarization: a case study of Indonesia, 1966–1989', PhD dissertation, Monash University, 1991.

—— 'Oil, IGGI and US hegemony: the global pre-conditions for Indonesian rentier-militarization', in Budiman (ed.), *State and civil society in Indonesia.*

—— 'The totalitarian ambition: intelligence organisations in the Indonesian state', in Budiman (ed.), *State and civil society in Indonesia.*

Taylor, John et al. (eds), *Repression and exploitation in Indonesia* (Nottingham: Spokesman Books, 1974).

Tim Lembaga Analisis Informasi, *Kontroversi Serangan Umum 1 Maret 1949* (Yogyakarta: Media Pressindo, 2000).

Tim Peniliti Sistem Pemilu, 'Laporan penelitian sistem pemilihan umum di Indonesia' (Jakarta: Lembaga Ilmu Pengetahuan Indonesia, 1995).

Tjahyadi Nugroho, *Soeharto Bapak Pembangunan Indonesia* (Semarang: Yayasan Telapak, 1984).

Tjokropranolo, *Panglima Besar TNI Jenderal Soedirman: pemimpin pendobrak terakhir penjajahan di Indonesia* (Jakarta: CV Haji Masagung, 1993).

Twang Peck Yang, *The Chinese business élite in Indonesia and the transition to independence* (Kuala Lumpur: Oxford University Press, 1998).

USCIA (US Central Intelligence Agency, Directorate of Intelligence), *Indonesia – 1965: the coup that backfired* (Intelligence report, December 1968).

Van der Eng, Pierre, 'Indonesia's economy and standard of living during the 20th century', in Grayson Lloyd and Shannon Smith (eds), *Indonesia today: challenges of history* (Singapore: Institute of Southeast Asian Studies, 2001), pp. 181–99.

Van der Kroef, Justus M., 'Indonesian communism since the 1965 coup', *Pacific Affairs* 43, 1 (1970), pp. 34–60.

—— '"Petrus": patterns of prophylactic murder in Indonesia', *Asian Survey* 25 (1985), pp. 745–59.

—— *Indonesia after Sukarno* (Vancouver: University of British Columbia Press, 1971).

Van Dijk, C., *Rebellion under the banner of Islam: the Darul Islam in Indonesia* (The Hague: Martinus Nijhoff, 1981).

Vatikiotis, Michael R. J., *Indonesian politics under Suharto: order, development and pressure for change* (London: Routledge, rev. edn, 1993; 3rd edn, 1998).

Volunteer Team for Humanity, 'Early documentation no. 1: the riot pattern in Jakarta and surroundings', 22 May 1998 (mimeo).

—— 'Early documentation no. 2: the plunder status of the riot', 9 June 1998 (mimeo).

Waddingham, John, 'Why the 1986 executions', *Inside Indonesia* 11 (1987), pp. 11–12.

Wanandi, Jusuf, 'Political development and national stability', in Crouch and Hill (eds), *Indonesia Assessment 1992.*

Ward, Ken, 'Indonesia's modernisation: ideology and practice', in Mortimer (ed.), *Showcase state.*

—— *The 1971 election in Indonesia: an East Java case study* (Clayton: Centre of Southeast Asian Studies, Monash University, 1974).

Way, Wendy (ed.), *Australia and the Indonesian incorporation of Portuguese Timor 1974–1976* (Canberra: Department of Foreign Affairs and Trade, 2000).

Weatherbee, Donald E., 'Indonesia in 1985: chills and thaws', *Asian Survey* 26, 2 (1986), pp. 141–9.

—— 'Interpretations of Gestapu, the 1965 Indonesian coup', *World Affairs* 132, 4 (1970), pp. 305–17.

Wertheim, W. F., 'Indonesia before and after the Untung coup', *Pacific Affairs* 39 (1966), pp. 115–27.

—— 'Suharto and the Latief trial: a painful revelation', *Tapol Bulletin* 29 (1978), pp. 5–7.

—— 'Whose plot? New light on the 1965 events', *Journal of Contemporary Asia* 9, 2 (1979), pp. 197–215.

White, Lawrence J., 'Problems and prospects of the Indonesian foreign exchange system', *Indonesia* 14 (1972), pp. 125–56.

Wibisono, Christianto, *Aksi² Tritura: kisah sebuah partnership10 Djanuari–11 Maret 1966* (Jakarta: Departemen Pertahanan Keamanan, 1970).

Wild, Colin and Peter Carey (eds), *Born in fire: the Indonesian struggle for independence* (Athens, Ohio: Ohio University Press, 1988).

Williams, Michael, 'China and Indonesia make up: reflections on a troubled relationship', *Indonesia* (special issue on 'The role of the Indonesian Chinese in shaping modern Indonesian life'), 1991, pp. 145–58.

Wimandjaja K. Liotohe, *Primadosa: Wimandjaja dan rakyat Indonesia menggugat imperium Suharto* (Jakarta: Yayasan Eka Fakta Kata, 1994).

Winters, Jeffrey A., '*Indonesia: the rise of capital*: a review essay', *Indonesia* 45 (1988), pp. 109–28.

—— *Power in motion: capital mobility and the Indonesian state* (Ithaca: Cornell University Press, 1996).

Wiwoho, B. and Bandjar Chaeruddin, *Memori Jenderal Yoga* (Jakarta: Bina Rena Pariwara, 1991).

Yani, A., *Ahmad Yani, sebuah kenang-kenangan* (Bandung: Karya Kelana, 1982?).

Yani, Amelia, *Profile of a soldier* (Singapore: Heinemann, 1990).

Yap Thiam Hien, 'Law, state and civil society', in Budiman (ed.), *State and civil society in Indonesia.*

Zifirdaus Adnan, '"Islamic religion: yes, Islamic (political) ideology: no!": Islam and the state in Indonesia', in Budiman (ed.), *State and civil society in Indonesia.*

Zwitser, H. L. and C. A. Heshusius, *Het Koninklijk Nederlandsch-Indisch Leger 1830–1950* ('s-Gravenhage: Staatsuitgeverij, 1977).

Index